Mike Meyers' Certification
Passport ★

A+
Certification
Second Edition

Mike Meyers
Martin Acuña

Osborne

New York · Chicago · San Francisco
Lisbon · London · Madrid · Mexico City
Milan · New Delhi · San Juan
Seoul · Singapore · Sydney · Toronto

The *McGraw·Hill* Companies

McGraw-Hill/Osborne
2100 Powell Street, 10th Floor
Emeryville, California 94608
U.S.A.

To arrange bulk purchase discounts for sales promotions, premiums, or fund-raisers, please contact **McGraw-Hill**/Osborne at the above address. For information on translations or book distributors outside the U.S.A., please see the International Contact Information page immediately following the index of this book.

Mike Meyers' A+® Certification Passport, Second Edition

7890 DOC DOC 019876

Book p/n 0-07-222915-2 and CD p/n 0-07-222916-0
parts of
ISBN 0-07-222914-4

Publisher Brandon A. Nordin	**Proofreader** Susie Elkind
Vice President & Associate Publisher Scott Rogers	**Indexer** Claire Splan
Editorial Director Gareth Hancock	**Computer Designers** Carie Abrew, Tara A. Davis
Project Editor Carolyn Welch	**Illustrators** Michael Mueller, Kathleen Edwards,
Acquisitions Coordinator Jessica Wilson	Melinda Lytle
	Series Design epic, Peter F. Hancik,
Technical Editor Jane Holcombe	and Kelly Stanton-Scott
Copy Editor Bob Campbell	**Cover Series Design** Ted Holladay

This book was composed with Corel VENTURA™ Publisher.

About LearnKey

LearnKey provides self-paced learning content and e-learning solutions to enhance personal skills and business productivity. LearnKey claims the largest library of rich streaming-media training content that engages learners in dynamic media-rich instruction complete with video clips, audio, full motion graphics, and animated illustrations. LearnKey can be found on the Web at www.LearnKey.com.

Dedicated with more love than I have words for to the most important bipeds in my life: lovely wife Anne and beautiful daughter Isabella, my inspiration and my reason for living, respectively. Because I'm an animal-friendly guy, I also want to dedicate this book to the other members of the Acuña household: Mijo, Pitbull Kitty, Mr. Mertle, and especially Chiquita Banana Boom-Boom Head, Demon Hound of the Apocalypse, for keeping me company those many nights I spent banging away on the keyboard long after everyone else had gone to sleep. Good doggy!

Acknowledgments

A lot of people have offered encouragement, given assistance, opened doors, taken chances, and otherwise earned my thanks. Thank you to my long-time friend and Editor-in-Chimp Scott Jernigan, for teaching me how to, you know, like, write good with words and stuff. Thank you to my mentor Mike Meyers, who sometimes blazed a trail for me to follow, and who sometimes shoved me out front with a machete and a compass. Thank you to Dudley Lehmer for leadership, vision, and being an excellent judge of character. Thank you to Edit Grrrl Cindy Clayton for laughs and word-fixery. Thank you to Roger Conrad for more laughs and for knowing stuff that I didn't know (and not being a jerk about it). Finally, to Janelle Meyers, David Biggs, David Dussé, Kathy Yale, Brandy Taylor, Jeremy Conn, Mike Smyer, Cary Dyer, the beauteous and punctual Bambi Thibodeaux, and all of the others at Totalsem, I just want to say thanks. So … *thanks.*

I owe thanks to my family: parents Ed and Margaret; brothers Ed Jr. and Michael; and sisters Elida, Elia, and Eloisa. During those aimless years when I couldn't decide whether I wanted to be a rock star/astronaut or a restaurateur/stuntman, every one of them, at one point or another, said, "You ought to look into computers. I think you'd be good with them." You were right!

The person I owe the most thanks to, however, is departed buddy Rex Applegate, Jr. Rex was an IT pro *nonpareil* long before I knew my ASCII text from a hole in the ground. Many years ago, Rex was able to explain to a newbie like me, in words I could understand, how to make the computer do what *I* wanted it to do instead of the other way around. I still remember what you said, Rex—"If it's made by man, you can do it." *Vaya con Dios,* bud. The next time we meet, the Bohemia's on me.

Of course, many thanks go to the folks at McGraw-Hill/Osborne who made this book possible: Nancy Maragioglio, our acquisitions editor, whose whip-cracking skills would put Indiana Jones to shame; Jessica Wilson, our acquisitions coordinator, who offered kind words of encouragement; and Carolyn Welch, our project editor, who kept up the gentle pressure while keeping wackier hours than we do! I hope this is the beginning of a beautiful friendship.

Contents

II Operating System Technologies 325

13 Networks: Wireless Networking 327

19 **Maintaining, Optimizing, and Troubleshooting Windows NT/2000/XP** 581

Check-In

May I see your Passport?

What do you mean you don't have a passport? Why, it's sitting right in your hands, even as you read! This book is your passport to a very special place. You're about to begin a journey, my friend, a journey towards that magical place called *certification*! You don't need a ticket, you don't need a suitcase—just snuggle up and read this passport—it's all you need to get there. Are you ready? Let's go!

Your Travel Agent: Mike Meyers

Hello! I'm Mike Meyers, president of Total Seminars and author of a number of popular certification books. On any given day, you'll find me replacing a hard drive, setting up a web site, or writing code. I love every aspect of this book you hold in your hands. It's part of a powerful book series called the Mike Meyer's Certification Passports. Every book in this series combines easy readability with a condensed format—in other words, the kind of book I always wanted when I went for my certifications. Putting a huge amount of information in an accessible format is an enormous challenge, but I think we have achieved our goal and I am confident you'll agree.

I designed this series to do one thing and only one thing—to get you the information you need to achieve your certification. You won't find any fluff in here. Martin and I packed every page with nothing but the real nitty gritty of the A+ Certification exams. Every page has 100 percent pure concentrate of certification knowledge! But we didn't forget to make the book readable, so I hope you enjoy the casual, friendly style.

My personal e-mail address is mikem@totalsem.com; Martin's e-mail is martin@totalsem.com. Please feel free to contact either of us directly if you have any questions, complaints, or compliments.

Your Destination: A+ Certification

This book is your passport to CompTIA's A+ Certification, the vendor-neutral industry standard certification for PC hardware technicians, the folks who build and fix PCs. To get A+ Certified, you need to pass two exams: *A+ Core Hardware* and *A+ Operating System Technologies*. The Core Hardware exam concentrates on the aspects of the PC that are not operating system-specific. This test is primarily a hardware identification and configuration exam, but explores everything from basic CPU and RAM topics, to SCSI and networking hardware. The first half of this book handles device installation, troubleshooting, and more hardware-specific topics in detail.

The Operating System Technologies exam concentrates on the organization, operation, function, and troubleshooting of Windows 9*x*/Me and Windows NT/2000/XP systems, with a significant understanding of the use of command prompts with these operating systems. This exam also includes very basic network and Internet configuration questions. The second half of this book delves deeply into OS topics, covering installation, configuration, troubleshooting, and more!

A+ Certification can be your ticket to a career in IT or simply an excellent step in your certification pathway. This book is your passport to success on the A+ Certification exams.

Your Guides: Mike Meyers and Martin Acuña

You get a pair of tour guides for this book, both me and Martin Acuña. I've written numerous computer certification books—including the best-selling *All-in-One A+ Certification Exam Guide*—and written significant parts of others, such as the first edition of the *All-in-One Network+ Certification Exam Guide*. More to the point, I've been working on PCs and teaching others how to make and fix them for a *very* long time, and I love it! When I'm not lecturing or writing about PCs, I'm working on PCs or spanking my friend Scott in Half Life or Team Fortress—on the PC, naturally!

Martin Acuña is a fellow geek whom I've known for years. He's been working on the front lines of the IT world since the big-haired 1980s, doing everything from simple PC repairs and upgrades to rolling out entire networks for businesses in the industrial, retail, and non-profit arenas. By his own estimation, Martin has built roughly "eleventy kabillion" PCs, and the number keeps on growing. Martin has contributed to my *All-in-One A+ Certification Exam Guide*, and is also the author of a successful series of online MCSE certification courses, and a self-described swell guy.

Why the Travel Theme?

The steps to gaining a certification parallel closely the steps to planning and taking a trip. All of the elements are the same: preparation, an itinerary, a route; even mishaps along the way. Let me show you how it all works.

This book is divided into 19 chapters. Each chapter begins with an *Itinerary* that provides objectives covered in each chapter, and an *ETA* to give you an idea of the time involved learning the skills in that chapter. Each chapter is broken down by objectives, either those officially stated by the certifying body or our expert take on the best way to approach the topics. Portable PCs appear in several A+ competencies, for example, but work best as a single chapter. Also, each chapter contains a number of helpful items to bring out points of interest:

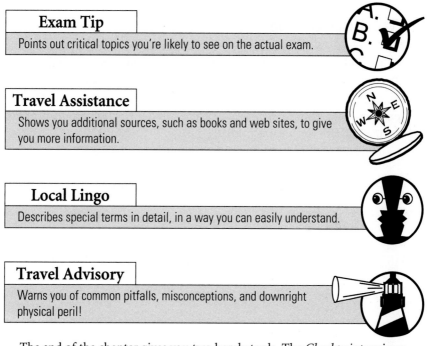

Exam Tip
Points out critical topics you're likely to see on the actual exam.

Travel Assistance
Shows you additional sources, such as books and web sites, to give you more information.

Local Lingo
Describes special terms in detail, in a way you can easily understand.

Travel Advisory
Warns you of common pitfalls, misconceptions, and downright physical peril!

The end of the chapter gives you two handy tools. The *Checkpoint* reviews each objective covered in the chapter with a handy synopsis—a great way to review quickly. Plus, you'll find end of chapter questions to test your newly acquired skills.

CHECKPOINT

But the fun doesn't stop there! After you've read the book, pull out the CD and take advantage of the free practice questions! Use the full practice exam to hone your skills and keep the book handy to check answers.

If you want even more practice, log on to http://www.osborne.com/passport, and for a nominal fee you'll get additional high-quality practice questions.

When you're acing the practice questions, you're ready to take the exam. *Go get certified*!

The End of the Trail

The IT industry changes and grows constantly, *and so should you*. Finishing one certification is just a step in an ongoing process of gaining more and more certifications to match your constantly changing and growing skills. Read the Career Flight Path at the end of the book to see where this certification fits into your personal certification goals. Remember, in the IT business, if you're not moving forward, you are way behind!

Good luck on your certification! Stay in touch!

Mike Meyers
Series Editor
Mike Meyers' Certification Passport

Core Hardware Service Technician

Ports and Connectors

	NEWBIE	SOME EXPERIENCE	EXPERT
ETA	2.5 hours	1.5 hours	1 hour

3

Mastering the craft of the PC technician requires that you learn the intricate details of numerous individual parts, connections, and settings. Even the most basic PC contains thousands of discrete hardware components, each with its own shape, size, electrical characteristics, and so on. Fortunately, it's much simpler than it seems! Computer makers have standardized many types of connections so that one connection can be used for a large number of devices. Once you recognize and know how to use a certain type of connector properly, you'll know how to use it on any type of PC.

This chapter describes the major connectors, plugs, and sockets that you'll find on a typical PC and spells out many of the amazing array of acronyms and abbreviations used by techs. The A+ Certification exams expect you to recognize a particular part simply by seeing what type of connector attaches to that part, so pay attention, folks!

Objective 1.01   Legacy Multifunction Ports

Good techs don't go around saying, "Just plug that *doohickey* into the *whatchamacallit* on the back of the PC," and you shouldn't either. These things have names, after all, so you should get into the habit of using them.

A cable has a *connector* at each end that plugs into a corresponding *port* on a PC. Connectors carry data and sometimes power between devices attached to the PC. Ports are the interfaces, the "doorways," that we use to connect devices to the PC. Connectors and ports can be either male or female, defined as having pins or having sockets.

The term "port" is one of the many that we'll see in the PC world that has more than one meaning. In addition to the sockets that are described in this chapter, ports are also *logical* interfaces used in networking, i.e., TCP/IP *port 80* corresponds to HTTP. You'll also hear the term used to describe the process of adapting a software program from one operating system to another, for example, *porting* an application from Windows to Macintosh. All of these are correct uses of the term port, but for the purposes of this chapter, we'll use it to mean the actual, physical ports on the PC that you can see and touch.

Let's start with the two ancient multifunction ports that linger on most modern PCs: serial ports and parallel ports. Most PC vendors support these *legacy* ports, although practically nobody is developing new devices that use them. Both types of ports support numerous types of devices.

Serial and parallel ports are technically known as DataBus ports, but techs usually shorten that name to *DB*. Note the *D* shape of the ports and connectors shown in the graphics that follow—this should help you remember the official term.

Serial Ports

Serial ports come in 9-pin and 25-pin varieties, as shown in Figure 1-1. Of the two, the 9-pin (five pins on the top row, four on the bottom) variety is much more common, although even those are rapidly disappearing from modern PCs.

Serial ports transfer data one *bit* (the smallest unit of data in the PC world) at a time, with a maximum throughput speed of 115 *kilobits per second* (Kbps). Devices that connect to the PC via the serial port include mice, external modems, label printers, personal digital assistants (PDAs), digital cameras, and so on.

Exam Tip
Make sure you know that serial ports transfer data one bit at a time.

All devices in a PC get assigned certain *system resources,* and serial ports are no exception. The CPU uses input/output (I/O) addresses to give commands to devices; some devices use an interrupt request (IRQ) to contact the CPU.

Travel Advisory
Chapter 10 covers these and other system resources in detail.

Most motherboards have at least one serial port—appropriately called Serial Port 1. By default, this port gets assigned the I/O address 3F8 and IRQ 4 (COM1). The rare Serial Port 2 on a PC gets I/O address 2F8 and IRQ 3 (COM2) by default.

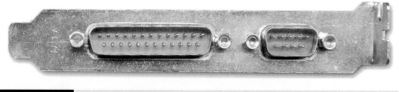

FIGURE 1.1   A 25-pin serial port and a 9-pin serial port

You can use the CMOS setup utility to change the resources assigned to devices built into the motherboard—such as serial ports. You can assign COM2 to serial port 1, for example, and COM1 to serial port 2. Further, you can enable or disable the serial port(s) in the CMOS setup utility to free up resources. Chapter 4 covers the CMOS setup utility in great detail.

Local Lingo

System setup utility   Many techs refer to the CMOS program as the *system setup utility*. The latter term happens to be more accurate as no modern PC uses a *complimentary metal-oxide semiconductor* chip to store CMOS information, but the older term has stuck. As one old tech said, looking me straight in the eye, "CMOS is CMOS, son."

Parallel Ports

Parallel ports are the 25-pin (13 on the top row, 12 on the bottom) female ports on the back of your PC, as shown in Figure 1-2. Folks often incorrectly refer to parallel ports simply as "printer ports," but many other devices use parallel ports, such as external CD-ROM drives, Zip drives, and scanners.

Parallel ports traditionally get I/O address 378 and IRQ 7 (LPT1), but as with the serial port assignments, modern motherboards give you the option of changing this setting.

Parallel ports are much more efficient than serial ports, transferring data eight bits, or one byte, at a time. Instead of a single-lane road, now you've got an eight-lane highway! Standard parallel ports have a total throughput speed of about 150,000 bytes per second, or 150 KBps.

Exam Tip

Parallel communications transfer data eight bits, or one byte, at a time.

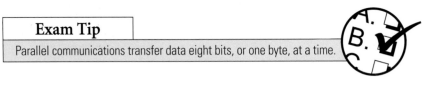

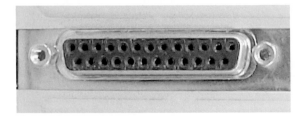

FIGURE 1.2   A 25-pin parallel port

Don't confuse a 25-pin serial port with a parallel port! Although they look very similar, 25-pin serial ports are always male, and the corresponding cable connector is always female; 25-pin parallel ports, in contrast, are always female, and parallel cable connectors are always male.

Technological advances, such as the Extended Capability Port (ECP) and the Enhanced Parallel Port (EPP) have improved throughput even further, to about ten times faster than a standard parallel port. These advances keep the parallel port from lumbering into obsolescence. See Chapter 12 for more details on parallel ports.

Objective 1.02 Standard Single-Function Ports

Every PC sports several single-function ports for connecting peripherals such as keyboards, monitors, and the like. With only a couple of exceptions, these standard ports support only a single type of device.

The Keyboard Port

Keyboards come in a variety of styles, from the plain-Jane, rectangular typewriter substitute to the exotically curved, multifunction gadget that's bristling with special function *hotkeys* and equipped with ports of its own. Regardless of their appearance, however, all keyboards enable you to do one thing—enter commands into your PC.

PCs have one of two single-function ports to accommodate a keyboard: a round, five-pin DIN—for Deutsche Industrie Norm—connector (often called an *AT-style connector*) or a six-pin mini-DIN (commonly called a *PS/2 connector*). Figure 1-3 shows the DIN and mini-DIN connectors.

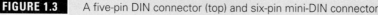
FIGURE 1.3   A five-pin DIN connector (top) and six-pin mini-DIN connector

Most PCs have a purple mini-DIN connector for the keyboard. AT-style keyboard ports are largely absent from modern computers, but you should be able to identify this kind of keyboard port. Keyboards are assigned the base I/O address of 60h ("h" designates "hexadecimal") and IRQ 1.

Keyboard connectors are always male and keyboard ports are always female, regardless of the pin type. Many keyboards come with adapters that enable you to plug a PS/2-style keyboard connector into an AT-style keyboard port, or vice versa.

The Mouse Port

Like keyboards, mice come in an array of sizes and shapes, and they use a variety of connectors to attach to the PC (see Figure 1-4). All mice enable you to manipulate the OS and applications.

Traditionally, mice plugged into one of the serial ports on the back of the PC, but most motherboards today have a dedicated mini-DIN mouse port. Aside from color, the green mouse port appears identical to the purple PS/2 keyboard port, but they're not interchangeable.

You can plug a PS/2 mouse connector into a PS/2 keyboard port, and vice versa, but they won't work. Mice go into mouse ports—keyboards go into keyboard ports.

Video Ports

Standard cathode ray tube (CRT) monitors connect to your PC using a 15-pin DB connector arranged in three rows of five pins each. The corresponding video port on the PC, as shown in Figure 1-5, accommodates only that connector. No other port on your PC looks like this one.

Exam Tip	
VGA, SVGA, and XGA monitors all have the DB connector with 15 pins in three rows.	

FIGURE 1.4   A serial mouse connector (left) and a PS/2 mouse connector

FIGURE 1.5   A female 15-pin DB connector

Many flat-panel liquid crystal display (LCD) monitors use a specially keyed, 24-pin Digital Visual Interface (DVI) connector that plugs into a DVI port on the back of your video adapter card, as shown in Figure 1-6. DVI comes in several varieties, such as analog—*DVI-A,* and digital—*DVI-D.* Chapter 9 covers monitors in more detail.

FIGURE 1.6   DVI connector for a flat-panel monitor

Local Lingo

Thin film transistor The most common LCD monitors use a technology called *thin film transistor* (TFT). Many techs erroneously refer to all LCD monitors as *TFTs*.

You might run into video cards with other connectors, such as an RG6 port that looks like a cable TV port. These types of connectors enable the PC to take an incoming cable TV or antenna signal or display the computer signal on a television screen. The RG6 port and connector both look male-oriented at first glance, but the female RG6 port has a single hole in the center that matches the single pin in the center of the male RG6 connector. Most connectors screw onto the port to secure the cable.

Audio Ports

At one time, audio was considered an extra add-on, but sound is standard issue on modern PCs. Most audio ports take the form of the popular mini-audio connectors commonly seen on the Sony Walkman or other similar gadgets. A PC typically has three color-coded sound ports: a green speaker output port, a pink microphone input port, and a blue auxiliary input port, as shown in Figure 1-7.

You will occasionally see variations, particularly on systems with high-performance sound cards. Some have separate outputs for each audio channel, or they may incorporate a special connector called a Sony/Phillips Digital Interface (S/PDIF), as shown in Figure 1-8. S/PDIF ports can be either mini-audio ports or the larger RCA-type connectors usually seen on consumer audio and video devices.

MIDI/Joystick Ports

Most PCs have an integrated female DB-15 port for connecting joysticks or other game controllers. These ports also support MIDI devices, such as a music

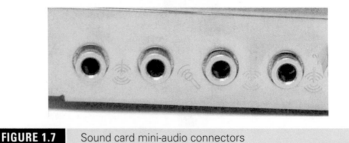

FIGURE 1.7 Sound card mini-audio connectors

FIGURE 1.8   S/PDIF connector

synthesizer keyboard, although you need a special breakout box to make the MIDI connection. Unlike DB-15 video connectors, MIDI/Joystick connectors have pins arrayed in two rows, with eight on the top and seven on the bottom, as shown in Figure 1-9.

Exam Tip
Make sure you know that the 15-pin DB connector can be used for both MIDI devices and joysticks.

Modem Ports

PC modem ports look identical to female telephone jacks and use standard, two-wire RJ-11 telephone cables and connectors (see Figure 1-10). The locking clips on the male RJ-11 connectors secure the cable into the port. Most modems also have an output port for a telephone.

FIGURE 1.9   MIDI/Joystick port

FIGURE 1.10 RJ-11 connectors on a modem

Network Interface Ports

Network interfaces come in three main varieties. Most network interface cards (NICs) have either an eight-wire RJ-45 port or a BNC port for the older coaxial cable networks, and some NICs have both types, as shown in Figure 1-11. RJ-45 connectors look like wider-than-normal RJ-11 telephone connectors and plug into the female RJ-45 ports in the same manner that RJ-11 telephone cables plug into a modem. BNC ports look very similar to an RG6 port for cable, but the cable is secured with a twist of the connector.

Local Lingo	
NIC	*Network interface cards* (NICs) enable PCs to connect to a network.

NICs that are older than ten years or so may use 15-pin Attachment Unit Interface (AUI) ports, as shown in Figure 1-12. Note that AUI ports look just like MIDI/Joystick ports, with eight pins arrayed on the top row and seven on the bottom. The two ports are not interchangeable.

Exam Tip	
Make sure you know the difference between RJ-11 connectors and RJ-45 connectors, and that you can easily tell the difference between the two at a glance.	

FIGURE 1.11 A NIC with both an RJ-45 port and a BNC port

FIGURE 1.12   NIC with AUI port

Objective 1.03   Modern Multifunction Ports

Modern PCs use one or more multifunction ports to supplement or replace the aged serial and parallel ports. All newer machines have *universal serial bus (USB)* ports; many have *IEEE 1394 (FireWire)* ports; and a few have a *small computer systems interface (SCSI)* port. All three come in at least two varieties and can be used to connect everything from printers to digital cameras.

USB

USB comes in two flavors, USB 1.1 and USB 2.0, the latter sometimes called *high-speed USB*. USB 1.1 ports transfer data at speeds up to 12 megabits per second (Mbps), making them much faster than parallel or serial communications. USB 2.0 is faster still, capable of bursts up to 480 Mbps. Note that despite the huge difference in speeds, USB 2.0 technology is fully backward-compatible with USB 1.1 devices. You can plug the latter into a 2.0 port, in other words, and they will work.

Travel Advisory
In the Spring of 2003, the USB standards committee implemented an interesting and rather annoying change to USB device and cable labeling. Because of the backward compatibility of USB 2.0 devices and controllers—they both can work with USB 1.1 devices and controllers, but run at the slower speed—the standards committee renamed all devices as USB 2.0. They distinguish between the various speeds described above as USB (~12 Mbps) and USB Hi-Speed (~480 Mbps). This name change has caused an amazing amount of confusion in the market place as you can well imagine. Be careful to recommend Hi-Speed devices and cabling if your clients want the hottest speed.

USB ports are female and rectangular-shaped. The four contact pins are mounted on a plastic protrusion that keeps you from inserting the USB cable improperly, as shown in Figure 1-13.

FIGURE 1.13   USB connectors

USB cables have two types of connectors, as shown in Figure 1-14. The rectangular *Type A* connector plugs into a USB port on your PC or hub. The square-shaped *Type B* connector plugs into the USB device.

FIGURE 1.14   USB cable with Type A and Type B connectors

Many current devices, such as keyboards, mice, joysticks, microphones, scanners, printers, modems, PDAs, digital cameras, lapwarmers, cupheaters, personal fans, lamps, and more connect to the PC via USB. Some devices even act as USB hubs with extra USB ports enabling you to connect other USB devices directly to them, such as the keyboard shown in Figure 1-15.

Travel Advisory
For more information about USB, visit http://www.usb.org/.

All Windows operating systems from Windows 95 *OEM Service Release 2 (OSR 2)* on support USB technology. Windows NT does not support USB, but Windows 2000 and Windows XP handle it very well.

Exam Tip
USB is supported by all Windows operating systems after Windows 95 OSR 2 but is not supported by the original release of Windows 95 or Windows NT.

USB devices are *hot-swappable,* which means that you can connect or disconnect them at any time without powering down your PC. USB technology enables you to connect up to 127 devices together in a series called a *daisy chain* while using only *one* IRQ address!

FIGURE 1.15   A keyboard that doubles as a USB hub

Exam Tip

Remember that you can hot-swap USB devices and daisy-chain up to 127 USB devices together.

Travel Advisory

For the purposes of the A+ Certification exams, you need to know that you can connect 127 devices together—but for real-life, on-the-job situations, it's a bad idea to hit this maximum. Some applications reserve bandwidth, and you could wind up with quite a mess. Too much of a good thing isn't good!

IEEE 1394

IEEE 1394 is an exciting communications technology created in a joint effort by Apple Computers, Texas Instruments, and the IEEE organization. The IEEE 1394 standard has been widely adopted not only by computer and peripheral makers, but also by manufacturers of home electronics such as digital video recorders.

Different manufacturers market IEEE 1394 technology under different trade names, such as *FireWire* (Apple), *iLink* (Sony), or *Lynx* (Texas Instruments), but they all refer to the same thing. Of these terms, FireWire is the most popular term among techs.

Local Lingo

FireWire, iLink, and Lynx   The terms *FireWire, iLink,* and *Lynx* all refer to the IEEE 1394 interface.

The original specification for FireWire—*1394a*—calls for data transfers of up to 400 Mbps. The current generation of FireWire—*1394b*—is capable of speeds up to a blinding 800 Mbps. What's even more impressive is that the design spec for FireWire states that speeds of up to 1600 Mbps are possible. FireWire technology is a very good match for video, external hard drives, backup storage devices, and other hardware that needs real-time data access. Like USB, FireWire is hot-swappable and supports daisy-chaining devices together.

You can connect up to 63 FireWire devices together while using only one set of I/O addresses, one IRQ, and one *direct memory access (DMA)* channel. Moreover, you can interconnect up to 1023 FireWire buses, which hypothetically means that you could connect *64,449* FireWire devices to a single PC!

FIGURE 1.16 FireWire (IEEE 1394) ports

FireWire ports are slightly taller than USB ports and are rounded on one end. The connector plugs are of course shaped to fit, as shown in Figure 1-16.

> **Travel Advisory**
>
> For more information regarding FireWire and the IEEE-1394 standard, visit http://www.ieee.org/.

SCSI

SCSI—amusingly pronounced "skuzzy"—has been around for a long time. Innovations in SCSI technology have kept SCSI competitive with other enhanced technologies such as USB and FireWire. Many higher-end PCs have built-in SCSI connectors, and SCSI controller cards are widely available to add SCSI ports to your system.

SCSI devices have a variety of interfaces—*SCSI-1, SCSI-2, Ultra SCSI, Wide Ultra SCSI,* just to name a few—but the 50-pin female SCSI-2 port shown in Figure 1-17 is the most common. You may also see 68-pin or 25-pin ports on some devices or PCs. Note that the very fine port sockets shown in the picture are matched to equally fine contact pins on the male SCSI-2 connector. Take it from me, these tiny pins bend and break easily, so handle with care!

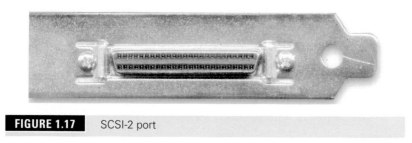

FIGURE 1.17 SCSI-2 port

Data throughput on SCSI varies from around 5 megabytes per second (MBps) for very early incarnations to 40–80 MBps for many current versions to 320 MBps and beyond for the latest and greatest implementation. Chapter 8 covers the amazing variety of SCSI devices and standards in detail.

Travel Advisory

For more information on SCSI, check out the SCSI Trade Organization at http://www.scsita.org/.

CHECKPOINT

✔**Objective 1.01: Legacy Multifunction Ports**   The 9-pin and 25-pin serial ports and the 25-pin parallel ports are used for connecting serial and parallel devices, respectively, to the PC. Serial devices transfer data one bit at a time, whereas parallel devices transfer data eight bits at a time.

✔**Objective 1.02: Standard Single-Function Ports**   Keyboards connect to the motherboard with 5-pin DIN (AT-style), 6-pin mini-DIN (PS/2), or USB connectors. Mice connect to the 9-pin serial bus in older systems; PS/2 or USB in newer systems. Make sure you remember the 15-pin, three-row DB port is for video; whereas the 15-pin, two-row port is for MIDI devices or joysticks or for the ancient AUI network connector. Finally, know the difference between the RJ-11 connectors for modems and the RJ-45 connectors for NICs.

✔**Objective 1.03: Modern Multifunction Ports**   USB enables you to hot-swap devices and daisy-chain up to 127 devices in one PC running Windows 95 OSR 2 or later. The Type A connector goes into the USB port; the Type B connector goes into the USB device. USB 1.1 (a.k.a., "normal" USB 2.0) is capable of throughput speeds up to 12 Mbps, while USB 2.0 (a.k.a., Hi-Speed USB 2.0) is good for up to 480 Mbps. IEEE 1394 is also known as FireWire, iLink, and Lynx. The 1394a version is capable of speeds up to 400 Mbps, and 1394b runs at up to 800 Mbps. Either version of IEEE 1394 enables you to connect up to 63 devices to a single IEEE 1394 port. Finally, the 50-pin ports used by SCSI-2 devices are the most common ones seen on the many SCSI technologies available today, but you might also see 68-pin, 25-pin, or other varieties.

REVIEW QUESTIONS

1. Which of these connectors can you use to connect a keyboard to a PC? (Select all that apply.)

   A. Mini-DIN

   B. 9-pin serial

   C. 25-pin parallel

   D. USB

2. Which of these connectors can you use to connect an SVGA monitor to a PC?

   A. 25-pin serial

   B. 9-pin serial

   C. 15-pin DB in two rows

   D. 15-pin DB in three rows

3. Which of the following ports can be found on network cards? (Select all that apply.)

   A. BNC

   B. RJ-45

   C. Parallel

   D. USB

4. How many pins does a parallel printer port have?

   A. 10

   B. 25

   C. 36

   D. 34

5. How is data transferred in serial communications?

   A. 10 bits at a time

   B. 1 bit at a time

   C. 1 byte at a time

   D. 16 bits at a time

6. How is data transferred in parallel communications? (Select all that apply.)

   A. 8 bits at a time

   B. 1 byte at a time

   C. 1 bit at a time

   D. 8 bytes at a time

7. If you daisy-chain 63 USB devices together, how many IRQs do you need?

   A. 63

   B. 21

   C. 1

   D. 2

8. If you try to connect a USB printer to a friend's PC, and the PC will not recognize the printer, what is most likely the problem?

   A. Your friend is using the first release of Windows 95.

   B. Your friend is using the latest version of Windows, which is incompatible with USB.

   C. The printer is out of ink.

   D. The system files on the PC are corrupted, and Windows needs to be reinstalled.

9. To what does a Type A USB connector connect?

   A. To a USB port on the PC

   B. To a USB device

   C. To a serial port on the back of your PC

   D. To a USB modem

10. What is the top data transfer speed possible under the IEEE 1394a standard?

   A. 50 megabits per second

   B. 800 megabits per second

   C. 400 megabits per second

   D. 400 megabytes per second

11. How many devices can you daisy-chain on a single FireWire connection?

   A. 65

   B. 127

   C. 63

   D. 1023

REVIEW ANSWERS

1. **A** **D**   Keyboards can use a USB or mini-DIN connector.

2. **D**   An SVGA monitor cable has a 15-pin connector in three rows.

3. **A** **B**   Network cards can have BNC ports, RJ-45 ports, or both.

4. **C**   Parallel printer port connectors have 36 pins or contacts.

5. **B**   Serial communications transfer data 1 bit at a time.

6. **A** **B**   Parallel communications transfer data 8 bits (1 byte) at a time.

7. **C**   Regardless of the number of USB devices that you daisy-chain together, you need only one IRQ—that is one of the biggest advantages of USB.

8. **A**   Out of all of the possible answers, **A** is the most likely. The first release of Windows 95 did not support USB.

9. **A**   The Type A connector on a USB cable connects to the USB ports on the back of your PC. USB devices have a Type B port.

10. **C**   The IEEE 1394a FireWire standard enables data transfers of up to 400 megabits per second.

11. **C**   You can daisy-chain up to 63 devices on a single FireWire port.

Maintenance and Safety Precautions

ETA	NEWBIE	SOME EXPERIENCE	EXPERT
	3 hours	2 hours	1 hour

There's more to keeping a PC running smoothly than launching an occasional ScanDisk or deleting some temporary Internet files. PCs are machines, and all machines need regular maintenance. This doesn't include changing the oil every 3000 miles, but it does include things like cleaning and dusting. Yes, *dusting*! Being a PC tech doesn't get you out of housework!

Further, don't be fooled by the benign appearance of a typical PC, monitor, or printer. Underneath that unassuming beige exterior lurk dozens of voltage-carrying wires and circuits. Any one of these can reach out and bite an unwary tech—sometimes with deadly effect.

Finally, you should appreciate that all PCs and PC components have a finite service life. Where do old monitors, batteries, and toner cartridges go to die?

This chapter covers the important cleaning and maintenance routines that you should follow to keep your system in optimal running condition. These routines take you into the very guts of your PC, so to prevent damage to your PC and to you, it's vital that you use the right tools and follow proper safety precautions. This chapter also goes over those precautions, and wraps up with a discussion on how to dispose of expired PC equipment properly.

Let's get started.

 Objective 2.01

Cleaning and Maintenance Procedures

To prolong the life of your PC, you must inspect and clean it regularly. Inspecting your PC alerts you to any dangerous or damaging conditions that exist, such as rust and corrosion, damaged connectors, damaged and improperly installed components, frayed cables, loose connections, and heat damage. Cleaning your PC rids it of the dirt, dust, and grime that build up from normal use. This does more than simply maintain a neat appearance; it helps to prevent two of the most damaging conditions, overheating and electrostatic discharge (ESD).

> ### Local Lingo
>
> **ESD**   *Electrostatic discharge* is a quick electrical charge that occurs when two objects with different electrical potentials come into contact with each other. More on this subject in the section "Electrostatic Discharge Precautions and Procedures" later in the chapter.

Your cleaning routine should include the PC and monitor case; the monitor screen; the keyboard and mouse; and any printers, hubs, scanners, and the like that are connected to the PC. Don't forget the inside of the PC case, the motherboard, component cards, drive devices, and power supply.

Let's look at the safest cleaning compounds and tools you can use to keep your PC looking and running its best, and then go over steps for properly cleaning and maintaining your PC, monitor, and peripherals.

Exam Tip
Make sure you know that regular cleaning of the PC will prolong the life of your components, help to prevent ESD, and help to prevent overheating.

Liquid Cleaning Compounds

Several kinds of liquid cleaners can be safely used on the PC, from plain water to specially formulated commercial compounds.

Clean or Soapy Water

Many cleaning chores require nothing more than a cloth dampened with some clean water. Common tap water is usually fine, but some local water is heavy with minerals and may leave a residue. If this is the case in your area, filtered or distilled water is a better choice.

If water alone cannot do the job, use a mild soap solution. Dish soap is best, but make certain that you dilute it thoroughly.

Denatured Alcohol

Denatured alcohol is used to clean electrical contacts and components such as the floppy disk drive heads. Make certain, however, that you never use alcohol on mechanisms such as motors or rubber drive belts. The alcohol dissolves the lubricants in motor bearings, and rubber belts may stretch or become brittle when exposed to alcohol.

Glass Cleaner

Glass cleaners such as Windex are usually safe to use on most metal and plastic surfaces on PCs. Ironically, they're not always recommended for use on a PC's glass surfaces, such as the monitor screen. Some monitor screens have special coatings that can be damaged by commercial glass cleaners. In particular, you should never use glass cleaner on an LCD display screen. You will melt the screen! Instead, use either clean water or a vinegar and water solution.

Vinegar and Water Solution

A solution of one part vinegar to four parts water is great for taking dirt, grime, and fingerprints off of surfaces such as your monitor screen, LCD screen, or scanner bed. Note that I mean plain white vinegar, not the fancier balsamic or red wine vinegar. Save those for your salads!

Fabric Softener

Some techs use a mixture of one part fabric softener to ten parts water to clean the plastic casing of their computer components. As a cleaning solution, it's not as good as mild soap and water, but as an antistatic solution it's excellent! Use it after the cleaning process to help protect your computer from the harmful effects of static electricity.

Commercial Computer Cleaning Solutions

If you want to save yourself the trouble of custom-brewing your own cleaning solution, try commercial products such as ComputerBrite or ComputerBath. These come in spray form and as premoistened towelettes (minus the lemon scent). All of these work just fine, although it's debatable if they work any better than homemade solutions. Still, if you don't want to lug a jug of white vinegar from job to job, commercial cleaners are a good alternative.

As a general rule, remember to read the labels of any commercial cleaning product before applying it to your PC. If you have any doubts about its safety, contact the manufacturer before using.

Cleaning Tools

Along with your trusty Phillips-head screwdriver and multimeter, no PC toolkit should be without the following cleaning tools: canned air, lint-free cloths, a small soft-bristled brush and swabs, and a nonstatic vacuum.

Canned Air

Canned air is used to loosen dirt and dust from delicate PC components. Canned air comes in a couple of forms: the liquid propellant kind and the kind that uses small cartridges of compressed CO_2. Both kinds can be found at computer stores, office supply stores, and camera shops.

You should follow three rules when using canned air:

- Never breath this stuff in. It's not that kind of air, and inhaling it can, quite literally, kill you!

- With the liquid propellant type of canned air, always keep the can upright. Tilting or turning the can upside down causes the liquid inside to come squirting out. This liquid causes frostbite to the tech and irreparable damage to any PC components that it touches.
- Don't shake canned air cans. They don't need to be shaken to work, and you run a small but real risk of the can exploding in your hand.

Lint-Free Cloths

Lint-free cloths like the type used for cleaning eyeglasses or cameras work well for general PC cleaning. These cloths are better than plain paper towels because they don't leave residue and won't scratch plastic surfaces. Make sure you never use "dry dusting" cleaning products in or on your computer. Products such as the Swiffer Sweeper use statically charged cloths to collect the dust. Static electricity and computers don't mix!

Brushes and Swabs

Soft-bristled brushes and lint-free swab applicators are used to clean dust and dirt from hard-to-reach areas, and to wipe grime from electrical contacts.

Some technicians use rubber pencil erasers to clean contacts; however, this is not recommended, because some erasers contain acids that can leave a residue or destroy your contacts. Plus, they may rub the metal coating completely off the contacts, so try to avoid using erasers.

Nonstatic Vacuums

Small, hand-held vacuums designed specifically for use on PCs (shown in Figure 2-1) are used to suck up dirt and dust loosened by your brush or canned air. Note that you should definitely *not* use a common household vacuum cleaner. These create static electricity and can toast your PC!

FIGURE 2.1   A nonstatic vacuum

Cleaning the Outside of the PC, Monitor, and Peripherals

This section discusses how to keep your PC dust- and dirt-free, but it's important that you understand how to protect your PC and yourself from damage before you start tugging on cables. Therefore, you should wait until you've finished this chapter before you follow any of the steps listed.

PC, Monitor, and Peripheral Covers

For everyday cleaning, wiping down the exterior of your PC, monitor, and peripherals with a lint-free cloth dampened, not soaked, with clean water should do the trick. Take care not to drip water or anything else onto or into your PC components.

If you're dealing with a buildup of grime, then use a mild soap solution. Harder cleaning chores, such as ink, crayon, and tape adhesive, should be dealt with using the vinegar and water solution mentioned earlier, denatured alcohol diluted with water, or commercial cleaners.

Use your canned air to blast dust and hair from air vents and other openings. When using canned air, remember the words of Cpl. Hicks from the *Aliens* movie, and use "short, controlled bursts." As a finishing touch, wipe down your PC and peripherals with the fabric softener and water solution. This helps prevent static, which helps keep dust buildup to a minimum.

Exam Tip
Read the label on any commercial cleaning solution before introducing it to your PC. If you have any doubts, contact the manufacturer before using.

Mouse

Use a damp cloth to clean the mouse cover, buttons, and ball. Use a swab dipped in denatured alcohol to loosen any dirt, lint, and hair wrapped around the tracking rollers. Tweezers are handy for picking the rollers clean. A quick blast of canned air is a good finishing touch.

Optical mice have no ball to clean, but they do have an optical sensor behind a recessed lens. It's important to keep this lens clean for optimal tracking. A lint-free swab dipped in denatured alcohol diluted with water does a good job.

Keyboard

Keyboards tend to accumulate the most grunge of any of your PC's components. Use canned air and a soft-bristled brush to lift out dirt, crumbs, hair, and other unmentionables from between the keys. Wipe down the exterior thoroughly with a dampened lint-free cloth. If necessary, use soapy water or one of the other cleaning solutions to remove stickier messes.

Be careful to avoid dripping cleaning liquids onto or into your keyboard. As a general rule, it's a good idea to let your keyboard air-dry for 48 hours before plugging it back into the PC.

Monitor

Before cleaning your monitor, let me emphasize again that you must make certain that your monitor is turned off and unplugged. This is life-or-death important, folks! Any CRT monitor stores enough voltage even when unplugged to zap an unwary tech with a potentially lethal jolt, so don't take any chances. It should also go without saying that you must never remove a monitor cover, but I'll say it anyway—*never remove your monitor cover*! I'll talk more about this in the section "Potential Hazards and Proper Safety Procedures" of this chapter.

Now, to clean your monitor cover, use a lint-free cloth dampened with either water or a mild soap solution. Canned air is good for removing dust from the air vents. Monitor screens sometimes take a little extra effort to remain clean and streak-free. The vinegar and water solution mentioned earlier works quite well, as do commercial cleaners. Make certain that you never spray cleaners directly onto the screen; always put the cleaner onto your lint-free cloth first.

Just a reminder: *never* use glass cleaners on LCD monitor screens. These will permanently damage the plastic coating!

Printers and Other Peripherals

Clean your printers, scanners, hubs, and any other attached peripherals as you do your PC and monitor. Use a lint-free cloth dampened with water or a mild soap solution for general upkeep. Remove stubborn dirt or grime with a vinegar and water mix or with a commercial cleaning solution. Use canned air and a soft-bristled brush to remove dirt, dust, and hair from air vents and from nooks and crannies that you can't reach with your cloth.

Travel Advisory	
Chapter 12 covers advanced printer cleaning and maintenance.	

Cleaning Contacts, Connectors, Motherboard, and Components

Once you've got the exterior of your PC and components in tip-top shape, it's time to do the same for your contacts, connectors, motherboard, and components. Before you go tugging on cables and removing the cover of your computer, make certain that you completely understand the guidelines discussed in the sections that follow for protecting your PC and yourself from electrical hazard.

Contacts and Connectors

Start by unplugging and inspecting your component cables from the back of your PC. Look for signs of dirt, rust, or corrosion on the contact pins or sockets. Believe it or not, but the main culprit in dirty contacts is you! Your skin contains natural oils, and touching the contacts while handling components leaves a small amount of oily residue on them. Given time, this residue leads to dirt and dust buildup, corrosion, and electrical interference.

The best way to protect your electrical components from becoming dirty is to avoid touching the contact pins, connectors, and sockets. If you must touch the contacts or pins, clean them immediately afterward with a lint-free swab dipped in denatured alcohol.

If there are signs of dirt on your contacts, use a lint-free swab dipped in denatured alcohol to loosen and remove it. You can also use a soft-bristled brush. If you see signs of rust or corrosion, you should replace the cable or component.

Motherboards and Components

Next, remove your PC cover to clean accumulated dust, dirt, and hair off your PC motherboard and component cards. Use canned air to loosen the dust and dirt from the delicate electrical components, and use a nonstatic vacuum to suck it up. Pay particular attention to your PC case air vents and the power supply intake and exhaust vents. Note also that dust tends to collect in the door openings of your floppy disk drive and CD-ROM drives, and inside your CPU heat sink.

Once you've cleaned the dust and dirt out, check to make sure that your component cards and cables are properly seated. Follow all of the proper precautions listed in the section "Electrostatic Discharge Precautions and Procedures" of this chapter to prevent ESD damage while working inside your PC case. When you've finished your inspection and maintenance, put the cover back on your PC and reattach your cables.

Objective 2.02   Component Protection and Storage

It's important that you know how to protect your computing environment from electrical power sags and power losses (called "brownouts" and "black-outs," respectively), power spikes, lightning strikes, and electromagnetic interference (EMI). This section discusses the causes of power disturbances and goes over protective steps. It then talks about properly storing PC components.

Brownouts

A *brownout* occurs when the supply of electricity drops dramatically but does not go out completely. During a brownout, you'll notice lights flickering or growing dim. When the power rises back up to its original level, your computer might not be able to handle the drastic change and damage may occur.

Blackouts

Blackouts occur when power is completely lost. The danger of a blackout is two-fold—first, you may have data loss or corruption when the power goes out, and second, your PC may receive electrical damage from the power surge when the electricity comes back on.

Power Spikes

Power spikes occur when the voltage on your power line rises suddenly to above-normal levels. Power spikes are extremely dangerous and can destroy PCs, monitors, and any other component plugged in to the affected power line.

Lightning

Lightning storms are an underrated hazard. Using a computer, or even leaving it plugged in during a lightning storm is asking for trouble. Keep in mind that no accessory can completely protect your PC from the damage caused by a lightning strike.

EMI

EMI is not caused by power grid fluctuations or storms, but by electrical noise created by voltage carried between power cables running near each other. EMI is also caused by excessively long power cables. The effects of EMI are power sags and surges that can lead to data loss and component damage.

> **Local Lingo**
>
> **EMI**   *Electromagnetic interference* occurs when two signals are close enough to each other to interfere with each other.

Saving Your PC from Electrical Problems

As you can see, any kind of power failure, sag, surge, or spike can cause irreversible damage to your PC and its components. Fortunately, many products on the market help you prevent this kind of damage.

Uninterruptible Power Supplies

An *uninterruptible power supply (UPS)* protects your PC from brownouts and blackouts. A UPS has built-in batteries that supply power to your PC when the electricity coming through the power line drops below a certain level. They usually have an integrated alarm that tells you when your PC is running on battery power. Many techs call a UPS a battery backup. Note that a UPS does not provide unlimited power for you to keep working while the city lights are out! A UPS gives you a short window of opportunity to save your data and shut the PC down properly.

> **Local Lingo**
>
> **Battery backup**   Uninterruptible power supplies are sometimes called *battery backups.*

UPSs come in two main varieties, *standby power systems (SPSs)* and *online UPSs.* Both of these protect your system in the event of a brownout or blackout, but they work differently and provide different levels of protection.

Standby Power Systems

An SPS actively monitors the electricity coming through the power line and begins supplying power as soon as the unit detects a sag. It takes a split second for the SPS to come online, however, and therein lies the main disadvantage. The brief lapse of time can result in data loss or damage before the SPS has kicked in.

Online UPS

An online UPS, in contrast, acts as a power source to the PC, using the electricity from the AC outlet simply to recharge its internal batteries. If you have an electrical brownout or blackout, your PC doesn't even flinch! Of course, as mentioned earlier, you don't have a tremendous amount of time to work while on batteries, but you certainly have a safe window to save your work and shut down properly before the UPS runs out of juice.

As an added bonus, most online UPS boxes act as power conditioners. That is, they regulate the flow of electricity to your PC to even out any fluctuations you might experience from your power line. An online UPS costs more than an SPS, but in the long run its benefits justify the expense.

Exam Tip
Don't plug a laser printer into a UPS. Printing draws massive amounts of electricity; it may interfere with the function of the UPS and prevent you from shutting down safely.

Surge Suppressors

Surge suppressors help to absorb power surges so that your computer does not feel their effects. They either come as separate modules or are integrated into the UPS. Good surge suppressors come with long-term or lifetime guarantees against damage to your PC. Avoid purchasing or using cheap surge suppressors. These are usually little more than power strips and provide virtually no protection against power spikes.

Unplug Your PC

Even if you have any or all of the layers of protection listed in the preceding sections, the only sure protection against severe threats such as lightning is to completely shut down and unplug your PC and peripherals. Leave no stone unturned: make sure that you unplug even your modem, because lightning can travel up the telephone line to give your system a shock. (I've seen it happen, folks!)

Exam Tip
Make sure you know that in the event of an electrical storm, the only way to protect your system is to completely unplug it, plus all peripherals with external power cords.

EMI Noise Filters

EMI can be controlled by using cables with a Mylar coating and through the use of special EMI noise filters. Noise filters can be purchased as stand-alone products or are sometimes integrated into an uninterruptible power supply.

As you can see, power fluctuations can wreak havoc on an unprotected PC, and not just in the obvious ways. Surges and sags can damage power supplies and components, and cause file corruption. The cost of a good UPS or surge suppressor is nothing compared to the cost in time and money caused by lost components or corrupted files that you may have to endure if you don't use either one.

Storing Components for Future Use

If you plan on storing computer components for future use, you still need to protect them from ESD, corrosion, and other damage.

Storage Environment

Even when your PC is not in use, heat, moisture, and dirt are still hazards. Heat causes plastics to fade and become brittle, moisture encourages rust and corrosion, and dirt is, well, *dirty.* For these reasons, PC components and peripherals should be stored indoors in a climate-controlled environment.

Electrical Precautions

It's important to take precautions to prevent electrical damage when storing PCs and components. Always store PC equipment away from high-voltage devices, and never store batteries of any kind for long periods of time. Old batteries leak or corrode, so if you are not planning on reusing them during their recommended lifetime, discard them and purchase new ones as needed.

The safest way to store your components for future use and to protect them from ESD is to put them in antistatic bags (discussed in the section "Electrostatic Discharge Precautions and Procedures"). For the ultimate in component safety, store the components in their manufacturers' original boxes and packaging. That should be encouraging news to the packrats among you!

Exam Tip	
Make sure you know that the safest way to store components for future use is in their original packaging or in an antistatic bag.	

Moisture

Moisture and PCs don't mix. It's important that you control moisture to keep rust and corrosion at bay and ensure that your components are still functional when you return them to service. The best thing to use is *silica-gel* packets, available from electronics stores and shipping supply companies. Place one or more small packets inside your component antistatic bags and inside your PC case.

Heed the manufacturers' warnings when using this stuff! It is poisonous, so don't eat it and don't get any in your eyes.

Objective 2.03   Electrostatic Discharge Precautions and Procedures

This chapter has mentioned the dangers of ESD numerous times. Now it's time for some details. ESD is one of the main enemies of your computer. To maintain your computer and to prolong the life of components, you need to learn about the effects of ESD and how to protect your computer from those effects.

What ESD Can Do

A prime example of ESD is the small shock you receive when you walk across a carpeted floor and then touch a metal doorknob. Zap! The small discharge doesn't do you any lasting damage, but such a seemingly harmless shock will destroy computer components. In fact, even discharges well below the level that you can feel will still damage or destroy PC components.

Types of ESD

ESD is caused by different conditions and factors. The cause of ESD is directly tied to the type of damage that is caused to the PC and components. ESD may cause *catastrophic* damage or gradual ESD *degradation.*

Catastrophic ESD Damage

Catastrophic ESD causes a computer component to fail immediately. When catastrophic ESD occurs, it will be obvious to you because, in all likelihood, you will be the one who caused it! Picture the scenario described a couple of paragraphs ago with you walking across a carpeted floor. Only this time, in place of the doorknob, picture an expensive RAID controller, video card, or hard disk full of vital data. Are you concerned yet?

ESD Degradation

ESD degradation occurs when the effects of ESD are cumulative. This is caused by situations where low levels of ESD occur repeatedly. Damage caused by ESD degradation is not immediately apparent in full force; instead, the effects gradually get more and more noticeable.

ESD degradation will cause your components to behave erratically and can make the original problem hard to recognize. This condition can eventually affect your other system components and cause them to fail also.

Exam Tip

Make sure that you understand what ESD is, how it can damage your PC, and how to protect against it.

Common ESD Protection Devices

ESD protection devices help to ensure a longer and more productive life for your PC components. These devices include antistatic wrist and ankle straps, antistatic mats, antistatic floor mats, antistatic bags, and antistatic sprays. Antistatic devices work by evening out the differences between your body's electrical potential and the electrical potential of your PC or PC component.

Local Lingo

Electrical potential   Everything has a certain *electrical potential*, or how charged it is relative to the *zero ground* of the Earth. Note the term *relative*. If your body has a +3000 volt charge and you touch a component that also has a +3000 volt charge (working in the International Space Station, perhaps?), no damage will occur. As far as you and the component are concerned, you're at the same electrical potential. Touch a component that has a –3000 volt charge, on the other hand, and watch the sparks fly!

One of the most important steps you can take to prevent the effects of ESD is grounding yourself before you handle PC components. Do this by touching a metal surface such as the exterior of the PC power supply before touching any of your system components.

Antistatic Wrist and Ankle Straps

Antistatic wrist and ankle straps, fondly called "nerd bracelets" by many techs, keep you at the same relative electrical ground level as the computer components on which you're working.

Antistatic straps wrap around your wrist or ankle with an elastic strap attached to a long grounding wire. On some models, the grounding wire attaches to a metal clip that you attach to a metal device in order to ground yourself. Figure 2-2 shows an antistatic wrist strap grounded to a computer chassis. Others have a prong that you plug into the ground wire of an electrical wall outlet.

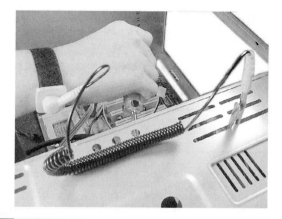

FIGURE 2.2   An antistatic wrist strap grounded to a computer

---

Exam Tip

Antistatic wrist and ankle straps use a one-megohm resistor that is suitable for protection only against very low level static electricity. They are unsuitable as protection against high voltage and can even make high-voltage situations more dangerous! Make sure that you always remove your antistatic strap before working on or near high-voltage components.

By the way, don't forget to remove your antistatic strap before walking away from your work area! Or if you forget frequently, try to leave a camcorder running so you'll have something funny to show at your next family reunion.

Antistatic Mats

Portable antistatic mats provide a work surface that dissipates ESD. They look very much like large place mats or those baby-changing mats that come with diaper bags. The thing that distinguishes them is that they have a small metal clip that you can attach an antistatic strap to in order to ground out ESD.

In addition to helping prevent ESD, these mats help keep your work area organized by giving you a place to put your tools and components while you work.

Antistatic Floor Mats

Antistatic floor mats are basically the same as portable antistatic mats, except much larger. Instead of placing them on top of your work area, you place your work area on top of the antistatic floor mat.

Antistatic Bags

Antistatic bags have a special coating or contain small filaments that help dissipate any static charge. Always store PC cards and peripherals components in antistatic bags when not in use and when transporting them—even if you're just going down the hall or across the room. Note that regular plastic or paper bags will *not* protect your components. In fact, plastic baggies conduct static electricity rather than preventing it, so don't use them!

Antistatic Spray

Special antistatic sprays dissipate static charges built up in your clothing. Commonly used to prevent unsightly static "cling," they are also good to use before you start working on PCs. Some folks also use these sprays to try to protect their work areas from the effects of ESD, but this is not an effective or recommended procedure. Never use these sprays directly on your components!

Fabric Softener Solution

As mentioned in the section "Cleaning and Maintenance Procedures" of this chapter, a mixture of one part fabric softener to ten parts water helps prevent static electricity from building up on your PC and monitor case. It won't protect against ESD, however, so always follow the proper precautions to ensure the life of your PC.

Travel Assistance

To learn more about ESD, be sure to visit http://www.ce-mag.com/esdhelp.html.

Objective 2.04

Potential Hazards and Proper Safety Procedures

While certain power issues can cause damage to your PC, it's even more important to remember that many hazards can injure you, the PC technician. Not least among these are high-voltage shocks and electrical fires. You need to make yourself aware of these hazards and of ways to prevent them from happening.

Potentially Dangerous or Hazardous ESD Situations

To maintain a safe work environment for yourself and your PC, it's important to consider that many conditions affect your level of ESD safety. Environmental conditions ranging from the weather around you to the clothes you wear can affect your ESD hazard level and how ESD manifests around you.

Weather Conditions

Good techs keep up with weather conditions. Believe it or not, but the temperature and humidity level *outside* can dramatically affect the risk of ESD *inside*. If the weather is cold and dry, the potential for a PC-killing zap is greatly increased. Take extra precautions to prevent ESD when the weather calls for it.

Clothing

Good techs don't just dress for success, but for safety too. Different fabrics have different electrical potentials. Natural fiber clothing, such as cotton or linen, is the best kind to wear when working on computers. The exception to this is silk, which is a good conductor of static electricity, making it a poor choice for wearing while working on PCs.

Synthetic fabrics have a tendency to *produce* static electricity, and you should avoid wearing them. If you needed an excuse to give the double-knit polyester leisure suit to charity, now you have one!

Shoes with rubber soles are the best to wear while working on PCs.

Hair

Long hair is another concern when working around computers, not just because of ESD, but because it can get tangled in any of the many sharp edges and protrusions on a typical PC. Tie long hair back and out of the way before working on a PC. You might also wish to use antistatic smoothing lotions. Hairspray can also help to prevent hair static to a certain extent.

Jewelry

Rings, bracelets, necklaces, watches, and other metal adornments can short out devices if touched on the wrong part of your PC. They can also scratch (or be scratched) by scraping against the PCs surfaces. Remember to remove jewelry and watches before working on or inside of your PC. Just remember to put your wedding ring back on before you head home to the spouse!

High-Voltage Equipment

The capacitors in PC power supplies, monitors, and laser printers carry very high voltages that can cause severe injury or death. Fortunately, high-voltage equipment is usually easy to identify because it is marked by a bright yellow warning sticker. Watch for these labels and heed them!

Further, anytime you work with a piece of high-voltage equipment, make sure the device is unplugged and that you have removed your antistatic wrist strap.

Power Supplies

In the old days, the conventional thinking was that you should leave the PC plugged in while working inside it to ensure electrical grounding. The opposite is true for modern PCs, because modern motherboards always have a small amount of voltage running anytime the PC is plugged in. Therefore, you should completely unplug the PC before servicing or you'll likely toast something!

Even unplugging PC power supplies does not make them safe enough to work on. The capacitors inside can hold a lethal charge even when unplugged, making them extremely risky to open. As the label says, "There are no user serviceable parts inside." With that in mind, the safest method of repairing power supplies is not to repair them at all. Better to dispose of them properly (as discussed in the section "Special Disposal Procedures and Environmental Protection Guidelines" of this chapter) and install a brand new power supply.

Exam Tip
As electricians will tell you, it's amperage (the amount of electricity) that's dangerous, not voltage. Power supplies have relatively low voltages, but high amperage. It's not worth the risk to attempt to service a power supply.

Monitors

Let's keep this section short and to the point—*never* open the case of a PC monitor! As with power supplies, they are not designed to be serviced by field PC techs. Damaged or malfunctioning monitors should be returned to the manufacturer for servicing or disposed of properly.

Fires

Thankfully, the risk of fire occurring inside your PC is relatively low. If, however, you do experience a computer fire, or any electrical fire for that matter, never try to extinguish it with water. This can cause the electrical current to travel up and straight into you! Instead, use a fire extinguisher certified for fighting electrical fires. These are type C and type ABC fire extinguishers.

> ### Exam Tip
> Make sure that you know that you need to use a type C or type ABC fire extinguisher to put out a fire in a computer.

Special Disposal Procedures and Environmental Protection Guidelines

Objective 2.05

Many computer components, such as batteries, CRTs, chemical solvents, and toner kits, contain harmful ingredients. Don't just throw these items in the garbage, as this is wasteful and possibly illegal. Many of these items can be recycled. If that's not an option, then you need to make sure that you dispose of them in accordance with environmental protection guidelines.

Remember that different cities and counties have different requirements for safe disposal of materials like PC components. Always check with the appropriate authorities before tossing that old 286 on the curb! Look in the government pages in your local telephone book, or your city's official web site for more information.

> ### Exam Tip
> Make sure you know the proper disposal procedures for each of the following items prior to taking the exam.

Batteries

Batteries often contain lithium, mercury, nickel-cadmium, and other hazardous materials. If they are thrown in the garbage and carried off to a landfill, they will contaminate the water and soil. Take batteries to a recycling center or send them back to the manufacturer. Most batteries have disposal instructions printed on them. Familiarize yourself with these instructions and follow them.

CRTs

Many CRT monitors contain lead. Lead is quite poisonous, so CRTs must be disposed of properly to avoid contamination. To dispose of nonfunctional CRTs, send them to a commercial recycler or contact your city's hazardous waste management department. They will give you the proper procedure for disposing of them.

Toner and Inkjet Cartridges

There are a couple of ways of dealing with depleted toner and inkjet cartridges. You can refill them yourself, which saves on environmental wear but can wreak havoc on your printer if not done properly. You can also check your yellow pages to see if commercial toner recyclers service your area. Alternatively, many toner cartridge manufacturers have a recycling program. Check with your vendor and see if this is an option for you.

Chemical Solvents and Cans

Chemical solvents or canned products for PC use (such as canned air mentioned earlier) contain harmful chemicals that should not be let loose in the environment. Instead, dispose of these through your city's hazardous waste program.

Material Safety Data Sheet

If you have any doubts or questions about how to handle and dispose of chemicals or compounds, remember that these come with a *material safety data sheet (MSDS)*. The MSDS documents any safety warnings about the product, safe methods of transportation, and safe disposal requirements. If an item comes without an MSDS, you can obtain one from the manufacturer or you can locate one on the Internet.

Travel Assistance
For more information about MSDSs, or to search for an MSDS, visit http://www.msdssearch.com/.

CHECKPOINT

✔**Objective 2.01: Cleaning and Maintenance Procedures**   You should regularly inspect and clean your PC and peripherals. Plain water or a solution of mild soap and water does a great job of cleaning most PC surfaces. Canned air, nonstatic vacuums, and soft-bristled brushes help maintain a clean PC. Electrical contacts get dirty from the oily residue from your fingers, so you should exercise care in handling components. Denatured alcohol is the best solution to use for cleaning drive heads and contacts.

✔**Objective 2.02: Component Protection and Storage**   A UPS protects your system against power sags, and a surge suppressor protects your system from power surges. Noise filters help prevent electromagnetic interference (EMI). In the event of a lightning storm, make sure you completely unplug the PC and any peripherals with external power cords. When storing components for future use, make sure to store them in a cool, dry place in antistatic bags or in their original packaging.

✔**Objective 2.03: Electrostatic Discharge Precautions and Procedures**   To help protect your system from the effects of ESD, always use an antistatic wrist strap or ankle strap unless working around high-voltage devices such as power supplies and CRTs. Antistatic mats, floor mats, and sprays can protect your work area.

✔**Objective 2.04: Potential Hazards and Proper Safety Procedures**   The capacitors in PC power supplies, monitors, and laser printers carry very high voltages that can cause severe bodily injuries. Don't touch them! This is especially true for CRT monitors, which carry *deadly* levels of electricity even after being unplugged.

✔**Objective 2.05: Special Disposal Procedures and Environmental Guidelines**   Batteries contain nasty chemicals, CRTs contain lead, and even seemingly innocuous toner cartridges have environmentally unfriendly chemicals. Always be sure to recycle batteries, monitors, and toner cartridges, or have them picked up as hazardous waste.

REVIEW QUESTIONS

1. What should you use to clean a mouse ball? (Select all that apply.)

   A. Glass cleaner

   B. Mild soapy water and a damp cloth

   C. Denatured alcohol

   D. Pencil erasers

2. After wiping down your keyboard with a mild cleaning solution, what should you do?

   A. Use canned air to dry it out.

   B. Use antistatic spray to give it a protective coating.

   C. Use a pencil eraser to clean the contact pins.

   D. Let it air-dry for 48 hours.

3. Which of the following products will do the best job of completely removing the dust from your computer? (Select all that apply.)

   A. Lint-free cloths

   B. Canned air

   C. Nonstatic vacuums

   D. Paint brushes

4. What type of fire extinguisher should you use to put out a PC fire?

   A. Type A

   B. Type B

   C. Type C

   D. Type D

5. When should you always remove your antistatic wrist strap?

   A. When working around high-voltage devices such as power supplies and CRTs

   B. When cleaning your PC

   C. When changing a toner cartridge in your printer

   D. You should never remove your antistatic wrist strap

6. If you use an antistatic wrist strap with a prong, where do you attach the prong?

   A. To the grounding wire of a wall outlet

   B. In the slot of a wall outlet

C. In a special hole that is incorporated into every PC case

D. Into the back of the power supply

7. If you do not receive an MSDS with a product, where can you obtain one? (Select all that apply.)

   A. The Internet

   B. The outside of the box the product came in

   C. The manufacturer

   D. Any good technical book

8. Which of the following should you avoid using on LCD displays?

   A. Distilled water

   B. Commercial glass cleaners

   C. Mild soap solution

   D. Vinegar and water solution

9. What are two proper ways to dispose of CRTs?

   A. Throw them in the garbage.

   B. Recycle them.

   C. Have them picked up by a hazardous waste program.

   D. There is no proper way to dispose of a CRT.

10. What should the conditions be like in the area where you store computer components? (Select all that apply.)

   A. Cool

   B. Warm

   C. Humid

   D. Dry

11. What weather conditions are most likely to be associated with ESD? (Select all that apply.)

   A. When it is cold

   B. When it is dry

   C. When it is hot

   D. When it is humid

12. How can you protect your PC in the event of a lightning storm?

   A. With a UPS

   B. With a suppressor

   C. By unplugging the PC and all of its components

   D. By turning off the PC

REVIEW ANSWERS

1. **B** You can clean a mouse ball with mild soapy water on a damp cloth. Make sure the mouse ball is dry before you put it back in the mouse.

2. **D** Let the keyboard air-dry for 48 hours before plugging it back into the computer.

3. **B C** Canned air loosens dirt and dust. Nonstatic vacuums remove the dust from your system.

4. **C** You would use a type C fire extinguisher to put out a PC or other electrical fire. If a choice on the exam is a type ABC, that type of fire extinguisher can be used also.

5. **A** You should always remove your antistatic wrist strap when working around CRTs and power supplies. The wrist strap provides a connection from the PC to your body, and wearing a wrist strap while working on either of these components could cause your body to absorb extremely high electrical charges, which could harm or kill you.

6. **A** If you are using an antistatic wrist strap with a prong, the prong should be attached in the wire ground of a wall outlet. The wire ground is the round hole—*never* place the prong in one of the slots, because they contain electricity.

7. **A C** If you do not receive an MSDS with a product, you can obtain one from the manufacturer or you can find one on the Internet. Technical books won't have MSDS information, and you won't find it on the outside of the box.

8. **B** Commercial glass cleaners such as Windex will melt LCD display screens. Use plain or mildly soapy water, or a vinegar and water solution to clean LCDs.

9. **B C** The proper way to dispose of CRTs is to either recycle them or have them picked up by a hazardous waste program. CRTs often contain lead, so you can't throw them in a landfill because they could contaminate the water supply.

10. **A D** The area where you store computer components should kept cool and dry. PC components do not like extreme heat, and condensation could cause corrosion.

11. **A B** ESD is most likely to occur when it is cold and dry.

12. **C** The only way to protect your system in the event of an electrical storm is to unplug it and all of its components. Simply turning off the machine or using a suppressor will not fully protect your system.

Motherboards, Power Supplies, and Cases

CHAPTER 3

	NEWBIE	SOME EXPERIENCE	EXPERT
ETA	5 hours	3 hours	2 hours

At the heart of all personal computers live certain core components. The *motherboard* provides the framework upon which every other component builds. The *power supply* provides current to feed the hungry motherboard and components and makes everything chug along happily. The PC case holds it all together. Don't think that all PC cases are created equal, however, as subtle differences between identical-looking cases can influence how difficult it is to upgrade and service the PC. Every good tech needs to understand these basic ingredients of the PC, including their common variants. Ready?

Objective 3.01 PC Motherboards

Every device in your computer system connects either directly or indirectly to the motherboard. Technicians often refer to the motherboard as the *system board*. Both terms are interchangeable, and questions on the A+ exam may be worded either way. You may also hear techs shorten the term *motherboard* to *mobo*.

> **Local Lingo**
>
> **System board**   Many PC techs call motherboards *system boards* or *mobos*.

Motherboards come in a variety of shapes and sizes, standardized into configurations called *form factors*. Regardless of their form factor, all motherboards have integrated sockets and connectors that enable you to plug in essentials such as the CPU, RAM, mass storage devices, component cards, and peripheral devices. This section examines common motherboard configurations and connections.

Motherboard Form Factors

Numerous form factors have come and gone, but the ones that dominate the PC world are AT (Advanced Technology) and ATX (AT Extended). Of these two standard form factors, ATX has all but completely supplanted AT on newer systems, but many servers and workstations currently chugging away out there still use the older AT form factor.

These form factors define the motherboard's size, its orientation, the location of built-in sockets and expansion slots, and so on. The motherboard's form factor is also directly tied to the type of power supply and case your PC uses. The two form factors are not interchangeable. That means that AT motherboards fit into AT cases and use AT power supplies, and ATX motherboards fit into ATX cases and use ATX power supplies. And never the twain shall meet.

AT

AT motherboards, which have been around since 1984, come in two variations: *Full AT* and *Baby AT*. Full AT motherboards range in size from approximately 9 × 13 inches to gargantuan models that could easily double as serving trays. Baby AT motherboards, as the name suggests, are scaled-down versions of Full AT motherboards designed to fit into smaller desktop PC cases. On either Full AT or Baby AT motherboards, the important connectors, mounting screw holes, and sockets are oriented identically. Baby AT motherboards can fit easily into Full AT cases, but the opposite is usually not true.

The only integrated port on an AT motherboard is a single DIN connector for the keyboard, located on the rear edge near the top. All other ports and peripheral devices hook up to the motherboard via *dongles* (special adapters that mount in an empty case slot opening) that plug into connectors on the motherboard called *headers*. Component cards for things such as sound and video plug in through integrated *expansion bus* sockets, which are described at the end of this section. Figure 3-1 shows a Baby AT motherboard.

Exam Tip
Few vendors still make AT motherboards today, but many systems humming away in offices and homes use them, so it's important for you to recognize this form factor and know its requirements.

ATX

ATX motherboards, shown in Figure 3-2, were introduced in 1996 and are approximately the same size as the Baby AT motherboard. Two visual cues can help you quickly distinguish between AT and ATX motherboards: the type of keyboard connector, and the number of integrated ports. ATX motherboards use mini-DIN (PS/2) connectors for the keyboard and mouse, and most have integrated serial, parallel, and USB ports. Many also feature onboard modem and NIC ports, MIDI/joystick ports, FireWire ports, sound, and video.

Two popular variations of the ATX form factor are *Micro ATX* and *Flex ATX*. These use the same power connections and have the same basic layout as ATX but are scaled to fit into much smaller ATX PC cases. Full-sized ATX motherboards will not fit into Micro ATX or Flex ATX cases.

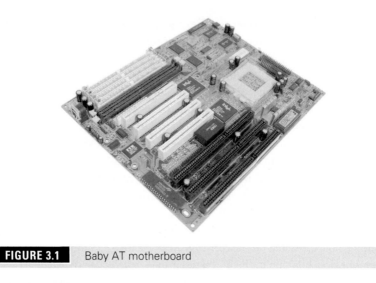

FIGURE 3.1 Baby AT motherboard

Motherboard Connectors and Ports

All motherboards have built-in sockets for vital PC components such as the RAM, CPU, and mass storage devices.

RAM Sockets

Modern motherboards typically have anywhere from one to four thin slots to accommodate the system RAM. The most common type of RAM supported nowadays is 184-pin *double data rate synchronous dynamic RAM (DDR SDRAM)*.

FIGURE 3.2 ATX motherboard

Sockets for the older 168-pin *dual inline memory module (DIMM)* RAM are also still common. Both types are usually black in color and have large white plastic retention clips on either end. The sockets for 72-pin *single inline memory module (SIMM)* RAM are white with small metal clips to hold in the RAM stick. By and large, SIMM RAM has been phased out, but you'll still see this type of memory on older systems, and many motherboards have sockets for both types of RAM (Figure 3-3). Newer motherboards designed for the Pentium 4 processors use *Rambus inline memory module (RIMM)* sockets. These are very similar to DIMM sockets, but they are keyed differently to prevent you from mistakenly inserting the wrong type of RAM into them.

Portable computers use two different types of reduced-size RAM sticks called *small outline DIMM (SO DIMM)* and *MicroDIMM*. Chapter 6 in this book goes into much greater detail about RAM, and Chapter 11 covers issues related to portables.

CPU Sockets

The CPU socket on an AT motherboard is located near the front edge of the board. The ATX motherboard layout is rotated 90 degrees compared to the AT, with the processor sitting near the top edge of the board. CPU sockets vary in appearance, depending on the type of processor that they support. Zero insertion force (ZIF) sockets are square and have a retention lever on one edge, as shown in Figure 3-4. Single edge contact (SEC) sockets are long and thin, similar in appearance to RAM sockets, as shown in Figure 3-5.

Many motherboards support two or more CPUs. Motherboards of this type are called *multiprocessor* motherboards. Chapter 5 of this book is devoted to CPUs.

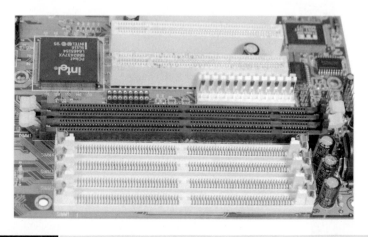

FIGURE 3.3   SIMM and DIMM RAM sockets

FIGURE 3.4   Zero insertion force (ZIF) CPU socket

FIGURE 3.5   Single edge contact (SEC) CPU socket

External Cache Memory

CPUs use Level 2 (L2) cache memory to store frequently accessed commands and data. Current CPUs have L2 cache incorporated into the microprocessor package, or *die,* but earlier systems had L2 cache on the motherboard. Some pre-Pentium systems enabled you to add L2 cache in slots on the motherboard; early Pentium systems generally had the cache soldered directly on the motherboard.

Support for Mass Storage Devices

In the old days before integrated motherboards, you had to install a controller card into an expansion slot to support mass storage drives. This hasn't been the case for years, however, and all current motherboards have built-in connectors and support for mass storage devices such as hard drives, CD and DVD media drives, and tape backup drives. Chapter 7 of this book gives the full scoop on mass storage devices, but the important connector sockets are described in the sections that follow.

IDE and EIDE

Integrated Drive Electronics (IDE) is the older implementation of modern Enhanced IDE (EIDE) technology for controlling mass storage devices. These controller sockets are also called AT Attachment (ATA) and ATA-2, respectively, though most techs simply call them "IDE" sockets. IDE controller sockets are rectangular in shape with two rows of 20 pins each. Modern motherboards have two IDE controller sockets, one designated as the Primary channel, and the other as the Secondary channel. Their color is either brown, white, or blue. Chapter 7 goes into more detail about IDE devices.

Serial ATA

Serial ATA (SATA) is the latest evolution of ATA technology. The main advantage of SATA mass storage devices is that they use a thin four-pin socket as opposed to the somewhat bulky forty-pin socket of the older IDE devices. Appropriately, they use a much thinner controller cable to connect the device to the motherboard, which increases airflow efficiency within the PC case.

SCSI

Although some high-end motherboards come with built-in support for SCSI drives and devices, for the most part, you need to install a SCSI controller card to get SCSI support. Chapter 8 goes into detail about SCSI technology.

The PC Expansion Bus

In the PC world, a *bus* is a pathway on the motherboard that enables components to communicate with the CPU. Common buses include Industry Standard Architecture (ISA), Peripheral Component Interconnect (PCI), Accelerated Graphics Port (AGP), USB, and FireWire. Collectively, these are referred to as the motherboard's *expansion bus.*

Component cards such as video and audio cards, and expansion cards such as SCSI, USB, and FireWire adapters, plug into the appropriate expansion bus slots to add functionality to the PC. Although completely integrated into the motherboard architecture, the different expansion buses operate at a different speed from the rest of the motherboard, as described in the sections that follow.

ISA

The ISA I/O bus was introduced with the first mainstream PC, the vaunted IBM PC (built around the Intel 8088 CPU). The initial ISA bus transferred data eight bits at a time and offered IRQs 0–7. Sixteen-bit ISA came out in 1984 and ran at 8.3 MHz, supporting IRQs 0–15; 16-bit ISA slots were backward-compatible with 8-bit ISA components.

Local Lingo
8088   The first mainstream PC was simply called the IBM PC, but most techs fondly call it the *8088*, in reference to the Intel CPU that it came with.

Figure 3-6 shows a motherboard with both 8-bit and 16-bit ISA slots. As you can see, they're very similar in appearance except for their respective lengths.

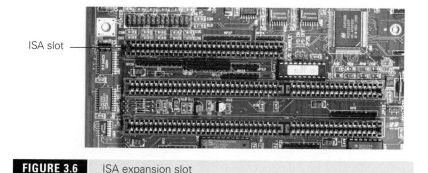

ISA slot

FIGURE 3.6 ISA expansion slot

Exam Tip

16-bit ISA slots support the use of either 8-bit or 16-bit ISA cards. Current PCs do not have ISA slots, but millions of PCs that you might be called upon to service certainly do. A+ Certified techs, therefore, know ISA.

PCI

The 32-bit PCI bus runs at half the speed of the processor (up to 33 MHz). At the time PCI was introduced in 1993, this bus was an excellent choice for graphics and video, but it has since been surpassed by other technologies. The PCI bus automatically configures PCI cards, which means the end of messing with manual configuration of IRQs and other resources. The small, white PCI slots shown in Figure 3-7 accept PCI cards.

AGP

The AGP bus was designed specifically for video and supports only video adapters. A subset of PCI, AGP provides a direct connection between the processor and the video card. Also like PCI, AGP is completely *plug and play* compatible.

AGP comes in 32-bit and 64-bit bus widths. The 32-bit–wide AGP bus operates at the speed of the processor's memory bus (up to 66 MHz), making it perfect for 3-D graphics. 32-bit AGP 4x can move data at blazing 1.07 megabytes per second using the maximum transfer rate formula. 64-bit 4x moves data at almost twice that speed, maxing out at 2.1 megabytes per second, and 64-bit AGP 8x handles speeds up to an amazing 4.2 megabytes per second!

AGP slots are brown and similar in size to PCI slots, as shown in Figure 3-8. However, AGP and PCI cards cannot use the same slots, and they are configured

FIGURE 3.7 PCI expansion slots

in such a way as to prevent an unwary tech from mistakenly plugging the wrong type of card into the socket.

Exam Tip

The most common bus architectures that you will see on modern computers are the ISA, PCI, and AGP.

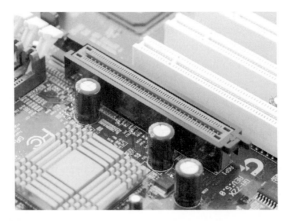

FIGURE 3.8 AGP expansion slot

USB

USB differs from the buses discussed so far in that it is an external bus that works with the PCI internal bus. Practically all ATX motherboards have built-in USB ports, or you can install an expansion card that offers the ports.

FireWire

Like USB, FireWire (IEEE 1394) is considered an external bus, but built-in support for FireWire has become more common on modern PC motherboards. Also like USB, FireWire readily permits expansion cards to be installed to add external FireWire ports to systems that don't have it. Many of these expansion cards have an additional FireWire port mounted internally, enabling you to connect FireWire mass storage devices that install inside the PC case just like regular IDE or SCSI devices.

> **Travel Advisory**
>
> Chapter 9 goes into greater detail about the functions of the PC expansion bus.

Objective 3.02 **PC Power Supplies**

The PC's power supply converts high-voltage alternating current, or AC, power into the lower-voltage direct current, or DC, power that your motherboard and disk drives need. Its internal fan also provides essential cooling for the PC components and drives.

Like motherboards, power supplies are designed for either AT or ATX motherboards and cases. The two different types are not pin-compatible or interchangeable, even if they are rated for the same wattage. That is, you cannot connect an AT-styled power supply to an ATX motherboard, or vice versa.

At first glance, the mass of multicolored wires exploding out the back end of a power supply can be intimidating. Take a closer look, however, and you'll see that for all the myriad bundles of wires, there are only a few types of connectors. All power supplies have at least these three types of power connectors: motherboard power connectors, *Molex* connectors, and *mini* connectors.

Motherboard Power

Everything on your motherboard needs electrical power to run. Power supplies use specialized connections to the motherboard to provide DC electricity to feed the needs of the various devices. As mentioned earlier, the two different motherboard form factors require different connectors, as described in the sections that follow.

AT Power Connectors

AT form factor power supplies use a pair of connectors—called P8 and P9—to provide juice to the AT motherboard. Each of these connectors has a row of teeth along one side and a small guide on the opposite side that help hold the connection in place, as shown in Figure 3-9.

Figure 3-10 shows the AT power plug on the motherboard.

P8 and P9 power connectors are *faced* (that is, they have a front and a back), so you cannot install them backward. Sometimes the small keys on P8 and P9 require that you angle the connectors in before snapping them down all the way. Figure 3-11 shows a technician angling in the P8 and P9 connectors.

Although you cannot plug P8 and P9 in backward, you certainly can reverse them by putting P8 where P9 should go, and vice versa. When connecting P8 and P9 to the motherboard, always keep the black ground wires next to each other. All AT motherboards and power supplies follow this rule. Be careful—incorrectly inserting P8 and P9 can damage both the power supply and other

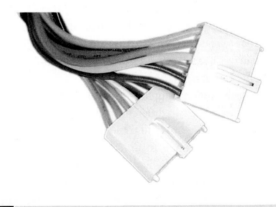

FIGURE 3.9   P8 and P9 connectors

FIGURE 3.10 A standard P8 and P9 connection

components in the PC. Figure 3-12 shows properly inserted P8 and P9 connectors.

Exam Tip

Remember the phrase "black to black" to help you remember to keep the black ground wires of the P8 and P9 connectors together.

FIGURE 3.11 Technician installing P8 and P9 connections

FIGURE 3.12   Installed P8 and P9. Note that the black ground wires on the connectors are together.

ATX Power Connector

Instead of the paired P8 and P9 connectors found on AT power supplies, ATX power supplies use a single type P1 power connector, as shown in Figure 3-13.

The white P1 socket shown in Figure 3-14 stands out clearly on the motherboard.

The P1 has a notched connector that allows you to insert it one way only—you cannot install the P1 connector incorrectly. Figure 3-15 shows a properly inserted P1 connection.

FIGURE 3.13   P1 connector

FIGURE 3.14   P1 socket

ATX12V Power Connector

Motherboards designed for the Pentium 4 and some Athlon XP CPUs have extra power requirements that call for an enhanced type of power supply—the ATX12V. A superset of the original ATX specification, the ATX12V sports a couple of additional types of power connectors, shown in Figure 3-16: a four-pin, 12-volt plug that's called the *P4* connector, and a six-pin auxiliary power plug, called the *P6* connector, that supplies additional 3.3- and 5-volt power.

FIGURE 3.15   Properly installed P1 connector

FIGURE 3.16   ATX12V P4 and P6 connectors

Peripheral Power

Devices like mass storage and media drives, floppy disk drives, Zip drives, and fans also draw power directly from the PC power supply. AT and ATX power supplies both have the Molex and mini connectors used by these devices.

Molex Connectors

The Molex connector shown in Figure 3-17 is used primarily for hard drives, CD and DVD media drives, and tape backup drives.

Figure 3-18 shows the arrangement of the wires on a Molex power connector. Note that Molex connectors have notches called *chamfers* that make installation relatively foolproof. These chamfers can be defeated if you push hard enough, however, so always inspect the Molex connection to ensure proper orientation

FIGURE 3.17   Standard Molex connector

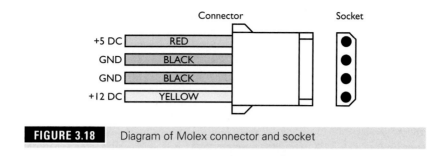

	Connector	Socket
+5 DC	RED	
GND	BLACK	
GND	BLACK	
+12 DC	YELLOW	

FIGURE 3.18 Diagram of Molex connector and socket

before you install. Installing a Molex connector backward almost always results in a toasted device.

Miniconnectors

The miniconnector shown in Figure 3-19 is used on 3.5-inch floppy drives. Miniconnectors make techs appreciate Molex connectors, especially after the tech fries his or her first floppy drive. It's amazingly easy to insert a mini plug incorrectly, and, as soon as you power on the PC, the yellow 12-volt wire will toast the poor 5-volt electronics on the drive! (The smell of ozone is so nice…) Worse, *there is no standardization* on floppy disk drives for the location or orientation of the mini port. One drive might have the port above the 34-pin data connection, for example, whereas another might have it to the left. A third drive will have it to the right of the data connection. You have to check before you turn on the power! The diagram in Figure 3-20 shows the correct orientation between the miniconnector and miniport on a floppy disk drive.

FIGURE 3.19 Standard miniconnector

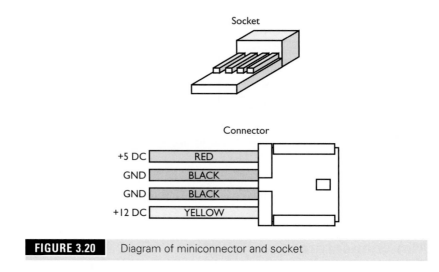

+5 DC	RED
GND	BLACK
GND	BLACK
+12 DC	YELLOW

FIGURE 3.20   Diagram of miniconnector and socket

Wattage

Power supplies are rated in watts. A PC requires sufficient wattage for the machine to run properly. The average desktop PC with two hard drives and a CD-ROM will need about 115 to 130 watts while running and up to 200 watts when booting up. Play it safe and buy power supplies in at least the 230- to 250-watt range. If your PC has extra drives or devices, plan on getting a higher-rated power supply such as a 300- or 400-watt model.

Sizes

Power supplies are available in a modest variety of shapes and sizes, usually tied to the form factor. Most desktop and minitower PCs use the standard ATX power supply. Full-tower cases usually require larger (roughly toaster-sized) power supplies, while smaller cases need special *low-profile* power supplies.

Travel Advisory

A power supply's size is not always a good indicator of its wattage. A good bit of advice is to always take the unit that you're replacing with you when shopping for power supplies. This saves you from making repeated trips.

Servicing Power Supplies

As noted in Chapter 2, PC power supplies are not made to be serviced by techs in the field. If you suspect that a power supply is malfunctioning, don't attempt to open it up and repair it yourself! Remove it and replace it with a new, compatible unit.

Objective 3.03 # PC Cases

A s you've probably surmised by now, PC cases also follow the AT and ATX form factor standards. AT PC cases use AT power supplies and support AT motherboards, and ATX cases are for ATX motherboards and power supplies. Aside from that, the basic size standards described in this section apply to both types of cases.

PC cases come in five basic sizes: low-profile (sometimes called *slimline*), desktop, minitower, mid-tower, and full-tower. You'd be hard-pressed to find any serious deviations from these size standards, but some PC and PC case makers have come up with interesting and innovative designs within those standards.

> ### Exam Tip
>
> The five case sizes listed above only apply to consumer or workstation PCs. Server PCs come in several different varieties, such as huge dual-power supply behemoths and rack-mounted systems too svelte to handle a normal expansion card. The A+ Certification exams test you only on the five consumer or workstation models.

Vendors such as Alienware offer myriad colors and exotic body styling. More important, these cases are outfitted with detailing that enhances the PC's function, such as additional cooling fans or liquid cooling systems, high-output power supplies, cable management systems, roomier interiors, screwless body panels (these require no tools to remove), and such welcome touches as front-mounted USB, FireWire, and MIDI/joystick ports.

Other design features that separate better PC cases from lower-quality models are finished edges (these prevent nasty scrapes both to your knuckles and to cables), quick-release drive bays, a detachable motherboard mount tray, and a removable front *bezel,* or faceplate, as shown in Figure 3-21. The more you work on PCs, the more you'll appreciate how these small features make it easier for you to service them.

If it's pure aesthetic flash you're looking for, case modification *(mod)* kits are available to trick up your boring beige box with neon and fiber-optic lighting,

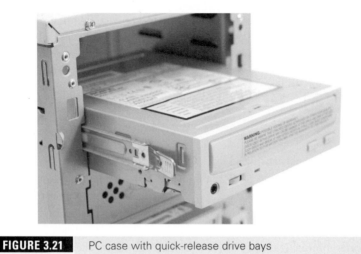

FIGURE 3.21   PC case with quick-release drive bays

see-through acrylic panels, special LED speed and temperature displays, and fancy multimedia control panels. These do nothing to enhance a PC's performance or reliability, or make them easier for techs to service, but they sure are cool to look at!

CHECKPOINT

✔**Objective 3.01: PC Motherboards**   The two most common types of motherboards are AT and ATX, although AT motherboards are largely phased out of modern PCs. ATX motherboards offer notable advantages, including integrated serial, parallel, and USB ports. Two popular variations of the ATX form factor are Micro ATX and Flex ATX. Current systems offer several expansion buses: PCI for general expansion cards, AGP for video, and USB and FireWire for external devices. The 32-bit PCI bus enables plug and play expandability and data throughput of 33 MBps.

✔**Objective 3.02: PC Power Supplies**   AT motherboards require P8 and P9 power connectors, oriented properly with the black ground wires next to each other. ATX motherboards use a single P1 connector. Hard drives, media drives, and tape backup drives use the larger Molex power connectors; floppy drives use the smaller miniconnector. AT and ATX power supplies are not interchangeable—AT motherboards require AT power supplies, and ATX motherboards require ATX power supplies.

✔**Objective 3.02: PC Cases** Like motherboards and power supplies, PC cases come in standard AT and ATX form factors. Beyond that, PC cases conform to five basic size standards; low-profile (slimline), desktop, minitower, mid-tower, and full-tower. Better PC cases feature bigger power supplies, better cooling, cable management systems, easy-to-remove body panels, front- mounted USB, FireWire, and MIDI/joystick ports, and detachable motherboard trays.

REVIEW QUESTIONS

1. What part of the PC is the framework on which everything builds?
   A. I/O buses
   B. Expansion slots
   C. The processor
   D. The motherboard

2. Which of the following motherboards are you most likely to see in modern PCs? (Select all that apply.)
   A. AT
   B. ATX
   C. Baby AT
   D. All of the above

3. If you have a PC with an AT motherboard and case and you decide you would like to upgrade the motherboard, can you replace it with an ATX motherboard?
   A. No
   B. Yes, if you reset the jumpers
   C. Yes, if you add more screw holes
   D. Yes, if you remove the integrated ports

4. What ports were integrated into the AT motherboard?
   A. Serial ports, parallel ports, USB ports, and mini-DIN ports
   B. A keyboard port
   C. Serial ports
   D. A mouse port

5. What type of connector attaches the AT power supply to the AT motherboard? (Select all that apply.)

A. P1

B. P2

C. P8

D. P9

6. What do you need to remember when connecting the AT power connectors to the motherboard?

A. Keep the red wires together

B. Keep the black wires together

C. Keep the brown wires together

D. It is impossible to put these connectors in wrong

7. The ATX motherboard is roughly the same size as the Baby AT motherboard, but it is rotated _____ degrees.

A. 45

B. 180

C. 60

D. 90

8. What type of connector attaches the ATX power supply to the ATX motherboard?

A. P1

B. P2

C. P8

D. P9

9. Which slots can an 8-bit ISA card use? (Select all that apply.)

A. 8-bit ISA

B. 16-bit ISA

C. PCI

D. AGP

10. What IRQs could a 16-bit ISA card theoretically use?

A. 0–4

B. 0–7

C. 0–15

D. 2–15

11. What do PCI slots look like?

    A. Small and white

    B. Small and brown

    C. Small and green

    D. Large and black

12. Which features will you find on a high-quality PC case that make it easier to service? (Choose all that apply.)

    A. Finished edges

    B. Screwless body panels

    C. Removable motherboard tray

    D. Fiber-optic lighting

13. Which of the following type of power supplies would you most likely install in a full-tower AT case?

    A. AT

    B. ATX

    C. ATX12V

    D. All of the above

14. Molex connectors supply to which devices? (Choose all that apply.)

    A. Hard disks

    B. CD and DVD media drives

    C. Tape backup drives

    D. Zip drives

15. What is the correct way to connect a miniconnector to a floppy disk drive?

    A. Yellow wire to the left

    B. Red wire on the left

    C. Black wire on the right

    D. There's no standard

REVIEW ANSWERS

1. **D**   The motherboard can be considered the cornerstone of the PC. All your system devices are either directly or indirectly attached to the motherboard, making it the most important part of your PC.

2. **B** **C**   Baby AT and ATX motherboards are still used in PCs today. The full AT motherboard has become obsolete.

3. **A**   You cannot replace an AT motherboard with an ATX motherboard using the same case. AT motherboards go into AT cases, and ATX motherboards go into ATX cases. There's nothing to stop an enthusiast from retrofitting an AT case to accept an ATX motherboard, of course, but that's definitely outside the scope of the A+ Certification exams.

4. **B**   The only port integrated into an AT motherboard is the keyboard (five-pin DIN) port. ATX motherboards provided us with more integrated ports.

5. **C** **D**   P8 and P9 connectors attach the AT power supply to the AT motherboard. It is important to remember to keep the black ground wires together.

6. **B**   You need to keep the black ground wires of the P8 and P9 connectors together, or you could destroy your motherboard.

7. **D**   ATX motherboards were roughly the same size as the Baby AT, but rotated 90 degrees. The processor is located near the rear of an ATX motherboard.

8. **A**   ATX power supplies connect to AT motherboards with a single P1 connector.

9. **A** **B**   Sixteen-bit ISA slots were backward-compatible, so an 8-bit ISA card could use a 16-bit slot as well as its own 8-bit ISA slot.

10. **C**   16-bit ISA cards theoretically could use IRQs 0–15, although in practice, most cards could use only a couple of IRQs.

11. **A**   PCI slots are easily recognizable because they are small and white.

12. **A** **B** and **C**   Finished case edges prevent scrapes to skin and cabling, and screwless body panels and removable motherboard trays make accessing the interior of the PC case easier. Fiber-optic lighting is neat to look at but offers no real benefit.

13. **A**   AT cases can accommodate only AT power supplies.

14. **A** **B** **C** and **D**   Molex connectors supply all of the listed devices.

15. **D**   There's no official standard for floppy disk drive power port orientation.

System BIOS and CMOS Setup Utility

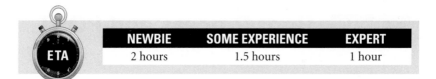

	NEWBIE	SOME EXPERIENCE	EXPERT
ETA	2 hours	1.5 hours	1 hour

In the seconds between the time that you press the power button and the desktop appears on your monitor, your PC goes through a series of ordered steps called the *boot process*. The vital components that drive the boot process are the System ROM, the System *basic input/output system (BIOS)*, and the *complementary metal-oxide semiconductor (CMOS)* memory chip and setup utility. The System ROM—for *read-only memory*—is the special memory chip that stores the BIOS programs. System BIOS is the collective name for the hundreds of tiny programs that tell your computer everything from what time it is to what *kind* of computer it is. The CMOS memory chip and the setup utility enable you to control important aspects of your PC configuration such as the boot device sequence and port assignments.

All PCs share these components in common and follow the same process when booting up. Understanding the boot process on one computer enables you to troubleshoot the boot process on any computer. Likewise, with only slight variations, BIOS and CMOS work the same on practically any PC. You will find yourself "entering CMOS" many times in your career as a PC technician, and the A+ exams expect you to demonstrate a deep understanding of the System ROM, System BIOS, and CMOS setup utility functions. Let's get started.

Objective 4.01   Boot Process and POST

The three main stages of the boot process are the power-on, *power-on self test (POST)*, and OS loading steps.

Power-On/CPU Wakes

You start the process by powering the system on, sending current to the motherboard and drive devices. Assuming there are no problems with your power supply, a special wire on the CPU called the *power good* wire is charged, telling it to wake up. The CPU then communicates with the System ROM chip and starts the BIOS programs.

POST

Unlike a person who wakes up knowing who they are and how many fingers they have, a computer literally rediscovers itself every time it powers up. This is done via the POST process. During POST, the System BIOS communicates with all essential hardware and, in essence, tells them to identify themselves. The devices—the keyboard, mouse, disk drives, RAM, display adapter, and so on—then run internal diagnostic routines and report back to the BIOS. If one of the devices reports an error condition back to the BIOS, then the BIOS reports this back to the user by using special POST *error codes.*

POST Error Codes

As you may have guessed, the POST process is the most vital of the steps in the boot process. It's during POST that any serious hardware errors come to light. The way that the PC communicates POST errors is through special sound codes called *beep codes* and through text or numeric messages displayed on your monitor.

Beep Codes

Beep codes vary according to the PC's BIOS manufacturer, although you'll find certain codes are common on most PCs. A single happy-sounding chirp at boot-up signals that all is well. A long, repeating beep signals a problem with RAM. A series of beeps—one long and three short—usually points to a problem with the video card. Specific beep code definitions are found in your PC's motherboard manual or on your BIOS manufacturer's web site.

Numeric and Text Codes

POST may also display numeric or text errors indicating the nature of a hardware problem. Numeric error codes are somewhat standardized into certain code *ranges.* For instance, an error code in the range 100–199 indicates a motherboard error, an error code in the 200–299 range indicates a RAM error, and so on. Table 4-1 lists the most common ranges of numeric error codes.

TABLE 4.1	Error Codes You Might Encounter During the POST

Error Code	Device
100 Series Error (Any error in the range 100–199)	Motherboard
200 Series Error (Any error in the range 200–299)	RAM
300 Series Error (Any error in the range 300–399)	Keyboard
400 Series Error (Any error in the range 400–499)	Monochrome video
500 Series Error (Any error in the range 500–599)	Color video
600 Series Error (Any error in the range 600–699)	Floppy drive
1700 Series Error (Any error in the range 1700–1799)	Hard drive

Exam Tip

Learn the series errors. On the exam if asked what a 301 error code is, you should remember that everything in the 300 series of error codes relates to the keyboard.

Text errors tend to be fairly direct statements, such as "Floppy Drive Failure" or "Keyboard error or no keyboard present," that display on your monitor and usually require you to press a key such as F1 to continue.

Some hardware problems prevent any POST errors from properly appearing on the display screen or coming through the system speaker. In these cases, a special hardware tool called a *POST card* comes in handy.

POST Cards

PC POST cards aren't the kind that you send snail-mail holiday greetings on. A POST card, shown in Figure 4-1, is a dedicated hardware component that plugs into an ISA or PCI expansion bus slot and displays POST codes coming from the System BIOS.

FIGURE 4.1   POST card error code readout

The POST card uses an LED display to present special POST code listings that the technician then interprets. Most POST cards come with documentation explaining the various error codes in general, but different BIOS manufacturers use different codes. You should go to the motherboard manufacturer's web site for information on the specific motherboard you're testing. You can also check the BIOS maker's web site for error code explanations.

OS Loads

During POST, the BIOS also locates the system boot device—such as the floppy disk, CD-ROM, or hard drive—that contains the OS boot files. Once the POST process completes successfully, the BIOS then passes control of the boot process over to the PC's OS. The exact loading process differs from one OS to the next (we'll look at this process in more detail in Chapter 13), but in general, one or more vital system files such as IO.SYS (in the case of Windows 9x) or NTLDR (in Windows 2000/XP) loads into memory and starts the ball rolling. Things move fast from there, as the OS loads its core files, drivers, and services into RAM. The next thing you know, you're looking at your desktop and hearing the soothing strains of the Windows Logon sound file.

Objective 4.02   System ROM

The System ROM chip stores the System BIOS programs and CMOS setup utility. System ROM is distinctively labeled with the BIOS maker's name, as shown in Figure 4-2. On older PCs, the BIOS programs were hard-coded onto the System ROM chip, meaning that the BIOS were unchangeable without replacing the entire ROM chip. Current motherboards use writable ROM chips such as *EEPROM* and *flash ROM*. Writable ROM chips enable you to install updated BIOS information without physically replacing the chip.

Many techs refer to the System BIOS as the *ROM BIOS*, and the A+ certification core hardware exam may use either term.

There's a big difference between System ROM chips and RAM that you need to appreciate. RAM is what's called *volatile* memory because RAM stores data only while the PC is powered on. System ROM memory, on the other hand, is *nonvolatile* memory and retains data even with the system powered off.

From a technician's standpoint, there's not much that you need to do to maintain the System ROM. System ROM requires no servicing beyond the usual

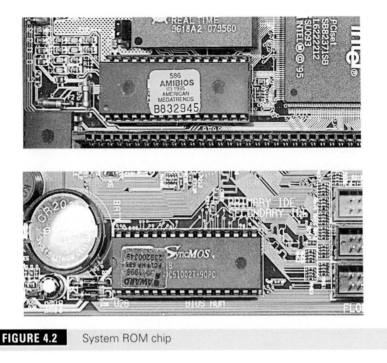

FIGURE 4.2   System ROM chip

blowing-out-the-dust type of PC case maintenance that should be part of your routine. Nor does the System ROM itself ever need to be updated, although the BIOS programs residing on it sometimes do. The only type of maintenance that you'll ever undertake on the System ROM is replacing the CMOS battery (described in the section below). Let's take a closer look at the System BIOS and CMOS setup utility.

Objective 4.03   # System BIOS and CMOS Setup Utility

You never deal directly with the many BIOS programs but instead interact with them only peripherally through the CMOS setup utility. Motherboard manufacturers don't actually write their own BIOS programs. Instead, they buy their BIOSes from third-party BIOS makers; among the largest makers are American Megatrends, or AMI, Award Software, and Phoenix Technologies.

There is a great deal of uniformity, however, so from a technician's point of view, there's not all that much of a difference between the various brands of BIOS software.

Likewise, PC CMOS setup utilities don't vary much from one brand to another—if you see one, you've seen them all! However, you may have to do more poking around to find the important settings you need if you move from a CMOS setup utility that you're familiar with to one that you're not. This section describes the important settings you need to familiarize yourself with.

System BIOS

What kinds of programs are in the BIOS? Frankly, there are far too many to list. Beyond the important POST routine programs described in the section "System ROM," literally hundreds of individual programs—some no more than 10 or 20 lines of code—reside in the System BIOS. They control things as mundane as whether the NUM LOCK key is engaged at startup, to things as exotic-sounding as the *SDRAM precharge control,* and beyond.

Unlike most types of PC software, BIOS programs rarely change. BIOS makers update BIOS programs only to fix known bugs (thus enhancing stability) and to add important functions such as compatibility with new hardware or hardware standards. For example, updating your BIOS might add support for the newer *Advanced Configuration and Power Interface (ACPI)* power management specification.

Travel Advisory

Motherboard manufacturers make new BIOS programs available to enhance stability and to add new functions.

Updating the System BIOS

Techs refer to updating System BIOS as *flashing the BIOS.* It's a simple procedure, but care must be taken to ensure that it's done correctly and without interruption. A BIOS flash procedure that gets interrupted usually results in a PC that won't boot and a motherboard that's rendered completely useless! Before flashing your BIOS, back up your important documents and update any system repair or Emergency Rescue diskettes. Do your best to make certain that the process isn't disturbed once you start.

BIOS makers provide updating utilities for their BIOS programs on their web sites. The correct steps to update a System BIOS are as follows:

1. Obtain the flashing program from the manufacturer's web site.
2. Turn your system off.
3. Insert a valid boot disk and boot to the A: prompt.
4. Insert the disk containing the flashing program and new BIOS into the floppy drive.
5. Run the flashing program according to your BIOS manufacturer's instructions, making certain to back up your current BIOS when prompted.
6. Restart your system when the update is complete.

That's all there is to it! Now let's take a look at the CMOS setup utility.

CMOS Setup Utility

The CMOS setup utility, stored in the system ROM, enables you to configure important System BIOS settings stored in the CMOS chip that's a part of the motherboard chipset's *Southbridge* circuitry on most PCs. These settings include port assignments, boot device sequence, power management, and a number of others, as described here.

Travel Advisory

The chipset is the circuitry built onto the motherboard that acts as the conduit between the CPU and the rest of the components on the PC. Chipset technology changes frequently, but in general, the chipset is split into two distinct pathways. The *Northbridge* connects the CPU to the system RAM and the AGP and PCI buses, while the *Southbridge* links the CPU to the "secondary" buses—USB, IDE, PS/2, etc.

Entering the CMOS Setup Utility

You can't enter the CMOS setup utility from within your operating system; you must do it during the early stages of the boot process. Different BIOS makers specify different methods for entering CMOS. The instructions for entering CMOS appear on your monitor screen during boot-up, as shown in Figure 4-3. Watch the messages carefully and press the proper key when prompted.

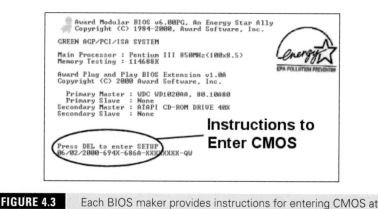

Award Modular BIOS v6.00PG, An Energy Star Ally
Copyright (C) 1984-2000, Award Software, Inc.

GREEN AGP/PCI/ISA SYSTEM

Main Processor : Pentium III 850MHz(100x8.5)
Memory Testing : 114688K

Award Plug and Play BIOS Extension v1.0A
Copyright (C) 2000 Award Software, Inc.

Primary Master   : WDC WD1020AA, 80.10A80
Primary Slave   : None
Secondary Master : ATAPI CD-ROM DRIVE 40X
Secondary Slave : None

Instructions to Enter CMOS

Press DEL to enter SETUP
06/02/2000-694X-686A-XXXXXXXX-QV

FIGURE 4.3   Each BIOS maker provides instructions for entering CMOS at boot-up.

Typically, AMI and Award have you press the DEL key when prompted. Phoenix might have you press the CTRL, ALT, and ESC keys simultaneously, or possibly F2. Check your motherboard documentation for the exact method on your PC.

The CMOS utility interface will remind you of a VCR programming interface (assuming you're old enough to remember VCRs). Navigation is usually by keyboard only (AMI provides mouse support), so you'll typically use your TAB and arrow keys to move around and your ENTER key to make selections. This also varies according to which BIOS you have on your PC. Navigation instructions should be prominent in the display somewhere. If you get stuck, remember that pressing the F1 key always brings up a Help menu.

Let's take a look at some of the more important CMOS settings.

Important CMOS Settings   The settings described here are important both in terms of the A+ exam and for your real-world PC configuration and troubleshooting experience. Get to know these settings! Always document any settings before you change them so that you can restore them to their previous configuration, if necessary. Remember that changing CMOS settings can seriously affect the way your PC operates, so if you're unsure of what the results of a change will be, it's best to leave it alone.

- **Parallel Ports**   CMOS automatically configures the built-in parallel ports in newer systems for the broadest compatibility with parallel devices (printers, scanners, Zip drives, and so on). You can manually configure the parallel ports in CMOS, if needed. For example, if the port isn't working properly due to a conflict with another device, you can reset the IRQ and the I/O address. You can also disable the port completely to free up its resources for other devices to use. Other settings include configuring the port as a Standard Parallel Port, Extended Capabilities Port (ECP), or Enhanced Parallel Port (EPP).

The Standard Parallel Port setting works fine for older printers and such, but it provides only *unidirectional* data flow, from the PC to the device. This isn't a problem for older devices, because they aren't made to send data back to the PC, but newer parallel devices are smarter and are able to communicate with the PC to report things like printer toner or ink levels, the status of print jobs, and so on. Also, other high-speed parallel devices such as external disk drives and removable media drives definitely need full-duplex (*bidirectional*) communication with the PC. For these devices, modern PCs offer spanking-fast options of either ECP or EPP mode, which are ten times faster than the traditional bidirectional mode.

ECP enables parallel devices, such as printers and scanners, to access *direct memory access (DMA)* channels. EPP enables devices other than printers and scanners, such as LAN adapters or disk drives, to access the DMA channels for devices.

Travel Advisory

Direct memory access channels enable devices to access RAM directly, thus making ultra high-speed data transfers possible.

Exam Tip

ECP and EPP are both ten times faster than regular bidirectional mode.

- **COM/Serial Ports**   Serial ports in newer systems are automatically configured through plug and play. The CMOS setup utility enables you to configure the IRQ and I/O addresses of serial ports if need be. You can also enable or disable serial ports in the CMOS to troubleshoot a device conflict. Disabling a COM/serial port frees up the port's resources for other devices to use.
- **Floppy Drive**   CMOS enables you to set floppy drive configurations, such as the size and capacity of the floppy drive. You can also configure your computer to boot from the floppy disk first, or to enable or disable the floppy drive controller.
- **Hard Drive**   Newer systems automatically detect your hard drive settings. In older systems, you may need to specify heads, cylinders, and sector values; drive type; and drive capacity.

- **Memory**   Modern PCs detect and configure RAM settings automatically, and there's typically little that you need to do in CMOS. Sometimes you may have to confirm RAM capacity after adding additional RAM to the PC. Some motherboards require that you manually enable support for the special types of error checking RAM such as *parity* RAM or *error correcting code* RAM. Be very careful with these settings! Enable these RAM settings only if you're certain that your system supports them. Enabling parity checking for nonparity RAM usually results in a nonbooting system. RAM is discussed in more detail in Chapter 6.

- **Boot Sequence**   Configuring the sequence by which the System BIOS searches for a boot device is one of the most common CMOS configuration settings that you will find yourself dealing with. The default boot device sequence on most PCs is floppy disk drive, CD-ROM drive, and then hard disk drive. One scenario where you would reconfigure this is when installing a new OS from a bootable CD-ROM disc. To do this, change the boot sequence to place the CD-ROM drive first on the list of boot devices.

- **Date and Time**   The computer's *real-time clock* is configured in the CMOS. The real-time clock is used by the operating system, as well as date- and time-oriented applications. If this clock starts losing time, you need to replace your CMOS battery.

Exam Tip

When the real-time clock starts losing time, it's time to replace the CMOS battery!

- **User and Supervisor Passwords**   A user-CMOS password enables you to set a degree of low-level security on the PC. With this setting configured, the user is required to enter a password during the early stages of the boot process. The PC will not boot without the correct password. In most CMOS utilities, you can also set supervisor passwords that prevent unauthorized persons from accessing the CMOS. Remember, however, that if you forget or lose the password, you'll be unable to access the CMOS!

Should you wind up locking yourself out of your PC by losing the CMOS password, you have a couple of ways to get access. Most motherboards store the CMOS password on a capacitor that's connected to a special jumper, usually labeled with the initials "PWD," a symbol of a lock, or some other icon indicating its function. Removing the shunt from this jumper for a few seconds discharges the capacitor, thus clearing any CMOS passwords. Check the motherboard's documentation for the exact instructions for your particular motherboard. The other method is to disconnect the AC power cable (remember that ATX systems always have a 5V trickle charge on the motherboard when plugged in) and unplug the CMOS battery for a few seconds. This clears your CMOS of all settings, including the offending password.

Exam Tip

Setting a jumper on the motherboard or removing and replacing the CMOS battery can clear CMOS passwords.

- **Plug and Play BIOS**   Plug and play is the technology that enables modern PCs to automatically recognize and configure plug and play–compliant hardware devices with IRQ and I/O address settings. To take advantage of plug and play, the BIOS, hardware, and OS all have to comply with the plug and play standards. All modern versions of Windows are plug and play.

  It's important to note that the OS plug and play settings always override the BIOS plug and play settings. This is to the good, actually, as the OS utilities give you more control over a device's settings if you have to do any manual tweaking. If you have a mixture of plug and play and non–plug and play hardware, it's a good idea to disable BIOS plug and play to minimize conflicting settings and deal with hardware strictly from within the OS.

- **Save & Exit Setup**   This option is the one that will make any changes you've configured in CMOS setup permanent. Use with caution! Typically, selecting this option brings up a confirmation prompt along the lines of "Are you really, really sure you want to make these changes? Y/N." Don't make any changes unless you're absolutely certain what the effect will be.

- **Exit Without Saving**   Of all the options on the CMOS setup menu, this one is your best friend! Exit Without Saving undoes any changes that you've made. Choosing this option brings up another "Are you sure Y/N?" type of confirmation prompt. Choose *Y* to take your leave of CMOS setup without doing any damage.

- **Restore Defaults** All CMOS setup utilities enable you to restore a default configuration if, for instance, you've made a change that had unexpected results.

- **Antivirus Protection** The antivirus function works at the BIOS level to prevent programs from overwriting the System BIOS settings stored on the System ROM. In some cases, such as when installing a new OS, it is necessary to disable this function.

- **Power Management** Configuring power management in CMOS tells the PC to let the BIOS handle power configuration settings such as turning the video and hard drives off after a certain amount of idle time or putting the PC into suspend mode. As with PnP, the power configuration set within Windows always overrides the CMOS power configuration setting.

- **Integrated Peripherals** Certain onboard devices such as serial ports and USB controllers can be disabled if they're not being used in order to free up system resources for other devices.

Replacing the CMOS Battery

Figure 4-4 shows two typical, motherboard-mounted CMOS batteries: the coin-shaped battery that you'll find on most modern PC motherboards, and the less common barrel-shaped battery that you may find soldered directly onto older motherboards. Some ancient motherboards use an external battery that mounts inside the PC case with Velcro and connects to the motherboard via a wire.

When CMOS batteries fail, they do so gradually. The first and best indicator that a PC's CMOS battery is dying is that the PC starts to lose time. If you notice that your PC's clock is running slow, or if you're consistently prompted to enter the date and time when you boot the PC, it's time to replace the CMOS battery.

Replacing the CMOS battery is as simple as sliding the old one out of the bracket and slipping the new one in its place. In the case of an external battery, you simply plug the wire's socket onto the appropriate contact pins on the motherboard.

A built-in capacitor preserves your current BIOS configuration during the battery-swapping process, but you may be prompted to manually reconfigure the date and time settings after swapping CMOS batteries.

It's vitally important that the voltage of the replacement battery match the original. Newer systems run on 3.6-volt batteries, while older ones typically use the 6-volt variety. Check your motherboard's documentation to determine the correct battery for your system.

FIGURE 4.4   CMOS batteries

CHECKPOINT

✔**Objective 4.01: Boot Process and POST**   After powering up, the System BIOS loads and runs the POST to test all the built-in and common devices in the PC. The POST gives you a beep code or text error message in the event of hardware failure.

✔**Objective 4.02: System ROM**   The System ROM chip stores the System BIOS programs and CMOS setup utility. System ROM is nonvolatile EEPROM or flash ROM memory that maintains data even while the PC is turned off through the use of a CMOS battery.

✔**Objective 4.03: System BIOS and the CMOS Setup Utility**   The System BIOS includes hundreds of small programs that establish communication between your PC hardware and the OS. System BIOS can be updated (*flashed*) to fix bugs or add new functions. The CMOS setup utility enables you to modify settings for built-in and common devices, serial and parallel ports, floppy and hard drives, and so on. You access CMOS by entering a key combination that's specific to your brand of BIOS. You should write down your CMOS settings before making any changes.

REVIEW QUESTIONS

1. Which of the following can you configure in the CMOS? (Select all that apply.)

    A. Parallel ports

    B. Serial ports

    C. Hard drive

    D. Video resolution

2. When should you update your System BIOS?

    A. When you upgrade your OS

    B. Every time you boot your computer

    C. Every time you defragment your computer

    D. To add functionality or fix known bugs

3. What should you do before making any changes to your CMOS settings?

    A. Reboot your computer

    B. Write down the current settings

    C. Remove all the cables from your PC

    D. Replace the BIOS

4. Why might you want to reconfigure the automatically set IRQ or I/O address of a port on your PC? (Select all that apply.)

    A. Device conflict

    B. Troubleshooting

    C. To free up system resources

    D. There's no way to reconfigure these settings

5. Which of the following devices can take advantage of ECP mode? (Select all that apply.)

    A. Scanners

    B. LAN adapters

    C. Disk drives

    D. Printers

6. Which of the following devices can take advantage of EPP mode? (Select all that apply.)

    A. Scanners

    B. LAN adapters

   C. Disk drives

   D. Printers

7. If your CMOS isn't capable of auto-detecting your hard drive, which of the following values do you need to specify? (Select all that apply.)

   A. Heads

   B. Cylinders

   C. Clusters

   D. Sectors

8. If your RAM doesn't support parity, how should the Parity Error Checking option in the CMOS be set?

   A. Enabled

   B. Disabled

9. By default, which of the following is the first device the BIOS searches for at startup?

   A. Hard drive

   B. CD-ROM drive

   C. Floppy drive

   D. All of the above

10. What do you need to do if the clock on your PC starts losing time?

   A. Replace your BIOS.

   B. Replace the CMOS battery.

   C. Replace your hard drive.

   D. Reinstall Windows.

11. If a user password has been set in the CMOS, what will happen?

   A. An unauthorized person will be unable to enter the CMOS settings program.

   B. The user must enter the correct password to boot the system.

   C. Nothing will happen.

   D. Only certain settings in the CMOS will be available to unauthorized users.

12. If you've set and forgotten a supervisor password for your CMOS, how can you get into the CMOS settings program? (Select all that apply.)

   A. Reboot the PC and press F1.

   B. Set a jumper on your motherboard to clear the password.

C. Reinstall Windows.

D. Remove and reinstall the CMOS battery.

13. At startup, where does your PC receive its first set of instructions?

A. Operating system

B. RAM BIOS

C. ROM BIOS

D. CMOS

14. If you're using Windows and set your PnP BIOS so the BIOS configures your PnP devices, what will happen?

A. Your BIOS will configure the devices.

B. Windows will configure the devices.

C. The devices will need to be configured manually.

D. None of the above.

15. If you boot your computer and receive a 301 error code, which of the following devices has a problem?

A. Floppy drive

B. Hard drive

C. Video

D. Keyboard

REVIEW ANSWERS

1. **A B C** Parallel ports, serial ports, and your hard drive are all configurable in the CMOS settings program.

2. **D** System BIOS should be updated only when a new BIOS version will fix a problem or add new functions.

3. **B** Before making any changes in the CMOS, you should write down the current CMOS settings. Taking the time to do this can save you from having to retrace your steps later.

4. **A B C** You might want to reconfigure the automatically set IRQ and I/O address settings of your ports if you're experiencing a device conflict, for troubleshooting purposes, or if you need to free system resources for other devices to use.

5. **A** **D**   Scanners and printers can take advantage of ECP mode. ECP mode runs at ten times the normal bidirectional mode and allows access to DMA channels.

6. **B** **C**   LAN adapters and disk drives take the best advantage of EPP mode. EPP mode runs at ten times the normal bidirectional mode and allows access to DMA channels.

7. **A** **B** **D**   If your CMOS cannot auto detect your hard drive, you need to specify the number of cylinders, sectors, and heads. In some cases, you also need to specify the hard drive's size.

8. **B**   If RAM doesn't support parity, the Parity Error Checking option in the CMOS settings program should always be disabled. If you enable this feature and your RAM doesn't support parity, your computer might not boot properly.

9. **C**   By default, at start up, your BIOS searches for your floppy drive first to boot. You can change the boot order in the CMOS, if necessary.

10. **B**   If the clock on your PC starts losing time, this is a good indication it's time to change the CMOS battery.

11. **B**   If a user password is set in the CMOS, the computer won't fully boot until the correct password is entered by the user.

12. **B** **D**   If you've set and forgotten a supervisor password in the CMOS, you can still enter the CMOS by setting a jumper on the motherboard to clear the password or by removing and reinstalling the CMOS battery.

13. **C**   At startup, your PC receives its first set of instructions from the System BIOS, also called ROM BIOS. There's no such thing as the RAM BIOS, a fact you should remember for the exam.

14. **B**   If you're using a PnP operating system, regardless of the settings made for the PnP BIOS, the operating system will override the settings.

15. **D**   All 300 series error codes refer to the keyboard, and therefore, if you receive a 301 error code, this means you're experiencing a keyboard problem.

CPUs

	NEWBIE	SOME EXPERIENCE	EXPERT
ETA	3 hours	2 hours	1 hour

The thing that enables a computer to compute is the microprocessor, or as most techs call it, the central processing unit (CPU). Everything else on the computer can be considered part of the CPU's life-support system. So what does the CPU do? If you believe the hyperbole of popular culture, the CPU is some sort of machine brain that's always on the verge of declaring "I think, therefore I am" and trying to take over the world. Don't let them kid you—computers don't think! What the CPU does, and does amazingly well, is add numbers. That's right—the CPU is really just a super-fast, super-powerful calculator!

As simple as that may sound, keep in mind that a CPU churns out *billions* of calculations every single second. These calculations make possible everything that your PC does: displaying your OS desktop, processing print jobs, grabbing web pages, and everything else you ask it to do. Of all the whiz-bang pieces of engineering that go into the PC, the CPU is by far the most impressive. The CPU has gone through many evolutions since its introduction over twenty years ago, but even the most advanced ones still operate in much the same manner as the old Intel 8088 that powered the very first IBM PC.

Today's desktop CPU market is dominated by two vendors; not surprisingly, Intel is one of them. The other major player is one-time Intel partner American Micro Devices, better known as AMD. Intel's CPU offerings include the Pentium line, the Celeron, the high-end Xeon, and the ultra-high-end Itanium processors. AMD gives us the Athlon, Duron, and Athlon XP product families, and the server-oriented Opteron processor.

Travel Advisory

Over the years, other companies have tried to get into the CPU business. Companies such as Cyrix, IDC, VIA, and Transmeta have all made CPUs, but with very limited success and very minor market shares.

The A+ Certification Core Hardware exam objectives concentrate on the aspects of the CPU that a tech has to know in order to service PCs in today's business world. First, a good PC tech must understand the basic internal components of a CPU and what they do. Second, a good tech must be able to identify and distinguish among the types of CPUs (from Intel and AMD) found in modern PCs. Third, a good tech knows how to install a CPU and its cooling system. This chapter covers all these subjects.

Objective 5.01   CPU Technology Overview

Most users and even many techs are unclear about the exact relationship be-tween the CPU and the rest of the PC's components. This is understandable given the complexity of CPU technology, but taken in overview, the process is ele-gantly simple. Let's start by defining the important techno-geek terms that apply to CPU operation, then look at how all these things work together (Figure 5-1). Then we'll look at CPU form factors, voltage, and cooling requirements.

In and Around the CPU

This section defines many of the CPU-related terms that you'll come to know and love during your career as a PC tech. Make sure you are comfortable with each of these!

Arithmetic Logic Unit (ALU)

The *arithmetic logic unit (ALU)* is the part of the CPU that actually processes data. The ALU takes data from the CPU *registers* (described next), processes it, and copies it back into the registers before moving on to the next batch of data.

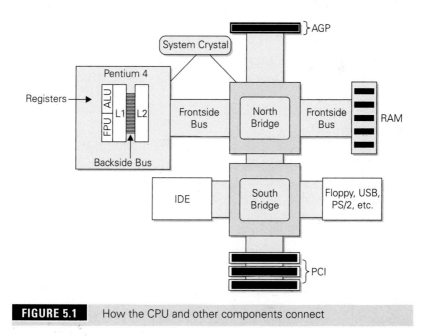

FIGURE 5.1   How the CPU and other components connect

Registers

Registers are memory circuits located inside the CPU that hold data before and after processing. In essence, the registers are the ALU's workbenches. Early Intel Pentium CPUs (Pentium I and Pentium MMX) used primarily 32-bit registers; modern CPUs use 64- and 128-bit register sizes.

Floating-Point Unit (FPU)

The *floating-point unit (FPU)* is the CPU component that handles calculations based on the IEEE *Floating Point Standard.* Without going off on a math tangent, the Floating Point Standard defines a set of codes for representing real numbers (numbers that can contain fractional parts) in CPU calculations. The FPU is the specialized CPU component that processes these types of mathematical calculations for applications that require it, such as graphics programs and 3-D games. The FPU on modern PCs is integrated with the CPU. Ancient, pre-Pentium CPUs relied on a separate FPU chip, sometimes called the *math coprocessor,* to handle FPU mathematics.

Pipeline

The term *pipeline* refers to the discrete series of steps that the CPU follows to process commands. The closest real-world analogy is the process you follow to do laundry. Rather than throw your clothes into a big pile and do everything at once, you go through an ordered series of steps; sort, wash, dry, iron, and fold. Early, pre-Pentium CPUs had only a single pipeline and thus could only process a single command at a time. The Pentium introduced *Dual Independent Bus Architecture*—dual pipelines that enabled the CPU to process two commands simultaneously. Later CPUs have even more pipelines and can thus process more commands at once.

Clock Speed

The CPU clock speed is a measurement of how many calculation cycles a CPU executes per second. One calculation cycle per second is equal to one hertz (Hz). Of course, nobody measures clock cycles in Hz, but rather in millions of calculation cycles per second, or megahertz (MHz). These days, it's more common to see clock speed measured in billions of cycles per second, or gigahertz (GHz).

Clock speed is determined by two things: the maximum speed of the CPU itself and the maximum speed that the motherboard is capable of handling. The CPU speed is determined by the manufacturer and is set at the factory. The motherboard clock speed is governed by an onboard component called the *system crystal.* The system crystal is simply a quartz crystal circuit that oscillates at a fixed frequency when fed current. It literally sets the tempo for the CPU, firing a small electrical charge with each oscillation onto a special wire on the CPU called the *CLK* (or *clock*) wire. Each beat from the system crystal onto the CLK wire equals one cycle on the CPU.

Multipliers

Clock *multipliers* are the mechanism the CPUs use to run at an even faster speed than that set by the system crystal clock. Early CPUs took the beat set by the clock and simply doubled it, thus enabling the CPU to run internally at twice the speed of the motherboard.

All modern CPUs use clock multipliers, so in reality, any CPUs has two speeds: the speed that it runs internally and the speed that it runs externally. When you see the advertised speed of a CPU—500 MHz, 1.8 GHz, 3 GHz, and so on—you're seeing the multiplied internal CPU speed, not the external speed that the CPU uses to talk to the rest of the PC. Multipliers run from x2 up to in excess of x20! Multipliers do not have to be whole numbers. You can find a CPU with a multiplier of x6.5 just as easily as you would find one with a multiplier of x7.

Cache Memory

To aid communication between the CPU and RAM, a special type of memory called *static RAM (SRAM)* is used. Normal system RAM is called *dynamic RAM (DRAM)*, because it can hold data for only a very short duration before it needs to be *refreshed*. SRAM cache memory, in contrast, never needs to be refreshed and is therefore much faster than DRAM. The *Level 1 (L1)* cache memory is the first and fastest cache and has been built into the CPU since even before the Pentium. L1 caches tend to run rather small, around 8–32 KB. Built-in caches are called *internal,* while caches on motherboards are called *external. Level 2 (L2)* cache memory is the second cache. It is always larger than the L1 cache (around 256 KB to 1 MB) and is usually slower. The L2 cache was external in the Pentium days, but all newer CPUs include onboard L2 cache memory. Believe it or not, we now have *Level 3 (L3)* cache memory. L3 caches are seen only on very high-end CPUs (Intel Xeon, Itanium) and are monstrous compared to the L1 cache, with sizes up to 3 MB and growing.

Local Lingo

Die   The ceramic package that holds the CPU is called the *die.* Components that are incorporated into the package, such as L2 cache memory, are referred to as being *on-die.*

Since SRAM is so much faster, why don't PCs use it for system RAM instead of DRAM? The answer is simple: cost. SRAM is roughly ten times more expensive than DRAM.

> **Exam Tip**
>
> DRAM is fast, cheap, and must be refreshed; SRAM is much faster, very expensive, and requires no refreshing.

Northbridge Chip

The *Northbridge* chip is a special memory controller circuit mounted on the motherboard that assists the CPU. The Northbridge chip connects the CPU to system RAM.

Frontside Bus

There are two distinct uses of the word *bus* inside your CPU. The *frontside* bus is the collective term for the physical pathways connecting the CPU, Northbridge chip, and RAM. The frontside bus consists of two parts: the *data bus* and the *address bus*. The data bus is the channel that the CPU uses to access data in RAM, and the address bus is the pathway that the CPU uses to talk to the Northbridge chip. Pentium processors and their equivalents have a 64-bit data bus and a 32-bit address bus. Starting with the Pentium Pro, a 36-bit address bus is available, but it's important to note that only 32 of those bits are used. Itanium and Opteron CPUs have a 64-bit address bus. The *backside* bus refers to the pathway that connects the CPU and the L2 cache.

Address Space

The number of wires on the address bus defines the maximum amount of RAM a CPU can theoretically address. This is called the *address space*. With a 32-bit address bus, the maximum amount of memory the CPU can address is 2^{32} or 4,294,967,296 bytes (4 GB).

Putting it All Together

You see now that the CPU is not an island unto itself, but just one component that interoperates with many other system components to perform the amazing feats of mathematical prowess that it does so well. The CPU is composed of several interlinked internal parts, including the ALU, FPU, registers, and L1 and L2 cache memory. The series of steps that the CPU follows to process commands is called the *pipeline*. Early CPUs used a single pipeline, meaning that they effectively processed only a single command at a time. Modern CPUs use multiple pipelines to process multiple commands at once.

The CPU is connected via the frontside bus to the Northbridge chip, which in turn connects it to system RAM. The backside bus connects the CPU to the L2 cache memory. The most important job of the Northbridge is to act as a memory manager. The CPU tells the Northbridge, via the address bus, which bytes of data it needs from RAM. The Northbridge responds by retrieving the requested data and placing it on the CPU's data bus. The Northbridge is also directly connected to the AGP bus and the Southbridge chip. The Southbridge chip acts as a helper for the Northbridge chip, connecting the Northbridge to the system's IDE channels; the PCI bus; the USB, PS/2, and serial buses; and all other "secondary" buses.

The CPU effectively runs at two different speeds: an internal speed at which it processes data and an external speed at which it sends and receives data from the rest of the system. The system crystal sets the clock speed for the entire system, measured in MHz. The CPU takes the system clock speed and multiplies it, so that the internal processing speed is two, four, six, or more times that of the system speed. The size of the address bus (determined by the number of wires used) dictates how much RAM the CPU can address.

CPU Packages

You should appreciate that the actual CPU microprocessor chip is only a thin square of silicon less than half the size of a postage stamp. What we think of as the CPU is actually the *CPU package.* The CPU package is the circuit board on which the microprocessor is mounted. The CPU package has integrated all of the electrical traces, wires, and contacts that enable the microprocessor to communicate with the motherboard's CPU socket. Different CPU packages are designed to work in different CPU sockets, as described in the following sections.

Pin Grid Array

Pin Grid Array (PGA) CPU packages are flat, square, and roughly two inches across with protruding contact pins arranged in rows on the bottom side. PGA CPUs plug into ZIF sockets, as described in Chapter 3. Figure 5-2 shows a typical PGA CPU package.

The type of ZIF socket that a PGA CPU uses is determined by the number of contact pins on the CPU package. At one time, PC manufacturers used coded socket numbering schemes, such as *Socket 4* to indicate a 273-pin CPU package. Intel simplifies things now by simply calling them *Socket X,* with *X* being the number of pins on the CPU package. Ergo, a *Socket 370* ZIF socket, as shown in Figure 5-3, accommodates an Intel 370-pin CPU package.

FIGURE 5.2   PGA CPU package (top and bottom)

Photo courtesy of AMD

Single Edge Contact

The *Single Edge Contact (SEC)* CPU package is rectangular, roughly five inches wide by two-and-a-half inches tall, with all contact pins mounted on the bottom edge. SEC packages are either fully or partially encased in a protective plastic cover. Although larger than the PGA CPU package, the SEC design takes up less space on the motherboard because it sits upright instead of flat, as shown in Figure 5-4.

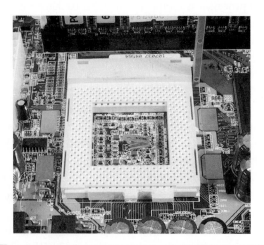

FIGURE 5.3   PGA Socket 370

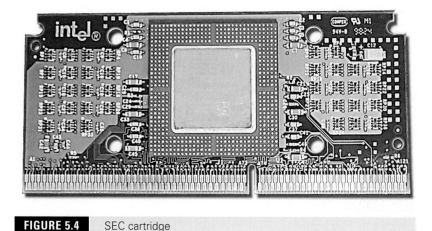

FIGURE 5.4   SEC cartridge

SEC packages come in a few variations. The Pentium II and early Celerons used a fully enclosed design called the *Single Edge Contact Cartridge (SECC)*. The Pentium III and Athlon used the semi-enclosed *SECC2* package. Later Celerons came in a package called *Single Edge Processor Package (SEPP)* that did away with the plastic casing.

All of these technologies are still found in functioning PCs, although they're not generally being made anymore. Intel SEC CPU packages use the *Slot 1* motherboard socket, with the exception of the Xeon, which uses a special socket called *Slot 2*. The AMD Athlon uses a variant of Slot 1 called *Slot A*. Even though both Intel and AMD have phased out the SEC CPU package in favor of the PGA package, it's still important for you to identify this type of CPU package.

CPU Voltage

CPUs have relatively low power requirements. Early Pentiums ran at 5 volts, but modern CPUs run at much lower voltages. When CPUs went to lower voltages, motherboards continued to run at 5 volts. As a result, motherboards required built-in voltage regulator circuits to control the flow of juice to the CPU. On older systems, you'll find special *voltage regulator modules (VRMs)* that are configured manually to control voltage to the CPU. Figure 5-5 shows a VRM slot. Manually configured VRMs are obsolete, as modern motherboards use VRMs that communicate directly with the CPU to automatically set the correct voltage.

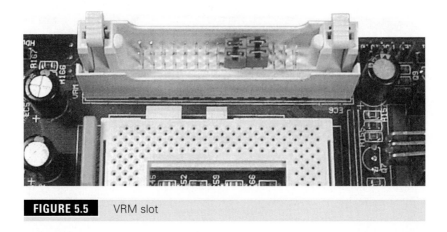

FIGURE 5.5   VRM slot

CPU Cooling

One factor is vitally important for all CPUs, regardless of who made them or what form factor they take: cooling. CPUs have no moving parts, but they nonetheless generate considerable heat. As you know by now, heat leads to system instability, lockups, and dead CPUs. CPU packages are made from high-tech thermal plastics and ceramics that dissipate heat, but they still can't provide enough relief without help. This help comes in the form of heat sink and fan assemblies and from liquid cooling systems.

Heat Sinks and Fans

The most common type of CPU cooling system is the heat sink and fan assembly. The heat sink is a finned alloy block that rests on the CPU package and draws heat away from the CPU chip. A powered CPU fan mounted on the heat sink increases air circulation, thus further dissipating heat. The heat sink must be affixed securely to the CPU package with special *thermal compound*. Figure 5-6 shows a typical PGA CPU package with a mounted heat sink and fan assembly.

Liquid Cooling Systems

Gamers, tweakers, and other high-performance PC enthusiasts have known about liquid cooling systems for some time, but such systems are now becoming popular in the mainstream. Liquid CPU cooling systems are similar to a car engine's cooling system: a pump circulates water through a set of hoses to a metal *cooling element* affixed to the CPU package. Heat from the CPU transfers to the water, and the heated water is then pumped away from the element and through a radiator-like *heat exchanger* unit where it is cooled before being circulated back to the CPU element. Very slick!

FIGURE 5.6   PGA package heat sink and fan assembly

Until recently, liquid cooling systems were strictly build-it-yourself affairs. Many techs resorted to using aquarium parts and hand-milling cooling elements out of solid metal blocks. Nowadays, ready-made kits are plentiful and many high-end PC cases have incorporated liquid cooling systems. Figure 5-7 shows the inside of a Koolance PC case with a built-in liquid cooling system. Note the top-mounted heat exchanger (it looks like a radiator grill). Not shown in the picture are three high-end fans on top of the case. Passive heat exchangers without fans are less desirable. The water reservoir sits in the bottom of the PC case. Figure 5-8 shows a close-up of the CPU cooling element. Copper is the best heat conductor, but other metals are also used.

In most cases, plain tap water is the coolant of choice, but if the local water in your area is high in mineral content, you should use distilled water. Special additives such as Water Wetter can increase water's cooling capacity and help prevent corrosion. Luminous dyes are also available, if you'd like your cooling water to glow in the dark. This adds nothing to performance, but it sure is cool to look at!

FIGURE 5.7 PC case with integrated liquid cooling system

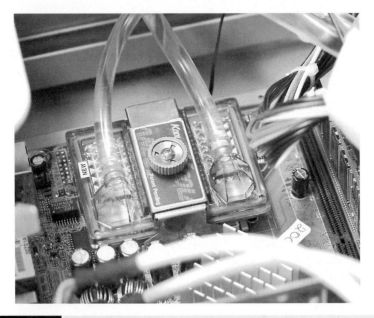

FIGURE 5.8 CPU cooling element

Are liquid cooling systems better than traditional heat sink and fan assemblies? The answer is a qualified yes. They definitely provide superior cooling, and they also keep the CPU at a consistent temperature even during times of peak activity, which may extend the life of the CPU. Plus, they're extremely quiet, thus appealing to use in home entertainment systems or sound-sensitive environments such as recording studios. On the other hand, they're considerably more expensive (roughly three times the cost of a heat sink and fan assembly). They're also more complicated to set up and maintain, and the extra cooling they provide doesn't necessarily boost performance. Consider also the added risk of having water circulating around inside your PC case. Even a small coolant leak could be disastrous!

Objective 5.02 CPU Specifications: Intel

This section takes a detailed look at the Intel line of CPUs. Intel has always been the dominant force in the CPU industry and, with the exception of AMD, practically monopolizes today's CPU market.

Pentium

Intel's popular Pentium processor line has now been around for over ten years. The original Pentium line had a 64-bit data bus and a 32-bit address bus, and came in speeds ranging from 60 to 166 MHz. Early Pentiums ran at 5 volts; later versions ran at the more modern standard of 3.3 volts.

Exam Tip
The Pentium processor was the first PC processor to have a 64-bit data bus.

Pentium Pro

Intel created the *Pentium Pro* in 1995 to compete in the high-end server market. This processor had a distinctive, rectangular 387-pin SPGA format and connected to the motherboard via Socket 8. The Pentium Pro had a 64-bit data bus, but instead of the 32-bit address bus of the Pentium line, it used a 36-bit address bus. Intel released the Pentium Pro in speeds of 150 to 200 MHz. All speeds used

3.3 volts DC with the exception of the 150-MHz version of the processor, which used 3.1 volts DC.

Pentium Pro CPUs could handle four pipelines simultaneously and, as a result, were capable of performing on average the equivalent of three simultaneous processes. In addition to a 16 K L1 cache, the Pentium Pro processor had an onboard L2 cache of 256 KB, 512 KB, or 1 MB. This new onboard L2 cache ran at the same speed as the processor, and thus provided an excellent boost in processing efficiency. The Pentium Pro is often regarded as the prototype of all Pentiums that followed until the Pentium 4.

Exam Tip
With the Pentium Pro, Intel introduced a 36-bit, rather than 32-bit, address bus into this and future lines of processors—but nobody used the extra wires for addressing memory. For the A+ exams, think in terms of 32-bit RAM support for all Pentium or later Intel processors (up to 4 GB) and you'll be safe.

Pentium II

Intel first introduced the Pentium II processor in 1997. The Pentium II was the first to use the SEC CPU package. The Pentium II processor has a 64-bit wide data bus and a 36-bit wide address bus (effectively 32-bit RAM support); it can address 4 GB of RAM. Intel shipped the Pentium II in speeds of 233, 266, 300, and 333 MHz, with a system bus speed of 66 MHz; the company later shipped Pentium II processors that ran on a 100 MHz bus at core speeds of 350, 400, and 450 MHz. The Pentium II contains 32 KB of L1 cache and a 512 KB L2 cache that runs at half the speed of the processor core.

Exam Tip
The first processor to break away from the PGA form factor and use the SEC (Single Edge Contact) form factor was the Pentium II.

The Pentium II's L2 cache was rather unique—it wasn't truly internal, as it sat on a separate part of the SEC package. But since it was on the cartridge, it wasn't external either. It was known as an on-chip cache, as opposed to the more common on-die cache. However, the difference from a performance standpoint made the Pentium II on-chip cache act like an internal cache, so we say the Pentium II had an internal cache—even though technically it wasn't.

Pentium III

Intel released the Pentium III processor in 1999. It initially came out in a 242-pin SEC package, but Intel eventually switched to the 370-pin PGA form factor. Pentium III processors came in a wide variety of core speeds and motherboard system speeds. Initially releasing a 450 MHz version with a 100 MHz system speed, Intel kept cranking up the speeds until the P-III topped out at 1.3 GHz with a 133 MHz system speed. Other variations exist as well. The Pentium IIIB introduced an onboard *Advanced Transfer Cache (ATC)* that greatly improved performance.

Like the Pentium II, Pentium III CPUs have a 64-bit data bus and a 36-bit address bus, and can handle up to 4 GB of memory.

Pentium 4

The Pentium 4 introduces radical improvements in the core processing technology, such as a 20-step pipeline and special instruction sets that enhance graphics, and up to eight data transfers per clock cycle. The Pentium 4 comes in two packages: a 423-pin design with a 256 KB L2 cache and a 478-pin model with double the L2 cache onboard. Speeds of the Pentium 4 currently range from a respectable 1.3 GHz to a blazing 3.06 GHz.

Table 5-1 summarizes the specifications of the Intel Pentium CPU line.

TABLE 5.1	Intel Pentium Family				
CPU	**Pentium**	**Pentium Pro**	**Pentium II**	**Pentium III**	**Pentium 4**
Generation	5th	6th	6th	6th	7th
External speed range	50–66 MHz (early), 66–75 MHz (later)	60–66 MHz	66–100 MHz	100–133 MHz	100–133 MHz (quad speed, 8X speed)
Internal speed range	60–200 MHz (early), 166–200 MHz (later)	150–200 MHz	233–450 MHz	450 MHz–1.26 GHz	1.3–3.06 GHz
Voltage	5 V, 3.3 V	3.1 V, 3.3 V	3.3 V	3.3 V	3.3 V
Multiplier range	x1–x3 (early), x2.5–x4.5 (later)	x2.5–x3	x3.5–x4.5	x4–x10	x13 and up
L1 cache	16 KB (early), 32 KB (later)	16 KB	32 KB	32KB	128 KB
L2 cache	None	256 KB, 512 KB, 1 MB	512 KB	256 or 512 KB	256 or 512 KB

TABLE 5.1	Intel Pentium Family *(continued)*				
CPU	**Pentium**	**Pentium Pro**	**Pentium II**	**Pentium III**	**Pentium 4**
L3 cache	None	None	None	None	None
Package	PGA	PGA	SEC	SEC-2, PGA	423-pin PGA, 478-pin PGA
Socket(s) used	Socket 4, Socket 5 (early), Socket 7 (later)	Socket 8	Slot 1	Slot 1, Socket 370	Socket 423, Socket 478
Max addressable RAM	4 GB	4 GB	4 GB	4 GB	4 GB

Celeron

The Celeron was originally a low-cost knockoff of the more powerful Pentium II design, but it's become very popular in its own right. As noted earlier, the first Celerons came in the SEP CPU package and ran at speeds of 266 and 300 MHz. Later Celerons use PGA packages that plug into Socket 370 motherboards and run at speeds up to 2.4 GHz.

The original Celeron had a bad reputation due to the fact that it had no onboard L2 cache, which seriously affected its performance. Intel quickly corrected this, and all Celerons now have a 128 KB L2 cache. Table 5-2 summarizes the specifications of the Intel Celeron CPU line.

TABLE 5.2	Intel Celeron Family		
CPU	**Celeron (Pentium II based)**	**Celeron (Pentium III based)**	**Celeron (Pentium 4 based)**
Generation	6th	6th	7th
External speed range	66 MHz	66–100 MHz	100 MHz (quad speed)
Internal speed range	266–700 MHz	533–700 MHz	850 MHz–2.4 GHz
Voltage	3.3 V	3.3 V	3.3 V
Multiplier range	x4–x10.5	x8–x11.5	x8.5–x20.5
L1 cache	32 KB	32 KB	32 KB
L2 cache	None (early), 128 KB (later)	128 KB	128 KB
L3 cache	None	None	None
Package	SEP, PGA	PGA	SEC, PGA
Socket(s) used	Slot 1, Socket 370	Socket 370	Slot 1, Socket 370
Max addressable RAM	4 GB	4 GB	4 GB

Xeon and Xeon MP

Just as the Celeron series are lower-end processors built around the Pentium core, the Xeon series of CPUs are Intel's high-end version. Although not that different on paper from the normal Pentium line, the Xeon is designed to offer strong multiprocessor support. Xeon processors are ideally suited for high-performance workstation and server systems that are capable of running two, four, or even eight CPUs. A version of the Xeon called the Xeon MP incorporates an on-die L3 cache of 512 KB, 1 MB, or 2 MB size.

Both the Pentium II- and Pentium III-based Xeons use a unique SEC package that snaps into a Xeon-only slot called *Slot 2*. Later versions use a 603-pin PGA package.

Table 5-3 summarizes the specifications of the Intel Xeon CPU line.

TABLE 5.3	Intel Xeon CPU Family		
CPU	**Xeon (Pentium II based)**	**Xeon (Pentium III based)**	**Xeon (Pentium 4 based)**	**Xeon MP**
Generation	6th	6th	7th	7th
External speed range	100 MHz	100–133 MHz	100–133 MHz (quad speed)	100–133 MHz (quad speed)
Internal speed range	400–450 MHz	500 MHz– 1 GHz	1.4–3.06 GHz	1.4–2 GHz
Multiplier range	x4–x4.5	x5–x7.5	x14–x28	x14–x20
L1 cache	32 KB	32 KB	12 KB	12 KB
L2 cache	512 KB–2 MB	256 KB, 512 KB, 1 MB, 2 MB	256 KB, 512 KB	256 KB, 512 KB
L3 cache	None	None	None	512 KB, 1 MB, 2 MB
Package	SEC	SEC	PGA	PGA
Socket(s) used	Slot 2	Slot 2	Socket 603	Socket 603
Max addressable RAM	4 GB	4 GB	4 GB	4 GB

Itanium and Itanium II

The Itanium CPU line is in a class of its own. The thing that separates the Itanium and Itanium II from all previous Intel CPUs is the inclusion of a 64-bit address bus. Remember that the number of wires on the address bus defines the maximum amount of RAM a CPU can address. With a 64-bit address bus, we will see CPUs that can address 2^{64} bytes of memory, or more precisely, 18,446,744,073,709,551,616 bytes of memory. Yes, you read that right—over 18 *quintillion* bytes! It's unlikely that you'll ever see this much RAM in one place in your lifetime, but just so you know, the technical term for a quintillion bytes is *exabyte (EB)*.

Travel Advisory

There have been a number of 64-bit CPUs before the Itanium, but they were not designed for the PC marketplace and they have had only a small amount of market share.

Before we go any further, let's clarify something—the numbers listed here are largely theoretical. Neither the Itanium nor the Itanium II currently uses the whole 64 bits of the address bus; that's simply the maximum that these processors are capable of using. The Itanium uses a 44-bit address bus, while the Itanium II uses 50 bits, for maximum address spaces of 17,592,186,044,416 bytes (17.5 terabytes, or TB) and 1,125,899,906,842,624 bytes (1.1 petabyte, or PB), respectively.

Physically, the Itanium packages are unique. The Itanium has a 418-pin *Pin Array Cartridge (PAC)* to help house its big Level 3 cache. The Itanium II uses a 611-pin form of PGA that Intel calls *Organic Land Grid Array,* or OLGA.

Table 5-4 sums up the specifications of the Intel Itanium and Itanium II.

TABLE 5.4	Intel Itanium Family	
CPU	**Intel Itanium**	**Intel Itanium II**
Generation	8th	8th
Physical address	44 bits	50 bits
Frontside bus width	64 bits	128 bits
External speed range	133 MHz (quad speed)	100 MHz (quad speed)
Internal speed range	733 MHz, 833 MHz	900 MHz, 1 GHz
Multiplier range	x6–x8.5	x9–x10
L1 cache	32 KB	32 KB
L2 cache	96 KB	256 KB

TABLE 5.4	Intel Itanium Family *(continued)*	
CPU	**Intel Itanium**	**Intel Itanium II**
L3 cache	2 MB, 4 MB	1.5 MB, 3 MB
Package	PAC	OLGA
Socket(s) used	Socket 418	Socket 611
Max addressable RAM	17.5 TB	1.1 PB

For the time being, one crucial factor relegates the Itanium CPUs to the rarified air of experimental or special-purpose computing—the fact that the 64-bit Itanium CPUs aren't backward compatible with 32-bit applications. An Itanium can run 32-bit applications, but only through special 64-bit emulation programs. Both the OS and the programs meant to take advantage of the Itanium's awesome processing power must be specifically programmed to run in a 64-bit environment.

Objective 5.03 CPU Specifications: AMD

AMD is Intel's only true competitor in the CPU market. AMD's line of processors are well-regarded in the PC world, equaling and in some cases surpassing the performance of their Intel counterparts. Additionally, their lower cost makes them a very appealing choice for those who want to produce a lower-cost PC without sacrificing quality. This section lists the important specifications for the AMD line of CPUs.

K5 and K6

The AMD K5 processor was released in 1995 and was a virtual clone of the Intel Pentium. The K5 had a 296-pin PGA that used Socket 7 to connect to the motherboard. K5 speeds ran from 75 to 116 MHz. Like the Pentium, the K5 had a 64-bit-wide data bus and the 32-bit address bus enabling it to address up to 4 GB of RAM. This processor used 3.52 volts of DC power and supported only 8 KB of L1 cache. Aside from markings on the chip, the K5 looked identical to a Pentium.

The K6 series also had a 296-pin PGA form factor, but used an enhanced socket 7 ZIF socket, called a Super Socket 7. Initially available in speeds of 166–266 MHz, these processors used 3.3 volts DC. By the end of production, the K6 series of processors had reached core speeds of 550 MHz with 1 MB of onboard L1 cache, and ran on only 2.2 volts DC. Table 5-5 lists specifications of the K5 and K6 line.

Athlon

The Athlon, introduced in 1999, was AMD's first serious step out from under Intel's shadow. Originally released at 500 MHz, speeds for the Athlon have climbed steadily; in fact, it was the first x86 processor to break the 1 GHz mark. Athlons have 128 KB of L1 cache, and either 256 KB or 512 KB of L2 cache.

Early Athlons were packaged in the Slot A SEC CPU package, which was almost identical to the Intel Slot 1 format; however, these two slots are *not* pin-compatible, and cannot be interchanged. The same is true of the Socket A, PGA-packaged version of the Athlon—it cannot be plugged into an Intel Socket 370 motherboard.

Another factor that separates the Athlon line from the Intel products is the way that the AMD CPUs effectively double the communication speed between the CPU and Northbridge. This "double data rate" makes the Athlon processors a natural match for high-performance DDR SDRAM, which is discussed in Chapter 6.

Like the Intel CPU line, the AMD Athlon line includes low-end and high-end variants of the basic (or "classic") Athlon. The Duron CPU is the chopped-down version of the Athlon that is quite popular on entry-level PCs. The Thunderbird Athlon gets a performance boost from a smaller, but more powerful, L2 cache. The Athlon XP pushes performance even further to match the Pentium 4-class Intel processors.

TABLE 5.5	AMD K5 and K6	
CPU	**K5**	**K6**
Generation	5th	6th
External speed range	50–75 MHz	66–100 MHz
Internal speed range	60–150 MHz	200–550 MHz
Multiplier range	x1.5–x2	x3–x5.5
L1 cache	16 KB	32 KB (K6, K6-2), 64 KB (K6-III)
L2 cache	None	None (K6, K6-2), 256 KB (K6-III)
L3 cache	None	None
Package	PGA	PGA
Socket(s) used	Socket 7	Socket 7
Max addressable RAM	4 GB	4 GB

This leads to an interesting point about how the Athlon line's speed ratings are advertised. AMD ignores clock speeds, and instead markets its CPUs using a number that matches the equivalent power of an Intel Pentium 4 processor. For example, the Athlon XP 1800+ actually runs at 1.6 GHz, but AMD claims that it processes as fast or faster than a Pentium 4 1.8 GHz CPU—ergo "1800+." This is called the Athlon's *P-Rating*.

Local Lingo

P-Rating   Athlon speed ratings are advertised according to their equivalent Pentium CPU speed (as determined by AMD). This is called a *P-Rating*.

Table 5-6 describes the specifications of the Athlon, Duron, Thunderbird Athlon, and Athlon XP CPUs.

TABLE 5.6   Athlon Family

CPU	Classic Athlon	Duron	Thunderbird Athlon	Athlon XP
Generation	6th	6th	6th	7th
External speed range	100 MHz (doubled)	100 MHz (doubled)	100–133 MHz (doubled)	133 MHz (dual speed)
Internal speed range	500 MHz–1 GHz	600 MHz–1.3 GHz	650 MHz–1.4 GHz	1.3 GHz (1500+)–2.16 GHz (3000+)
Multiplier range	x5–x10	x3.5–x14	x3.5–x14	x13–x16.5
L1 cache	128 KB	128 KB	128 KB	128 KB
L2 cache	512 KB	64 KB	256 KB	256 KB, 512 KB
L3 cache	None	None	None	None
Package	SEC	PGA	PGA	462-pin PGA
Socket(s) used	Slot A	Socket A	Socket A	Socket A
Max addressable RAM	4 GB	4 GB	4 GB	4 GB

AMD Duron Processors

AMD released the Duron processor, shown in Figure 5-9, to compete on the lower end of the CPU spectrum with Intel's Celeron CPU. Basically a cut-down Athlon, the Duron has the same 128 KB of L1 cache, but has only 64 KB of L2 cache. Other improvements (such as a 200-MHz frontside bus) make the Duron slightly faster than a comparative Celeron. The Duron debuted at 600 MHz, and has continued to climb in clock speed ever since. Durons come in a Socket A PGA form factor.

Opteron

The Opteron is AMD's server-level 64-bit CPU offering. Although not quite on par with the latest Itanium CPUs in terms of sheer processing muscle, the Opteron possesses a couple of features that make it somewhat more compelling than the Itanium. One of these is the use of an internal processing technology called *HyperTransport*. This is essentially an onboard Northbridge chip and memory controller that enables the Opteron to transfer data internally at an astounding 6.4 GB per second!

More importantly, the Opteron contains internal instruction sets that make it backward compatible with 32-bit applications. This is in direct contrast to the Itanium's 64-bit-only operating mode, and makes the Opteron an attractive choice to those who aren't fully committed to making the jump to the 64-bit world. Table 5-7 describes the specifications of the Opteron CPU.

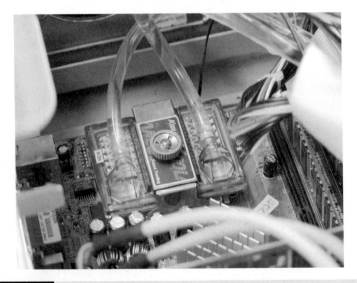

FIGURE 5.9   AMD Duron

TABLE 5.7	AMD Opteron
CPU	**AMD Opteron**
Generation	8th
Physical Address	40 bits
Frontside Bus Width	128 bit
External Speed Range	6.4 GB/Second (HyperTransport)
Internal Speed Range	1.4–1.8 GHz
Multiplier Range	x14–x20
L1 Cache	128 KB
L2 Cache	1 MB
L3 Cache	None
Package	PGA
Socket(s) used	Socket 940

Travel Advisory

The AMD64 and AMD64 FX CPUs are not covered on the A+ exam!

Objective 5.04 Installing CPUs

Installing a CPU is only slightly more complicated than installing any other component; however, there are a number of things to take into consideration before you pop the cover off of your PC case. It should be clear by now that you can't just slap any CPU into your PC and expect it to work!

The most important consideration is motherboard compatibility. You've got to make certain that your motherboard is matched to the right brand and model of CPU, running at the right speed, and configured for the right voltage. If you're performing a CPU upgrade, you may find that you have to replace not only the CPU, but also the motherboard, RAM, and possibly even the PC case.

After you choose your new CPU, you need to install it. Surprisingly, installing a CPU is a fairly trivial step—assuming you have the right CPU, of course! You also need to provide proper cooling for the CPU; typically, replacing a CPU also means replacing the heat sink and fan assembly with new ones that match the new processor. If you're using a liquid cooling system, you've got to make sure that your CPU cooling element fits properly on your new CPU, and that the system has enough cooling capacity to keep the temperature of your new CPU under control.

Once you've confirmed these things, you're ready to do some PC brain surgery. Let's look at the procedure now.

Compatibility Issues

The key to a successful CPU installation is making sure that the processor and motherboard are compatible. The motherboard's documentation is the best source for compatibility information. The motherboard manual should contain some sort of chart listing the CPUs that it supports. Most motherboards are also packaged with a CD-ROM that contains needed drivers and help files—you may find an updated list of compatible CPUs there.

Because Intel and AMD CPUs are not pin-compatible, all motherboards made since the mid-1990s support *either* Intel CPUs *or* AMD CPUs—not both. Once you know which brand of processor your motherboard takes, the next step is to match the model. The type of CPU socket that the motherboard uses (SEC or PGA) determines which model of Intel or AMD CPU you can install. Many motherboards accept more than one model of CPU into a compatible socket; for example, most Intel motherboards will take either a Pentium or Celeron processor. Remember that some CPU models use more than one socket type. For instance, the Pentium 4 model comes in two socket varieties: Socket 423 and Socket 478. Make certain that you know which one you need before you make a decision!

Once you've narrowed your choices down to a particular brand and model, you need to determine which CPU speed your system can support. The maximum speed of a particular CPU that a motherboard can handle is determined by the chipset and BIOS, and is listed along with the other information in the motherboard documentation. Sometimes you can upgrade the speed of CPU that a motherboard can handle by updating (flashing) the BIOS. Your motherboard maker's web site is the best place to find out if this is an option for you.

It's less common to have to ensure that your CPU runs at the right voltage for the motherboard. As mentioned earlier in this chapter, modern motherboards automatically adjust voltage to match the CPU. If you happen to come across a motherboard and CPU combination that requires you to set the voltage manually, be certain that you set it correctly! Improper voltage settings will send your brand-new CPU up in smoke. Check the motherboard documentation for this information.

Cooling Issues

When purchasing a CPU, you generally have a choice of buying the *boxed* or *unboxed* version. There's no difference between the actual CPUs, but boxed packages include all documentation and drivers, and also come with a heat sink and fan assembly preinstalled. Unboxed CPUs include *only* the CPU itself, meaning that you have to download documentation and drivers from the manufacturer's web site and provide your own cooling system.

Whether you go with a traditional heat sink and fan assembly or a fancy liquid cooling system, make certain that they're configured specifically for your CPU brand and model. Cooling systems have to fit very tightly onto the CPU package, and installing the wrong one can crack the ceramic die.

Heat sinks are made of either copper or aluminum alloy, and come with either thick or thin heat-dissipating vanes. The thin-vaned ones provide better cooling, but are more expensive and more delicate. Make certain that you get one that's matched to your CPU package and to the fan that you're installing. Never install a heat sink without first putting a thin layer of thermal compound on the CPU. The same rules apply when using a liquid cooling system. Make certain that the metal cooling element is matched to your CPU package, and that you use thermal compound.

Local Lingo

Thermal Paste   Thermal compound is sometimes called *thermal paste* or *heat dope.*

The fan you choose should be powerful enough to provide sufficient airflow for your CPU. Fans are rated in *cubic feet per minute,* or CFM. Typical fans for PGA CPUs are rated at about 22 CFM. More cooling capacity is better, as you can't over-cool a CPU, but you can certainly under-cool one! The fan's documentation should tell you if it's compatible with your CPU. You should also check to make sure that there's sufficient clearance inside your PC case. The heat sink and fan assembly should be clear of any obstructions that might hinder airflow, and shouldn't touch any other components or cards.

If you're using a liquid cooling system, follow the maker's instructions to ensure proper fit and finish, and be sure to test the system beforehand to ensure that there are no leaks and that the pumps and fans are in good working order.

CPU Physical Installation

Now that we've got the preliminaries out of the way, let's look at the steps to install a CPU. Before you begin, power down the PC and unplug the power cable. Put the PC case on your antistatic mat, if you have one. Make sure you've got enough room and light to work and remove the cover from your PC case. Strap on your nerd bracelet and ground yourself, and you're ready to go.

PGA Package

PGA-packaged CPUs fit into square ZIF sockets, such as Socket 478 (for Intel CPUs) or Socket A (for AMD CPUs). Follow these steps to install:

1. Lift the CPU release lever arm.

2. Locate the orientation mark on the corner of the CPU and socket. They are usually marked with an arrow or raised dot. Double-check the orientation by looking at the pin configuration—the CPU and socket should be oriented so that the corner (or corners) with missing pins align.

3. Holding the CPU by its edges, position it over the socket and gently set it in place. If the pins and socket holes are oriented correctly, the CPU should drop right in without any force (*zero* insertion force—get it?). If the CPU doesn't fit easily into the socket, you're doing it wrong! Make certain that it's oriented correctly and try again. When seated, the CPU package should sit flush with the socket mount with no pins showing.

4. Lower and lock the release lever into place.

That's all there is to it. The next step is to install the cooling system, but first let's look at the installation steps for an SEC-packaged CPU.

SEC Package

SEC-packaged CPUs are somewhat easier to install than PGA CPUs, but there is also a bit more variety in SEC mounting hardware. Some use levered or latched brackets to secure the CPU package, while others simply snap into place without any additional support.

1. If necessary, lift the CPU release arm or latch out of the way.

2. Locate the orientation guide ridge in the SEC socket and align the CPU.

3. Gently press the CPU assembly into the socket until it seats firmly.

4. If needed, lower the release arm or latch into place.

Installing the Cooling System

If you opted for a boxed CPU, then the cooling assembly should have come preinstalled, requiring no extra effort on your part. Unboxed CPUs, of course, require you to install the cooling system separately. Heat sink and fan assemblies take a bit of force and finesse to mount properly—more than you might think! A small flat-headed screwdriver will help.

PGA Package

Heat sink and fan assemblies for PGA-packaged CPUs usually come as a unit, but if not, you should attach the fan to the heat sink before installing them onto the CPU.

1. If your CPU has thermal paste preapplied, remove and discard the protective tape. If not, then apply a thin film of thermal paste to the raised center of the CPU package.

2. Align the mounting bracket hardware on the heat sink and fan assembly with the mounting notches on the CPU socket.

3. Attach the mounting bracket to one side of the CPU socket.

4. Using your screwdriver as a lever, press down on the mounting bracket on the other side of the CPU socket and snap the bracket into place. If this makes you nervous, don't worry—that's normal. Most techs are surprised by the amount of force needed to mount the heat sink and fan assembly into place.

5. The last step is to plug the fan's power cable into the appropriate socket or header on the motherboard. Check your motherboard documentation for this information.

SEC Package

Part of the attraction to SEC-packaged CPUs is that the package itself acts as a heat sink, meaning that the additional heat sink and fan assembly can be less bulky and less powerful (thus a bit quieter). Many types of SEC CPUs have fans integrated into the CPU housing. Others require that you install a separate fan.

1. Apply thermal compound to the CPU, or remove the protective tape from any pre-applied compound.

2. SEC heat sink and fan assemblies attach to the CPU package by four spring-loaded locking pins or with screws. Align the pins or screws on

the assembly with the corresponding mounting holes on the CPU package.

3. Push the locking pins or screws through the mounting holes on the CPU package and secure them into place.

4. Plug the CPU fan into the socket on the motherboard, and you're done.

Installing a Liquid Cooling System

For all the differences between traditional heat sink and fan assemblies and the more modern liquid cooling systems, the essential installation steps are very similar.

1. Follow the manufacturer's instructions to attach the hoses from the coolant reservoir tank to the CPU cooling element and the heat exchanger unit. Make certain that all hoses are secure and crimped properly.

2. Fill the coolant reservoir with the recommended amount of distilled water.

3. Apply a small amount of thermal compound to the CPU.

4. If your liquid cooling system uses a separate CPU temperature sensor on the cooling element, attach it to the appropriate slot or groove and secure it with the supplied metal tape.

5. Mount the cooling element to the CPU with the attached bracket and secure it in place with the tension screw. Be careful not to overtighten the screw.

6. You're ready to go!

Testing CPU Installation

The moment of truth has arrived! Confirm that you haven't accidentally unseated any other components inside the PC, then reattach your power cable and boot the system.

Assuming you've done everything correctly, your system will start without any undue alarms or errors. If, however, something has gone wrong, look (and listen) for the following signs:

- It's normal for the CPU fan speed to fluctuate, but if the fan doesn't spin at all for more than five seconds or so, turn the system off and make sure that the fan is plugged in correctly.

- If the fan is spinning but the PC doesn't boot, make certain that any jumpers governing speed or voltage are set correctly.

- If, after a few minutes, you hear a loud alarm, this is an indication that the system is overheating. Turn it off immediately and check your fan installation to make sure you've got good CPU/heat sink contact and that the fan is functioning properly.

- If the system does not boot and the fan does not spin, check to ensure that the CPU is seated properly and that no other components or cables have been unseated or disturbed.

CHECKPOINT

✔**Objective 5.01: CPU Technology Overview**   Modern CPUs have two speeds: an external speed set by the PC's system crystal clock and an internal speed set by multiplying the system speed by a factor of 2 or greater. CPU makers advertise the faster internal speed of their processors rather than the external speed. The frontside bus connects the CPU, Northbridge chip, and RAM. The backside bus connects the CPU and L2 cache memory. Most CPUs use a 32-bit address bus and can address up to 4 GB of RAM. Desktop CPU packages include the Single Edge Contact (SEC) form factor and the Pin Grid Array (PGA), and their variants. Modern motherboards have built-in voltage regulators to control the flow of electricity to the CPU; older motherboards require a voltage regulator module (VRM). Essential CPU cooling is provided by heat sinks and fan assemblies, and by liquid cooling systems.

✔**Objective 5.02: CPU Specifications: Intel**   Early Pentium processors in-troduced Dual Pipeline Architecture and could handle two sets of instruc-tions at once. Later versions of the Pentium can handle even more pipelines simultaneously. The Pentium Pro CPUs were the first to have an onboard L2 cache and the first to use a 36-bit address bus. The Pentium III introduced the Advanced Transfer Cache. The Pentium 4 uses a 20-step pipeline and can handle up to eight data transfers per clock cycle. The Xeon CPU is enhanced for multiprocessor support and uses a special proprietary socket called Slot 2. The Itanium CPU is the first to incorporate a 64-bit address bus, but in ac-tuality only 44 or 50 bits are used. Only applications programmed for a 64-bit environment run on the Itanium CPU.

✔**Objective 5.03: CPU Specifications: AMD**   Athlon CPUs come in both Slot A and Socket A configurations; Durons use only Socket A. Slot A looks like Slot 1, and Socket A looks like Socket 370, but neither is pin-compatible with the Intel-based connections. The Athlon uses a special communication scheme between the CPU and Northbridge that effectively doubles the bus speed. AMD markets the clock speed of its CPUs using the equivalent of what an Intel CPU runs at rather than the actual clock speed, e.g., the 1.6-GHz Athlon XP is advertised as the 1800+ due to the fact that (according to AMD) it processes data at the same rate as an Intel 1.8-GHz CPU. AMD's 64-bit CPU, the Opteron, differs from the 64-bit Itanium in that it is fully backward compatible with 32-bit applications.

✔**Objective 5.04: Installing CPUs**   Motherboards are made to accommodate a narrow range of CPU types. The CPU's form factor, speed, and voltage must be compatible. Installing CPUs is physically very simple, but you must be careful not to damage the CPU pins or package. Proper cooling is absolutely essential. Use thermal compound between the CPU and the heat sink and fan assembly, or between the CPU and cooling element if using a liquid cooling system.

REVIEW QUESTIONS

1. Which of the following CPUs will fit into a Socket 7 ZIF socket?
   A. Pentium Pro
   B. Pentium
   C. AMD K6
   D. Duron

2. Which processor was the first to have a 64-bit data bus?
   A. Pentium
   B. Pentium II
   C. Pentium Pro
   D. Athlon

3. What socket type does a Pentium Pro processor fit into?
   A. Socket 7
   B. Socket 4
   C. Socket 9
   D. Socket 8

4. Which of the following processors was the first to use an internal L2 cache?

   A. Intel Pentium II

   B. Intel Pentium Pro

   C. AMD Duron

   D. Cyrix MII

5. What is the purpose of the system crystal?

   A. Controls voltage to the CPU

   B. Sets the base clock speed of the motherboard

   C. Holds data before and after processing by the ALU

   D. Aids communication between the CPU and RAM

6. How do Pentium II processors connect to the motherboard?

   A. Socket 7

   B. Socket 8

   C. Slot 1

   D. Slot A

7. What form factor did the Pentium II processor use?

   A. PGA

   B. SEC

   C. SPGA

   D. All of the above

8. Which of the following are advantages liquid cooling systems provide over heat sink and fan assemblies? (Choose two.)

   A. Superior CPU cooling

   B. Lower cost

   C. Maintains consistent temperature even under peak CPU activity

   D. Simpler to set up and maintain

9. Which processor connected to the motherboard using the Socket 370 ZIF socket?

   A. Pentium Pro

   B. AMD Duron

   C. Pentium II

   D. Pentium III

10. Which processor connects to the motherboard using Slot A?

    A. Pentium II

    B. AMD Duron

    C. Pentium III

    D. AMD Athlon

11. What does the backside bus connect?

    A. The CPU and the Northbridge chip

    B. The Northbridge chip and RAM

    C. The CPU and L2 cache memory

    D. The CPU and RAM

12. The main difference between the Itanium and the Opteron is that

    _____.

    A. The Itanium is a 32-bit processor, while the Opteron is a 64-bit processor.

    B. The Itanium can run only 64-bit code, while the Opteron can run both 32-bit and 64-bit code.

    C. The Itanium is made by AMD, while the Opteron is made by Intel.

    D. The Itanium fits in Slot 1, while the Opteron fits in Slot A.

13. How does SRAM cache memory differ from DRAM? (Choose two.)

    A. SRAM is faster than DRAM.

    B. SRAM never needs to be refreshed.

    C. SRAM is less expensive than DRAM.

    D. SRAM can be installed only internally on the CPU.

14. If you have a 133-MHz system bus and your CPU runs at 2.53 GHz, what is the CPU multiplier?

    A. 12

    B. 14

    C. 17

    D. 19

REVIEW ANSWERS

1. **B** **C** The Pentium MMX and AMD K6 CPUs both fit into Socket 7 ZIF sockets, as do most of the earlier Pentiums, the K5, and the Cyrix 6x86 and M-II processors.

2. **A** The Pentium was the first x86 processor to have a 64-bit-wide data bus.

3. **D** Pentium Pro processors connect to the motherboard using Socket 8.

4. **B** The first processor to have an integrated L2 cache was the Pentium Pro. Before this, all L2 cache was located on the motherboard.

5. **B** The system crystal sets the base clock speed of the motherboard.

6. **C** Pentium II processors connect to the motherboard using Slot 1.

7. **B** The Pentium II Processor had an SEC form factor. This Single Edge Contact design fit into Slot 1.

8. **A** **C** Liquid cooling systems provide superior CPU cooling and maintain a consistent CPU temperature, but are costlier and more complex to install and maintain than traditional heat sink and fan assemblies.

9. **D** Pentium III processors connected to the motherboard using the Socket 370 ZIF socket. The later Celeron processors also use Socket 370.

10. **D** The AMD Athlon processor connects to the motherboard using Slot A. Slot A looks similar to Slot 1, but it isn't pin-compatible with Slot 1.

11. **C** The backside bus is the pathway that connects the CPU and cache memory.

12. **B** The AMD Opteron is able to run 32-bit or 64-bit applications; the Intel Itanium is 64-bit only.

13. **A** **B** SRAM cache memory is much faster than DRAM because it never needs to be refreshed. It is also considerably more expensive. SRAM caches can be mounted internally on the CPU itself or externally on the motherboard.

14. **D** A 133-MHz clock speed multiplied by 19 equals a 2.53-GHz internal CPU speed.

RAM

	NEWBIE	SOME EXPERIENCE	EXPERT
ETA	1.5 hours	1 hour	45 minutes

PC users are curious people, and before long one of them is going to ask you, the learned PC tech, "Where do my programs actually run?" Without hesitation, you answer, "In your system RAM, of course!" and if you're like most techs, you continue to talk about how RAM works until their eyes glaze over and they ask you to go away.

Nonetheless, it's a fair question. Many PC users are under the misapprehension that programs run directly off of the PC's hard drive. This is, of course, impossible, because even the fastest hard drive simply can't keep up with even the slowest CPU. Instead, programs must be copied to a super-fast medium that's capable of supplying the CPU with the data that it needs to run an application at a speed that it can use: this is the function of RAM. Launching an application loads the necessary files from the hard disk into RAM, where the CPU—via the Northbridge—can grab the specific data that it needs to run the program.

Not long ago, RAM was a precious commodity in the PC world, and even a small upgrade would set you back hundreds of dollars. Things have changed dramatically for the better, so nowadays adding more RAM is often your best upgrade option for a sluggish PC. This doesn't mean that you can just grab any type of RAM that you can get your hands on and stick it in your system. You've got to match the motherboard with the right type of RAM, running at the right speed.

In most cases, installing RAM is literally a snap, but don't take the installation procedure for granted. RAM is perhaps the most sensitive component on the system when it comes to the dreaded *ESD*. Safe handling is absolutely vital. Once you've successfully installed RAM, you may find that your work isn't done. Memory errors come in many shapes and sizes, and when things go wrong with RAM, you can pretty much plan on canceling any appointments you had for the rest of the day if you don't know what to do.

In this chapter, you'll learn how to identify types of RAM, how to handle RAM safely, how to install RAM correctly, what to look for when you suspect a RAM error, and what steps you can take to correct RAM errors.

Objective 6.01   RAM Overview

In this section, we'll look at the various physical RAM form factors (sometimes called *packages*) and types of RAM that are referenced on the A+ exam.

RAM Form Factors

RAM form factors have gone through several evolutionary steps since the introduction of the first PC. Manufacturers originally installed RAM directly onto the motherboard, as shown in Figure 6-1, but this took up too much room and made upgrading difficult.

The next step was to put RAM memory chips onto special removable circuit boards that fit into sockets on the motherboard. Most techs simply call these circuit boards RAM *sticks*. These RAM sticks are what we use today: the SIMM, the DIMM, and the RIMM.

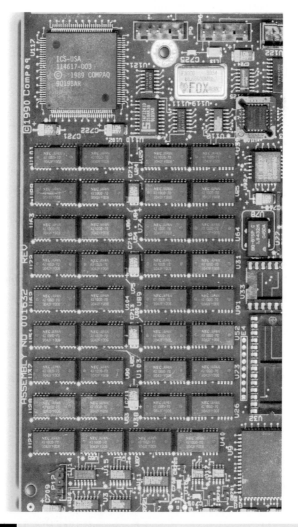

FIGURE 6.1   RAM soldered onto an ancient motherboard, now part of the Total Seminars Tech Museum

SIMM

Single inline memory modules (SIMMs) used to be the most common form of memory, but you won't see them on any PCs manufactured in the last few years. SIMM RAM sticks come in either 30-pin or 72-pin layouts. There's no real significance to the number of pins as far as PC techs are concerned—the important difference is in the bit-width. The 30-pin SIMMs put out 8 bits of data on the data bus at one time, which makes them 8 bits wide. Their capacity ranges from 1MB to 16MB. The 72-pin SIMMs are 32 bits wide and are available in sticks of up to 64MB. Figure 6-2 shows two SIMMs.

DIMM

Dual inline memory modules (DIMMs) are the ones you're most likely to run into these days, including two popular variants used in laptops, *MicroDIMMs* and *small outline DIMMs (SO DIMMs)*. DIMMs for desktop PCs look similar to SIMMs but are wider and longer. DIMMs have either 168 or 184 pins, are 64 bits wide, and range in capacity from 8 MB to 512 MB. Figure 6-3 shows 184-pin and 168-pin DIMMs.

MicroDIMM RAM comes in 144-pin packages. The SO-DIMM variant come in 72- and 144-pin configurations. One important difference is that the 72-pin version is 32-bit, while the 144-pin version is 64-bit. MicroDIMMs and SO DIMMs otherwise come in the same capacities as their full-sized counterparts.

RIMM

The other popular type of RAM, usually found on high-performance PCs, is the *RIMM*. Technically, the term RIMM doesn't stand for anything, but most techs use it as an acronym for *Rambus inline memory module*. It's more accurate to call this type of memory *RDRAM,* for *Rambus dynamic RAM,* but since RIMM is the common term, that's the one we'll use. RIMMs come in capacities of up to

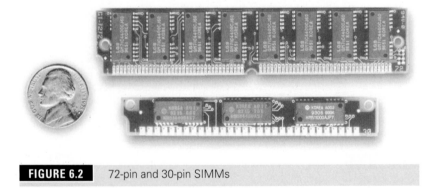

FIGURE 6.2   72-pin and 30-pin SIMMs

FIGURE 6.3   184-pin (top) and 168-pin DIMMs

512 MB. RIMM sticks look like DIMMs but have 184 pins. Figure 6-4 shows a typical RIMM stick. Note that the memory chips themselves are covered by a thin metal shield called a *heat spreader.* This shield does exactly what it sounds like: it helps dissipate heat generated by the RIMM memory chips. Do not attempt to remove the heat spreader!

RAM Types

As Chapter 5 described, there are two main types of RAM, static RAM (SRAM) and dynamic RAM (DRAM). SRAM is faster than DRAM, because it never needs to be refreshed; however, it is also much more expensive. SRAM is therefore reserved for special purposes, such as L1, L2, and L3 system cache memory. DRAM used for system memory needs to be refreshed every few nanoseconds (ns), and during this time it is inaccessible to the CPU. This interval is called a *wait state.* Faster RAM has a shorter wait state. The paragraphs that follow describe the popular types of DRAM available on the PC market today.

FIGURE 6.4   184-pin RDRAM RIMM

> **Exam Tip**
>
> SRAM doesn't need to be refreshed, but it costs more than other RAM solutions and so is used primarily for cache. DRAM requires periodic refreshing and is used for system memory.

EDO

Extended data out RAM (EDO) works by grabbing large chunks of data to feed to the CPU. EDO RAM is asynchronous, meaning that it runs at a speed independent of the system clock speed. EDO RAM is sold in 72-pin SIMMs and 168-pin DIMMs and has access times of 50–60 ns.

SDRAM

Synchronous dynamic RAM (SDRAM)—the current RAM of choice in most systems—delivers data in high-speed bursts. SDRAM runs at the speed of the system bus (thus, *synchronously*) and has access times in the 8–10 ns range. However, manufacturers don't rate SDRAM speeds in ns, but rather in MHz. SDRAM is rated according to the highest speed data bus it runs on, such as 66, 100, or 133 MHz. Hence, we have PC66, PC100, and PC133 SDRAM. To avoid confusion, most RAM manufacturers label SDRAM with both nanosecond and a megahertz ratings. SDRAM DIMMs have a special chip called the *serial presence detect* (SPD) chip. The SPD chip identifies a DIMM's size, its speed, and a number of other more technical bits of information to the system.

> **Exam Tip**
>
> SDRAM transfers data in high-speed bursts and is measured in megahertz, not in nanoseconds.

The most common form of SDRAM uses a 168-pin DIMM (dual inline memory module). SDRAM for laptops comes in two reduced-size varieties, 72-pin and 144-pin SO DIMMs, and MicroDIMMs.

DDR SDRAM

The latest motherboards support double data rate (DDR) SDRAM. DDR SDRAM operates in a similar fashion to modern CPUs, taking the base bandwidth speed of the system bus and multiplying it. DDR SDRAM comes in designations ranging from 266 MHz (aka PC2100) to 433 MHz (PC3500). High-end motherboards have dual memory access channels, effectively doubling the already doubled throughput of DDR SDRAM. DDR SDRAM comes in a 184-pin DIMM package for desktops or either a 200-pin SO DIMM or a 172-pin MicroDIMM for laptops.

RDRAM

RDRAM, developed by Rambus, Inc., uses special Rambus channels that have data transfer rates of 800 MHz. If that's not fast enough for you, you can also double the channel width for faster speeds. When the channel rates are doubled, RDRAM can reach data transfer speeds of up to 1.6 GHz. RDRAM is more expensive than SDRAM and is supported only on systems that use Northbridge chips that support it.

VRAM

Although not used for system memory, video RAM (VRAM) is referenced on the A+ certification core hardware exam. VRAM is used, as you may have guessed, on video cards. VRAM is a very fast type of DRAM that is *dual-ported,* meaning that it can be read from and written to at the same time. This enables the video adapter's onboard video processor to access it at the same time that the CPU is writing new data into it.

WRAM

Another type of video RAM is window RAM, or WRAM. Developed by Samsung, WRAM is also dual-ported. WRAM is even faster than VRAM because of its ability to address large blocks (or *windows*) of memory.

Error-Checking RAM: Parity and ECC

High-end, mission-critical systems often use special *parity* or *error-correcting code (ECC)* RAM. These types of RAM use special circuitry to detect and, in some cases, correct errors in data. Parity RAM, the older technology, used a dedicated parity chip mounted on the RAM stick that added an extra bit—the parity bit—to each byte of data. Parity checking was useful in the early days of desktop computers when DRAM had a relatively high failure rate, but today's DRAM is so dependable that very few PCs still support parity.

ECC RAM contains circuitry that not only detects errors but corrects it on-the-fly without causing interruption to system processes. ECC RAM is common on performance-enhanced workstations and server systems.

Note that the PC's motherboard and BIOS must be designed to support either parity or ECC RAM. Most motherboards that are designed for parity or ECC RAM can be configured in BIOS to disable error checking, thus enabling you to install RAM that is not parity or ECC RAM.

Memory Addressing

RAM is made up of millions of individual storage circuits, similar to the cells of a spreadsheet table. Each cell stores one bit of data, and any cell that holds data is charged into the "on" position, or in the binary terms that the PC understands, it's set to "1." Cells that don't have any data are "off," represented as a "0." This binary numbering scheme is the key to how the CPU uses RAM.

CPUs read data one byte at a time, so it takes eight individual cells to equal one addressable block of memory. Referring back to Chapter 5, we know that the number of wires on the address bus determines how much RAM a CPU can address, the formula being 2^X, with X being the number of wires on the address bus. Modern CPUs use 32 wires on the address bus (they function at 32 bits wide), ergo they can address 2^{32} bytes of RAM. You guessed it, that equals just over four billion individual addresses, or 4 GB of RAM.

Travel Advisory

Every CPU since the Pentium II has 36 address wires, so you'll often see this number crop up in tech discussions. Although the modern CPU has 36 wires, they function with only 32. Until very recently, PCs have not needed more than 4 GB of RAM. This is changing, however, and new operating systems will take advantage of the extra address wires. As far as the A+ exams go, however, think in terms of the *functional* address bus as 32-bits wide.

The CPU taps out the binary address of the RAM bytes that it wants by turning specific wires in the address bus on and off. The Northbridge chip responds by retrieving the data stored in those cells and placing it on the data bus for the CPU.

Memory Banks

Manufacturers arrange memory slots on motherboards in electronic groups of one, two, or four RAM slots, according to the type of RAM and type of processor. These groupings, called *memory banks,* match the width of the processor's data bus. On a Pentium or later motherboard, for example, each bank is 64 bits wide. So, a single 168-pin DIMM slot makes up a single bank, but you'd need two 72-pin SIMM slots to make a bank. The exception to this is dual-channel DDR SDRAM, which requires two DIMM slots to be filled. Banking RAM enables the processor to access as much RAM as it can handle at one chunk, thus making data access as efficient as possible.

The basic rule on banking is you need to fill a bank completely with the identical type and speed of RAM. Mixing different types of RAM almost always results in errors, and some systems even have problems if you mix RAM from different manufacturers. To determine the number of RAM modules needed to complete a bank, divide the width of the external data bus by the bit width of the RAM.

A single RIMM RAM stick usually makes a complete bank, but unused RIMM sockets can't be left empty. Instead, use a special RIMM *terminator,* called a *continuity RIMM (CRIMM)* stick, to fill any unpopulated RIMM sockets.

Memory banks should be either completely filled or completely empty. Although some manufacturers created motherboards that could run with half banks filled (for example, a Pentium running on a single 72-pin SIMM), most motherboards follow the banking rule closely. You need to have at least one bank of RAM in your PC for it to boot properly. Trying to boot your PC with absolutely no RAM results in an annoying loud beep and a PC that won't boot, as we'll look at in section 6.03.

Objective 6.02 Handling and Installing RAM

It's important for you to follow the proper RAM handling and installation procedures to prevent damage to your PC. In the following section, you will learn the proper way to handle RAM, how to install RAM, and how to confirm RAM installation.

Handling RAM

RAM is extremely sensitive to ESD, so take precautions while transporting, handling, and installing RAM. Always store RAM in antistatic bags or sleeves when it's not installed on a PC. If you have spare RAM lying around, always keep it labeled with the type, size, and speed so that you can identify it later. Don't take a RAM stick out of its bag before you actually need to install it. If the conditions are right, even carrying an unprotected stick of RAM across the room can cause a buildup of ESD sufficient to zap it into oblivion, so keep your RAM wrapped! Review the ESD safety guidelines in Chapter 2, under "Component Protection and Storage," for more information.

This should be obvious, but I'll say it anyway—don't handle RAM roughly. It *can* break! Handle RAM by the edges, and avoid touching the contacts or circuits.

Installing RAM Modules

This section covers the procedures for installing DRAM modules on your PC. Remember that on modern systems, a small trickle charge runs through the motherboard even when it's turned off, so before you work on your PC, shut it down and unplug the power cable from the wall. If you're installing RAM on a portable PC, you must also remove the battery.

Clear yourself a work area and set your PC on an antistatic mat, if you have one, and remove the cover. Strap on your *nerd bracelet* (otherwise known as an *antistatic wrist strap*) and clip it to the system chassis to ground yourself and you're ready to go.

Installing DIMMs and RIMMs

DIMM and RIMM sticks need to go into their sockets vertically. You'll note on the motherboard that the guide notches on the sockets match up to the notches on the RAM to prevent you from inserting it the wrong way. Glance back up at Figures 6-3 and 6-4. All three RAM sticks pictured are the same size—roughly 5 inches wide—but the notches enable you to install each only in the proper slot.

Before you install a DIMM or RIMM into a slot, make sure that the RAM retention clips at either end of the socket are pushed completely outward. Holding your RAM by the edges, position it above the RAM socket and press it straight down into the slot with gentle pressure. When the RAM is fully inserted, the retention clips will swing up and engage the retention notches in the outside edges of the RAM. Snap the clips firmly into place, and you're done. Figure 6-5 shows properly seated DIMM RAM.

Barring ESD, there's not a lot to go wrong with installing DIMMs or RIMMs. The main thing to look for is improper seating. If the retention clip doesn't engage fully, then your RAM stick isn't inserted completely. Double-check your positioning, and insert the RAM again. If it doesn't go in easily, you're not in the right position.

To remove a DIMM or RIMM, push the retention clips on the socket outward. These clips act as levers to raise the RAM stick out of the socket so that you can then pull it all the way out.

Installing SIMMs

Installing SIMM RAM is slightly trickier. To insert a SIMM, first insert it into place in the RAM socket at an angle—not straight up and down like a DIMM or RIMM—and then snap it into the vertical position.

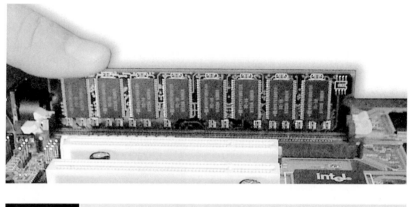

FIGURE 6.5   Properly seated DIMM

Also note that there are no clearly demarcated guide notches on a SIMM; the only guide is a single notch taken out of one end of the stick. Still, like DIMMs and RIMMs, SIMM RAM goes in only one way, so if it doesn't go in easily, stop what you're doing and double-check your orientation.

To install SIMM RAM, first determine which end of the stick has the guide notch. Then position the RAM stick in the RAM socket at approximately a 45-degree angle and insert it until it seats. Now pivot the SIMM upward until it snaps into place (see Figure 6-6).

To remove a SIMM, gently push the retention clips outward until you can unseat the RAM stick, and then pivot it downward and lift it out.

Just to keep things interesting for us techs, some older low-profile systems use SIMMs that are configured so that the installation procedure is actually the *opposite* of what was just described. That is, the SIMM is inserted into the RAM socket vertically and locked into position at an angle.

Confirm RAM Installation

Once you've got your RAM installed, confirm that your PC recognizes it by booting up and checking the RAM count message (see Figure 6-7).

Older systems may require you to confirm the RAM amount in BIOS manually, but modern systems automatically detect the RAM size and configure the system accordingly. You rarely need to reconfigure BIOS RAM settings.

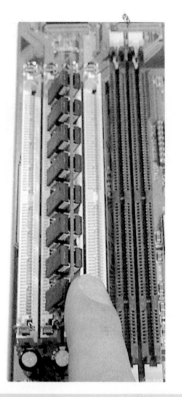

FIGURE 6.6   Installing a SIMM

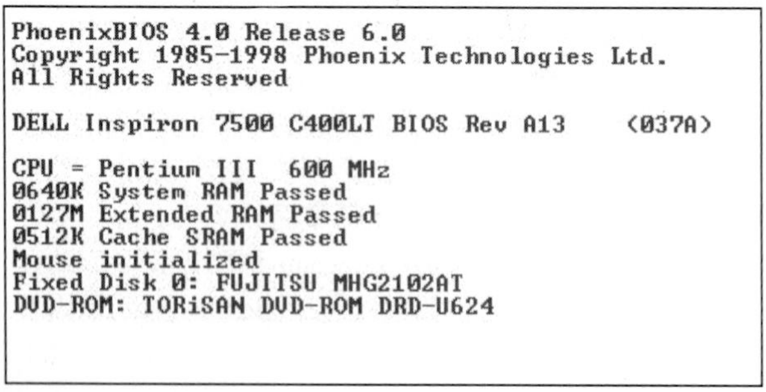

```
PhoenixBIOS 4.0 Release 6.0
Copyright 1985-1998 Phoenix Technologies Ltd.
All Rights Reserved

DELL Inspiron 7500 C400LT BIOS Rev A13     (037A)

CPU = Pentium III   600 MHz
0640K System RAM Passed
0127M Extended RAM Passed
0512K Cache SRAM Passed
Mouse initialized
Fixed Disk 0: FUJITSU MHG2102AT
DVD-ROM: TORiSAN DVD-ROM DRD-U624
```

FIGURE 6.7   Confirm RAM installation by checking RAM count at startup

Objective 6.03 # Troubleshooting RAM Errors

Your first task is to determine whether or not the error is, indeed, RAM-related. Once you've done that, you can begin the process of pinpointing the cause and taking corrective measures. The following section lists symptoms of false and genuine RAM errors, causes of errors, and corrective measures that you should take.

False Memory Errors

A lot of system errors get blamed on memory when they don't really have anything to do with RAM. If you've used any version of Windows prior to Windows 2000, then you've surely seen the infamous *Out of memory* error pop up. "How can this be?" you may have asked yourself, "I've got *plenty* of RAM!"

As you may have guessed, that particular error doesn't have anything to do with the amount of RAM your PC has. It's actually Windows' way of telling you that your system resources are running low, which is a different matter altogether.

Other errors that mimic RAM errors are things such as *page faults, exception errors,* the dreaded *Blue Screen of Death,* the system slowdown or freeze, and the ever-popular spontaneous reboot. These are often tied to other factors, such as a badly fragmented hard disk, an overtaxed CPU, or a faulty application or driver. Overheating as a result of dust and dirt accumulated inside the PC case or a failed cooling fan is also a common culprit. Finally, a dying power supply can cause any or all of the random types of errors.

Common Symptoms of RAM Errors

The majority of genuine memory errors happen after you've made a change to your PC's hardware and restart the system and it goes through the POST routine. Common startup errors include the following:

- System won't boot, accompanied by a loud, continuously repeating beep
- System boots, but the display screen is blank
- System boots, misreports RAM size
- System boots, reports memory or address error

Once you've determined that the error you're getting is a genuine RAM error, you can determine the cause and take corrective measures.

Common Causes of RAM Errors

Genuine RAM-related system errors are generally the result of one of three things: a RAM configuration error, a RAM installation error, or a faulty RAM component.

Configuration errors are the most common and are usually simple to correct. A configuration error typically means that you've installed the wrong type or speed of RAM, or that you didn't follow all of the rules about properly banking or terminating the RAM. It might also mean that your system's motherboard is incompatible with the installed RAM due to hardware or BIOS issues. BIOS configurations that include RAM *shadowing,* which copies the contents of BIOS into RAM for quick access, can also cause memory errors and system lockups.

Improper installation is also pretty common, though most techs don't like to admit it! This can mean you didn't fully seat or snap a RAM stick into its socket, or it can mean that some other related factor, such as dirt, dust, or corrosion on the RAM contact pins or socket, is causing a problem. Installation errors may also mean that while you were installing RAM, you accidentally unseated another hardware component or cable.

Faulty RAM is less common, but it does happen. Sometimes it comes out of the factory that way, but it's more likely that the RAM was damaged somehow during transport or storage. Don't forget that our old enemy ESD can cause good RAM to go bad in no time flat.

Corrective Measures

Since the vast majority of RAM errors are due to misconfiguration, improper installation, or faulty components, the remedies are fairly simple. Your first step is to confirm that your RAM configuration is correct. Is the RAM compatible with your PC? Is it the right type and the right speed? Your best resource is your motherboard's documentation, and the motherboard manufacturer's web site. Check for any known issues with the type or amount of RAM that you've installed, and make certain that you've got the latest version of the system BIOS installed. If your BIOS has shadowing enabled, disable it. Your RAM manufacturer's web site is a good place to turn. Some manufacturers have configuration utilities available for download. Take advantage of these resources.

Once you've confirmed that your RAM configuration is correct, the next step is to confirm that you've installed it correctly. Remove and inspect the RAM and RAM sockets for dirt or corrosion, and clean as necessary. Then reinstall the RAM and test the system again.

If neither of these steps corrects the error, then your last option is to remove and replace the RAM. Try to use RAM that you know is good, such as RAM taken from another working system of the same configuration. If the error reoccurs after you've installed known good RAM, then you know that it's unlikely that the RAM is at fault. If the error goes away after you swap RAM sticks, then you've probably got bad RAM.

You may wonder if there's a better way to test RAM sticks than swapping them around from PC to PC. Practically speaking, there's not. Dedicated RAM testing devices exist, but they cost as much as a whole new PC system! Until a cheaper alternative comes along, you're stuck with doing it the old-fashioned way.

Table 6-1 helps you quickly recognize and remedy common RAM errors.

TABLE 6.1   Typical RAM Errors and Troubleshooting Steps

Symptom	Probable Cause	Corrective Measures
Computer won't start, accompanied by beeps	Configuration, installation, faulty or damaged RAM	Confirm that your RAM configuration is correct for your PC. Check that RAM is properly seated and terminated. Replace RAM.
Computer starts, but screen is blank	Configuration or installation	Confirm that your RAM configuration is correct for your PC. Check that RAM is properly seated and terminated. Check that other internal components weren't dislodged during RAM installation.
Computer starts but misreports the amount of RAM	Configuration	Confirm that your RAM configuration is correct for your PC. Check that RAM is installed following banking rules. Update system BIOS.
Computer reports a *Memory mismatch* error at startup	Configuration	Confirm that your RAM configuration is correct for your PC. Enter your system's CMOS settings utility and manually confirm or enter the correct amount of RAM.

TABLE 6.1 Typical RAM Errors and Troubleshooting Steps *(continued)*

Symptom	Probable Cause	Corrective Measures
Computer reports a memory error, e.g., *Memory failure at xxxxx*	Configuration, faulty or damaged RAM	Confirm that all RAM is supported by motherboard. Perform RAM maintenance or replace with known good RAM.
Computer locks up or spontaneously reboots	Faulty or damaged RAM or *other*	Perform RAM maintenance or replace with known good RAM. Check power supply. Disable BIOS shadowing.
Computer reports Registry error	Faulty or damaged RAM	Perform RAM maintenance or replace with known good RAM.
Computer reports general protection faults, page faults, or exception errors	Faulty or damaged RAM or *other*	Restart PC. Uninstall any recently installed applications or drivers. Perform RAM maintenance or replace with known good RAM.

CHECKPOINT

✔**Objective 6.01: RAM Overview** DRAM requires periodic refreshing, unlike SRAM, but costs substantially less. SDRAM improves on EDO DRAM by running at the speed of the data bus and moving data in high-speed bursts. Modern CPUs use 32 wires on the address bus and can address 4 GB of RAM. The basic rule on banking is you need to fill a bank completely with identical (type and speed) RAM modules. The two most common styles of error-checking RAM are the old-style parity SIMMs and the newer error-correcting code (ECC) DIMMs. Parity SIMMs had an extra bit per byte of data that functioned as a low-level error-checking feature. ECC uses much more sophisticated error-checking electronics than parity and can correct data errors on-the-fly.

✔**Objective 6.02: Handling and Installing RAM** RAM is very sensitive to ESD, so always keep it in an antistatic bag or package until you're ready to install it. Make certain to orient the RAM boards properly using the motherboard socket's guide notches, and be sure to lock the RAM into place. Following installation, confirm the RAM count during bootup. Older PCs may require you to enter BIOS to confirm the RAM amount.

✔**Objective 6.03: Troubleshooting RAM Errors**   Many errors that are not directly related to memory mimic RAM errors. Genuine RAM errors are caused by improper RAM configuration, improper RAM installation, and faulty or damaged RAM. Always check your motherboard documentation for the correct RAM configuration. Make certain that RAM is properly seated and banked, and that you don't accidentally unseat other components or cables during RAM installation. If you suspect faulty or damaged RAM, swap it out with known good RAM of the same type and speed.

REVIEW QUESTIONS

1. Which type of RAM never needs periodic refreshing?

   A. SRAM

   B. DRAM

   C. FPM RAM

   D. EDO RAM

2. Which type of RAM module has 168 pins?

   A. SIMMs

   B. DIMMs

   C. RIMMs

   D. None

3. Which RAM module is available with two different numbers of pins?

   A. SIMMs

   B. DIMMs

   C. RIMMs

   D. SRAM

4. What RAM module was created to work ‘ pecifically with RDRAM?

   A. SIMMs

   B. DIMMs

   C. RIMMs

   D. EDO RAM

5. Which type of RAM is used mainly for cache memory?

   A. SRAM

   B. DRAM

   C. EDO RAM

   D. SDRAM

6. What is stored in RAM?

   A. Currently running programs

   B. Programs that aren't running

   C. Nothing is stored in RAM

   D. Hardware information

7. Which type of RAM requires the use of Rambus channels?

   A. SRAM

   B. DRAM

   C. SDRAM

   D. RDRAM

8. Which type of RAM is measured in megahertz?

   A. SRAM

   B. SDRAM

   C. DRAM

   D. VRAM

9. Which types of RAM can be both read from and written to at the same time? (Choose two.)

   A. DRAM

   B. VRAM

   C. SRAM

   D. WRAM

10. How do you determine how much RAM you need to fill a memory bank?

    A. The width of the external data bus divided by the bit width of the RAM

    B. The width of the external data bus multiplied by the bit width of the RAM

    C. The width of the external data bus plus the bit width of the RAM

    D. The width of the external data bus subtracted from the bit width of the RAM

11. Which of the following statements about memory banks is true?

    A. You should use different sizes of RAM in a memory bank.

    B. You should use different speeds of RAM in a memory bank.

    C. All RAM in a memory bank should be the same speed.

    D. You don't need to fill an entire memory bank.

12. What were parity chips used for?

    A. Error checking for RAM

    B. To increase the speed of RAM

    C. To increase the capacity of RAM

    D. To speed up Windows

13. What is a CRIMM used for?

    A. Error-checking

    B. Termination

    C. To synchronize RAM with the system clock

    D. To identifies the RAM to the system BIOS

REVIEW ANSWERS

1. **A** SRAM requires no refreshing, thus it incurs no CPU wait states.

2. **B** Dual inline memory modules (DIMMs) have 168 pins. SIMMs have 30 or 72 pins, and RIMMs have 184 pins.

3. **A** SIMMs are available in both 30-pin and 72-pin sizes.

4. **C** RIMMS were created for the insertion of RDRAM. RDRAM requires the use of Rambus channels and RIMM slots on the motherboard.

5. **A** SRAM is used mainly for cache memory because it's extremely expensive, but it doesn't need to be refreshed.

6. **A** Currently running programs are stored in RAM. When you start a program, part of the program is taken from the hard drive and placed into RAM to make your access speeds quicker.

7. **D** RDRAM requires the use of Rambus channels. RDRAM also requires you to have RIMM slots on your motherboard.

8. **B** SDRAM is measured in megahertz. Manufactures started including a nanosecond access speed setting after confusion occurred regarding the speed of the SDRAM.

9. **B** **D** WRAM and VRAM can be both read from and written to at the same time. The increased speed makes these types of RAM excellent for video.

10. **A** The amount of RAM needed to fill a memory bank is determined by the width of the external data bus divided by the bit width of the RAM.

11. **C** All RAM in a memory bank should be the same speed. If it isn't, the PC might not boot properly and might have memory error messages.

12. **A** Parity chips were used to check RAM for errors.

13. **B** CRIMMs are used to terminate RDRAM.

IDE Mass Storage Devices

	NEWBIE	SOME EXPERIENCE	EXPERT
ETA	3 hours	2 hours	1 hour

Computers need a way to store data permanently. In the past, different types of storage media have been used for this purpose—punched paper ribbons and cards, magnetic tape reels and cartridges, and so on. Today we use magnetic hard drives and optical devices such as CD-ROM, CD-RW, DVD-ROM, and DVD-RW drives. This chapter concentrates on the most common type of mass storage device, the one on which PC techs spend the largest amount of time: the hard drive.

Mass storage devices have gone through a variety of standards and interfaces over the years. Two standards, the *Integrated Drive Electronics (IDE)* standard and the *AT Attachment (ATA)* standard, both introduced around 1990, currently dominate the world of desktop PC mass storage devices. The *Small Computer System Interface (SCSI)* also has a large user base, but is mainly reserved for high-end workstations and file server systems (Chapter 8 is dedicated to SCSI technology). A newer standard, called *Serial ATA (SATA),* is making inroads in the PC world and is expected to be extremely popular as the technology develops.

This chapter reviews the specifications for IDE/ATA and SATA mass storage devices and gives you details about cabling, interfaces, and setup procedures.

Objective 7.01   How Hard Drives Store Data

If you're like most techs, you've never seen the inside of a hard drive. After all, they're not made to be serviced in the field, and in fact, opening a hard drive's casing is a sure way to render it completely unusable. If, however, you happen to have an old hard drive that's ready for the trash heap, you can better appreciate how data is stored on hard drives by opening it up and having a look around.

Physical Structure

Inside a hard drive is a short stack of polished metal disks called *platters*. The platters are attached to a spinning cylindrical core that is driven by a small but powerful motor. The platters turn at an extremely high speed—7200 RPM is typical on modern hard drives. The platters are coated with a highly sensitive magnetic substance that stores the binary ones and zeros that make up your system's data. A motorized arm tipped with tiny read/write heads navigates the platters, riding on a cushion of air created by the disk's spinning action. Figure 7-1 shows the exterior and the interior of a typical IDE hard drive.

FIGURE 7.1 Outside and inside views of a typical hard drive

In order to be useful, data must be organized in a fashion that the system can understand. This organization is referred to as the drive's *geometry*.

Geometry

A hard drive's geometry isn't something that you, the learned PC tech, can determine with the naked eye, but your PC sees it just fine! The three main characteristics that make up a disk's geometry are the *cylinders, heads,* and *sectors per track*. Collectively, techs call these the *CHS* settings.

Cylinders

Data is recorded onto the platters in a series of magnetic rings called *tracks*. Each platter has tracks on the top and bottom surfaces, and each track on one platter is matched up to a track on every other platter in the stack. A stack of tracks is referred to as a *cylinder.*

The best way to visualize cylinders is to picture a tube, such as a soup can with the top and bottom cut out. Then picture another can of a slightly wider diameter placed around the first can, then another, bigger can placed around that can, and so on thousands of times.

Heads

The term *heads* literally describes the tiny read/write components that put data on and take data off the data tracks on each platter. A platter needs two heads, one for the top surface and one for the bottom. A hard drive that has a stack of four platters, therefore, needs eight heads. Note, however, that a hard drive can have additional heads that it uses for special purposes.

Sectors per Track

Imagine cutting wedges from the stack of platters, the way you would a birthday cake or a pizza. Each slice on any given track is called a *sector*. Each sector stores exactly 512 bytes of data. The sector is the universal "atom" of all hard drives—you can't divide data into anything smaller than a sector. The total number of sectors on each track is a constant for a hard drive—all tracks for Drive X have 63 sectors, for example. You would refer to this geometry as 63 sectors per track, often expressed as *sectors/track*.

Configuring Geometry

You'll recall from Chapter 4 (under "System BIOS and CMOS Setup Utility") that the PC's CMOS setup utility stores information that the system needs to use hardware such as mass storage devices. In order to be recognized by the system, a hard drive's geometry has to be entered into CMOS. Back in the old days, techs had to enter the CHS settings into CMOS by hand. Thanks to standardized drive technology, modern motherboard BIOS chips can recognize IDE drives and set them up in CMOS through a process called *autodetect*. Later in this chapter, I'll go into more detail about configuring a hard drive's geometry.

Capacity

To determine hard drive capacity, you simply multiply all of the basic drive units together. As an example, let's look at the numbers for an IDE drive that has 13,328 cylinders, 16 heads, and 63 sectors per track. $16,383 \times 16 \times 63 = 16,514,064$. Now multiply that by 512 (representing the number of bytes per sector) for a total capacity of 8,455,200,768 bytes, or roughly 8.4 GB.

Partitions and File Systems

Are the CHS settings all there is to data storage? Obviously not! That would be too easy. Before data can be stored on a hard drive, the drive must be configured with a *partition* and a *file system*. A partition is an electronic, logical division of the physical hard drive space. A partition can encompass the entire disk's available space, or it can be a smaller portion of the disk. Partitions are configured to support a specific type of file system—a sort of index of what goes where—through a process called *formatting*.

Windows 9*x*/Me systems—meaning Windows 95, 98, 98 SE, and Me—support two types of file systems. *File Allocation Table* 16 (FAT16, called simply FAT in Windows NT/2000/XP) and FAT32. The difference between the two is, appropriately, that FAT16 is 16-bit and FAT32 is 32-bit. Windows versions based on the NT core OS kernel—Windows NT Workstation and Server, Windows 2000 Professional and Server, and Windows XP Home and Professional—also support an advanced file system called *New Technology File System (NTFS)*. A later section of this chapter goes into detail on partitioning and formatting hard drives.

Exam Tip

Windows NT Workstation and Server support FAT16 and NTFS, but not FAT32. Windows 2000 and XP support all three file systems.

Objective 7.02

IDE, EIDE, and SATA Interface Standards

Hard drives connect to the PC expansion bus through interfaces that conform to defined standards. The IDE/ATA standards define mass storage devices with integrated controller circuitry that enables parallel data communication with a PC's IDE/ATA expansion bus, and the two terms are used interchangeably. The original IDE/ATA standards have undergone multiple improvements since their inception, as described in the sections that follow.

Local Lingo

IDE devices   Although modern hard drives conform to various EIDE/ATA standards, they are most commonly called simply "IDE" devices.

IDE/ATA

You won't find IDE hard drives on the market anymore, but the technology that supports them is still in use today and is referenced on the A+ Core Hardware examination. The original IDE standard was quite revolutionary, but it also had some important limitations. IDE was originally designed to support only hard drives, not optical mass storage devices such as CD-ROM drives. Plus, only a single IDE hard drive controller channel, using IRQ 14, was supported (although two hard drives, jumpered to *master* and *slave*, could be installed). Further, drive detection and configuration was, in technical terms, a pain.

Capacity was very limited on early IDE hard drives. The largest of the original IDE drives had 1024 cylinders, 16 heads, and 63 sectors per track, translating into a total capacity of 504 megabytes. Although this was a huge number for its day, computer programmers soon wrote applications and operating systems to fill that space. To address these issues, manufacturers developed *Enhanced IDE (EIDE)* technology.

Exam Tip
The original IDE hard drives had a capacity limit of 504 MB.

Enhanced IDE/ATA-2 (and Beyond)

Sometimes called *ATA-2,* the new standard broke the IDE capacity barrier of 504 MB using one of two methods: *sector translation—logical block addressing (LBA)* or *enhanced CHS (ECHS).* The EIDE standard supports hard drives up to 8.4 GB. EIDE also supports a secondary IDE controller channel and a wider range of devices, including AT Attachment Packet Interface (ATAPI) devices such as CD-ROM, CD-RW, DVD-ROM, and DVD-RW drives. Techs usually refer to IDE and EIDE devices simply as IDE devices.

Improvements to the EIDE standard don't stop there, and in fact the ATA standard is now up to ATA-6. Improvements and extensions to the standard have added support for technologies such as *self-monitoring, analysis, and reporting technology (SMART,* for short), *direct memory access (DMA—*a technology that enables the EIDE device to bypass the CPU to access RAM) modes, drive security, error-checking, and others. In the mid-1990s, an extension to the standard—called *INT13 extensions—*was created. INT13 extensions allow for a maximum hard drive size of up to 137 GB.

Exam Tip
Without INT13 extension support, you won't be able to format and partition more than 8.4 GB on your hard drive, regardless of how large it is.

Serial ATA

Even with these improvements in capacity and performance, problems that plagued the earliest incarnations of IDE/ATA are also inherent in the latest and greatest versions. Foremost among these are power requirements, limits to the devices' cable length, the fact that they're not hot-swappable, and the fact that the technology has simply reached the limits of what it can do in terms of throughput.

Serial ATA (SATA) addresses these issues. SATA creates a point-to-point connection between the SATA device—hard drive, CD-ROM, CD-RW, DVD-ROM, DVD-RW, and so on—and the SATA controller. At a glance, SATA devices look identical to standard EIDE devices. Take a closer look at the cable and power connectors, however, and you'll see significant differences (see Figure 7-2). Because SATA devices send data serially instead of in parallel, the SATA interface needs far fewer physical wires—seven instead of the 80 wires that is typical of EIDE—resulting in much thinner cabling.

This might not seem significant, but the benefit is that thinner cabling means better cable control and better airflow through the PC case, resulting in better cooling. The power cable is also smaller, in keeping with the significantly reduced power requirement of 500 millivolts (mV), a fraction of the five-volt power requirement of IDE drives.

FIGURE 7.2   SATA hard drive controller (left) and power (right) connections

Further, the maximum SATA device cable length is almost twice that of an IDE cable—one meter (39.4 inches) instead of 18 inches. Again, this might not seem like a big deal, unless you've struggled to connect an IDE hard drive installed into the top bay of a full-tower case to a controller located all the way at the bottom!

SATA devices are also hot-swappable, meaning that they can be plugged into or removed from the PC without having to shut down. This makes SATA a natural fit for *redundant array of independent* (or sometimes *inexpensive*) *disks (RAID)* technology on OSes that support it.

The big news, however, is in data throughput. As the name implies, SATA devices transfer data in serial bursts instead of in parallel, as IDE devices do. Typically, you don't think of serial devices as being faster than parallel, but in this case, that's exactly the case. A SATA device's single stream of data moves much faster than the multiple streams of data coming from a parallel IDE device—theoretically up to 30 times faster!

SATA devices currently have a rated maximum data burst throughput rate of 150 MBps (megabytes per second). Granted, this isn't much of an immediate gain over current IDE speeds, but the SATA technology specification calls for eventual throughput speeds of up to 600 MBps! Obviously, the potential for greatly improved performance is the biggest draw to SATA.

SATA is backward-compatible with current IDE standards, and thus no updates to the OS software or special drivers are required. Adapters enable you to plug IDE drives into SATA sockets on the motherboard. Keep in mind, however, that these adapters slow throughput by as much as 50 percent, so if you have a choice in the matter, it's best to use "native" SATA drives and controllers.

Objective 7.03 Installing IDE and SATA Hard Drives

For all of their physical, logical, and electronic complexity, hard drives are surprisingly simple to install. This section describes how to hook up your power connection and IDE controller cables properly, and how to set your jumpers to designate a drive as a *stand-alone, master*, or *slave* drive.

Power Connection

The four-wire, five-volt Molex power connector is keyed with special chamfers to prevent you from plugging it in the wrong way. However, these chamfers can be defeated if you press hard enough. An incorrectly connected power cable results in a toasted hard drive, so double-check your orientation before plugging the power cable into the drive.

Looking at the hard drive from the top down, the red power wire should be the farthest from the drive's edge, and the yellow wire should be the closest to the edge, as shown in Figure 7-3.

Controller Cable

IDE devices connect to the motherboard or controller card with a 40-pin ribbon cable that has three connectors: one that plugs into the IDE controller socket on the motherboard (or IDE controller card) and two that plug into the IDE devices. As mentioned earlier, IDE controller cables should be no longer than 18 inches to avoid undue signal attenuation and electrical noise interference. Note that you *can* purchase custom-made cables that are longer, but these are not recommended, as they can lead to data corruption.

All modern motherboards provide two IDE sockets (or *channels*) supporting up to four total IDE devices (one master and one slave drive per channel). Many IDE controller cable connectors are keyed to prevent you from installing them

FIGURE 7.3   Properly connected power cable on an IDE drive

the wrong way, but unfortunately these are not universally implemented. The better way to make sure that your IDE controller cable is oriented properly is to use the colored stripe running down one edge of the cable as your guide. The colored stripe indicates the edge with the power pin (pin 1) on the cable connector. Simply match pin 1 on the controller cable connector to pin 1 on the controller and you're good to go. The colored stripe should be closest to the red wire on the Molex power connector, as shown in Figure 7-4.

You can connect the variously-named later IDE drives (Ultra DMA, ATA 4/Ultra ATA 66, ATA/66, and ATA/100 and 133) using a typical 40-pin ribbon cable, but to achieve speeds beyond 33 MBps, these drives require a special IDE cable with 80 conductors instead of 40. Note that the 80-conductor cable, as shown in Figure 7-5, still has only 40 pins. The difference between the 80-conductor cable and the 40-conductor cable is that every pin in the 80-conductor cable has its own ground conductor.

When you have two EIDE controllers on a motherboard or controller card, the system distinguishes between them as *primary* and *secondary.* The resources for each controller (I/O range, IRQ) must be configured for each controller in CMOS. Each controller can handle up to two devices, jumpered as master, slave,

FIGURE 7.4   Properly oriented IDE cable and power connection

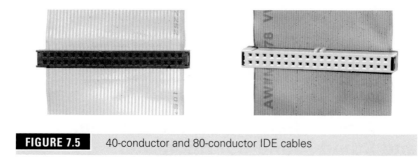

FIGURE 7.5   40-conductor and 80-conductor IDE cables

or sometimes *stand-alone* (described next). Figure 7-6 shows typical EIDE controllers on a motherboard.

Some motherboards have two different speeds of hard drive controllers. In these cases, the primary IDE controller (IDE1) is typically the faster of the two, such as ATA/66, 100, or 133, while the secondary IDE controller (IDE2) is the slower ATA/33. If this is the case on your PC, make sure to plug the 80-conductor IDE controller cable into the primary IDE channel to get top speed out of your hard drive. Usually, the faster hard drive controller is colored a bright blue or red rather than the run-of-the-mill brown, white, or black of the slower hard drive controller. Note that motherboards with this dual-speed IDE arrangement are no longer being made today, although you'll find them in existing systems.

FIGURE 7.6   Primary and secondary EIDE controllers

Exam Tip

IDE devices connect to the system board using a 40-pin ribbon cable. Orient the colored stripe on the IDE cable with pin 1 both on the system board or controller card and on the drive.

IDE Jumper Settings: Master, Slave, and Stand-Alone Configuration

As previously noted, you can install two IDE devices onto each controller cable. IDE uses jumpers to distinguish the devices. You can set the jumpers to be master, slave, or sometimes stand-alone. Stand-alone, appropriately, designates that the device is the only device on the cable, but this configuration option is not universally adopted. If you are installing only a single hard drive on a drive controller cable and it doesn't offer the stand-alone configuration option, set it as the master drive instead. If you install two devices on the cable, then one *must* be configured as the master device, and the other as the slave. You cannot have two master devices or two slave devices on the same controller cable. Figure 7-7 shows two hard drives—one jumpered as the master drive, and the other as the slave drive.

FIGURE 7.7	Two hard drives configured as master drive (bottom) and slave drive (top)

In the early days of IDE, controllers wouldn't handle devices configured as slave if the cable didn't also have a master, and you never set a CD-ROM drive as master and a hard drive as slave. Current motherboards are more forgiving, however. Nearly any configuration other than two masters or two slaves on a cable works fine.

It doesn't matter in which order you install devices on the IDE cable unless you're using *cable select* configuration (described in the next section). The arrangement of hard drives does, however, affect how the OS assigns drive letters, as you'll discover when I describe how to partition and format hard drives. Also, if you have only one device, you should plug it into the connector at the end of the cable rather than in the middle. If you leave the unattached end of the IDE cable dangling, it actually acts as an antenna and can pick up electrical noise, causing signal interference.

IDE Jumper Settings: Cable Select

The cable select configuration option simplifies IDE device installation for systems that support it. With cable select configuration, you don't need to set drives to master or slave configuration. Instead, setting them to cable select (sometimes abbreviated as *c/sel* or *cs*) indicates that the drive on the last IDE connector is designated as the master, and the drive on the middle connector is the slave.

Note that in order to support cable select configuration, you must use a cable select cable. Cable select cables are distinguished from normal IDE cables by a tiny hole through one pin.

SATA Drives

If your motherboard doesn't have SATA controller sockets (and most current ones don't), special host adapters enable you to add SATA functionality via a PCI card. Some of these offer sockets for up to eight SATA drives, and many offer both ATA and SATA sockets.

Installing SATA hard drives is even easier than IDE devices because there's no master, slave, or cable select configuration to mess with. In fact, there are no jumper settings to worry about at all, as SATA supports only a single device per controller channel. Simply connect the power and plug the controller cable in as shown in Figure 7-8—the OS automatically detects the drive and it's ready to go!

CMOS Settings

After you physically install a hard drive, its geometry must be entered into the CMOS through the CMOS setup program. Without this information, the hard

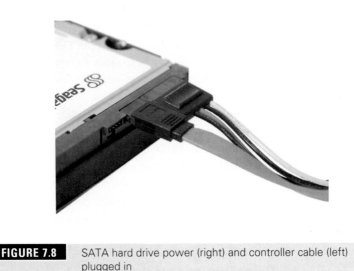

FIGURE 7.8 SATA hard drive power (right) and controller cable (left) plugged in

drive won't work. You no longer have to enter the hard drive's type, size, or geometry into CMOS manually, thanks to the autodetect function. All modern hard drives have their CHS values stored inside their onboard circuitry. How your PC retrieves this information depends on how you have the CMOS setup utility configured.

Modern CMOS setup utilities enable you to set the hard drive type one of two ways. You can set it to *Auto*—meaning that the autodetection function runs each time the PC boots, thus detecting any new device's configuration—or you can set it to query the device once and save the geometry information in CMOS. This option is usually called *User,* but this may vary according to which company made your system BIOS. This option shaves a few seconds off of the time it takes the PC to boot. Once the hard drive type is determined, the CHS and size settings are automatically configured. Figure 7-9 shows a typical CMOS setup screen with disk configuration data entered.

You should familiarize yourself with the numerous additional settings and options in CMOS. You can enable or disable the primary and secondary controllers, for example, and specify the drive mode (LBA, Normal, or Large). Many CMOS setup utilities enable you to toggle Block mode (a method of transferring large chunks of data on a single clock cycle) on or off (on by default for newer systems and drives), and even manually configure Ultra DMA modes. For the most part, techs can safely use all the automatic settings with newer systems and drives.

Autodetect provides one other great service for techs: it enables you to learn quickly whether your physical configurations are correct. If you install and

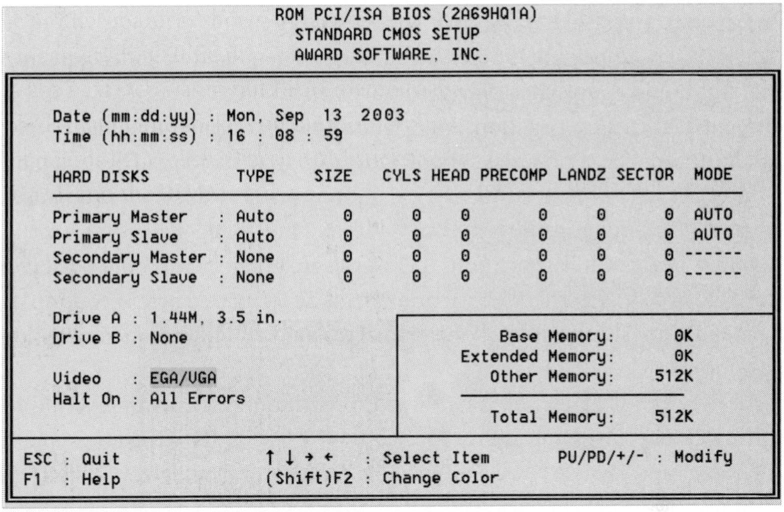

```
                    ROM PCI/ISA BIOS (2A69HQ1A)
                       STANDARD CMOS SETUP
                       AWARD SOFTWARE, INC.

   Date (mm:dd:yy) : Mon, Sep  13  2003
   Time (hh:mm:ss) : 16 : 08 : 59

   HARD DISKS          TYPE    SIZE   CYLS HEAD PRECOMP LANDZ SECTOR  MODE

   Primary Master   : Auto      0      0    0      0      0     0    AUTO
   Primary Slave    : Auto      0      0    0      0      0     0    AUTO
   Secondary Master : None      0      0    0      0      0     0   ------
   Secondary Slave  : None      0      0    0      0      0     0   ------

   Drive A : 1.44M, 3.5 in.
   Drive B : None                   ┌──────────────────────────────
                                    │      Base Memory:      0K
   Video   : EGA/UGA                │  Extended Memory:      0K
   Halt On : All Errors             │     Other Memory:    512K
                                    │      Total Memory:    512K

   ESC : Quit           ↑ ↓ → ←  : Select Item    PU/PD/+/-  : Modify
   F1  : Help          (Shift)F2 : Change Color
```

FIGURE 7.9 Hard drive configuration in CMOS

configure a drive but it fails to show up in autodetect, this almost invariably means that something's wrong with the physical setup. You can usually easily correct this by making certain that your cables are completely plugged in and oriented the right way, and that your jumpers are set properly.

Objective 7.04 # Partitioning and Formatting

Once you install a hard drive with the proper jumpers, cabling, and CMOS settings, you must complete two more tasks before the drive can hold data: partitioning and formatting. Chapter 16 of this book covers the specifics of partitioning and formatting in Windows 9x/Me and Windows NT/2000/XP in detail, but here's a quick overview of the process.

Partitioning

Partitioning establishes the framework upon which your file system is built. Using special partitioning utilities, you can configure your hard drive with up to four partitions—either four *primary* partitions, or three primary plus one *extended* partition. Partitioning creates a partition table and a drive letter for each partition.

Primary and Extended Partitions

There are some important differences between primary and extended partitions that you should appreciate. Only a primary partition can be made bootable by setting it as the *active* partition. An extended partition cannot be made active, and thus cannot be configured to boot. Only a single partition can be designated as the active partition. An extended partition is made usable by further subdividing it into numerous *logical* drives—up to 24 of them, depending on your configuration. Extended partitions themselves are not formatted, but the logical drives created on the extended partition must be formatted before you can use them. A PC must have at least one primary partition, but extended partitions are optional.

All Windows OSes come with utilities for partitioning a hard drive. Windows 9*x*/Me PCs use the FDISK utility, located on the system boot diskette supplied with the setup CD-ROM (see Figure 7-10). Windows NT uses a tool called Disk Administrator, and Windows 2000/XP systems use the built-in Computer Management console's Disk Management utility (see Figure 7-11), an updated version of Disk Administrator.

Travel Advisory

Windows assigns drive letters sequentially by default, with primary partitions getting letters first, according to position on the controller (primary master, then primary slave, and so on), followed by (in order) logical drives, SCSI hard drives, and removable media drives. Disk Administrator and Disk Management enable you to assign any available letter to any mass storage device. This can lead to some funky drive settings in Windows NT/2000/XP, where a primary hard drive partition can have a letter that's sequentially after the lowly CD or DVD drive!

How to Partition Using FDISK

As an example of how FDISK works, let's look at the procedure for partitioning a completely blank hard drive on a new PC. Before you do, however, remember that FDISK is a powerful tool capable of wiping out an entire drive's data in only a few seconds. Use FDISK as described next only if you're certain that you can do so safely!

1. Boot the PC using the Windows 9*x* boot diskette (remember to set your floppy disk drive as the first bootable device in CMOS).

2. Type **fdisk** at the command prompt.

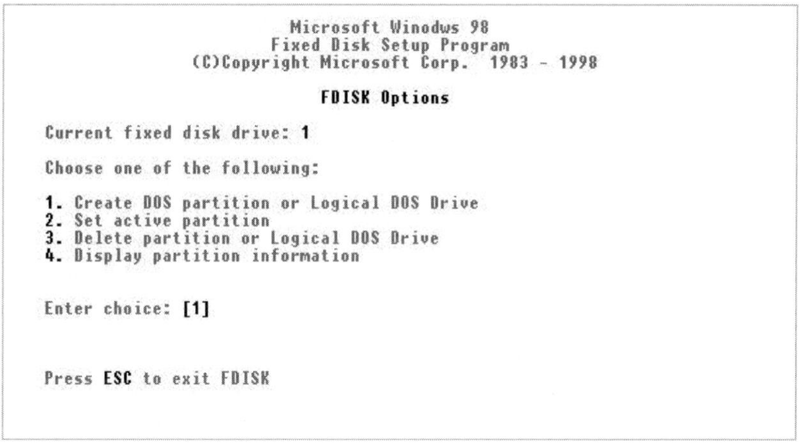

```
                    Microsoft Winodws 98
                  Fixed Disk Setup Program
         (C)Copyright Microsoft Corp.  1983 - 1998

                      FDISK Options

    Current fixed disk drive: 1

    Choose one of the following:

    1. Create DOS partition or Logical DOS Drive
    2. Set active partition
    3. Delete partition or Logical DOS Drive
    4. Display partition information


    Enter choice: [1]



    Press ESC to exit FDISK
```

FIGURE 7.10   FDISK utility

3. You are presented with an option menu with four choices: create DOS
partition or logical DOS drive, set active partition, delete partition or
logical DOS drive, or display partition information. Note that if your
system has more than one physical hard drive, you'll have a fifth choice
of switching between fixed disks.

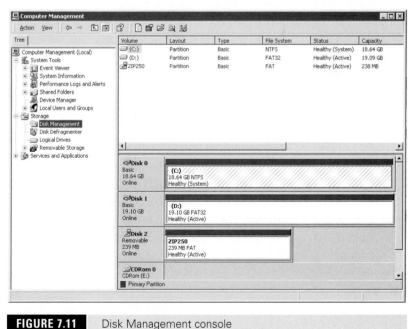

FIGURE 7.11   Disk Management console

4. Choose to create a new partition. You are presented with a submenu listing the following choices: create a primary partition, create an extended partition, or create a logical drive in an extended partition.

5. Choose the option to create a primary partition. You are then asked if you want to use the maximum available space for your new partition. Choose Yes to partition the entire disk with a single primary partition. If you choose No, you can enter a partition size smaller than the entire disk. This is a good option if you want to leave some free space on your hard drive so that you can create additional partitions at a later time.

6. Since this is the first partition created on your new hard drive, you are prompted to set the partition as the active partition. Do this and follow the remaining prompts to complete the partitioning process.

Once partitioning is complete, you simply need to reboot the system. The next step is to format the partition, as described in the following section. For now, let's look at how you create a partition in Windows 2000/XP.

How to Partition Using Disk Management

The old FDISK tool has been dumped in Windows 2000/XP and replaced with the powerful and flexible Disk Management utility (part of the Computer Management Microsoft Management Console, or MMC). This example assumes that you want to create a partition on a new, second hard drive installed on a system that has an operating Windows 2000 OS. Follow these steps to create a new partition:

1. To access the Disk Management console, select Start | Programs | Administrative Tools | Computer Management.

2. Expand the Storage branch in the left-hand pane to access the Storage management tools, and then highlight the Disk Management folder icon to connect to the Local Disk Management service.

3. Alternate-click an unallocated section of the disk and select Create Partition to start the Create Partition Wizard (see Figure 7-12). Then just follow the prompts from the wizard to select a partition type (primary, extended, or logical), specify partition size, assign a drive letter or path (mount the partition to a folder), and format the partition with a file system.

FIGURE 7.12 The Create Partition Wizard in Windows 2000 Disk Management

Formatting

Formatting creates a file system for the drive—essentially a big spreadsheet that tracks what piece of data is stored in which location. As described earlier, Windows supports three different file systems—FAT, FAT32 (not supported on Windows NT), and NTFS (Windows NT/2000/XP only). Each of these file systems has its own benefits and drawbacks, as described in the sections that follow.

FAT

FAT's strength is that it is supported by all Microsoft operating systems, but aside from that, FAT has some considerable limitations. For instance, FAT does not support disk partitions larger than 2.1 GB, and it offers no local, file-level security. The main reason to keep FAT around is for backward compatibility with older operating systems. Also, in the Windows world, removable devices such as 1.44-MB floppy disks, Zip disks, and USB drives are always formatted with FAT.

FAT32

FAT32 is the improved, 32-bit version of FAT that was introduced with Windows 95 OSR2. FAT32 supports partitions as large as 2 TB. FAT32 is also more efficient at storing data than FAT16. However, like FAT16, FAT32 has no mechanism for controlling local security.

Support for FAT32 is a new feature to Windows 2000; Windows NT version 4.0 and earlier does not support FAT32. You should note that Windows 2000's Disk Management tool lets you create FAT32 partitions of only up to 32 GB—to get the full capacity, you have to use FORMAT, which I'll describe in a moment.

NTFS

Windows 2000/XP operate well on FAT- and FAT32-formatted disks, but to get the full benefits of these operating systems, you need NTFS. Put simply, NTFS is the way to go in Windows 2000/XP. Why? How about the fact that NTFS supports partitions as large as 2 TB? How about built-in compression and encryption capabilities that enable you to conserve disk space and secure files against prying eyes? How about support for disk quotas—a method of limiting the amount of disk space a user can use—and dynamic disk configurations that enable you to add space to existing partitions on the fly? Oh, and the last three big reasons to use NTFS:

1. Security
2. Security
3. Security

NTFS supports local security, and without that, you have no true control over your resources. That reason alone is worth the price of admission!

How to Format a Partition

Windows enables you to format partitions either from the command line, using the FORMAT command, or from within the OS using My Computer. You can also use the Disk Management console in Windows 2000/XP.

Using FORMAT   Syntax for FORMAT is as follows: **format** *drive* [**/v:***label*]. For example, to format a hard drive with the letter D:, open a command line window and type **format d:**. You are warned that all data will be lost; press the **Y** key to proceed, or **N** to cancel (see Figure 7-13). Note that the *label* parameter switch is optional, but useful if you want to assign the drive a distinct, user-friendly name in addition to its drive letter. Windows 2000/XP also offer the /fs: *file system* parameter switch, which enables you to specify whether to format the partition with FAT or NTFS. Note that Windows 2000 automatically formats partitions of 2 GB or less with FAT, and greater than 2 GB with FAT32.

Using My Computer   All versions of Windows enable you to alternate-click a partition in My Computer or Windows Explorer and select Format from the drop-down menu (see Figure 7-14).

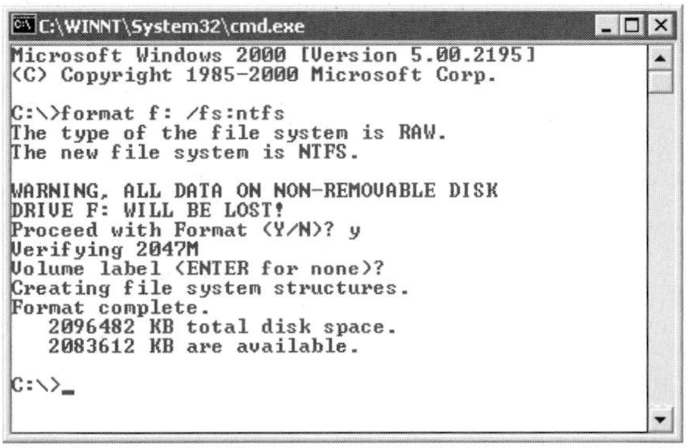

```
C:\WINNT\System32\cmd.exe                          _ □ ×
Microsoft Windows 2000 [Version 5.00.2195]
(C) Copyright 1985-2000 Microsoft Corp.

C:\>format f: /fs:ntfs
The type of the file system is RAW.
The new file system is NTFS.

WARNING, ALL DATA ON NON-REMOVABLE DISK
DRIVE F: WILL BE LOST!
Proceed with Format (Y/N)? y
Verifying 2047M
Volume label (ENTER for none)?
Creating file system structures.
Format complete.
   2096482 KB total disk space.
   2083612 KB are available.

C:\>_
```

FIGURE 7.13   Using the format command from a Windows 2000 command
line window

Using Disk Management   Windows 2000/XP offer a third way to format a
partition—the Disk Management utility. Start the console as described earlier
in this section, and alternate-click an unformatted partition to start the formatting dialog (shown in Figure 7-15). Then select Format from the pop-up menu,
enter a volume label (optional), select a file system from the drop-down menu, and
specify any other options. Then click OK.

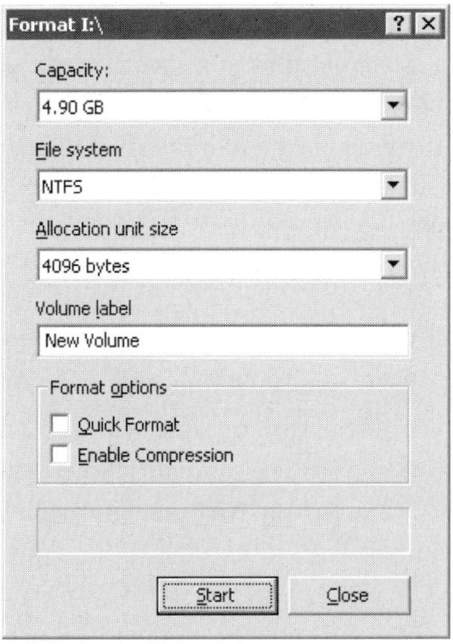

```
Format I:\                                    ? ×

  Capacity:
  ┌─────────────────────────────────────┐ ▼
  │ 4.90 GB                             │
  └─────────────────────────────────────┘

  File system
  ┌─────────────────────────────────────┐ ▼
  │ NTFS                                │
  └─────────────────────────────────────┘

  Allocation unit size
  ┌─────────────────────────────────────┐ ▼
  │ 4096 bytes                          │
  └─────────────────────────────────────┘

  Volume label
  ┌─────────────────────────────────────┐
  │ New Volume                          │
  └─────────────────────────────────────┘

  ┌─ Format options ──────────────────────┐
  │   □ Quick Format                      │
  │   □ Enable Compression                │
  └───────────────────────────────────────┘

  ┌───────────────────────────────────────┐
  │                                       │
  └───────────────────────────────────────┘

              ┌──────────┐   ┌──────────┐
              │  Start   │   │  Close   │
              └──────────┘   └──────────┘
```

FIGURE 7.14   Using My Computer in Windows 2000 to format

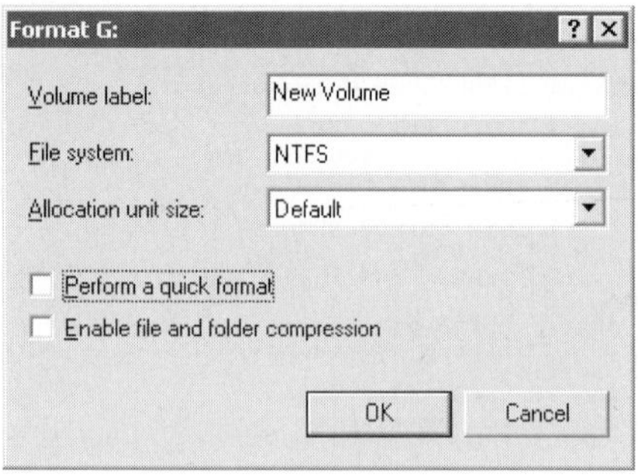

Format G:	? X
Volume label:	New Volume
File system:	NTFS ▼
Allocation unit size:	Default ▼

☐ Perform a quick format
☐ Enable file and folder compression

| OK | Cancel |

FIGURE 7.15 Windows 2000 Disk Management Format dialog box

CHECKPOINT

✔ **Objective 7.01: How Hard Drives Store Data**   Hard drives store data on magnetically charged metal platters that spin at an extremely high rate of speed (typically 7200 RPM). Special read/write heads float over the platters on a cushion of air created by the spinning motion. A hard drive's geometry consists of the cylinders (data tracks that permeate each platter), heads (two read/write heads per platter, plus any special reserved heads), and sectors (individual 512-byte slices of the cylinder data tracks). Collectively, these settings, called CHS, must be entered into CMOS before the hard drive can be used. Modern hard drives store all CHS settings in their onboard circuitry. CMOS programs automatically detect and read this data from the disk. Capacity is figured by multiplying the cylinders, heads, and sectors together, and then multiplying that number by 512.

✔ **Objective 7.02: IDE, EIDE, and SATA Standards**   IDE hard drives connect to the controller via a 40-pin ribbon cable, with pin 1 of the drive aligned to pin 1 on the controller. The IDE standard allowed two drives—jumpered master and slave—limited to 504 MB capacity each, but only a single IDE drive controller channel. The Enhanced IDE standard offers significant improvements over IDE. EIDE added a second controller channel, thus enabling up to four drives or other EIDE devices (such as ATAPI CD-ROM drives) to connect to the two drive controllers. LBA and ECHS broke the 504-MB limit, and INT13 Extensions broke the 8.4-GB limit. Serial ATA devices use only a small fraction of the power required by IDE devices. SATA devices currently offer only marginally better data throughput (150 MBps), but the SATA standard calls for eventual speeds of up to 600 MBps). SATA devices are hot-swappable.

✔**Objective 7.03: Installing IDE and SATA Hard Drives** Keep the red power wire on the five-volt power connector closest to the colored pin 1 wire of the IDE controller cable. If you have only a single device on a controller cable, set it to either master or stand-alone. If you have two devices, one must be set as master and the other as slave. Use autodetect to enter CHS data for drives into CMOS, if possible. Autodetect gives you the added bonus of testing your connectivity and jumper settings. If you set things up incorrectly, the drive won't autodetect. Use cable select to simplify installation if your system supports it. With cable select, the master drive goes on the end of the cable, and the slave drive goes on the middle connector.

✔**Objective 7.04: Partitioning and Formatting** FDISK in Windows 9x and Disk Management in Windows 2000 enable you to create up to two partitions on a drive—primary and extended—and then to create logical drives in the extended partition. A hard drive must have an active partition to be bootable. Windows 2000/XP support three drive formats: NTFS, FAT32, and FAT. Windows 9x (from 95 OSR2 on) and Windows Me support two drive formats: FAT32 and FAT16. DOS, as well as all earlier versions of Windows, could handle only FAT16.

REVIEW QUESTIONS

1. Which of the following statements regarding master/slave configurations is true?

   A. You need a slave device to have a master device.

   B. You need a master device to have a slave device.

   C. EIDE systems can have two slaves, but only one master on a single cable.

   D. EIDE systems cannot have two masters or two slaves on a single cable.

2. What does the FDISK utility do?

   A. It sets up the file allocation tables.

   B. It sets up the master/slave configuration.

   C. It partitions a hard drive.

   D. It separates a hard drive into clusters.

3. How many pins on the ribbon cable are used to connect an IDE drive?

   A. 36

   B. 40

   C. 60

   D. 80

4. How many pins does an 80-conductor EIDE cable use for data transfer?

   A. 36

   B. 40

   C. 60

   D. 80

5. If autodetect doesn't see your newly installed hard drive, what can you suspect as the most probable reason?

   A. There's some problem with connectivity or jumper settings.

   B. There's some problem with your System BIOS.

   C. The hard drive is dead.

   D. There's no problem.

6. What must you do to the Windows 2000 OS to prepare for installing SATA devices?

   A. Update the BIOS.

   B. Install SATA drivers.

   C. Nothing needs to be done.

   D. You cannot install SATA devices on a PC running Windows 2000.

7. How many EIDE drives can you install in a system that uses EIDE technology?

   A. 1

   B. 2

   C. 3

   D. 4

8. Where do you place the master hard drive on a standard, non-cable select EIDE cable?

   A. It must go at the end of the cable.

   B. It must go in the middle of the cable.

   C. It doesn't matter.

   D. EIDE cables are for floppy drives.

9. Where do you place a slave device on a cable select EIDE cable?

    A. It must go at the end of the cable.

    B. It must go in the middle of the cable.

    C. It doesn't matter.

    D. Slave devices aren't attached to the EIDE cable.

10. What was the capacity limitation of the original IDE standard?

    A. 504 MB

    B. 512 MB

    C. 528 MB

    D. 8.4 GB

11. The red stripe on the IDE cable corresponds to which pin?

    A. Pin 0

    B. Pin 1

    C. Pin 40

    D. Pin 80

12. How should you configure a new CD-ROM drive on a system using modern EIDE technology?

    A. Configure it as master.

    B. Configure it as slave.

    C. Configure it as either master or slave; it doesn't matter.

    D. A CD-ROM drive can be set only to stand-alone.

13. Which of the following terms is *not* a common EIDE drive jumper setting?

    A. Master

    B. Stand-alone

    C. Slave

    D. Secondary

14. What is the maximum number of logical drives you can configure using FDISK?

    A. 1

    B. 2

    C. 4

    D. 24

15. What is the maximum size of a FAT32 partition on Windows 95 OSR2?

    A. 2.1 GB

    B. 32 GB

    C. 504 MB

    D. 2 TB

REVIEW ANSWERS

1. **D**   EIDE systems cannot have two masters or two slaves on a single cable.

2. **C**   FDISK partitions a hard drive. You can create up to four partitions on a hard drive. You can also create an extended partition with logical drives on it.

3. **B**   An IDE ribbon cable has 40 pins.

4. **B**   An 80-conductor EIDE cable uses only 40 pins for data transfers. The difference between the 40-conductor and 80-conductor cables is that each pin in the 80-conductor cable has its own ground wire.

5. **A**   Some problem exists with connectivity or jumper settings.

6. **C**   SATA is backward compatible with current IDE standards. Nothing needs to be done to the OS to get SATA devices to work on Windows 2000.

7. **D**   You can connect up to four IDE/EIDE devices in a system that uses EIDE technology.

8. **C**   With non-cable select cables, the jumper settings on the drives determine whether the drivers are master or slave. Position on the cable doesn't matter.

9. **B**   Place the device that you want to act as slave in the middle of the cable select EIDE cable.

10. **A**   IDE had a capacity limitation of 504 MB. EIDE technology broke this limitation.

11. **B**   The red stripe on the IDE connector corresponds to pin 1.

12. **C**   Early EIDE technology required CD-ROM drives to be configured as slave. Modern EIDE controllers can handle CD-ROM drives as master or slave drives.

13. **D** Secondary is a term used to describe the second EIDE controller on the motherboard.

14. **D** You can configure up to 24 logical drives using FDISK. Drives A: and B: are reserved for floppy drives.

15. **D** Windows 95 OSR 2 introduced FAT32, which supports partitions as large as 2 TB.

SCSI Mass Storage Devices

	NEWBIE	SOME EXPERIENCE	EXPERT
ETA	3 hours	2 hours	1 hour

A company called Shugart Systems introduced the Small Computer System Interface (SCSI) in 1979 as a system-independent means of mass storage. SCSI can best be described as a miniature network inside your PC. While SCSI theoretically supports any type of peripheral device, it makes the most sense for mass storage devices, such as hard drives, tape drives, removable drives, external cluster storage devices, and CD and DVD media.

Since their introduction, SCSI mass storage devices have held a distinct advantage over IDE devices in terms of performance and reliability. Over the years, the speed gap between the two technologies has closed considerably, but most techs will still tell you that if you have mission-critical storage needs, SCSI is the way to go.

> **Local Lingo**
>
> **Skuzzy**   SCSI is amusingly pronounced "skuzzy."

Objective 8.01   Fundamentals of SCSI

SCSI manifests itself through a SCSI *chain,* a series of SCSI devices linked together on the SCSI controller cable, which plugs into the SCSI *host adapter.* The host adapter is the controller card device that attaches the SCSI chain to the PC's expansion bus. Figure 8-1 shows a typical SCSI host adapter.

The typical host adapter card has two connections: one for attaching SCSI devices externally and the other for internal SCSI drives. The external connector is shown at the left of the Figure 8-1, and the external connector is shown at the top of the figure. Figure 8-2 shows a SCSI ribbon cable.

SCSI has a reputation for being difficult to configure. While this reputation is far from deserved, there are two important SCSI configuration issues that you must understand to ensure a successful installation. The first is the SCSI *ID number,* and the second is the SCSI device *termination.* If either of these is misconfigured, your SCSI installation will fail. Let's have a closer look at each of these issues.

FIGURE 8.1   SCSI host adapter

SCSI IDs

As mentioned earlier, you can view the SCSI interface as a miniature network within a desktop computer. Just as individual nodes on a network need to be uniquely identified in order to communicate with each other, individual SCSI components each require a unique identifier—the ID number—in order to communicate with the SCSI host adapter and the rest of the PC (see Figure 8-3).

FIGURE 8.2   Typical SCSI cable

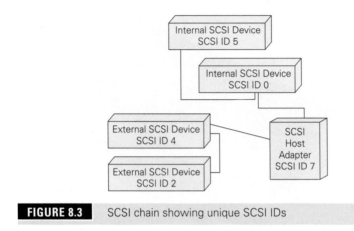

FIGURE 8.3   SCSI chain showing unique SCSI IDs

The values for ID numbers range from 0 to 7 in early SCSI implementations, and 0 to 15 in later versions. The SCSI standard sets the priority of the SCSI IDs at 0 for the highest, and then 1, 2, and so on. A device with a higher-priority SCSI ID runs marginally faster than lower-priority devices, although in the real world you'll never notice the difference.

SCSI ID numbers are similar to many other hardware settings in a PC in that no two devices can share the same ID number. A SCSI device can have any SCSI ID, as long as no two devices connected to a single host adapter share the same ID.

No rules apply to the order of SCSI ID assignment. It doesn't matter which device gets which number—any SCSI device can have any SCSI ID as long as no two have the same ID. Most host adapter manufacturers set their devices to use SCSI ID 0, 7, or 15.

You typically set a SCSI ID for a particular device by configuring jumpers on it. Figure 8-4 shows a SCSI hard drive's jumper settings.

Exam Tip

The term *SCSI ID* is often used interchangeably with the term *SCSI address*—you'll need to know them both.

It's important to note that even though the SCSI standard allows SCSI IDs to run from 0 to 7 or even 0 to 15, not all SCSI *devices* are designed to use every possible SCSI ID. For example, it's common for SCSI Zip drives to have settings for only SCSI ID 5 and 6.

Other SCSI devices use various means to set their SCSI IDs. Instead of a jumper, some use DIP switches or rotary wheels; in fact, for many modern SCSI

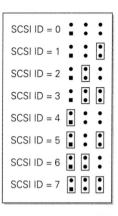

FIGURE 8.4   SCSI hard drive jumper settings

devices, you set the ID using device configuration software rather than any physical means. Always check the device's documentation or consult the maker's web site for explicit instructions on how to set the SCSI ID. Regardless of the method, remember that SCSI IDs are set at the device level, not centrally by the controller.

Termination

SCSI devices are designed so that they can be easily daisy-chained together in strings of up to either eight or sixteen devices (including the host adapter), depending on the implementation. Data signals travel through the chain until they reach the end of the line, but what happens then? If the chain isn't terminated, then the signal reflects back up the wire in the form of an electrical echo. As you can probably imagine, this echo causes interference with the original data signal, resulting in data corruption and loss. Terminating the SCSI chain solves this problem.

Termination simply means putting a device—a *terminator*—on each end of the chain to prevent the data signal from echoing back up the wire. Terminators are what's known as *pull-down resistors* and can manifest themselves in a number of different ways. SCSI terminators are either *passive* or *active*. The difference is that active SCSI terminators have built-in voltage regulators. Some of the high-speed implementations of SCSI require active terminators.

SCSI termination rules are actually quite simple. You must terminate *both* ends of the SCSI chain. If this isn't done correctly, your SCSI devices won't work. Figure 8-5 shows a few examples of SCSI chains with various combinations of internal and external devices connected to a SCSI host controller, along with their appropriate terminations.

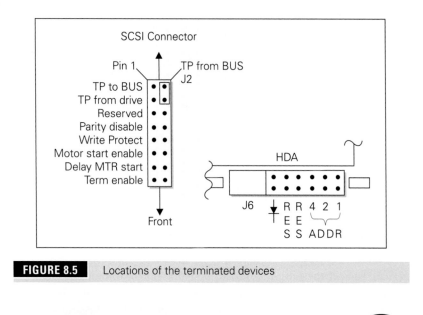

SCSI Connector

Pin 1
TP to BUS
TP from drive
Reserved
Parity disable
Write Protect
Motor start enable
Delay MTR start
Term enable

TP from BUS
J2

Front

HDA

J6   R R 4 2 1
     E E
     S S ADDR

FIGURE 8.5   Locations of the terminated devices

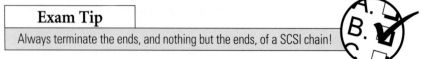

Exam Tip
Always terminate the ends, and nothing but the ends, of a SCSI chain!

SCSI devices employ a variety of technologies to set termination. Most SCSI devices have terminators built in, which you configure via jumpers or switches. If the SCSI devices don't have built-in terminators, they must be terminated with add-on resistor components that snap onto the end of the chain. Figure 8-6 shows a hard drive that's terminated using a jumper setting.

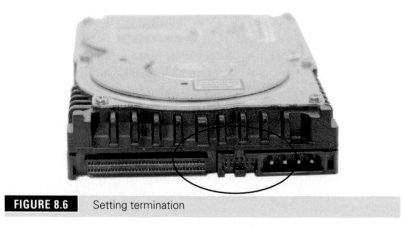

FIGURE 8.6   Setting termination

Hard drive with removable terminating resistors

The hard drive in Figure 8-7 has terminating resistors inserted. They must be removed to unterminate the drive. The Zip drive in Figure 8-8 uses a slide for termination.

Some host adapters set termination using software. Figure 8-9 shows a typical host adapter configuration program.

Be careful when terminating a SCSI device! Improper termination can, in some situations, damage or destroy SCSI hardware. Later in the chapter I'll discuss SE, HVD, and LVD SCSI—be sure to read and understand this information to avoid expensive mistakes. Unlike setting SCSI IDs, termination can be a little tricky. But before we can discuss the different types of termination options, you must understand the different types of SCSI.

FIGURE 8.8 Zip drive with termination slide at left (note SCSI ID slide at right)

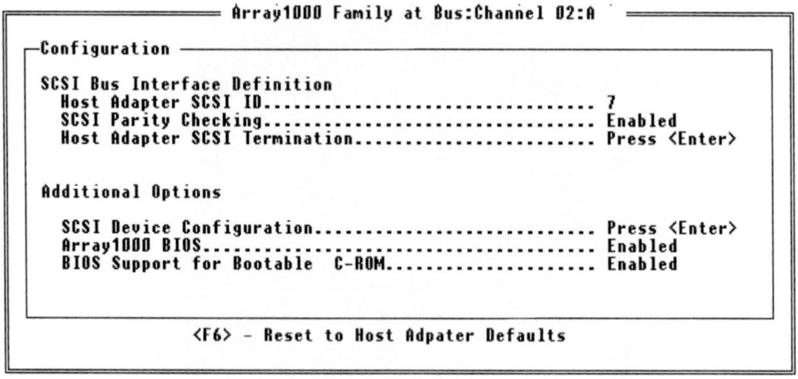

```
═════════════ Array1000 Family at Bus:Channel 02:A ═════════════
┌─Configuration ──────────────────────────────────────────────────┐
│                                                                  │
│  SCSI Bus Interface Definition                                   │
│    Host Adapter SCSI ID................................... 7      │
│    SCSI Parity Checking................................... Enabled│
│    Host Adapter SCSI Termination.......................... Press <Enter>│
│                                                                  │
│                                                                  │
│  Additional Options                                              │
│                                                                  │
│    SCSI Device Configuration.............................. Press <Enter>│
│    Array1000 BIOS......................................... Enabled│
│    BIOS Support for Bootable  C-ROM....................... Enabled│
│                                                                  │
│                                                                  │
└──────────────────────────────────────────────────────────────────┘
         <F6> - Reset to Host Adpater Defaults
```

FIGURE 8.9   Software termination setting

Objective 8.02   **SCSI Types**

SCSI has been around for quite a while and has seen a number of standards over the years. These different standards are usually called *SCSI types* and sometimes called *SCSI flavors*—the terms are interchangeable. The American National Standards Institute (ANSI) governs the creation and adoption of SCSI types. To date, three SCSI types have been recognized, all of which enjoy wide support. Each improved version invariably provides some degree of support for earlier versions.

SCSI-1

The *SCSI-1 standard* defined an 8-bit, 5 MHz bus capable of supporting up to eight SCSI devices, but it was fuzzy in describing many aspects of SCSI. As a result, many manufacturers of SCSI devices had different opinions as to how to implement those standards. So, SCSI-1 was more of an opinion than a standard.

In 1986, SCSI began to appear on IBM-compatible PC machines and everyone seemed to have a proprietary SCSI device. The key word here is "proprietary," meaning that only the company that produced, designed, manufactured, and sold the device supported it. SCSI was being used in PCs for stand-alone devices, such as hard drives, and each device came with its own host adapter. Makers of SCSI devices had no interest in chaining their particular device with anyone else's. Each SCSI device had its own command set, and no two command sets were the same. It was often impossible to get one vendor's SCSI hard drive to work with another vendor's SCSI adapter card.

SCSI-1 supported up to eight devices (including the host adapter) on the SCSI chain, but they transferred data through a parallel path only 8 bits wide. For most PCs using SCSI-1 devices, an 8-bit pathway wasn't much of a bottleneck. Although the devices themselves weren't capable of high-speed data transfers, neither were the 80286-based machines of the time. SCSI-1 devices seemed fast by comparison. Plus, the only common hard-drive interface competition was the ST-506 controller, and 8-bit SCSI was far faster!

SCSI-2

In contrast with its predecessor, the *SCSI-2 standard* is quite detailed and applies common rules on command sets and cabling. One of the more important parts is the definition of 18 commands that must be supported by SCSI-2-compliant devices. This set of commands, called the common command set (CCS), made the job of hooking up devices from various manufacturers less of a nightmare. The CCS also introduced new commands for addressing devices besides hard drives, including CD-ROM drives, tape drives, and scanners. Finally, SCSI-2 incorporated a new feature called *command queuing*, which enabled a SCSI device to accept multiple commands at once.

> **Travel Assistance**
>
> Check out http://www.paralan.com for some great details on the SCSI-2 standard, as well as SCSI in general.

SCSI-2 also defined permitted types of connectors. Before SCSI-2, no true standard existed for SCSI connectors, although a few types became de facto standards. The new SCSI-2 connector standard ensured that any two SCSI-2-compliant devices could be physically connected. SCSI-2 also provided a more detailed specification for terminations.

The plethora of data bus widths and data transfer speeds is the most confusing part of the SCSI-2 standard. SCSI-2 defined two optional 16-bit and 32-bit buses called *wide SCSI*, and a new, optional 10 MHz speed called *fast SCSI*. SCSI-2 devices could now be 8-bit (narrow), 16-bit (wide), or 32-bit (also called *wide*), and they could be 5 MHz (slow, the standard) or 10 MHz (fast). This adds up to six subflavors of SCSI-2. Table 8-1 shows the various combinations, plus the SCSI-1 standard for comparison.

Even though SCSI-2 defined a 32-bit SCSI bus, it was almost completely ignored by the industry because of its high cost and a lack of demand. In the real world, wide SCSI means 16 bits wide.

TABLE 8.1	SCSI Bus Widths and Speeds	
SCSI Type/Bit Width	**5 MHz (Standard)**	**10 MHz (Fast)**
SCSI-1: 8-bit	5 MBps	NA
SCSI-2: 8-bit	5 MBps	10 MBps
SCSI-2: 16-bit (wide)	10 MBps	20 MBps
SCSI-2: 32-bit (wide)	20 MBps	40 MBps

Fast SCSI-2 transfers data in *fast synchronous* mode, meaning the SCSI device being talked to (the target) doesn't have to acknowledge (ack) every individual request (req) for data from the host adapter (initiator). Using this mode doubles the transfer speed, from approximately 5–10 MBps for narrow and 10–20 MBps for wide. However, experience has shown that external fast SCSI devices rarely provide this "fast" performance unless the SCSI cable provides proper shielding and electrical impedance or "load." Cables that do provide proper shielding and load are generally a bit more expensive, but you need them to achieve truly "fast" performance.

SE, HVD, and LVD SCSI

SCSI-1 devices were all *single-ended (SE)*, meaning they communicated each bit of information through only one wire. This one wire was measured or referenced against the common ground provided by the metal chassis and, in turn, by the power supply of the system. The big problem with SE SCSI is line noise, called *common-mode noise*, usually spread through either the electrical power cables or the data cable. An SE SCSI device is vulnerable to common-mode noise because it can't tell the difference between valid data and noise. When noise invades the data stream, the devices must resend the data. The amount of noise generated grows dramatically with the length of a SCSI cable, limiting the total length of an SE SCSI chain to about six meters, depending on the type of SCSI.

To achieve much longer SCSI chains, SCSI-2 offered an optional solution called *High Voltage Differential (HVD)* SCSI (formerly called *differential* SCSI). HVD devices employ two wires per bit of data: one wire for the data bit and one for the inverse of the data bit. The inverse signal takes the place of the ground wire in the single-ended cable. By taking the difference of the two signals, the device can reject the common-mode noise in the data stream. This allows for much longer SCSI chains, up to 25 meters.

Unfortunately for techs, there are few apparent differences between SE and HVD SCSI devices. The connectors and cabling seem identical. This is a bit of a problem because under no circumstances should you try to connect SE and

HVD devices on the same SCSI chain! At the very least, you'll probably fry the SE device and, if the HVD device lacks a security circuit to detect your mistake, you'll probably smoke it as well.

Don't panic! Although HVD SCSI devices exist, they are rare and usually found only in aging high-end servers. SE SCSI devices and controllers still reign. The makers of HVD SCSI know the danger and will clearly label their devices.

The problems of cable length versus cost led manufacturers to come up with a second type of differential SCSI called *Low Voltage Differential (LVD)*. LVD SCSI requires less power than HVD and is compatible with existing SE SCSI controllers and devices. LVD devices can sense the type of SCSI and then work accordingly. If you plug an LVD device into a single-ended chain, it acts as a single-ended device. If you plug an LVD device into LVD, it runs as LVD. LVD SCSI chains can be up to 12 meters in length. The safety, ease of use, and low cost of LVD has made it quite popular in higher-end PCs and servers.

SCSI-3

SCSI technology didn't stand still with the adoption of SCSI-2. Manufacturers have made significant improvements in SCSI-2, particularly in increased speeds and easier configuration. The T-10 SCSI committee collected these improvements and created a working set of standards collectively called *SCSI-3*. SCSI-3 devices have many names and technologies, such as *Ultra2 or Wide Ultra*.

One of the more popular and widely adopted features of SCSI-3 is that wide SCSI can control up to 16 devices on one chain. Each device gets a number from 0 through 15, instead of 0 through 7. Many people think this feature is part of SCSI-2 because wide, 16-device control came out quickly after the SCSI-2 standard was adopted.

The terms Ultra and Fast-20 are used by many SCSI component manufacturers to define a high-speed 20 MHz bus speed. Ultra2 and Fast-40 define a 40 MHz bus speed, and Ultra3 and Fast-80 define an 80 MHz bus speed. The narrow and wide SCSI types still exist. Table 8-2 compares the possible speeds for these two widths.

TABLE 8.2 Narrow SCSI vs. Wide SCSI

SCSI Type/Bit Width	8-bit (Narrow)	16-bit (Wide)
Ultra SCSI (FAST20)	20 MBps	40 MBps
Ultra2 SCSI (FAST40)	40 MBps	80 MBps
Ultra3 SCSI (FAST80)	80 MBps	160 MBps

The SCSI-3 standard also includes optional hot swap capabilities, a feature that is extremely useful in mission-critical systems that can't afford unscheduled downtime, and is already popular for high-end SCSI drives.

With the development of SCSI-3 standards and devices, you might assume older SCSI-2 devices would go away, but this hasn't been the case. Manufacturers continue to produce SCSI-2 devices and controllers, and put them into the marketplace right alongside the higher-end SCSI-3 devices and controllers.

SCSI Developments

Given that the latest versions of IDE mass storage technology match or exceed their SCSI counterparts, some argue that SCSI is on its way to obsolescence. Don't believe it! SCSI device manufacturers are not sitting idle, and the latest developments in SCSI technology show that SCSI will be with us for a long time.

Ultra320 SCSI

The latest and greatest SCSI standard makes some interesting changes to the tried-and-true technology. Ultra320 SCSI doubles the clock speed, pumping performance up over the previous high mark of 160 MBps to 320 MBps. For the first time, the SCSI protocol itself has been revised. Dubbed *packetized* SCSI, the revised protocol reduces processing overhead, resulting in increased performance. Packetized SCSI also allows the transfer of multiple commands or data from multiple I/O processes in a single connection. Further, Ultra320 SCSI offers improved reliability through *cyclical redundancy checking (CRC)* error control on data, commands, and status. Ultra320 SCSI is fully backward-compatible with earlier SCSI implementations.

Serial Attached SCSI

Serial-Attached SCSI (SAS) is the industry's response to Serial ATA. SAS was actually developed in cooperation with the SATA II working group to leverage the technological advancements that brought us SATA.

Like current IDE devices, SCSI devices communicate in parallel. SAS is, as you've probably guessed, a serial version of SCSI. Like SATA, SAS is a point-to-point interface that uses a reduced-size data cable and has reduced power consumption demands. SAS isn't expected to compete with either parallel SCSI or SATA, but rather to complement both of those technologies as an enterprise-level storage solution. For the time being, details about SAS speeds and other specifications are hard to come by, as the standard is still being finalized, but available data suggests that SAS will achieve throughput speeds of 1.5 GBps!

As far as the CompTIA A+ core hardware exam is concerned, however, Table 8-3 summarizes the current SCSI picture.

The following notes apply to Table 8-3:

1. The listed maximum bus lengths may be exceeded in point-to-point and engineered applications.

2. Use of the word "Narrow," preceding SCSI, Ultra SCSI, or Ultra2 SCSI, is optional.

3. LVD wasn't defined in the original SCSI standards for this speed. If all devices on the bus support LVD, then 12-meter operation is possible at this speed. However, if any device on the bus is singled-ended only, then the entire bus switches to single-ended mode and the distances in the single-ended column apply.

4. Single-ended isn't defined for speeds beyond Ultra.

5. HVD (differential) isn't defined for speeds beyond Ultra2.

6. After Ultra2, all new speeds are wide only.

TABLE 8.3 Current SCSI Picture

SCSI Trade Association Terms	Bus Speed (MBps)	Bus Width (bits)	Max. Bus Lengths Meters[1]			Max. Device Support
			SE	LVD	HVD	
SCSI-1[2]	5	8	6 [3]		25	8
Fast SCSI-1[2]	10	8	3 [3]		25	8
Fast Wide SCSI	20	16	3 [3]		25	16
Ultra SCSI[2]	20	8	1.5 [3]		25	8
Ultra SCSI[2]	20	8	3			4
Wide Ultra SCSI	40	16	[3]		25	16
Wide Ultra SCSI	40	16	1.5			8
Wide Ultra SCSI	40	16	3			4
Ultra2 SCSI[2,4]	40	8	[4]	12	25	8
Wide Ultra2 SCSI[4]	80	16	[4]	12	25	16
Ultra3 SCSI or Ultra160[6]	160	16	[4]	12 [5]		16
Ultra320	320	16	[4]	12 [5]		16

(Table courtesy of the SCSI Trade Association—http://www.scsita.org)

Objective 8.03 Internal vs. External SCSI Devices

Most SCSI controllers have connectors for both external and internal devices, so you can have a single SCSI chain that contains both types of devices. The SCSI chain does not distinguish between internal and external devices as far as setup is concerned. Every device needs a SCSI ID and termination. Only terminate the ends of the chain. If you have one external device and one internal device attached to a controller, that puts the controller in the middle. You would terminate the two devices, but not the controller.

The one significant difference between the two types of SCSI devices lies in the cabling. Internal SCSI devices use ribbon cables, while external devices use a thick insulated cable similar to a printer cable. The cable plugs into a connector port on the SCSI device. Most external SCSI devices have two ports—an input and an output—to allow for daisy chaining, as shown in Figure 8-10. External SCSI devices also need their own power supply.

FIGURE 8.10 An external SCSI device, with two ports visible

Objective 8.04   # SCSI Cabling

There's no such thing as official SCSI-1, SCSI-2, Ultra SCSI, or any other flavor of SCSI cable or connector, although manufacturers generally follow similar guidelines today. Which cable you need depends on whether the device is internal or external, what types of connectors are available, and the type of SCSI you use.

Types of SCSI Cables

The most common kind of SCSI cable is type A (see Figure 8-11), which has 50 wires and is used for 8-bit data transfers under both the SCSI-1 and SCSI-2 standards. Type A is also used for 8-bit Fast SCSI-2.

In the earliest days of SCSI-2, 16-bit data transfers required a different type of cable, inventively known as type B. It had 68 wires and was used in parallel with the 50-wire type A cable. Because the industry was so underwhelmed by this dual-cable concept, the B cable quietly and quickly disappeared, to be replaced by the type P cable (see Figure 8-12). Like its predecessor, this cable has 68 wires and transfers data at 16 bits. Unlike type B cable, type P cable can be used alone.

Some of the higher-end SCSI-3 host adapters and drives use an 80-pin cable called an SCA 80 (and no, it has nothing to do with Renaissance festivals). The extra wires enable you to hot swap the drives, but that's about it. The drives work fine using either 68-pin cables and an adapter, or their own 80-pin cable.

| **FIGURE 8.11** | Type A SCSI cable |

FIGURE 8.12 Type P SCSI cable

Types of External Connectors

All external connectors on SCSI devices are female. The types of external connectors are as follows:

- 50-pin Centronics, an obsolete SCSI-1 connector (see Figure 8-13)
- 50-pin HD (High Density) SCSI-2 (Figure 8-14)
- 68-pin HD DB, used for wide SCSI-2 and SCSI-3 (Figure 8-15)
- 25-pin standard D-type (looks like a parallel connector), used for SCSI-2, most commonly on Macintosh systems and many removable drives (Figure 8-16)

Exam Tip

Make sure you know what types of connectors are used for both narrow and wide SCSI, and make sure you know your cable lengths!

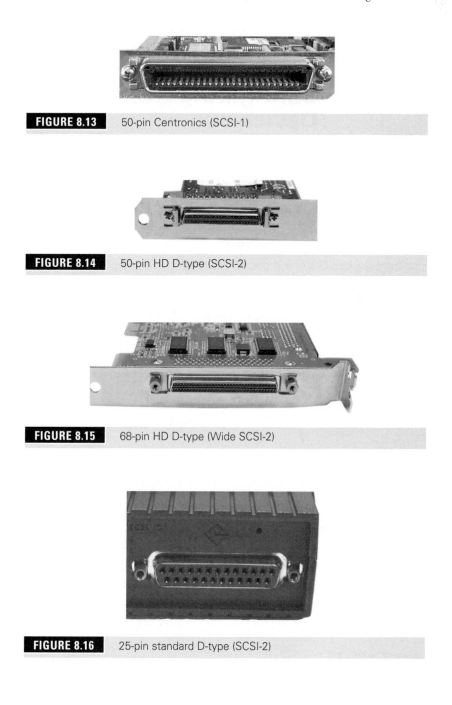

FIGURE 8.13 50-pin Centronics (SCSI-1)

FIGURE 8.14 50-pin HD D-type (SCSI-2)

FIGURE 8.15 68-pin HD D-type (Wide SCSI-2)

FIGURE 8.16 25-pin standard D-type (SCSI-2)

Objective 8.05   Proper Procedures for Installing and Configuring SCSI Devices

Today's world of plug and play makes installing SCSI devices almost trivial. All modern versions of Windows (Windows 9x/Me, Windows 2000/XP) come with a special set of drivers that will recognize most SCSI devices. As long as you do the physical installation properly, you shouldn't encounter any problems with the installation of a SCSI device.

Some high-end PCs have built-in SCSI, but for the most part you can count on installing an add-on SCSI host adapter card. Many SCSI devices come with host adapter cards, but these tend to run on the cheap side, so you would do well to spend a little extra cash on a higher-end host adapter. Adaptec is the big name in SCSI host adapters, and with good reason. Adaptec host adapters have a well-deserved reputation for reliability, so if you have a choice in the matter, it's hard to go wrong with this brand.

Travel Assistance

Check out the Adaptec web site for great host adapters and great SCSI info! http://www.adaptec.com.

Make sure you get the right host adapter for your needs. If you have wide SCSI devices, get a wide host adapter. If you have narrow SCSI devices, get a host adapter that supports narrow devices. If you have both wide and narrow types, you can get host adapters that support both, or two separate host adapters (assuming you've got available expansion bus slots). If you're installing a giant-sized tape drive, make sure you get a SCSI controller that has INT13 extensions built in, just as you would for a hard drive larger than 8.4 GB. While you're shopping, don't forget that a given host adapter supports only certain speeds and terminations—it's well worth your time to make certain that all of your devices are compatible with your host adapter!

Once you've got your SCSI devices and host adapter card in hand, and you've confirmed that they're all compatible, you should set your IDs and terminations before you physically install them. This is a lot easier than trying to get at the tiny switches and jumpers once the components are tucked away inside your PC case! Take a few extra minutes to write down your settings and even sketch out your device arrangement. You'll be glad you did when it's time to add another device to the chain six months down the line!

Once you've taken care of the preliminaries, installing SCSI devices is exactly like installing any other device. Power down your PC, unplug the power cable, and pop the cover off. Strap on your nerd bracelet and go to it—making sure that you follow all of the rules about ESD and that you seat all components properly!

Some techs like to slap the entire SCSI chain together at one time and hope for the best, but it's smarter to install the host adapter card first and boot the system to make certain that it's recognized and functional before you connect your SCSI devices. Also, don't forget your terminators! While most techs remember to terminate the SCSI devices, they often forget to terminate the host adapter when it's the end of the chain. Host adapters are as much a part of the SCSI chain as any other device and also need termination. Fortunately, most good host adapters now have an autotermination feature, so they can automatically terminate themselves when they detect they're at the end of the chain.

After you install the SCSI devices, power up the system and confirm installation. SCSI host adapters typically have their own boot environment that enables you to configure the adapter defaults and perform troubleshooting tasks such as scanning the SCSI chain. Typically, you are prompted during boot-up to press a key (such as F2 or F6) to enter the host adapter configuration utility, but most of the time you don't need to use it unless you need to make a change to the adapter's SCSI ID or run the scanning utility. In Windows, check Device Manager to see that your hardware is recognized and functional without any conflicts. Figure 8-17 shows a Windows 2000 system with a SCSI host adapter, Zip drive, and hard drive connected.

Troubleshooting SCSI Address/Termination Conflicts

Objective 8.06

You'll always know when you get a SCSI address or termination conflict because the SCSI device won't be visible to your system! When this happens, invariably during a new installation, it's a sure sign that the SCSI ID, termination settings, or both are incorrect. Fortunately, the diagnosis is fairly easy: you

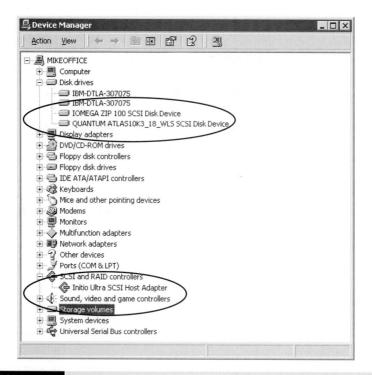

FIGURE 8.17   Windows 2000 Device Manager showing three devices (including host adapter) on a SCSI chain

run a SCSI chain scanning utility. Good host adapters—yes, such as Adapter—have this utility built right into them. Reboot the system and press the appropriate key when prompted to start the diagnostics utility. Check your hardware manual for instructions on how to run the utility.

If your host adapter didn't come with a chain-scanning utility—and most low-end adapters don't—you'll need to acquire one to best troubleshoot your conflict. Most host adapter makers give these programs away free, or you can often find one in a good PC diagnostic tool. Whatever the case, get one and use it. It usually tells you the problem instantly. If you forgot to terminate properly, the scanning software won't show any devices on the chain. If you see only a few devices, you probably put a terminator somewhere other than on the end of the chain. Turn the system off, reset the termination, and try again.

That same scanning program will usually tell you if two devices are set with the same SCSI ID. When you scan the chain, it'll look like you have only one device, but it has cloned itself. Literally every SCSI ID will show the same device, repeated over and over, as if there were only one! Unfortunately, the scanning software doesn't tell you which devices are actually using the same ID, so you must dismantle everything and recheck all the SCSI ID settings. How's that for motivation to double-check your settings before installing SCSI devices? As the saying goes, *measure twice, cut once.*

CHECKPOINT

✔**Objective 8.01: Fundamentals of SCSI**   No two SCSI devices on the same SCSI chain can share the same ID number. The rule with SCSI is you must terminate both ends of the SCSI chain. Do not terminate devices that aren't on the ends of the cable.

✔**Objective 8.02: SCSI Types**   SCSI-1 supported up to eight devices on a chain and transferred data in 8-bit parallel. SCSI-2 comes in narrow (8-bit), wide (16-bit or 32-bit), standard (5 MHz), and fast (10 MHz) varieties. SCSI-3 comes in a variety of flavors, usually called Ultra SCSI or some close variation.

✔**Objective 8.03: Internal vs. External SCSI Devices**   Internal SCSI devices use ribbon cables, while external devices use an insulated cable. Regardless of whether a device is internal or external, each device needs a SCSI ID. If a device sits on the end of the SCSI chain, it needs termination.

✔**Objective 8.04: SCSI Cabling**   SCSI-1 and SCSI-2 use 50-pin type A cables for internal connections. Fast SCSI-2 uses a 68-pin type P cable. External cables provide more variety. SCSI-1 used 50-pin Centronics or HD DB connectors. Normal SCSI-2 uses 50-pin HD DB or 25-pin DB. Fast SCSI uses 68-pin HD DB connectors. SCSI-3 uses 68-pin or 80-pin internal cables and 68-pin external cables.

✔**Objective 8.05: Proper Procedures for Installing and Configuring SCSI Devices**   Set jumpers and termination properly for all devices prior to installation. You should install and confirm function of the SCSI host adapter before connecting SCSI devices.

✔**Objective 8.06: Troubleshooting SCSI Address/Termination Conflicts**
Use the host adapter scanning utility to check improper addressing or termination settings. If the scan returns settings that seem odd, check the devices for proper settings.

REVIEW QUESTIONS

1. Which of the following statements are true about SCSI IDs? (Select all that apply.)

   A. They must follow the SCSI chain in sequence.

   B. No physical order requirement exists for the use of SCSI IDs.

   C. The device itself is where the SCSI IDs are set, either via software or with physical jumpers, shunts, or DIP switches.

   D. The host adapter dynamically assigns SCSI IDs for a device when its ROM is accessed at boot-up.

2. Judy is worried that her SCSI chain might be too long to work properly. What is the maximum length for narrow and normal (slow) SCSI-2 chains?

   A. 0.5 meters

   B. 1 meter

   C. 3 meters

   D. 6 meters

3. Which of the following connectors might be something other than a valid SCSI connector?

   A. 50-pin Centronics

   B. 50-pin HD D-type

   C. 68-pin HD D-type

   D. 25-pin parallel

4. How many devices can be connected on a fast/narrow SCSI-2 bus, including the host adapter?

   A. Six

   B. Seven

   C. Eight

   D. Nine

5. A client calls you on the phone and tells you that he installed a new external SCSI CD-RW onto a system that has an internal SCSI hard drive and SCSI CD-ROM already installed. Now none of the SCSI devices work. You instruct the client to run the SCSI chain scanning utility that came with the SCSI host adapter. He then tells you that the utility shows all of the SCSI devices configured with identical SCSI IDs. What is the likeliest cause?

    A. The external SCSI CD-RW device isn't properly terminated.

    B. The external SCSI CD-RW's ID is duplicated.

    C. You cannot connect more than two devices to a single SCSI host adapter.

    D. The SCSI host adapter has become unseated.

6. SCSI devices can be classified into two groups. What are they?

    A. Stand-alone

    B. Internal

    C. External

    D. Variable

7. Which of the following is true about SCSI chains?

    A. SCSI chains must have at least three devices.

    B. SCSI chains must have a terminator at each end.

    C. SCSI chains must have at least one SE and one HVD device.

    D. SCSI chains must have a terminator on each device.

8. Edwina wants to add a CD-ROM drive to her system. She plugs it in to the SCSI host adapter, sets the termination properly, and boots up the system. The host adapter doesn't recognize the CD-ROM. What did Edwina forget to do?

    A. Install ASPI drivers.

    B. Turn off the host adapter's ROM.

    C. Verify that the CD-ROM drive has a unique SCSI ID.

    D. Nothing, she just needs to boot two more times for the CD-ROM drive to kick in.

9. Dave wants to boot to his SCSI hard drive. What ID number must he use for the drive?

    A. He must set it to the highest possible ID.

    B. He should set it to one ID number lower than any EIDE drives in the system.

    C. He needs to set it to whatever ID number the host adapter dictates.

    D. It doesn't matter; the system looks for the active partition.

10. How should you place terminations on a SCSI chain with one internal hard drive and one external CD-RW drive?

    A. Terminate the hard drive only.

    B. Terminate the SCSI host adapter card.

C. Terminate both the hard drive and CD-ROM drive.

D. Terminate the SCSI host adapter card, hard drive and CD-ROM drive.

REVIEW ANSWERS

1. **B** **C**   SCSI IDs can be used in any order and SCSI devices IDs are set at the device level.

2. **D**   Narrow, slow SCSI has a maximum chain length of six meters.

3. **D**   Some SCSI devices use a 25-pin connector that looks exactly like a 25-pin parallel connector. Don't mix the two!

4. **C**   Narrow SCSI-2 supports a maximum of eight devices.

5. **B**   A single SCSI device ID "cloning" itself to every device indicates that two or more SCSI devices are configured with the same SCSI ID. Since the problem popped up only after the client added a new external SCSI CD-RW device, chances are that device is the culprit.

6. **B** **C**   All SCSI devices are either internal or external.

7. **B**   All SCSI chains must be terminated at each end.

8. **C**   The CD-ROM and the host adapter are almost certainly using the same SCSI ID.

9. **C**   Most SCSI host adapters reserve ID 0 for bootable devices, but this setting can usually be changed. IBM host adapters traditionally reserve ID 6 for bootable devices. The key factor, however, is to match the drive ID to your host adapter's setting for bootable devices.

10. **C**   Both ends of the SCSI chain must be terminated, which in this case means the last internal device (the hard drive) and the last external device (the CD-RW drive).

Expansion Bus, System Resources, and Installing Peripheral Devices

	NEWBIE	SOME EXPERIENCE	EXPERT
ETA	3 hours	2 hours	1 hour

One of the many things that make PCs so useful is their amazing versatility. Modern PCs support a wide array of peripheral devices and attachments that expand their capabilities and boost performance.

Peripherals attach to the PC via the *expansion bus*, which we introduced back in Chapter 3. The term "expansion bus" is collectively used to describe the different pathways that are used to gain access to the system's CPU and RAM.

Once you've physically installed a device, you also need to assign it a set of *system resources* for it to function properly. System resources include the device's I/O address, IRQ settings, and DMA channels. Modern plug-and-play devices make configuring system resources largely a nonissue, but many legacy devices still require the hands-on approach.

The CompTIA core A+ hardware exam expects you to know how to install and configure add-on peripheral devices both through the magic of Plug and Play (PnP) and the "old-fashioned" way. This chapter explains what you need to know to meet these objectives. Let's get started.

Objective 9.01 Expansion Bus: Internal and External

As you'll recall, a *bus* is a pathway on the motherboard that enables components to communicate with the CPU and other system resources. The expansion bus is the pathway that enables you to plug new devices and device controllers into the motherboard. This pathway can be split up into two groups—the internal expansion bus and the external expansion bus. The internal expansion bus includes the Peripheral Component Interconnect (PCI) bus, the Accelerated Graphics Port (AGP) bus, and on older systems, the Industry Standard Architecture (ISA) bus. Other, specialized internal buses, such as Audio/Modem Riser (AMR) and Communication Network Riser (CNR) also pop up on some systems. The external expansion bus includes the Universal Serial bus (USB) and the IEEE 1394 (FireWire) bus.

Internal Expansion Bus

As described in Chapter 3, PCI and AGP are the predominant types of internal expansion buses found on modern PCs. ISA and Enhanced ISA slots are still found on some systems, however, so you can also expect to support them for the time being. You should also expect to support proprietary buses such as AMR and CNR as well. This section describes these internal expansion bus technologies.

PCI

Peripheral devices that plug into the PCI bus include video adapters; sound cards; network interface cards (NICs); modems; I/O cards that add additional parallel or serial ports; controller cards such as SCSI, SATA, or IDE controllers; USB and FireWire controllers; and specialized devices such as video capture cards and TV tuners. Figure 9-1 shows typical PCI slots.

Although the PCI bus is no longer on the cutting edge of PC technology, it is still going strong due to its flexibility, strength, and universal adoption by computer makers (even Apple!). Among the many qualities and features that keep PCI relevant are flexibility, scalability, self-configuration, IRQ steering, bus mastering, and speed.

- **Flexibility**   The PCI bus is what we call a "mezzanine" bus. It sits between the frontside bus (which you'll recall from Chapter 5) and any other expansion bus. This means that the PCI bus, along with any devices attached to it, is able to work independently or with any other expansion bus, such as ISA. The other bus type doesn't need to be PCI-aware, because the PCI bus handles all communications. You should recall from Chapter 5 that the motherboard's Southbridge chip handles communication between the Northbridge chip and the PCI bus. Many Southbridge chips actually control or *bridge* communication between the PCI bus and other buses; hence, the Southbridge is sometimes referred to as the *PCI bridge.*

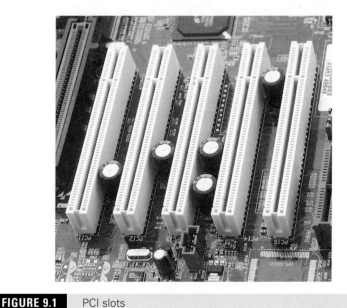

FIGURE 9.1   PCI slots

Travel Advisory

Most of the latest motherboards use the Southbridge chip to control the PCI bus, but on some older motherboards, the duties are split between the Northbridge and Southbridge chips. In either case, the Southbridge handles communication between the PCI bus and ISA.

- **Scalability**   The PCI specification enables variations within the PCI bus itself. Manufacturers are able to create devices that run at 32 bits and 33 MHz (the current standard) or bump that up to 64 bits and 66 MHz, or mix and match bit-widths and speeds to produce devices running at 64 bits and 33 MHz, all of which interoperate flawlessly.

- **Self-configuration**   PCI works with PnP devices and operating systems to enable hands-off configuration of system resources (I/O addresses, IRQ settings, and DMA channels). The PCI standard defines configuration settings (even for multiple occurrences) of virtually every device commonly in use today, as well as some not-yet-common devices. The intelligent PCI mezzanine bus interrogates PCI cards as they are installed and assigns them preset system resources. We'll go into more detail about PnP in the section "Installing Peripheral Devices."

- **IRQ steering**—PCI does not use IRQs in the classic sense; instead, it uses shareable "Interrupt Channels" labeled "INTA," "INTB," "INTC," and "INTD." This enables several devices to use the same IRQ. The makers of the PCI devices configure these interrupt channels at manufacture, and only on the most rare of occasions do we need to change them.

- **Bus mastering**   Devices attached to the PCI bus are able to "talk among themselves," so to speak, via bus mastering. This means the PCI devices can communicate directly with each other, while other devices, such as ISA, must pass all communications through the CPU.

- **Speed**   Finally, the PCI bus uses an accelerated transfer mode called *burst mode* that enables it to communicate more efficiently with system RAM. Essentially, the PCI bus recognizes when bits of data written to its buffer are addressed for consecutive blocks of memory. It then sends the data along in grouped packets instead of individual bytes. Burst mode is a powerful feature, but as the name implies, it is not intended for sustained high-speed transfers.

As you can plainly see, the PCI bus is one of the most intelligently engineered features of modern PCs. One of the areas where it falls short, however, is in handling the demands of high-end video. For that, PCs use a high-powered subset of PCI, the AGP bus.

AGP

The popularity of advanced 3-D games created a need for fast and powerful video adapters capable of handling their intense demands. AGP was developed to answer the call. The AGP bus is dedicated for video adapters only—no other component plugs into an AGP slot, and most current motherboards support only a single AGP slot, shown in Figure 9-2. The latest AGP specification (AGP 3.0) calls for support for multiple AGP sockets.

AGP slots today run at 32 bits and 66 MHz, and use clock multiplying (called *strobing,* and represented as 2x, 4x, and so on) in the same way that CPUs do to increase performance. AGP has several technological advantages over PCI, including the efficiency of the bus itself, internal operations, and capability to handle 3-D texturing.

First, AGP currently resides alone on its own personal data bus, connected directly to the Northbridge. This is important because more advanced versions of AGP outperform every bus on the system except the frontside bus! Second, AGP takes advantage of pipelining commands, similar to the way CPUs pipeline. Third, AGP has a feature called *sidebanding*—basically, a second data bus that enables the video card to send more commands to the Northbridge while

FIGURE 9.2 AGP slot

receiving other commands at the same time. Further, the AGP 3.0 standard allows for more than one AGP device, although motherboard manufacturers are sticking with a single slot, at least on the typical PC motherboard.

Modern video processors can do amazing things, rendering scenes in video games, for example, that seem real enough to pull you into the illusion. But this process is phenomenally complicated. Look at the wall in the room you're in right now. It might seem regular at first glance, but look again, this time noticing the subtle or not-so-subtle shadows and highlights, the scuff marks or nail holes. Note the curves of a light switch cover. Almost any video card can display a still photograph that captures the irregularities of that wall, but imagine what it would take to create such a complex picture and make it both interactive and changeable on the fly. What would it take to make a scuff mark appear if your character kicks the wall, or have all the shadows and light change if your character flicks on a lighter?

Video processors use pre-made sets of *textures*—like photos of a wall in different phases, with fresh paint, nail marks, handprints, and so on—to make the backgrounds. Then they apply *effects* such as lighting, shadows, smoke, distance, curves, and so forth to enhance the realism.

AGP video adapter cards come equipped with massive amounts of onboard video memory (256 MB or more!) that are used mainly to store 3-D textures. AGP also provides a pathway to the PC's main system memory so that the video card can use it to store even more textures. Called *system memory access,* this feature is very popular among video card manufacturers.

Table 9-1 lists the AGP standards.

TABLE 9.1	AGP Specifications						
AGP Standard	**Bus Speed**	**Bus Width**	**Strobe Multiplier**	**Throughput**	**Voltage**	**System Memory Access**	**Multiple AGP Support**
AGP 1.0	66 MHz	32 bits	1x, 2x	264 MBps (1x) 528 MBps (2x)	3.3 V	No	No
AGP 2.0	66 MHz	32 bits	2x, 4x	528 MBps (2x) 1 GBps (4x)	1.5 V	Yes	No
AGP 3.0	66 MHz	32 bits	4x, 8x	1 GBps (4x) 2.1 GBps (8x)	1.5 V and 0.8 V	Yes	Yes

ISA

Development for the ISA bus has halted for a number of years now, and you would be hard-pressed to find new ISA components on any computer store shelf. Most modern motherboards, in fact, no longer include ISA slots. Of course, that doesn't mean that you'll never run into systems that have both ISA and PCI sockets onboard (called *transitional* motherboards). Some components, such as sound cards and NICs, run perfectly well in ISA sockets because of their relatively low demands. Figure 9-3 shows ISA slots on a transitional motherboard.

Other Buses

Some low-cost and low-profile desktop PCs sport one of two different slots designed for modems, sound, or networking. Audio/Modem Riser (AMR) slots handle modems and sound, as you might expect from the name, and Communication and Networking Riser (CNR) slots do NICs and occasionally sound. Both slots are much smaller than a PCI slot, as you can see from the photo of a CNR slot in Figure 9-4. Although both of these buses conform to industry standards, the types of devices that use these buses are always proprietary to the particular system, meaning that replacements must be obtained directly from the manufacturer.

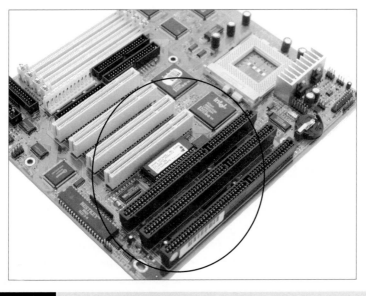

FIGURE 9.3   ISA slots on transitional motherboard

FIGURE 9.4   CNR slot

Typically, AMR manifests as a small, 46-pin socket, while CNR sockets are 30 pins wide. The two are not interchangeable, although either type of socket may provide audio capabilities.

By its nature, the internal expansion bus is made to accommodate internally installed devices. Installing new devices means opening up the PC case and all the precautions and procedures that that entails. Further, devices can't be added to the internal expansion bus while the system is running—that is, it's not *hot-swappable.* Plugging in a PCI device while the system is powered up spells disaster! The two popular external expansion buses, USB and FireWire, address both of these issues and more.

External Expansion Buses

USB and FireWire devices are easily connected to external ports, even while the system is running. Both of these external buses are completely PnP, requiring virtually no intervention on your part to configure the device's resources (although you may have to install special drivers in some cases). USB and FireWire make it easy for your PC to interface with the many types of consumer electronics available today, such as digital cameras and camcorders, PDAs, audio equipment, and cell phones, as well as PC keyboards, mice, joysticks, scanners, NICs, and mass storage devices.

USB

All modern PCs have built-in USB ports, as shown in Figure 9-5. On those older systems that lack them, you can easily install USB controller cards to add them, assuming that your OS is Windows 95 OSR2 or later (earlier versions of Windows 95 and Windows NT 4 do not support USB).

USB ports manifest in Windows as a *USB root hub*, as shown in Device Manager (Figure 9-6). The onboard controller circuitry for the USB port, called the *USB universal host controller,* handles the devices on the USB root hub.

Typically, there's nothing more to installing a USB device than plugging it in. The device draws power from the USB port through two of its four connection wires, with the other two being used to transfer data. The PC will recognize the device and prompt you to install any needed drivers. Be careful here, though, because quite a few USB devices require you to install the drivers *before* you install the device. Read the documentation before you plug it in!

Travel Assistance
For more information about USB, visit www.usb.org or revisit Chapter 1.

FireWire

Originally created in a joint effort by Apple Computers, Texas Instruments, and the IEEE organization, FireWire is increasingly popular in the PC world. Although mainly used to connect digital video cameras, storage devices, and other gadgets that require fast transfer of massive amounts of data, FireWire is also

FIGURE 9.5   USB ports on the back of a PC

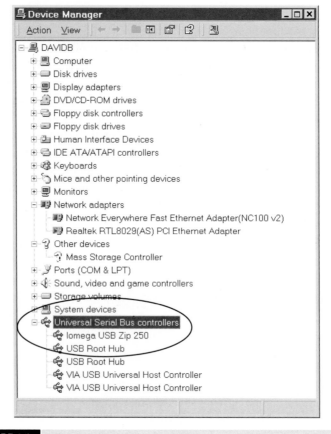

FIGURE 9.6   Device Manager showing USB bus

compatible with home electronics equipment such as television and home audio. FireWire is also being developed as a full-blown networking solution. Figure 9-7 shows FireWire ports on the back of an add-on peripheral card.

As discussed in Chapter 1, the speeds of the FireWire standard (IEEE 1394a) and the faster USB standard (Hi-Speed USB 2.0) are roughly the same, running at 400 and 480 Mbps, respectively. The big difference, however, is that FireWire

FIGURE 9.7   FireWire ports

is able to consistently sustain its throughput rate, but USB only reaches its maximum transfer rate during data bursts.

> **Local Lingo**
>
> **FireWire, iLink,** and **Lynx** The terms FireWire, iLink, and Lynx all refer to the IEEE 1394 interface.

> **Travel Assistance**
>
> For more information regarding FireWire and the IEEE 1394 standard, visit www.ieee.org.

Now that the internal and external expansion buses have been described in detail, it's time to examine how installed devices are assigned system resources.

Objective 9.02 System Resources: I/O, IRQ, and DMA

Every device in your PC needs a method to talk to the CPU to function properly. If the mouse moves, it needs a way to tell the CPU that it has moved so that the CPU can, in turn, talk to the video card to show the new mouse position. If the hard drive wants to send a file to RAM, it needs a way to tell the CPU that the data is ready so that the CPU can move the file off the hard drive and into RAM. Equally, the CPU needs a way to talk to the devices to get them to do whatever they should do, such as the video card updating the location of the mouse pointer on the monitor. You get the idea.

To do this, the inventors of the PC created a group of wonderful little functions known collectively as *system resources*. System resources break down into three types: I/O addresses, interrupt requests (IRQs), and direct memory access channels (DMAs). Let's look at each of these in detail to appreciate how they work.

> **Local Lingo**
>
> **System resources** "System resources" is the collective name for I/O addresses, IRQs, and DMA channels used by devices in a PC.

Back in the pre-PnP days, you had to go through some pretty painful steps to get a device to work in a PC. Manually configuring jumpers, flipping tiny DIP switches, running configuration software, and sometimes spending tons of time on trial and error were all par for the course. In today's world of PnP, however, many techs have never had the "opportunity" to experience this ordeal, and might even argue that this topic isn't important. Frankly, this opinion misses a key point. Yes, the ability to snap in a new device and have it work automatically is wonderful, but as any experienced PC tech can tell you, it *doesn't* work every time!

Understanding how system resources work together to enable hardware devices to run properly is absolutely vital for an accomplished PC tech. Let's start by examining how system resources relate to the CPU's external data bus and address bus.

I/O Addresses

You understand that the CPU uses the external data bus to transfer lines of programs between memory and the CPU. The external data bus also enables data to travel back and forth from peripheral devices to the CPU. The CPU uses the address bus to access programs in memory. This raises two related questions: First, how does the CPU know how to talk to a particular device? Second, how does a particular device know the CPU is talking to it?

The address bus holds the answers to these questions. When IBM first designed the PC, it assigned groups of unique binary addresses on the address bus for each device in the computer. The CPU uses a special wire, called the input/output memory (IO/MEM) wire, to notify devices that it's using the address bus to communicate with a particular device instead of RAM.

The original IBM 8086 CPU address bus had 20 wires, but when the IO/MEM wire had voltage, only the first 16 wires were monitored by the devices. The same principal applies today, even on modern CPUs. You might have a Pentium 4 with a 32-bit address bus, but the moment the CPU places a voltage on the IO/MEM wire, the RAM takes a nap and every device watches the first 16 wires on the address bus, waiting to see if one of their binary addresses comes up.

All devices, both those embedded on the motherboard (like the keyboard controller) and those inserted into expansion slots (like a video card), respond to unique binary patterns encoded into them. Every device gets a number of patterns, not just one pattern! Each different pattern of 16 ones and zeros is a unique command for that device. For example, the keyboard controller has four unique patterns. The hard drive controller responds to 16 unique commands, each telling the hard drive to perform a certain function. If the CPU lights up the

IO/MEM wire and puts the pattern 0000000111110000 onto the address bus, the hard drive controller sends back a message describing its error status. All the different patterns used by the CPU to talk to the devices inside your computer are known as the *I/O addresses*. Figure 9-8 shows this process.

I/O addresses function inside the PC as long strings of ones and zeroes, but tech people use *hexadecimal* notation—a type of binary shorthand—to display specific addresses. The starting I/O address for the floppy drive controller is 0000 0011 1111 0000, for example, but appears in print as 03F0. Each hexadecimal character takes the place of four binary characters. Even I/O addresses that appear to be regular decimal numbers—the secondary hard drive controller, for example, uses I/O address 0170—are hexadecimal representations of a binary number.

Travel Assistance

For a detailed explanation of hexadecimal notation, surf on over to "The Dreaded Hex" Tech File at Total Seminars. Go to www.totalsem .com and click on the Tech Forums. You'll find the Tech Files there. Enjoy!

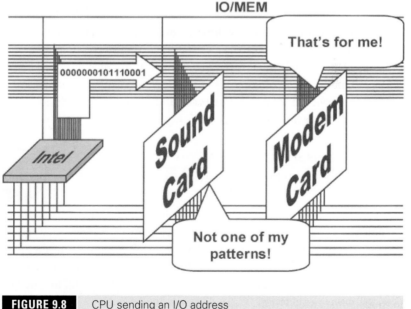

FIGURE 9.8   CPU sending an I/O address

The Rules of I/O Addresses

Three basic rules apply to I/O addresses: all devices have I/O addresses, all devices use more than one address, and two devices cannot have the same I/O address in a single system. What's amazing for the PC industry is these three rules apply universally.

- **All devices must have I/O addresses**   The CPU uses I/O addresses to talk to everything in your computer. Every device in your computer either has a preset I/O address or you must give it one. Basic devices in the computer have preset I/O addresses. The primary hard drive controller channel on a motherboard, for example, always gets the preset I/O addresses of 01F0–01F7. A sound card, in contrast, has to have I/O addresses configured when you install it into a system.

- **All devices use more than one I/O address**   All devices respond to more than one pattern of ones and zeroes. That is why each device is assigned one or more ranges of addresses. The CPU uses different I/O addresses within a device's range to give various commands to that device; and each device must also have one or more I/O addresses to respond to the CPU. For example, the hard drive's I/O address range is 01F0–01F7. If the CPU sends a 01F0 pattern, it asks the hard drive controller if an error exists anywhere. The command 01F1 is a totally separate command. No device has only a single I/O address.

- **Once a device has an I/O address, no other device can use that address**   When you install an expansion card in your system, you must know the I/O addresses currently taken. You then must make certain the sound card uses I/O addresses that no other device uses. Every device in your computer has an I/O address. No two devices can share any I/O addresses, or they won't work.

Travel Advisory
If two devices share an I/O address, the PC will lock up!

You need to determine, therefore, the I/O addresses in use in a particular PC. Fortunately, most of the I/O addresses were set up by IBM a long time ago, so this isn't a tough call. When IBM released the PC to the public domain, they provided a list of I/O addresses that manufacturers must use to make components and systems IBM-compatible. This list, shown in Table 9-2, is still followed by every PC in the world today.

| TABLE 9.2 | I/O Address Device List |

I/O Address Range	Usage
0000–000F	DMA controller
0020–002F	Master IRQ controller
0030–003F	Master IRQ controller
0040–0043	System timer
0060–0063	Keyboard
0070–0071	CMOS clock
0080–008F	DMA page registers
0090–009F	DMA page registers
00A0–00AF	Slave IRQ controller
00B0–00BF	Slave IRQ controller
00C0–00CF	DMA controller
00E0–00EF	Reserved
00F0–00FF	Math coprocessor
0170–0177	Secondary hard drive controller
01F0–01F7	Primary hard drive controller
0200–0207	Joystick
0210–0217	Reserved
0278–027F	LPT2
02B0–02DF	Secondary EGA
02E8–02EF	COM4
02F8–02FF	COM2
0378–037F	LPT1
03B0–03BF	Mono video
03C0–03CF	Primary EGA
03D0–03DF	CGA video
03E8–03EF	COM3
03F0–03F7	Floppy controller
03F8–03FF	COM1

Techs have a few quirks when discussing I/O addresses that you need to know to "talk the talk" when it comes to I/O addresses:

- Sixteen-bit I/O addresses are always represented by four hexadecimal numbers, such as 01F0. When discussing I/O addresses, however, most techs drop the leading zeros. Techs refer to address 01F0, for example, as 1F0.

- Also, most techs use only the first I/O address in a range for a device— called the *I/O base address*—when discussing that device. The entire range of I/O addresses is always implied. If the hard drive uses the I/O addresses of 1F0–1F7, for example, the I/O base address is 1F0.

- Finally, when discussing any hex value, many people put a lowercase *h* on the end to show you it's a hex value. For example, some people will show the I/O base address for the floppy controller as 3F0h. Glance at Table 9-2 one more time and list the base addresses for some of the devices in "tech speak"—mono video is 3B0h; primary EGA is 3C0h; and so on.

Take a close look at the I/O address map one more time. Notice there are neither I/O addresses for sound cards nor I/O addresses for network cards. In fact, IBM mapped out the I/O addresses for only the most common devices. So, if you want to install a sound card, what I/O addresses are available? Look at I/O base address 210h, and then look at the next I/O base address—you'll note that it's 278h. All the I/O addresses between these two are open for use, so plenty of unused addresses exist!

> ## Exam Tip
>
> Don't bother memorizing all the I/O addresses! Just make sure you know the ones for common devices such as floppy drives, hard drives, and LPT and COM ports.

IRQs

The CPU can now communicate with all the devices inside the computer using I/O addresses, but a small problem still exists. I/O addressing enables two-way communication, but the CPU must initiate all communication. So far, the devices can only "speak when spoken to." A device can't send its own message to the CPU to get the CPU's attention. So, how does a device initiate a conversation with the CPU? For example, how does the mouse tell the CPU it has moved? How does the keyboard tell the CPU somebody just pressed a key? The PC needs some kind of mechanism to tell the CPU to stop doing whatever it's doing and talk to a particular device.

This mechanism is called *interruption*. Every CPU in the PC world has a special wire designated as the interrupt (INT) wire. If this wire is charged, the CPU will stop what it's doing and deal with the device. The INT wire is lit up when needed by the intermediary between the PC devices and the CPU, the Northbridge and Southbridge chipset.

The chipset connects to the INT wire of the CPU on one side and has another 15 wires called *interrupt requests (IRQs)* that extend out from the chip into the motherboard. Every device that needs to interrupt the CPU gets an IRQ. If a device needs to interrupt the CPU, it lights its IRQ wire and the chipset then lights the INT wire on the CPU. Whenever the INT wire lights up, the CPU talks to the chipset via its I/O addresses to determine which device has interrupted. The chipset tells the CPU which IRQ is lit, and this enables the CPU to know which routine to run.

The Rules of IRQs

IRQ setup and use in a system follows a somewhat vague pair of rules:

- First, almost every device needs an IRQ. This includes devices built into the motherboard as well as devices that use the expansion bus slots.

- Second, under almost all circumstances, no two devices can share an IRQ.

| Travel Advisory |
| If two devices share an IRQ, the system will invariably lock up. |

For the most part, PnP BIOS routines and devices make IRQ assignment automatic, but A+ techs should understand the settings in case something goes awry. To prevent devices from sharing IRQs, IBM gave an IRQ map to card manufacturers so that they would know which IRQs to use for certain types of devices, just as IBM did for I/O addresses (refer to Table 9-3).

The devices listed in parentheses are the ones that commonly use these IRQs but are *not* listed in the original IRQ map. Note the strange IRQ 2/9—this is a holdover from the early PC days where two chips were needed to control all the IRQs. Called the *cascade,* this still exists for backward compatibility. Don't worry about why this takes place. Just know that IRQ 2 and IRQ 9 are really the same IRQ.

| **TABLE 9.3** | Default IRQs |

IRQ Wire	Default Function
IRQ 0	System timer
IRQ 1	Keyboard
IRQ 2/9	Open for use (PCI steering)
IRQ 3	Default COM2, COM4
IRQ 4	Default COM1, COM3
IRQ 5	LPT2 (sound cards)
IRQ 6	Floppy disk drive
IRQ 7	LPT1
IRQ 8	Real-time clock
IRQ 10	Open for use
IRQ 11	Open for use (USB)
IRQ 12	Open for use (PS/2 mouse port)
IRQ 13	Math coprocessor
IRQ 14	Primary hard drive controller
IRQ 15	Secondary hard drive controller

These settings are somewhat flexible. If a device that uses a certain IRQ isn't present, then another device can use that IRQ. For example, if you don't have a secondary hard drive controller, you can use IRQ 15 for another device.

Exam Tip

Memorize the IRQ chart!

PCI Devices and IRQs

PCI devices do not use classic IRQs but rather use dynamically assigned interrupt channels A–D. To support older programs and legacy devices, however, the PCI bus sometimes has to make the PCI devices appear to support classic IRQs. All this stuff happens in the background and does not affect techs often, but it looks weird in Device Manager. Figure 9-9 shows Device Manager listing devices by their resources—note that all six PCI devices are shown using IRQ 9!

Windows systems use a feature called *IRQ steering* to make peace between PCI and legacy expansion cards. The OS will take over an IRQ and reserve it for PCI devices, then seemingly put quite a few PCI devices on that single IRQ. You might have a sound card, USB controller, and network card all using IRQ 9, as in the preceding example, and all devices are working just fine.

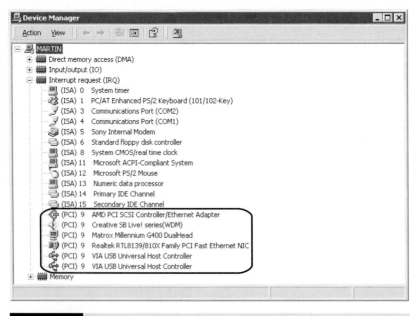

FIGURE 9.9   Device Manager showing six PCI devices using the same IRQ

The devices don't actually use the IRQ when communicating with PCI devices or the chipset, but if a program needs a classic IRQ, the chipset does a quick bit of digital sleight-of-hand. The PCI network card that uses interrupt channel C magically appears to the old program as using IRQ 11. The PCI chipset handles the actual interface between the device and the old program and all works out fine—the program runs, the network card works, and the end user is happy.

Also, notice that some of these IRQs are assigned to COM and LPT ports. Odds are good you've seen these pop up occasionally—so let's make sure you know what they do!

COM and LPT Ports

IRQs and I/O addresses weren't invented for the IBM PC. Mainframes, minicomputers, and pre-PC microcomputers all used IRQs and I/O addresses. When IBM designed the PC, it wanted to simplify the installation, programming, and operation of devices. Because virtually every peripheral needs both an IRQ and an I/O address, IBM created standard preset combinations of IRQs and I/O addresses. For serial devices, the preset combinations are called *COM ports*. For parallel devices, they are called *LPT ports*. The word "port" is used to describe a "portal," or two-way access—*not* the physical connection port.

Ports simplify installation of many devices. Look at modems, for example. Many modems don't have a setting for IRQs or I/O addresses; instead, you set their COM port. Most people don't realize that when they select a COM port, they actually assign the IRQ and I/O address. If you set a modem to COM1, for example, you set that modem's IRQ to 4 and the modem's I/O address to 3F8.

Table 9-4 lists the preset combinations of I/O addresses and IRQs.

No doubt you noticed that COM ports 1 and 3, and 2 and 4 share IRQ settings, which would seem to run counter to the rules. Actually, it *is* possible for two or more devices to use the same IRQ as long as they never talk at the same time!

If you configure more than one device to use the same IRQ and they *do* try to use it at the same time, you'll know it because the computer will lock up. Luckily,

TABLE 9.4	Preconfigured System Resources for COM and LPT Ports	
Port	**I/O Address**	**IRQ**
COM1	3F8	4
COM2	2F8	3
COM3	3E8	4
COM4	2E8	3
LPT1	378	7
LPT2	278	5

this doesn't break anything, so just set one device to another IRQ to correct the problem and try again.

Local Lingo
COM and **LPT** COM and LPT ports are preset combinations of IRQs and I/O addresses.

Physical Ports vs. I/O Ports

This is a point that confuses a lot of folks, and you'll frequently hear techs describe the 9-pin DB serial connection on the back of their PC as the COM port, or the 25-pin Centronics connector as the LPT port. This is not correct! The connector is physical; the port is logical, simply an I/O address with an IRQ assigned to it. To clarify this idea, think about the telephone sitting on your desk. Would it be correct for someone to point to it and declare, "That's an 867-5309"? No it wouldn't, the correct thing to say is, "That's a telephone with the number 867-5309 assigned to it."

Now let's look at the COM and LPT port settings used in a typical PC.

COM and LPT Port Settings

Even though IBM dictated a specific I/O address and IRQ for a particular COM or LPT port, you can change the IRQ as long as the device can handle it and the software that talks to that device knows about the change. So you can change, say, the IRQ setting for COM1 from 4 to 5 if the hardware and software enable it. As an example, let's look at a typical PC that has two built-in serial ports. You can change the COM port settings by accessing the CMOS, as shown in Figure 9-10.

Note that the physical serial connector port 1 is set to I/O address 3F8 and IRQ 4. This translates into COM1, but you can change that serial port to any of the following settings:

- 3F8/IRQ 4: standard COM1
- 2F8/IRQ 3: standard COM2
- 3F8/IRQ 5: COM1 I/O address combined with the nonstandard IRQ 5
- 2F8/IRQ 5: COM2 I/O address combined with the nonstandard IRQ 5

You see, therefore, that COM1, COM2, and so forth often refer specifically to the I/O address, but not necessarily to the IRQ. Many motherboards, for example, show the default serial port settings as COM1/IRQ 4 or COM2/IRQ 3. We know by definition that COM1 uses IRQ 4 and COM2 uses IRQ 3. Why do they do this? Why don't they simply show COM1 and COM2? Why add the IRQs if

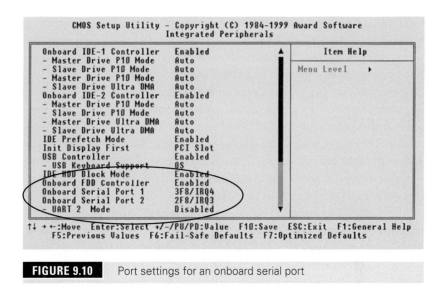

```
              CMOS Setup Utility - Copyright (C) 1984-1999 Award Software
                              Integrated Peripherals
┌─────────────────────────────────────────────────┬──────────────────────────┐
│  Onboard IDE-1 Controller    Enabled        ▲    │      Item Help           │
│  - Master Drive PIO Mode      Auto               │                          │
│  - Slave Drive PIO Mode       Auto               │  Menu Level    ▶         │
│  - Master Drive PIO Mode      Auto               │                          │
│  - Slave Drive Ultra DMA      Auto               │                          │
│  Onboard IDE-2 Controller     Enabled            │                          │
│  - Master Drive PIO Mode      Auto               │                          │
│  - Slave Drive PIO Mode       Auto               │                          │
│  - Master Drive Ultra DMA     Auto               │                          │
│  - Slave Drive Ultra DMA      Auto               │                          │
│  IDE Prefetch Mode            Enabled            │                          │
│  Init Display First           PCI Slot           │                          │
│  USB Controller               Enabled            │                          │
│  - USB Keyboard Support       OS                 │                          │
│  IDE HDD Block Mode           Enabled            │                          │
│  Onboard FDD Controller       Enabled            │                          │
│  Onboard Serial Port 1        3F8/IRQ4           │                          │
│  Onboard Serial Port 2        2F8/IRQ3           │                          │
│  - UART 2  Mode               Disabled      ▼    │                          │
├─────────────────────────────────────────────────┴──────────────────────────┤
│ ↑↓ ←→:Move  Enter:Select  +/-/PU/PD:Value  F10:Save  ESC:Exit  F1:General Help│
│      F5:Previous Values  F6:Fail-Safe Defaults  F7:Optimized Defaults        │
└─────────────────────────────────────────────────────────────────────────────┘
```

FIGURE 9.10   Port settings for an onboard serial port

any decent A+ Certified tech already knows this? In this day of COM ports that easily change to nonstandard IRQs, the motherboard folks separate the COM port from the IRQ, ensuring that you won't accidentally create an unintentional conflict.

Exam Tip
Memorize the I/O addresses and IRQs for the LPT ports!

The combination of I/O address and IRQ is the cornerstone of CPU-device communication. But there's one more aspect of this communication that we must discuss—the concept of DMA.

DMA

CPUs do a lot of work. They run the BIOS, operating system, and applications. CPUs handle interrupts and access I/O addresses. They are busy little chips!

From a user's perspective, however, the most important thing that the CPU deals with is data. CPUs constantly manipulate data: they move data from one place in RAM to another, from peripheral devices to RAM, and from RAM to peripherals. This is obviously a necessary function, but it's also a function that eats up cycles of the CPU's time that could be better spent doing other things. So, why not make devices that access memory directly, without involving the CPU? The process of accessing memory without using the CPU is called *direct memory access (DMA)*.

DMA enables the system to run background applications without interfering with the CPU, as shown in Figure 9-11. This is excellent for doing mundane things like creating background sounds in games and other multimedia applications, and for accessing floppy disk drives and hard drives.

Handling DMA is another function of the motherboard's chipset. The chipset keeps more than one device from accessing the external data bus at the same time, and it makes certain that the CPU always has priority access to the bus when it needs it. The chipset sends data along the external data bus when the CPU is busy and not using the external data bus. This is perfectly acceptable because the CPU accesses the external data bus only a small percentage of the time, usually only 5 percent of the time on a Pentium or later CPU.

The chipset links to the CPU via a wire called the *HRQ* wire. The chipset uses the HRQ wire to inform the CPU when the external data bus is going to be busy. The chipset has eight wires, called *DMA requests (DRQs)*, that lead to the DRAM refresh circuitry and ISA slots. DRQs were, and still are, more commonly known as *DMA channels*. If a device wants to perform a DMA data transfer, it must activate its assigned DMA channel.

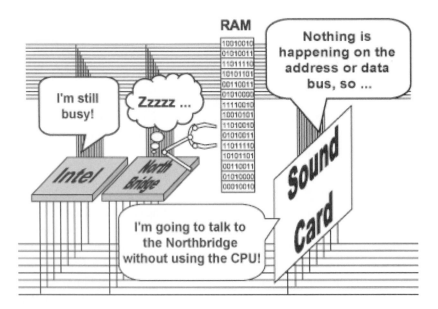

FIGURE 9.11   DMA in action

Local Lingo

DMA channel and **DRQ** The terms "DMA channel" and "DRQ" mean the same thing and can be used interchangeably.

In the early days, PCs used two cascaded DMA controller chips for a total of seven DRQs, and modern chipsets retain this structure for backward compatibility. The cascade made DRQ 0 and DRQ 4 the same wire, just like IRQ 2/9. DRQs work exactly like IRQs, with all the same rules—such as that no two devices can share the same DMA channel.

Exam Tip

Don't bother memorizing DMA channels; just make sure you understand what DMA does!

DMA Limitations

DMA, as originally designed by IBM, has some serious limitations. First, DMA is designed to run from cards installed on the ISA bus. As a result, DMA is limited to a maximum speed of roughly 8 MHz. Second, the first DMA functions could handle only byte-wide (8-bit) data. Although this wasn't a problem in the first IBM PC, as PCs moved from 8088s through 286s, 386s, and 486s, it was often faster to skip 8-bit DMA and just wait for the CPU to move data.

The chipsets in later systems enabled 16-bit data transfers. If a device wants to use 8-bit transfers, it should use the lower DMA channel: 0 through 3. If a device wants to use 16-bit transfers, it should use a high DMA channel: 5 through 7. But even 16-bit data transfers ran at 8 MHz, which made them too slow for modern systems. This slowness relegated "classic" DMA to low-speed, background jobs like floppy drive access, sound creation, and tape backup. A new process called *bus mastering*, however, has created a resurgence in the use of DMA in modern systems.

Bus Mastering Most devices today that use DMA do so without accessing the chipset or the CPU. These devices are known as *bus masters*. Bus mastering devices skip the chipset altogether—they have circuitry that enables them to watch for other devices accessing the external data bus and can get out of the way on their own. Bus mastering has become extremely popular in hard drives. All of today's EIDE and SATA hard drives take advantage of bus mastering. Hard drive bus mastering is hidden under terms such as *Ultra DMA* and, for the most part, is totally automatic and invisible.

Who Uses Classic DMA?

Are there still devices that use classic DMA? On most systems, sound cards and floppy drives use classic DMA, as do some printers and other parallel devices. Table 9-5 shows the traditional DMA channel map.

So, in a nutshell, that's how the system configures resources for installed devices. This is important for PC techs to understand, but it's not terribly hands-on, is it? Now let's look at the practical application of these principles—installing peripheral devices.

Objective 9.03 Installing Peripheral Devices

Although it's important to understand the *whys* of I/O addresses, IRQs, and DMA (the "big three"), we need to discuss the *hows* of installation, configuration, and troubleshooting these big three. Today's plug-and-play card installation makes problems more rare, but problems still occur often enough to warrant a good understanding of I/O addresses, IRQs, and DMA. The best way to do this is to gain a solid methodology to ensure that you can set up any device in any PC with a minimum of effort and a maximum of speed.

First, let's look at how Plug and Play technology makes our jobs as techs easier, then we'll discuss the best methods to follow when installing peripherals.

Local Lingo	
Plug and Play	Plug and Play is almost always abbreviated to the simple *PnP*.

TABLE 9.5	DMA Channels	
DMA Channel	**Type**	**Function**
0	8-bit	None
1	8-bit	Open for use
2	8-bit	Floppy drive controller
3	8-bit	Open for use
5	16-bit	Open for use
6	16-bit	Open for use
7	16-bit	Open for use

Plug and Play

Plug and Play consists of a series of standards designed to enable devices to self-configure. PnP is a broad standard, crossing over every type of expansion bus. In theory, PnP makes device installation trivial—you simply install a device and it automatically configures its I/O address, IRQ, and DMA with no user intervention. Unfortunately, given the amazing variety of devices currently used in PCs all over the world, PnP has yet to reach this worthy goal—but it's getting close!

Identifying PnP

For PnP to work properly, the PC needs three items. First, you need a PnP BIOS. If you have a Pentium or later computer, you have a PnP BIOS. You can verify this by watching the boot process and seeing if it's advertised. Figure 9-12 shows a typical PnP BIOS. This type of BIOS will also have a reference in the CMOS, as shown in Figure 9-13.

Second, you need a PnP operating system, such as Windows 9x/Me or Windows 2000/XP. Older operating systems, such as Windows NT can use PnP devices with the help of special device drivers and utility programs.

Last, of course, you need a PnP device. This part is the easiest to ensure, because nobody makes non-PnP devices anymore! Every modem, every NIC, every sound card, video card, controller card, what-have-you, fully supports PnP.

Keep in mind, however, that even though new devices are guaranteed to be PnP, there's still a huge base of non-PnP devices—techs call them *legacy* devices—already installed on systems humming away under desks in offices all over the world. Sooner or later, you'll run into these devices, and CompTIA expects you to know what to do with them.

```
  Award Modular BIOS v6.00PG, An Energy Star Ally
  Copyright (C) 1984-2000, Award Software, Inc.

GREEN AGP/PCI/ISA SYSTEM

Main Processor : Pentium III 850MHz(100x8.5)
Memory Testing : 114688K

Award Plug and Play BIOS Extension v1.0A
Copyright (C) 2000 Award Software, Inc.

  Primary Master   : WDC WD1020AA, 80.10A80
  Primary Slave    : None
Secondary Master   : ATAPI CD-ROM DRIVE 40X
Secondary Slave    : None


Press DEL to enter SETUP
06/02/2000-694X-686A-XXXXXXXX-QW
```

FIGURE 9.12 PnP BIOS shown at boot

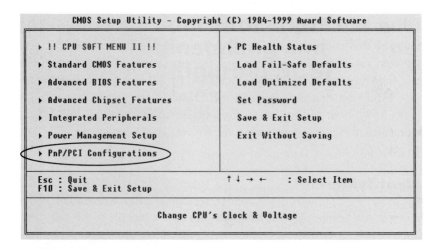

FIGURE 9.13   Award BIOS PnP screen reference in CMOS

How do you quickly tell if a given device is PnP or not? You have two options: one option is to simply drop the card into a system and see if the BIOS recognizes the device as PnP, as shown in Figure 9-14.

If the BIOS fails to recognize the device, it *still* could be PnP, but you need to take a close look at the card itself. Look for jumpers on the card that set the I/O address and IRQ, as in Figure 9-15.

Once you see the I/O address and IRQ setting jumpers, you can probably assume it's a legacy device. Some cards, however, have the capability to switch between PnP and legacy by moving a jumper or by running a special configuration program that came with the device. Figure 9-16 shows a modem that could switch between PnP and legacy.

```
        CMOS Setup Utility - Copyright (C) 1984-1999 Award Software
                              IRQ Resources
  ┌──────────────────────────────────────────┬──────────────────────────┐
  │  IRQ-3   assigned to     PCI/ISA PnP      │      Item Help           │
  │  IRQ-4   assigned to     PCI/ISA PnP      │                          │
  │  IRQ-5   assigned to     Legacy ISA       │                          │
  │  IRQ-7   assigned to     PCI/ISA PnP      │  Menu Level  ▶           │
  │  IRQ-9   assigned to     PCI/ISA PnP      │                          │
  │  IRQ-10  assigned to     PCI/ISA PnP      │  Legacy ISA for devices  │
  │  IRQ-11  assigned to     PCI/ISA PnP      │  compliant with the      │
  │  IRQ-12  assigned to     PCI/ISA PnP      │  original PC AT bus       │
  │  IRQ-13  assigned to     PCI/ISA PnP      │  specification, PCI/ISA   │
  │  IRQ-14  assigned to     PCI/ISA PnP      │  PnP for devices         │
  │                                            │  compliant with the      │
  │                                            │  Plug and Play standard  │
  │                                            │  whether designed for    │
  │                                            │  PCI or ISA bus          │
  │                                            │  architecture            │
  └──────────────────────────────────────────┴──────────────────────────┘
```

FIGURE 9.14   Legacy device recognized in BIOS

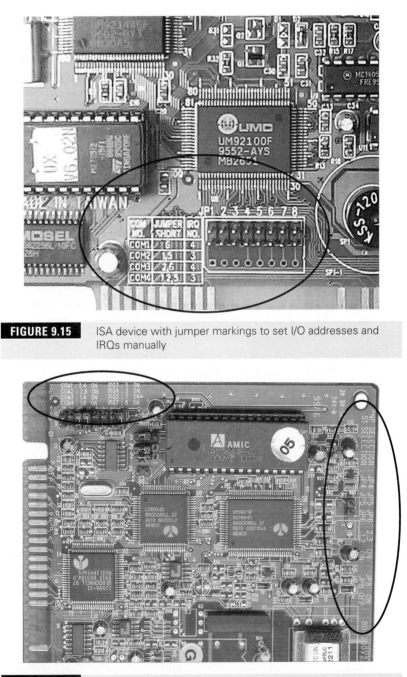

FIGURE 9.15   ISA device with jumper markings to set I/O addresses and IRQs manually

FIGURE 9.16   Modem with legacy or PnP option (jumpers open for PnP, jumpers closed for legacy)

How PnP Works

Let's look at a hypothetical scenario to learn how PnP works. To do this, assume you have a machine with a PnP BIOS, a PnP OS (Windows 2000, for this example), and a mix of PnP and legacy devices. When you install a new PnP card, such as a fax/modem, PnP goes through a fairly standard process, the majority of which takes place during the boot process. Let's watch as PnP boots, allocating system resources to devices in the system.

The PnP BIOS takes over immediately after the POST, first telling all PnP devices to "be quiet" so that the BIOS can find any legacy ISA devices.

The PnP BIOS must then determine the resources used by legacy devices to see what's left over for the PnP devices. Basically, you can go two ways—the BIOS can try to find the ISA devices by querying a special list it keeps (more on this shortly), or you can tell the BIOS what system resources the legacy device uses and the BIOS will work around those resources. You can determine what the BIOS will do by going into CMOS setup and changing the PnP settings.

Figure 9-17 shows the PnP/PCI Configurations screen from a typical Award BIOS. The left side of the screen contains the PnP settings. Two items enable you to direct how BIOS will perform its resource search: the Reset Configuration Data option and the Resources Controlled By setting. It's easier to explain them in the reverse order from how they appear on the screen.

The Resources Controlled By setting enables you to select between Auto and Manual. If you set this to Auto, the BIOS defers all system resource determination to the OS. If you set it to Manual, you must manually set all the IRQ and DMA information to either PCI/ISA PnP or Legacy ISA. Never use the manual setting unless your system contains legacy devices. If you do have legacy devices,

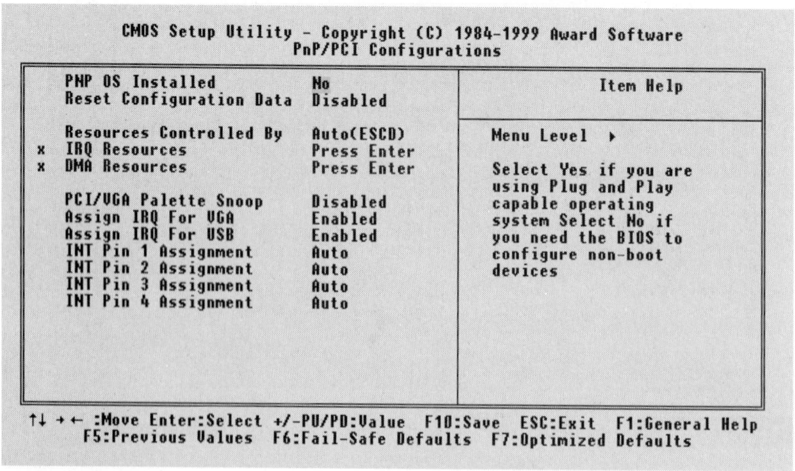

```
          CMOS Setup Utility - Copyright (C) 1984-1999 Award Software
                            PnP/PCI Configurations
┌─────────────────────────────────────────────┬─────────────────────────────┐
│  PNP OS Installed           No               │        Item Help            │
│  Reset Configuration Data   Disabled         │                             │
│                                              │                             │
│  Resources Controlled By    Auto(ESCD)       │  Menu Level  ▶              │
│ x IRQ Resources             Press Enter      │                             │
│ x DMA Resources             Press Enter      │  Select Yes if you are      │
│                                              │  using Plug and Play        │
│  PCI/UGA Palette Snoop      Disabled         │  capable operating          │
│  Assign IRQ For UGA         Enabled          │  system Select No if        │
│  Assign IRQ For USB         Enabled          │  you need the BIOS to       │
│  INT Pin 1 Assignment       Auto             │  configure non-boot         │
│  INT Pin 2 Assignment       Auto             │  devices                    │
│  INT Pin 3 Assignment       Auto             │                             │
│  INT Pin 4 Assignment       Auto             │                             │
│                                              │                             │
└─────────────────────────────────────────────┴─────────────────────────────┘
 ↑↓ →← :Move  Enter:Select  +/-PU/PD:Value  F10:Save  ESC:Exit  F1:General Help
      F5:Previous Values  F6:Fail-Safe Defaults  F7:Optimized Defaults
```

FIGURE 9.17   Award BIOS PnP/PCI Configurations screen

you'll find the manual setting easier to use because you know what IRQ and DMA settings the legacy devices use because of jumper settings, and so on.

The second item in CMOS setup that concerns the BIOS search is the Reset Configuration Data option. To understand this option, you need to understand the function of what techs call the *device list*.

Every PnP BIOS keeps a list of all system resources used, usually on the CMOS or Flash ROM. Interestingly, no official name exists for this storage area—although most folks call it the *extended system configuration data (ESCD)* list. The PnP standard doesn't define the physical location of this data, but the standard strictly defines the PnP BIOS routines. In other words, the PnP standard doesn't care where the BIOS stores the information, just how the BIOS must respond when queried.

In the example, assume the IRQ and DMA resources are manually configured in CMOS. The PnP BIOS then refers to this list to determine which resources are already used. Now that the BIOS knows which resources are available, it can "wake up" each PnP device, asking the device which system resources it needs, as you can see in Figure 9-18.

You can't give just any available system resource to a PnP device. Each PnP device has an internal list of acceptable system resources from which the BIOS must choose. If a device can use only IRQs 3, 5, or 7, for example, then the BIOS can't allocate IRQ 10 to the device; it must choose from the device's list. As each PnP device calls for certain resources, the BIOS allocates those resources to the PnP device.

So, taking the example shown earlier, PnP 1 might get I/O 310–31F, IRQ 2/9, and DMA 1; PnP 2 might get I/O 220–227 and IRQ 11. The BIOS then adds them to the device list.

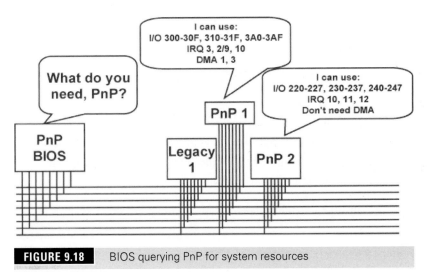

FIGURE 9.18 BIOS querying PnP for system resources

Sometimes adding another piece of equipment can confuse the PnP settings. For example, if you have a PnP device that needs a resource already taken by another device, you need to make the system reallocate the resources. That's where the Reset Configuration Data option comes into play, by making the PnP BIOS reconfigure all the devices. This is most often done when you install a device that the system refuses to recognize.

The OS can also update and edit the device list. Unlike the BIOS, Windows makes a strong attempt to find the IRQs and DMAs for legacy devices through its own system information program. This program runs automatically at boot and when the Add New Hardware (or Add/Remove Hardware) Wizard is run from the Control Panel.

Once the OS takes over, it queries the PnP BIOS to determine if you have installed a device. If it discovers a new device, the operating system then updates its own system resource information, makes changes to the resources if necessary, and depending on the OS, may prompt the user for the device driver.

Even with an occasional legacy device, PnP works magnificently most of the time. On the more rare occasions when something goes wrong, a tech who lacks knowledge about system resources might find it difficult to fix the problem. Chapter 17 goes into details of how to diagnose and troubleshoot devices. For now, however, let's concentrate on the installation process.

Installation Methods

Many technicians look at the concept of device installation from one of two extremes. On one side, we have techs who take the seat-of-the-pants approach and simply drop a device in the PC and hope it will work (frequently skipping important safety precautions). The other extreme comes from the overly cautious techs who (usually because of a bad past installation experience) insist on full data backups, OS updates, and other extravagant rituals before cracking open the PC case. The best plan is to strive for somewhere between these two extremes with a quick, efficient methodology that minimizes risk to your system.

Use a three-step system of device installation:

1. Know the device you're installing.
2. Install the thing, taking all of the appropriate safety precautions.
3. Confirm installation with the built-in OS tools to make sure that installation went without a hitch.

Let's look at each step in detail.

Know the Device You're Installing

Save yourself frustration and repeated trips by learning all you can about the device before you ever set foot in the local computer store.

- Is the device compatible with your motherboard?
- Is the device compatible with your OS?
- Are the correct drivers available for your OS?

If your component is new, then it'll be either a PCI or AGP device. This practically guarantees compatibility with any system manufactured in the last few years. Check the device's documentation and check the web site for the device to see that you have the correct drivers. Windows 9x/Me systems are very forgiving (some would say promiscuous) about the type of hardware that they will accommodate, but Windows NT/2000/XP systems are *much* pickier about the kind of hardware that they'll support. Always take the time to visit Microsoft's web site and check the definitive hardware compatibility resource for those operating systems—the *Hardware Compatibility List.*

Travel Assistance

Microsoft's Windows 2000/XP Hardware Compatibility List can be found at www.microsoft.com. Do a search for the HAL and it should pop up quickly.

Install the Device

This step varies depending on whether you install a PnP or legacy device, but regardless of which type of device you're installing, the same safety precautions and preliminary steps apply.

Safety Precautions and Preliminary Steps   Always completely shut down and unplug the computer. Make certain that you have enough room and light to work. Move the PC to a workbench if necessary. Use an antistatic mat and a wrist strap, and make certain that you remove watches or jewelry.

If you're adding a new device, then you don't need to take any special steps to prepare your OS for installation. If you're replacing an existing device with a newer device, however, you should be certain to remove any currently installed drivers before installing the new ones to prevent conflicts. In Windows 9x/Me, simply select the device driver that you want to uninstall and click the Remove button. In Windows 2000/XP, right-click the device driver that you want to uninstall and select Uninstall. Many devices, especially ones that come with a lot of applications, will have an Uninstall option in the Add/Remove Programs applet on the Control Panel.

Once you've taken these precautions, you're ready to pop the top (or side, as the case may be) off of your PC and get to work.

Installing PnP Devices   First, locate an empty PCI or AGP slot and remove the metal slot cover. If there is a card currently installed in the slot that you want to use, first remove the screw from that card's back plate. Then carefully grab the outside edge of the card with one hand and the back edge with the other, slowly wiggling the card out. A well-seated card can take some serious tugging—don't be afraid to give it a little muscle, but be sure to touch only the edges of the card. Handling the chips on the board can cause them to fail. Figure 9-19 shows both the correct and incorrect ways to handle a card.

Place the card that you've removed in an antistatic bag. Now remove the new card from its antistatic bag. Holding it by the edges, line the card up over the slot and push it slowly but firmly into place, as shown in Figure 9-20.

If the card resists at all, check that the pins are properly aligned with the slot. A properly aligned card snaps firmly into place and stays in the slot without any support from you. Some techs don't finish securing the card in the slot with a screw until after they've confirmed that the OS recognizes it. Don't be that guy! Always secure peripheral cards completely before you power the system back up—the slightest movement to an unsecured card can lead to a toasted device.

After you've secured the device, but *before* you close the case, reconnect the power cables and start the computer and verify that the new device is working properly. After all, if you take the time to put the cover back on the PC immediately after installing a new card, *Murphy's Law of Computer Problems* guarantees that you'll have a problem with the card that requires you to open the darn thing

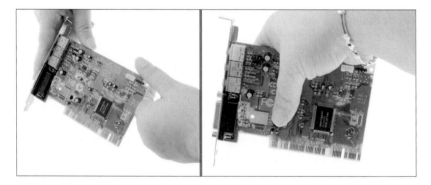

FIGURE 9.19   Handling a PCI card correctly (left) and incorrectly (right)

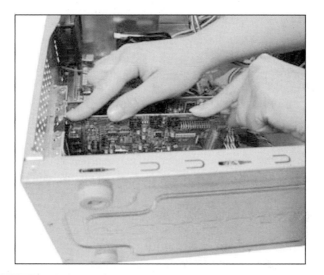

FIGURE 9.20   Pushing the card into place in the slot

back up again. When the card has proved itself by running properly and doing whatever it's designed to do, you can put your PC case back on with some degree of confidence.

Always save your antistatic bags! In fact, avoid throwing away any hardware packaging for at least a few months. If you can return a card in its original box with all the trimmings, the store will be much more likely to take it back.

Installing Legacy Devices   The basic installation steps are the same as for PnP devices, but with a few additional twists. Before you install the device, you have to determine and assign the proper system resources.

First, run Device Manager to determine the available resources for the system. All versions of Device Manager enable you to view the devices by resource.

Once you determine the available resources, you must configure the device to use those resources. To do this, you might have to set jumpers or flip switches before physical installation, or run a special setup program after physical installation.

After you configure the legacy device's system resources, you still need to inform Windows of the legacy device by running the Add/Remove Hardware Wizard.

Installing USB/FireWire Devices   Installing USB and FireWire devices onto the external expansion bus is simplicity itself. Locate an available USB or FireWire connector port on your PC (or on a USB or FireWire hub) and plug the cable into it. Then simply plug the other end of the cable into the USB or FireWire device. The OS will recognize the device immediately, prompting you to install any drivers (if necessary). Follow the prompts and insert the device's driver disk or CD-ROM, and you're done!

Verify Installation

Go into Device Manager and verify the device is working properly. Assuming Device Manager shows the device working properly, put the device to work by making it do whatever it's supposed to do. If you installed a printer, print something. If you installed a scanner, scan something. If it works, you're done!

Ah, if only it always worked this easily. Many times, the Device Manager shows us a problem. First, it might not even show the new device. In that case, verify you inserted the device properly and the device has power, if necessary. Run the Add/Remove Hardware Wizard and see if Windows recognizes the device. If the Device Manager doesn't recognize the device at this point, you have one of two problems:

1. The device is physically damaged, and you must replace it.

2. The device is legacy, and you failed to configure its system resources properly.

Using the Device Manager as a Troubleshooting Tool

The Device Manager rarely fails to see a device. More commonly, device problems manifest themselves in Device Manager via error symbols—a black *!*, a red *X*, a blue *I*, or a green *?*.

- A black exclamation point (!) on a yellow circle indicates a missing device, one Windows does not recognize, or a device driver problem. The device might still work with this error.
- A red *X* indicates a disabled device. This usually points to a system resource conflict or a damaged device. The device won't work with this error.
- A blue *I* on a white field indicates a PnP device on which someone has configured the system resources manually. This merely provides information and doesn't indicate an error with this device.
- A green question mark (?) indicates Windows doesn't have the correct driver but has successfully installed a compatible driver. The device

works but may lack certain functions. This error symbol only appears with Windows Me.

The *!* symbol is the most common error symbol, and it's usually the easiest to fix.

First, double-check the device's connections. Second, try reinstalling the driver with the Update Driver button. To get to the Update Driver button, click the desired device and select Properties. In the Properties dialog box, select the Driver tab. On the Driver tab, click the Update Driver button.

These troubleshooting steps correct the majority of simple installation errors. We'll examine more complicated matters in Chapter 17.

CHECKPOINT

✔ **Objective 9.01: Expansion Bus: Internal and External**   The expansion bus enables you to add peripheral devices to the PC to expand functionality and increase performance. Internal expansion buses include the PCI, AGP, and ISA/Enhanced ISA buses, as well as proprietary technologies such as AMR and CNR. External expansion buses are USB and IEEE 1394 (FireWire).

✔ **Objective 9.02: System Resources: I/O, IRQ, DMA**   All peripheral devices need system resources to function. System resources include input/output (I/O) addresses, interrupt (IRQ) settings, and direct memory address (DMA) channels. I/O addresses are unique address settings that enable a CPU to identify not only specific devices, but also specific functions of those devices. IRQs are physical wires that enable devices to get the CPU's attention. DMA channels enable devices to access system memory directly without going through the CPU.

✔ **Objective 9.03: Installing Peripheral Devices**   Ensure successful peripheral device installation by making certain that the device is compatible with your motherboard and operating system, that you have the correct device drivers, and that you follow all safety precautions. Plug and play enables compliant systems and hardware to self-configure system resource settings. Legacy devices usually require manual configuration. Rely on Device Manager to assist you in troubleshooting and diagnosing installation and driver problems. Pay attention to the errors or warnings marked next to any device.

REVIEW QUESTIONS

1. What is the definitive source for determining peripheral device compatibility in Windows 2000/XP?

    A. Microsoft Hardware Compatibility List

    B. Microsoft Windows Component Guide

    C. Tom's Hardware Guide

    D. All peripheral devices are compatible with Windows 2000/XP

2. When installing a USB device on a computer system with a USB-compatible OS and BIOS, it is sometimes necessary to _____ before the device will work.

    A. Reboot the system

    B. Manually configure system resources

    C. Install a device driver

    D. Flash the system BIOS

3. A new device has been installed in a Windows Me system. On reboot, the device isn't functioning. When inspecting the device in the Device Manager, you notice a black exclamation point in a yellow circle. This tells you:

    A. The device isn't working properly

    B. The device driver is corrupted

    C. The device isn't getting power

    D. The device is destroyed

4. COM2 is configured with which settings by default?

    A. I/O address 3F8, IRQ 4

    B. I/O address 2F8, IRQ 3

    C. I/O address 3E8, IRQ 4

    D. I/O address 2E8, IRQ 3

5. Joey comes to you perplexed, carrying a motherboard with three types of expansion slots. The one closest to the CPU is obviously AGP, and the next four white slots are PCI. But there's a third type of slot that's about half the size of a PCI slot and sports a tiny expansion card modem. What type of slot is that most likely to be?

    A. AMR

    B. ISA

    C. PCI-2

    D. Modem

6. In which type of expansion bus slot would you most likely find a SATA controller card?

    A. ISA

    B. PCI

    C. CNR

    D. AGP

7. If a device doesn't plug and play in Windows 98, where can you assign system resources?

    A. In the Print folder

    B. In the Device Manager

    C. At the command prompt

    D. From the Start menu

8. You install a new device on your PC, then go into Device Manager to see whether it appears there. The new device is listed, but you notice a red *X* next to it. What does the red *X* signify?

    A. This device is disabled.

    B. This device isn't recognized by Windows.

    C. This device isn't installed.

    D. This device is enabled with restrictions.

9. IRQ 0 maps to which device?

    A. System timer

    B. Keyboard

    C. Default COM2, COM4

    D. Floppy disk drive

10. The AGP bus connects directly to the system's _____ .

    A. Frontside bus

    B. Backside bus

    C. Southbridge

    D. Northbridge

REVIEW ANSWERS

1. **A** The Hardware Compatibility List on Microsoft's web site is the definitive source for a listing of peripheral devices that are guaranteed to work on Windows 2000/XP.

2. **C** You must sometimes install drivers for a USB device before it will work.

3. **A** The exclamation point only tells you the device isn't working properly. It can't tell you *why* the device isn't working properly.

4. **B** COM2 is configured with I/O address 2F8, IRQ 3 by default.

5. **A** The little slot is most likely an Audio/Modem Riser (AMR) slot.

6. **B** PCI offers the best option from the choices listed.

7. **B** Device Manager is the tool for configuring devices and assigning resources, even for non-PnP devices.

8. **A** A red *X* on a Device Manager shows the device is disabled.

9. **A** IRQ 0 maps to the system timer.

10. **D** The AGP bus connects directly to the Northbridge.

Printers

	NEWBIE	SOME EXPERIENCE	EXPERT
ETA	6 hours	4 hours	2 hours

A good twenty-first-century tech understands the various types of printers and printer connections, and can diagnose and troubleshoot printing problems to keep users up and running with all those paper documents. In most office and repair situations, you almost always get tagged, not as the PC repair person, but as the *computer person,* and *everyone* knows that printers are included in that description!

Objective 10.01 Printers

Printers are one of the most common types of PC peripherals. The A+ exam has traditionally stressed this area. This chapter helps you identify the different printer types, connections, configurations, and common troubleshooting issues.

Dot Matrix Printers

Dot matrix technology uses a series or matrix of pins to create dots on a piece of paper arranged to form characters. The speed at which a dot matrix printer prints is measured in the number of characters it can produce per second. The print head mechanism pushes each pin into the ribbon, which then strikes the paper. The original dot matrix print heads had 7 pins, while newer, letter-quality print heads use 24 pins to produce near letter quality (NLQ) documents. Figure 10-1 shows a typical dot matrix printer.

Dot matrix printers are called *impact* printers because the printing mechanism physically strikes the page. The continual motion of the pins through the print head creates a ton of heat, so avoid touching the print head after printing a handful of pages or more. The print head can give you a nasty burn!

Paper moves through a dot matrix printer using a *tractor feed* mechanism, as shown in Figure 10-2. Spoked wheels located on each side of the paper feed mechanism move the paper. The spokes on the outer edges of the wheels fit into holes on the sides of specially designed *continuous form* paper. As the wheels turn, they pull the paper through the printer.

Because impact printers physically strike the page, you can use them to create multipart forms with ease. Many offices and government agencies use them for that very reason. Although impact printers have been replaced in most homes and offices by newer, sexier inkjet and laser printers (discussed in the sections that follow), they still retain a substantial portion of the market in their niches.

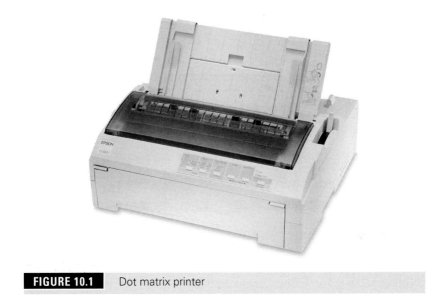

FIGURE 10.1 Dot matrix printer

Inkjet Printers

Inkjet printers create printouts by squirting ink out of special inkjet cartridges. They use both black and colored ink cartridges, and they can combine ink colors to create a wide range of hues. Inkjet printers use either liquid ink cartridges or solid, wax-based ink cartridges. Figure 10-3 shows a typical inkjet printer.

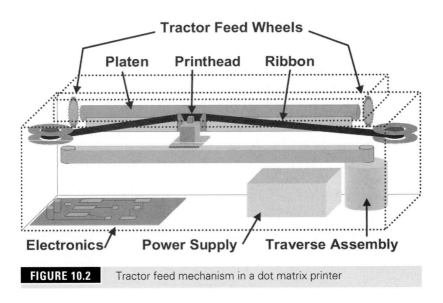

FIGURE 10.2 Tractor feed mechanism in a dot matrix printer

FIGURE 10.3   Typical inkjet printer

Inkjet printers are *nonimpact* printers because their print mechanism never actually touches the paper. Because they process an entire page at a time before starting to print it, they are referred to as *page* printers. Inkjet printers use a *friction feed* mechanism to feed paper through the printer. Sheets of paper are stacked in the paper tray, where small rollers press down to create friction and pull a sheet of paper through the printer.

Most liquid inkjet printers and all solid inkjet printers use a thermal process to eject ink onto the paper. The printing element heats up, boiling the ink in the case of liquid inkjet printers, and melting it in the case of solid inkjet printers. A tiny bubble of ink forms on the end of the print nozzle. Once the bubble becomes sufficiently enlarged, it pops, at which point electrically charged plates deflect the ink onto the paper. Sounds kind of messy, but it's actually precise. An inkjet print head contains between 300 and 600 nozzles, each about the diameter of a human hair. Figure 10-4 illustrates a typical inkjet print head. When the inkjet cartridge is not in use, pump pressure keeps the ink from leaking out the nozzle.

Epson printers use a different, proprietary inkjet technology featuring a special *crystal* at the back of the ink reservoir that flexes when an electric current is applied to it. When the crystal flexes, it forces a drop of ink out of the nozzle. The way it flexes determines the size and placement of the resulting drop.

A common problem with inkjet printers is the tendency for the ink inside the jets to dry out when it's not used, even for a relatively short time. To counter this problem, all inkjet printers move the print head to a special park position that keeps the ink from drying. Aside from replacing the inkjet cartridges and print

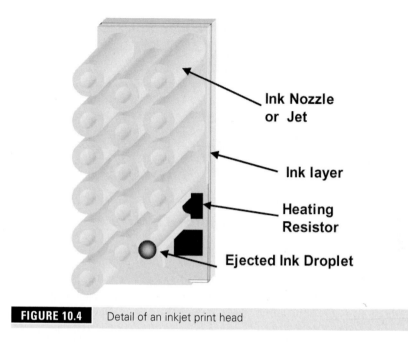

Ink Nozzle
or Jet

Ink layer

Heating
Resistor

Ejected Ink Droplet

FIGURE 10.4 Detail of an inkjet print head

heads, there's not much to do by way of maintenance. In some cases, you may need to replace the rubber paper rollers or tracking belts, but for the most part any serious repairs are simply not cost effective. The low cost of new inkjet printers makes them more of a candidate for replacement than repair.

Dye-Sublimation Printers

The term *sublimation* means to cause something to change from a solid form into a vapor and then back into a solid. This is exactly the process behind dye-sublimation printing (sometimes called *thermal dye transfer* printing).

The dye-sublimation technique uses a roll of heat-sensitive plastic film embedded with page-sized sections of cyan, magenta, and yellow dye (some also have a section of black dye). A print head containing thousands of heating elements, capable of precise temperature control, moves across the film, vaporizing the dyes and causing them to soak into specially coated paper underneath before cooling and reverting to a solid form. The process requires one pass per page for each color. Some also utilize a final finishing pass that applies a protective laminate coating to the page. Figure 10-5 shows how a dye-sublimation printer functions.

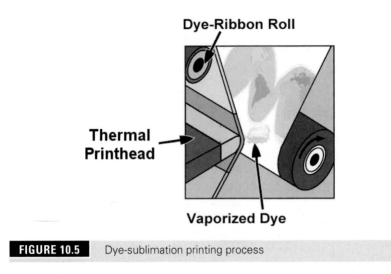

FIGURE 10.5   Dye-sublimation printing process

Documents printed through dye-sublimation display *continuous tone* images, meaning that each pixel dot is a blend of the different dye colors. This is in contrast to the *dithered* images of other print technologies, which use closely packed, single-color dots to simulate blended colors. Dye-sublimation printers produce high-quality color output that rivals professional photo lab processing. They are used mainly for photo printing, high-end desktop publishing, medical and scientific imaging, or other applications where fine detail and rich color is more important than cost and speed. Smaller, specialized printers called *snapshot* printers use dye-sublimation specifically for printing photos at a reduced cost (~200 USD) compared to their full-sized counterparts (~1000+ USD). Still, when you can get a high-end six-ink inkjet printer for the same price and have the versatility to print documents with speed and low expense and high-quality photographs, the snapshot printers become less desirable.

Thermal Printers

There are two kind of thermal printers that you'll see in use. The first is the *direct thermal* printer and the other is the *thermal wax transfer* printer.

Direct thermal printers use a heated print head to burn dots into the surface of special heat-sensitive paper. If you remember the first generation of fax machines, you're already familiar with this type of printer. You don't see many fax machines of the direct thermal type in the workplace anymore, but you will often see this type of printer used in retail point-of-sale areas as receipt printers.

Thermal wax printers work similarly to dye-sublimation printers, except that instead of using rolls of dye-embedded film, the film is coated with colored wax.

The thermal print head passes over the film ribbon and melts the wax onto the paper. Unlike dye-sublimation printers, however, thermal wax printers don't require special papers and so are more flexible and somewhat cheaper to use.

Also in contrast to dye-sublimation printers, thermal wax printers don't offer continuous tone output, using color dithering instead. This means that their output isn't quite as good as dye-sublimation printers, but it is still quite good.

Laser and LED Printers

Laser printers rely on the photoconductive properties of certain organic compounds. *Photoconductive* means that particles of these compounds, when exposed to light (that's the *photo* part), will conduct electricity. Laser printers use lasers as a light source because of their precision. LED printers work exactly the same way laser printers work, except that they use tiny LEDs as a light source instead of lasers. Both types of printers are usually simply called a laser printer. Unlike inkjet printers, the relatively high initial cost of laser printers makes their repair a practical and popular option. Figure 10-6 shows a typical laser printer.

Like inkjet printers, laser printers are nonimpact page printers. The print mechanism never touches the paper, and they image the entire page before transferring it to paper. Some laser printers support *duplex* printing, which enables you to print on both sides of the paper, either through a built-in mechanism or an add-on duplexing tray device. Modern laser printers are capable of resolutions as high as 2400 × 2400 dpi.

FIGURE 10.6   Typical laser printer

Until recently, one of the limitations of laser printing was that color wasn't available—at least, not without spending prohibitively big bucks! Lately, however, the price of laser printing in color has dropped dramatically, so you can expect to see full-color laser printers deployed in the workplace and referenced on the CompTIA core A+ exam.

Laser Printer Parts

Laser printers have many components, and the A+ exams expect you to know them. Let's run through the list.

Toner Cartridge Components   Many manufacturers incorporate laser printer components such as the image drum and fuser assembly (both described in the text that follows) into the toner cartridge (see Figure 10-7). While this makes replacement of individual parts nearly impossible, it also greatly reduces maintenance costs. Those parts most likely to break are replaced every time you replace the toner cartridge.

Travel Assistance

If you're looking for a company that sells laser printer parts, try The Printer Works—a large mail-order outfit with very knowledgeable sales folks. Like an auto parts store, they can often help you determine the problem, and then sell you the part. The Printer Works is on the Web at http://www.printerworks.com.

FIGURE 10.7   Laser printer's toner cartridge

Toner   The *toner* in a laser printer is a fine powder, made up of plastic particles bonded to iron particles. The reservoir in the toner cartridge where the toner is stored is called the *hopper*. The *toner cylinder* charges the toner with a negative charge of between ~200 and ~500 volts. Because that charge falls between the original uniform negative charge of the photosensitive image drum (~600 to ~1000 volts) and the charge of the particles on the drum's surface hit by the laser (~100 volts), particles of toner are attracted to the areas of the photosensitive drum that were hit by the laser, that is, to the areas with a positive charge *relative to* the toner particles.

Travel Advisory

Watch out for toner spills, as the super-fine toner particles make quite a mess. They'll stain your clothes as badly and permanently as ink and, worse, can prove toxic if inhaled. Don't sniff any toner!

The Photosensitive Drum   The *photosensitive drum* (sometimes called the *image drum*) is an aluminum cylinder coated with particles of photosensitive compounds (see Figure 10-8). The drum itself is grounded to the power supply, but the coating is not. When light hits these particles, whatever electrical charge they may have had drains out through the grounded cylinder.

As noted previously, most printer component manufacturers incorporate the image drum into the toner cartridge so that both components are replaced when the cartridge runs out of toner. Some makers, such as Okidata, use

FIGURE 10.8   Toner cartridge with photosensitive drum exposed

long-life image drum components that are replaced separately from the toner cartridge.

The photosensitive image drum is extremely light sensitive and should not be exposed for longer than a few seconds. Bright lights such as direct sunlight can permanently damage an image drum. Image drums sometimes become dirty from dust or spilled toner. In these cases, the drum can be wiped clean with a dry, lint-free cloth. Keep in mind, however, that if you scratch the drum, the scratch will appear on every page printed from that point on!

Erase Lamp   The *erase lamp* exposes the entire surface of the photosensitive drum with light, making the photosensitive coating conductive. Any electrical charge present in the particles bleeds away into the grounded drum, leaving the surface particles electrically neutral.

Primary Corona Wire   The *primary corona wire,* located close to the photo sensitive drum, never touches the drum. When the wire is charged with an extremely high voltage, an electric field (or corona) forms, allowing voltage to pass to the drum and charge the photosensitive particles on its surface. The *primary grid* regulates the transfer of voltage, ensuring the surface of the drum receives a uniform negative charge of between ~600 and ~1000 volts.

Transfer Corona Wire   To transfer the image from the photosensitive drum to the paper, the paper must be given a charge that will attract the toner particles off the drum and on to the paper. The *transfer corona wire* applies a positive charge to the paper, drawing the negatively charged toner particles to the paper. The paper, with its positive charge, is also attracted to the negatively charged drum. To prevent the paper from wrapping around the drum, a *static charge eliminator* removes the charge from the paper.

Transfer corona wires are prone to grime buildup and should be cleaned regularly using a special tool supplied with your printer. You should never touch the transfer corona wire with your bare fingers, as oils from your skin attract dirt and cause corrosion.

Laser or LED   The *laser* is the printer's writing mechanism. Any particle on the drum struck by the laser becomes conductive, allowing its charge to be drained away into the grounded core of the drum. In this way, the laser *writes* a positive image onto the drum. Particles struck by the laser are left with a ~100 volt negative charge, compared to the ~600 to ~1000 volt negative charge of the rest of the drum surface.

Some printers use an array of powerful LEDs in place of a laser beam to write the image onto the photosensitive image drum. Aside from this difference, LED printers work identically to laser printers.

Fuser   In most printers, the *fuser* assembly (sometimes called the *fuser pad*) is outside the toner cartridge, but it can be an integrated component. After the static charge eliminator has removed the paper's static charge, the toner is still merely resting on top of the paper. The toner must be fused to the paper to make the image permanent. Two rollers—a pressure roller and a heated roller—work together to fuse the toner to the paper. The pressure roller presses against the bottom of the page, while the heated roller presses down on the top of the page, melting the toner into the paper. The heated roller has a nonstick coating to prevent the toner from sticking to it.

The laser printers' fuser pad assembly has probably been responsible for more burned fingers than any other PC component. Use caution when working around the fuser assembly of a laser printer!

The Laser Printing Process

Let's put these steps together to see how a typical laser printer does its job. Remember, some brands of laser printers may depart from this exact process, although most do work in exactly this order. The printing process contains six steps, in this order:

1. Clean
2. Charge
3. Write
4. Develop
5. Transfer
6. Fuse

Exam Tip

Know the order of a laser printer's printing process! To help you keep the steps in order, remember: Careful Computer Weenies Don't Trade Files!

Step 1: Clean the Drum   Before printing each new page, the drum must be returned to a clean, fresh condition, so the printing process begins with the physical and electrical cleaning of the photosensitive drum. All residual toner left over from printing the previous page is removed, usually by a rubber cleaning blade that scrapes the surface of the drum. If residual particles remain on the drum, they appear as random black spots and streaks on the next page. The physical cleaning mechanism either deposits the residual toner in a debris cavity or recycles it by returning it to the toner cartridge hopper. Damage to the drum during the physical cleaning process causes a permanent mark to be printed on every page.

The printer must also be electrically cleaned, as shown in Figure 10-9. One or more erase lamps bombard the surface of the drum with the appropriate wavelengths of light, causing the surface particles to discharge into the grounded drum. After the cleaning process, the drum should be completely free of toner and have a neutral electrical charge.

Step 2: Charge the Drum   Electrically charging the drum makes it receptive to new images. The corona wire applies a uniform negative charge to the entire surface of the drum, normally between ~600 and ~1000 volts.

Step 3: Write the Image   Next the laser writes a positive image on the surface of the drum, as shown in Figure 10-10.

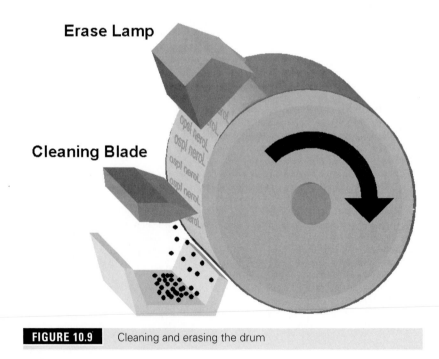

FIGURE 10.9   Cleaning and erasing the drum

Primary
Corona

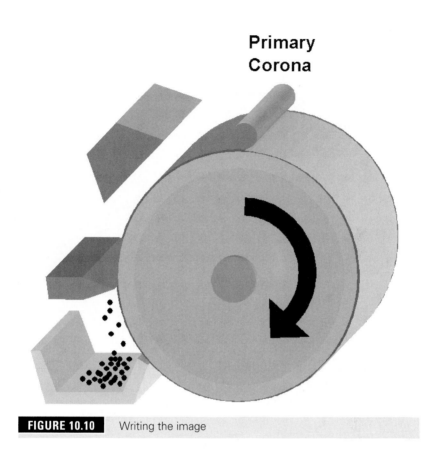

FIGURE 10.10   Writing the image

Step 4: Develop the Image   Every particle on the drum hit by the laser will release most of its negative charge into the drum. Those particles are then positively charged relative to the toner particles and will attract them, creating a developed image on the drum.

Step 5: Transfer the Image   To transfer the image from the drum onto the paper, the transfer corona charges the paper with a positive charge. Once in proximity to this positive charge, the negatively charged toner particles leap from the drum to the paper. Then the static charge eliminator removes the paper's positive charge, leaving the particles resting on the paper.

Step 6: Fuse the Image   For the final step in the process, the fuser melts the toner onto the paper (see Figure 10-11). The printer then ejects the final printed copy, and the process begins again with the physical and electrical cleaning of the printer.

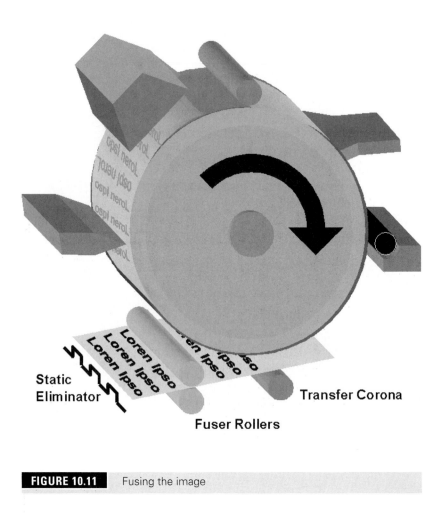

Static Eliminator

Transfer Corona

Fuser Rollers

FIGURE 10.11   Fusing the image

Travel Advisory

The heated roller of the fuser produces enough heat to melt some types of plastic media, particularly overhead transparency materials. Never use transparencies in a laser printer unless they are specifically designed for use in laser printers. Use of non-approved materials can seriously damage a laser printer and void the warranty!

Other Laser Printer Components

Although the majority of the printing activity takes place within the toner cartridge, many other parts of the laser printer are hard at work outside the cartridge, as you can see in Figure 10-12.

Power Supplies   All laser printers have at least two separate power supplies. The first power supply is called the *primary power supply* or sometimes just the *power supply*. The primary power supply powers the motors that move the paper, the system electronics, the laser, and the transfer corona.

The second power supply is the *high-voltage* power supply. It usually powers only the primary corona. The extremely high voltage of this power supply makes it one of the most dangerous devices in the world of PCs! Therefore, it's imperative that—except when inserting a new toner cartridge or paper—you *always turn off* a laser printer before you open it!

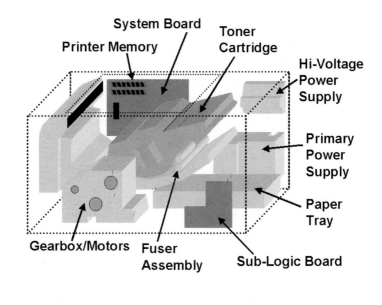

System Board
Toner
Cartridge
Printer Memory
Hi-Voltage Power Supply
Primary Power Supply
Paper Tray
Gearbox/Motors   Fuser Assembly   Sub-Logic Board

FIGURE 10.12   Inside a laser printer

Turning Gears   A laser printer performs many mechanical operations. The paper must be picked up, fed through, and kicked out of the printer. The photosensitive roller must be turned and the laser, or a mirror, must be moved from left to right. The toner must be evenly distributed, and the fuser assembly must squish the toner into the paper. All these functions are performed by complex gear systems. In most laser printers, these gear systems are packed together in discrete units powered by their own solenoid motors. These units are generically called *gear packs* or *gearboxes*. Most laser printers have two or three gearboxes. These are relatively easy to remove and replace in the rare case when one of them fails.

System Board   Every laser printer has at least one electronic board containing the main processor, the printer's ROM, and the RAM it uses to store the image before it's printed. Many printers divide these functions among two or three boards dispersed around the printer. The printer may also have an extra ROM chip and/or a slot where you can install an extra ROM chip, usually for special functions such as PostScript printing. When the printer doesn't have enough RAM to store the image before it prints, it generates a Memory Overflow error. Solve this condition by adding more RAM.

Travel Advisory

Adding RAM is usually a simple job—just snapping in a SIMM stick or two—but getting the *right* RAM is important. Call the printer manufacturer and ask what type of RAM you need. Although most printer companies will happily sell you their expensive RAM, most printers can use generic DRAM like the kind you use in your PC.

Network Interface   Recognizing that most offices share networked printers, many manufacturers include integrated network interface cards (NICs) on some printers. These printers have built-in print server software that enables them to be plugged directly into an available network plug instead of attached to a PC.

Ozone Filter   The coronas inside laser printers generate *ozone* (O_3). While the amount generated isn't harmful to humans, high concentrations of ozone will damage printer components. To counter this problem, most laser printers have a special ozone filter that must be replaced periodically. The best time is when you replace the toner cartridge, and in fact many toner cartridges come packaged with a new ozone filter.

Sensors and Switches Every laser printer contains a large array of sensors and switches. The sensors are used to detect a broad range of conditions such as paper jams, empty paper trays, or low toner levels. Many sensors are really tiny switches that detect conditions like open doors. Most of the time, these sensors and switches work reliably, but they can occasionally become dirty or broken and send a false signal to the printer. Simple inspection is usually sufficient to determine if a problem is real or just the result of a faulty sensor or switch.

Duplexer *Duplexers* are mechanical paper feeding devices that enable you to print on both sides of a sheet of paper. If your printer doesn't have a built-in duplexing mechanism, you can usually purchase one as an add-on component. Depending on the make and model of your printer, the duplexer may attach onto the front or back of the printer, or may take the place of the paper tray.

Finishers Some printers also include components called *finishers* that do things like collate, staple, and bind printed documents. Typically, these functions are beyond the capabilities of all but high-end, commercial printers.

Exam Tip	
Know and understand the various laser printer components!	

Objective 10.02 Printer Connections and Configurations

As a technician, you should know how to connect and configure parallel, serial, USB, and network printers.

Serial Printers

Older or specialized printers (such as label printers) sometimes connect to the PC via a 9- or 22-pin serial port. Serial cables can reach lengths of up to 25 feet without significant EMI or crosstalk problems.

Parallel Printers

Although the parallel port is being overtaken by USB, it remains the connection type most identified with computer printers.

The Parallel Port

The parallel port was included in the original IBM PC as a faster alternative to serial communication. The IBM engineers considered serial communication, limited to one bit at a time, to be too slow for the high-speed devices of the day, such as dot matrix printers. Like so much of the technology used in PCs today, the standard parallel port has been kept around for backward compatibility.

The speed of a standard parallel port has remained the same, despite speed improvements in almost every other part of the PC. The maximum data transfer rate of a standard parallel port is approximately 150 KBps. Standard parallel ports aren't capable of true bidirectional communication. Standard parallel communication on a PC relies heavily on software, eating up a considerable amount of CPU time.

Despite the "standard" label, the lack of standardization remains a source of incompatibility problems for some parallel devices. Because manufacturers are not required to adhere to a single standard for electromagnetic shielding on the cables to protect against EMI and crosstalk, for example, parallel cables longer than six feet are not recommended.

The IEEE 1284 Standard

In 1991, a group of printer manufacturers proposed to the Institute of Electrical and Electronics Engineers (IEEE) organization that a committee be formed to devise a standard for a backward-compatible, high-speed, bidirectional parallel port for the PC. The committee was the IEEE 1284 committee, hence the name of the standard. The IEEE 1284 standard attempts to deal with both the poor performance and the lack of standardization of standard parallel ports, while maintaining backward compatibility.

The IEEE 1284 standard requires the following:

* Support for all five modes of operation (Compatibility, Nibble mode, Byte mode, EPP, and ECP)
* A standard method for negotiation to determine which modes are supported both by the host PC and by the peripheral device
* A standard physical interface (the cables and connectors)
* A standard electrical interface (termination, impedance, and so forth)

Because only one set of data wires exists, all data transfer modes included in the IEEE 1284 standard are *half-duplex*; that is, data is transferred in only one direction at a time.

Compatibility Mode/Centronics Mode   The standard parallel port used in the original IBM PC is often referred to as a *Centronics* port. This connection normally manifests itself as a female DB-25 (25-pin) connector on the PC and as a female Centronics 36-pin connector on the printer.

The pins or wires on the DB-25 connector are assigned various tasks. Four control wires are used for control and handshaking signals going from the PC to the printer. Five status wires are used for handshaking signals from the printer to the PC, and for standardized signals from the printer to the PC, such as out of paper, busy, and offline. Only eight wires are used for passing data, and that data travels in only one direction: from the PC to the printer. The remaining eight wires are used as grounds.

The advantage to Centronics mode is backward compatibility, but its disadvantages are clear. Data passes in only one direction, from the PC to the peripheral device, or forward. In addition, the CPU must constantly poll the status wires for error messages and handshaking signals, using up significant numbers of CPU clock cycles. Centronics-mode transfers are limited to approximately 150 KBps.

Nibble Mode   *Nibble mode* is the simplest way to transfer data in the reverse direction—from the printer to the PC. Nibble mode requires no special hardware and can normally be used with any standard parallel port (that is, it doesn't require an IEEE 1284 parallel port). When used in concert with compatibility/Centronics mode, it provides a limited form of bidirectional communication using any parallel port.

All parallel ports have five status wires designed to send signals from the peripheral to the PC. Using four of these wires at a time, we can transfer a byte (eight bits) of data in two pieces, one nibble (four bits) at a time. Nibble mode is even more software-intensive than compatibility/Centronics mode, eating up many CPU clock cycles. This intensive use of CPU time, combined with the limitation of passing data in small chunks, limits Nibble-mode data transfers to approximately a whopping 50 KBbps.

Byte Mode/Enhanced Bidirectional Port   *Byte mode* enables reverse direction (peripheral to PC) parallel communication by using extra hardware that handles the negotiation between the PC and the peripheral. With *Byte mode*, two-way communication can achieve speeds approaching the speed of the one-way Centronics data transfers, approximately 150 KBps. Parallel ports capable of Byte-mode transfers are sometimes referred to as *enhanced bidirectional ports.* Byte mode is often supported by parallel ports and devices that don't support the entire IEEE 1284 standard.

Enhanced Parallel Port (EPP)

The *Enhanced Parallel Port (EPP)* protocol outperforms the standard parallel port while retaining backward compatibility. EPP is used primarily by peripherals *other* than printers, such as hard drives, CD-ROM drives, and scanners, which require constant two-way communication with the PC. The EPP protocol offers high-speed, two-way data transfers with relatively little overhead. Hardware handles the handshaking and synchronization between the peripheral device and the PC, allowing the CPU to transfer data to and from the port with a single command. Data transfers using the EPP protocol can approach the speed of an ISA bus, transferring between 500 KBps and 2 MBps.

Extended Capabilities Port (ECP)

The *Extended Capabilities Port (ECP)* protocol is designed to provide high-performance parallel communication for operations that involve moving large chunks of data but don't require much monitoring. Examples of this are a print job going out to a printer or an image coming in from a scanner. In contrast to EPP, once an ECP data transfer has begun, the software that initiated the transfer (a printer driver, for example) cannot monitor the progress of the transfer. The software must wait for a signal that shows the transfer was completed. This reduces the number of clock cycles used by the transfer to a bare minimum.

ECP ports use a data compression method called *run-length encoding (RLE).* With RLE, data can be compressed by a ratio of up to 64:1. This enhances performance significantly because printers and scanners deal with *raster* graphics, which tend to compress well. For RLE to work, both the device and the parallel port must support it. Note that RLE compression isn't actually part of the IEEE 1284 standard but instead is part of Microsoft's standard for implementing the ECP protocol.

Like EPP, the ECP standard provides a great degree of flexibility to hardware manufacturers. As long as the parallel port and devices respond to the standardized ECP commands, manufacturers can enhance performance any way they want. Because data transfers that use ECP don't require manipulation of the data, many manufacturers have added special capabilities to the ports, especially *Direct Memory Access (DMA)* channels, something never seen on any other form of parallel port.

<table>
<tr><td colspan="2">

Local Lingo
</td></tr>
</table>

Raster graphics Raster graphics is another term for bitmapped graphics, which refers to the way an image is represented in a computer's memory. Bitmapping means dividing an image into rows and columns of dots, and recording a value for each dot as one or more bits of data.

Vector graphics Rather than bitmapping to represent images on computers, mathematical formulas can be used to record the various parameters of an image. Because they're recorded as formulas, vector images can easily change size without looking different. Vector images are used to create scalable fonts.

Some parallel modes are more appropriate for some types of devices than for others. With the highest throughput of all the parallel modes, ECP excels at handling large blocks of data via DMA channels, making it ideal for printers and scanners. External devices that must frequently switch back and forth between read and write operations, such as external CD-ROMs, are better served by EPP's capability to change the direction of the data flow without additional handshaking and overhead. Because Centronics mode and Nibble mode are controlled through software, any parallel port ever made for an IBM PC can do both. If the parallel port lacks appropriate hardware support, however, expensive devices capable of high-speed communication using Byte mode, ECP, or EPP must slow down to the speed of the parallel port. Check the parallel port settings in CMOS, as shown in Figure 10-13, to verify that a parallel port is set to the appropriate mode.

```
                    ROM PCI/ISA BIOS (2A69KS21)
                      INTEGRATED PERIPHERALS
                       AWARD SOFTWARE, INC.

   IDE HDD Block Mode        : Enabled    onboard Parallel Port : 378/IRQ7
   IDE Primary Master P10    : Auto       Parallel Port Mode    : EPP
   IDE Primary Slave  P10    : Auto
   IDE Secondary Master P10  : Auto
   IDE Secondary Slave  P10  : Auto
   IDE Primary Master UDMA   : Auto
   IDE Primary Slave  UDMA   : Auto
   IDE Secondary Master UDMA : Auto
   IDE Secondary Slave  UDMA : Auto
   On-Chip Primary   PCI IDE : Enabled
   On-Chip Secondary PCI IDE : Enabled
   USB Keyboard Support      : Disabled
   Init Display First        : PCI Slot

   Onboard FDC Controller    : Enabled   ESC : Quit   ↑↓ → ← : Select Item
   Onboard Serial Port 1     : Disabled  F1  : Help     PU/PD/+/-  :Modify
   Onboard Serial Port 2     : 2F8/IRQ3  F5  : Old Values (Shift)F2:Color
   UR2 Mode                  : Standard  F7  : Load Setup Defaults
```

FIGURE 10.13 Parallel port settings in CMOS

USB Printers

USB is the most common type of printer connection found on newer printers. USB printers can connect to a USB port on the back of your PC or to a USB hub. As with any USB device, you can add or remove a USB printer at any time without powering down your machine. Because printers require a lot of power, they use the USB interface only to talk to the PC. USB printers require a separate power source.

Many USB printers are capable of communicating directly with other USB devices such as digital cameras, enabling you to print out photos without going through the PC.

FireWire Printers

Many newer printers offer a FireWire interface as well as parallel and USB. Like USB printers, they require a separate power source. Like USB-enabled printers, FireWire printers enable you to connect directly to and print directly from many digital cameras.

Infrared Printers

Some printers are capable of wireless communication with laptop PCs and PDAs through an integrated infrared port. Infrared printing uses the *Infrared Data Association (IrDA)* protocol incorporated into all modern versions of Windows and popular PDA OS platforms such as Palm and PocketPC.

Typically, no special configuration is required to get infrared printing to work. Simply point the infrared-equipped PC or PDA in the direction of the printer's infrared transceiver and a link should be established automatically. Infrared devices are capable of communicating at speeds up to 4 MBps, so printing is fairly fast. However, range is limited to a maximum of one meter (just over 39 inches) and is line-of-sight only, meaning that there can be nothing between the sending and receiving infrared transceivers.

Networking Printers

You can set up a printer in two different ways on a network: you can configure the printer as a *shared printer* connected to a PC, or it can be plugged directly into a network port.

Shared Printers

A shared printer is attached to a computer on the network, referred to as a *print server*. The print server shares its printer with other computers on the network and processes incoming print jobs. The computers on the network can use the shared printer only if the print server is on the network and has given the other computers permission to access its printer.

Network Printers

Network printers attach to the network either through an integrated NIC or through a dedicated network print server device such as HP's JetDirect print server. Network printers are equipped with powerful processors and massive amounts of RAM, as well as built-in print server software and configuration utilities. Network-capable printers are typically configured through a special utility supplied by your printer manufacturer (or sometimes through a web browser–based utility) from a networked workstation. Some have built-in keypads and display screens that let you configure them directly.

Objective 10.03 Troubleshooting

It's the rare business that has a dedicated printer technician on staff. As an A+ certified PC tech, most businesses expect your problem-solving skills to extend beyond the computer to the printer as well. Printer-related errors come in a variety of forms, and troubleshooting them can range from pleasingly simple to headache-inducingly complex. When troubleshooting printers, try the obvious first, and then graduate to more advanced troubleshooting techniques. This section describes common printer errors and solutions.

Exam Tip
Know the basic troubleshooting procedures for all printer types.

Feed and Output

Printers often develop problems with the paper-feed mechanism. When paper-feed problems occur, the paper can become jammed in the feed mechanism, halting the printing process.

Problems with Friction Feed Mechanisms

The most common problem with friction-feed mechanisms is usually caused by user error: too much paper in the paper tray! This causes the feed mechanism to pick up several sheets of paper and try to send them through the printer at the same time, resulting in a paper jam. Most paper trays have a line or symbol on the edge to show the maximum allowed paper in the paper tray at one time.

Another cause of this type of error is static electricity. Static buildup in friction-feed mechanisms causes pages to stick together, which again results in several pages being fed through the printer at the same time. To prevent paper jams caused by static, fan the stack of papers on a desk or other surface before placing them in the paper feed tray. This loosens the pages and reduces the static cling.

Believe it or not, but not having enough paper in the paper tray also causes feed errors. If the paper level is too low, the rollers can have trouble catching hold of the top sheet. If sufficient paper seems to be in the tray, check to see if you're using recycled paper, which can sometimes be thinner than normal paper and harder for the rollers to grab.

To fix a paper jam, turn off the printer, then open it and gently extract the paper. Whenever possible, move the paper in the direction it would normally go. Remember your physics, and pull slowly and gently. This minimizes the likelihood that you'll rip off the exposed part of the paper. Also, pulling too hard can damage the rollers in the feed mechanism. Some printers won't continue printing after you fix the problem until you press the Online or Reset button.

Problems with Tractor-Feed Mechanisms

Impact printers' tractor-feed mechanisms require you to line up the spokes on the wheels with the holes in the paper. If the holes on either side of the paper aren't lined up evenly, the text might print diagonally on the page. If the holes are uneven, the paper will crease, wrinkle, and jam.

Because they use continuous form paper, tractor-feed printers can require a bit of skill to position the paper properly. Each model of printer has its own special way of positioning the paper vertically, making trial and error an essential part of this process. If you get this wrong, your top and bottom margins will be off, and sometimes lines of text will even split across two sheets of paper.

Printer Errors

Printing errors centered on the printer itself can be a bit more complicated to troubleshoot than paper feeding errors. Sometimes printer errors are accompanied by error messages from either the PC or the printer itself. Other times, you'll have to investigate a bit further to get to the root of the problem.

Out-of-Paper Errors

The cause of a *Paper Out* error should be pretty obvious: no paper is in the printer. To correct this problem on a tractor-feed printer, lift the printer's lid and carefully feed the first sheet onto the tractor wheels. To fix this problem on a friction-feed printer, simply add paper to the paper tray.

Input/Output Errors

Input/Output errors occur when the computer is unable to communicate with the printer. When troubleshooting an Input/Output error, start with these possibilities:

- Is the printer plugged in?
- Is the printer turned on?
- Are all cables firmly connected?
- Is the proper driver for your printer installed? If so, could it have become corrupted?
- Are the IRQ and I/O settings for the printer correct?

If all these check out, try restarting the printer, the PC, or both. Simply restarting can sometimes fix a multitude of problems. If the printer still produces the Input/Output error, connect the printer to another computer. If the printer does not work on the other computer, you know you have a printer problem. If it works fine on the other computer, you have a configuration problem.

Incorrect Port Mode Errors

An *Incorrect Port Mode* error indicates the parallel port you connected the printer to isn't using the correct port mode. If you receive this error, use the CMOS settings program to change the port mode to one that's compatible with your printer.

No Default Printer Errors

A *No Default Printer* error indicates that no printer has been installed or that you haven't set a default printer. To set a default printer:

1. Click the Start button.
2. Select Settings.
3. Select Printers. The Printers dialog box will appear.
4. Alternate-click the icon of the printer you want to set as the default.
5. Select Set As Default from the Shortcut menu.

If no printer has been installed, follow these steps:

1. Click the Start button.

2. Select Settings.

3. Select Printers. The Printers dialog box will appear.

4. Double-click the Add Printer icon and follow the instructions.

Toner Low and Ink Low Errors

When the toner cartridge in a laser printer runs low, it issues a warning before the cartridge runs out completely. Replace the cartridge as soon as you see the error to avoid half-finished or delayed print jobs. You should also replace inkjet cartridges promptly to prevent clogged print nozzles.

Consumable Refills   Ink and toner refill kits are much less expensive than purchasing new cartridges and may seem like an economic solution to the consumable problem. However, because you're reusing the original cartridge components, such as the pump and heating element, you risk damaging your printer. Purchasing new cartridges is more economical than fixing your laser printer because of damage caused by old cartridges.

Remanufactured laser toner cartridges, however, are usually safe to use and reliable. Many laser toner manufacturers even have their own recycling programs.

Print Quality

Depending on the printer type you're using, several factors might affect print quality.

Dot-Matrix Print Quality Issues

One downside to dot matrix is the need for ongoing maintenance. Keep the *platen* (the roller or plate on which the pins impact) and the print head clean. Be sure to lubricate gears and pulleys according to the manufacturer's specifications. Never lubricate the print head, however, because the lubricant will smear and stain the paper.

White Bars on Text   White bars going through the text point to a dirty or damaged print head. Try cleaning the print head with a little denatured alcohol. If the problem persists, replace the print head. Print heads for most printers are readily available from the manufacturer.

Chopped Text   If the characters look chopped off at the top or bottom, the print head probably needs to be adjusted. Follow the manufacturer's instructions for proper adjustment.

Pepper Look   If the paper is covered with dots and small smudges—the "pepper look"—the platen is dirty. Clean the platen with a soft cloth.

Faded Image   If the image is faded and you know the ribbon is good, try adjusting the print head closer to the platen.

Light to Dark   If the image is okay on one side of the paper but fades on the other, the platen is out of adjustment. Platens are difficult to adjust, so your best plan is to send it to the manufacturer's local warranty/repair center. The money you'll spend is far cheaper than the frustration of trying to do it yourself!

Inkjet Print Quality Issues

Inkjet printers are more complicated than dot-matrix printers, which also means more things can go wrong.

Unclear Images   If an inkjet printer is producing unclear images, the ink cartridges are probably running low on ink and need to be replaced.

Blank Printouts   If an inkjet printer is producing blank printouts, either the ink level is low or the nozzles have become clogged. First check the ink and replace the cartridge if it's low. If the ink is at an acceptable level, the nozzles have probably become clogged. To unclog the nozzles, dip a cotton swab in denatured alcohol and gently wipe away any dried ink.

Confetti Printouts   Printouts with ink speckles, or *confetti*, always indicate an ink problem. Over time, ink can escape into the body of an inkjet printer, eventually finding its way onto subsequent printouts. To fix or prevent speckling, clean the insides of the printer with a damp cloth.

Wrong Colors in Printouts   If an inkjet produces printouts using the wrong colors, check for low ink in one or more cartridges, or a dirty nozzle. First check the ink cartridges. If they're full, clean the nozzles with a cotton swab dipped in denatured alcohol.

Smudges on Printouts   Smudges on printouts are most often caused by the user touching the printout before the ink has completely dried. Other causes include dirty printers and worn-out nozzles. Worn-out nozzles cannot be fixed. You must replace the ink cartridges if the nozzles have become worn out.

Laser Print Quality Issues

Laser printers usually manifest problems by creating poor output. One of the most important tests you can do on any printer—not only a laser printer—is called a *diagnostic print page* or an *engine test page*. You can print a test page by holding down the Online button as the printer is started or by selecting the menu option on the printer's operator panel. You can also select Start | Settings | Printers in Windows and issue the test page command from the printer's Properties dialog box. The A+ exam is *very* concerned that you understand laser printer maintenance. Make sure you know the causes and solutions for their various maintenance problems.

Blank Paper   Blank sheets of paper usually mean the printer is out of toner. If the printer does have toner and nothing prints, print a diagnostic print page. If that's also blank, remove the toner cartridge and look at the imaging drum inside. If the image is still there, you know the transfer corona or the high-voltage power supply has failed. Check the printer's maintenance guide to see how to zero in on the bad part and replace it.

Ghosting   Sometimes ghost images appear at regular intervals on the printed page. Either the imaging drum hasn't fully discharged and is picking up toner from a previous image, or a previous image has used up so much toner that either the supply of charged toner is insufficient or the toner hasn't been adequately charged.

Light Ghosting vs. Dark Ghosting   A variety of problems can cause both light and dark ghosting, but the most common source of *light ghosting* is *developer starvation*. If you ask a laser printer to print an extremely dark or complex image, it can use up so much toner that the toner cartridge won't be able to charge enough toner to print the next image. The proper solution is to use less toner by doing the following:

- Lowering the resolution of the page (print at 300 dpi instead of 600 dpi)
- Using a different pattern
- Avoiding 50 percent gray scale and dot-on/dot-off patterns
- Changing the layout, so gray scale patterns don't follow black areas
- Making dark patterns lighter and light patterns darker
- Printing in landscape orientation

- Adjusting print density and Resolution Enhancement Technology (RET) settings
- Printing a completely blank page immediately prior to the page with the ghosting image and as part of the same print job

Low temperature and low humidity can aggravate ghosting problems. Check your users' manual for environmental recommendations.

Dark ghosting can sometimes be caused by a damaged drum. It can be fixed by replacing the toner cartridge. Light ghosting cannot be solved in this way. Switching other components usually won't fix ghosting problems because they're a side effect of the entire printing process.

Vertical White Lines   Vertical white lines are usually caused by clogged toner. Clogs prevent the proper dispersion of toner on the drum. Try shaking the toner cartridge from side-to-side to dislodge the clog or, if that doesn't work, replacing the toner cartridge.

Blotchy Print   This is most commonly because of uneven dispersion of toner—especially if the toner is low. Try shaking the toner from side to side. Also be sure the printer is level. Finally, make sure the paper isn't wet in spots. If the blotches are in a regular order, check the fusing rollers and the photosensitive drum for foreign objects.

Spotty Print   If spots appear at regular intervals on the printout, the printer's drum may be damaged or toner may be stuck to the fuser rollers. Try wiping off the fuser rollers. Check the drum for damage. If the drum is damaged, you must get a new toner cartridge.

Embossed Effect   If your prints have an embossed effect (like putting a penny under a piece of paper and rubbing it with a pencil), a foreign object is almost certainly on a roller. Use regular water with a soft cloth to try to remove it. If the foreign object is on the photosensitive drum, you'll have to use a new toner cartridge.

Incomplete Characters   Incompletely printed characters on laser-printed transparencies can sometimes be corrected by adjusting the print density. Remember to use only materials approved for use in laser printers.

Creased Pages   Laser printers have up to four rollers. In addition to the heat and pressure rollers of the fusing assembly, rollers are designed to move the paper from the source tray to the output tray. These rollers crease the paper to avoid curling, which would cause paper jams in the printer. If the creases are noticeable, try using a different paper type. Cotton bond paper is usually more susceptible to noticeable creasing than other bonds. You might also try sending the output to the face-up tray, which eliminates one roller. No hardware solution exists to this problem. This is simply a side effect of the process.

Warped, Overprinted, or Poorly Formed Characters   Poorly formed characters can indicate either a problem with the paper (or other media) or a problem with the hardware.

Incorrect media causes a number of problems. Avoid too rough or too smooth paper. Paper that's too rough interferes with fusing of characters and their initial definition. If the paper is too smooth (like some coated papers, for example), it might feed improperly, causing distorted or overwritten characters. While you can purchase laser printer–specific paper, all laser printers will run acceptably on standard photocopy paper. Because paper picks up humidity from the air, don't open a ream of paper until you're ready to load it into the printer. Always fan the paper before loading it into the printer—especially if the paper has been left out for more than a few days.

The durability of a well-maintained laser printer makes hardware a rare source of character-printing problems, but it is a possibility. Fortunately, checking the hardware is easy. Most laser printers have a self-test function, often combined with a diagnostic printout, that's quite handy to verify those "Is it the printer or is it the computer?" questions. Run the self-test to check for connectivity and configuration problems. Possible solutions:

- Replace the toner cartridge, especially if you hear popping noises.
- Check the cabling.
- Replace the data cable, especially if bends or crimps exist, or objects are resting on the cable.
- If you have a Front Menu Panel, turn off Advanced Functions and High Speed Settings to determine if they aren't working properly or aren't supported by your current software configuration (check your manuals).

If these solutions don't work, the problem might not be user serviceable. Contact an authorized service center.

General Print Quality Issues

Now that you understand some of the print quality issues that can affect the individual printer types, you need to understand the print quality issues that can affect all three. Let's look at the most common print problems in Windows.

Print Job Never Prints   If you press the Print button, but nothing comes out of the printer, check the obvious things first. Is the printer on? Is it connected? Is it online? Does it have paper? Assuming the printer is physically in good order, the next step is to check the print server's print *spooler* status.

The print spooler is the hard disk space reserved for channeling print jobs from the PC to the printer. You can see the spooler status either by double-clicking the printer's icon in the Printers applet or by clicking the tiny printer icon in the System Tray if it's present (if you're having a problem, it's almost always there).

Print spoolers can overflow or become corrupt because of a lack of disk space or too many print jobs. The Printers window shows all the pending print jobs and enables you to delete, start, or pause print jobs. The best answer is usually to delete the print jobs and try again.

Incorrect Page Size   A print job that comes out sized incorrectly usually points to a user mistake in setting up the print job. Check the Print dialog box for incorrect print parameters. Also check the Page Setup option in the relevant application. Make sure the user is setting up the page properly.

If you know the page is set up correctly, recheck the printer drivers. If necessary, uninstall and reinstall the print drivers. If the problem persists, you might have a serious problem with the printer's print engine, but that is a possibility only when you continually get the same strangely sized printouts using a number of different applications.

Garbage Characters in Printout   Misaligned or garbage printouts invariably point to a corrupted or incorrect driver. Make sure you're using the right driver and then uninstall and reinstall the printer driver. If the problem persists, it's possible that you're asking the printer to do something it cannot do. For example, you might be printing to a PostScript printer with a PCL driver. Check the printer type to verify you haven't installed the wrong type of driver for that printer! Try some of these diagnostic avenues:

- Make sure the printer cables are attached firmly and haven't become loose.
- Turn the power to the printer off, and then on again.
- To check the basic communication between the PC and the printer, try printing a plain text file—Notepad is excellent for this.
- Restart your computer. Many Windows and application problems can be resolved simply by restarting your system.
- Reinstall your printer drivers. Drivers occasionally become corrupted and might need reinstalling.

- Check your resource settings for the parallel or USB port to verify no resource conflicts exist.
- Connect the printer to a different computer. If the printer continues producing garbage characters on the second computer, you know the problem lies within the printer.
- Try printing a smaller document. If you can print a smaller document, the problem may be insufficient memory in the printer. Insufficient memory can be remedied by adding more RAM to the printer.

Printer Not Responding   If the printer isn't responding, check the easy things first. Make sure the printer is turned on, and the cables are securely and correctly attached. Make sure the printer is online. Make sure the application you're printing from is sending the print job to the correct printer. Try to print a test page. Try attaching it to a new computer. If nothing works, your printer might have to go to a printer repair facility.

Objective 10.04 Preventive Maintenance

Printers are more mechanical in nature than most PC components and so require regular maintenance to stay in top running form. Paper dust, toner, and ink deposits are the root of many printer problems. Paper dust can jam gears and causes ESD. Excess ink or toner causes poor-quality printouts. Cleaning your printer regularly can prevent many problems from occurring.

This section describes the procedures for cleaning dot matrix, inkjet, and laser printers. On all types of printers, be sure to turn the power off and unplug all cables from the printer before servicing. You should also wait a few minutes after shutting the printer down to allow the print heads and fuser components to cool down and the onboard capacitor circuits to discharge.

Exam Tip
Know the proper cleaning procedures for all printer types.

Cleaning Dot Matrix Printers

Follow these steps to clean a dot matrix printer:

1. Remove the plastic casing and carefully pull the print head away from the platen.

2. Inspect the ribbon and replace it, if necessary.

3. Loosen paper dust from the printer by using compressed air and remove it with an antistatic vacuum.

4. Clean the print head with denatured alcohol.

5. Remove paper from the platen.

6. Inspect the carriage belt and replace it, if it's worn or cracked.

After you finish cleaning the printer, lubricate the gears and pulleys—*not* the print head itself! Never lubricate the print head, or your printouts will appear stained. Reassemble the printer in reverse order and run a test printout.

Cleaning Inkjet Printers

To clean liquid or solid inkjet printers, follow these steps:

1. Remove the plastic housing and ink cartridges.

2. Loosen paper dust from the printer by using compressed air and remove it with an antistatic vacuum.

3. Wipe off the ink cartridges with a damp cloth.

4. Wipe excess ink from the inside of the printer with a damp cloth.

5. Clean the platen.

6. Inspect the carriage belt and replace it, if necessary.

Once you're finished, reassemble the printer and run a test printout.

Cleaning Thermal and Dye-Sublimation Printers

To clean thermal-based printers such as thermal wax and dye-sublimation printers, follow these steps:

1. Remove the wax or dye ribbon cartridge.

2. Loosen paper dust from the printer by using compressed air and remove it with an antistatic vacuum.

3. Wipe off the ribbon cartridges with a damp cloth.

4. Wipe excess ink residue from the inside of the printer with a damp cloth.

5. Use compressed air to loosen dust from the drive gears and remove it with an antistatic vacuum.

6. Be careful not to disturb the thermal print head!

Once you're finished, reassemble the printer and run a test printout.

Cleaning Laser Printers

To clean a laser printer, follow these steps:

1. Remove and wipe off the toner cartridges.

2. Loosen paper dust from the printer by using compressed air and remove it with an antistatic vacuum.

3. Use the special tool supplied with the printer to clean the transfer corona wire. You can also wipe the wire down with a swab and denatured alcohol.

4. On LED printers, use a clean, lint-free cloth to clean the LED array window. Many toner kits come with a special one-use cleaning pad for this purpose.

5. Clean the fusing rollers and replace the roller pad.

6. Replace the ozone filter.

7. Clean the rubber guide rollers with clean water.

When you finish, carefully reassemble and reconnect the printer and run a test printout.

CHECKPOINT

✔ **Objective 10.01: Printers** Know the types of printers—dot matrix, inkjet, dye-sublimation, laser—and how each one works. Understand the laser printing process and know its six discrete steps in the order they occur.

✔ **Objective 10.02: Printer Connections and Configurations** Five types of printer connections exist: serial, parallel, USB, FireWire, and NIC. You should know the various connectors for the first four types and the requirements for accessing a printer over a network.

✔**Objective 10.03: Troubleshooting**　　Common printer problems include paper jams and problems with paper-feed mechanisms, I/O errors, No Default Printer errors, low toner/ink, a huge variety of print-quality issues, and nonresponsive printers.

✔**Objective 10.04 Preventive Maintenance**　　The A+ Core Hardware exam expects you to know the proper cleaning procedures for each printer type, including dot matrix, ink jet, and laser. In general, you will vacuum up small particles, clean appropriate surfaces and mechanisms, and where needed, replace certain parts such as ribbons, belts, and filters.

REVIEW QUESTIONS

1. What are the six steps of the laser printer process?

   A. Paper In, Charge, Develop, Transfer, Fuse, Paper Out

   B. Clean, Charge, Write, Develop, Transfer, Fuse

   C. Charge, Clean, Write, Transfer, Print, Fuse

   D. Clean, Charge, Develop, Transfer, Write, Fuse

2. What type of feed mechanism do dot matrix printers use?

   A. Tractor feed

   B. Friction feed

   C. Paper feed

   D. Spoke feed

3. Which printer types use friction-feed mechanisms?

   A. Dot matrix

   B. Laser

   C. Inkjet

   D. Dye sublimation

4. What is the maximum recommended length for a parallel printer cable?

   A. 10 feet

   B. 25 feet

   C. 6 feet

   D. 3 feet

5. Garbage characters are appearing in a printout. What's the problem?

   A. The printer is old and needs to be replaced

   B. You have the wrong language set up for the printer

    C. The printer needs to be cleaned

    D. The computer isn't communicating correctly with the printer

6. What does the primary corona wire in a laser printer do?

    A. Cleans the drum

    B. Charges the drum

    C. Creates the image on the drum

    D. Transfers the image from the drum to the paper

7. What do inkjet printers use to deflect ink onto a page?

    A. A print head

    B. Electrically charged plates

    C. Fusers

    D. Rollers

8. Which parallel port mode is the fastest?

    A. Centronics

    B. Byte mode

    C. ECP

    D. EPP

9. Dye-sublimation printers use what to transfer ink to the paper surface?

    A. Impact print head

    B. Thermal print head

    C. Electrically charged plates

    D. Print nozzles

10. What can cause ghosted images to appear in printouts from a laser printer?

    A. The writing stage of the laser printer process has failed

    B. The charging stage of the laser printer process has failed

    C. The transferring stage of the laser printer process has failed

    D. The cleaning stage of the laser printer process has failed

11. Which part of a dot matrix printer is most dangerous?

    A. The print head

    B. The ribbon

    C. The feed mechanism

    D. The wheels

12. Which part of a laser printer is the most dangerous?

   A. Laser

   B. Primary corona

   C. Fuser

   D. High voltage power supply

13. Which printer connection is the slowest?

   A. Parallel

   B. USB

   C. Serial

   D. Network

14. Which type of printer can create carbon copies?

   A. Laser

   B. Inkjet

   C. USB

   D. Dot matrix

15. What component of a laser printer transfers the image from the drum to the paper?

   A. Primary corona

   B. Fusing rollers

   C. Transfer corona

   D. Friction feed

REVIEW ANSWERS

1. **B**   The steps of the laser printer process are Clean, Charge, Write, Develop, Transfer, Fuse.

2. **A**   Dot matrix printers use a tractor-feed mechanism.

3. **B C**   Both inkjet and laser printers use a friction-feed mechanism.

4. **C**   The maximum length for a parallel printer cable is six feet. Cables any longer are subject to crosstalk and EMI.

5. **D**   Garbage characters in a printout mean the computer isn't communicating correctly with the printer. One possible reason for this is incorrect or corrupted drivers.

6. **B**   The primary corona wire charges the drum after it has been cleaned.

7. **B** Electrically charged plates deflect ink onto the paper.

8. **C** ECP is the fastest parallel port mode.

9. **B** Dye-sublimation printers use a thermal print head to vaporize dyes and transfer them to paper.

10. **D** Ghosted images in laser-printer printouts indicate the cleaning stage of the laser printer process has failed.

11. **A** The print head on a dot matrix printer gets very hot and can burn you.

12. **D** The high voltage power supply inside the laser printer can pack a lot of punch and give you a terrible shock. Be very careful inside a laser printer.

13. **C** Serial is the slowest type of printer connection.

14. **D** Dot matrix printers are impact printers and can create carbon copies.

15. **C** The transfer corona in laser printers transfers the image from the drum to the paper.

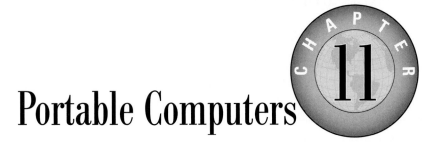

Portable Computers

	NEWBIE	SOME EXPERIENCE	EXPERT
ETA	2 hours	1 hour	1/2 hour

The computing world today differs vastly from that of earlier years; this is perhaps most evident in the world of portable computers. The term "portable" acts as an umbrella term describing a number of different devices. Generally speaking, *portable* refers to any of the three most common types of mobile computing devices: *laptop computers, handheld computers,* and *personal digital assistants* (*PDAs*). Advances in display screen technology, battery life, CPU muscle, and networking capabilities have prompted many folks to opt for portables in addition to, and sometimes instead of, desktop PCs.

Laptops range in size from sleek and thin so-called *ultra-portables* with displays around eleven inches across and weighing only five pounds or so, to gigantic *desktop replacement* systems with displays of seventeen inches or more and tipping the scales at over fifteen pounds. You'll also hear some laptop computer models described as *notebook* or *subnotebook* computers, but these are marketing terms and not really cut-and-dried official definitions. The thing that distinguishes laptops from handhelds or PDAs is that they run a standard, full-function version of Windows and enable users to input data through full-sized keyboards and interact with the desktop using a built-in *touchpad.*

Handheld computers, as the name implies, are smaller and lighter than laptops, with display screens usually no more than about ten inches across and weighing in at around three to five pounds. Handheld computers use a specialized version of the Windows OS such as Windows CE. Handheld computer users may input data and interact with the desktop either using a scaled-down keyboard or through a pen-like *stylus* and touch-sensitive screen with specialized handwriting recognition software.

PDAs are the smallest form factor. Once considered mere gadgets that only hardcore geeks could love, PDAs are now powerful enough and sport enough features to make them truly useful. Sometimes called *palmtop computers,* PDAs fit literally into the palm of your hand with display screens no more than about three inches across and weighing only a few ounces. PDAs also use specialized operating systems, such as Windows Pocket PC or Palm OS, and most use stylus-based input, although some also have tiny keyboards.

The CompTIA Core A+ Certification exams expect you to be familiar with the special quirks and support requirements for all of these devices and know how to get them to interact with each other seamlessly. Let's get started.

Objective 11.01 Configuration

For years, portable PC makers engineered entirely proprietary components for each system model they developed. For the most part, this proprietary attitude still prevails, but some standardization has crept in, making it easier to repair or upgrade the system using parts from third-party vendors instead of sometimes-expensive OEM parts. The following sections highlight the most common components.

RAM

Modern laptop RAM modules are standardized into two form factors: *MicroDIMM* and *small outline DIMM*, or *SO DIMM*. MicroDIMM RAM comes only in the 114-pin variety. SO DIMM RAM comes in either 72- or 114-pin varieties. The important difference between the two types of SO DIMM RAM is that 72-pin SO DIMMs are 32-bit, while the 114-pin variety are 64-bit. Aside from those differences, RAM in laptops is configured exactly the same as in desktop PCs. Figure 11-1 shows typical SO DIMM RAM.

Handheld computers and PDAs aren't as standardized as laptops, so upgrading the built-in memory on these types of portables usually means that you must use manufacturer-supplied RAM if it's possible at all. You can upgrade storage capacity, on the other hand, using add-on flash memory cards of the type used on digital cameras and other electronic devices.

FIGURE 11.1   SO DIMM RAM

Hard Drives

ATA hard drives in the 2.5-inch drive format now rule in laptops. Although much smaller than regular ATA drives, they use the same features and configurations. Figure 11-2 shows a laptop's hard drive (left) compared to a standard 3.25-inch desktop hard drive.

Some manufacturers might use special settings, such as requiring the drive to use the cable select setting instead of master or slave configuration, but otherwise these types of hard drives are installed, partitioned, and formatted in exactly the same way as their larger 3.25-inch brethren.

CPUs

Both Intel and AMD have long sold specialized, modular CPUs for laptops, yet many folks don't realize they can easily upgrade many systems by removing the old module and replacing it with a new one, as shown in Figure 11-3. Always follow the manufacturer's specifications when upgrading a laptop CPU!

FIGURE 11.2   A 2.5-inch laptop hard drive (left) and a standard desktop hard drive

FIGURE 11.3   Modular laptop CPU

Typically, CPUs can't be replaced on handheld computers or PDAs. A call to your vendor's tech support line or a visit to their web site can tell you whether or not you can replace a portable's processor.

Other Devices

Some laptop manufacturers take advantage of the *mini PCI* expansion bus to enable you to add components that didn't come pre-installed, such as modems, NICs, wireless Bluetooth adapters, and sound cards. Figure 11-4 shows a tech adding an expansion card to the mini PCI bus in a laptop.

Other devices, such as video adapters, are usually soldered directly onto the laptops' motherboard, but some vendors enable you to replace these units. The best way to determine your repair and upgrade options for a laptop is to make a call to the vendor's tech support line or visit its web site.

PC Cards

The majority of portable laptop and handheld computers accept devices through the *PC Card* slot. PC Cards are hot-swappable devices, roughly the size of a credit card, that add a variety of functions to portable computers. Although originally visualized as memory cards, today PC Cards hold modems, NICs,

FIGURE 11.4 Installing an expansion card on the mini PCI bus

hard drives, digital cameras, sound cards, SCSI controllers, and any number of other devices. Figure 11-5 shows a few PC Card devices.

Local Lingo

PCMCIA The PCMCIA (Personal Computer Memory Card International Association) organization defines the standards for PC Card devices.

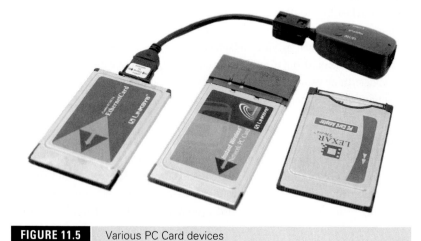

FIGURE 11.5 Various PC Card devices

PCMCIA Card Sizes

PC Card devices come in three different physical sizes, as determined by the PCMCIA Organization. They are Type I, Type II, and Type III. The PCMCIA standard recommends, rather than mandates, that certain sizes of cards perform certain functions, but most PC card makers follow these recommendations. Table 11-1 describes the typical functions for which each PC Card type is used.

The only difference among these three types is the thickness of the card. All PC Cards share the same 68-pin interface, and assuming the slot is able to accept the card, any PC Card will work in that slot. Type II cards are by far the most common type of PC Cards. Most laptops have two Type II slots—one above the other—so they can accept two Type I or II cards or one Type III card, as shown in Figure 11-6.

Many PC Card makers advertise a Type IV slot. This slot is not part of the PCMCIA standard. The Type IV slot is used to describe any PC Card thicker than the Type III.

PCMCIA Standard

The PCMCIA standard defines two levels of software drivers to support PC Cards. The first, lower level is known as socket services. *Socket services* are device drivers used to support the PC Card socket, enabling the system to detect when a PC Card is inserted or removed, and providing the necessary I/O to the device. Socket services are standardized and are handled by the System BIOS. Windows itself handles all card services and has a large pre-installed base of PC Card device drivers, although most PC Cards come with their own drivers.

The second, higher level of software drivers, known as *card services,* recognizes the function of the particular PC Card in the slot and provides the specialized drivers necessary to make the card work.

PC Card devices are completely plug and play and take advantage of technologies such as *Advanced Power Management (APM)* and DMA when

TABLE 11.1	Types of PC Cards			
PC Card Type	**Length**	**Width**	**Thickness**	**Typical Function**
Type I	85.6 mm	54.0 mm	3.3 mm	Flash memory
Type II	85.6 mm	54.0 mm	5.0 mm	I/O devices (modem, NIC, etc.)
Type III	85.6 mm	54.0 mm	10.5 mm	Hard drives

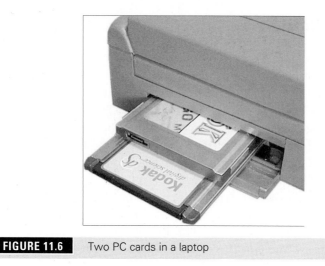

FIGURE 11.6   Two PC cards in a laptop

matched with a compatible computer system. The PCMCIA standard also enables PC Cards to perform multiple functions simultaneously, meaning that a single PC Card device may serve as a NIC and a modem at the same time.

PC Card devices operate at fairly low voltage. The original PCMCIA standard called for PC Card devices to operate at 5 volts. The latest release of the standard adds support for 3.3-volt operation. A physical keying mechanism prevents you from inserting a 3.3-volt device into a 5-volt socket.

CardBus

The newest type of PC Card is called *CardBus*. CardBus provides a 32-bit multiplexed address/data path operating at PCI local-bus speeds of up to 33 MHz. CardBus uses the synchronous burst-transfer orientation of PCI and what is essentially a PCI bus protocol. This means CardBus devices are capable of acting as system-bus masters. This compares to PC Cards, which use an 8- or 16-bit interface operating at ISA bus speeds (8 MHz) and an ISA-like asynchronous protocol.

A single CardBus card can perform up to eight functions. Regular PC Cards can perform a maximum of two functions. An example of a two-function PC card is a modem/network PC card. Thanks to CardBus, don't be surprised if you can purchase a modem/network/ISDN/sound/SCSI combo card.

CardBus uses the same form factors and the same 68-pin connector as a regular PC Card. This allows a regular PC Card to work in a CardBus slot; however, a CardBus card won't work in a regular PC card socket. In fact, because CardBus uses 3.3-volt power instead of the regular 5-volt PC card power, CardBus cards have special keying that prevents you from accidentally plugging one into a regular PC Card socket.

Finally, for CardBus to operate, the laptop should be running Windows 95 OSR2 or later. Practically all modern portable computers have at least one CardBus slot in addition to any standard PC Card slots.

USB Portable Storage

Although not strictly limited to use on portable computers, USB portable storage drives, usually called *thumb drives* or *flash drives,* are very popular among laptop computer users. Figure 11-7 shows a typical USB portable storage drive.

Ranging in capacity from 8 MB to over 2 GB, USB portable storage drives provide a fast and convenient way to back up and transport files between systems.

USB portable storage drives use Flash memory and operate at the speed of the USB bus—up to 480 MBps using Hi-Speed USB 2.0. USB portable storage drives plug directly into an available USB port and are instantly recognized by all modern versions of Windows as a removable storage device. USB portable storage drives come from the factory formatted with FAT to ensure compatibility with all popular operating systems. Windows 2000/XP enable you to format USB portable storage drives with NTFS to take advantage of NTFS' security and compression features.

Features that you may find on USB portable storage drives include security software (enabling you to "lock" drives formatted with FAT against unauthorized usage), e-mail clients, backup software, and even MP3 music players.

Objective 11.02 Power Management

In early portable computers, every component drew power continuously, whether or not the system needed that device at that time. The hard drive

FIGURE 11.7   USB portable storage drive

would continue to spin whether or not it was being accessed, for example, and the screen would continue to display, even when nobody was actively using the system. Modern systems use specialized hardware, the BIOS, and the OS itself to enable *power management* functions.

System Management Mode

Intel's 386SX CPU was the first to employ power management features. These new features, collectively called *System Management Mode (SMM)*, allowed the CPU to slow down or stop its clock without erasing the register information and supported power saving in peripherals. From its humble beginnings in the 386SX, SMM slowly started to show up in more CPUs and is now common.

Using only a power-saving CPU meant power management was relegated to special sleep or doze buttons that would stop the CPU and all the peripherals on the laptop. To take real advantage of SMM, you must also have a specialized BIOS and operating system. To this end, Intel proposed the Advanced Power Management (APM) specification in 1992 and the *Advanced Configuration and Power Interface (ACPI)* standard in 1996.

Requirements for APM/ACPI

APM and ACPI require four features to function fully:

- The first requirement is an SMM-capable CPU, which virtually all CPUs now are.
- The second requirement is an *APM-compliant BIOS*, which enables the CPU to shut off the peripherals as desired.
- The third requirement is devices that will accept being shut off. These devices are usually called *Energy Star* devices, which signals their compliance with the EPA's Energy Star standard. To be an Energy Star device, a peripheral must have the capability to shut down without actually turning off.
- Finally, the system's operating system must know how to request that a particular device be shut down and the CPU's clock be slowed down or stopped.

ACPI goes beyond the APM standard by supplying support for hot-swappable devices, always a huge problem with APM. This feature aside, it's a challenge to tell the difference between an APM system and an ACPI system at first glance.

APM/ACPI Levels

The APM specification defines five different power usage operating levels for a system: Full On, APM Enabled, APM Standby, APM Suspend, and Off. These levels are left intentionally fuzzy to give manufacturers considerable leeway in their use.

- **Full On**   Everything in the system running at full power. No power management.

- **APM Enabled**   CPU and RAM running at full power. Power management enabled. An unused device may or may not be shut down.

- **APM Standby**   CPU is stopped. RAM still stores all programs. All peripherals are shut down, although configuration options are still stored, so you won't have to reinitialize the devices to get back to APM Enabled state.

- **APM Suspend**   Everything in the PC is shut down or at its lowest power consumption setting. Many systems use a special type of Suspend called *Hibernation,* where critical configuration information is written to the hard drive. Upon a wake-up event, the system is reinitialized and the data is read from the drive to return the system to the APM Enabled mode. The recovery time between Suspend and Enabled states is much longer than the time between Standby and Enabled states.

- **Off**   When in the Off state, your computer or device is powered down and inactive. Data and operational parameters may or may not be preserved.

ACPI handles all these levels, plus a few more, such as *Soft Power On/Off,* which enables you to define the function of the Power button.

Configuration of APM/ACPI

You configure APM/ACPI via CMOS settings or from within Windows. As with other CMOS settings, Windows settings override CMOS settings. Although the flexibility of APM/ACPI standards can cause some confusion among different implementations, some settings are usually part of CMOS configuration. First, CMOS can initialize power management, which enables the system to enter the APM Enabled mode. CMOS configuration often includes options for setting time frames for entering Standby and Suspend modes, as well as settings to determine which events take place in each of these modes. Finally, many CMOS versions include settings to determine wake-up events, such as directing the system to monitor a modem or a particular IRQ, as you can see in Figure 11-8.

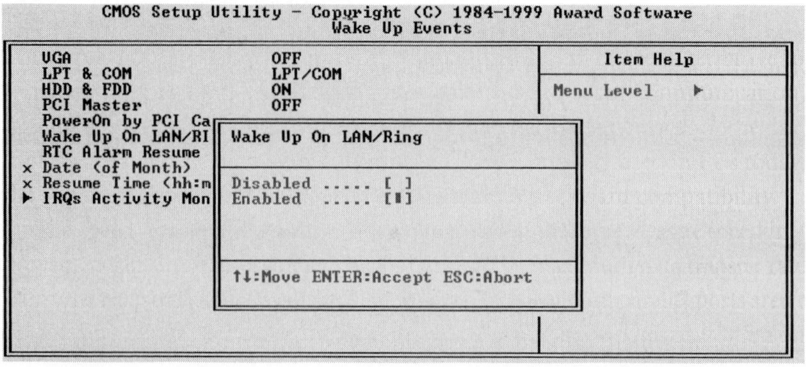

```
     CMOS Setup Utility - Copyright (C) 1984-1999 Award Software
                          Wake Up Events
 ┌─────────────────────────────────────────────────┬──────────────────────┐
 │  UGA                    OFF                       │    Item Help         │
 │  LPT & COM              LPT/COM                   │                      │
 │  HDD & FDD              ON                        │  Menu Level    ►     │
 │  PCI Master             OFF                       │                      │
 │  PowerOn by PCI Ca┌──────────────────────────┐   │                      │
 │  Wake Up On LAN/RI│ Wake Up On LAN/Ring       │  │                      │
 │  RTC Alarm Resume  │                          │  │                      │
 │ x Date (of Month) │                           │  │                      │
 │ x Resume Time (hh:m│ Disabled  ..... [ ]      │  │                      │
 │ ► IRQs Activity Mon│ Enabled   ..... [■]      │  │                      │
 │                    │                          │  │                      │
 │                    │                          │  │                      │
 │                    │                          │  │                      │
 │                    │ ↑↓:Move ENTER:Accept ESC:Abort│                    │
 │                    └──────────────────────────┘  │                      │
 └─────────────────────────────────────────────────┴──────────────────────┘
```

FIGURE 11.8   Setting a wake-up event in CMOS

A true ACPI-compliant CMOS provides an ACPI setup option. Figure 11-9 shows a typical modern BIOS that provides this setting.

APM/ACPI settings can be found in two areas in Windows 9x. Because the monitor is one of the biggest power users on a computer, a great place to start the power management configuration process is in the Control Panel. Select Display | Settings tab | Advanced Settings.

With the exception of adding the Suspend option to the Start button, Windows 9x hides the APM/ACPI Standby and Suspend features. Instead, Windows provides individual control for the big power eaters—monitors, PC Cards, and hard drives—and makes its own assumptions for everything else in the PC.

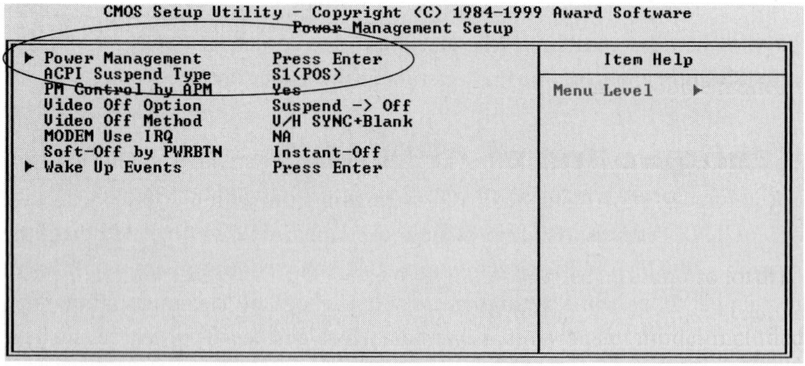

```
     CMOS Setup Utility - Copyright (C) 1984-1999 Award Software
                        Power Management Setup
 ┌─────────────────────────────────────────────────┬──────────────────────┐
 │  ► Power Management     Press Enter              │    Item Help         │
 │    ACPI Suspend Type    S1(POS)                  │                      │
 │    PM Control by APM    Yes                      │  Menu Level    ►     │
 │    Video Off Option     Suspend -> Off           │                      │
 │    Video Off Method     U/H SYNC+Blank           │                      │
 │    MODEM Use IRQ        NA                        │                      │
 │    Soft-Off by PWRBTN   Instant-Off              │                      │
 │  ► Wake Up Events       Press Enter              │                      │
 │                                                   │                      │
 │                                                   │                      │
 │                                                   │                      │
 │                                                   │                      │
 └─────────────────────────────────────────────────┴──────────────────────┘
```

FIGURE 11.9   CMOS with ACPI setup option

These controls can be found in the Power section of the Control Panel, as shown in Figure 11-10.

Windows 2000/XP systems support the same power conservation functions, plus they add another option called *Hibernation*. Note that in Windows 2000/XP, the Suspend option is called *Standby* but otherwise operates the same as Suspend in Windows 9x.

One of the drawbacks to using Suspend (or Standby) is that the computer system's memory is still active. If the PC completely loses power while in Suspend mode, any unsaved work is lost. Hibernation solves this problem. When Hibernation kicks in, the contents of RAM are written to a file on the hard drive, called HIBERFIL.SYS, and the system shuts down. Restarting the system causes the system state to be restored from the HIBERFIL.SYS file exactly as it was when the system shut down.

To take advantage of Hibernation, you must have enough free disk space to accommodate the contents of RAM. In other words, if your system has 512 MB of RAM, you need at least that much free space on your hard drive.

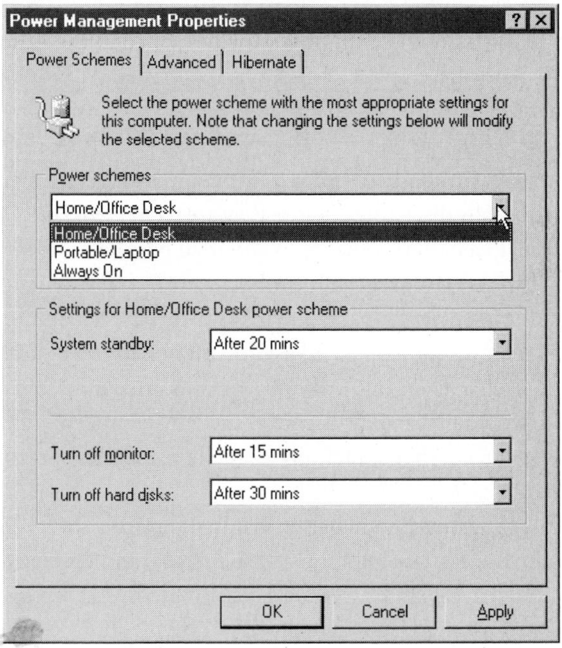

Power Management Properties

Power Schemes | Advanced | Hibernate

Select the power scheme with the most appropriate settings for this computer. Note that changing the settings below will modify the selected scheme.

Power schemes

Home/Office Desk

Home/Office Desk
Portable/Laptop
Always On

Settings for Home/Office Desk power scheme

System standby: After 20 mins

Turn off monitor: After 15 mins

Turn off hard disks: After 30 mins

OK | Cancel | Apply

FIGURE 11.10   Power management controls

Objective 11.03   Batteries

The thing that makes portable computers portable is their mobile power source, the battery. Different types of batteries all have different benefits and needs.

Three types of batteries are commonly used in portable PCs, handhelds, and PDAs: *nickel-cadmium (Ni-Cd), nickel-metal hydride (NiMH),* and *lithium-ion (Li-Ion).* Another type of portable power source called a *fuel cell* battery is finding its way into the PC market but currently is not common. Let's investigate each of these types.

Nickel-Cadmium (Ni-Cd)

Ni-Cd batteries were the first type of battery able to provide portable computers with the steady supply of voltage that they need and were widely used in early portable PCs. However, Ni-Cds were far from an ideal solution. For one thing, they weren't capable of holding a sufficient charge to power the computer for more than a couple of hours even under the best of conditions. Real-life usage with frequent hard drive and CD-ROM activity drained Ni-Cd batteries in about half that time. Another problem that plagued Ni-Cds is something called *battery memory.*

Battery memory is a tendency for Ni-Cd batteries to "remember" the level at which they are usually discharged before they are recharged. For example, if you consistently use up a battery's charge to about 70 percent of its capacity before hooking it up to a charger, eventually the battery will start behaving as if it *needs* to be recharged at 70 percent capacity, thereby wasting the remaining 30 percent!

To prevent memory problems, a Ni-Cd battery had to be discharged completely before each recharging. Another fix was to purchase a *conditioning* charger, which would first totally discharge the Ni-Cd battery and then generate a special reverse current that electrically cleaned the internal parts of the battery. This is referred to as *deep cycling* the battery.

Another knock against Ni-Cd batteries is that they're not very robust. Ni-Cd batteries would, at best, last for about 1000 charges, and far fewer if they were subjected to rough use. Ni-Cds were also sensitive to overcharging—a very real danger because Ni-Cd chargers aren't very "smart" about determining how much of a charge the battery requires. Ni-Cds were also extremely susceptible to high temperatures, so storing your laptop in the trunk of a car for more than a few hours would usually result in a dead battery.

Ni-Cd batteries didn't stop causing trouble after they died. The highly toxic metals inside the battery made it unacceptable to simply throw them in the trash. Ni-Cd batteries must be disposed of via specialized disposal companies—most recycling centers and many battery manufacturers and distributors are glad to take them. For the most part, Ni-Cd batteries aren't used in computer devices much anymore, although you'll still find them in many consumer electronics devices.

Nickel Metal Hydride (NiMH)

NiMH batteries were the next generation of mobile PC batteries and are still quite common today. Basically, NiMH batteries are like Ni-Cd batteries without most of the headaches. NiMH batteries are much less susceptible to memory problems, are less susceptible to overcharging (because they take advantage of *smart battery* technology, explained in the next section), and last longer between rechargings. Like Ni-Cd batteries, however, NiMH batteries don't tolerate heat well and have limited capacity.

While they're considered nontoxic to the environment, it's still a good idea to do a special disposal. Unlike Ni-Cds, NiMH batteries usually respond best to shallow recharges, or *topping off*, as opposed to a complete discharge/recharge. NiMH batteries are popular replacement batteries for Ni-Cd systems.

Lithium Ion (Li-Ion)

The most common type of battery used today is Li-Ion. These batteries are extremely powerful, are completely immune to memory problems, and provide power for twice as long on a charge as Ni-Cd or NiMH batteries (up to four hours on systems using power management). They also carry a charge longer than Ni-Cd or NiMH batteries when not in use, and it's not unusual to be able to power up a laptop that's been sitting idle for days or even weeks!

Li-Ion batteries are susceptible to overcharging damage and in fact will explode if they're overcharged! For this reason, all Li-Ion batteries use *smart battery* technology (explained next) and have built-in circuitry to prevent accidental overcharging. Lithium batteries can be used only on systems designed to use them; and they can't be used as replacement batteries for the older types.

Smart Batteries

To provide better maintenance for laptop batteries, manufacturers have developed a new type of battery technology called the *smart battery*. NiMH and Li-Ion batteries incorporate smart battery technology. With previous, non-smart batteries, the computer had to make a guess at the battery's capacity and charge state. Smart batteries contain built-in circuitry that communicates with the computer to tell it when they need to be charged, conditioned, or replaced.

Fuel Cell Batteries

The biggest problem with current PC battery technology is that manufacturers have pretty much reached the limits of what they can do in terms of capacity and storage life. To address this, a new type of battery called a *fuel cell* has been developed, but it is still not widely available.

Fuel cell batteries use a replenishable liquid fuel source to produce electricity without the need for charging. Chemical reactions between the fuel solution, oxygen, and metal catalysts within the battery housing produce instant electricity. Once the charge in the battery is spent, instead of hooking it up to a recharging device, you simply replace the fuel supply and you're ready to go.

The type of fuel cell battery designed for portable computers uses *direct methanol fuel cell (DMFC)* technology. A fuel mixture of liquid methanol and water is packaged in removable fuel cartridges that are simply plugged into the battery housing. Current DMFC batteries are capable of providing slightly more battery life than Li-Ion batteries, topping out at roughly five hours of juice. DMFC batteries can carry a charge indefinitely when not used. The exciting thing about this technology, however, lies in what's coming down the line. Next-generation DMFC batteries are said to run for up to ten hours, with some capable of forty hours of operation!

Battery Maintenance Guidelines

In general, remember five basic rules to safely extend the life of your portable computer's battery.

- First, always store batteries in a cool place. Although a freezer might sound like an excellent storage place, moisture, metal racks, and foodstuffs make it a bad idea.
- Second, use only conditioning chargers for your Ni-Cd and NiMH batteries—they'll last longer.
- Third, keep battery contacts clean with a little alcohol or a dry cloth.
- Fourth, *never* handle a battery that has ruptured or broken—battery chemicals are extremely dangerous.
- Fifth, always recycle old batteries.

Objective 11.04 Docking Stations and Port Replicators

Until recently, it was almost always true that a person who owned a portable PC also had a desktop PC. You could take your portable to a job site or on a trip—and that was cool—but when you wanted to get real work done, you used your desktop computer. To keep these multiple-PC users on the near side of sanity, Microsoft and other vendors provide a number of handy tools such as the Microsoft Briefcase to assist you in synchronizing the data on your laptop with the data on your PC.

The power of laptops has gotten great enough, and the cost low enough, to tempt many people to forgo the desktop PC entirely and replace it with a laptop. While simple on the surface, this solution presents a number of challenges. For example, a laptop computer selected for its light weight and portability might be uncomfortable to work on for extended periods because of its small screen and keyboard. It may also be inconvenient to have to reattach printers, network cables, modem cables, scanners, and other devices to the portable computer every time you wish to transport it.

Recognizing this problem, manufacturers of portable PCs provide devices called *docking stations* and *port replicators.* The docking station is a base that sits on your desk and has connections for printers, mice, display monitors, and so on. Further, many docking stations have integrated hardware devices that might not exist on the laptop, such as floppy disk drives, CD or DVD media drives, additional hard drives, network connections, and so on. A special port connector on the back or bottom of the laptop, shown in Figure 11-11, matches up to a connector on the docking station.

Simply lock the laptop into place and the attached peripherals come to life. Figure 11-12 shows a typical laptop connected to a docking station.

| **FIGURE 11.11** | Docking station port connector |

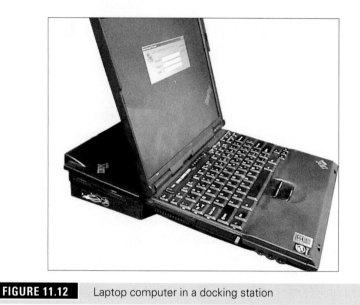

FIGURE 11.12 Laptop computer in a docking station

Port replicators are similar in function and design to docking stations, except that they don't offer any additional devices or connections. Port replicators are simply a convenient way of collecting all of your I/O port connectors—keyboard, mouse, printer, and so on—into a single device that connects to the appropriate piece of hardware on your desktop.

Hardware Profiles

Docking stations provide fantastic convenience, but there's a catch—the laptop has to know what hardware is available on the docking station and be able to use that equipment. By the same token, once the laptop is disconnected, it must know what hardware *isn't* available anymore. Windows handles this problem via *hardware profiles.*

A hardware profile is a preconfigured list of devices Windows automatically enables or disables in the Device Manager, depending on what devices the system detects. The user can also manually choose a profile from a list at boot-up, as shown in Figure 11-13.

The manual method has become less prominent because smarter laptops can detect their current state and easily choose the proper profile via the plug and play process. Both Windows 9x/Me and Windows 2000/XP configure their hardware profiles in the System Properties applet. Figure 11-14 shows the hard-

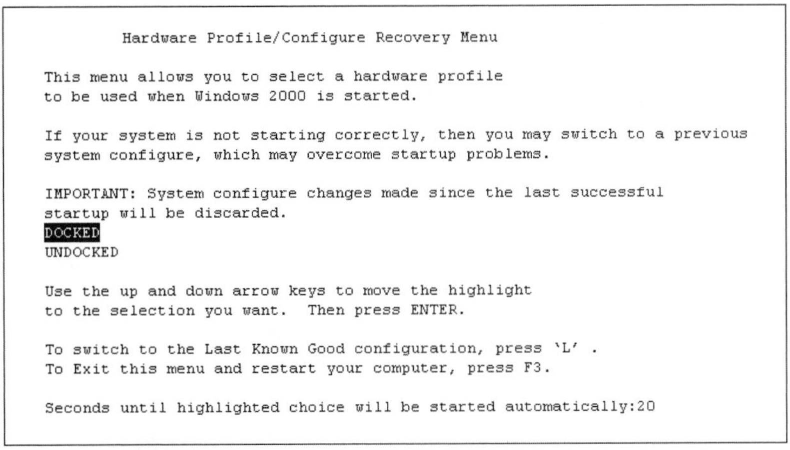

```
            Hardware Profile/Configure Recovery Menu

This menu allows you to select a hardware profile
to be used when Windows 2000 is started.

If your system is not starting correctly, then you may switch to a previous
system configure, which may overcome startup problems.

IMPORTANT: System configure changes made since the last successful
startup will be discarded.
DOCKED
UNDOCKED

Use the up and down arrow keys to move the highlight
to the selection you want.  Then press ENTER.

To switch to the Last Known Good configuration, press 'L' .
To Exit this menu and restart your computer, press F3.

Seconds until highlighted choice will be started automatically:20
```

FIGURE 11.13   Boot-up hardware profile list

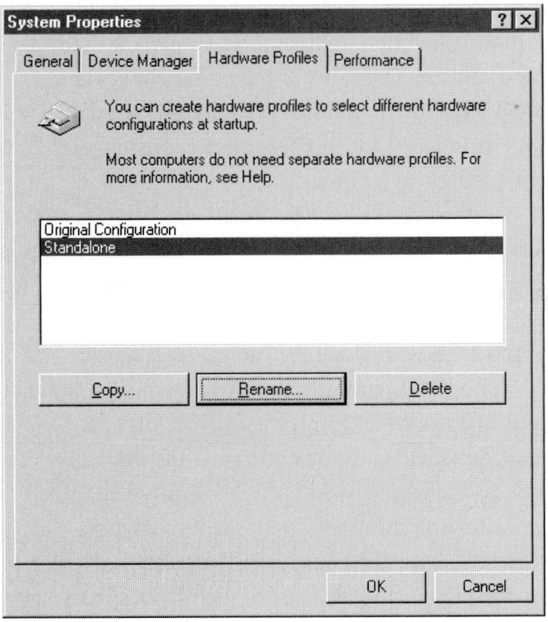

System Properties

General | Device Manager | Hardware Profiles | Performance

You can create hardware profiles to select different hardware configurations at startup.

Most computers do not need separate hardware profiles. For more information, see Help.

Original Configuration
Standalone

Copy...   Rename...   Delete

OK   Cancel

FIGURE 11.14   Hardware profiles

ware profiles for a laptop running Windows 98. One profile is for what this user calls *Stand-alone*—not connected to the docking station. The other hardware profile is used when the laptop is connected to the docking station.

In theory, you can create hardware profiles for any system, but in reality, hardware profiles are for laptops. In fact, the hardware profiles features in Windows 2000/XP simply assume that if you use hardware profiles, you're using a laptop. The only trick to hardware profiles is that some devices show as disabled in the Device Manager, depending on which profile is active. Don't panic if you see a red *X* on a device in Device Manager on a laptop—this might only mean a particular device isn't being used by the current profile!

Objective 10.05 Handheld Computers and PDAs

Handheld computers and PDAs are listed separately from portable laptops because they run different operating systems specifically designed for their particular platform. The most popular run either the Palm OS or one of Microsoft's chopped-down versions of Windows designed specifically for portables. These include Windows CE (and the most recent version, Windows CE .NET), Pocket PC (or, as it's now called, Windows Mobile), and a special mobile version of Windows XP called XP Embedded. The Palm OS is better suited to users who simply want an information manager and editor. Windows versions offer more in the way of multimedia, including music and video recording and playback.

Popular models of PDAs include the Palm Zire, Tungsten, and M-series (running Palm OS), HP's iPAQ (running Pocket PC), and many others. Handhelds running versions of Windows CE include the HP Jornada, NEC MobilPro, and others. Currently, handheld computers running the Embedded version of Windows XP are special-purpose devices used in industrial and retail inventory control, diskless workstations, information kiosks, and the like.

Handhelds and PDAs use the same type of batteries that laptop computers use, the most common being Li-Ion. Because of their reduced functionality, these devices are able to get significantly more working time out of batteries, typically in the 7- to 10-hour range. Popular microprocessors include Motorola's DragonBall series, the Texas Instruments ARM-based processor, and the Intel XScale processor running at speeds ranging from 16 MHz up to over 400 MHz. RAM capacity varies from 8 MB to about 128 MB. Devices running Window CE or Pocket PC typically require the more powerful hardware.

Most have color displays, run specialized productivity and communication applications (such as Microsoft Pocket Word and Pocket Outlook), and accept add-on components such as modems, network adapters, Bluetooth adapters, digital cameras, and *global positioning satellite (GPS)* systems, among many others.

Handhelds and PDAs aren't meant to replace desktop or laptop systems running full versions of Windows, but to augment them. They enable you to transport and edit important files and contact lists, manage appointments and tasks, take memos, and even access corporate networks and the Internet while away from your desk. Data is kept consistent between your desktop and your PDA or handheld through *synchronizing*.

Synchronizing Handhelds and PDAs

Synchronizing your handheld computer or PDA with your desktop or laptop PC transfers data between the two systems, keeping them, as the name implies, in sync with each other. Synchronizing software supplied by the vendor of the handheld or PDA, such as Palm's HotSync Manager or Microsoft ActiveSync, handles communication between the devices.

Synchronizing Software

In addition to acting as a conduit between your PC and handheld computer or PDA, the synchronization software enables you to do such things as install applications and configure synchronization preferences and profiles. It also provides you with an alternate interface to the device's data. Figure 11-15 shows ActiveSync's Sync Options configuration screen, which enables you to specify which data to synchronize between the PDA and the PC.

Synchronizing Hardware

PDAs and handhelds connect to the PC through a special *sync cable* or *cradle* that attaches to the serial port or an available USB port. The cable or cradle, in turn, connects to contacts on the portable device to transfer data into and out of the PDA or handheld. The advantage of a sync cradle over a cable is that it also acts as a battery charger for the portable device—sync cables only sync the data.

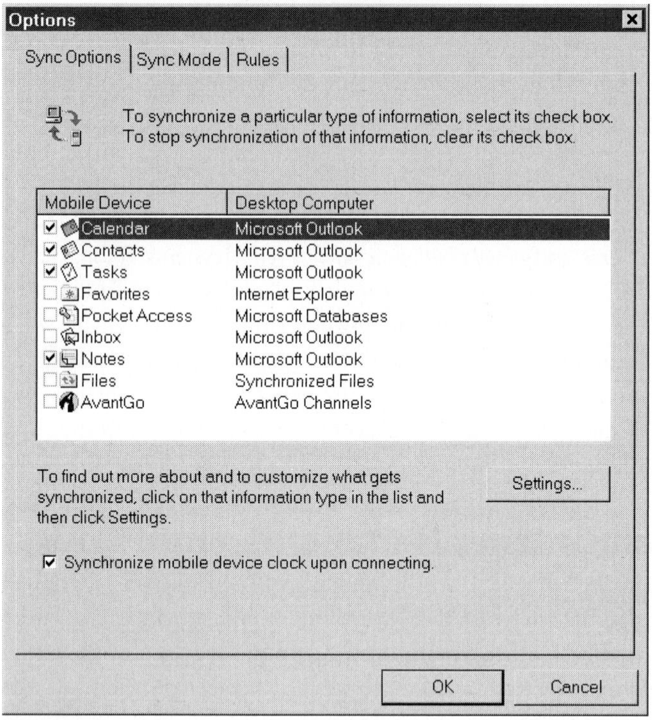

FIGURE 11.15 ActiveSync Sync Options configuration screen

The synchronizing process can be initiated by pressing a button on the sync cable or cradle. Figure 11-16 shows a PDA synchronizing with a laptop PC.

Synchronization is also possible through remote and wireless connections such as infrared, modem, 802.11-based wireless Ethernet, and Bluetooth, provided that your device has the appropriate hardware available. The key points of these wireless technologies will be discussed in Chapter 13, but generally speaking, you simply configure your PDA or handheld to use the alternate connection to synchronize instead of the sync cable or cradle.

For example, to configure Palm OS-based devices to synchronize via infrared, select HotSync from the System menu, and then choose Connection to change the synchronization configuration to IR to a PC/Handheld. Pocket PC devices are configured similarly—select Start, then ActiveSync, and then Tools to change the default synchronization setting to infrared or other. Figure 11-17 shows these options on a Handspring Visor and a Compaq iPAQ.

FIGURE 11.16 PDA synchronizing with laptop

Configuring devices to use a modem, a wireless 802.11-based Ethernet connection, or Bluetooth is very similar, except that you must specify the name and IP address of the computer that you wish to sync up with.

FIGURE 11.17 Changing synchronization settings on Palm OS and Pocket PC

CHECKPOINT

✔**Objective 11.01: Configuration** Most portables are made up of proprietary components, although if you look hard enough, you can find modular replacement components. Know how to replace or upgrade RAM, hard drives, modular CPUs, and video cards, as well as PCMCIA (PC) and CardBus cards. Also know the three types of PC Cards and how they differ from one another.

✔**Objective 11.02: Power Management** Understand the APM (Advanced Power Management) and ACPI (Advanced Configuration and Power Interface) standards. The five power usage operating levels defined by the APM specification are Full On, APM Enabled, APM Standby, APM Suspend (Hibernate), and Off. The biggest advantage of ACPI is that it supports hot-swappable devices.

✔**Objective 11.03: Batteries** Three types of batteries are commonly used in mobile PCs: Nickel-Cadmium (Ni-Cd), Nickel-Metal Hydride (NiMH), and Lithium-Ion (Li-Ion). The most common type used today is Li-Ion. Modern Li-Ion batteries provide about four hours of continuous use and can carry a charge for days or weeks when not in use. The most common type of fuel cell battery uses direct methanol fuel cell (DMFC) technology. Instead of being recharged, fuel cell batteries use replenishable liquid fuel cartridges. Current DMFC batteries provide about five hours of use; future generations are said to provide up to forty hours of juice.

✔**Objective 11.04: Docking Stations and Port Replicators** Docking stations enable laptops to maintain consistent connections to resources such as networks, printers, and mass storage drives. Laptops that connect to docking stations use hardware profiles to determine what devices are available. A hardware profile is a list of devices that Windows automatically enables or disables in the Device Manager, depending on what devices the laptop detects. Port replicators are similar to docking stations, except that they simply duplicate the ports that exist on your laptop.

✔**Objective 11.05: Handheld Computers and PDAs** Handheld computers and PDAs are distinguished from portable laptops by the fact that they run either a specialized version of Windows (such as Windows CE) or the Palm OS. Handhelds and PDAs enable you to transport and edit data from your desktop or laptop PC and synchronize changes using special synchronizing software and hardware. Sync cables are used only to synchronize data between devices. Sync cradles synchronize data and also provide a power source for recharging your devices' batteries.

REVIEW QUESTIONS

1. Which of the following is not true about PC Cards?
   A. Socket Services need to be set to detect whether a card is installed.
   B. PCMCIA services must be set up in CMOS.
   C. Card Services need to be set up to detect the function of the card installed.
   D. PC Cards are hot-swappable.

2. How many Type III cards can typically fit into a laptop at one time?
   A. 1
   B. 2
   C. 3
   D. 4

3. How do you correct the battery memory condition in a Ni-Cd battery? (Choose two.)
   A. Use a conditioning charger.
   B. Place the battery in a freezer overnight.
   C. Completely discharge the battery before recharging it.
   D. Recharge the battery any time its capacity drops below 50 percent.

4. NiMH batteries can be used as replacements for what type of battery?
   A. Ni-Cd batteries
   B. Li-Ion batteries
   C. DMFC fuel cell batteries
   D. NiMH batteries can be used only as replacements for other NiMH batteries

5. What is the difference between a docking station and a port replicator?
   A. Port replicators can provide connections and devices that don't exist on the laptop; docking stations provide only connections that exist on the laptop.

   B. Docking stations can provide connections and devices that don't exist on the laptop; port replicators provide only connections that exist on the laptop.

   C. Docking stations work only on Windows laptops; port replicators only work on laptops running the Macintosh OS.

   D. There is no difference between docking stations and port replicators.

6. How many Type II cards can typically fit into a laptop at one time?

   A. 1

   B. 2

   C. 3

   D. 4

7. Which of the following is not possible?

   A. Having two Type II cards in a laptop at one time

   B. Having a Type I card and a Type II card in a laptop at one time

   C. Having two Type I cards in a laptop at one time

   D. Having a Type II card and a Type III card in a laptop at one time

8. Which of the following are valid methods to synchronize a PDA with a laptop computer? (Choose all that apply.)

   A. Sync cable or cradle

   B. Infrared

   C. Wireless Ethernet (with the appropriate network adapter)

   D. Wireless Bluetooth (with the appropriate Bluetooth adapter)

9. Which of the following is *not* a recommended maintenance procedure for laptop batteries?

   A. Keep the contacts clean using alcohol or a dry cloth.

   B. Store them in the freezer if they won't be used for a long period of time.

   C. Recycle them according to the manufacturer's specifications.

   D. Store them in a cool place.

10. How many pins do PC Cards have?

   A. 30

   B. 40

   C. 68

   D. 168

REVIEW ANSWERS

1. **B**   There's no need to set up PCMCIA services in CMOS.

2. **A**   Only one Type III PC Card can fit into a laptop at a time because of the thickness of these cards.

3. **A** **C**   Use a conditioning charger or completely discharge a battery before recharging to correct battery memory.

4. **A**   NiMH batteries can be used as replacements for Ni-Cd batteries.

5. **B**   Docking stations enable the laptop to use connections and devices such as removable storage drives and network connections that may not exist on the laptop. Port replicators simply duplicate the existing ports.

6. **B**   A typical laptop can fit two Type II cards at the same time.

7. **D**   If you use a Type III card, no other card will fit into the socket.

8. **A** **B** **C** **D**   All of these methods are valid for synchronizing a PDA with a laptop computer, assuming that they are equipped with the appropriate hardware.

9. **B**   Storing batteries in the freezer for a long period of time isn't advisable because of the presence of moisture, metal racks, and food.

10. **C**   There are 68 pins on PC cards and sockets.

Networks: Wired Networking

	NEWBIE	SOME EXPERIENCE	EXPERT
ETA	3 hours	2 hours	1 hour

No PC is an island. To truly experience the power of computers, you have to hook them up to other computers. Networking is the name of the game, and Windows PCs play the game very well indeed! Networking enables different users to share resources such as printers, scanners, files, and Internet connections. Computer networks are an integral part of any business environment. Not only that, but more and more multi-computer homes are using networks to get the most out of their PC investment.

Networks range in size from the smallest and simplest network of all—two computers connected together—to the largest and most complex network of all—the Internet. As an A+ certified PC tech, you'll have many opportunities to put your networking knowledge to use. This chapter runs you through the basics of networking hardware, topologies, and protocols.

Travel Advisory

This chapter touches briefly on the software components needed for a functional network, but you'll find the majority of that discussion in Chapter 17, "Networking in Windows."

Objective 12.01 Networking Components for the PC

Networks need hardware to move data between computers. The network adapter, or *network interface card (NIC)*, links the PC to the rest of the networking hardware. NICs come in wired and wireless varieties, meaning that they either use physical network cabling (such as Ethernet or Token Ring) or some sort of wireless technology (such as infrared or radio waves) to transfer data. Next, you must install appropriate networking software—a network *client*, and one or more protocols. These enable your PC to access network services and resources.

Installing Network Adapters and Drivers

Installing a NIC into any version of Windows is usually a no-brainer, because most NICs today are completely plug and play. For the most part, this is simply a matter of turning off the PC, installing the card into an available expansion bus slot, and turning the system on again. If you are using a USB or PC Card NIC, then you don't even need to turn the system off! Simply insert it into the slot and wait for Windows plug and play to do its thing.

After the NIC is detected by Windows, supply the appropriate driver, and you're ready to go. The only trick is to remember that you should use the driver diskette that comes with the NIC, even if Windows offers to use its own drivers. Vendor-supplied NIC drivers are usually more up to date than the versions that ship with Windows.

All the issues discussed with respect to installing devices also hold true for NICs. If the NIC shows up in the Device Manager, you're done with this step. If it doesn't, you follow the normal hardware troubleshooting steps to resolve the problem. Figure 12-1 shows a typical network adapter, nicely installed in Windows 2000 Device Manager.

Legacy NICs might require you to configure system resources (I/O address, IRQ, DMA, and so on) manually. Some NICs require that you configure jumpers or DIP switches to set resources, but most are configurable through vendor-supplied setup utilities. This usually means that you have to boot the system into DOS or Safe Mode Command Prompt Only. Once configured with resources, install the device drivers using the Windows Control Panel's Add New

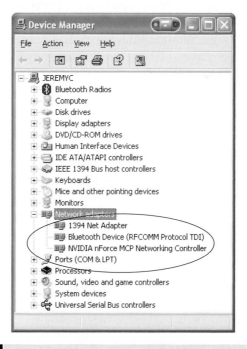

FIGURE 12.1   Windows 2000 showing a NIC installed

Hardware applet (also known as Add/Remove Hardware, in Windows 2000/XP). When prompted for a driver, instead of telling the applet to search for a driver, click the Have Disk button and insert the driver diskette or CD-ROM.

Legacy NICs are especially difficult to install on Windows NT/2000/XP systems due to those operating systems' compatibility requirements. Always confirm that the NIC you install is on the Hardware Compatibility List (HCL) before you crack the PC case open!

> ### Travel Advisory
> If the Hardware Compatibility List (HCL) does not contain the NIC, don't even bother to try to install the legacy card under Windows NT/2000/XP.

Keep in mind that many of the low-cost, no-name-brand Ethernet NICs use a driver called *NE2000-compatible*. Most of the time, the card then installs itself with a series of preset resources. Always verify that these settings don't wind up causing a resource conflict, because it's not unusual for these settings to be wrong!

The Link Between Networking Hardware and Data Packets

At this point, you've got all of the hardware in place that you need to access a network. There's more to it, of course, but we'll save the rest of this discussion for the operating system section of this book. Before we move on, however, let's briefly talk about the link between networking hardware and the data packets that they send out.

Every NIC in the world has a built-in identifier called a *Media Access Control (MAC)* address. The MAC address is a binary address that is unique for every network card. Yup, that's right! Every network card in the world has a unique MAC address. The MAC address is 48 bits long, giving over 281 *trillion* individual MAC addresses, so there are plenty of MAC addresses to go around. Note that on the vast majority of NICs, the MAC is hard-coded on to the card's circuitry and can't be reset. Some (very few) NICs permit you to configure this value in the card properties.

> ### Local Lingo
> **Packet**　A container for data that includes the MAC address of the sending NIC.
>
> **Frame**　A commonly used synonym for packet.

All the many varieties of data packets share certain common features.

- First, packets contain the MAC address of the network card to which the data is being sent.
- Second, they have the MAC address of the network card that sent the data.
- Third is the data itself (at this point, we have no idea what the data is—software handles that question), which can vary in size depending on the type of packet.
- Finally, there is some type of data check to enable the receiving network card to verify if the data was received in good order (Figure 12-2).

A detailed understanding of how data packets are assembled, addressed, sent out over the network, and then retrieved and reassembled at the other end isn't necessary for the CompTIA A+ Core PC Tech exam. That's what the Network+ exam is for! Just be sure that you understand that each data packet is "tagged" with the physical MAC address of the hardware that it originates from.

At this point, you're ready to plug a piece of network cable into the PC and connect to the network, right? But how does the PC communicate with another PC? You need software for that, specifically client services and software protocols. Let's glance at them now.

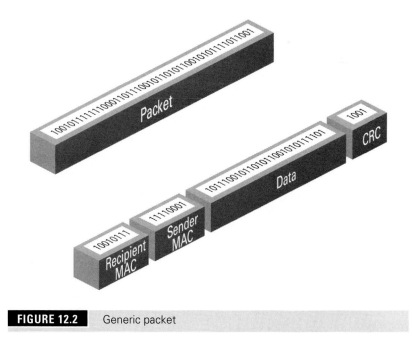

FIGURE 12.2 Generic packet

Client Service

The *client service* is the component that enables your computer to see and be seen on the network. If using NetBEUI or TCP/IP, use the *Client Service for Microsoft Networks.* NetWare users need to install the *Client Service for NetWare Networks.* Like the network protocols, the client service is also installed by default when you add a network adapter onto the PC.

Generally, there's not any configuration that you need to do, unless your network uses a nonstandard *Name Service Provider,* such as the *DCE Cell Directory Service.* This is rare, however, so typically all you have to do with the client service is to install it and let Windows handle it from there. Note that in Windows NT, the client service is called the *Workstation* service.

Software Protocols

Protocols handle the details of data transfer, such as making sure the sending PC packages the data properly in uniformly understood *packets,* and that the receiving PC knows how to put the data back together. Each protocol uses its own unique "language" for a packet, so packets created with one protocol cannot be read by another machine that does not have that protocol installed.

So which protocol should you use? It depends on the type of network you're running. For instance, if your network has servers running Novell's NetWare network operating system, then chances are you'll need the IPX/SPX protocol. Windows networks may use Microsoft's NetBEUI protocol, and networks using Macintosh systems may use AppleTalk. Note that most modern computer networks use the TCP/IP protocol. Why? Well, all modern computer systems, whether they're Windows, Macintosh, NetWare, or UNIX/Linux, are able to use it, so there's no platform-proprietary nonsense to have to wrestle with. Plus, TCP/IP is the *de facto* standard protocol for the Internet.

In a business environment, you'll typically work with network technicians who can tell you which protocol or protocols to install. Windows also helps by automatically installing certain protocols when you install hardware devices that will use them. For instance, Windows 95 automatically installs both the IPX/SPX and NetBEUI protocols whenever a network adapter is installed. Windows 98 and Windows 2000 automatically install TCP/IP. Should you need to install another protocol, go to the Network window in the Control Panel, select Add Protocol, and choose the protocol you want to install, as shown in Figure 12-3.

Depending on the protocol that you're using, you may also have to configure other settings. For example, you may have to configure a *network name* before you can access a NetBEUI network: AppleTalk may need you to set a *zone* name; IPX/SPX might require you to set the correct *network number* and *frame type;*

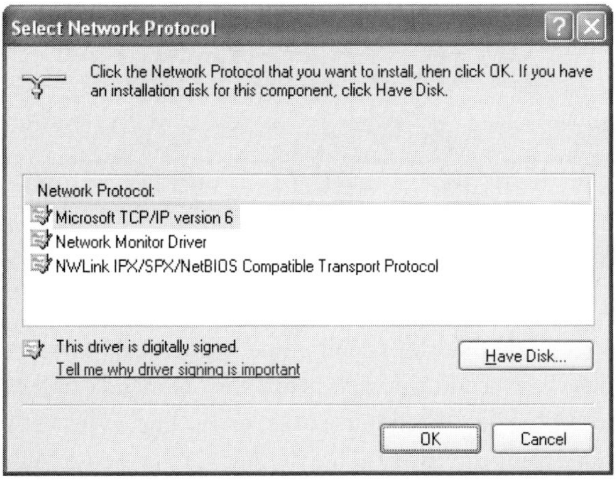

Select Network Protocol   [?][X]

Click the Network Protocol that you want to install, then click OK. If you have
an installation disk for this component, click Have Disk.

Network Protocol:
Microsoft TCP/IP version 6
Network Monitor Driver
NWLink IPX/SPX/NetBIOS Compatible Transport Protocol

This driver is digitally signed.
Tell me why driver signing is important   [Have Disk...]

                                              [OK]   [Cancel]

FIGURE 12.3   Adding a network protocol

and finally, TCP/IP may require that you configure a unique *IP address* and *subnet mask.* We'll touch on these subjects in Chapter 19.

Objective 12.02   Network Topologies

Even though most networks share the same basic look and feel, the way the data moves around inside those wires may be quite different from one network to the next. The *topology* of a network describes these different configurations of the cabling between computers.

Networks today use two main types of topologies: *bus* topology and *ring* topology. Other hybrid topologies that are popular are *star ring* and *star bus* topologies. Each of these topologies has advantages and disadvantages. The best topology for a specific situation depends on a variety of factors, including cost, speed, ease of installation, the physical position of the PCs, and the number of PCs in the network.

Bus Topology

The first type of topology was bus topology. Bus topology means all the PCs are connected via *single cable* that runs to all the PCs. Bus topologies look something like Figure 12-4.

Bus Topology

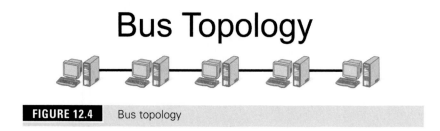

Bus topology

Bus topology works like a big telephone party line: all devices must first listen to see if anyone else is sending packets before they can send a packet. If the cable is not being used, the device sends its packet on the line. Every network card on the bus sees and reads the packet. This is called Carrier Sense Multiple Access/Collision Detection (CSMA/CD).

Sometimes two cards do talk at the same time. This is called a *collision,* and the cards themselves arbitrate to see who gets to resend its frames first.

Reflection and Termination

Data packets manifest as tiny electrical signals tapped out onto the network wire. Any time a device sends electrical voltage along a wire, some voltage bounces back or reflects when it reaches the end of the wire. This *reflection* poses a big problem for a bus topology network. As soon as one PC sends a packet, that packet will bounce off the end and back up the wire, making the cards that want to send data wait for no reason.

Worse, the endlessly reflecting packets create what's called a *packet storm,* which prevents other networked PCs from sending data. To prevent a packet storm, every bus network needs a device called a *terminator* plugged into each end of the bus cable. A terminator is a resistor that absorbs the signal, thus preventing reflection.

This need for termination is a weak spot in bus topology. If the cable breaks anywhere, a packet storm is instantly created and no device can send data, even if the break isn't between the devices exchanging data.

Ring Topology

A *ring topology* connects all the PCs together on a single cable, much like bus topology. As the name implies, however, this bus functions like a ring.

Ring topologies use a transmission method called *token passing.* In token passing, a minipacket, called a *token,* constantly passes from one card to the next in one direction, as shown in Figure 12-5. If one PC wants to talk to another, it

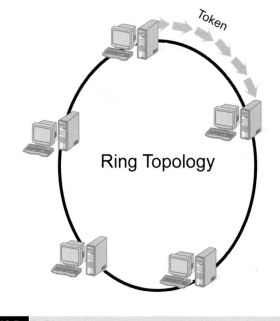

FIGURE 12.5 Ring topology uses token passing scheme

must wait until it gets the token. The PC's NIC then attaches data to the token and sends the packet back out the ring. If another PC wants to send data, it must wait until a free token (one that doesn't have an attached packet) comes around.

Because ring topologies use token passing, we tend to use the term *token ring* when describing ring networks. There were a few exceptions where a ring topology used features other than token passing, but they were few and are long gone. All current ring networks use an IBM-trademarked version of token passing called, rather appropriately, *Token Ring*. So, if it is a ring topology, it's Token Ring.

Star Ring

Token Ring topology was, if not invented, perfected and packaged by IBM. Token Ring actually uses a topology called *star ring*. Instead of running a ring of cable all around the LAN, the ring is stored inside a special box called a Multistation Access Unit (MSAU). We often just call it a *MAU* or *token ring hub* (although Token Ring techs would have a heart attack if you said it within earshot of them). Although Token Ring is a ring, it looks more like a star, as you can see in Figure 12-6.

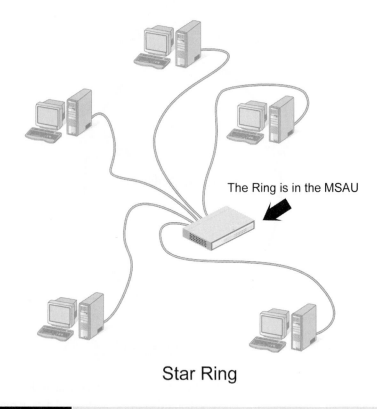

The Ring is in the MSAU

Star Ring

FIGURE 12.6   Star ring topology—the ring is inside the MSAU

Star Bus

The star configuration used in Token Ring made it dependable and easy to expand. This led to a variation of the bus topology called *star bus* topology. Imagine if you were to take a bus network and shrink the bus down so that it would fit inside a hub, as in Figure 12-7.

The bus topology would sure look a lot like a star, wouldn't it? This type of star bus topology is the single most popular topology today. Cheap and centralized, a star bus network does not go down if a cable breaks. True, the network would go down if the hub itself failed, but that doesn't happen often. Even if a hub fails, replacing a hub in a closet is much easier than tracing a bus running through walls and ceilings trying to find a break!

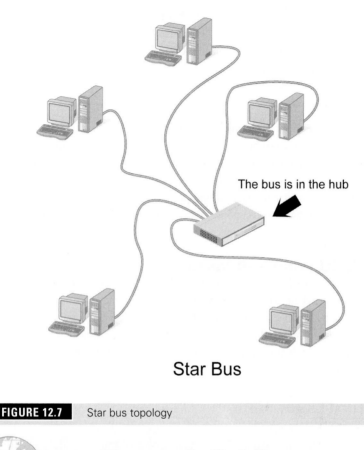

Star Bus

| FIGURE 12.7 | Star bus topology |

Objective 12.03 Network Cabling Standards

Now that we've looked at how PCs are made network-ready, we need to examine the connective components of networking. In the vast majority of networks, physical network cabling is the medium by which data packets are moved from one PC to the other. Wireless alternatives exist, as we'll see in Chapter 13, but at some point even wireless networks connect to a wired network "backbone."

Wired (and even wireless) networking hardware—the cabling, hubs, switches, routers, repeaters, and patch panels—must conform to standards defined by the IEEE organization. The two predominant standards are *Ethernet* and the previously mentioned *Token Ring.*

Ethernet

Ethernet is, by far, the more popular of the two networking standards. The Ethernet standard—now controlled by the *802* committee of the IEEE standards body—has appeared in several physical forms, such as 10Base5, 10-and 100-BaseT, 100BaseFX, and 802.11*x* wireless. There are significant differences between the forms, mainly in terms of cabling media and data throughput, but it's all Ethernet. This means that with the right hardware, you can mix and match without losing the ability to communicate.

Thick Ethernet—10Base5

The original Xerox Ethernet specification defined a specific type of cabling for the first Ethernet networks. This type of cable is called *thick Ethernet.* Thick Ethernet, also known as *ThickNet,* is a thick coaxial cable—about half an inch in diameter—manufactured under the *Belden 9580* standard. Belden is a *big* cable manufacturer, and their internal part number (9580) for thick Ethernet is a popular way to define ThickNet.

Local Lingo

Coaxial cable (Coax)   Coaxial cable consists of a center cable (core) surrounded by insulation. This, in turn, is covered with a shield of braided cable. The inner core actually carries the signal, and the shield effectively eliminates outside interference. The entire cable is then sheathed by a protective insulating cover.

ThickNet networks use a true bus topology, which means that all PCs attach to a single cable called the *segment.* ThickNet supports up to 100 devices hooked to one segment. The maximum length of one segment is 500 meters. 10Base5 networks have a maximum data throughput speed of 10 Mbps.

One of the important quirks of ThickNet to keep in mind is that devices must connect to the cable in some multiple of 2.5 meters. This is to reduce noise due to signal oscillation. ThickNet cabling is clearly marked every 2.5 meters to ensure proper device connection. Devices connect to ThickNet by means of a *vampire connector.* The vampire connector has sharp teeth that literally pierce the cable sheathing and contact the cable core when clamped into place.

ThickNet network adapters are different from other types of network adapters. They have both external and internal components: the external *transceiver* is integrated into the vampire connector and passes the network signal to the network adapter card installed in the PC via a cable. The cable from the vampire connector/transceiver to the PC network adapter must be no more than 50 meters. ThickNet connects to a PC's network card via a 15-pin male connector called an *Attachment Unit Interface (AUI)* or *DIX* (Digital, Intel, Xerox) connector. ThickNet uses a bus topology, as just mentioned, so it needs terminators. As you might guess, the 50-Ohm ThickNet terminator must be placed on each end of the segment.

ThickNet is on its way out for a number of reasons. It's expensive, it's difficult to work with, and it's slow. Nonetheless, ThickNet has a large installed user base, so for that reason, the A+ Core Hardware exam expects you to know how it works.

Thin Ethernet—10Base2

Thin Ethernet, also known as *ThinNet*, or *802.3*, is an inexpensive alternative to ThickNet. ThinNet cable is much easier to handle than ThickNet cable and is used in many small networks.

ThinNet uses a specific type of coax called RG-58. RG stands for *Radio Grade*, which is an industry standard for measuring coax cables. This type of coax looks similar to the coax used with common cable television boxes, called RG-6, but it's quite different. The RG rating should be clearly marked on the cable. If it isn't, it will say something like ThinNet or 802.3 to let you know you have the right cable.

While ThinNet also runs at 10 Mbps on a true bus topology, it has several big limitations that thick Ethernet doesn't share. Thin Ethernet supports only 30 devices per segment, and each segment can be no more than 185 meters long. On the plus side, cabling with ThinNet is a snap compared with ThickNet. The cable is much thinner and more flexible than for ThickNet. In addition, the transceiver is built into the ThinNet network card, so ThinNet does not require an external transceiver. Each ThinNet network card is simply connected to the bus cable with a T connector.

Exam Tip	
Know the ThinNet (10Base2) numbers—10 Mbps speed, 30 devices per segment, and 185-meter segment maximum length.	

The ThinNet cable has twist-on, barrel-type connectors called *British Naval Connectors (BNC)*, which attach to the T connector, as shown in Figure 12-8.

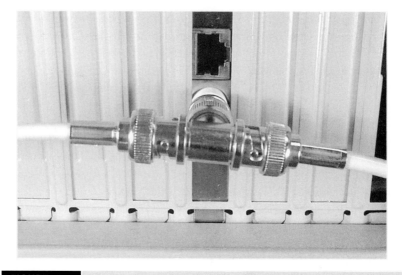

FIGURE 12.8   BNC connectors plugged into T connector

Termination is handled by twisting small, specialized terminators onto the un-used end of the T connector on the machines at the ends of the chain.

When installing ThinNet, it's important that one of the terminators be grounded. Special terminators can be grounded to the case of the PC, but be sure the PC is also grounded! You *must* use a T connector! You cannot simply plug the end of the ThinNet cable into the network adapter.

To add another PC to the network, simply remove the terminator from the last PC, add another piece of cable with another T connector, and add the termi-nator on the new end. Adding a PC between two systems is also easy: unhook one side of a T connector and add another PC and cable in between.

ThinNet, like its heavyweight cousin, is on its way out. Very popular for a time in *small office/home office (SOHO)* networks, the fact that it uses a bus to-pology where any wire break means the whole network goes down makes 10Base2 unacceptable in a modern network.

10ˣBaseT

Most modern Ethernet networks employ one of two technologies (and some-times both), *10BaseT* or *100BaseT*. As the numbers in the names would suggest, 10BaseT networks run at 10 Mbps and 100BaseT networks run at 100 Mbps. Both standards are about to be eclipsed by Gigabit Ethernet, or 1000BaseT, which runs at 1 Gbps. The segment length (the distance from the PC to a hub) for all three is limited to 100 meters. All three technologies—collectively abbreviated as 10ˣBaseT—connect via a type of cable called *unshielded twisted pair (UTP)*.

UTP cables come in categories that define the maximum speed at which data can be transferred (also called *bandwidth*).

Local Lingo

CAT 1–6 levels Experienced networking techs refer to the different types of cabling as *"CAT x,"* as opposed to *"Category x,"* as in, "Yo, Frankie! Toss me that coil o' CAT 5, alright?"

CAT Levels UTP cable comes in seven major categories (CATs) of two-pair cables. You can find the CAT level clearly marked on a cable. Table 12-1 shows the speeds.

These categories are established by the Telecommunication Industry Association/Electronic Industries Alliance (TIA/EIA) and are under the TIA/EIA-568 specification. Currently, just about everybody uses CAT 5 cable (or the slightly superior CAT 5e). Although most networks run at 10 Mbps, the industry standard has shifted to networks designed to run at 100 Mbps or faster. Of the two-pair cables, only CAT 5 handles these speeds, so everyone installs CAT 5 or better even if they are running at speeds where CAT 3 or CAT 4 would do. Consequently, it's hard to get anything but CAT 5, CAT 5e, or CAT 6 cables.

A number of wire makers are pushing UTP with even higher ratings. A good example is Belden Wire and Cable's DataTwist 350 cable, designated to run as fast as 350 Mbps. These new cables tend to get names like "CAT 6a" and "CAT 7," but these are marketing labels and not official CAT designations.

TABLE 12.1	Standard CAT Types
Ethernet Cable Category	**Typical Bandwidth Throughput and Usage**
CAT 1	Data speeds up to 2 Mbps. Standard phone line.
CAT 2	Data speeds up to 4 Mbps. Rarely used.
CAT 3	Data speeds up to 16 Mbps. Phone and small network use.
CAT 4	Data speeds up to 20 Mbps. Rarely used.
CAT 5	Data speeds up to 100 Mbps. Phone and data. The most common Ethernet network cable in use.
CAT 5e	Data speeds up to 1 Gbps.
CAT 6	Data speeds up to 10 Gbps; best for new installations.

The 10ˣBaseT cabling standard requires two pairs of wires: a pair for sending and a pair for receiving. 10ˣBaseT cables use a connector called an *RJ* connector. The RJ designation was invented by Ma Bell years ago and is still used today. Currently, you see only two types of RJ connectors: *RJ-11* and *RJ-45*, as shown in Figure 12-9.

RJ-11 connectors should look familiar. RJ-11 is the connector that hooks your telephone to the telephone jack. It supports up to two pairs of wires, though most phone lines use only one pair (the other pair is used to support a second phone line). RJ-11 connectors aren't used in any common network installation, although some proprietary "out of the box" network solutions use the telephone lines already installed in a building to transmit data. These types of networks aren't very popular, however.

RJ-45 is the standard for UTP connectors. RJ-45 has connections for up to four pairs of wires and is visibly much wider than RJ-11. The #1 pin on an RJ-45 jack is the first one on the *left* when pointing the jack away from you with the clip facing *down.*

Exam Tip

Know the 10ˣBaseT numbers and names—10, 100, or 1000 Mbps data transfers; 100-meter segment length; RJ-45 connectors; and UTP cabling.

Two standards exist for CAT 5/6 cabling: the TIA/EIA *568A* and the TIA/EIA *568B.* Both are acceptable. The only truly critical thing is to use the *same* standard on each end of the cable, but your life will be much simpler if you choose one standard and stick with it. The wires in UTP cabling are color-coded to make standardization easy. Table 12-2 shows the official TIA/EIA standard colors as they correspond to the wire number.

FIGURE 12.9   RJ-11 (left) and RJ-45 (right)

TABLE 12.2	UTP Cabling Color Chart	
Pin #	**568A**	**568B**
1	White/Green	White/Orange
2	Green	Orange
3	White/Orange	White/Green
4	Blue	Blue
5	White/Blue	White/Blue
6	Orange	Green
7	White/Brown	White/Brown

Fiber-Optic Ethernet

Fiber-optic cable is an attractive networking solution for a number of reasons. First, because it uses light instead of electricity, fiber-optic cable is immune to electrical interference and "crosstalk." Second, fiber-optic signals travel much farther than copper cabling: up to 2000 meters (compared with 100 meters for 10BaseT or 100BaseT). Third, fiber-optic cabling and hardware has become quite affordable in recent years. Last, fiber-optic technology is only slightly more difficult to work with than standard Ethernet, and in some cases even easier.

There are two standards for using fiber-optic cable with Ethernet. In either case, the cabling is the same and it's called *62.5/125 multimode fiber-optic.* All fiber Ethernet networks require two of these cables. Figure 12-10 shows the two most popular types of connectors.

The two fiber-optic standards are called *10BaseFL* and *100BaseFX.* As you can guess by the names, the biggest difference is the speed of the network (some important differences occur in the way hubs are interconnected, and so on).

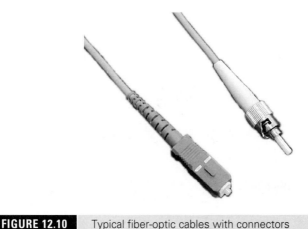

FIGURE 12.10   Typical fiber-optic cables with connectors

Combining and Extending Ethernet

Because the many technologies involved in Ethernet follow the 802.3 standards, you can get hardware to combine different networks, thus increasing compatibility and range. Many 10BaseT hubs, for example, have a ThinNet BNC connector so that you can hook a small 10Base2 network into a star bus network. That saves you from having to add new NICs and run new cabling for the older network.

Combo Cards   Because 10BaseT uses the same language as 10Base2 or 10Base5, you can find Ethernet combo network cards that support two or even three different type of connections. Further, most current 100BaseT NICs are actually 10/100 NICs and are able to automatically adjust to either 10 Mbps or 100 Mbps speeds, depending on the rest of the network hardware.

Repeaters   Ethernet networks have limited lengths, as noted earlier, but various devices enable you to break that limitation. A *repeater* is an electronic device that amplifies the signal on a line, thus enabling you to extend the useful length of a network segment. Networks use two different types of repeaters.

The first type is a dedicated box that takes input from one segment, amplifies it, and then passes it to another segment. Figure 12-11 shows a photo of a common repeater for 10Base2.

The 10^{x}BaseT hub, also a repeater, can enable a maximum separation of 200 meters between PCs on a 10^{x}BaseT network.

Hubs   In a 10^{x}BaseT network, each PC connects to a 10^{x}BaseT hub or switch. These devices have multiple connections called *ports,* one per connected device. To add a device to the network, simply plug another cable into the hub or switch, as in Figure 12-12.

FIGURE 12.11   Ethernet repeater

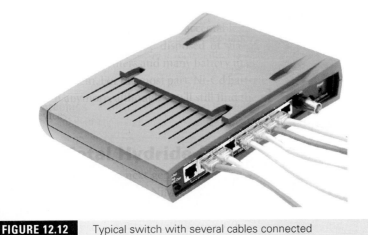

FIGURE 12.12 Typical switch with several cables connected

The primary functional difference between a hub and a switch is that a switch ends collisions on an Ethernet network, which means that each PC gets to use the full bandwidth available. Bottom line? Swap out your old hubs for newer switches and you'll dramatically improve your network performance.

Networks running 10°BaseT use the star bus topology. The hub or switch holds the actual bus and allows access to the bus through the ports. Using a star bus topology creates a robust network: the failure of a single node will not bring down the entire network.

The maximum distance from the hub or switch to any device is 100 meters. No more than one PC can be hooked to each segment, and the maximum number of PCs that can be hooked to any one hub or switch is 1024. You'll be hard pressed, though, to find a hub or switch with that many connectors. Most hubs and switches come with 4, 8, 16, 32, or 64 ports. 10BaseT hubs and switches act as repeaters, amplifying the signals between devices hooked into the network. They need power to provide this amplification, so make sure the hubs and switches are plugged in to a good power source.

Although just about every 10°BaseT network worth its salt uses a switch of sorts to connect the PCs, in a desperate pinch you can hook two 10°BaseT network cards together without a hub. Just connect the two PCs together with a *crossover cable*! Crossover cables work great as a quick way to network two PCs. You can make a crossover cable by making one end TIA/EIA 586A and the other TIA/EIA 568B.

> **Local Lingo**
>
> **Patch cable**   A specific length (usually short, but can be up to 100 feet) of cable terminated at each end with a plug or socket. Also called a patch cord.

> **Travel Advisory**
>
> To expand a network, technically called *scaling*, you simply add more hubs or switches. Hubs and switches are connected together by a normal patch cable through an integrated port called an *uplink port*, which performs the same action as a crossover cable.

Token Ring

"Token Ring" is a confusing term. The problem is Token Ring refers to two related, but different, things. First, *Token Ring* is a topology. Second, Token Ring is a set of network standards developed by IBM that define a complete network system. Token Ring is completely incompatible with Ethernet and is considered a competitor to Ethernet.

Token Ring runs at either 4, 16, or 100 Mbps, depending on the type of Token Ring network cards you buy. Token Ring was originally based around the IBM Type 1 cable. *Type 1 cable* is a two-pair, shielded twisted pair (STP) cable designed to handle speeds up to 20 Mbps. Today, Token Ring can use either STP or UTP.

STP Types

STP cables also have certain categories. These are called *types* and are defined by IBM. The most common types are shown in Table 12-3.

TABLE 12.3   STP Cable Categories

STP Type	Description
Type 1	Standard STP with two pairs—the most common STP cable
Type 2	Standard STP plus two pairs of voice wires
Type 3	Standard STP with four pairs
Type 6	Patch cable—used for connecting hubs
Type 8	Flat STP for under carpets
Type 9	STP with two pairs—Plenum grade

Local Lingo

Plenum grade cabling   Normal network cabling used for patching network equipment uses a PVC coating—or *cladding*—that gives off toxic fumes when burned. Plenum grade cabling is a type of cabling with special cladding that doesn't give off toxic fumes when burned. Plenum grade cabling is usually required by law when stringing cable through ceilings or behind walls. These areas are known as the *plenum space.*

Token Ring Connectors

The Type 1 Token Ring connectors are not RJ-45. Instead, IBM designed a unique *hermaphroditic* connector, called either an IBM-type Data Connector (IDC) or a Universal Data Connector (UDC). These connectors are neither male nor female: they are designed to plug into each other, as seen in Figure 12-13.

Token Ring network cards use a nine-pin female connector. A standard Token Ring cable has a hermaphroditic connector on one end and a nine-pin connector on the other. Token Ring can also be used with CAT 3, 4, 5, 5e, and 6 UTP, or fiber-optic cable. When combined with UTP, Token Ring uses an RJ-45 connector, so from a cabling standpoint, Token Ring UTP and Ethernet UTP look the same. Many Token Ring network cards are combo cards. This means they come with both a nine-pin connection for STP and an RJ-45 connection for UTP.

As discussed earlier, Token Ring uses a star-ring topology, so it also uses a hub. A Token Ring hub is *not* interchangeable with an Ethernet hub. IBM has a special name for its hubs. They are called either MAUs or MSAUs. Unfortunately, they are also sometimes just called hubs (usually by Ethernet people who don't know any better).

- Token Ring can support up to 260 PCs using STP and up to 72 PCs using UTP.
- Using UTP, the maximum distance from any MAU to a PC is 45 meters.
- Using STP, the maximum distance from any MAU to a PC is 100 meters.

FIGURE 12.13   Hermaphroditic IDC/UDC connector

Token Ring also uses repeaters. Token Ring repeaters can be used only between MAUs. With a repeater, the functional distance between two MAUs increases to 360 meters (with UTP) and 720 meters (with STP).

Travel Advisory

It would be unfair not to give at least a token nod to the possibility of making direct cable connections using the parallel or serial ports on a pair of PCs. All versions of Windows have complete support for allowing two, and no more than two, systems to network together using either parallel or serial cables. You need crossover versions of IEEE 1284 cables for parallel and RS-232 cables for serial. Given the incredibly slow speeds of parallel and especially serial cable transmission compared to those of Ethernet and Token Ring, direct cable connections should never be used unless there is no other viable alternative.

CHECKPOINT

✔**Objective 12.01: Networking Hardware for the PC**   Network Interface Cards (NICs) send data on to the network cabling as discrete chunks called data packets, also called frames. Every NIC has a unique 48-bit MAC address. PCs also need a client service and a common protocol. Popular protocols include NetBEUI, IPX/SPX, AppleTalk, and TCP/IP.

✔**Objective 12.02: Network Topologies**   Bus topology refers to a network in which all computers are physically connected by a single length of cable. Each end of the cable must be terminated. Ring topology also refers to a network in which a single length of cable connects all computers, except the ends are joined, thus making, appropriately, a ring.

✔**Objective 12.03: Network Cabling Standards**   ThickNet (10Base5) supports up to 100 devices hooked to a segment of no more than 500 meters. ThinNet (10Base2) uses RG-58 coaxial cables and supports 30 devices hooked to a segment of no more than 185 meters. Ethernet (10BaseT, 100BaseT) uses UTP cabling (usually CAT 5) with RJ-45 connectors. Ethernet hubs and repeaters enable a maximum separation between PCs of 200 meters. Token Ring refers to both the standard star ring topology and the network standards. Token Ring networks use STP, UTP, or fiber-optic cabling, and moves data at 4, 16, or 100 Mbps.

REVIEW QUESTIONS

1. To provide a computer a physical and electronic connection to a network, what must be installed?

   A. A hub

   B. A router

   C. A NIC

   D. A bridge

2. What is the maximum distance for a 10BaseT segment?

   A. 1000 meters

   B. 330 meters

   C. 185 meters

   D. 100 meters

3. Which of the following is needed to configure a plug and play NIC in a Windows 2000 system?

   A. CMOS

   B. Device driver

   C. Configuration software

   D. DMA

4. José wants to extend his 10Base2 network beyond its maximum segment distance. Which of the following does he need?

   A. Converter

   B. Expander

   C. Repeater

   D. Extender

5. Everything worked fine on your 10BaseT, star bus topology network yesterday, but today, no one can connect to the server. The server seems to be in good running order. Which of the following is the most likely problem?

   A. A hub is malfunctioning.

   B. Someone changed all the passwords for server access.

   C. Someone's T connector has come loose on the bus.

   D. The server's cable is wired as TIA/EIA 568A, and all the others are wired as TIA/EIA 568B.

6. What is the minimum specification of cable types for 100BaseT networks?

   A. Category 2

   B. Category 3

   C. Category 4

   D. Category 5

7. How far apart can two PCs that share the same 10BaseT hub be placed?

   A. 1000 meters

   B. 330 meters

   C. 200 meters

   D. 100 meters

8. Which component(s) prevent reflection on a bus topology network?

   A. Terminator

   B. Crossover cable

   C. Uplink port

   D. Multiple Station Access Unit

9. What is special about plenum grade network cabling?

   A. Plenum grade cabling doubles bandwidth throughput speed.

   B. Plenum grade cabling increases the maximum length of Ethernet network segments from 100 meters to 185 meters.

   C. Plenum grade cabling does not give off toxic fumes when burned.

   D. Plenum grade cabling has no special qualities: it is simply a marketing term.

10. What must be used to set IRQs on legacy ISA network interface cards with no jumpers?

   A. COMS

   B. Device Manager

   C. Configuration software

   D. DIP switches

REVIEW ANSWERS

1. **C**   A system must have a network interface card (NIC) to participate in any type of network.

2. **D**   10BaseT has a maximum distance of 100 meters.

3. **B**   Plug and play requires only the proper driver.

4. **C**   José needs a repeater.

5. **A**   Although someone might have changed all the passwords or the cables during the night, a bad hub is the most probable answer.

6. **D**   100BaseT requires CAT 5 or better rated cabling.

7. **C**   As each system can be 100 meters from the hub, any two systems can be up to 200 meters apart.

8. **A**   A terminator is a resistor that absorbs voltage from the bus topology cable to prevent reflection.

9. **C**   Unlike normal network cabling, plenum grade cabling doesn't give off toxic fumes when burned. It is usually required by law when stringing cable into a building's plenum space.

10. **C**   Although some cards still use jumpers, most NICs use software-based resource settings.

PART

II

Operating System Technologies

Networks: Wireless Networking

	NEWBIE	SOME EXPERIENCE	EXPERT
ETA	3 hours	2 hours	1 hour

One of the biggest hurdles to setting up a wired network is the wires. Most businesses frown on having CAT5 cabling running down every hall and along every wall, so wiring a building for networking means installing cabling up into ceiling crawlspaces and down behind walls and paneling. Any tech who's had to do this more than a few times can tell you that "pulling cable" is an unpleasant chore even under the best conditions. In many cases, installing network cabling is impractical, and in some cases, it may even be prohibited, such as in a building that's designated as historical. Thankfully, developments in wireless technology give us a number of alternatives to traditional wired networks.

Objective 13.01   Wireless Networking Basics

A wireless network eliminates the need for the network cabling that connects the PCs to each other in a typical wired network. Instead of a physical set of wires running between networked PCs, servers, printers, or other *nodes,* wireless networks use either radio waves or beams of infrared light to communicate with each other.

Different kinds of wireless networking solutions have come and gone in the past. The types of wireless radio wave networks you'll find yourself supporting these days are those based on the most common implementation of the IEEE 802.11 wireless Ethernet standard—*Home Radio Frequency (HomeRF)* and *Wireless Fidelity (Wi-Fi)*—and those based on the newer *Bluetooth* technology. Wireless networks using infrared light are limited to those that use the *Infrared Data Association* protocol (IrDA).

Exam Tip

The A+ exams currently focus on Wi-Fi and IrDA. You might run into some HomeRF devices in the field and certainly will work with Bluetooth devices, so we mention both technologies in this chapter.

Wireless devices use the same networking protocols and client that their wired counterparts use, but the basic networking scheme differs. You'll recall from Chapter 12 that Ethernet bus devices use the *Carrier Sense Media Access/Collision Detection (CSMA/CD)* to communicate on the same network media without stepping on each other's data packets. Wireless devices use a variation called *Carrier Sense Media Access/Collision Avoidance (CSMA/CA)*.

If two networked systems in a CSMA/CD network attempt to transmit data at the same time, the two packets collide, thereby canceling each other out. This collision is detected by each network node, which responds by generating a random "timeout" period. When the timeout period expires, the nodes then retransmit the data packet, counting on the randomness of their respective timeouts to prevent another collision. Not very elegant, but it gets the job done.

Wireless devices use the CSMA/CA networking scheme, meaning that instead of dealing with collisions after they occur, they proactively take steps to avoid collisions in the first place. Wireless nodes listen in on the wireless medium to see if another node is currently broadcasting data. If so, then it waits a random amount of time before retrying. However, wireless Ethernet offers the option of using the *Request to Send/Clear to Send (RTS/CTS)* protocol. When enabled, a transmitting node that determines that the wireless medium is clear to use sends an RTS frame to the receiving node. The receiving node responds with a CTS frame, telling the sending node that it's okay to transmit. Then, once the data is sent, the transmitting node waits for an acknowledgment (ACK) from the receiving node before sending the next data packet. Very elegant, but keep in mind that using RTS/CTS introduces significant overhead to the process and can impede performance.

Let's look now at the components you need to network wirelessly.

Wireless Networking Components

Wireless networking capabilities of one form or another are built into many modern computing devices. Infrared *transceiver* ports have been standard issue on portable computers, PDAs, and high-end printers for years, although they're curiously absent from many of the latest Tablet PCs. Figure 13-1 shows the infrared transceiver ports on a laptop computer and a PDA.

FIGURE 13.1   Infrared transceiver ports on a laptop and PDA

Wireless Ethernet and Bluetooth capabilities are increasingly popular as integrated components can easily be added using PCI or PCMCIA add-on cards. Figure 13-2 shows a PCI card that accepts a wireless PCMCIA Ethernet card.

You can also add wireless network capabilities using external USB wireless network adapters, as shown in Figure 13-3.

Wireless network adapters aren't limited to PCs. Many handheld computers and PDAs have wireless capabilities built in or available as add-on options. Figure 13-4 shows a PDA accessing the Internet through a wireless network adapter card.

To extend the capabilities of a wireless Ethernet network, such as by connecting to a wired network or sharing a high-speed Internet connection, you need a *wireless access point (WAP)*. A WAP centrally connects wireless network nodes in the same way that a network hub connects wired PCs. Many WAPs also act as

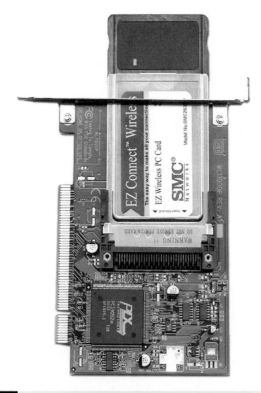

FIGURE 13.2　　Wireless PCMCIA NIC inserted into PCI add-on card

FIGURE 13.3   External USB wireless NIC

high-speed switches and Internet routers, such as the Linksys device shown in Figure 13-5.

Wireless Networking Software

In terms of configuring wireless networking software, there's very little that you need to do. Wireless network adapters are plug and play, so any modern version

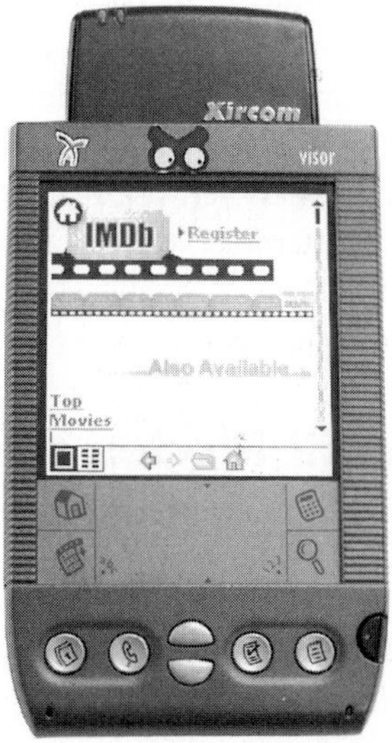

FIGURE 13.4   PDA with wireless capability

FIGURE 13.5 Linksys device that acts as wireless access point, switch, and DSL router

of Windows will immediately recognize one when installed into a PCI or PCMCIA slot, or a USB port, prompting you to load any needed hardware drivers.

You will, however, need a utility to set parameters such as your *Service Set Identifier (SSID)*, also called a *network name*. Windows XP has built-in tools for configuring these settings, but for previous versions of Windows, you need to rely on configuration tools provided by the wireless network adapter vendor. Figure 13-6 shows a typical wireless network adapter configuration utility.

Using this utility, you can determine your link state and signal strength, configure your wireless networking *mode* (discussed in the next section), set security encryption and power saving options, and so on.

Wireless Network Modes

The simplest wireless network consists of two or more PCs communicating directly with each other *sans* cabling or any other intermediary hardware. More complicated wireless networks use a WAP to centralize wireless communication and bridge wireless network segments to wired network segments. These two different methods, or *modes*, are called *ad hoc* mode and *infrastructure* mode.

Ad Hoc Mode

In ad hoc mode, sometimes called peer-to-peer mode, each wireless node is in direct contact with each other node in a decentralized free-for-all, as shown

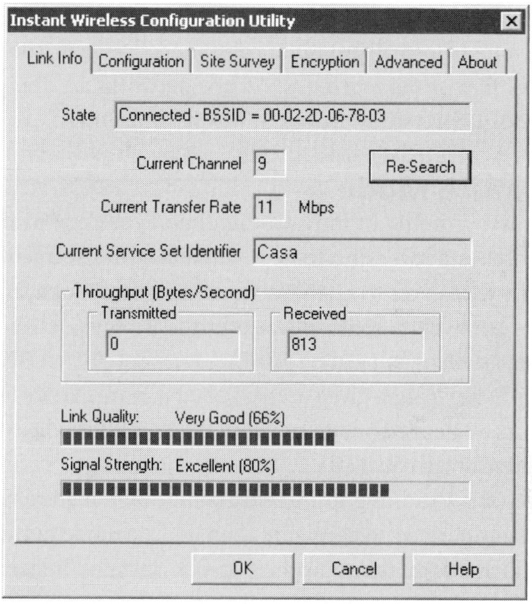

FIGURE 13.6 Wireless configuration utility

in Figure 13-7. Two or more wireless nodes communicating in ad hoc mode form what's called an *Independent Basic Service Set (IBSS)*.

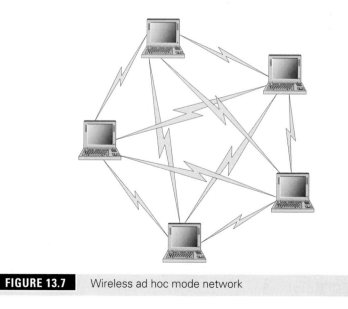

FIGURE 13.7 Wireless ad hoc mode network

Ad hoc mode networks are easier to configure than infrastructure mode networks and are suited for small groups of computers (less than a dozen or so) that need to transfer files or share printers. Ad hoc networks are also good for temporary networks such as study groups or business meetings.

Infrastructure Mode

Wireless networks running in infrastructure mode use one or more WAPs to connect the wireless network nodes to a wired network segment, as shown in Figure 13-8. If you plan on setting up a wireless network for a large number of PCs or need to have centralized control over the wireless network, then infrastructure mode is what you need.

A single WAP servicing a given area is called a *Basic Service Set (BSS)*. This service area can be extended by adding more WAPs. This is called, appropriately, an *Extended Basic Service Set (EBSS)*.

Wireless networks running in infrastructure mode require more planning and are more complicated to configure than ad hoc mode networks, but they also give you finer control over how the network operates. Infrastructure mode is better suited to business networks or networks that need to share dedicated resources such as Internet connections and centralized databases.

Wireless Networking Security

One of the major complaints about wireless networking is that it offers weak security. In many cases, the only thing you need to do to access a wireless network

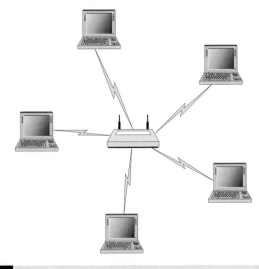

FIGURE 13.8   Wireless infrastructure mode network

is walk into a WAP's coverage area and turn on your wireless device! Further, data packets are floating through the air instead of safely wrapped up inside network cabling. What's to stop an unscrupulous PC tech with the right equipment from grabbing those packets out of the air and reading that data?

Wireless networks use three methods to secure access to the network itself and secure the data that's being transferred. The SSID (network name) parameter ensures that only wireless network devices configured with the same SSID are permitted access to a particular network. You can tighten security even further by employing *MAC filtering,* to create a list of the machines that are permitted to access a network. Enabling wireless encryption through either *Wireless Equivalency Privacy (WEP)* or *Wi-Fi Protected Access (WPA)* ensures that the data packets themselves are secure while in transit.

SSID

One of the main security weaknesses with wireless networks is that out of the box there's *no* security configured at all! Wireless devices *want* to be heard, and WAPs are usually configured to broadcast their presence to their maximum range, and welcome all other wireless devices that respond.

Configuring a unique SSID name is the very least that you should to do secure a wireless network. The default SSID names are well-known and widely available online. This is intended to make setting up a wireless network as easy as possible, but conversely it creates a security hole you could drive a bullet train through!

Each node and WAP in a wireless network must be configured with the same unique SSID name. This SSID name is then included in the header of every data packet broadcast in the wireless network's coverage area. Data packets that lack the correct SSID name in the header are rejected.

Travel Advisory

Most WAPs broadcast their SSIDs by default, creating a security breach. Detecting the SSID of a wireless network is a hacker's first step toward using that network without permission. You need additional security to make a wireless network secure.

MAC Filtering

Most WAPs also support MAC address filtering, a method that enables you to limit access to your wireless network using the physical, hard-wired address of the units' wireless network adapters. MAC filtering is a handy way of creating a type of "accepted users" list to limit access to your wireless network. A table stored in the WAP lists the MAC addresses that are permitted to participate in that wireless network. Any data packets that don't contain the MAC address of a node listed in the table are rejected.

WEP

The next step up in wireless security is enabling WEP encryption. Enabling WEP encryption ensures that data is secured while in transit over the airwaves. WEP encryption uses a standard 40-bit encryption to scramble data packets. Many vendors also support 104-bit encryption. Note that some vendors advertise 128-bit encryption, but they actually use a 104-bit encryption key. WEP provides a level of authentication based on the wireless node's MAC address. Note that it performs no *user* authentication at all.

One important note to consider is that WEP doesn't provide complete end-to-end encryption, because WEP encryption is stripped from the data packets at the lowest networking levels. For true end-to-end encryption, you need to upgrade to WPA.

WPA

WPA is designed to address the weaknesses of WEP, and functions as a sort of security protocol upgrade to WEP-enabled devices. WPA offers security enhancements such as an encryption key integrity-checking feature, and user authentication through the industry-standard *Extensible Authentication Protocol (EAP)*. The use of EAP is a huge security improvement over WEP's MAC address authentication scheme. After all, MAC addresses are fairly easy to "sniff" out (with the right hardware), because they're transmitted in unencrypted, clear-text format. User names and passwords are encrypted and therefore much more secure. WEP also provides true end-to-end data packet encryption.

Even with these enhancements, WPA is intended only as an interim security solution until the IEEE 802.11i security standard is finalized and implemented.

Wireless Networking Speed

Wireless networking data throughput speeds are dependent on several factors. Foremost is the standard used by the networked wireless devices. Depending on the standard used, wireless throughput speeds range from a measly 2 MBps to a respectable 54 MBps.

Another factor affecting speed is the distance between wireless nodes (or between wireless nodes and centralized WAPs). Wireless devices dynamically negotiate the top speed at which they can communicate without dropping too many data packets. Speed decreases as distance increases, so the maximum throughput speed is achieved only at extremely close range (less than about 25 feet). At the outer reaches of a device's effective range, speed may decrease to around 1 MBps before it drops out altogether.

Finally, throughput speed can be affected by interference from other wireless devices operating in the same frequency range, such as cordless phones and baby monitors, as well as by solid objects. So-called *dead spots* occur when something capable of blocking the radio signal comes between wireless network nodes. Large electrical appliances such as refrigerators are *very* effective at blocking wireless network signals! Other culprits include electrical fuse boxes, metal plumbing, and air conditioning units.

Wireless Networking Range

Wireless networking range is hard to define, and you'll see most descriptions listed with qualifiers such as "*around* 150 feet" or "*about* 300 feet." This is simply because, like throughput speed, range is greatly affected by outside factors. Interference from other wireless devices affects range, as does interference from solid objects. The maximum ranges listed in the next section are those presented by wireless manufacturers as the theoretical maximum ranges. In the real world, you'll see these ranges only under the most ideal circumstances. True effective range is probably about half what you see listed.

Range can be increased in a couple of ways. First, you can install multiple WAPs, to permit "roaming" between one WAP's coverage area and another's— this is the EBSS described earlier in this chapter. Second, you can install a signal booster that increases a single WAP's signal strength, thus increasing its range.

Objective 13.02 # Wireless Networking Standards

To better understand wireless networking technology, let's take a brief look at the various wireless networking standards. First, we'll look at 802.11-based wireless networking and then talk about Infrared and Bluetooth.

IEEE 802.11–Based Wireless Networking

The IEEE 802.11 wireless Ethernet standard defines methods by which devices may communicate using spread-spectrum radio waves. *Spread-spectrum* broadcasts data in small, discrete chunks over the different frequencies available within a certain frequency range. All of the 802.11-based wireless technologies broadcast and receive at 2.4 GHz (with the exception of 802.11a, which uses 5 GHz).

802.11 defines two different spread-spectrum broadcasting methods: *direct-sequence* spread-spectrum (DSSS) and *frequency-hopping* spread-spectrum (FHSS). DSSS sends data out on different frequencies simultaneously, while FHSS sends data on one frequency at a time, constantly shifting (or *hopping*) frequencies. DSSS uses considerably more bandwidth than FHSS—around 22 MHz as opposed to 1 MHz. DSSS is capable of greater data throughput, but is also more prone to interference than FHSS. HomeRF wireless networks are the only type that use FHSS; all other 802.11-based wireless networking standards use DSSS.

The original 802.11 standard has been extended to the 802.11*a,* 802.11*b,* and 802.11*g* variations used in Wi-Fi wireless networks, and also *hybridized* (combined with another wireless communication technology) to form the *Shared Wireless Access Protocol (SWAP)* used in HomeRF networks.

Wi-Fi Wireless Networking Standards

Wi-Fi is currently by far the most widely-adopted type of wireless networking. Not only do thousands of private businesses and homes have wireless networks, but many public places such as coffee shops and libraries also offer Internet access through wireless networks.

Technically, only wireless devices that conform to the extended versions of the 802.11 standard—802.11a, 802.11b, and 802.11g—are Wi-Fi certified. Wi-Fi certification comes from the Wi-Fi Alliance (formerly the Wireless Ethernet Compatibility Alliance, or WECA), a nonprofit industry group made up of over 175 member companies who design and manufacturer wireless networking products. Wi-Fi certification ensures compatibility between wireless networking devices made by different vendors. First-generation devices that use the older 802.11 standard are not Wi-Fi-certified, and so may or may not work well with devices made by different vendors.

Wireless devices can communicate only with other wireless devices that use the same standard. The exception to this is 802.11g, which is backward compatible with 802.11b (although at the slower speed of 802.11b). The following paragraphs describe the important specifications of each of the popular 802.11-based wireless networking standards.

802.11   Devices that use the original 802.11 standard are a rarity these days. You're most likely to find them in service on some brave early adopter's network.

802.11 was hampered by both slow speeds (2 MBps maximum) and limited range (about 150 feet, tops). However, 802.11 employed some of the same features that are in use in the current wireless standards. 802.11 uses the 2.4 GHz broadcast range, and security is provided by the use of industry-standard WEP and WPA encryption.

802.11a   Despite the "a" designation of this extension to the 802.11 standard, 802.11a was actually developed *after* 802.11b. 802.11a differs from the other 802.11-based standards in significant ways. Foremost is that it operates in a different frequency range, 5 GHz. This less-popular frequency range means that 802.11a devices are less prone to interference from other devices. 802.11a also offers considerably greater throughput than 802.11 and 802.11b, reaching speeds up to 54 MBps! Range, however, suffers somewhat, topping out at about 150 feet. Despite the superior speed of 802.11a, it isn't widely adopted in the PC world.

802.11b   Currently the reigning king of wireless networking standards, 802.11b is practically ubiquitous. The 802.11b standard supports data throughput of up to 11 MBps—on par with older wired 10BaseT networks—and offers a range of up to 300 feet under ideal conditions. 802.11b networks can be secured through the use of WEP and WPA encryption. The main downside to using 802.11b is, in fact, that it's so popular. The 2.4 GHz frequency is already a crowded place, so you're likely to run into interference from other wireless devices.

802.11g   The latest and greatest version of 802.11, 802.11g, offers data transfer speeds of up to 54 MBps, equivalent to the 802.11a standard, and the wider 300-foot range of 802.11b. More importantly, 802.11g is backward compatible with 802.11b, meaning that an 802.11g WAP can service both 802.11b and 802.11g wireless nodes. Table 13-1 maps the important differences between the different versions of the 802.11 standard.

HomeRF

HomeRF, as the name implies, is intended for home use, not for use in large business network environments. It is easy to set up and maintain but doesn't offer much in the way of range (about 150 feet, maximum). Speed on early HomeRF devices was also nothing to write home about, clocking in at a maximum of 2 MBps, but the later version 2.0 of the HomeRF standard bumps that up to a respectable 10 MBps and provides full backward-compatibility with the earlier HomeRF technology. Also, because HomeRF devices use the FHSS spread-spectrum broadcasting method, they are less prone to interference and somewhat more secure than Wi-Fi devices.

TABLE 13.1 802.11 Versions

Standard	802.11	802.11a	802.11b	802.11g
Max. Throughput	2 MBps	54 MBps	11 MBps	54 MBps
Max. Range	150 feet	150 feet	300 feet	300 feet
Frequency	2.4 GHz	5 GHz	2.4 GHz	2.4 GHz
Security	SSID, MAC filtering, Industry-standard WEP, WPA	SSID, MAC filtering, Industry-standard WEP, WPA	SSID, MAC filtering, Industry-standard WEP, WPA	SSID, MAC filtering, Industry-standard WEP, WPA
Compatibility	802.11	802.11a	802.11b	802.11b, 802.11g
Spread-spectrum method	DSSS	DSSS	DSSS	DSSS
Communication mode	Ad hoc or infrastructure	Ad hoc or infrastructure	Ad hoc or infrastructure	Ad hoc or infrastructure
Description	The original 802.11 wireless standard. Only seen on first-generation wireless networking devices.	Products that adhere to this standard are considered "Wi-Fi Certified." Eight available channels. Less prone to interference than 802.11b and 802.11g.	Products that adhere to this standard are considered "Wi-Fi Certified." Fourteen channels available in the 2.4 GHz band (only 11 of which can be used in the U.S. due to FCC regulations). Three nonoverlapping channels.	Products that adhere to this standard are considered "Wi-Fi Certified." Improved security enhancements. Fourteen channels available in the 2.4 GHz band (only 11 of which can be used in the U.S. due to FCC regulations). Three nonoverlapping channels.

HomeRF wireless networks use the SWAP protocol, a hybrid of the *Digital Enhanced Cordless Telecommunications (DECT)* standard for voice communication and the 802.11 wireless Ethernet standard for data. HomeRF uses seven channels in the 2.4 GHz range, six dedicated to voice communication, the remaining one for data.

HomeRF uses a proprietary 56-bit (128-bit in version 2.0) encryption algorithm instead of the industry-standard WEP and WPA that 802.11 uses. Also, instead of an SSID name, HomeRF uses what they call a *Network ID (NWID)*, instead. It serves the same purpose as an SSID but is somewhat more secure.

Infrared Wireless Networking

Wireless networking using infrared technology is largely overlooked these days, probably due to the explosion of interest in the newer and faster wireless standards. This is a shame, because infrared provides an easy and reasonably fast way to transfer data, often without the need to purchase or install any additional hardware or software on your PC.

Infrared Data Association Standard

Communication through infrared devices is enabled via the *Infrared Data Association (IrDA)* protocol. The IrDA protocol stack is a widely-supported industry standard and has been included in all versions of Windows since Windows 95. Apple computers also support IrDA, as do Linux PCs.

Speed- and range-wise, infrared isn't very impressive. Infrared devices are capable of transferring data at speeds ranging from about 115 KBps up to 4 MBps. Not too shabby, but hardly stellar. The maximum distance between infrared devices is very limited—only one meter. Infrared links work on a direct line-of-sight basis, and are susceptible to interference. An infrared link can be disrupted by anything that breaks the beam of light—a badly placed can of Mountain Dew, a coworker passing between desks, or even bright sunlight hitting the infrared transceiver can cause interference.

Infrared is designed to make a point-to-point connection between two devices in ad hoc mode only. No infrastructure mode is available. You can, however, use an infrared access point device to enable Ethernet network communication using IrDA.

Infrared devices operate at half-duplex, meaning that while one is talking, the other is listening—they can't talk and listen at the same time. IrDA has a mode that emulates full-duplex communication, but it's really half-duplex.

Security-wise, the IrDA protocol offers exactly nothing in the way of encryption or authentication. Infrared's main security feature is the fact that you have to be literally within arm's reach to establish a link.

Clearly, infrared is not the best solution for a dedicated network connection, but for doing a quick file transfer or print job without getting your hands dirty, it'll do in a pinch. Table 13-2 lists infrared's important specifications.

Bluetooth

Bluetooth wireless technology is named for Harald Bluetooth, a Danish king from the ninth century. This information isn't on the CompTIA core A+ exam, but it's a pretty common question, so now you can sound knowledgeable when some user asks you!

When it was first introduced, there was some confusion among PC techs about what Bluetooth technology was for. Since then, much of the confusion has been cleared up. Bluetooth is designed to create small wireless *personal area networks (PANs)* that link PCs to peripheral devices such as PDAs and printers; input devices such as keyboards and mice; and even consumer electronics such as cell phones, home stereos, televisions, and home security systems. Bluetooth is *not* designed to be a full-function networking solution, nor is it meant to compete with either Wi-Fi or HomeRF. If anything, Bluetooth is poised to replace infrared as a way to connect PCs to peripherals.

The IEEE organization has made Bluetooth the basis for its forthcoming 802.15 standard for wireless PANs. Bluetooth uses the FHSS spread-spectrum broadcasting method, switching between any of the 79 frequencies available in the 2.45 GHz range. Bluetooth hops frequencies some 1600 times per second, making it highly resistant to interference. Bluetooth transfers data at speeds ranging from 723 KBps to 1, count 'em *1*, MBps, with a maximum range of 10 meters (~33 feet). Some high-powered Bluetooth devices can reach a whopping 2 MBps throughput speed with a maximum range of up to 300 feet, but these are uncommon.

TABLE 13.2	Infrared
Standard	**Infrared (IrDA)**
Max. Throughput	Up to 4 MBps
Max. Range	1 meter (39 inches)
Security	None
Compatibility	IrDA
Communication mode	Point-to-point ad hoc
Description	IrDA is good for very short range data transfers between devices.

Objective 13.03   Configuring Wireless Networking

The mechanics of setting up a wireless network don't differ much from those for a wired network. Physically installing a wireless network adapter is the same as installing a wired NIC, whether it's an internal PCI card, a PCMCIA card, or an external USB device. Simply install the device and let Plug and Play handle detection and resource allocation. Install the device's supplied driver when prompted, and you're practically done. Unless you're using Windows XP, you also need to install the wireless network configuration utility supplied with your wireless network adapter so that you can set your communication mode, SSID, and so on.

As mentioned earlier, wireless devices want to talk to each other, so communicating with an available wireless network is usually a no-brainer. The trick is to configure the wireless network so that only specific wireless nodes are able to use it and to secure the data that's being sent through the air.

Wi-Fi and HomeRF

Wi-Fi and HomeRF wireless networks both support ad hoc and infrastructure operation modes. Which mode you choose depends on the number of wireless nodes you need to support, the type of data sharing they'll perform, and your management requirements.

Ad Hoc Mode

As mentioned earlier, ad hoc mode is best used for small offices, home offices, study groups, meetings, or any other type of workgroup environment where you don't need centralized control over the network. Ad hoc wireless networks don't need an access point, so they are also somewhat cheaper to set up than infrastructure mode networks.

The only requirements in an ad hoc mode wireless network are that each wireless node be configured with the same network name (SSID), and that no two nodes use the same IP address. You may also have to select a common channel for all ad hoc nodes. The only other configuration steps to take are to make sure that no two nodes are using the same IP address (this step is usually unnecessary if all PCs are using DHCP) and that the File and Printer Sharing service is running on all nodes.

Figure 13-9 shows a wireless network configuration utility with ad hoc mode selected.

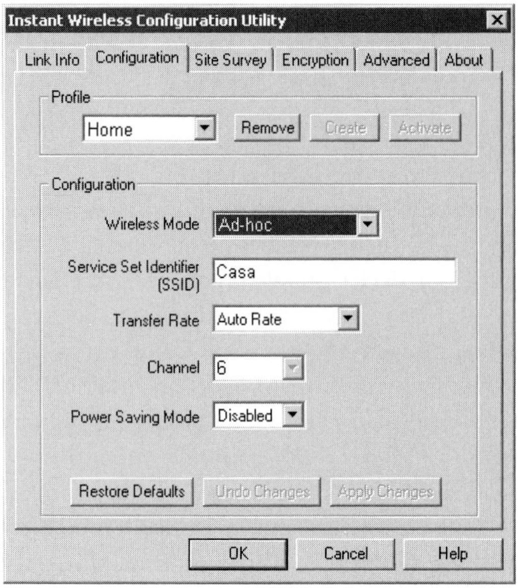

FIGURE 13.9 Selecting ad hoc mode in a wireless configuration utility

Infrastructure Mode

Infrastructure mode is better suited to larger network environments where centralized network control is important. Typically, infrastructure-mode wireless networks employ one or more WAPs connected to a wired network segment, a corporate intranet or the Internet, or both.

As with ad hoc-mode wireless networks, infrastructure-mode networks require that the same SSID be configured on all nodes and access points. Figure 13-10 shows a wireless network access point configuration utility set to Infrastructure mode.

Depending on the capabilities of your WAP, you may also configure DHCP options, filtering, and so on.

Access Point SSID Configuration WAPs have an integrated web server and are configured through a browser-based setup utility. Typically, you fire up your web browser on one of your network client workstations and enter the WAP's default IP address, such as 192.168.1.1, to bring up the configuration page. You will need to supply an administrative password, included with your WAP's documentation, to log in (see Figure 13-11).

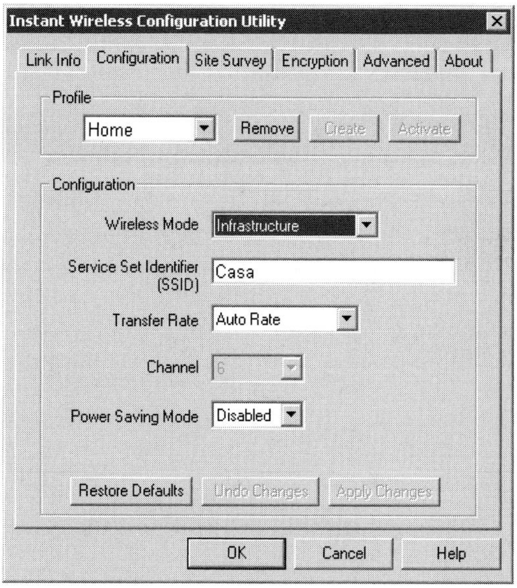

FIGURE 13.10   Selecting infrastructure mode in a wireless configuration utility

Setup screens vary from vendor to vendor and from model to model. Figure 13-12 shows the initial setup screen for a popular Linksys WAP/router.

Configure the SSID option where indicated, and you're in business! Channel selection is usually automatic, but you can reconfigure this option if you have particular needs in your organization (such as if you have multiple wireless networks operating in the same area). Remember that it's always more secure to configure a unique SSID than it is to accept the well-known default one.

FIGURE 13.11   Security login for Linksys wireless access point

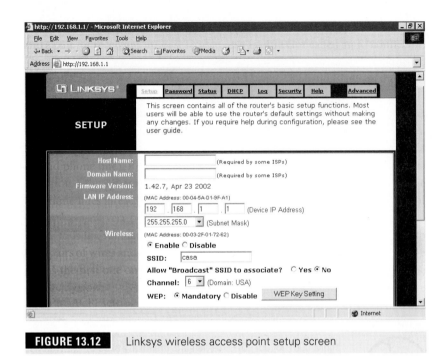

FIGURE 13.12   Linksys wireless access point setup screen

You should also make sure that the option to allow broadcasting of the SSID is disabled. This ensures that only wireless nodes specifically configured with the correct SSID can join the wireless network.

MAC Filtering   Increase security even further by using MAC filtering. This builds a list of wireless network clients that are permitted access to your wireless network because of their unique MAC address.

Figure 13-13 shows the MAC filtering configuration screen on a Linksys WAP. Simply enter the MAC address of a wireless node that you wish to allow (or deny) access to your wireless network.

Encryption   Enabling encryption ensures that data packets are secured against unauthorized access. Set up encryption by turning encryption on at the WAP and then generating a unique security key. Then configure all connected wireless nodes on the network with the same key information. Figure 13-14 shows the WEP key configuration dialog for a Linksys access point.

You have the option of automatically generating a set of encryption keys or doing it manually—save yourself a headache and use the automatic method. Select an encryption level—the usual choices are either 64-bit or 128-bit—

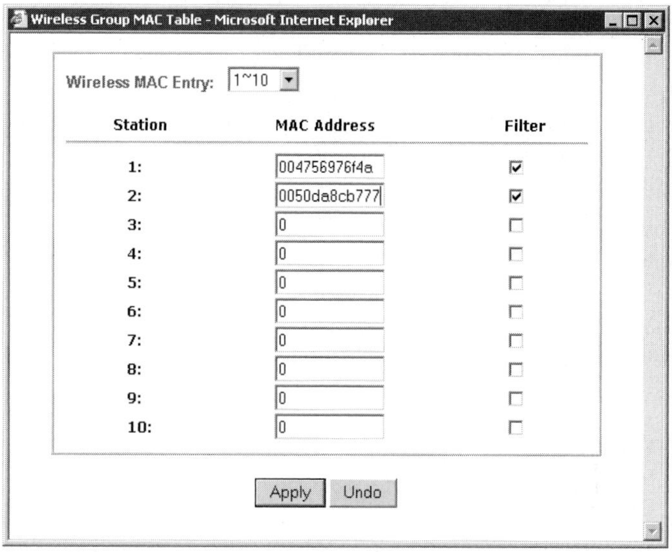

FIGURE 13.13   MAC filtering configuration screen for a Linksys wireless access point

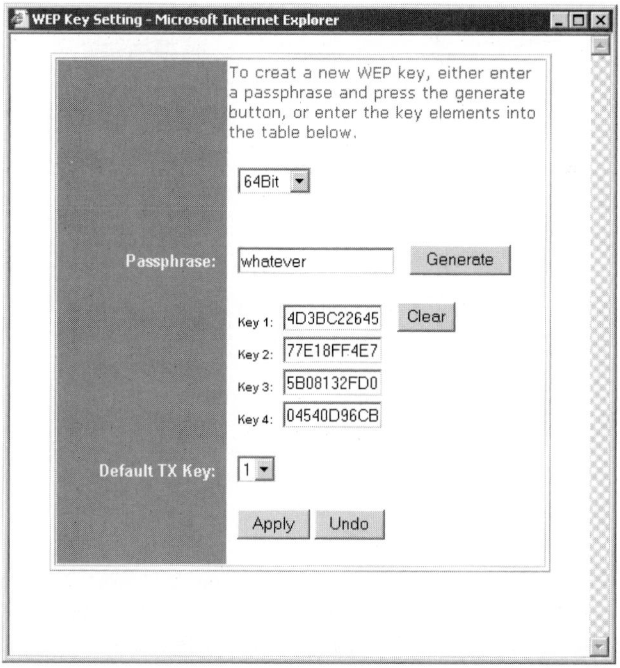

FIGURE 13.14   Encryption key configuration screen on Linksys wireless access point

and then enter a unique passphrase and click Generate (or whatever the equivalent button is called on your access point). Then select a default key and save the settings.

The encryption level, key, and passphrase must match on the wireless client node or communication will fail. Many WAPs have the ability to export the encryption key data onto a floppy disk for easy transfer to a client workstation. You can also manually configure encryption using the vendor-supplied configuration utility, as shown in Figure 13-15.

WPA encryption, if supported by your wireless equipment, is configured in much the same way. You may be required to input a valid user name and password to configure encryption using WPA.

Infrared

IrDA device support is very solid in the latest version of Windows—in fact, there's not much for us techs to configure. IrDA links are made between devices dynamically, without user interaction. Typically, there's nothing to configure on an infrared-equipped PC. Check your network settings to ensure that you've got the IrDA protocol installed and enabled, and you should be good to go (see Figure 13-16).

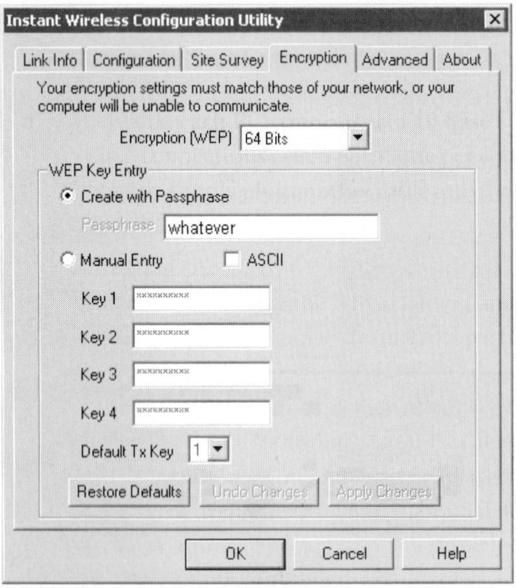

FIGURE 13.15 Encryption screen on client wireless network adapter configuration utility

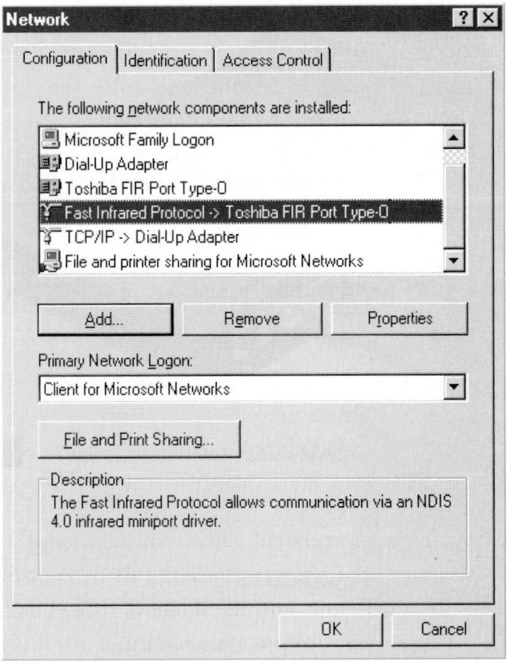

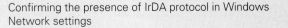

FIGURE 13.16 Confirming the presence of IrDA protocol in Windows Network settings

As far as infrared networking goes, your choices are somewhat limited. Infrared is designed to connect only two systems together in ad hoc mode. This can be done simply to transfer files, or with a bit more configuration, you can configure the two PCs to use IrDA in *direct-connection* mode. You can also use a special infrared access point to enable Ethernet LAN access via IrDA.

Transferring Files via Infrared

File transfers via IrDA are as simple as can be. When two IrDA-enabled devices "see" each other, the sending (primary) device negotiates a connection to the receiving (secondary) device, and *voilà*. It's just point and shoot!

Figure 13-17 shows Windows 2000's Wireless Link applet. Use this to configure file transfer options and the default location for received files.

You can send a file over the infrared connection via any of the following actions:

- Specify a location and one or more files using the Wireless Link dialog box.

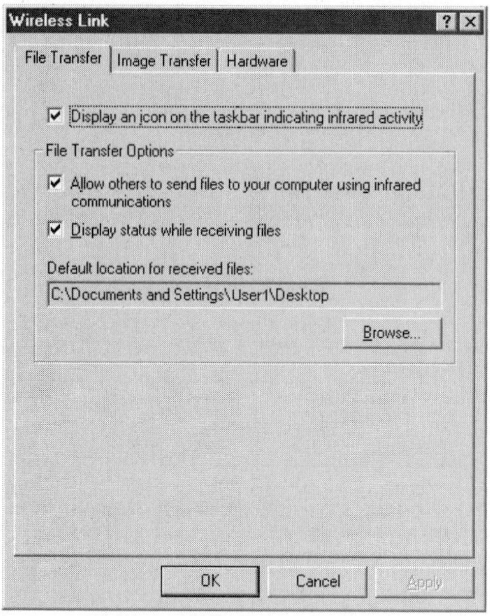

FIGURE 13.17   Windows 2000 Wireless Link applet

- Drag and drop files onto the Wireless Link icon.
- Using Windows Explorer or My Computer, right-click a file (or selection of files), and then select Send To Infrared Recipient.
- Print to a printer configured to use an infrared port.

Networking via Infrared

Direct network connections between two PCs using infrared are similar to using a null-modem cable to connect two PCs together via a serial port. Modern versions of Windows use wizard-driven dialogs to make this type of connection extremely easy. Figure 13-18 shows the Windows 2000 Network Connection wizard. Simply select the Connect Directly To Another Computer radio button and follow the prompts, choosing your infrared port as the connection device.

An infrared access point combines an infrared transceiver with an Ethernet NIC and translates the IrDA protocol into an Ethernet signal, enabling you to log on to your network and access resources. Figure 13-19 shows a laptop accessing an Ethernet LAN through an infrared access point.

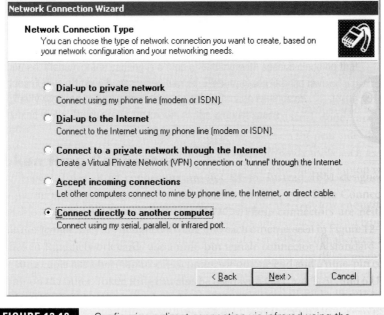

FIGURE 13.18   Configuring a direct connection via infrared using the Network Connection wizard

FIGURE 13.19   Laptop using infrared access point

CHECKPOINT

✔**Objective 13.01: Wireless Networking Basics**   Wireless networks operate much like their wired counterparts, eliminating the network cabling by using either radio waves or infrared light as a network medium. Wireless NICs usually require configuration software supplied by the manufacturer. Windows XP systems have wireless NIC configuration software built in. Wireless networks operate in ad hoc (decentralized) or infrastructure (centralized) fashion. Security is enabled using SSID identification, MAC filtering, and WEP or WPA encryption. Speeds range from 2 MBps to 54 MBps.

✔**Objective 13.02: Wireless Networking Standards**   Wireless networks are based around three standards, IEEE 802.11x (and its variant, HomeRF), Infrared Data Association (IrDA), and Bluetooth. Of these, 802.11b (11 MBps throughput) is the most popular. 802.11g (54 MBps throughput) is becoming the most popular and is backward compatible with 802.11b. 802.11a (54 MBps throughput) is incompatible with any of the other standards. Infrared is line-of-sight only and tops out at 4 MBps. Bluetooth is not a true networking standard, due to its limited range (30 feet) and slow speed (1 MBps). Bluetooth enables you to wirelessly connect a PC to its peripheral devices and synchronize the PC with wireless PDAs.

✔**Objective 13.03: Configuring Wireless Networking**   Ad hoc mode is the simplest way to network wireless computers but offers no fine control over shared resources. Infrastructure mode requires more planning, and wireless access point (WAP) hardware. Wireless access points are configured using built-in browser-based utilities.

REVIEW QUESTIONS

1. Which wireless networking technology uses the 5 GHz frequency range?
   - **A.** 802.11
   - **B.** 802.11a
   - **C.** 802.11b
   - **D.** 802.11g

2. The original 802.11 wireless specification enables a maximum throughput speed of ___?
   - **A.** 2 MBps
   - **B.** 11 MBps

    C. 54 MBps

    D. 4 MBps

3. Which of the following use DSSS spread-spectrum broadcasting? (Choose all that apply.)

    A. HomeRF

    B. 802.11a

    C. 802.11g

    D. 802.11b

4. What is the maximum range of current Bluetooth devices?

    A. 1 meter

    B. 3 feet

    C. 10 meters

    D. 300 feet

5. What function does CSMA/CA provide that CSMA/CD does not?

    A. Data packet collision detection

    B. End-to-end data packet encryption

    C. Data packet collision avoidance

    D. Data packet error checking

6. Why should you configure a unique SSID for your wireless network?

    A. A unique SSID enables backward compatibility between 802.11g and 802.11b.

    B. A unique SSID boosts wireless network range.

    C. A unique SSID boosts wireless network data throughput.

    D. A unique SSID prevents access by any network device that does not have the same SSID configured.

7. What is the maximum speed of IrDA?

    A. 115 KBps

    B. 2 MBps

    C. 4 MBps

    D. 11 MBps

8. Which of the following advantages does WPA have over WEP? (Choose all that apply.)

    A. End-end data packet encryption

    B. EAP user authentication

    C. Encryption key integrity checking

    D. 128-bit data encryption

9. What hardware do you need to enable wireless PCs to connect to resources on a wired network segment in infrastructure mode?

    A. An access point

    B. A router

    C. A hub

    D. A bridge

10. What do you call a wireless Ethernet network in infrastructure mode with more than one access point?

    A. BSS

    B. EBSS

    C. PAN

    D. PICONET

REVIEW ANSWERS

1. **B**   802.11a operates in the 5 GHz frequency range.

2. **A**   Early 802.11 wireless networks ran at a maximum of 2 MBps.

3. **B** **C** **D**   HomeRF uses FHSS. 802.11a, 802.11b, and 802.11g use DSSS.

4. **C**   Current Bluetooth devices have a maximum range of 10 meters (~30 feet).

5. **C**   CSMA/CA uses the RTS/CTS protocol to provide data packet collision avoidance.

6. **D**   A unique SSID prevents wireless devices that do not have the same SSID from accessing the network.

7. **C**   4 MBps is the maximum data throughput speed of IrDA.

8. **A** **B** **C**   WPA upgrades WEP to provide end-to-end data packet encryption, user authentication via EAP, and encryption key integrity checking.

9. **A**   A wireless access point enables you to connect wireless PCs to a wired network segment.

10. **B**   A wireless network with more than one access point is called EBSS, Extended Basic Service Set.

Operating System Fundamentals

	NEWBIE	SOME EXPERIENCE	EXPERT
ETA	3 hours	2 hours	1 hour

In this section of the book, we begin to veer away from the nuts-and-bolts side of the PC and start examining the thing that makes a Windows PC a Windows PC. That thing is the *operating system (OS)*. It's the OS that truly brings a PC to life and makes it a useful, even essential, tool for everyone from an actuary to a zoologist. Without an OS, even the most high-end computer is reduced to being nothing more than a slick-looking cup holder.

In this chapter, we'll examine the general functions of an OS and look at how an OS manifests. Then we'll focus our attention on the most popular OS in the world, Microsoft Windows, and learn how to identify its characteristics and understand the features and functions common to all available versions. Let's get started.

Objective 14.01 Characteristics of the Operating System

All OSs share certain common characteristics. First of all, all operating systems have some degree of "CPU specificness" (Hey, I just invented a new word!). Second, all operating systems must have their own specifically written applications. Third, all operating systems take control of the PC after the POST and keep that control until you shut down the system.

CPU-Specific

The OS must understand important aspects of the CPU, such as the amount of memory the CPU can handle, what modes of operation it is capable of performing, and the commands needed to perform any operation. For that reason, an OS only works with a particular type of processor. The Intel and AMD "x86" line of CPUs heavily dominates today's PCs, but other platforms use different CPUs that are completely incompatible with the Intel and AMD lines. The most obvious example of the latter is the Motorola Power PC, the CPU inside Macintosh computers.

> **Travel Advisory**
>
> When Microsoft introduced Windows NT, they separated the OS into two portions: the Windows Executive and the Hardware Abstraction Layer (HAL). By inserting different HALs, Windows NT could run on different processors. However, the huge popularity of 80x86 processors motivated Microsoft to drop this feature on later versions.

Application Compatibility

Next, just as an OS has to be matched to a particular CPU, application programs have to be written for particular OSs. Whoever makes an OS always provides a "rule book" that tells programmers how to write programs for a particular OS. These rule books are known as *application programming interfaces (APIs)*. Many applications are able to function on more than one OS through porting.

Local Lingo

Porting   Porting means to rewrite an application to use another operating system's API. Many of today's development platforms such as Microsoft C# make this porting very easy to do.

PC Control

Further, an OS takes control of the PC immediately following the POST process (described in Chapter 4) and controls all aspects of the PC operation. The OS continues running until you manually reboot or turn off the PC. You cannot exit from the OS unless you also turn off the PC.

Objective 14.02 Common Operating System Functions

All operating systems are not created equal, but every OS provides certain functions.

- First, it must communicate, or provide a method for other programs to communicate, with the hardware of the PC.
- Second, the OS must create a user interface—a visual representation of the computer on the monitor that makes sense to the people using the computer.
- Third, the OS, via the user interface, must enable users to determine the available installed programs and run, use, and shut down the program of their choice.
- Fourth, the OS should enable users to add, move, and delete the installed programs and data.

Those four things—communicate with hardware, provide a user interface, provide a structure for access to applications, and enable users to manipulate programs and data—are common to any OS. Let's take a look at each of these in more detail.

Communicating with Hardware

It's up to the OS to access the hard drives, respond to the keyboard, and output data to the monitor. The OS works with the system BIOS to deal with these devices. If users want to access the hard drive to retrieve a program, the OS takes the request and passes it to the appropriate hard-drive BIOS instruction that tells the drive to send the program to RAM. If for some compelling reason the BIOS lacks the capability to perform its function, the OS should bypass the system BIOS and talk to the piece of hardware directly. Most recent OSs, including Windows, skip the system BIOS and talk directly to almost every piece of hardware.

Installing and configuring hardware devices was discussed in Chapter 9, so you should recall that hardware devices need their own programs to enable them to communicate with the OS device drivers. OS makers provide development tools for hardware makers to create driver software for their products.

Creating a User Interface

Unless you happen to speak the binary language of computers fluently enough to keep up with the millions of calculation cycles per second that the CPU routinely handles, you need some other way to enter commands. The OS creates a way for you to do this through the *user interface (UI)*.

The UI might be a *command prompt* that enables you to use a keyboard to type simple instructions into the system, or it might be a graphical *desktop* that you interact with using a pointer device such as a mouse, trackball, touchpad, joystick, or even using handwriting or voice commands. Whatever the UI's manifestation, they all do the same thing—enable you to control the computer. The "Operating System Interfaces" section of this chapter covers OS implementations in more detail.

Accessing and Supporting Programs

In addition to creating an environment for a user to interact with the PC, the OS creates the environment that enables users to interact with application programs.

In the old days, computers only ran one program at a time, but modern PCs are *multitasking* machines and must run two, three, ten, or any number of programs or processes concurrently. As with hardware, the OS must also determine the state of running programs and either correct error states or alert the user when a program has stopped responding.

Additionally, the OS enables you to install new programs and remove old ones with relative ease. Properly written programs should integrate with the OS seamlessly. It's when badly written or "buggy" programs are installed that we see problems.

Organizing and Manipulating Programs and Data

In order for programs and data to be useful, the OS must organize them into a logical structure. Fortunately, all OSs share the same basic organization method. All programs and data are stored as files. We can define a file as "a discrete piece of data organized in such a way that when the CPU loads it, it knows what to do with it." All files have two-part names: the first part is the unique identifier (A+_Passport_Ch14), and the second part called an extension that defines the type of data. (.DOC is the universal extension for Microsoft Word files). We combine these to give the complete filename (A+_Passport_Ch14.DOC). Executable files all have the extension, EXE or COM.

Files are useless if you can't organize them. All OSs share the same basic "directory-tree" organization. Each storage device has a name and an icon. We then subdivide each storage device into discrete folders or directories that contain related files. Windows makes a number of folders for the OS itself, but we may make our own for whatever use we decide.

Speaking of making folders, all of these files and folders are useless unless we can manipulate them. The OS enables users to create, manipulate, and arrange files on the storage devices. Common functions of this sort include copying data, moving data, and deleting data.

One of the greatest challenges to OS designers is making all of these functions comprehensible to users. Over the years, OSs have gone through vast changes trying to use the monitor to show you the system in such a way that you could do these manipulations. The "face" of the OS, the way you see the OS on the screen, is the user interface. The user interface has evolved from the dark days of the first PCs to the newest of today's systems.

Objective 14.03 Operating System Interfaces

All operating system user interfaces for the PC manifest in two ways, through a *command line interface* and through a *graphical user interface (GUI)*. Undoubtedly, the GUI is more familiar to most users, but the command line has by no means become obsolete.

Command Line Interface

Mainframes and minicomputers of old all used the classic command line interface for many years before the advent of the GUI, and it is still used to this day. While it's true that you won't find modern PCs that use this type of interface exclusively, all modern OSs—Windows, Macintosh, and the many flavors of Linux—enable users to "drop down" to a command prompt to enter instructions. In fact, many higher-level functions and utilities can *only* be run from a command line environment; therefore, it's not only relevant but important for techs to understand how to talk to the PC from the command line!

Microsoft's venerable *MS-DOS* OS is probably the first example that pops to mind when we talk about command line–based OS interfaces. Still considered by many to be an elegant OS, DOS is the first OS that most old-school PC techs encountered. Many of the commands that we first learned in DOS, such as COPY, DIR, ATTRIB, and others, are still used today. In fact, it's not uncommon for folks to (incorrectly) refer to the Windows command line interface as a *DOS window*.

Accessing the Command Line Interface

The command line interface program (also called the *command interpreter*) manifests as a simple text *prompt*—so-called because of the blinking text *cursor* character that prompts you for input. Anytime you've booted the PC using a floppy boot disk or gone into one of the command line modes from the advanced Windows OS boot menu, you've seen the good old C:\> prompt.

You can also access a command line interface from within Windows. Steps for doing so vary from version to version, but in general you can find the shortcut to the command line interface program, COMMAND.EXE in Windows 9*x*/Me, and CMD.EXE in NT/2000/XP, in the Accessories folder of your Start menu. Most techs, however, simply start it from the Run menu; e.g., Start | Run | *cmd*, as shown in Figure 14-1. (Note that you would type *command* rather than *cmd* in Windows 9*x*/Me.)

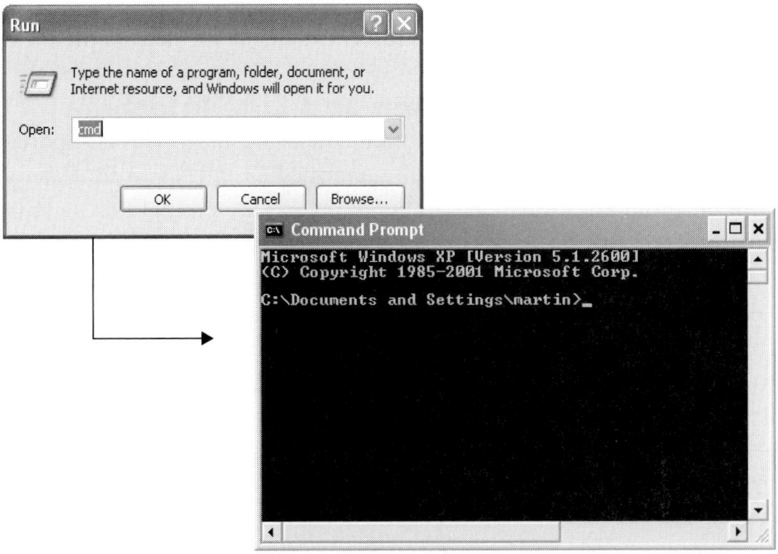

FIGURE 14.1 Type "cmd" in the Run dialog box to open a command line interface window in Windows XP.

Exam Tip

The location of the shortcut to the command line interface program varies depending on your version of Windows. Most versions place it on the Start menu under the Programs | Accessories submenu. Windows 2000/XP calls the shortcut *Command Prompt,* while Windows 9*x*/Me calls the shortcut *MS-DOS prompt,* but don't be fooled! You're not loading DOS when you click this shortcut, you're simply loading the COMMAND.EXE command line interface program into its own window.

Issuing Instructions Using the Command Line

The command line accepts only very specific commands. These commands must follow a very specific command *syntax.* Valid command line commands also vary from one OS to another, and even among different versions of the same OS. For a complete list of instructions, simply type **help** at the command prompt and press the ENTER key. For details on the various *switches* and *parameters* that apply to a particular command, type **help** followed by a space and the command name (e.g., **help attrib**).

For the moment, you can concentrate on the handful of commands that you're most likely to use. Table 14-1 lists a few of the more important commands that work in all versions of Windows command lines. I've also included the older forms of the commands for reference. You might see these on the exams.

Navigating Using a Command Line Interface

The command prompt is always *focused* on a specific folder. This is important because any commands you issue are performed *on the files in the folder* on which the prompt is focused. For example, if you see a prompt that looks like C:\>, you know that the focus is on the root directory of the C: drive.

As noted in Table 14-1, you change the command prompt's focus to another folder by typing **cd** followed by the target folder's name. To see which files are contained in a particular folder, use the **dir** command. Figure 14-2 shows the command prompt focused on the **Documents and Settings\martin\Desktop** folder of the C: drive.

Travel Advisory

In Windows 9*x*/Me, you must enclose long folder names in quotation marks. For example, we would type **cd "Documents and Settings"** instead of the way it is shown in the figure.

The **cd** command is *not* used to move between drives. To get the prompt to switch its focus to another hard disk drive, removable drive, or partition, just

TABLE 14.1	Common Command Line Interface Commands

Command	Description
cd	Changes the focus of the command prompt from one folder (directory) to another. The older form of the command is **chdir**.
copy	Copies files from one folder to another.
del	Permanently deletes files. The command **erase** works as well.
dir	Displays a listing of the files and folders (subdirectories) in a directory.
exit	Closes the command line interface program.
md	Creates a new folder. The older form of the command is **mkdir**.
move	Moves files from one folder to another.
rd	Deletes (removes) a folder. The older form of the command is **rmdir**.
ren	Renames files. You can spell it out as well, using **rename** as the command.
tree	Graphically displays the structure of a path.
ver	Displays the version of Windows.

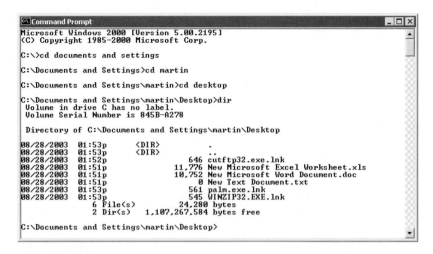

```
Command Prompt                                                   _ □ ×
Microsoft Windows 2000 [Version 5.00.2195]
(C) Copyright 1985-2000 Microsoft Corp.

C:\>cd documents and settings

C:\Documents and Settings>cd martin

C:\Documents and Settings\martin>cd desktop

C:\Documents and Settings\martin\Desktop>dir
 Volume in drive C has no label.
 Volume Serial Number is 845B-A278

 Directory of C:\Documents and Settings\martin\Desktop

08/28/2003  01:53p    <DIR>          .
08/28/2003  01:53p    <DIR>          ..
08/28/2003  01:52p               646 cutftp32.exe.lnk
08/28/2003  01:51p            11,776 New Microsoft Excel Worksheet.xls
08/28/2003  01:51p            10,752 New Microsoft Word Document.doc
08/28/2003  01:51p                 0 New Text Document.txt
08/28/2003  01:53p               561 palm.exe.lnk
08/28/2003  01:53p               545 WINZIP32.EXE.lnk
               6 File(s)         24,280 bytes
               2 Dir(s)   1,107,267,584 bytes free

C:\Documents and Settings\martin\Desktop>
```

FIGURE 14.2 Command prompt indicating focus on C:\Documents and Settings\martin\Desktop

type the target drive letter followed by a colon. If, for example, the command prompt is focused at the C:\Documents and Settings\martin\Desktop directory and you want to copy a file from the floppy disk drive (drive A:), just type **a:** and press the ENTER key and the command prompt will point to the floppy drive.

Note that navigation commands aren't case sensitive. Typing **c:** and typing **C:** followed by the ENTER key both get you to the root drive.

Running Applications from the Command Line Prompt

Executing applications from the command line environment is done in the same way as running the built-in Windows command line utilities. Simply navigate to the folder containing the application and type the name of the executable file. Valid files have an extension of **.exe** or **.com**, but typically you don't need to enter the file extension, just the filename.

Graphical User Interface

The GUI implementation of an OS is by far the more familiar to most users. Instead of using a character-based interface to run programs and administer files, you see files, folders, and programs represented as tiny graphics called *icons* arranged in a workspace called the *desktop*. You use a mouse or other pointing device to manipulate icons by selecting them with a *pointer*. Figure 14-3 shows a typical GUI, the venerable Windows 98.

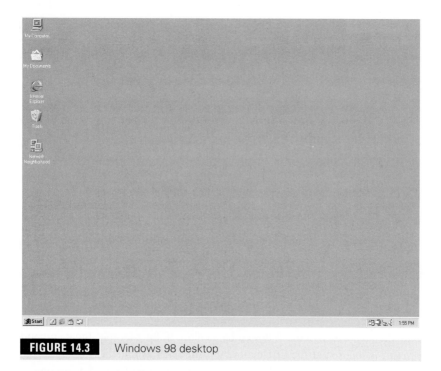

FIGURE 14.3 Windows 98 desktop

Modern versions of Windows, Windows NT/2000/XP, are pure GUI-based OSs. Accessing vital OS functions and programs is, of course, possible through a command line interface in these OSs, but the command line interface is a function of the GUI, and not the GUI itself. The focus of the CompTIA A+ exam is squarely on Microsoft Windows, so that's what we'll concentrate on as well. The next section looks at the features of Windows that are common to all versions.

Objective 14.04 Common Microsoft Windows Features

All versions of Windows share certain characteristics, configuration files, and that nebulous quality called *look and feel*. You'll find the same or similar utilities in almost all versions, and once you master one interface—both GUI and command line interface—you've pretty much got them all knocked.

This section covers the essentials: where to find things, how to maneuver, and common utilities. We'll get to the underlying structure of the two families of

Windows in the subsequent two sections of this chapter. Let's look at the common user interface, tech-oriented utilities, and typical OS folders.

User Interface

Windows offers a set of utilities or interfaces that every user should know how and why to access. Let's take a quick tour of the typical Windows GUI.

> ## Exam Tip
>
> If you're new to Windows and would like a feel for the basics of manipulating folders, resizing windows, and the like, surf on over to the Tech Files at www.totalsem.com and grab a copy of "Essential Windows." The A+ Certification OS Technologies exam tests you on basic user skills.

Login Screen

Every version of Windows supports multiple users on a single machine, and thus the starting point for any tour of the Windows user interface starts with the login screen. The login screen for Windows 9*x*/Me offers no security for the system—you can simply press the ESC key to bypass the screen and access the OS. Windows NT/2000/XP, in contrast, offer a high degree of security. In fact, you can't access any of these OSs without logging in with a valid user account. Figure 14-4 shows a Windows 2000 welcome screen.

Note that you're required to press the CTRL-ALT-DELETE key combination—the infamous *three-fingered salute*—in order to log into Windows 2000. This is a holdover from Windows NT, designed as a security measure. Windows XP changes the login procedure somewhat in a simple workgroup environment. One version of the Windows XP login screen presents you with a list of user accounts stored on the PC, enabling you to simply choose one to log in with, as shown in Figure 14-5. You still, of course, have to supply a valid password.

FIGURE 14.4 Windows 2000 welcome screen

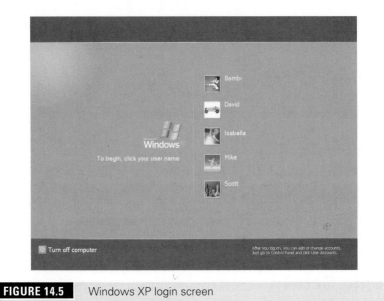

FIGURE 14.5   Windows XP login screen

Travel Advisory

Windows XP Professional has two very different login methods. The one shown in Figure 14-5 shows Windows XP configured to log in to a Workgroup. If you log in to a Windows Domain, you get a screen almost identical to the one shown for Windows 2000. See Chapter 17 for details on Workgroups and Domains.

Once you log into the system, you're presented with your user account's desktop, described in the next section.

Desktop

The Windows desktop is your main interface to the OS. The desktop is the workspace where you launch applications, input and manipulate data, configure hardware, and of course, watch videos and play games. Figure 14-6 shows a typical Windows XP Professional desktop.

The desktop is a highly customizable environment, enabling you to personalize virtually every aspect, including settings like the background wallpaper and default sound effects, screen resolution and color schemes, and language settings and accessibility options.

Windows systems enable different users to create different desktop environments (usually called *profiles*) that are loaded when a user logs on to the PC.

FIGURE 14.6   Windows XP Professional desktop

Every Windows desktop, however, still shares a few common features, such as several default folder shortcut icons and the *taskbar*. The paragraphs that follow describe the typical desktop icons you'll find on a Windows PC.

My Computer

The folder called My Computer enables you to quickly access all drives, folders, and files on the system. Note that Windows XP does not include My Computer on the desktop. You can readily access it through the Start menu. To open My Computer, simply double-click the My Computer icon on the desktop. When opened, My Computer shows you all the drives on the system, as shown in Figure 14-7.

The left side provides details of whatever icon you currently have highlighted. Microsoft calls this the web view. For example, Figure 14-7 has the C: drive highlighted, so the left side provides details about that drive. If you use Windows 95 or Windows NT, or if you choose to turn off this option in Windows 98/Me or Windows 2000/XP, you get a less sophisticated window, but you still have the same access to the system's drives, folders, and files.

Windows assigns different icons to different types of files according to their file type extensions, such as .EXE or .JPG. As you look at these icons on your own screen, you may note that you don't see any extensions—that's because later versions of Windows hides them by default. Revealing your file extensions requires a different process in each version of Windows.

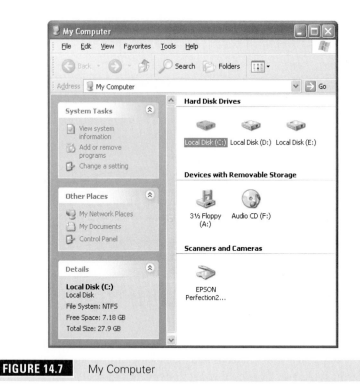

FIGURE 14.7 My Computer

If you have Windows 95 or NT, click View | Options to open the Options menu. Click the View tab and uncheck the *Hide MS-DOS file extensions for file types that are registered* check box (in Windows 95) or the *Hide file extensions for known file types* (in NT). While you're there, let's change one other item that will help later. Click the *Show All Files* radio button, too. All of your file extensions appear!

If you have Windows 98, it's exactly the same process, except Windows 98 calls the Options menu the File Options menu. Windows Me/2000/XP, of course, also have to do things a little differently. For Windows 2000/XP, click Tools | Folder Options, and then click the View tab. You need to do three jobs here. First, click the *Show hidden files and folders* radio button; second, uncheck *Hide file extensions for known file types*; and third, uncheck *Hide protected operating system files*. Click the *Apply to All Folders* button (just called *Apply* in Windows Me). A Windows XP View tab should look like Figure 14-8 when you are done. All file extensions and previously hidden system files (such as BOOT.INI and NTLDR) are viewable now.

In every version of Windows before XP, Windows Explorer acted like a separate and distinct tool from My Computer. Windows XP has merged the two into

Folder Options

General | View | File Types | Offline Files

Folder views

You can apply the view (such as Details or Tiles) that you are using for this folder to all folders.

[Apply to All Folders] [Reset All Folders]

Advanced settings:

- ☑ Display the full path in the address bar
- ☐ Display the full path in the title bar
- ☐ Do not cache thumbnails
- 📁 Hidden files and folders
  - ○ Do not show hidden files and folders
  - ⦿ Show hidden files and folders
- ☐ Hide extensions for known file types
- ☐ Hide protected operating system files (Recommended)
- ☐ Launch folder windows in a separate process
- ☑ Remember each folder's view settings
- ☐ Restore previous folder windows at logon
- ☐ Show Control Panel in My Computer

[Restore Defaults]

[OK] [Cancel] [Apply]

| **FIGURE 14.8** | Windows XP View tab |

a single tool, but you can still get the Explorer-like interface by alternate-clicking on a folder and selecting Explore from the pop-up options menu, or by holding down the WINDOWS key on your keyboard and pressing the E key.

My Documents

Windows 98, Windows Me, and Windows 2000 provide a special shortcut icon to the logged-on user's My Documents folder on the desktop (Windows XP does not). Newer Windows programs, such as Microsoft Office 2003 and Jasc Paint Shop Pro 8, store their files in My Documents unless you explicitly tell them to use a different folder.

As with My Computer, most Windows XP installations do not show the My Documents folder on the desktop—you can access it readily through the Start menu, or you can add it to your desktop.

Each version of Windows since Windows 98 seems to add more folders like My Documents to cover a whole host of other functions. For example, Windows XP Professional comes with My Documents, My Pictures (that offers filmstrip and thumbnail views of the pictures therein), My Music (with Media Player ready to play any file), My Videos (again, Media Player), and more.

Recycle Bin

The Recycle Bin shows up on the desktop of all versions of Windows. As you probably know, Windows doesn't completely erase items when you delete them from your drives. Instead, the file, folder, icon, or what-have-you is copied into the Recycle Bin folder, where it stays and one of three things occurs:

- You manually empty the Recycle Bin.
- You restore the item.
- The Recycle Bin grows larger than a preset amount and the file is permanently deleted to make room for more recently deleted files.

It's important to note that these rules only apply when you're dealing with fixed disk drives. Files deleted from removable disks, such as floppy disks or USB thumb drives, don't go to the Recycle Bin when you delete them—once they're deleted, they're gone for good!

Configure Recycle Bin behavior by alternate-clicking its icon and selecting Properties from the pop-up menu. Figure 14-9 shows the Recycle Bin configuration options.

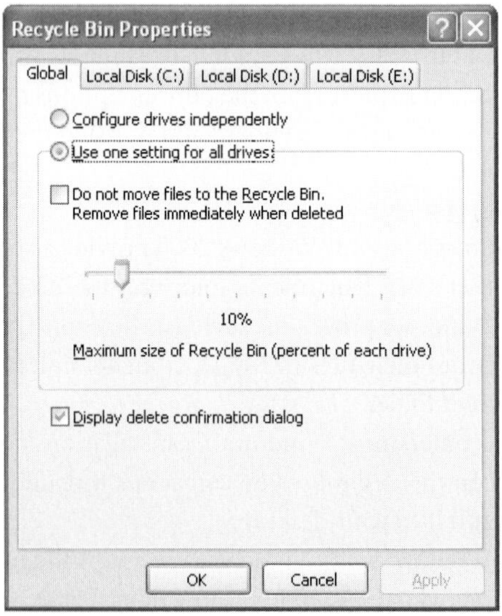

FIGURE 14.9   Recycle Bin Properties dialog box

> **Exam Tip**
>
> Everything in Windows has a properties setting. You can access the properties by alternate-clicking and selecting Properties. From here on, when I say "access properties," you know I mean to alternate-click and then select the word "Properties." You may also access properties by highlighting the object and pressing the ALT-ENTER key combination.

Important options include:

- **Configure drives independently**   This option enables you to set limits on the amount of disk space reserved for the Recycle Bin for each hard disk drive or partition. The default setting is to reserve the same percentage of disk space for each drive or partition.

- **Do not move files to the Recycle Bin**   This setting effectively disables the Recycle Bin, meaning that any items deleted are unrecoverable. Use this option with caution!

- **Maximum size of Recycle Bin**   Displayed in percentage (10 percent is the default), this is the amount of disk or partition space reserved for deleted items.

Internet Explorer

Most versions of Windows place a shortcut icon to Microsoft's web browser, Internet Explorer, on the desktop. In keeping with its Spartan look, Windows XP puts an icon for Internet Explorer on the Start menu, but not on the desktop.

Taskbar

The taskbar, by default, runs along the bottom of all Windows desktops and has up to four sections (depending on the version of Windows and your configuration): the Start Menu button, the *Quick Launch* area, the *active programs* area, and *System Tray* area.

Like the rest of the desktop, the taskbar is fully customizable, enabling you to do things like move it to any edge of your monitor screen (by clicking and dragging it with your pointer), add and remove icons to the Start menu and Quick Launch area, and hide the taskbar altogether when not in use.

Start Menu

The Start button, probably the most clicked-upon button on all Windows systems, is located on the far left-hand side of the taskbar. Clicking the Start button opens the Start menu, as shown in Figure 14-10, as does pressing either the

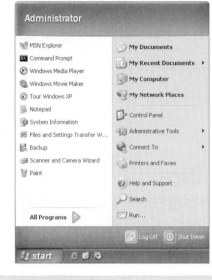

FIGURE 14.10   Windows 2000 Start menu

WINDOWS key (if your keyboard has one) or the CTRL-ESC key combination. Knowing these keyboard shortcuts is handy if you come upon a system that is configured to hide the taskbar.

Different programs may also add their own shortcut icons to the Start menu when you install them, or you can add and remove shortcut icons as you wish. Later versions of Windows automatically hide menu icons that are rarely used (you can disable this option).

Quick Launch Area

If, like most users, you install a lot of applications on your Windows system, you will soon wind up with a crowded Start menu that requires you to navigate through several tiers of menu options before you locate the icon you're looking for. The Quick Launch area of the taskbar addresses this by enabling you to place icons for your most frequently used programs where they're always visible and available.

As shown in Figure 14-11, the Quick Launch area of the taskbar is located just to the right of the Start button. Note that neither Windows 95 nor any version of Windows NT has the Quick Launch area on the taskbar.

FIGURE 14.11   Taskbar Quick Launch area

Active Programs Area

The bulk of the taskbar is taken up by the active programs area. This is where icons representing currently running applications show up. The active programs area enables you to keep track of, and quickly toggle between, running programs. Clicking the icon of a running program brings that program to the top of the desktop if it was running in the background. You can also quickly close a running program by alternate-clicking on its icon in the active programs area and selecting Close from the pop-up menu. Figure 14-12 shows the active programs area of a taskbar with several applications running.

System Tray

Looking all the way to the right end of the taskbar, you'll see the area called the System Tray. At the very least, the System Tray displays the current system time. The System Tray also shows icons for applications and services that are configured to launch automatically at system startup, or for system controls (such as the volume control) that you want to have quick access to. Figure 14-13 shows a typical Windows XP System Tray.

Different systems show different icons in the system tray, depending on how they're configured, but you'll usually see icons for things like PDA synchronizing software utilities, antivirus software, UPS control and configuration software, etc., as well as icons for currently running processes such as print jobs. In fact, many programs aggressively want to launch at startup automatically and install an icon into your System Tray. You can, of course, control this behavior, as described in the next section.

Configuring the Taskbar

All versions of Windows make it easy to control how your taskbar and Start menu behave. To get to the configuration options, alternate-click anywhere on the taskbar and select Properties from the pop-up submenu. This will open the Taskbar and Start Menu Properties dialog box (shown in Figure 14-14), enabling you to configure settings such as the size of the icons displayed on the Start menu, showing or hiding the system clock, and enabling or disabling *Personalized Menus* (this option hides seldom-used icons from the Start menu), as well as advanced settings: controlling which program icons are listed on the Start menu, what programs reside in the Startup folder (these are launched automatically at system startup), and so on.

FIGURE 14.12   Taskbar Active Programs area

FIGURE 14.13 System Tray

Network Neighborhood/ My Network Places

Systems tied to a network, via either a network cable, modem, or wireless connection, have an icon for the Network Neighborhood (or as Windows Me/2000/XP call it, My Network Places) on the desktop. Network Neighborhood/My Network Places can be thought of as My Computer for the network. Use Network Neighborhood/My Network Places to browse shared resources on the local network, or on remote networks such as web sites or *File Transfer Protocol (FTP)* servers. Figure 14-15 shows a typical Windows 2000 My Network Places folder.

OS Files and Folders

As mentioned earlier, one of the characteristics of an OS is that it organizes data stored on the hard disk drive. This includes organization of the vital OS files

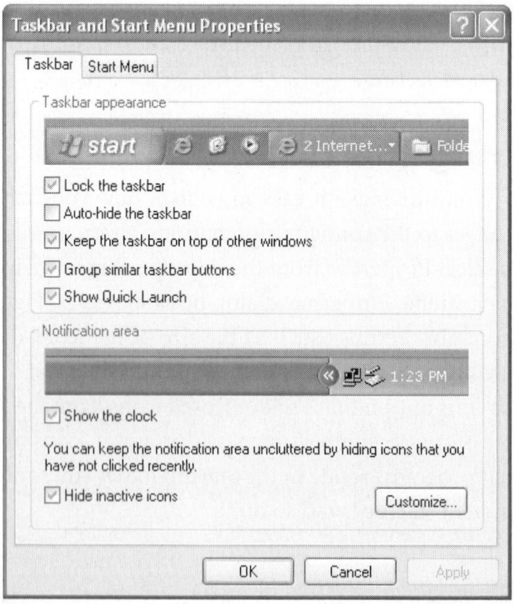

FIGURE 14.14 Taskbar and Start Menu Properties dialog box

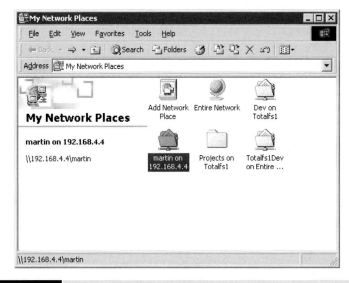

FIGURE 14.15   Windows 2000 Professional My Network Places folder

themselves. Each modern version of Windows organizes essential files and folders in a similar fashion:

- All have a primary system folder for storing most Windows internal tools and files.
- All use Registry files that keep track of all the hardware loaded and the drivers that enable you to use that hardware.
- Finally, every version has a virtual memory file, enabling more robust access to programs and utilities.

Let's take a more detailed look at these aspects of Microsoft Windows.

System Folder

Evidently, you can't simply go around calling the folder where Windows installs the operating system files "The folder where Windows installs the operating system files." Instead, *SystemRoot* is the tech name given to the folder in which the latest versions of Windows is installed. The SystemRoot folder for Windows NT/2000 is named WINNT by default. Windows 9*x*/Me and XP call the SystemRoot folder WINDOWS by default. Note that unlike Windows 9*x*/Me, Windows NT/2000/XP can be installed on any primary, active partition.

It's handy to know about SystemRoot. You'll find it cropping up in many other tech publications, and it can also be specified when adjusting certain

Windows settings in NT, XP, and 2000, to make sure that they work under all circumstances. When used as part of a Windows configuration setting, the term is often written as *%SystemRoot%* (the percent signs indicating that the SystemRoot is a variable parameter).

Travel Advisory

Here's a handy trick. If you don't know where Windows was installed on a particular system, go to a command prompt, type **cd %systemroot%**, and press the ENTER key. The prompt will change focus to the directory in which the Windows OS files are stored. Slick!

Naturally, things are done differently in Windows 9*x*/Me. *WinDir* is the Windows 9*x*/Me equivalent of SystemRoot when used at a command prompt, as in the Advisory above. The WinDir folder in Windows 9*x*/Me is called *Windows* by default and is always located on the root drive (e.g., C:\Windows). Note that for backward compatibility, NT, 2000, and XP support using either SystemRoot or WinDir commands.

Exam Tip

Windows NT/2000/XP can be installed on any primary, active partition. Without using third-party tools, Windows 9*x*/Me can only be installed on the root C: drive.

Registry

The Registry is a database that stores everything about your PC, including information on all the hardware in the PC, network information, user preferences, file types, and virtually anything else you might run into with Windows. Almost any form of configuration done to a Windows system involves editing the Registry. In fact, the Control Panel applets that you know and love are really simply user-friendly Registry editing tools!

The Registry in Windows 9*x*/Me is composed of two binary files, SYSTEM.DAT and USER.DAT. These files reside in the system folder (\%WinDir%). The Registry in Windows NT/2000/XP is considerably more complicated. The numerous Registry files (called *hives*) are stored in the \%SystemRoot%\System32\config folder.

Accessing the Registry The main way to access the Registry is through the Control Panel. You can get to the Control Panel in several ways. Double-click the My Computer icon on your desktop, and double-click the Control Panel icon. Alternatively, select Start | Control Panel (XP) or Settings | Control Panel (9x/Me, NT, 2000). Figure 14-16 shows the Windows XP Professional Control Panel sporting the Classic View (preferred by four out of five techs world wide). You can switch to Category View (the default) by selecting the appropriate option (top left).

Under normal circumstances, everything necessary to configure the system is handled from the Control Panel, and very few occasions require direct Registry access. However, all good techs should know how to access, navigate, and when necessary edit the system Registry. Microsoft provides us with tools for doing this—the *Registry Editor.*

The Registry Editor comes in two versions, the 16-bit version and the 32-bit version. The 16-bit version, called *regedit,* works in either Windows 9x/Me or Windows NT/2000/XP. The 32-bit regedit only works on 32-bit versions of Windows. By and large, either version is used identically to edit Registry hives and keys, but most techs using Windows NT/2000/XP wind up toggling between the two versions due to subtle but important differences. The 16-bit version of the Registry Editor has a superior searching capability for locating a particular Registry entry, but the 32-bit version has the ability to save and print Registry *subkeys,* and to set security permissions on Registry entries.

FIGURE 14.16   Windows XP Professional Control Panel

> **Travel Advisory**
>
> Windows XP combines REGEDIT and REGEDIT32 into a single
> 32-bit program that has the search power of the old REGEDIT.
> You can type either **regedit** or **regedt32** at a command prompt
> in XP and you'll get the same program.

Launch either version of the Registry Editor by going to Start | Run and typing in the appropriate name. Figure 14-17 shows the 16-bit (top) and 32-bit versions of Registry Editor.

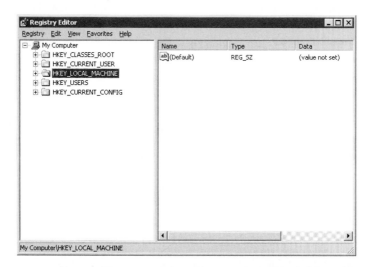

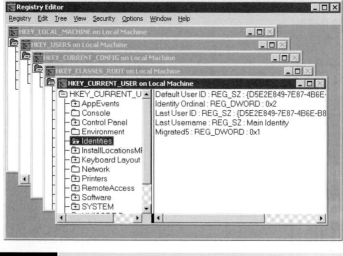

FIGURE 14.17   16-bit (top) and 32-bit versions of Registry Editor

Exam Tip

The Registry files are binary. You cannot edit the Registry with Edit, Notepad, or any other text editor as you could with SYSTEM.INI. You must use the Registry Editor tool.

Registry Components   The Registry is what's called a *hierarchical* database, organized in a tree structure similar to the folders in the PC. Open the Registry Editor (16-bit version), and you'll see six main subgroups or root keys:

- HKEY_CLASSES_ROOT
- HKEY_CURRENT_USER
- HKEY_LOCAL_MACHINE
- HKEY_USERS
- HKEY_CURRENT_CONFIG
- HKEY_DYN_DATA (Not present on Windows NT/2000/XP)

Try opening one of these root keys, and note that more subkeys are listed underneath them. Many subkeys also have other subkeys or values. The secret to understanding the Registry is to understand the function of the six root keys first. Each of these root keys has a specific function, so let's take a look at them individually.

- **HKEY_CLASSES_ROOT**   This root key defines the standard *class objects* used by Windows. A class object is a named group of functions. Pretty much everything that has to do with files on the system is defined by a class object.
- **HKEY_USERS and HKEY_CURRENT_USER**   Windows can be configured to support more than one user on the same PC, storing personalized information such as colors, screen savers, and the contents of the desktop. HKEY_USERS stores all the personalization information for all users on a PC. HKEY_CURRENT_USER stores the current user settings, like fonts, icons, and colors on systems that are set up to support multiple users.
- **HKEY_LOCAL_MACHINE**   This root key contains all the data for a system's non-user-specific configurations. This includes every device in your PC, including devices that you have removed.
- **HKEY_CURRENT_CONFIG**   If values in HKEY_LOCAL_MACHINE have more than one option, such as two different monitors, this root key defines which one is currently being used. Because most people

have only one type of monitor and similar equipment, this area is almost never touched.

● **HKEY_DYN_DATA** This is Registry data stored in RAM to speed up system configuration. A snapshot of all hardware in use is stored here. It is updated at boot and when any changes are made in the system configuration file. This key is not present in Windows NT/2000/XP systems.

Exam Tip

Make sure you know the default root keys of the Windows Registry.

Virtual Memory

Windows uses *virtual memory* as an extension of system RAM. Virtual memory is a section of physical hard disk drive space that's used as a temporary storage box for running programs. When the PC starts running out of real RAM, when, for instance, one program needs more resources, the system moves inactive programs from RAM to the virtual memory area on the hard disk drive, thus opening more space in RAM for programs currently active. This process is fully automated, requiring no user intervention. All versions of Windows use virtual memory, although they may call it different things, such as the *swapfile* or *pagefile*.

Local Lingo

Virtual memory, swapfile, pagefile Virtual memory, swapfile, and pagefile all refer to the same thing: space on the hard disk drive reserved as temporary storage for running programs.

The swapfile in Windows 9x/Me is called WIN386.SWP, and it usually resides in the \Windows folder, but that can be changed. In Windows NT/2000/XP, the file is called PAGEFILE.SYS. You can often find it in the root directory of the C: drive, but again, that can be changed. In both cases, the swap file is going to be a hidden, system file, which means that you'll have to change your folder viewing options to see them.

Because swapping programs between RAM and virtual memory takes time and CPU cycles, you may notice a reduction in performance if there's a lot of "paging" activity. To counter this performance hit, there are a few things you can do:

- Because virtual memory is only brought heavily into play when there's not enough RAM to accommodate running programs, you can decrease paging by adding more RAM to the system.

- Change the size of the virtual memory. The general rule of thumb is that the size of virtual memory should be 1.5 times the amount of installed system RAM on a Windows 9x/Me system (i.e., a system with 256 MB of RAM should have a virtual memory size of 384 MB). However, this is more of a guideline than a hard and fast rule. As you increase system RAM, you actually need less virtual memory space, and conversely, a system with too little RAM needs more virtual memory. Don't bother to change the size of the virtual memory on Windows 2000 or XP machines. Windows does a great job without tweaking.

- Change the location of the pagefile. If you have more than one physical hard disk drive, you can increase performance by moving the pagefile from the system disk—the disk that has Windows installed on it—to another hard disk drive.

We'll talk more about how to increase system performance later in this book.

CHECKPOINT

✔**Objective 14.01: Characteristics of the Operating System**   Operating systems are made to work on a particular type of CPU platform. Microsoft Windows runs on the Intel and AMD x86 CPU family. Some OSs, such as Linux and Microsoft Windows NT, can operate on more than one type of processor. Software applications are likewise made to work on one type of OS (although some are ported to operate on more than one OS). The OS takes over control of the PC after POST and continues to run until you exit the OS or shut down the system. An OS must be flexible enough to enable you to install new hardware and software.

✔**Objective 14.02: Common Operating System Functions**   Functions that are common to any OS include: communicating with hardware, creating a user interface (a means for the user to issue instructions to the PC and retrieve information from it), enabling users to access application programs, and enabling users to create and manipulate data.

✔**Objective 14.03: Operating System Interfaces** The user interface manifests in two ways: a text-only command line interface and an icon-driven graphical user interface (GUI). Microsoft DOS is an example of a text-only command line interface OS, and modern versions of Microsoft Windows are GUI-based OSs. GUI versions of Windows also offer command line interface access to the OS.

✔**Objective 14.04: Common Microsoft Windows Features** Different versions of Windows offer different features, but all versions have a common feature set. The Windows user interface is the same or similar in all versions of Windows; it includes the login screen, the desktop, and the taskbar. On networked systems, Windows places either the Network Neighborhood or My Network Places (depending on your version of Windows) icon on the desktop. All versions of Windows use common OS files and folders, such as the system folder (the folder where the Windows OS files are stored), the Registry, and the virtual memory swapfile or pagefile.

REVIEW QUESTIONS

1. What is the best way to access the Registry Editor in Windows 9x/Me?
   A. Start | Programs | DOS prompt icon. Type **edit**.
   B. Start | Programs | Registry Editor.
   C. Start | Run | Type **regedit** and click OK.
   D. Start | Run | Type **regedt32** and click OK.

2. Which of the following is not a Registry root key in Windows NT/2000/XP?
   A. HKEY_CURRENT_MACHINE
   B. HKEY_CLASSES_ROOT
   C. HKEY_CURRENT_USER
   D. HKEY_DYN_DATA

3. An employee reports that he accidentally deleted a file from his USB thumb drive and cannot find it in the Recycle Bin. What can you do to correct this?
   A. Tell the employee to open My Computer and click Tools | Folder Options. Then click the View tab and select the View Hidden Files And Folders radio button.

    B. Tell the employee to open My Computer, and click View | Options to open the Options menu. Click the View tab and uncheck the Hide MS-DOS File Extensions For File Types That Are Registered check box.

    C. Alternate-click the Recycle Bin icon and select Properties from the pop-up menu. Select the Do Not Move Files To The Recycle Bin check box.

    D. You cannot correct this.

4. Which of the following commands entered in the Start | Run dialog box will start the Windows XP 32-bit command interpreter? (Choose all that apply.)

    A. CMD

    B. COMMAND

    C. WINNT32

    D. CMD32

5. The mouse on your PC stops responding. The PC is configured to automatically hide the taskbar and Start menu. How can you access the Start button without the mouse? (Choose all that apply.)

    A. Press the WINDOWS key on the keyboard.

    B. Press the CTRL-ALT-DEL key combination on the keyboard.

    C. Press the CTRL-ESC key combination on the keyboard.

    D. Press the ALT-F4 key combination on the keyboard.

6. What are the major functions of an operating system (OS)?

    A. An OS provides a method for other programs to communicate.

    B. An OS creates a user interface.

    C. An OS enables users to add, move, and delete installed programs and data.

    D. All of the above.

7. Which of the following shows a typical command line prompt?

    A. A:\\

    B. D:/>

    C. C:\>

    D. C://

8. Which of the following best describes the operating system's user interface?

    A. It enables the system to communicate with peripheral devices.

B. It provides a means for the user to enter commands and retrieve data.

C. It provides a display of the system hardware to the user.

D. It provides error handling or notification displays when communicating with hardware.

9. To manipulate and organize data and programs, which of the following must the OS do? (Select all that apply.)

   A. Identify all the data and programs on the system and organize them in a binary-code format.

   B. Provide a method to identify data according to the type of program that uses that particular data.

   C. Provide a naming system for each drive.

   D. Give the user an interface to assign drive letters to drives.

10. What type of memory stores running programs in a swapfile on a hard disk drive?

   A. Extended memory

   B. Flash memory

   C. Virtual memory

   D. Random access memory

REVIEW ANSWERS

1. **C**   Start | Run | Type **regedit** and clicking OK will start the Registry Editor in Windows 9*x*/Me.

2. **D**   HKEY_DYN_DATA is not a valid Registry root key in Windows NT/2000/XP.

3. **D**   Files deleted from removable drives are not stored in the Recycle Bin.

4. **A B**   In Windows XP, typing **cmd** or **command** at the Start | Run dialog box starts the 32-bit command line interface.

5. **A C**   Pressing the WINDOWS key or the CTRL-ESC key combination brings up the Start menu.

6. **D**   All of the above.

7. **C**   C:\> is a typical prompt.

8. **B**   The user interface enables users to input instructions and retrieve data.

9. **B** **C**   The user must have some method to know which data files are used by particular programs. Further, the OS must provide a naming system for every drive.

10. **C**   Virtual memory holds the swapfile (or pagefile).

Operating Systems: Windows in Detail

	NEWBIE	SOME EXPERIENCE	EXPERT
ETA	3 hours	2 hours	1 hour

Now that we've covered the basics of what an operating system is and what it can do, as well as the basic feature set of Microsoft Windows, it's time to dig deeper. This chapter looks under the hood of the Windows OS at the nitty-gritty files, folders, and functions that are usually hidden from the typical user's eyes but that are vitally important for techs to understand.

Many versions of Windows have come and gone, and in fact, many different versions are currently on the market. The CompTIA A+ core OS exam is primarily focused on the versions of Windows that a PC tech is likely to service in the workplace or home—those derived from the roots of Windows 95 (what we've been calling Windows 9*x*/Me) and those based on the Windows NT *kernel*, or core OS code. These include Windows NT Workstation, Windows 2000 Professional, and Windows XP Home and Professional. As described in the preceding chapter, there are many similarities between the Windows versions, but more importantly, there are many differences that affect the way the PC operates and the way that you approach servicing and troubleshooting scenarios.

With that in mind, let's begin by looking at the structure of Windows 9*x*/Me and then look at Windows NT/2000/XP in detail. Let's get started.

Objective 15.01 Windows 9*x*/Me Structure

Microsoft debuted Windows 95 as its first stand-alone GUI operating system. Subsequent versions include Windows 95A, 95 OSR2, 98, 98 Second Edition (SE), and Millennium Edition (Me). Windows 95 was built on the experience Microsoft had with DOS and with its first attempt at a GUI, Windows 3.*x*. Windows 3.*x* was great for its time but was not a true OS; rather, it was a graphical shell that required DOS to interact with the PC hardware.

Because of this lineage, Windows 9*x*/Me has a complex structure that retains elements—files and configuration utilities—from the previous operating system and graphical shell. This set of legacy files and utilities enables Windows 9*x*/Me to support a very wide variety of hardware and applications, even stuff that dates back prior to Windows 3.*x*! It also means that a lot of files can be configured incorrectly, so a tech needs to understand how the legacy "fileage" influences the graphical OS of Windows 9*x*/Me.

Windows 9*x*/Me is not just a polished-up combo of DOS and Windows 3.*x*, but rather, it has a complex set of operating system files and utilities all of its own. Windows 9*x*/Me has both 16-bit components—those that sprung from

DOS and Windows 3.*x*—and 32-bit components—the native Windows 9*x*/Me code. Let's look at the legacy structures of Windows and then turn to the graphical OS. We'll finish this section with a brief discussion about the differences among the various versions of Windows 9*x*/Me.

DOS Protected Mode Interface

Windows 9*x*/Me is really two products: a *DOS protected-mode interface (DPMI)* and a protected-mode GUI. *Protected-mode* in this context means 32-bit, rather than 16-bit. The improved DOS part of Windows 9*x*/Me looks and acts pretty much exactly like good old DOS, although you can't easily access it in Me. Windows 9*x*/Me first starts the DOS aspect of Windows and then fires up the GUI. This means that you do not have to use the GUI to boot to Windows 9*x*! (You can't do this in Windows Me. You have to boot to the GUI.) This is important because many PC repair functions, particularly for the hard drive, are handled at a C:\ prompt. Do not confuse booting Windows 9*x* without the GUI with running a command prompt window inside Windows 9*x*/Me! Let's look at the main aspects of Windows' DPMI.

FAT32

Later versions of Windows 95 and all versions of Windows 98, Me, and 2000/XP support the powerful FAT32 file format, enabling partitions up to 2 terabytes (TB) in size on FAT32-formatted hard disk drives. Before FAT32, the old FAT16 format had a maximum partition size of only 2.1 gigabytes (GB).

Core Files

DPMI is composed of three main files: IO.SYS, MSDOS.SYS, and COMMAND .COM, although you may not have COMMAND.COM in some circumstances. Even though the names are the same as the true DOS equivalents, the functions have changed dramatically.

IO.SYS   IO.SYS tells the PC how it is set up. IO.SYS is a binary file, and as such, not editable using text editors. IO.SYS is the first file loaded when your Windows 9*x*/Me system boots and as such, has a number of jobs to do.

When the computer boots up and says "Starting Windows 95" or "Starting Windows 98," press the F8 key (for Windows 98, press the left CTRL key) and the Windows boot menu appears. One of the many jobs of IO.SYS is to check to see if the F8 key (left CTRL key in Windows 98) has been pressed as Windows loads. If it has, the Windows boot menu loads. Let's take a look at the Windows boot menu.

The Windows boot menu provides a method for technicians to choose from a number of boot methods "on the fly" to enable many different trouble-shooting scenarios. Be warned that not all systems show the same boot options. Figure 15-1 shows a boot menu from a typical Windows 98 system.

Although some of these options may seem obvious, others could do with a bit of explaining. Here's a list of the common boot menu options for Windows 9*x*:

- **Normal**   This boots Windows normally.
- **Logged**   This logs the boot process in a file called BOOTLOG.TXT on the root drive.
- **Safe mode**   This boots Windows into *Safe mode*, Windows' troubleshooting GUI mode with only minimal drivers and services loaded. (You can automatically boot into Safe mode by pressing the F5 key at boot.)
- **Safe mode with network support**   This boots Safe mode but still loads the network drivers so that you can access the network. This option appears only on networked systems—that does not include dial-up networking!
- **Step-by-step confirmation**   Similar to the old DOS F8 step-by-step boot method, this includes a number of auto-loading features that are normally invisible.
- **Command prompt only**   This processes all startup files but does not start the GUI. You can type **WIN** from the **C:** prompt to start the GUI, if desired.

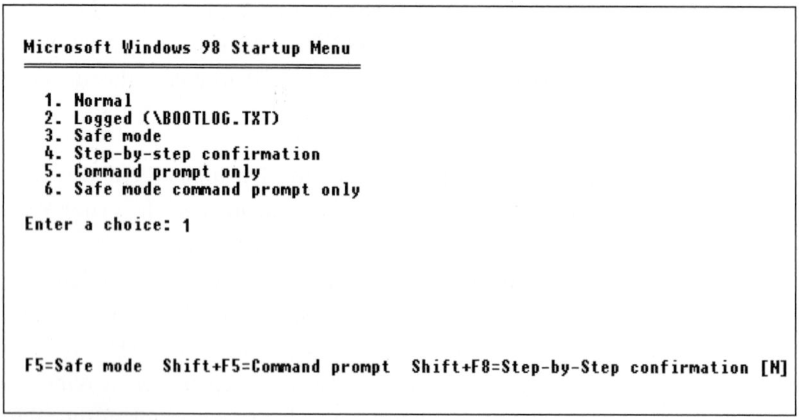

```
Microsoft Windows 98 Startup Menu
================================

   1. Normal
   2. Logged (\BOOTLOG.TXT)
   3. Safe mode
   4. Step-by-step confirmation
   5. Command prompt only
   6. Safe mode command prompt only

Enter a choice: 1




F5=Safe mode   Shift+F5=Command prompt   Shift+F8=Step-by-Step confirmation [N]
```

FIGURE 15.1   Windows 98 boot menu

- **Safe mode command prompt only**   This skips all startup files to get to a C: prompt. You must reboot to start Windows.

- **Previous version of MS-DOS**   If you installed Windows over a true DOS system, Windows keeps the original DOS boot files in the root directory with the extension DOS and shows this option. You may boot to them. Do not use this option if you do not have a previous version of DOS or if the version of Windows uses FAT32.

Exam Tip

Take the time to become familiar with the ways you can enter the advanced Boot Menu, and the options you have once you get there.

Just to keep things interesting, Windows Me offers only a subset of the boot menu options. You do not get any of the command prompt options, so it is impossible to boot to a command prompt only in Windows Me. You can get a command prompt—but only from within Windows Me.

MSDOS.SYS   MSDOS.SYS is a read-only text file in the root directory of the boot drive. MSDOS.SYS is used as a startup options file.

In earlier versions of Microsoft Windows, MSDOS.SYS was an important part of the OS kernel, but in modern versions, MSDOS.SYS is just a text file that replaces many of the AUTOEXEC.BAT and CONFIG.SYS functions that the system needs before the GUI kicks in. A good Windows 9x tech should be comfortable editing an MSDOS.SYS file, so let's take a moment to see the contents of MSDOS.SYS.

MSDOS.SYS is opened using any text editor, such as Notepad. MSDOS.SYS has *hidden, system,* and *read-only* attributes by default, so you'll need to turn them off to see what's in this file. Notice that MSDOS.SYS is organized just like an INI file with groups and options under each setting.

The following options shown in Table 15-1 must be placed in the [Options] group. Each of the examples shows the default setting, but other settings are listed.

The options shown in Table 15-2 must be in the [Paths] group.

Don't kill yourself trying to memorize all these features! Do take the time to appreciate that MSDOS.SYS is now a text file, and make sure you know how to edit it if need be. Take some time to appreciate what it does and does not do. Does it load device drivers or TSRs? No. Does it provide a number of boot options? Yes. Think about how some of these options might come in handy in a troubleshooting scenario.

TABLE 15.1	MSDOS.SYS [Boot] Section Options

Option	Description
BootConfig=1	This enables the computer to boot up a particular hardware configuration. For example, BootConfig=2 would start configuration 2.
SystemReg=1	This loads the system Registry (0 = don't load).
BootSafe=0	This option does not force the machine to boot in Safe mode (1 = force Safe mode).
DRVSpace=1 or DBLSpace=1	This loads DoubleSpace or DriveSpace disk drive compression drivers (0 = don't load).
BootWin=1	This boots Windows (0 = DOS). This is a dangerous option and should never be used unless you installed a true DOS before you installed Windows and you have only FAT16 partitions!
BootWarn=1	This shows the "You Are in Safe mode" warning message (0 = don't show) when booted into Safe mode.
BootKeys=1	This specifies using the function keys (like F8) at boot (0 = no keys). Nice for keeping nosy users out of places they shouldn't go.
BootGUI=1	This specifies booting the Windows 9x GUI (0 = DOS prompt only).
Network=1	This shows boot in Safe mode, with a networking menu option available (0 = don't show).
BootMenu=0	This does not automatically load boot menu at boot (1 = show menu).
BootMenuDefault=1	This shows the default boot menu option if you don't pick one. Choices are: Normal 2 = Logged to Bootlog.txt 3 = Safe mode 4 = Safe mode with network support (if network settings are enabled) 4 (if no networking) or 5 (if networking enabled) = Step-by-step 5 (no networking) or 6 (networking) = Command prompt 6 (no networking) or 7 (networking) = Safe mode command prompt 7 (no networking) or 8 (networking) = Previous version of MS-DOS (if BootMulti=1)
DoubleBuffer=1	This loads VFAT's double buffer (0 = don't load). Obsolete command for older SCSI drives.
BootMulti=0	This is for dual-boot systems. If set to 0, the boot menu will not prompt for the previous version of MS-DOS in the boot menu. If set to 1, you will see the option "Previous version of MS-DOS." Don't mess with this option unless a) you installed on top of DOS and b) you did not use FAT32.
Logo=1	This shows an animated logo (0 = don't show).
LoadTop=1	This loads COMMAND.COM at the top of 640K (0 = load at the bottom).
BootDelay=X	This specifies how long the computer waits, in seconds, after showing "Starting Windows 9x." Many techs set this to "0" to make booting faster.
AutoScan=1	This option specifies whether ScanDisk runs automatically when you reboot after a crash. If you set this to 0, ScanDisk will not run. Set to 1 means the system will prompt you before running, and set to 2 means Windows will run ScanDisk without asking your approval (although it will prompt before making changes/fixes). This is usable only in OSR2 and later versions of Windows 9x.

TABLE 15.2	MSDOS.SYS [Paths] Section Options
Option	**Description**
UninstallDir=C:\	This specifies where to find the Windows 9x uninstall file.
WinDir=C:\WINDOWS	This specifies the location of the Windows GUI files.
WinBootDir=C:\WINDOWS	This specifies the location of the Windows files needed to boot. It is normally the same as the WinDir directory.
HostWinBootDrv=C	This is always the C: drive.

COMMAND.COM   COMMAND.COM is still there and, as described previously, provides the prompt enabling users to input instructions. COMMAND.COM is no longer required if the system will always run in the GUI mode. But if a C:\ is ever needed, or if the system needs to use an AUTOEXEC.BAT file, COMMAND.COM must be present in the root directory.

Configuration Files

Windows 9x/Me can use the two DOS-era configuration files, CONFIG.SYS and AUTOEXEC.BAT, for loading legacy device drivers and *terminate and stay resident (TSR)* programs. You'll see both files come into play to load CD-ROM drivers in Windows 9x/Me Startup disks, for example, and in systems that run older applications. For the most part, though, the files sit empty in the root directory of the C: drive.

Two DOS-era memory management files can appear in CONFIG.SYS— HIMEM.SYS and EMM386.EXE—although Windows 9x/Me loads both files automatically in the protected-mode GUI phase. HIMEM.SYS provides access to the memory beyond the first 1 MB of space and thus is required by Windows 9x/Me in order to load the graphical portions of the operating systems. EMM386.EXE was a great utility for its day, enabling us to (among other things) play classic games such as DOOM and Red Baron, and providing a tool for fine-tuning memory addresses. EMM386.EXE is obsolete in modern computers.

Exam Tip
Windows 9x/Me PCs require HIMEM.SYS in order to load the graphical portion of the OS.

Legacy GUI Files

After the DPMI-level OS files and configuration files and utilities load, WIN.COM runs and initiates the graphical portion of the operating system. During the loading process, Windows incorporates the legacy INI files to provide support for any ancient applications you might load on a Windows 9*x*/Me system. (The same holds true for Windows 2000/XP, although not for NT 4.0.)

Windows 3.*x* used text files with the extension INI to initialize just about everything from device drivers to applications to Windows itself. Both the Windows OS and Windows applications created initialization files. Although Windows 9*x*/Me and Windows 2000/XP rely much less on INI files, knowing how to edit an INI file is crucial to repairing all Windows PCs.

Two legacy INI files in particular, SYSTEM.INI and WIN.INI, bear further discussion. Note that all INI files are broken up into logical sections called *groups*. Each group starts with a word or words in square brackets, called a *group header*—for instance, [*mswindows*]. Following each group header are the settings for that group. They are organized with the syntax *item=settings*.

SYSTEM.INI

SYSTEM.INI was the CONFIG.SYS of Windows 3.*x*. All the resources were initialized there, as well as a number of global settings that defined how resources were to be used. We often edited this file on Windows 3.*x* systems to tweak a large number of settings. The SYSTEM.INI file was absolutely required to run a Windows 3.*x* system.

You still find SYSTEM.INI on all Windows 9*x*/Me systems today. Keeping the SYSTEM.INI file enables backward compatibility with older Windows 3.*x* applications that still look for a SYSTEM.INI file to load or determine critical settings. All Windows 9*x*/Me systems still require SYSTEM.INI, even though the settings are no longer critical.

WIN.INI

WIN.INI was the AUTOEXEC.BAT of Windows 3.*x*. It defined all the personalized settings of Windows, such as fonts, screen savers, and display colors, and how resources interacted with applications. WIN.INI was also the dumping ground for settings that did not have a home anywhere else.

This file was often manually edited. Windows 3.*x* didn't require WIN.INI to boot, but you lost a lot of functionality without it. Windows 9*x*/Me systems rarely have a WIN.INI file unless an installed application makes one.

> **Exam Tip**
>
> Know how to edit SYSTEM.INI and WIN.INI on Windows systems. You can use EDIT.EXE, NOTEPAD, or SYSEDIT to edit AUTOEXEC.BAT, CONFIG.SYS, and INI files. Binary system files such as USER.DAT cannot be edited with a text editor. Also, know why the INI files exist on Windows 9x/Me systems and when they are needed!

WIN.INI has two problem areas that can cause trouble on modern systems: LOAD= and RUN=. These lines automatically load programs when Windows starts, acting like a hidden Startup group. If you find that a program keeps running but it isn't in a Startup group, check here to see if one of these lines is starting the program.

Windows 9x/Me GUI Files

Assuming a Windows 9x/Me device driver is available, you don't need CONFIG.SYS to load device drivers anymore. So, assuming Windows 9x/Me drivers are available, you do not need CONFIG.SYS. In addition, Windows has its own startup methods, so you probably don't need AUTOEXEC.BAT or WIN.INI either.

The lowest levels of Windows 9x/Me are the device drivers—either real-mode drivers loaded at CONFIG.SYS or AUTOEXEC.BAT, or protected-mode drivers loaded with the GUI. After the device drivers comes the *virtual memory manager (VMM)*, which supports memory usage at both the DPMI and GUI levels. At the DPMI level, VMM does little more than load a simple command line. When the GUI is loaded, VMM takes advantage of the power of 386 protected mode to create *virtual machines,* one for Windows 9x/Me and one for each DOS program running in Windows 9x/Me.

When the GUI is running, the main functions of Windows 9x/Me are handled by the kernel, user, and *graphical device interface (GDI)* modules. These files—KRNL386.EXE, USER.EXE, and GDI.EXE—reside in the C:\Windows\ System folder. Most functions run in full 32-bit protected mode, although they provide support for 16-bit real mode.

At the top of the Windows 9x/Me architecture is the user interface—the programs you actually *see* on the screen: the icons, windows, and toolbars. Windows 9x/Me can use the default interface, the Windows 3.x interface, or even other shells.

Objective 15.02 Major Differences among Versions of Windows 9x/Me

The following sections detail a few of the more outstanding updates implemented with the different versions of Windows 9x/Me.

A Great Startup Disk

A *startup disk* is simply a special bootable floppy disk that contains a number of handy utilities to help you fix a system that won't boot Windows. You cannot start Windows from a startup disk, so you can't run any graphical programs—but both Windows 95 and Windows 98 enable you to make a startup disk with enough tools that can run from an **A:** prompt to fix many common problems.

One huge problem with the Windows 95 startup disk is that it does not support a CD-ROM drive. In many cases, you need to access the CD-ROM in order to install programs, so you have to go through a rather painful process to make the Windows 95 startup disk access the CD-ROM. The Windows 98/SE/Me startup disk automatically supports almost every type of CD-ROM drive made.

FAT32

The first version of Windows 95 (Windows 95A) supported only FAT16 file systems for hard drives. Microsoft introduced FAT32 with Windows 95 version B, also called OSR2.

System Information Tool

The System Information tool provides a handy snapshot of your system in a fairly easy-to-read format. The System Information tool is located under Start | Programs | Accessories | System Tools. You can also start it at a command prompt by typing **MSINFO32**. Think of the System Information tool as a "*read-only* Device Manager" in that you get to see all of the resource and driver information provided by Device Manager in a report format, as shown in Figure 15-2.

Additionally, the System Information tool provides a launch point for almost every utility used by Windows 98 SE/Me. Look under the Tools menu option to find many other tools (Figure 15-3). When you're not sure where to find a utility in Windows 9x/Me, MSINFO32 is the tool to check first!

| FIGURE 15.2 | System Information tool |

Windows Update

Microsoft constantly provides free updates to its OSs. Updating Windows 95 gave the best techs a bad case of the jitters because the updating order had to be carefully monitored. Windows 98/SE/Me eliminates this problem completely

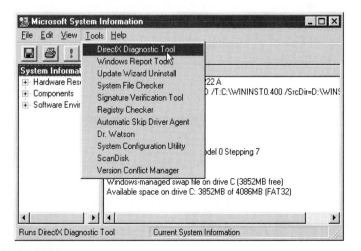

| FIGURE 15.3 | Starting the DirectX Diagnostic Tool from the System Information Tools menu |

with the Windows Update utility. This web-based utility inspects your system and provides a simple method to update your system safely (Figure 15-4).

Disk Cleanup

Windows 98/SE/Me has a Disk Cleanup utility that enables you to clean out unnecessary files (Figure 15-5). What makes this tool particularly handy is that it will automatically start when your drive reaches a certain minimum. Although third-party utilities such as Norton CleanSweep do a better job, Disk Cleanup works perfectly well for most systems.

Active Desktop

Windows 98 SE/Me come with a vastly improved version of Internet Explorer that includes the amazing Active Desktop, enabling the Desktop to load active web pages directly. Why bother opening a browser when that often-accessed web page sits on your Desktop, ready for instant viewing? New, even more powerful versions of Internet Explorer have since been released.

Internet Connection Sharing

The biggest improvement Microsoft included with Windows 98SE was Internet Connection Sharing (ICS), a way to enable multiple PCs to share a single dial-up connection through a local area network (LAN).

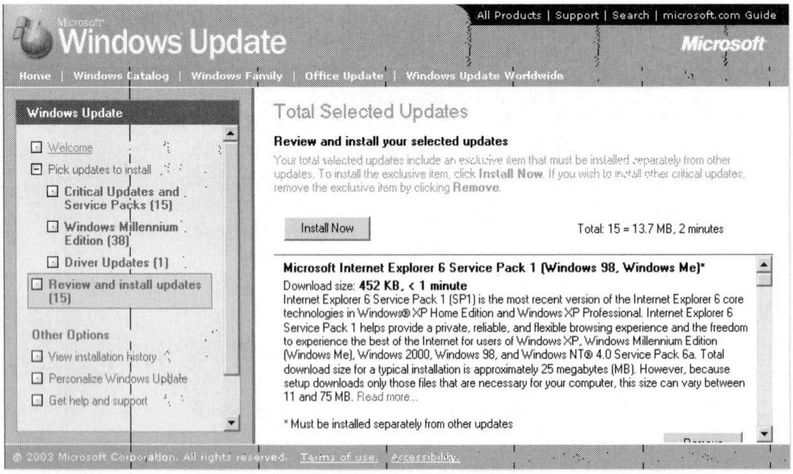

FIGURE 15.4 Windows 98 Update utility

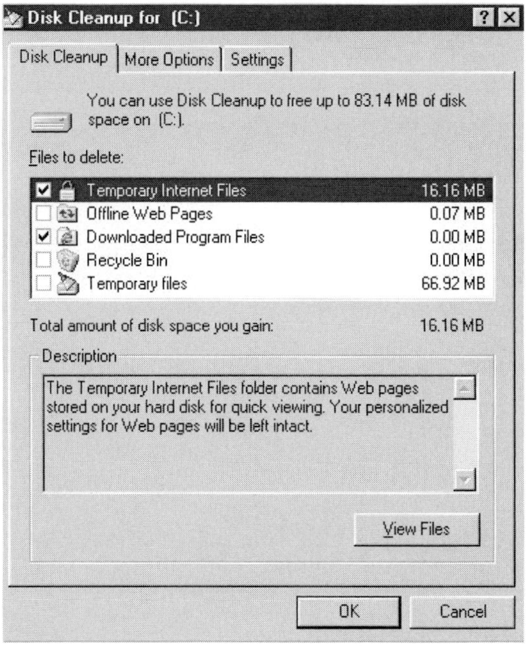

FIGURE 15.5   Windows 98 Disk Cleanup utility

System Restore

The most important enhancement that Windows Me has over its older siblings is a feature called System Restore. System Restore enables you to create Restore Points—snapshots of your system files and configurations at a particular moment—so that you can restore your PC to this pristine state if you install something later that makes it unhappy. You use this feature right before installing a big office suite, for example, or an aggressive program like Real Media. Figure 15-6 shows System Restore in action.

But Underneath...

All of the extra functions in Windows 98, 98 SE, and Me do not eliminate the fact that in nearly every aspect, these later OSs are identical to Windows 95. The installation process, install functions, and troubleshooting procedures vary little among the versions.

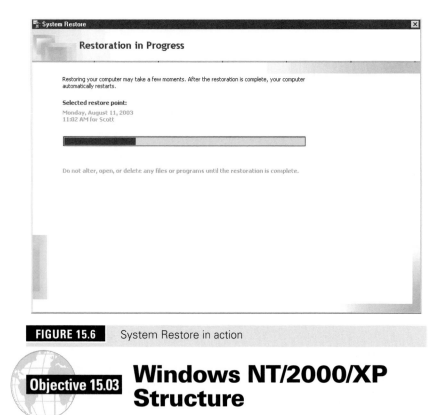

System Restore

Restoration in Progress

Restoring your computer may take a few moments. After the restoration is complete, your computer automatically restarts.

Selected restore point:
Monday, August 11, 2003
11:02 AM for Scott

Do not alter, open, or delete any files or programs until the restoration is complete.

FIGURE 15.6	System Restore in action

Objective 15.03 Windows NT/2000/XP Structure

In 1996, Microsoft released Windows NT 4.0, a true 32-bit, GUI OS. With NT, Microsoft offered a rock-solid, high-performance OS that offered scalability and, above all else, security. Windows NT's successors, Windows 2000 and Windows XP, share all of basic features of Windows NT, so the discussion that follows applies to all versions of operating systems based on the Windows NT *core*.

From the outside, Windows NT and 2000 look pretty much just like Windows 9*x*/Me, and users of those OSs generally have little trouble switching over to the heavy-duty version of Windows. So what's different? Plenty! Windows NT has so many features beyond Windows 9*x*/Me that it takes a moment to decide where to start! Let's begin with the organization of the OS.

Travel Advisory

Windows XP radically changed the appearance of Windows from its "classic" environment, but don't be fooled! Under the candy-colored skin, Windows XP is using the same basic engine designed for Windows NT.

Subsystems

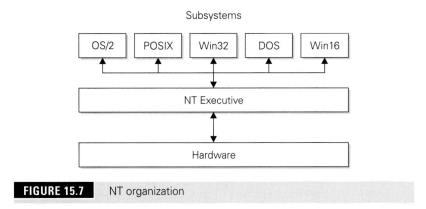

FIGURE 15.7 NT organization

OS Organization

NT/2000/XP takes an *object-oriented* approach to the OS, separating the OS into three distinct parts: the hardware drivers, the core NT Executive, and the subsystems, as shown in Figure 15-7.

Windows NT was designed to support different CPU platforms beyond the *x*86, such as DEC Alpha, MIPS, and PowerPC. To achieve this, the NT Executive holds the *Hardware Abstraction Layer (HAL)*, a special type of hardware driver that separates the system-specific device drivers from the rest of the NT system (Figure 15-8).

Travel Advisory

Even though NT, 2000, and XP all use the same structure, Microsoft dumped support for other CPUs in 2000 and XP. So, while 2000 and XP *could* support other CPUs, Microsoft has dropped this capability.

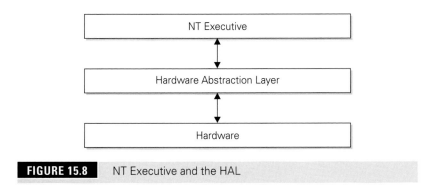

FIGURE 15.8 NT Executive and the HAL

The robustness of NT/2000/XP comes from the separation of running processes into myriad subsystems. NT is fully POSIX-compliant (a UNIX thing) and has support for OS/2, DOS, and 16- and 32-bit Windows applications via these numerous subsystems. Windows 2000/XP keeps all the same supports, with the exception of OS/2 (Figure 15-9).

Multiprocessing

Windows NT/2000/XP is the only Microsoft OS to support *symmetric multiprocessing (SMP)*, providing support for systems with up to two CPUs (in Windows NT Workstation, 2000 Professional, and XP Professional). Server versions of Windows NT/2000/XP offer support for up to 32 CPUs (depending on the version)!

Travel Advisory
Windows XP Home edition does not support SMP.

Note that applications must be written to take advantage of SMP in order to get any kind of performance boost. Many high-end graphics applications, database programs, and (of course) 3-D games are designed for SMP.

New Technology File System (NTFS)

From the beginning, Microsoft designed and optimized every aspect of Windows NT/2000/XP for multiuser, networked environments. This is most evident in the file system. Whereas all previous Microsoft OSs used either FAT16 or FAT32 formats, NT, 2000, and XP use a far more powerful file system appropriately called *NT File System (NTFS)*.

Exam Tip	
Windows NT supports FAT16, NTFS, and HPFS (for OS/2). Windows 2000 supports FAT16, FAT32, and NTFS.	

NTFS offers the following features:

- Redundancy
- Backward compatibility
- Recoverability
- Security

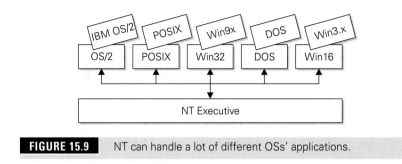

FIGURE 15.9 NT can handle a lot of different OSs' applications.

Each of these features is described in the following paragraphs.

Redundancy

NTFS uses a *Master File Table (MFT)* to keep track of hard disk drive contents. An NTFS partition keeps a backup copy of the most critical parts of the MFT in the middle of the disk, reducing the chance that a serious drive error can wipe out both the MFT and the MFT copy. Whenever you defrag an NTFS partition, you'll see a small, immovable "chunk" in the middle of the drive; that's the backup MFT.

Backward Compatibility

For all its power, NTFS is amazingly backward compatible. You can copy DOS or Windows 9*x*/Me programs to an NTFS partition.

Recoverability

Accidental system shutdowns, reboots, and lockups in the midst of a file save or retrieval wreak havoc on most systems. NTFS avoids this with *transaction logging*. Transaction logging determines incomplete file transactions and restores the file to the original format automatically and invisibly.

Not related to NTFS but since we're on the topic of recoverability, Windows NT/2000/XP all support a startup option called *Last Known Good Configuration*. Choosing Last Known Good Configuration provides a way to recover from problems such as a newly added driver that may be incorrect for your hardware. Note that the Last Known Good Configuration option does not solve problems caused by corrupted or missing drivers or files, but it is handy for turning back the clock (so to speak) to before you installed a bad driver.

Windows NT/2000/XP restores system information from the HKLM\System\CurrentControlSet Registry key. Select Last Known Good Configuration during startup by pressing the SPACEBAR when prompted in Windows NT, or by pressing F5 during startup in Windows 2000/XP and selecting Last Known Good Configuration from the Advanced Startup Options menu.

Security

NTFS truly shines with its powerful security functions. When most people hear the term "security," they tend to think about networks. NTFS security works perfectly in a network environment, but for the moment, let's just pretend that only one Windows NT/2000/XP system exists in the entire world. Three different people use this computer. Each person has one personal folder that they don't want others using the same computer to access.

On a Windows 9x/Me system, anyone who can get in front of the keyboard of a system can access any folder; the password only allows him or her on the network. This is not so with Windows NT/2000/XP! Each user must log on to the system with a valid user account and password, and each user is *only* able to access areas of the physical hard disk drive that their account is given *permissions* to.

Let's look at three major features of NTFS security: accounts, groups, and permissions.

> ### Exam Tip
>
> Don't confuse Windows 9x/Me login passwords with screensaver passwords! If you walk up to a Windows 9x/Me system that prompts for a password, it has nothing to do with the login password. Screensaver passwords for Windows 9x/Me systems are set under the Screensaver tab of the system's Display Properties dialog box. Windows NT/2000/XP do not have this separate password problem. They use the login password for the screensaver too, so you only need to remember your login password to access a Windows NT/2000/XP system that uses a screensaver password.

Accounts   To use a Windows NT/2000/XP system, you must have a valid account and password. Without that account, you cannot use the system. Every Windows NT/2000/XP system has a "super" account called *administrator*. The administrator account is used to configure important system settings and manage other user accounts. When you first install a Windows NT/2000/XP system, it prompts you for a password for the administrator account. As you might imagine, this account has access to everything—a dangerous thing in the wrong hands!

> ### Travel Advisory
>
> Do *not* lose the password for the administrator account! Doing so may require that you reinstall Windows.

Groups A *group* is simply a collection of accounts that share the same access capabilities. A single user account can be a member of multiple groups. Groups make Windows administration much easier by enabling you to assign levels of access for a file or folder to a group instead of individual accounts. This way, all members of that group are given access *en masse* instead of needing to set up access one by one. Users can be added to or removed from groups at will. Windows NT/200/XP provide several built-in groups, which vary from version to version, but six are noteworthy: Administrators, Power Users, Users, Backup Operators, Everyone, and Guests. These built-in groups have a number of preset abilities, as described here:

- **Administrators** Any account that is a member of this group has complete administrator privileges. It is very common for the primary user of a Windows 2000 system to have his or her account in the Administrators group.
- **Power Users** Power users are almost as powerful as administrators, but they cannot install new devices or access other users' files or folders unless the file or folder specifically provides them access.
- **Users** Users cannot edit the Registry or access critical system files. They can create groups, but they can manage only the ones they create.
- **Backup Operators** Backup Operators have the same rights as users, but they can run backup programs that access any file or folder—for backup purposes only.
- **Everyone** This account applies to any user that can log on to the system. You cannot edit this group.
- **Guests** Someone who does not have an account on the system can log on using the Guest account if the system has been set up to enable that feature. This group is used in certain network situations.

Travel Advisory

You can create new groups, but you cannot delete the built-in groups.

Windows XP diverges a lot from Windows NT/2000 on user accounts. XP Professional offers all the accounts listed but then adds other specialized types, such as Help Services Group and Remote Desktop Users. Computer Administrators can do anything, as you might suspect. Limited Users can access only certain things and have limits on where they can save things on the PC.

NTFS Permissions   In the NT/2000/XP world, every folder and file on an NTFS partition has a list that contains two sets of data. First, the list details every user and group that has access to that file or folder. Second, the list specifies the level of access that each user or group has to that file and folder. The level of access is defined by a set of restrictions called "permissions."

- **Permissions**   These define exactly what a particular account can or cannot do to the file or folder and are thus quite detailed and powerful. You can make it possible, for example, for a person to edit a file but not delete it. You can create a folder and not allow other people to make subfolders. NTFS file and folder permissions are so complicated that entire books have been written on them! Fortunately for us, the A+ Certification exams only test your understanding of a few basic concepts of NTFS permissions: Ownership, Take Ownership permission, Change permissions, Folder permissions, and File permissions.

- **Ownership**   When you create a new file or folder on an NTFS partition, you become the *owner* of that file or folder. A newly created file or folder by default gives full permission to everyone to access, delete, and otherwise manipulate that file or folder. Owners can do anything they want to the files or folders they own, including changing the permissions to prevent others from accessing them.

- **Take Ownership**   One special permission, however, called Take Ownership, enables anyone with that permission to do just that— seize control of a file or folder. Administrator accounts have Take Ownership permission for everything. Note the difference here between owning a file and accessing a file. If you own a file, you can prevent anyone from accessing that file. Note, however, that the administrator can easily edit the file permissions to grant themselves access to any files that they've been locked out of.

- **Change Permissions**   Another important permission for all NTFS files and folders is the Change permission. An account with this permission can give or take away permissions for other accounts.

- **Folder Permissions**   In Windows NT/2000/XP, every folder in an NTFS partition has a Security tab. Every Security tab contains two main areas. The top area shows the list of accounts that have permissions for that resource: the lower area shows exactly what permissions have been assigned to that account. Figure 15-10 shows the NTFS permissions for a folder called MIKE.

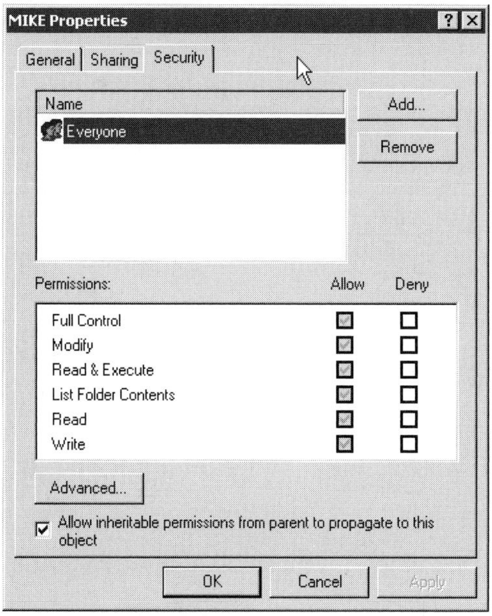

FIGURE 15.10 NTFS permissions

Windows NTFS permissions are quite powerful and quite complex. The list of permissions shown in the permission area, for example, is not really permissions, but rather preset combinations of permissions that cover the most common types of access. Click the Advanced button, and then click View/Edit to see the real NTFS permissions; Microsoft calls them *special permissions* (Figure 15-11). Even the most advanced NT/2000/XP support people rarely need to access these.

Don't panic about memorizing special permissions; just appreciate that they exist and that the permissions we see in the Security tab cover the vast majority of our needs. Standard permissions for a folder are shown in Table 15-3.

* **File Permissions** File permissions are quite similar to Folder permissions. Take a look at the list of file permissions shown in Table 15-4.

Permissions are *cumulative,* and they accumulate according to *inheritance.* There is an inheritance relationship between a folder and the files or subfolders that it contains. Permissions that are configured on a folder are passed down, or inherited, to the contents of that folder by default. This means that if you have Full Control on a folder, you get Full Control on the files in that folder.

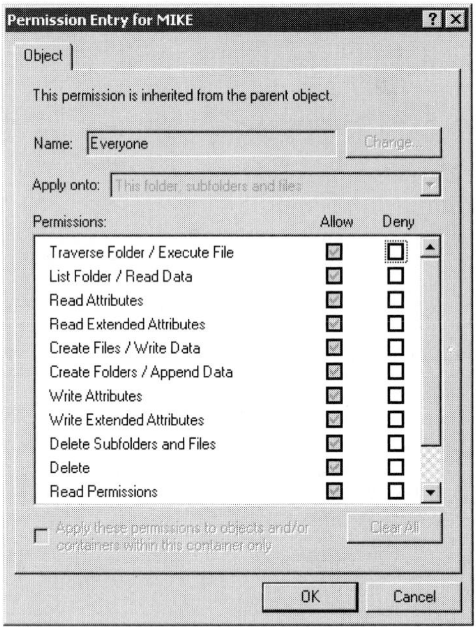

FIGURE 15.11 Special permissions

TABLE 15.3 Folder Permissions

Permission	Description
Full Control	Enables you to do anything you want!
Modify	Enables you to do anything except delete files or subfolders.
Read & Execute	Enables you to see the contents of the folder and any subfolders.
List Folder Contents	Enables you to see the contents of the folder and any subfolders. (This permission seems the same as the Read & Execute permission, but is only inherited by folders.)
Read	Enables you to read any files in the folder.
Write	Enables you to write to files and create new files and folders.

TABLE 15.4 File Permissions

Permission	Description
Full Control	Enables you to do anything you want!
Modify	Enables you to do anything except take ownership or change permissions on the file.
Read & Execute	If the file is a program, you can run it.
Read	If the file is data, you can read it.
Write	Enables you to write to the file.

If you look at the bottom of the Security tab, you'll see a little check box that says, "Allow inheritable permissions from parent to propagate to this object." In other words, any files or subfolders created in this folder get the same permissions for the same users/groups that the folder has. This enables you to stop a user from getting a specific permission via inheritance. Windows 2000 and XP (unlike NT) provide explicit Deny functions to each option.

Exam Tip

Don't bother memorizing all of these NTFS permissions! Simply appreciate that NTFS enables NT/2000/XP to provide a tremendous level of security. Windows 9x/Me uses the far more primitive FAT16 or FAT32 file systems. These file systems provide almost no security. If you want powerful, flexible security, you need Windows NT/2000/XP with NTFS. Note that although you can install Windows NT on a drive with FAT (i.e., FAT16), and Windows 2000/XP on a drive with FAT16 or FAT32 file systems, neither file system provides any security, so forget about permissions if you use them. Only NTFS offers file and folder security.

System Partition vs. Boot Partition

One of the more confusing aspects of the Windows NT/2000/XP family lies in the way Microsoft distinguishes between what they call the *system partition* and the *boot partition*. Only a few vital files are required to start the boot process, and these files are stored on the system partition. This is the first active, primary partition on the system: by default, this is the C:\ drive. The boot partition, interestingly, is *not* the partition that the OS boots *from*, but rather the partition that the OS boots *to*. The boot partition is the partition that holds the OS files themselves (in the \WINNT folder).

The system partition and the boot partition *can* be the same partition (and if your hard disk drive has only one partition, then they are the same), but they don't have to be. During Windows NT/2000/XP setup, you can specify any partition as your boot partition. In fact, on systems with more than one OS installed—*multiboot* systems—Microsoft highly recommends that you install each OS on its own partition.

As an example, let's say you've got a system with a single hard disk drive split into two partitions, C: and D:, with Windows 98SE installed on the C: drive (i.e., C:\Windows) and Windows 2000 installed on the D: drive (i.e., D:\WINNT). The C: drive is called the system partition, and the D: is called the boot partition. Get it?

Would it make more sense to call the partition with the essential files necessary to boot the boot partition and the partition that stores the OS SystemRoot the system partition? Yes it would, but that's not the way Microsoft does it!

Critical Boot Files

Unlike the thousands of files that are necessary to support the Windows NT/2000/XP GUI, only a very small handful of files are needed to start the system, as shown in Table 15-5.

Of the files listed, NTLDR, BOOT.INI, and NTDETECT.COM are the "big three." Any Windows NT/2000/XP system uses these files. As with other vital system files, they are hidden and read-only by default.

The Boot Process

When you sit down and power the machine on, the first thing that happens is that the computer system BIOS loads the underlying programs that fire up the computer. We've gone into this process previously, in Chapter 4, so we'll skip ahead to the last thing the BIOS does: load the Windows NT/2000/XP *Master Boot Record (MBR)* data into memory.

1. The MBR contains code that locates the system bootable partition.

2. From the system partition, NTLDR executes and gets the operating system startup process rolling.

TABLE 15.5	Boot Files and Locations

File	Location
NTLDR	System partition root (e.g., "C:\")
BOOT.INI	System partition root (e.g., "C:\")
BOOTSECT.DOS	System partition root (e.g., "C:\"). Only needed on multiboot systems with Windows 9x/Me.
NTDETECT.COM	System partition root (e.g., "C:\")
NTBOOTDD.SYS	System partition root (e.g., "C:\") This file is used only if system partition is on SCSI disk with BIOS disabled
NTOSKRNL.EXE	%*SystemRoot*%\System32 (e.g., "C:\WINNT\ System32")
HAL.DLL	%*SystemRoot*%\System32 (e.g., "C:\WINNT\ System32")
SYSTEM	%*SystemRoot*%\System32\Config (e.g., "C:\WINNT\ System32\Config")

3. This brings us to the BOOT.INI file. NTLDR locates and reads the BOOT.INI file for information such as which operating system to launch, where to find the appropriate files to launch that system, and boot menu items.

4. The boot menu displays.

5. NTDETECT.COM launches.

6. NTOSKRNL.EXE runs and the HAL is loaded.

7. Low-level system device drivers load.

8. Operating system kernel and subsystems load and initialize.

9. Any remaining drivers and services are loaded, and Windows 2000 is up and running.

Let's go back to the BOOT.INI file for a moment. For a seemingly innocuous text file, BOOT.INI actually serves a couple of very important purposes in the Windows NT/2000/XP startup process.

BOOT.INI

A typical BOOT.INI file looks something like this:

```
[boot loader]
timeout=30
default=multi(0)disk(0)rdisk(0)partition(1)\WINNT
[operating systems]
multi(0)disk(0)rdisk(0)partition(1)\WINNT="Microsoft Windows 2000
Professional"
```

It doesn't *look* very important, does it? What, then, is so interesting about BOOT.INI? Well, for one thing, the BOOT.INI file is what Windows NT/2000/XP uses to do things like locate the boot partition and operating system. *That* could be considered important!

As you can see, the BOOT.INI file has two sections, the "boot loader" section and the "operating systems" section. The boot loader section specifies how long to display the boot menu at startup ("timeout=30"), and which operating system to load as the default if a selection is not made ("default=multi(0)disk(0)rdisk(0)partition(1)\WINNT "). The operating system section tells NTLDR where to find the operating system, and even what text will be displayed in the menu ("Microsoft Windows 2000 Professional").

Windows setup creates the BOOT.INI file during installation, and is particular to that computer system's configuration. For instance, on a dual-boot system with Windows 9*x*/Me as the other operating system, you could expect to see the operating systems section of the BOOT.INI file read as follows:

```
[operating systems]
multi(0)disk(0)rdisk(0)partition(2)\WINNT="Microsoft Windows 2000
     Professional"
/fastdetect
C:\="Microsoft Windows 98"
```

Pretty straightforward stuff, with the possible exception of the *ARC path* statements (e.g., "multi(0)disk(0)rdisk(0)partition(2)\WINNT"). What is the ARC path?

ARC Path in BOOT.INI The *Advanced RISC Computing (ARC)* path in BOOT.INI is used by NTLDR to determine which disk contains the operating system. Interestingly, Windows 2000/XP no longer support RISC processors, but we're not going to worry about that. What we do need to know about the ARC path is how to translate it. Table 15-6 shows the definition for each parameter of an ARC path statement.

For example, let's look at that first BOOT.INI ARC path statement again:

```
multi(0)disk(0)rdisk(0)partition(1)\WINNT="Microsoft Windows 2000
Professional"
```

We now see that the statement indicates the following:

* **multi(0)** is an EIDE controller or a SCSI controller with the BIOS enabled.

* **disk(0)** is 0, since the multi option is indicated.

TABLE 15.6 ARC Path Statement Parameters

Parameter	Description
multi(x)	Specifies SCSI controller with the BIOS enabled, or non-SCSI controller. x=ordinal number of controller.
scsi(x)	Defines SCSI controller with the BIOS disabled. x=ordinal number of controller.
disk(x)	Defines SCSI disk that the operating system resides on. When *multi* is used, x=0. When *scsi* is used, x= the SCSI ID number of the disk with the operating system.
rdisk(x)	Defines disk that the operating system resides on. Used when operating system does not reside on a SCSI disk. x=0-1 if on primary controller. x=2-3 if on multichannel EIDE controller.
partition(x)	Specifies partition number that the operating system resides on. x=cardinal number of partition, and the lowest possible value is 1.

- **rdisk(0)** specifies that the first disk on the controller is being used.
- **partition(1)** specifies that the system partition is on the first partition.
- **\WINNT** indicates the folder that is used to store the system files.
- **"Microsoft Windows 2000 Professional"** is the text displayed in the boot menu.

BOOT.INI Switches   If the need arises, you can modify the BOOT.INI file in any text editor. The following switches shown in Table 15-7 are valid.

Why would you ever want to edit the BOOT.INI? The first example that comes to mind may be of interest if you are used to the Windows NT boot menu. The default Windows NT boot menu offers the choice of booting into VGA mode, which means that only the base video drivers are loaded. This is a particularly handy option if you are troubleshooting a suspected video driver issue. This option is not available by default in the Windows 2000 boot menu. By adding the following line to your BOOT.INI file, you can bring that option back:

```
multi(0)disk(0)rdisk(0)partition(1)\WINNT="Microsoft Windows 2000
Professional [VGA
Mode]" /basevideo
```

Or, suppose you wanted to see the list of drivers that are loaded during startup (again, as in Windows NT). You would modify the BOOT.INI file with the "/sos" parameter switch to have Windows 2000/XP show you all of the steps.

Don't forget, you can also edit the boot menu text to display whatever text you choose. For instance, you may wish to edit the boot menu text to read "Microsoft Windows 2000 Professional, now with 20% more FREE!!!"

Before you open up Notepad, however, there are two important things to keep in mind. The BOOT.INI file is marked with the System and Hidden file

TABLE 15.7	BOOT.INI Switches

Parameter Switch	Description
/basevideo	Boots using standard VGA driver
/fastdetect=[comx,y,z]	Disables serial mouse detection on all COM ports if port not specified. Included by default
/maxmem:n	Specifies amount of RAM used when a memory chip may be bad
/noguiboot	Boots Windows without displaying graphical startup screen
/sos	Displays device driver names as they load
/bootlog	Enable boot logging
/safeboot:minimal	Boot in safe mode
/safeboot:minimal(alternateshell)	Safe mode with command prompt
/safeboot:network	Safe mode with networking support

attributes. You must remove these attributes before you can do anything with it. Also, editing the BOOT.INI file incorrectly may result in your system failing to start. Minor details!

Take the time to memorize the primary boot files and the boot process for Windows NT/2000/XP. Most boot errors are easily repaired if you know which files are used for boot and in which order they load.

Major Differences among Versions of Windows NT/2000/XP

Objective 15.04

Unlike the Windows 9x/Me family, the Windows NT/2000/XP line has far more features in common than they do different. Unlike the baby steps that took us from Windows 95 to Windows 95 OSR2, to Windows 98, to Windows 98 SE, and finally to Windows Me, the jump between Windows NT and Windows 2000 was *huge*. Microsoft took the rock-solid foundation of Windows NT and added features to make Windows 2000 substantially more user- and hardware-friendly, as well as incorporating a number of important innovations that were refined even further in Windows XP.

The following sections detail a few of the more outstanding updates implemented with the versions of Windows 2000 and Windows XP.

Improved User Organization

Windows 2000/XP offer a highly structured environment designed to enhance file and folder security on shared workstations. The biggest change over NT is the creation of the \Documents and Settings folders that contain all the user information on a system, assigning them default data and program folders. Note that each user in Figure 15-12 has his or her own tree in the file system.

Combined with NTFS, this user organization provides a wall between users. All can access the shared folders and the installed programs, but one user cannot access the My Documents of another user.

Plug and Play

One of Windows NT's biggest failings was in the area of hardware support. Without plug and play functionality, adding new hardware to a Windows NT system often proved to be a headache-inducing nightmare. Although later service packs of Windows NT provided rudimentary plug and play support,

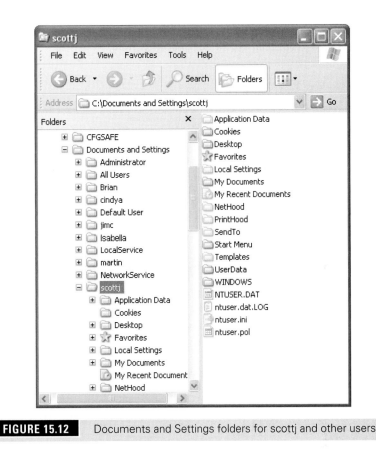

FIGURE 15.12   Documents and Settings folders for scottj and other users

Windows 2000/XP pack complete plug and play support. Windows 2000/XP also have Device Manager and the Add New Hardware Wizard, making device installation a breeze. Plus, when you need a snapshot of all your devices, you can go to the System Information tool, just like in Windows 9x/Me.

NTFS5

Windows 2000/XP come with a new type of NTFS called NTFS 5.0 (the NTFS that came with NT 4.0 was called NTFS 4.0). NTFS 5.0 adds four improvements: encryption, mount points, disk quotas, and dynamic disks.

Easier Administration

Windows NT supported the use of the Microsoft Management Console (MMC) for a few tools, but in Windows 2000/XP, the MMC is the default shell for all the important utilities. The MMC provides a uniform environment for the numerous *snap-ins* that are supplied by Microsoft, and also by third-party vendors. Figure 15-13 shows the MMC loaded with the *Services* snap-in.

Recovery Console

While neither NT, 2000, or XP has a pure command line environment, Windows 2000 introduces a rudimentary DOS-like command line interface called the Recovery Console (RC) to help troubleshoot startup problems. RC can be loaded from the Windows 2000/XP installation CD-ROM, or installed on the hard disk drive to load as an option from the advanced boot menu. RC supports about two dozen commands such as CHKDSK (checks the hard disk integrity), FIXBOOT (writes a boot sector to the system partition), and FIXMBR (writes a new Master Boot Record), among others. We'll come back to the RC in Chapter 19.

Files and Settings Transfer Wizard

It used to be that swapping out your primary hard drive for a bigger one was a huge hassle. Not the actual hard disk drive installation—that was the quick and easy part for any good tech—but then you had to go through the laborious

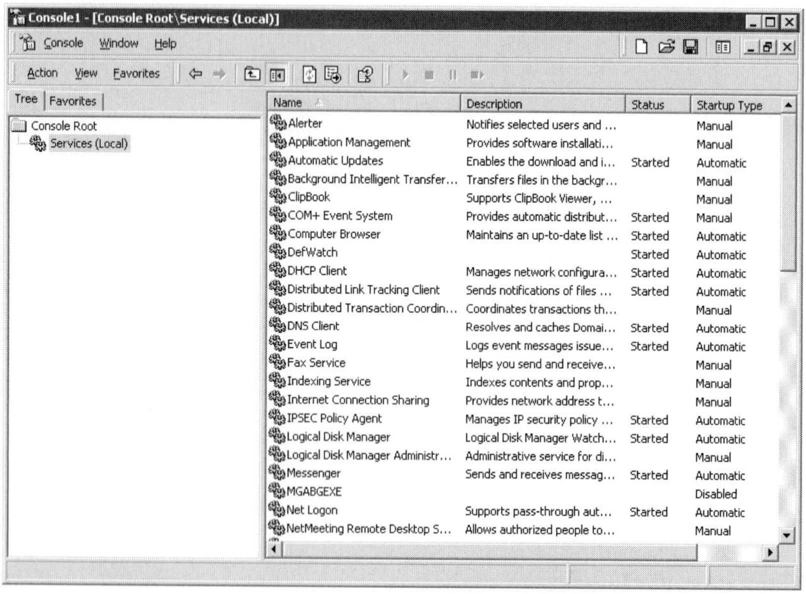

FIGURE 15.13   Windows MMC with Services snap-in loaded

process of reinstalling Windows, reinstalling your applications, and then copying over all of your files, settings, backgrounds, and so on. What a mess! And if things didn't go as planned, you simply lost a bunch of stuff.

Microsoft introduced the Files and Settings Transfer Wizard (FST Wizard) in Windows XP, and now changing systems is a simple, efficient process. Here's how it works. Before you dismantle your current system, you run the wizard from the XP CD-ROM (Figure 15-14).

The FST Wizard prepares your old drive to transfer its settings. Then you install Windows XP on the new hardware and connect the old hard drive to the new and run the FST Wizard again. This time, choose the appropriate drive and transfer everything over (Figure 15-15).

System Restore and Driver Rollback

Windows XP's *System Restore* feature enables you to take a snapshot of the system state at any one time and then, if things go awry with an installation or bad download, restore the PC to a previous time when all was well.

Windows XP also includes the new *Driver Rollback* feature, which enables you to roll back individual device drivers for pieces of hardware. Want to try out those beta drivers for your video card but you wisely shy away from the potentially horrible outcome if they don't work? With Driver Rollback, you can install what you want and then return to the old drivers if the new ones give you fits. It's a great boon to hardware enthusiasts and general users alike. It's definitely a boon to techs! Figure 15-16 shows the feature in action.

FIGURE 15.14   Files and Settings Transfer Wizard

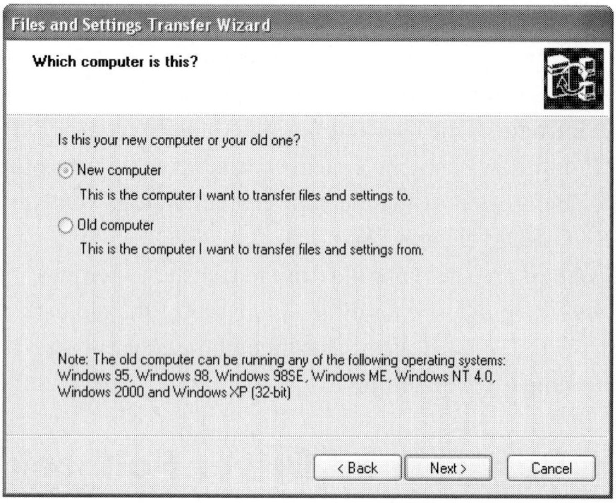

FIGURE 15.15 Selecting source or destination drive

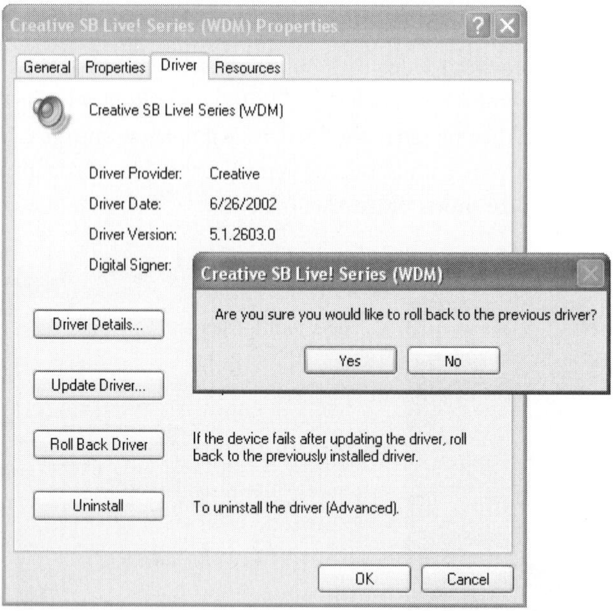

FIGURE 15.16 Windows XP driver rollback

Remote Assistance

In the past, one of the most common misconceptions among computer users was that it was possible for you, the learned PC tech, to take control of their computer remotely to run diagnostics and troubleshoot problems when they called you for support. Yes, specialized software like PC Anywhere made this level of control possible, but not everybody has it installed by default. With Windows XP's *Remote Access* feature, you *can* run tests just as if you were sitting in front of the PC!

Remote Access gives you the ability to take control of any Windows XP PC remotely, over a local area network or even over the Internet. You have to get invited to help and be granted permission to take the driver's seat remotely, but in practice this feature is incredibly useful. Figure 15-17 shows Remote Assistance in action.

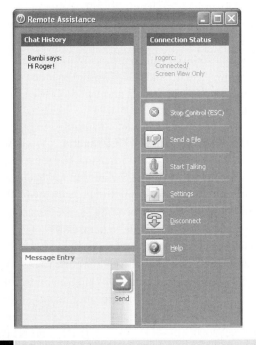

| FIGURE 15.17 | Remote Assistance |

CHECKPOINT

✔**Objective 15.01: Windows 9x/Me Structure**   Windows 9x/Me 32-bit mode is called protected mode. It's not necessary to boot the Windows GUI to boot to Windows 9x/Me. Later versions of Windows 9x/Me support FAT32 and long filenames. IO.SYS tells the system how to start up. MSDOS.SYS is an editable text file that is used as a startup options file. COMMAND.COM provides a text-based command interface. SYSTEM.INI still appears on modern systems, to enable backward compatibility with legacy applications.

✔**Objective 15.02: Major Differences among Versions of Windows 9x/Me**   Windows 95's startup floppy diskette lacked support for CD-ROM drives. Windows 98, SE, and Me's startup disk offers support for many types of CD-ROM drives. The first version of Windows 95 (Windows 95A) supports only FAT16. Windows 95 OSR2 is the first Microsoft OS to support FAT32. Important tools introduced with Windows 98 include the System Information tool, Windows Update, and Disk Cleanup. Windows 98 SE introduced Internet Connection Sharing (ICS), and Windows Me introduced the System Restore feature.

✔**Objective 15.03: Windows NT/2000/XP Structure**   Windows NT/2000/XP is a true 32-bit, GUI OS that gets its robustness by separating the hardware drivers, the core NT Executive, and the subsystems. Windows NT/2000/XP support multiprocessing, or running the PC with two CPUs (Server versions support up to 32 CPUs, depending on the version). Windows NT/2000/XP support an advanced file system called NTFS. NTFS enables file-level security and compression. The version of NTFS that ships with Windows 2000/XP, NTFS5, also natively supports file encryption and disk quotas. NTFS file and folder permissions enable you to configure specific levels of access for specific users and groups. The system partition is what Microsoft calls the hard disk drive partition that stores the vital boot files for Windows NT/2000/XP—NTLDR, BOOT.INI, and NTDETECT.COM. The boot partition is what Microsoft calls the partition that stores the OS files (in the \WINNT folder by default). NTLDR starts the OS boot process following the BIOS startup routine. BOOT.INI tells NTLDR where to find the OS files.

✔**Objective 15.04: Major Differences among Versions of Windows NT/2000/XP**
Windows 2000 introduces the Documents and Settings folder for storing user
files and settings. Windows 2000 also introduced support for plug and play
(lacking in Windows NT). The Microsoft Management Console (MMC) is
the default tool interface in Windows 2000/XP. Windows XP introduces the
Files and Settings Transfer Wizard, which makes moving user files from one
hard disk drive to another running Windows XP a snap. Windows XP also
supports System Restore, Driver Rollback, and Remote Assistance.

REVIEW QUESTIONS

1. What is the first version of Windows to support Internet Connection
   Sharing (ICS)?

   A. Windows 95 OSR2

   B. Windows XP

   C. Windows 2000

   D. Windows 98 SE

2. Which of the following is *not* an advantage of running Windows 2000
   on NTFS as opposed to FAT32?

   A. Security

   B. Encryption

   C. File naming

   D. Compression

3. John's Windows 2000 system can also boot to Windows 98. What file
   does the NT loader read to know what OS to boot to?

   A. MSDOS.SYS

   B. BOOTLOG.TXT

   C. NTOSKRNL.EXE

   D. BOOT.INI

4. Which feature of Windows Me enables you to revive a PC that crashes
   hard after installing some new applications?

   A. Command Line Interface

   B. Driver Rollback

   C. System Recovery

   D. System Restore

5. You update a device driver on a Windows NT 4.0 Workstation, but after you reboot, the PC refuses to finish loading the GUI. What should you do to correct the problem?

   A. Reinstall Windows NT.

   B. Start the PC and load the Last Known Good Configuration.

   C. Start the PC and run CHKDSK from the Recovery Console.

   D. Start the PC and run SCANDISK from a DOS command line.

6. Which of the following files is not necessary for Windows NT/2000 systems using IDE hard disk drives and drive controllers?

   A. NTLDR

   B. NTBOOTDD.SYS

   C. NTDETECT.COM

   D. BOOT.INI

7. You create a new local account for a user on a Windows XP Professional PC. In which folder are the user's files and settings stored by default?

   A. \User Documents

   B. \My Documents

   C. \Documents and Settings

   D. \Files and Settings

8. What character is placed at the beginning of a line in WIN.INI to prevent a driver from loading?

   A. A semicolon (;)

   B. A question mark (?)

   C. A forward slash (/)

   D. A comma (,)

9. Which of the following files can be edited using SYSEDIT? (Choose three.)

   A. AUTOEXEC.BAT

   B. CONFIG.SYS

   C. WIN.INI

   D. USER.DAT

10. What does Microsoft call the partition on the hard disk drive that stores the Windows NT Workstation NTLDR, BOOT.INI, and NTDETECT.COM files?

   A. Boot partition

   B. System partition

   C. Protected Mode partition

   D. Extended partition

REVIEW ANSWERS

1. **D**   Windows 98 SE is the first version to support ICS.

2. **C**   NTFS and FAT share basically the same file naming rules.

3. **D**   BOOT.INI tells the NT loader (NTLDR) where to find the OS files.

4. **D**   System Restore enables you to return a Windows Me (or Windows XP) system to a state previous to it becoming unstable.

5. **B**   Last Known Good Configuration enables you to return the system to a state before you loaded the bad driver.

6. **B**   NTBOOTDD.SYS is necessary only for systems using SCSI host adapters.

7. **C**   \Documents and Settings is the default storage folder for user files and settings in Windows 2000 and XP.

8. **A**   semicolon (;) prevents a line in WIN.INI from loading.

9. **A** **B** **C**   BAT, .SYS, and .INI files are text files that are editable with text editors such as Sysedit or Notepad. Binary files such as USER.DAT can't be edited with text editors.

10. **B**   The partition that stores the vital boot files for Windows NT/2000/XP (NTLDR, BOOT.INI, and NTDETECT.COM) is called the system partition. Go figure!

Installing and Upgrading Windows

	NEWBIE	SOME EXPERIENCE	EXPERT
ETA	3 hours	2 hours	1 hour

425

One of the many tasks you may be called on to do for users is to install or update their computer to a new version of Windows. The version of Windows you are most likely to install these days is Windows XP, but there is still a very real chance that you will be called upon to install or reinstall earlier versions like Windows 98 or Windows 2000. With that in mind, we'll look at the steps involved in installing all versions that you're likely to run into in the real world.

Before you can install, you gotta prepare—so we'll talk about that first. Let's look at the steps that you must take prior to popping in the installation CD-ROM for any version of Windows, and then get specific with Windows 9x/Me, NT Workstation, 2000, and XP.

Objective 16.01 Windows Installation/Upgrade Overview

Installing or upgrading an OS is like any good story: it has a beginning, a middle, and an end. In this case, the beginning is the several tasks you need to do before you actually do the installation/upgrade. If you do your homework here, the installation process is a breeze, and the post-installation tasks are minimal. In the next section, we'll discuss preparation tasks, describe a generic Windows installation, and then outline the tasks you need to do after the installation.

Preparing for Installation or Upgrade

Preparation involves a number of steps but they usually go pretty fast, and skipping them can cause you gobs of grief later when you're in the middle of installing and things blow up. Okay, so maybe there won't be a real explosion, but the computer may well lock up and refuse to boot into anything usable. With that in mind, let's look at the nine tasks you need to complete *before* you insert that CD-ROM.

1. Identify hardware requirements.
2. Verify hardware and software compatibility.
3. Decide whether to perform a clean installation or an upgrade.
4. Determine how to back up and restore existing data, if necessary.
5. Select an installation method.
6. Determine how to partition the hard disk and what file system to use.

7. Determine your computer's network role.

8. Decide on your computer's language and locale settings.

9. Plan for postinstallation tasks.

Let's take a look at each of these tasks in more detail.

Identify Hardware Requirements

Identifying hardware requirements helps you to decide whether a computer system is a reasonable host for a particular operating system. Requirements include the CPU model, the amount of RAM memory, the amount of free hard disk space, and the video adapter, display, and other storage devices that may be required to install and run the operating system.

Hardware requirements are stated as minimums, or more often these days, as recommended minimums. Although you could successfully install an operating system on a computer with hardware that only met the old minimum requirements that Microsoft published, they were not realistic specs for actually accomplishing work! For example, the original minimum CPU requirement for Windows 2000 is a Pentium 133 MHz with 64 MB of RAM! While it's true that the OS *will* install and *will* run on a system with that configuration, it certainly wouldn't be much fun to work on!

With the last few versions of Windows, Microsoft has published *recommended* minimums that are much more realistic. You will find the published minimums on the packaging and at Microsoft's web site (www.microsoft.com).

Verify Hardware and Software Compatibility

Assuming your system meets the minimum hardware requirements, you next need to find out how well Windows supports the brand and model of hardware and the particular application software you intend to use under Windows. The two basic sources for this information are Microsoft, and the manufacturer of the device or software.

If you're installing Windows 2000 or XP, the Setup Wizard automatically checks out your hardware and software and reports any potential conflicts. You can also run the compatibility checker manually prior to installation. However, the wise PC tech doesn't wait until she is ready to install to check this out. With any flavor of Windows, and even with Windows XP, do your homework before you even open the case of the installation CD-ROM!

For a list of compatible hardware, go to Microsoft Windows Hardware and Drivers Central, shown in Figure 16-1, at www.microsoft.com/whdc/hcl/search.mspx, for the definitive *Hardware Compatibility List (HCL)* (with disclaimer).

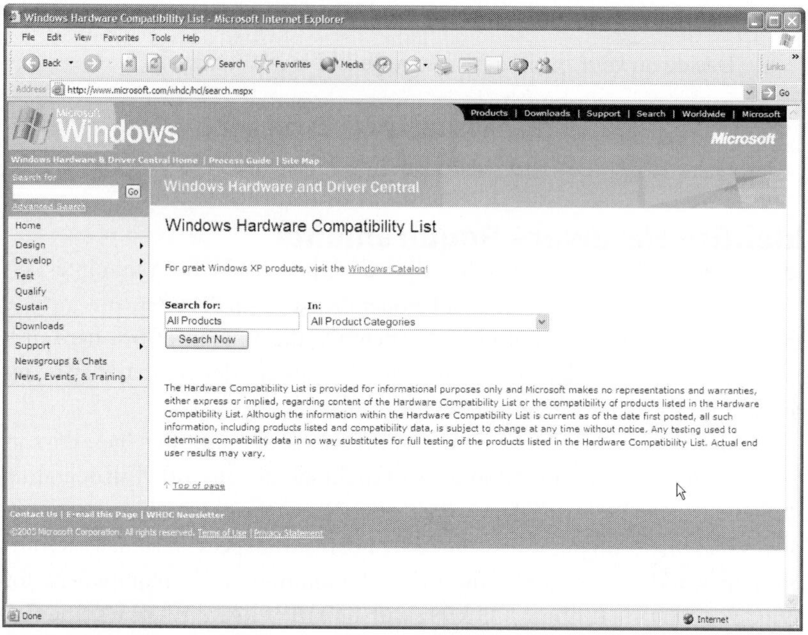

FIGURE 16.1   Windows Hardware and Driver Central

When preparing to upgrade to a different version of Windows, check with the manufacturers of the applications already installed in the previous OS. If there are software compatibility problems with the versions you have, the manufacturer should provide upgrade packs that can be installed during the upgrade process.

Decide Whether to Perform a Clean Installation or an Upgrade

A *clean installation* of an OS involves installing it onto an empty hard drive partition with no previous OS installed. An *upgrade installation* is an installation of Windows that overwrites an earlier installed version, inheriting all previous hardware, software, and user settings.

You may think the choice between doing a clean installation and an upgrade installation is simple: you do a clean installation on a brand new computer with an empty hard drive, and you do an upgrade if there's a preexisting OS installation. It isn't necessarily so!

Clean Installation A typical clean installation begins with a completely empty hard disk. The advantage to doing a clean installation is that you don't carry problems from the old OS over to the new one, but the disadvantage is that you have to reinstall all applications and reconfigure the desktop and each application to the user's preferences.

A variation of a clean installation is a *multiboot installation.* That is, you can install the new OS in a different directory or a different disk partition, leaving the old OS intact and usable. You can use the boot menu to select which OS to start up. The most compelling situation that calls for a multiboot installation is the "try before you buy" scenario, where your company acquires an evaluation version of an OS product to test out on a few specific systems (that already are in use with a previous version of Windows) before you make a huge investment in new OS software for the whole organization. Another reason to install a multiboot system is for the use of support personnel who handle help requests involving a variety of OS platforms.

Upgrade Upgrade installations leave the old OS intact with all its settings and installed software. The core OS files are overwritten with newer versions in the same directory used for the old installation. This is why, for instance, even though the default SystemRoot folder for a Windows 2000 installation is \WINNT, it is called \WINDOWS on a system that has been upgraded from Windows 9*x*/Me.

Hardware configuration settings are preserved, unless there's a conflict between the hardware and the new OS (remember that Windows 2000 and XP are picky about the hardware that they support). In that case, the hardware may be disabled by the new OS. Installed software stays put, as well as all user accounts and user-specific settings like desktop environment, browser bookmarks, and so on.

Exam Tip

Before starting an OS upgrade, make sure you have shut down all other open applications, including things like virus programs running in the background!

To begin the upgrade of Windows, you must run the appropriate program from the CD-ROM. The program used to upgrade an older version of Windows 9*x* to a newer one (for example, Windows 95 to Windows 98) is the same as the installation program: SETUP.EXE. Run WINNT32.EXE to start an upgrade to Windows 2000 or XP from a version of Windows 9*x*/Me, and WINNT.EXE to start the Setup program for an upgrade from DOS or Windows 3.*x*.

You can also start an upgrade to Windows 2000 or XP by booting from the CD, as you would do with a clean installation. Then, to do an upgrade, you indicate that Windows 2000 or XP should install into a directory that already contains an installation of Windows. You will be asked whether it is an upgrade or a new installation. If you select new installation, it will remove the existing OS before installing.

Upgrade Paths   Although clean installations can be performed on any machine that meets the hardware requirements, upgrade installations require compatible OS installations. You cannot simply upgrade *any* older version of Windows to *any* newer version! Upgrades have to follow an upgrade *path*. Sometimes you must upgrade to an intermediate version of Windows before you can upgrade to a newer version. Table 16-1 lists possible upgrade paths for the various versions of Windows.

TABLE 16.1   Window Upgrade Paths

Original OS	Upgrade Path
Windows 3.*x*	Windows 95 Windows 98
Windows 95	Windows 98 Windows 98SE Windows 2000 Professional
Windows 98	Windows 98SE Windows 2000 Professional Windows XP Home Edition Windows XP Professional
Windows 98SE	Windows 2000 Professional Windows XP Home Edition Windows XP Professional
Windows ME	Windows XP Home Edition Windows XP Professional
Windows NT Workstation 4.0	Windows 2000 Professional Windows XP Professional (Service Pack 5 required)
Windows 2000 Professional	Windows XP Professional
Windows XP Home Edition	Windows XP Professional
Windows XP Professional	No upgrade path (currently)

Determine How to Back Up and Restore Existing Data, If Necessary

If you're doing a multiboot or upgrade installation, it's always a good idea to back up existing user data *just in case*. Yes, most of the time, these types of installations go just fine, or if there is an error, it's minor and recoverable. However, if an installation goes awry enough, you could have to repartition and reformat the disk from scratch, resulting in a total loss of existing data.

If you're working in a networked environment, then there's a good chance that vital user data and documents are backed up on a network server. Check with the network administrator to be sure. If the user saves data locally, or is not connected to a network, then plan on doing a backup to some kind of removable media, such as CD- or DVD-R/RW disks or magnetic data tapes. You will, of course, need the appropriate CD or DVD "burner," or tape backup drive installed on the system. Many newer backup devices can easily be connected to the system via USB or FireWire. In fact, some of the newer backup devices use USB- or FireWire-connected hard disk drives instead of removable media, so you have a lot of backup options available.

Select an Installation Method

It used to be that you really only had one way to perform a Windows OS installation—by feeding a short stack of floppy disks, one by one, into the PC and swapping them out when prompted. Not so anymore! Installation options these days include simple CD-ROM-based, attended installations, CD-ROM-based unattended (scripted) installations, network-based installations, *Remote Installation Services (RIS)* installations, imaged (cloned) installations…, the list goes on and on.

The method you choose depends on several factors. Do you have a large number of installations to "roll out," or just a few? Do you have network resources available, such as disk space to store CD images, and a network infrastructure that will support huge file transfers without interrupting other network services? Do you have the appropriate disk imaging or remote installation software available? What kind of hardware do the "target" systems (the PCs you're installing Windows onto) have?

The following paragraphs describe the various installation methods.

CD-ROM-Based Installation   Typically, if you're only installing Windows onto a few systems, then it's easiest to simply perform the installation from the CD-ROM. The biggest drawback to this method is that it's time-consuming and requires that you be physically in front of the PC to fill in the blanks when the

Setup routine prompts you for information. This process can be sped up by using a text-based script called an *answer file* that fills in the Setup prompts for you.

The CD-ROM–based method can be used to perform both clean and upgrade installations. In the case of a clean installation, you boot directly to the CD-ROM and run the setup program—called SETUP in Windows 9x/Me, and either WINNT or WINNT32 in Windows 2000/XP. Upgrade installations are run from within your present OS.

Any modern PC should be able to boot directly to the installation CD-ROM, but if your system can't, you can use a bootable floppy disk (or set of disks) to get the ball rolling. Windows 98 provides a special floppy boot disk for this purpose. It boots into DOS and then runs the setup program from the CD-ROM via a line in AUTOEXEC.BAT. Windows 2000 and Windows XP do not come with bootable floppy disks; however, you can create a set of setup boot diskettes (four are required for Windows 2000, six for Windows XP).

The Windows 2000 utility to create these diskettes is called MAKEBOOT.EXE or MAKEBT32.EXE, depending on whether you need the 16-bit version or 32-bit version. Use the 16-bit version if you're running the utility from within DOS or Windows 3.x, and the 32-bit version from any other version of Windows. You can find it in the \BOOTDISK directory on the CD-ROM. If you need to make bootable diskettes for Windows XP, you must go online, to Microsoft's *Knowledge Base*. The Knowledge Base is a huge collection of articles on every conceivable aspect of every piece of software Microsoft has ever made, including all types of installation, troubleshooting, and compatibility problems. Its URL is support.microsoft.com (note there's no "www"). To see the Knowledge Base article on creating the disks, search on its article number: 310994. This article provides links for several versions of the program needed to create the diskettes.

CD-based upgrade installations are very straightforward. From within your current OS, you simply insert the CD-ROM for the new OS and wait for the Setup program to start, then follow the prompts. Just in case your system isn't set to autostart programs from inserted CD-ROMs, you can manually start the appropriate Setup program by clicking Start | Run, entering the drive letter of your CD-ROM drive, and then typing the name of the Setup program (SETUP, WINNT, OR WINNT32); for example, D:\i386\WINNT32.

Network Installation   To install Windows on a large number of PCs, it's more efficient to use the network installation method. With a network installation, you don't need the actual Windows installation CD-ROM present. Instead, you copy the important setup files from the CD-ROM to a shared network folder. You then start Setup by booting the target PC and navigating to the network source folder, then execute the appropriate Setup program.

You can use this method to perform clean or upgrade installations. Naturally, the target PC must have a NIC and networking software installed. If you're performing an upgrade installation, then this probably isn't a problem, but clean installations are trickier. You must use a DOS boot diskette that also has a networking client and drivers for your NIC. Microsoft has instructions on their Knowledge Base for creating this kind of boot diskette, or many NIC manufacturers can provide instructions for how to create a network boot diskette with their products.

Imaged Installation   A *disk image* is a complete bit-by-bit copy of a hard disk partition. This includes not only the OS, but also any applications and settings, such as the desktop environment and language settings. Imaged installations are particularly good if you need to make certain that all PCs in your organization have the same programs and settings preconfigured.

Unfortunately, disk imaging is not a native function of any Windows OS (yet). Disk imaging requires special third-party software, such as Norton's Ghost, which is available from Symantec, PowerQuest's Drive Image 2002, and Acronis' True Image. Hardware-based disk copiers, such as the ICS Image MASSter, perform the same function, except that they require you to remove the source hard disk drive from the PC.

Remote Installation Services Installation   Beginning with Windows 2000 Server, Microsoft added Remote Installation Services (RIS), which can be used to initiate an attended or scripted installation based on a network image of the Windows 2000 Professional installation CD-ROM. The target system connects to the RIS server via the network and downloads the installation image. Unlike in a network installation, however, the target PC doesn't need to boot into an OS; instead, it downloads a boot image from the RIS server as well as the OS installation files.

Note that RIS can be used only to perform clean installations, not upgrades. RIS can also be used only to install Windows 2000 and XP, in a Windows 2000 Server–based *Active Directory* domain network.

Determine How to Partition the Hard Disk and What File System to Use

On a clean installation, you need to decide ahead of time how to partition the disk space on your hard disk drive, including the number and size of partitions and the file system you will use.

FAT   If you choose to format your disk with either version of FAT, the Windows 2000/XP Setup Wizard will automatically format it with FAT16 if the partition is less than 2GB, and FAT32 if the partition is greater than 2GB. Support for FAT32 is a feature new to Windows 2000. Windows NT versions 4.0 and earlier do not support FAT32.

NTFS   The version of NTFS that comes with Windows 2000/XP (NTFS5) has a few advancements over the older NTFS from Windows NT (NTFS4). Windows 2000/XP can only create NTFS5 volumes; it cannot make the older NTFS4 volumes. NTFS5 offers the most options for your Windows 2000/XP OS installation. Using NTFS5, you can do the following new functions that NTFS4 could not do:

- Assign disk quotas to users to limit the amount of hard disk space they can use.
- Encrypt files and folders on the hard disk.
- Support Windows 2000 Dynamic Disk configurations.

Unless you are configuring your system for multiple-boot options, NTFS is the best way to go. If upgrading from Windows NT 4.0 Workstation to either Windows 2000 or Windows XP, all existing NTFS4 partitions will be upgraded to NTFS5 automatically during the installation.

> **Travel Advisory**
>
> If you want to dual-boot between NT 4.0 and 2000, you must first install Windows NT Service Pack 4, which contains an updated Ntfs.sys driver that enables Windows NT 4.0 to read from and write to NTFS volumes in Windows 2000. However, the new features of NTFS5 will be disabled when you boot from Windows NT 4.0.

If you are not planning a multiboot installation, use the most advanced file system your version of Windows supports—FAT32 in Windows 9x/Me and NTFS in Windows NT/2000/XP. If you are planning a multiboot configuration, then the lowest common denominator rule applies, at least for the system volume, and for any volumes you want usable by the oldest OS. Once you know which file system you are using, deciding the size and number of partitions will follow, because if you decide to use FAT16 you will have the size limitations of FAT16 to deal with.

Determine Your Computer's Network Role

A Windows computer can have one of several network membership *roles*: *stand-alone, workgroup,* or *domain.*

- Stand-alone simply means that the PC doesn't participate in any workgroup or domain. Any version of Windows can be installed on a stand-alone computer.

- Workgroup membership means that the PC belongs to a group of networked computers that lack centralized administrative control. Each member of a workgroup manages its own resources. All of the versions of Windows covered by the A+ exam can be members of a workgroup. This is the only role that a Windows 9*x*/Me or XP Home computer can play on a network. Workgroups are also called *peer-to-peer* networks.

- A domain is a secured, centralized network environment in which all user and computer accounts reside on one or more *domain controllers.* These are Windows NT, 2000, or 2003 Server systems that are specially configured to manage shared resources and access. Domains are sometimes called *client/server* networks. You'll learn more about domains in Chapter 17.

Decide on Your Computer's Language and Locale Settings

The locale settings include properly displaying date and time information, and using the proper math separators and currency symbols for various locales. These settings are especially important for Windows 2000 and Windows XP because these versions have greatly increased support for various spoken languages and locale conventions.

Plan for Postinstallation Tasks

Once the OS is installed, your work is not done! Here are a few of the postinstallation tasks you should complete:

- Install the latest *patches* and *service packs* for your OS. These are available freely from Microsoft. Patches (also called *hotfixes*) are small software fixes made to address specific problems with the OS, such as security, stability, or performance issues. Service packs are collections of updates that not only fix known problems but also add new features and functions to the OS.

- Check to see if you need to install updated drivers for your system hardware. Hardware drivers, particularly those for devices like video adapters, change often, adding new features and fixing bugs present in older versions. Generally speaking, you should use the latest version available. Visit your hardware component manufacturer's web site for the latest driver software.

- Install any applications (word processing, spreadsheet, database, etc.) required for the work the user of the computer needs to do.

- Finally, don't forget to restore any data backed up before installation/upgrade. Your method of restoring will depend on how you backed up the files in the first place. If you used a third-party backup program, you will need to install it before you can restore those files, but if you used Windows Backup, you are in luck, because it is installed by default. If you did something simpler, like copying to a CD-R or network location, all you have to do is copy the files back to the local hard disk.

Performing the Installation/Upgrade

Installation for all versions of Windows goes through two distinct phases—the *text mode* phase and the *graphical* phase. During text mode, the computer inspects the hardware and displays the *End User License Agreement (EULA)*. You must accept the EULA for setup to continue. During text mode, you can partition your hard disk. The last thing that happens in text mode is that Setup copies files to the local hard disk for running the graphical portion.

When the text mode phase is complete, the computer reboots and the graphical portion of installation begins. During graphical mode, you are prompted to enter the product key, located on the CD-ROM jewel case or envelope. Most techs learn the hard way that these covers tend to disappear when you need them most, so it's a good idea to write the product code directly on the CD-ROM disc itself. Just don't use a ballpoint pen! They'll scratch the surface of the disc, thus rendering it unusable. Most of the installation process takes place in the graphical portion. This is where you select configuration options and optional Windows components.

Once the graphical portion of installation completes, the PC reboots again and you're just about ready to go. Windows XP, as you probably know, requires that you *activate* the OS by either connecting to Microsoft's activation servers via the Internet—this process is automated, if you choose it—or manually entering an activation code acquired from Microsoft. If you choose not to activate, you'll be reminded again in a few days. Failure to activate within 30 days results in a disabled OS!

Now let's walk through the specific steps for installing Windows. First, we'll cover Windows 9x/Me, then Windows NT/2000/XP.

Objective 16.02 Installing and Upgrading Windows 9*x*/Me

The A+ exam is very interested in your ability to install Windows 9*x*/Me on a blank (unpartitioned) drive and to upgrade a Windows 95 system to a Windows 98 one. This section covers both of these situations and assumes a stand-alone system without networking.

Preparing to Upgrade/Install

Most Windows upgrades and installations fail for the simple reason that the tech fails to perform a few basic checks before installing/upgrading Windows 9*x*/Me. In the first section of this chapter, we looked at the nine key steps for a successful upgrade/installation. Follow these few steps—they work! Now let's focus here on specific things you need to know for successfully installing Windows 9*x*/Me.

Minimum Requirements

Microsoft defines some fairly low hardware requirements for Windows 9*x* and Windows Me. To make things more confusing, different types of Microsoft documentation give different values. The minimums listed in the left column of Table 16-2 are the "official-as-of-this-week" figures, but you'll find these requirements laughably low. Even Microsoft admits this, but it is possible to run (maybe a better term would be "walk") Windows 9*x* with this minimum hardware configuration. In the right column are listed minimums that are more appropriate when you plan to get real work done.

> **Exam Tip**
>
> Make a point to save any data when upgrading, as Windows installations do fail occasionally. In some cases, a failed installation destroys everything on the drive!

Setup Disk

Windows 98 Second Edition and Windows Me installation CD-ROMs are bootable, but Windows 95 and Windows 98 installation CD-ROMs are not, requiring you to use a bootable floppy disk to start the process. All versions of Windows 9*x*/Me, however, include a bootable floppy disk as part of the package.

| | **TABLE 16.2** | Windows 9x/Me Hardware Requirements |

Component	Minimum for a Windows 9x/Me Computer	Recommended for a Windows 9x/Me Computer
CPU	486DX/66 CPU	Intel Pentium II CPU
Memory	24 MB of RAM	64–128 MB of RAM
Hard disk	Hard drive space up to 400 MB—the average Windows installation takes 200MB	4 GB of available hard disk space
Display	Video capable of 640 × 480 @ 16 colors	SVGA- or higher-resolution video adapter
Other	A mouse, CD-ROM, and sound card	A mouse, CD-ROM, and sound card

FAT16 or FAT32?

You need to decide ahead of time what type of partition you will want to use. Although you should almost always pick FAT32 for both clean installs and upgrades, three situations exist that might make you want to keep at least one FAT16 partition.

1. First, consider whether you might want to boot to the previous version of MS-DOS to support a DOS program that will not run in Windows, even in a DOS box.

2. Second, you might have a version of Windows 95 that simply doesn't support FAT32.

3. Third, you might want to set up multiboot functions where FAT16 is the only type of formatting supported by all operating systems. For example, dual-booting with Windows NT Workstation.

Except in those rare cases, you should choose to use FAT32.

Many techs are aware of partition *conversion* tools, such as CVT.EXE (used at a command prompt) or the CVT1.EXE (Windows-based, select Programs | Accessories | System Tools | Drive Converter) utility that comes with Windows 98. These tools enable you to convert a FAT16 drive to FAT32 without losing data.

With such handy conversion tools, why bother worrying about using FAT16 or FAT32? Don't forget the 2GB partition size limitation of FAT16. A brand-new 30GB drive will need a lot of drive letters. Also, the convert tools have been known to fail disastrously, albeit rarely. Better to play it safe and decide ahead of time!

Exam Tip

You can upgrade from Windows 95 to Windows 98 and from any 9*x* version to Windows Me.

The Windows 9*x*/Me Installation/ Upgrade Process

Your clean installation of Windows will begin with the text mode (described earlier) and after at least one reboot, continue into graphics mode. Since we've already covered the general steps, let's focus on what is unique about the Windows 98 and Windows Me installation/upgrade process.

Text Mode

Before you can install any version of Windows 9*x*/Me, the hard disk drive that will receive the operating system needs to be properly prepared.

Windows 95 and 98 require that you use the FDISK utility, found on the bootable floppy disk, to partition your drive prior to the start of the installation process—you can format a newly created partition during the setup process, as shown in Figure 16-2. Windows Me is a different kind of bird. You don't need to use the FDISK utility, because Windows Me can partition *and* format a hard disk drive during the setup process.

```
Microsoft Windows 98 Setup
====================================

   Setup needs to configure the unallocated space on your
   hard disk to prepare it for use with Windows. None of
   your existing files will be affected.

   To have Setup configure the space on your hard disk for you,
   choose the recommended option.

 ┌──────────────────────────────────────────────────────────┐
 │ Configure unallocated disk space (recommended).          │
 │  Exit Setup.                                             │
 └──────────────────────────────────────────────────────────┘

   To accept the selection, press ENTER.
   To change the selection, press the UP or DOWN ARROW key,
   and then press ENTER.



ENTER=Continue   F1=Help   F3=Exit
```

FIGURE 16.2 Windows 98 Setup detects an unformatted drive.

Follow the instructions on this screen and work your way through the partitioning and installation process, using the UP ARROW and DOWN ARROW keys to move from choice to choice and the ENTER key to make selections. Once the blank drive is formatted, the Install and the Upgrade processes become virtually identical. If you're upgrading, just boot normally into Windows 95 and toss in the upgrade disk to see the upgrade prompt, as shown in Figure 16-3.

Exam Tip

If you are not using the Windows 98 startup boot disk, your startup disk must support the CD-ROM or you won't get a CD-ROM drive letter!

A common installation trick is to copy the contents of the \WIN9*x* folder from the CD-ROM to a folder on your hard drive. Copying the installation files to your hard drive does two things:

1. First, it makes the installation of Windows faster, as CD-ROMs are very slow.

2. Second, Windows is notorious for needing the original CD-ROM virtually every time you make a change to the system's configuration.

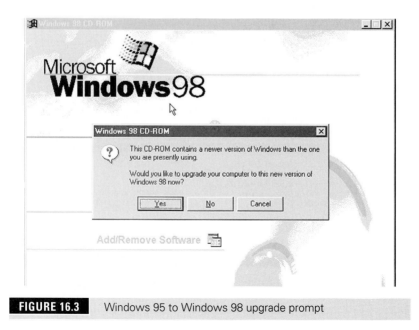

FIGURE 16.3   Windows 95 to Windows 98 upgrade prompt

Windows will remember where it was installed from and will prompt you to "Insert the Windows Installation CD-ROM." If you put the files in a folder on a local drive and then install from there, Windows will remember that and will immediately go straight to those files, saving you the hassle of trying to find the Installation CD-ROM.

At the end of the text mode portion, the setup program performs a quick ScanDisk and checks for video and mouse. Then the program loads a few critical files needed for installation, and initiates the first of many reboots.

Graphical Mode

After the initial command prompt installation process, Windows shifts into a graphical mode with the Install Setup Wizard. This wizard begins by installing a second set of critical installation files. It then uses these files first to verify that you have sufficient hard drive space, and then to prompt you for input on various Windows options. Let's look at the setup prompt screens.

Prompt for Component Options   Windows Setup prompts you to install with options that look like Figure 16-4. For most users, a Typical installation is the safest bet. Once they become familiar with the many options of the Windows installation, however, most folks prefer to use the Custom option. The Compact option is rarely used; it simply skips too many features that most users want. Never worry

FIGURE 16.4   Windows 98 Setup Options: Typical, Portable, Compact, and Custom

about this screen; you can always add or remove components after Windows installs by using the Add/Remove Programs applet in the Control Panel.

Prompt for Product Key Windows 95 used to wait until near the end of the installation process to ask for the product key, driving techs crazy when they realized they had spent the last two hours installing just to discover that their key was missing. Beginning with Windows 98, the Setup program is kind enough to ask for the key early in the process, saving considerable inconvenience when you're juggling 23 different CD-ROMs all in the wrong cases, and trying to punch in the correct product key.

Prompt for Installation Directory Clean installations will always prompt for an installation directory, recommending C:\WINDOWS, as shown in Figure 16-5.

Use this default unless compelled not to. When upgrading from Windows 95 to Windows 98, you must use the same folder that contains the Windows 95 files, or Windows 98 will simply perform a clean installation, leaving you with a useless copy of Windows 95 on your system, and requiring you to reinstall all your applications.

Prompt for Startup Disk The *startup disk* created here differs in two ways from the Windows 9*x*/Me setup boot disk. First, it does not include the option to

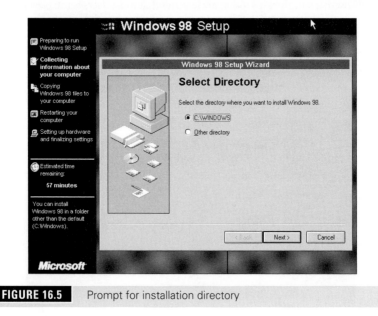

FIGURE 16.5 Prompt for installation directory

run Setup from the Startup menu. Second, this startup disk creates a RAM disk to which it copies a bunch of handy utilities. So, even if you have the setup boot disk, you will still want a startup disk. If you don't already have a startup disk, you can make one now if you would like. All startup disks for the same version of Windows are identical. If you choose not to make a startup disk, simply click Cancel when given the opportunity.

Network Options   One of the final steps of setup is network configuration. Since we're assuming a stand-alone installation, we'll save a discussion of network options for Chapter 17.

Save System Files   This option applies only when upgrading from an earlier version of Windows. You are given the opportunity to save the Windows system files. If you save these files, you may uninstall Windows 98 or Windows Me from the computer by using the Add/Remove Programs | Windows Setup tab in the Control Panel.

Hardware Detection   The point where the hardware detection phase begins varies between Windows 95 and Windows 98/Me. They all work the same way, but Windows 98/Me are a bit more automated.

Windows first tries to find legacy devices (Windows 95 "cheats" by asking you if you have a sound card or a network card) and then kicks in the Plug and Play hardware detection functions, searching for and configuring the detectable hardware on the system, as shown in Figure 16-6.

In a completely Plug and Play environment, this step is simply a matter of watching the installation process take place. As Windows detects devices, it will load the appropriate device drivers if it has them. If not, it will prompt you for a driver disk.

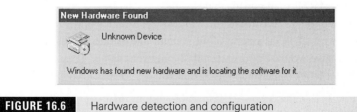

New Hardware Found

Unknown Device

Windows has found new hardware and is locating the software for it.

FIGURE 16.6   Hardware detection and configuration

Installing Windows NT 4.0 Workstation

Objective 16.03

When all is right with the world, installing Windows NT 4.0 Workstation takes only a little more effort than installing Windows 95 and follows almost all the same steps. Although it's unlikely that you'll ever experience the thrill of spending a day installing Windows NT, the OS has a very large installed base and thus a need for techs to service it, so you need to know a few of the quirks.

First off, you'll most likely install Windows NT on an older machine, not anything new, so hardware compatibility shouldn't be too much of a problem. This is good, because one of the major hassles with NT is that it is *not* Plug and Play-capable. To deal with hardware issues, you should use hardware that is on the NT Hardware Compatibility list (HCL), a list you can find on the installation CD—a file called HCL.HLP in the SUPPORT folder—or at www.microsoft.com.

You can test for specific hardware incompatibility by using the NT Hardware Qualifier (NTHQ) program that comes on the installation CD, in the \SUPPORT\HQTOOL folder. The folder contains a batch file called MAKEDISK.BAT that will create a bootable floppy disk with the NTHQ tool. Create the floppy, boot to it, and then run the program to test the system.

Second, do yourself a huge favor and don't bother trying to install NT on a system that falls anywhere near the listed system requirements. Throw as much RAM into the system as the motherboard will support and go with at least a mid-range Pentium CPU. Table 16-3 shows the minimum and my recommended minimums for an NT Workstation.

Third, NT supports FAT (a.k.a., FAT16) and NTFS 4 file systems, as you'll recall from Chapter 15. Unless you have a compelling need for FAT16, go with NTFS. You'll get all the security and stability the file system offers, plus you can use partitions larger than two gigabytes.

Fourth, Windows NT assumes you will connect to a network, but offers you a chance to set up the PC as a stand-alone system. The second step in the installation process gives you the option to skip the network setup.

Finally, NT is very old, which means that you desperately need to patch it immediately after installation. Microsoft released six Service Packs for NT and a host of patches between packs. Luckily, you only need to install Service Pack 5, as it contains all the fixes in the previous ones.

Windows NT is not an upgrade candidate for any OS. You cannot upgrade to Windows NT from any version of Windows 9*x*.

TABLE 16.3	Windows NT Workstation Hardware Requirements	

Component	Minimum for a Windows NT Workstation Computer	Recommended for a Windows NT Workstation Computer
CPU	Intel 80486 25 MHz	Intel Pentium 150 MHz
Memory	12 MB	64 MB
Hard disk	128 MB	2 GB hard disk with 1 GB of free space
Network	None	Modern PCI network card
Display	Video adapter and monitor with VGA resolution	Video adapter and monitor with SVGA resolution, capable of high color (16-bit) display
CD-ROM	12x (not required if installing over a network)	24x (not required if installing over a network)
Floppy disk drive	High Density	High Density
Keyboard and mouse	Keyboard and Microsoft Mouse or compatible pointing device	Keyboard and Microsoft Mouse or compatible pointing device

Installing Windows NT is not something that most techs will ever do in the twenty-first century, but if you run into a situation where you need to have in-depth knowledge of the subject, surf on over to www.totalsem.com for Brian Schwarz's "Installing Windows NT" Tech File.

Installing and Upgrading to Windows 2000 Professional

Objective 16.04

Although it's no longer the latest and greatest product from Microsoft, Windows 2000 Professional is still widely adopted in the business world. Plan on supporting it for years to come.

Because Windows 2000 is completely Plug and Play-compliant, installing Windows 2000 Professional is closer in experience to installing Windows 9x/Me. You insert the CD-ROM, access the setup routine, and go! However, given the inherently more complex nature of the Windows 2000 OS, there are a few twists involved.

Preinstallation Tasks

Preinstallation tasks for Windows 2000 are similar to those for Windows 9x/Me; however, because hardware compatibility is so much more important with Windows 2000, it's particularly important to pay attention to the minimum specs and (especially) the HCL.

Hardware Requirements

The minimum specs represent what Microsoft says you need to install the Windows 2000 Professional OS. Windows 2000 Professional will install and run on a system with the minimum specifications, but you need to take these numbers and at least double them if you want to be happy with your system's performance!

A more realistic recommendation for a useful Windows 2000 Professional computer system is shown in Table 16-4.

If your system(s) exceeds the recommended configuration, all the better!

Hardware Compatibility List (HCL)

In addition to meeting the minimal specifications, your hardware also needs to be supported by the Windows 2000 OS. The HCL is the definitive authority as to whether your component is compatible with the OS. Items on the HCL have

TABLE 16.4	Windows 2000 Professional Hardware Requirements	
Component	Minimum for a Windows 2000 Professional Computer	Recommended for a Windows 2000 Professional Computer
CPU	Intel Pentium 133 MHz	Intel Pentium II 350 MHz
Memory	64 MB	128 MB
Hard disk	2 GB with 650 MB of free space	6.4 GB hard disk with 2 GB of free space
Network	None	Modern PCI network card
Display	Video adapter and monitor with VGA resolution	Video adapter and monitor with SVGA resolution, capable of high color (16-bit) display
CD-ROM	12x (not required if installing over a network)	24x
Floppy disk drive	High Density	High Density
Keyboard and mouse	Keyboard and Microsoft Mouse or compatible pointing device	Keyboard and Microsoft Mouse or compatible pointing device

been extensively tested with Windows 2000 and are guaranteed by Microsoft to work with your installation.

Travel Advisory

If you contact Microsoft's technical support staff, one of the first things they ask is if all of your systems' components are on the HCL.

The HCL is located in the \SUPPORT folder on the Windows 2000 CD-ROM (HCL.TXT), but for the most current list, visit the Windows 2000 page at the Microsoft web site.

Travel Assistance

Microsoft Windows Hardware Compatibility List:
http://www.microsoft.com/whdc/hcl/search.mspx.

Upgrading Issues

Here are some of the issues that you should be aware of before performing an upgrade:

- Remember to check the upgrade path table before starting an upgrade installation. You can upgrade directly to Windows 2000 Professional from Windows 9x/Me (all versions) and Windows NT Workstation 4.0.

- Because of Registry and program differences between Windows 9x/Me and Windows 2000, you might need upgrade packs (or migration DLLs) for your Windows 9x/Me applications. Not only does Windows 2000 have hardware issues, it also does not like a lot of Windows 9x/Me software!

- Windows 2000 does not support applications that make use of *Virtual Device Drivers (VxDs)*. VxDs enable applications to access hardware directly, bypassing the OS altogether—something not permitted by Windows 2000! Many older games and multimedia applications use VxDs, which makes this a potentially serious issue.

- Third-party disk compression applications are not supported by Windows 2000.

- Third-party power management applications are also likely to cause problems with a Windows 2000 installation.

Obviously, it's worth your time to take a few extra steps before you pop in that CD-ROM! If you plan to upgrade rather than run a clean installation, follow these steps first:

1. Check out the Hardware and Software Compatibility web site or run a compatibility report using the *Compatibility Checker* utility provided with Windows 2000 Professional. The utility generates a detailed list of potentially problematic devices and applications. You can run the utility as follows: Insert the Windows 2000 Professional CD-ROM and, from your current OS, open a command prompt or use the Start | Run box to run the WINNT32.EXE program from the Windows 2000 Professional CD-ROM with the CHECKUPGRADEONLY switch added. The command line will look like this: d:\i386\winnt32 /checkupgradeonly (where *d*: is the CD drive.) Note that the Compatibility Checker runs automatically when you do a clean installation.

2. Have an up-to-date backup of your data and configuration files handy.

3. Perform a "spring cleaning" on your system by uninstalling unused or unnecessary applications and deleting old files.

4. Perform a disk scan and a disk defragmentation.

5. Uncompress all files, folders, and partitions.

6. Perform a current virus scan, and then remove or disable all virus-checking software.

7. Disable virus checking in your system CMOS.

8. Last, keep in mind that if worse comes to worst, you may have to start over and do a clean installation anyway. This makes step 2 exceedingly important! Back up your data!

The Windows 2000 Installation/Upgrade Process

Like your clean installation of Windows 9x/Me, your clean installation of Windows 2000 will begin with the text mode and, after a reboot, continue into graphics mode. Again, we'll limit this discussion to what is unique about the Windows 2000 installation/upgrade process.

Disk Partition Options

The first thing that the Setup program does is to examine your hard disk to determine its existing partition and file system configuration. You then get the option of either installing onto an existing partition (if any) or creating a new partition for installation.

By default, the first active partition (the C: drive) is where the Windows 2000 system files are copied. The boot partition is where your OS files are located. Typically, Windows creates a folder called C:\WINNT for a clean installation. An upgrade installation will overwrite your current OS files in their current location (that is, \WINNT if upgrading from Windows NT, and \WINDOWS if upgrading from Windows 9x). Microsoft recommends that your boot partition be at least 1GB in size.

Travel Advisory

The system and boot partition do not have to be separate partitions! In fact, on most systems, the system and the boot partition are the same partition.

File System Options

At the heart of any OS is the system by which you create and organize your files. Windows 2000 supports FAT16 and FAT32, just like Windows 9x/Me, but also supports its own native NTFS. We've covered the relative benefits and drawbacks of each file system, so your decision at this point should be pretty clear. Unless you have a compelling reason to stick with FAT or FAT32, NTFS is the way to go.

Networking Options

As with previous versions of Windows NT, the Windows 2000 line is optimized for networking with other computer systems. By default, Windows 2000 installs the Client for Microsoft Networks, the File and Printer Sharing for Microsoft Networks service, and the TCP/IP protocol (called the Internet Protocol by Windows 2000). You are also given the option of joining either a workgroup or a domain.

Note that even if, like now, you're installing Windows 2000 as a stand-alone PC, you have to specify one or the other networking option. Go ahead and let Setup configure the machine as part of a workgroup (with the default name of *Workgroup*). This can easily be changed later. Chapter 17 covers networking terminology and concepts in detail.

Language and Locale Settings

Windows 2000 can easily be configured to support multiple languages and regional input settings for such things as keyboard layout, currency, time/date display, and numbering.

Installing and Upgrading to Windows XP Professional

Objective 16.05

You'll prepare for a Windows XP installation just as you did for previous installations of Windows. Run through the preinstallation tasks, check out hardware requirements and hardware and software compatibility, check the HCL (or, as it's called in XP, the *Windows Catalog*), and off you go!

XP Hardware Requirements

Hardware requirements are higher than in previous versions of Windows but quite in line with even a modestly priced computer today. Microsoft XP runs on a wide range of computers, but you need to be sure that your computer meets the minimum hardware requirements, as shown in Table 16-5. Also shown is my recommended minimum for a system running a typical selection of business productivity software.

TABLE 16.5	Windows XP Hardware Requirements	
Component	**Minimum for a Windows XP Computer**	**Recommended for a Windows XP Computer**
CPU	Any Intel or AMD 233 MHz or higher processor	Any Intel or AMD 300 MHz or higher processor
Memory	64 MB of RAM (though Microsoft admits XP will be somewhat crippled with only this amount)	256 MB of RAM or higher
Hard disk	1.5 GB of available hard drive space	4 GB of available hard drive space
Network	Video card that supports DirectX 8 with at least 800 × 600 resolution	Video card that supports DirectX 8 with at least 1024 × 768 resolution

TABLE 16.5	Windows XP Hardware Requirements *(continued)*

Component	Minimum for a Windows XP Computer	Recommended for a Windows XP Computer
CD-ROM	Any CD-ROM or DVD-ROM drive	Any CD-ROM or DVD-ROM drive
Keyboard and mouse	Keyboard and Microsoft Mouse or compatible pointing device	Keyboard and Microsoft Mouse or compatible pointing device

Hardware and Software Compatibility

You'll need to check hardware and software compatibility before installing Windows XP Professional—either as an upgrade or as a new installation. Luckily, you have two tools for determining whether your hardware is compatible: the Windows Catalog and the *Upgrade Advisor* on the XP CD.

Windows Catalog

Windows XP's Windows Catalog performs the same function as Windows 2000's HCL. It is a searchable list of hardware and software that is known to work with Windows XP. The URL for this exact page is so long, it looks like a typing test. Here is another way to get to it through a shorter URL. First, connect to www.microsoft.com/windowsxp/compatibility/. On the Compatibility page, select the link labeled Discover the Windows Catalog.

Once at the Windows Catalog page, you can search on specific hardware or software products, or browse through the catalog of hardware and software products that will work with Windows XP.

Upgrade Advisor

Windows XP supports a wide range of hardware and software, even some rather old "no name" computers, but you should be proactive when planning an installation. Fortunately, the *Upgrade Advisor* is the first process that runs on the XP installation CD-ROM.

The Upgrade Advisor examines your hardware and installed software (in the case of an upgrade) and provides a list of devices and software that are known to have issues with XP. Figure 16-7 shows the Upgrade Advisor in action.

The Upgrade Advisor can also be run separately from the Windows XP installation. You can run it from the Windows XP installation CD-ROM, or if you want to find out about compatibility for an upgrade before purchasing Windows XP, connect to the Windows XP Compatibility page (www.microsoft.com/

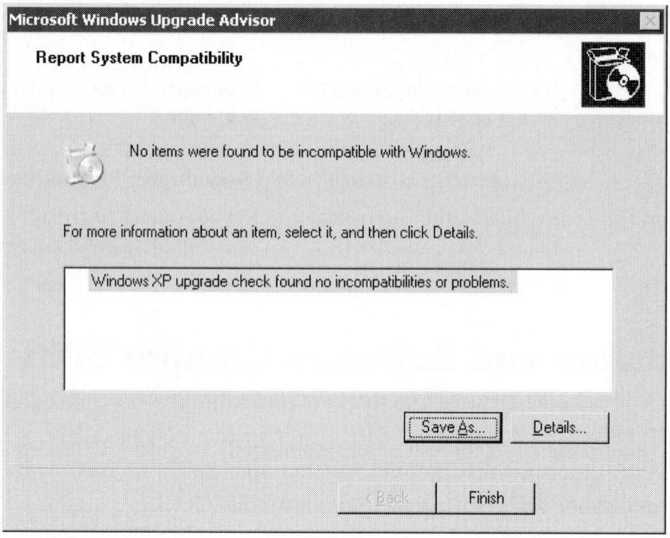

FIGURE 16.7 Windows XP Professional Upgrade Advisor

windowsxp/compatibility) and select Upgrade Advisor. Follow the instructions on the following page to use the online Upgrade Advisor.

Travel Advisory
Be sure to follow the Upgrade Advisor's suggestions!

Booting into Windows XP Setup

The Windows XP CDs are bootable, and Microsoft no longer includes a program to create a set of setup boot disks. This should not be an issue, because PCs manufactured in the last several years have the ability to boot from CD-ROM. This system BIOS setting, usually described as "boot order," is controlled through a PC's BIOS-based setup program.

In the unlikely event that your lab computer can't be made to boot from CD, you can create a set of six (yes, *six!*) Windows XP setup boot disks using a program downloaded from Microsoft's web site.

Registration Versus Activation

During setup, you will be prompted to register your product and to activate it. Many people confuse activation with registration. These are two separate operations.

Windows Registration

Registration is informing Microsoft of the official owner or user of the product, providing contact information such as name, address, company, phone number, e-mail address, and so on. Registration is still entirely optional.

Windows Activation

Activation is Microsoft's way of ensuring that each license for Windows XP is used solely on a single computer. It's also more formally called *Microsoft Product Activation (MPA)*.

Activation is mandatory, but you may skip this step during installation. You will have 30 days in which to activate the product, during which time it will work normally. If you don't activate it within that time frame, it will be disabled. Don't worry about forgetting, because once it's installed, Windows XP frequently reminds you to activate it with a balloon message over the tray area of the taskbar. The messages even tell you how many days you have left.

Activation Mechanics   Here is how product activation works. When you choose to activate, either during setup or later when XP reminds you to do it, the product ID code that you entered during installation is combined with a 50-digit value that identifies your key hardware components to create an installation ID code. You must send this code to Microsoft, either automatically if you have an Internet connection, or verbally via a phone call to Microsoft. Microsoft then returns a 42-digit product activation code. If you are activating online, you don't have to enter the activation code; it will happen automatically. If you are activating over the phone, you must read the installation ID to a representative and enter the resulting 42-digit activation code into the Activate Windows By Phone dialog box.

No personal information about you is sent as part of the activation process. Figure 16-8 shows the dialog box that will open when you start activation by clicking the reminder message balloon.

The Windows XP Installation Process

Installing XP is simple. The wizard will guide you through every step of the process. The onscreen directions are correct and clear. Very few decisions will need

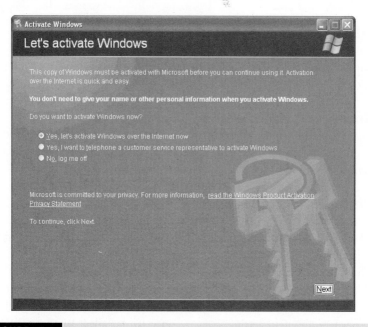

FIGURE 16.8   Activation will take just seconds with an Internet connection.

to be made. If you are in doubt about a setting, pressing ENTER will likely perform the correct action.

Overall, the installation process takes about an hour. Most of that time will be spent watching the screen. Feel free to walk away as the installation is taking place. If input is needed, the installation program will stop and wait until you click the correct buttons. The following steps describe a clean installation of Windows XP.

Text Mode

Insert the Windows XP CD and boot the computer. After inspecting your hardware configuration, XP setup will show the blue character mode setup screen and copy files to your computer. After the files are copied, you will be prompted to remove the CD and reboot the system. Windows setup will start, load system devices, and display the Welcome To Setup screen shown in Figure 16-9.

Press ENTER to start the installation of XP. Read and accept the *End User License Agreement (EULA)*. If your hard disk is unpartitioned, you will need to create a new partition when prompted. Figure 16-10 shows the dialog screen that enables you to select the size of your partition. You can either accept the default

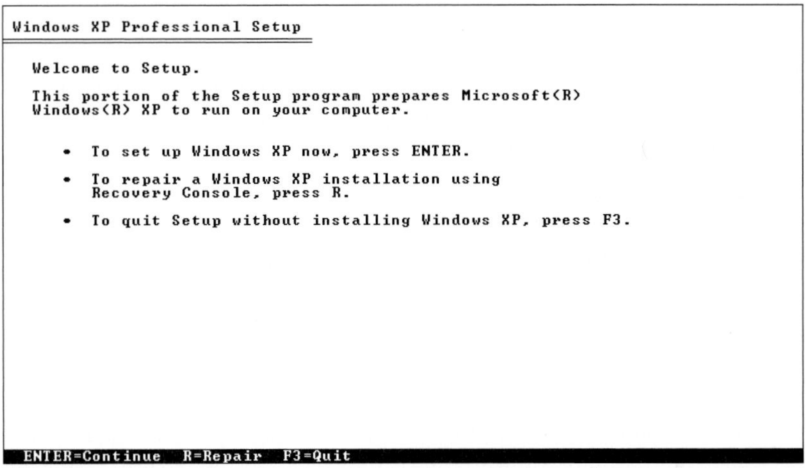

```
Windows XP Professional Setup

  Welcome to Setup.

  This portion of the Setup program prepares Microsoft(R)
  Windows(R) XP to run on your computer.

     •  To set up Windows XP now, press ENTER.

     •  To repair a Windows XP installation using
        Recovery Console, press R.

     •  To quit Setup without installing Windows XP, press F3.



  ENTER=Continue   R=Repair   F3=Quit
```

FIGURE 16.9   Windows XP Welcome To Setup screen

size for the partition or enter a smaller value in the highlighted box. For this example, we wanted a 2 GB (2048 MB) partition.

Next, you will select the partition on which to install XP, and then you need to decide which file system format to use for the new partition. If you have been reading this book carefully, you will choose to format the partition using the NTFS file system.

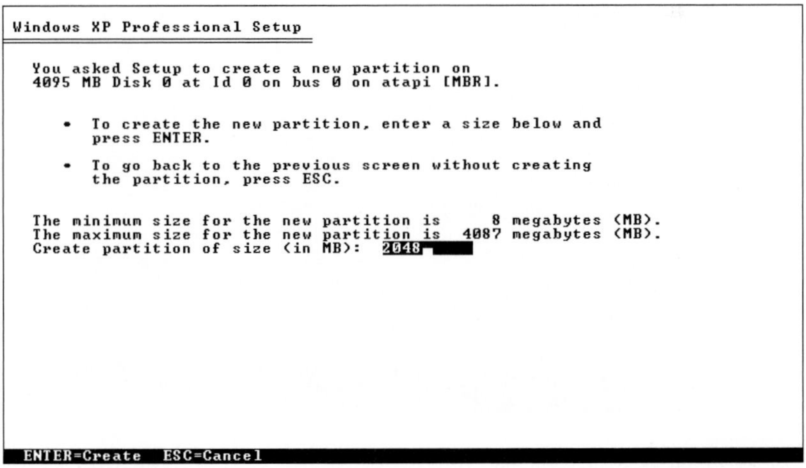

```
Windows XP Professional Setup

  You asked Setup to create a new partition on
  4095 MB Disk 0 at Id 0 on bus 0 on atapi [MBR].

     •  To create the new partition, enter a size below and
        press ENTER.

     •  To go back to the previous screen without creating
        the partition, press ESC.

  The minimum size for the new partition is      8 megabytes (MB).
  The maximum size for the new partition is   4087 megabytes (MB).
  Create partition of size (in MB):  2048




  ENTER=Create   ESC=Cancel
```

FIGURE 16.10   Enter the partition size

Now, Setup is ready to copy files to the newly formatted partition, displaying another progress bar. On a clean installation, Setup creates a folder named \Windows (as opposed to \WINNT, as in NT and 2000) in C:\ into which it installs the OS, creating appropriate subfolders below this folder.

Graphical Mode

After it completes copying the base set of files to this location, your computer reboots, and the graphical mode of Windows XP Setup begins. On the left of the screen shown in Figure 16-11, uncompleted tasks have a white button, completed tasks have a green button, and the current task has a red button.

The following screens ask questions about a number of things Setup needs to know. Just answer them appropriately. They include the desired region and language the computer will operate in, your name and organization for personalizing your computer; and a valid product key for Windows XP. Be sure to enter the product key exactly, or you will be unable to continue.

Next, you need to give your computer a name that identifies it on a network. Check with your system administrator for an appropriate name. In addition to a valid name for your computer, you need to create a password for the Administrator user account. This will be the password that allows you to modify and fix the computer. Next, set the date, time, and time zone.

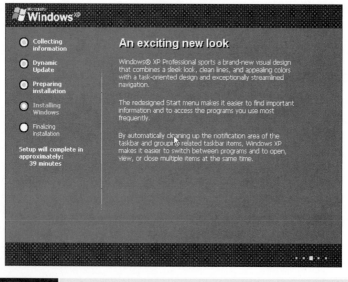

FIGURE 16.11   Beginning of graphical mode in Windows XP Setup

If a network card was detected, the network components will be installed and you'll have an opportunity to configure the network settings. On the Network Settings page, select Typical Settings. Once the networking elements are installed, you need to configure the network. Relax; XP will do most of the work for you. Unless you have specific instructions from your network administrator, the default settings are the preferred choices.

After the files required for the final configuration are copied, XP will reboot again. During this reboot, XP determines your screen size and applies the appropriate resolution. This reboot can take several minutes to complete, so be patient. Once the reboot is complete, you must log on as the Administrator. Balloon messages may appear over the tray area of the taskbar. A common message concerns the display resolution. Click the balloon and allow Windows XP to automatically adjust the display settings.

Another message reminds you that you have 30 days left for activation. When you do a single install, you should test it for a few days before activating, in case you need to make any significant changes in the hardware. You don't need to worry about accidentally forgetting to activate the OS—Windows XP aggressively reminds you every chance it gets.

So what happens if, for some reason, you miss the 30-day deadline? Nothing traumatic: no sirens or explosions, but the OS will no longer let you log on! Instead, it simply displays the activation screen, thus giving you the chance to complete activation (but nothing else).

Once you've completed the Windows XP installation and should have a desktop with the default background (called *Bliss*), as shown in Figure 16-12.

CHECKPOINT

✔**Objective 16.01: Windows Installation/Upgrade Overview**   Prior to installing any version of Windows, you need to accomplish several important tasks. These include identifying hardware requirements, verifying compatibility, picking an installation type (clean or upgrade) and method, backing up data (if needed), preparing disk storage, determining your PC's network role, and planning postinstallation tasks. Clean installations start with a blank hard disk partition and create a completely new Windows OS. Upgrade installation overwrite currently existing Windows installations with a newer version but preserve current user settings and applications. OS upgrade installations follow specific upgrade paths.

FIGURE 16.12 Windows XP desktop with Bliss background

✔**Objective 16.02: Installing and Upgrading Windows 9x/Me** Windows 9x/Me must be installed on hard disk drives formatted with FAT16 or FAT32. Partitioning and formatting is done using a DOS bootable diskette that has the FDISK utility. Installation goes through two distinct phases: text mode and graphical mode. It is during graphical mode that you input information such as component options, product key, installation directory, network options, and so on.

✔**Objective 16.03: Installing Windows NT 4.0 Workstation** Because Windows NT does not have Plug and Play capability, hardware compatibility is a much more important issue than it is in Windows 9x/Me. Always confirm that your hardware is on the Hardware Compatibility List (HCL) before proceeding. You cannot upgrade any version of Windows 9x/Me to Windows NT.

✔**Objective 16.04: Installing and Upgrading Windows 2000 Professional** Unlike Windows NT, Windows 2000 is completely Plug and Play-compliant, so installation proceeds much as it does in Windows 9x. It is, however, still important to confirm that your hardware is on the HCL. The Compatibility Checker utility examines your system and alerts you to any potential hardware and software conflicts. You can upgrade to Windows 2000 from any version of Windows 9x/Me.

✔**Objective 16.05: Installing and Upgrading Windows XP Professional**

Windows XP provides the Upgrade Advisor utility to examine your system and alert you to any potential conflicts or problems. The main difference between installing Windows XP Professional and any other version of Windows is product activation. Windows XP requires you to activate the OS, either through Microsoft's activation servers on the Internet, or manually by calling Microsoft and acquiring an activation key number. If you do not activate the OS, it will disable itself after 30 days.

REVIEW QUESTIONS

1. Which file system should you use when you install Windows ME on a 30GB hard drive?

   A. FAT

   B. FAT16

   C. FAT32

   D. NTFS

2. The computers in your company are currently running Windows NT 4.0. The hardware meets the requirements for Windows 2000 Professional. How should you upgrade these computers to Windows 2000 Professional?

   A. Upgrade the computers directly to Windows 2000 Professional.

   B. Upgrade the computers to Windows 98, then to Windows 2000 Professional.

   C. Install the latest service pack for Windows NT 4.0, and then upgrade to Windows 2000 Professional.

   D. Install Microsoft BOB, and then upgrade to Windows 2000.

3. Which of the following computer systems will need to be upgraded before you can install Windows 2000 Professional on it?

   A. Computer 1: Pentium 166 MHz, 96 MB RAM, 3.2 GB HD

   B. Computer 2: Pentium II 433 MHz, 128 MB RAM, 500 MB HD

   C. Computer 3: Celeron 333 MHz, 64 MB RAM, 1.3 GB HD

   D. Computer 4: AMDK6 266 MHz, 64 MB RAM, 6.4 GB HD

4. After upgrading a computer system from Windows 98 to Windows XP Professional, you notice that the modem no longer works, even after you manually attempt to install the driver. What is the first thing you should check before making a call to technical support?

   A. Check the Windows XP Hardware Compatibility List (HCL).

   B. Check the Windows XP Approved Vendors List (AVL).

   C. Remove the modem and check the jumpers to make sure it is configured for Plug and Play detection.

   D. Check the modem manufacturer's web site for an updated driver.

5. You have configured a laptop computer system to dual-boot between Windows 98 and Windows 2000 Professional. The system has a single FAT32 partition on a 3.2 GB hard disk. By default, where did Setup install the Windows 2000 Professional system files?

   A. C:\WINDOWS

   B. C:\WIN2K

   C. D:\WINNT

   D. C:\WINNT

6. Which of Windows 2000 Professional's features would be unavailable in the previous dual-boot configuration?

   A. File and folder compression and encryption

   B. Multiple user profiles

   C. Internet Connection Sharing (ICS)

   D. Advanced Power Management's Hibernation feature

7. Which of the following applications should you remove from a Windows 98 computer system before performing an upgrade to Windows XP Professional?

   A. Third-party antivirus software

   B. Third-party disk compression software

   C. Microsoft applications not specifically written for Windows XP

   D. Netscape Communicator

8. What command-line switch can you add to WINNT32.EXE to generate a compatibility report prior to performing an upgrade installation of Windows 2000 Professional?

   A. /SCANDISK

   B. /COMPATIBILITY

    C. /CHECKUPGRADEONLY

    D. /CHKDSK

9. Which of the following processes take place during the text mode phase of Windows XP Professional installation. (Choose three.)

    A. You accept the EULA.

    B. You partition the hard disk drive.

    C. You format the hard disk drive.

    D. You enter the product key.

10. Jon attempted to install a clean version of Windows 98 SE onto a drive, but received the following error message:
"Windows has detected that Drive C: does not contain a valid FAT partition."
What could be the problem? (Select all that apply.)

    A. Jon forgot to partition the hard drive.

    B. Jon forgot to format the hard drive.

    C. The drive was already formatted as NTFS.

    D. The drive was already formatted with FAT32.

REVIEW ANSWERS

1. **C** FAT32

2. **A** Upgrade the computers directly to Windows 2000 Professional. There is no need for any intermediate steps—the upgrade to Windows 2000 Professional from Windows NT 4.0 is a direct path. Just be sure that the system meets the minimum hardware specifications for Windows 2000 Professional.

3. **B** Computer 2: Pentium II 433 MHz, 128 MB RAM, 500 MB HD. Windows 2000 Professional needs at least 650 MB of HD space to install.

4. **A** Windows XP Hardware Compatibility List (HCL). If the component is not on the HCL, it is incompatible with the Windows XP OS.

5. **D** C:\WINNT. C:\WINNT is the correct default location where Setup installs the Windows 2000 Professional system files.

6. **A** File and folder compression and encryption. Windows 2000 Professional must be installed on an NTFS partition in order to compress or encrypt files and folders.

7. **B**   Third-party disk compression software. Windows 2000 does not support applications that attempt to take control of hardware.

8. **C**   /CHECKUPGRADEONLY. Running WINNT32.EXE /CHECKUPGRADEONLY will generate a compatibility report indicating any problematic hardware or applications prior to installation.

9. **A B C**   You enter the product key during the graphical mode of installation.

10. **A C**   Jon forgot to partition the hard drive or the drive was already formatted as NTFS.

Networking
in Windows

	NEWBIE	SOME EXPERIENCE	EXPERT
ETA	5 hours	3 hours	2 hours

Every modern Windows operating system assumes it will be part of a network, straight out of the box. Windows XP practically *requires* you to log into the Internet for Product Activation, just to use the OS beyond 30 days! Arguably, you can't have a stable, well-functioning PC today without connecting to the Internet, the biggest network of all.

Once you finish a successful installation or upgrade of the operating system, as you did in Chapter 16, you should install and configure networking even before bothering to install drivers for any component except the motherboard. No matter how well intentioned, Microsoft engineers simply cannot produce a bug-free OS on the first try. It's just too huge a project with too many variables on hardware and applications. It's almost surprising that they do as good a job as they do. Regardless, you need to patch your operating system and update drivers on every PC. You get those patches and drivers from a central server on a local area network (LAN) or directly from Microsoft and other vendors on the Internet.

At this point in the book, you've covered the hardware aspects of connecting to a LAN or directly to the Internet. You have an NIC or modem for the PC that handles splitting data into packets and putting the packets back together at the destination PC. You've got a cabling standard to connect the NIC to a hub/switch or MSAU, thus making that data transfer possible; or a wireless standard such as 802.11g that connects the NIC to a WAP and thus to the greater network. Or, you have a telephone cable that enables you to dial into an *Internet Service Provider (ISP)*, a company that connects you to the Internet. Chapter 12 discussed the need for software protocols to create an interface between the hardware and the operating system, requiring you to install NetBEUI or TCP/IP, for example.

Let's turn to the software side of connection in detail now, setting up a LAN first, and then connecting to the Internet through dial-up or via a LAN.

Objective 17.01 Network Operating Systems

In a classic sense, a *network operating system (NOS)* communicates with the PC hardware—of whichever hardware protocol—and makes the connections between multiple machines on a network. The NOS enables one or more PCs to act as a server machine and share data and services over a network—to share *resources*, in other words. You then need to run software on client computers to enable those computers to access the shared resources on the server machine.

Every Windows OS is an NOS and enables the PC to share resources and access shared resources. But it doesn't come out of the box ready to work on all networks! You need to configure Windows to handle all three tasks to make all this work: install a network protocol to communicate with hardware, enable server software to share resources, and install client software to enable the PC to access shared resources.

All NOSes are not alike, even among Windows versions. Before you can share resources across a network, you must answer a number of questions. How do you make that happen? Can everyone share his or her hard drives with everyone else? Should you place limits on sharing? If everyone needs access to a particular file, where will it be stored? What about security? Can anyone access the file? What if someone erases it accidentally? How are backups to be handled? Different NOSes answer these questions differently.

Network Organization

All NOSes can be broken into three basic organizational groups: client/server, peer-to-peer, and domain-based. All Windows PCs can function as network clients and servers, so this muddies the waters a bit. Let's take a look at traditional network organization.

Client/Server

The client/server solution to all the resource-sharing questions is to take one machine and dedicate it as a resource to be shared over the network. This machine will have a dedicated NOS optimized for sharing files. This special OS includes powerful caching software that enables high-speed file access. It will have extremely high levels of protection and an organization that permits extensive control of the data. This machine is called a *dedicated* server. All of the other machines that use the data are called *clients* (because it's what they usually are) or *workstations*.

The client/server system dedicates one machine to act as a "server." Its only function is to serve up resources to the other machines on the network. These servers do not run Windows 9x or Windows XP. They use highly sophisticated and expensive NOSes that are optimized for the sharing and administration of network resources. The most popular NOS that fits within the client/server concept is Novell NetWare.

A NetWare server is not used directly by anyone. It does not run Windows; it runs only Novell NetWare. Novell NetWare just *serves* shared resources; it does not run programs like Excel or CorelDRAW. Many network administrators will even remove the keyboard and monitor from a Novell NetWare server to keep people from trying to use it. NetWare has its own commands and requires substantial training to use, but in return, you get an amazingly powerful NOS!

> **Travel Advisory**
>
> The terms "client" and "server" are, to say the least, freely used in the Windows world. Keep in mind that a client generally refers to any process (or in this context, computer system) that can request a resource or service, and a server is any process (or system) that can fulfill the request.

Client/server NOSes like Novell NetWare provide excellent security for shared resources. Do you remember the NTFS permissions used by Windows NT, 2000, and XP? Novell NetWare has a similar level of permissions, but because it is client/server, only the servers have this file protection.

Peer-to-Peer

Some networks do not require dedicated servers—every computer can perform both server and client functions. A peer-to-peer network enables any or all of the machines on the network to act as a server. Peer-to-peer networks are much cheaper than client/server networks, because the software costs less and does not require you to purchase a high-end machine to be the dedicated server. The most popular peer-to-peer NOSes today are Windows 9x/Me and Windows 2000/XP. As long as the total number of machines on the network stays relatively low, no problem occurs. As the number of machines begins to go past 20–30, the entire network begins to slow down. If one file is being shared heavily, even five or six machines can bring the entire system to a crawl.

Security is the other big weakness of peer-to-peer networks. Each system on a peer-to-peer network maintains its own security. The Windows 9x/Me NOS has traditionally been weak in the area of network security. When a Windows 9x/Me system shares a resource such as a folder or printer, it has only three levels of network permissions from which to choose:

- Read-Only
- Full Access
- Depends on Password

Microsoft did this on purpose. If you want real security, you need to buy Windows NT, 2000, or XP. But even a network composed only of Windows XP machines requires you to place a local account on every system. So, even though you get better security in a Windows XP Professional peer-to-peer network, system administration entails a lot of running around to individual systems to create and delete local users every time someone joins or leaves the network. In a word: bleh.

Windows peer-to-peer networks organize the networked systems into *workgroups,* which is little more than a pretty way to organize systems to make navigating through Network Neighborhood a little easier (Figure 17-1). In reality, workgroups have no security value.

Peer-to-peer remains very popular; the price—usually free because it comes with Windows—combined with its tremendous ease of use makes peer-to-peer the NOS of choice for smaller networks that do not need the high level of protection and greater speed provided by client/server network operating systems.

Exam Tip

Know the difference between client/server and peer-to-peer.

Domain-Based

Client/server networks, especially NetWare, dominated networking for many years. In order to access earlier versions of a NetWare server, you needed an

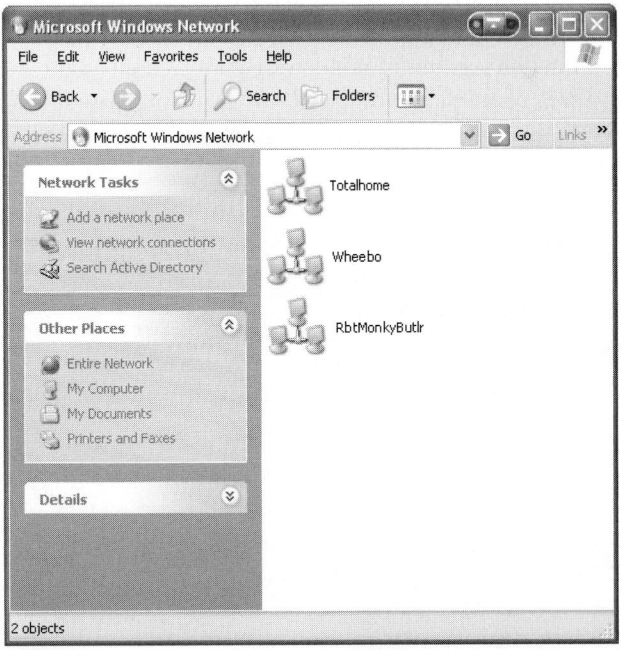

FIGURE 17.1   Multiple workgroups in a network

account on that server. Each serving system stores a database of its accounts and passwords. If you want to access a server, you must log on. When only one server exists, the logon process takes only a second and works very well. The trouble comes when your network contains multiple servers. In that case, every time you access a different server, you must repeat the logon process. In larger networks containing many servers, this becomes a time-consuming nightmare not only for the user, but also for the network administrator. Imagine if Tom Smith decides to quit the company. The network administrator must walk up to each server and delete his account—a major hassle.

A domain-based network provides an excellent solution for the problem of multiple logins. In a domain-based environment, one or more servers hold the security database for all systems. This one database holds a single list of all users and passwords. When you log on to your computer or to any computer, the logon request goes to this single system, called the *domain controller,* to verify the account and password.

No version of Windows covered by the A+ Certification exams can run as a domain controller. You need a copy of one of Microsoft's server NOSes to do that, such as Windows NT Server, 2000 Server, or 2003 Server. The server versions of Windows look and act very similar to the workstation versions but come with extra programs to enable them to take on the role of domain controller, among other things. A quick glance at the options you have in Administrative tools enables you to see how much more complicated the server versions are than the workstation versions of Windows. Figure 17-2 shows the Administrative Tools options on a typical Windows XP workstation. These should be familiar to you. Figure 17-3 shows the many extra tools you need to work with Windows 2000 Server.

FIGURE 17.2   Administrative Tools in Windows XP Professional

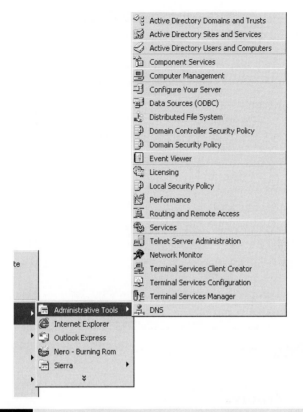

Active Directory Domains and Trusts
Active Directory Sites and Services
Active Directory Users and Computers
Component Services
Computer Management
Configure Your Server
Data Sources (ODBC)
Distributed File System
Domain Controller Security Policy
Domain Security Policy
Event Viewer
Licensing
Local Security Policy
Performance
Routing and Remote Access
Services
Telnet Server Administration
Network Monitor
Terminal Services Client Creator
Terminal Services Configuration
Terminal Services Manager
Administrative Tools ▶   DNS
Internet Explorer
Outlook Express
Nero - Burning Rom
Sierra ▶

FIGURE 17.3   Administrative Tools in Windows 2000 Server

Every Windows NT/2000/XP system contains a very special account called *administrator*. This one account has complete and absolute power over the entire system. When you install Windows NT, 2000 or XP, you must create a password for the administrator account. Anyone who knows the administrator password has the ability to read any file and run any program. As you might imagine, you should keep the administrator password secret to all but the highest level of administrators. Equally important, losing the administrator password usually requires completely reinstalling Windows NT or 2000—so don't lose it!

Any Windows 9x/Me system may also log into and access a Windows domain and share folders and printers although Windows 9x/Me's use of non-NTFS file systems makes its sharing security much weaker than what you get with Windows NT, 2000, or XP systems. We usually add Windows 9x/Me systems to a domain simply as clients. To set up or change a Windows 9x system's workgroup membership, use the Identification tab in the Network Neighborhood properties (Figure 17-4).

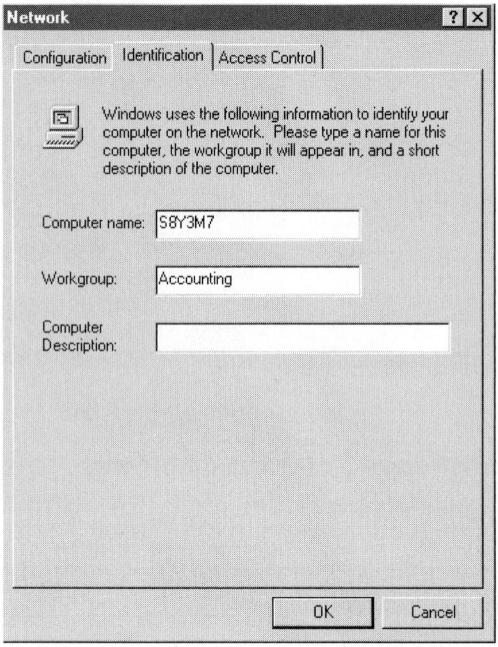

FIGURE 17.4   Changing the workgroup in Windows 98

Travel Advisory

Windows XP Home addition does not have the ability to log into a domain!

Making or changing a domain membership takes a little more effort, and each version of Windows does it differently. In Windows 9*x*, click the properties for Client for Microsoft Networks, check Log On To Windows NT Domain (even if this is a Windows 2000 domain), and then enter the domain name as shown in Figure 17-5. In Windows NT, open the properties for Network Neighborhood. You'll find the Identification tab here. Click the Change button to get to a screen that looks and functions similar to the screen in Windows 98. Windows 2000, as usual, makes the process a little easier. Open the properties for My Computer and select the Network Identification tab. This shows your current selection. While we're talking about logging into domains, it's nice to compare this to Windows XP Professional's method for logging into a domain. Although substantially the same process, Windows XP calls the tab Computer Name and renames a few of the buttons (Figure 17-6).

Clicking the Network ID button opens the Network Identification Wizard, but most techs just use the Properties or Change button to change the computer's

Entering a domain name in Windows 98

name (Figure 17-7). These buttons do the same thing as the Network ID button, but the wizard does a lot of explaining that you don't need if you know what you

Computer Name tab in Windows XP Professional

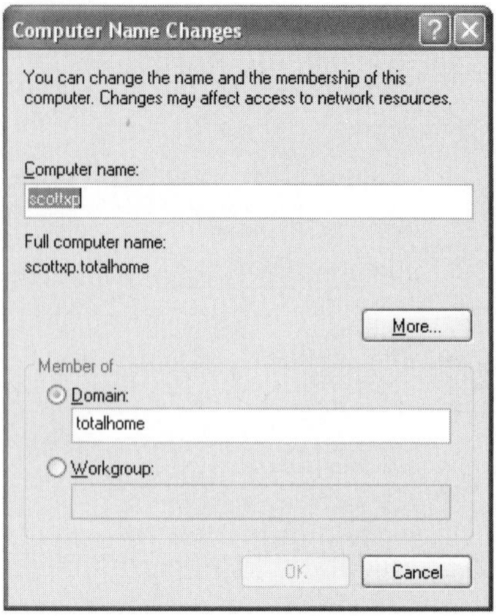

FIGURE 17.7   Windows XP Computer Name Changes dialog box

want to do. Make sure you have a good domain account, or you won't be able to log into a domain.

Computer Names

Whether your system is a client or a server, in the Windows world it must have a name. The computer's name is used by the network to identify the system. The traditional naming system used in Microsoft networks is called NetBIOS. When you install a Windows 9x system, the name you give your computer is the NetBIOS name—this is the name that will show up in Network Neighborhood. NetBIOS is an old way of naming computers; Windows has replaced it with the much more modern DNS system. You'll see more on both later in this chapter.

Objective 17.02 Installing and Configuring a LAN

You've got the basics, now let's install a network. You need to install an NIC, including proper drivers. You must install client software so that the PC can see and be seen on the network. The NIC needs to run a properly configured network protocol that matches that of other machines. And finally, you must enable File and Print Sharing to turn the PC into a server and make its resources available for other users across the network.

Plus, of course, you need to connect the PC to the network hub or switch via some sort of cable (preferably CAT 6 with Gigabit Ethernet cranking through the wires, but that's just me!) or through a wireless standard. When you install an NIC, by default, Windows 2000 and XP Professional install the TCP/IP protocol (configured for DHCP), the Client for Microsoft Networks, and File and Printer Service upon setup. Other versions of Windows require you to jump through a couple more hoops and install some or all of this stuff to get connectivity.

Installing an NIC

The NIC is your computer system's link to the network and installing one is the first step required to connect to a network. You did this in Chapter 12, so there's no need to run through the steps here. NICs are manufactured to operate on specific media and network types, such as 100BaseT Ethernet, 802.11b (wireless), or 16 MBps Token Ring. Follow the manufacturer's instructions for installation procedures. If your NIC is of recent vintage, it will be detected, installed, and configured automatically by Windows 2000 or Windows XP. Installing an NIC into any other Windows OS will require special drivers for that version of Windows from the manufacturer. You can usually download them from the Internet, but if you haven't connected to the Internet yet (because your NIC is sitting next to the PC), that won't help you here! The driver disk is therefore very important.

Travel Advisory

If you have the option, you should save yourself potential headaches and troubleshooting woes by acquiring new, name-brand NICs for your Windows installation. This is especially true with Windows XP.

Configuring a Network Client

To establish network connectivity, you need a network client installed and configured properly. You need a client for every type of server NOS to which you plan to connect on the network. Let's look at the two most used, for Microsoft and Novell networks.

Client for Microsoft Networks

Installed as part of the OS installation, the Client for Microsoft Networks rarely needs configuration, and in fact, few configuration options are available.

1. In Windows XP, click Start, then alternate-click My Network Places and select Properties. In Windows 2000, select Start | Settings | Network And Dial-up Connections. In Windows 9x/Me, go to the Control Panel and double-click the Network applet, or alternate-click Network Neighborhood and double-click My Network Places.

2. Double-click the Local Area Connection icon. Click the Properties button, highlight Client For Microsoft Networks, and click Properties.

3. Note that the Windows Locater service is specified as the Name Service Provider for the Remote Procedure Call (RPC) service by default.

4. The only configuration option available is to click the Name Service Provider pull-down menu and select DCE Cell Directory Services. If you do so, you will need to enter an address in the Network address field.

Travel Advisory

Do not change the name service provider!

Client Service for NetWare

Client Service for NetWare provides access to file and print resources on NetWare servers. The NetWare server must be running Novell Directory Services (NDS) or bindery security (NetWare versions 3.x or 4.x). Client Service for NetWare supports some NetWare utilities and NetWare-aware applications. Once installed, Client Service for NetWare offers no configuration options.

Configuring Simple Protocols

Protocols come in many different flavors and perform differently on the network. Some, such as NetBEUI, lack elements that allow their signals to travel through routers, making them nonroutable (essentially, this protocol is unsuitable for a large network that uses routers to retransmit data). The network protocols supported by Windows include NetBEUI, NWLink (IPX/SPX), and TCP/IP. Windows XP drops support for NetBEUI. This section looks at installing and configuring the simple protocols used by Windows 9x/Me and NT/2000, NetBEUI and NWLink.

NetBEUI

NetBEUI is very easy to configure, since no network or logical addresses are needed. Generally, all that is needed to establish a connection between computer systems using NetBEUI is a NetBIOS computer name.

To install the NetBEUI protocol in any version of Windows except XP, follow these steps:

1. In Windows 2000, select Start | Settings | Network And Dial-up Connections, and then double-click the Local Area Connection icon to bring up the Local Area Connection Status dialog box (Figure 17-8). In Windows 9*x*/Me, open the Control Panel and double-click the Network applet.

2. Click the Properties button to bring up the Local Area Connection Properties dialog box (Figure 17-9).

3. Click the Install button. In the Select Network Component Type dialog box, highlight Protocol and click Add (Figure 17-10).

4. In the Select Network Protocol dialog box, select NetBEUI Protocol and click OK (Figure 17-11). You will be prompted to reboot the system to make the changes take effect.

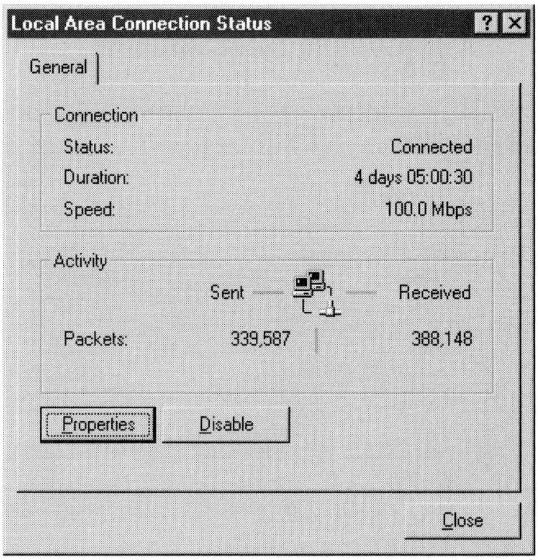

FIGURE 17.8   Local Area Connection Status dialog box in Windows 2000

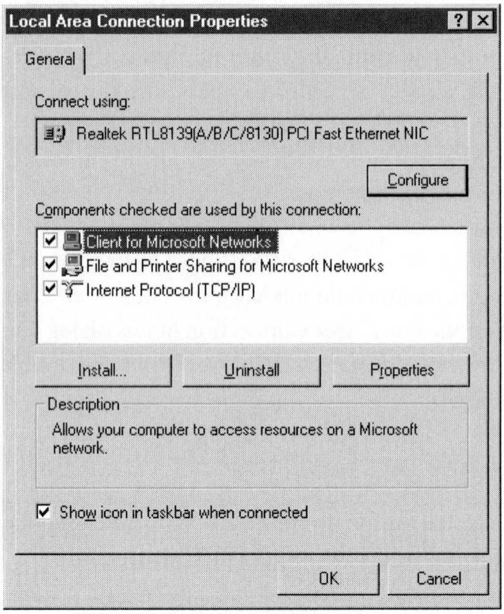

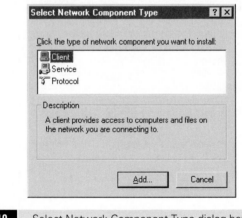

FIGURE 17.9 Local Area Connection Properties dialog box in Windows 2000

FIGURE 17.10 Select Network Component Type dialog box in Windows 2000

| **FIGURE 17.9** | Selecting NetBEUI protocol |

NWLink (IPX/SPX)

NWLink is Microsoft's implementation of the IPX/SPX protocol. The Microsoft version of NWLink includes an element for resolving NetBIOS names.

NWLink packages data to be compatible with client/server services on NetWare networks, but it does not provide access to NetWare File and Print Services. For this, you also need to install the Client Service for NetWare, as noted in the preceding section.

Follow the same steps used to install NetBEUI to install NWLink, except choose NWLink rather than NetBEUI when you make your final selection. Note that Windows 9*x* calls the protocol IPX/SPX-Compatible Protocol. You'll be prompted to reboot after adding the protocol.

NWLink is a relatively easy protocol to configure. Normally, the only settings you may need to specify are the internal network number and the frame type (usually, however, the default values are sufficient).

- The internal network number is used to identify NetWare servers.
- The frame type specifies how the data is packaged for transport over the network. For computers to communicate by NWLink, they must have the same frame types. By default, the frame type is set to Auto Detect.

Travel Advisory

When NWLink is set to Auto Detect the frame type, it will detect only one type, searching in the following order:

802.2

802.3

802.5

To configure NWLink properties manually, follow these steps:

1. In Windows XP, select Start | Control Panel and open the Network Connections applet. Double-click the Local Area Connection. In Windows 2000, select Start | Settings | Network And Dial-up Connections, and double-click the Local Area Connection icon. Finally, in Windows 9x/Me, go to the Control Panel and double-click the Network applet.

2. Click Properties, highlight NWLink IPX/SPX/NetBIOS Compatible Transport Protocol, and click Properties.

3. In the NWLink IPX/SPX/NetBIOS Compatible Transport Protocol properties dialog box, set the internal network number and frame type (Figure 17-12).

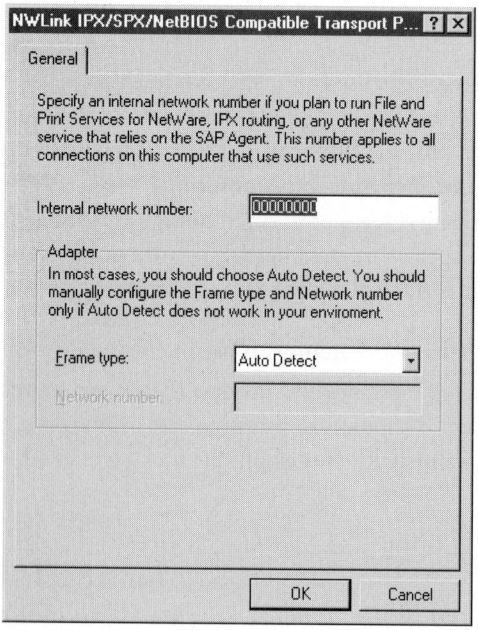

NWLink IPX/SPX/NetBIOS Compatible Transport P...

General

Specify an internal network number if you plan to run File and Print Services for NetWare, IPX routing, or any other NetWare service that relies on the SAP Agent. This number applies to all connections on this computer that use such services.

Internal network number: `00000000`

Adapter

In most cases, you should choose Auto Detect. You should manually configure the Frame type and Network number only if Auto Detect does not work in your enviroment.

Frame type: `Auto Detect`

Network number:

OK   Cancel

FIGURE 17.10   Configuring NWLink

Configuring TCP/IP

This final section on protocols covers TCP/IP, the primary protocol of the modern networks, including the Internet. For a PC to access the Internet, it must have the TCP/IP protocol loaded. TCP/IP has become so predominant that most network folks use it even on networks that do not connect to the Internet. Although TCP/IP is very powerful, it is also a bit of a challenge to set up. So whether you are installing a modem for a dial-up connection to the Internet or setting up 500 computers on their own private *intranet,* you must understand some TCP/IP basics. Let's go through the basic sections of the protocol and then look at specific steps to install and configure TCP/IP.

Network Addressing

Any network address must provide two pieces of information. It must uniquely identify the machine, and it must locate that machine within the larger network. In a TCP/IP network, the *IP address* identifies the PC and the *subnet mask* helps determine in which subnet within the network the machine resides.

IP Addresses   In a TCP/IP network, every system has a unique IP address. An *IP address* consists of four sets of eight binary numbers (octets) separated by a period. This is called *dotted-octet notation.* Here's a typical IP address:

```
202.34.16.11
```

Written in binary form, you'd get an address like

```
11001010.00100010.00001000.00001011
```

But the TCP/IP folks decided to write the decimal equivalents:

```
00000000 = 0
00000001 = 1
00000010 = 2
...
11111111 = 255
```

The IP address is the unique identification number for your system on the network. Part of the address (the network ID) identifies the network, and another part (the Host ID) identifies the local computer (host) address on the network. For example, my computer's IP address is 192.168.4.23. On my network (these are usually different on all networks), my network ID is 192.168.4 and my host ID is 23. A traditional TCP/IP network divides IP addresses into classes, which correspond with the potential size of the network: Class A, Class B, and Class C. Class A addresses were intended for huge organizations, such as major multinational corporations. Class C networks were targeted for LANs. The crushing need for more

IP addresses for the Internet pretty much blew the class structure out of the water, but here it is to satisfy your curiosity:

- Class A networks use the first octet to identify the network address, and the remaining three octets to identify the host.
- Class B networks use the first two octets to identify the network address, and the remaining two octets to identify the host.
- Class C networks use the first three octets to identify the network address, and the last octet to identify the host.

Table 17-1 lists range (class) assignments.

Travel Advisory

The 127 address range (i.e., 127.0.0.1) is reserved for network testing (loopback) operations.

Subnet Mask   The *subnet mask* is a value that distinguishes which part of the IP address is the network address and which part of the address is the host address. The subnet mask blocks out (or "masks") the network portions (octets) of an IP address. Certain subnet masks are applied by default, as shown in Table 17-2.

For example, the Class B IP address 131.190.4.121 with a subnet mask of 255.255.0.0 is distinguished as follows:

- The first two octets (131.190) make up the network address.
- The last two (4.121) make up the host address.

The A+ Certification exams do not require you to configure IP addresses and subnet masks, but you should know what they are and how to find them on a PC.

TCP/IP Services

TCP/IP is a very different type of protocol. Although it supports File and Print Sharing, it adds a number of special sharing functions unique to it. These are

TABLE 17.1	Class A, B, and C Addresses		
Network Class	**Address Range of First Octet**	**Number of Network Addresses Available**	**Number of Host Nodes (computers) Supported**
A	1–126	126	16,777,214
B	129–191	16,384	65,534
C	192–223	2,097,152	254

TABLE 17.2	Subnet Masks for Class A, B, and C Networks

Class	Subnet Mask
Class A	255.0.0.0
Class B	255.255.0.0
Class C	255.255.255.0

lumped together under the umbrella term of TCP/IP services. The most famous TCP/IP service is called the Hypertext Transfer Protocol (HTTP), the language of the World Wide Web. If you want to surf the Web, you must have TCP/IP. But TCP/IP supplies many other services beyond just HTTP. Using a service called Telnet, you can access a remote system as though you were actually in front of that machine. Another example is a handy utility called *Ping*. Ping enables one machine to check whether it can communicate with another machine. Figure 17-13 shows an example of Ping running on a Windows 2000 system. Isn't it interesting that many TCP/IP services run from a command prompt? Good thing you know how to access one! There are plenty of other services that I'll show you in a moment.

The goal of TCP/IP is to link together multiple networks (which we'll call *local area networks, or LANs*) to make an entire *wide area network (WAN)*. LANs are usually linked together via some type of telephone service, ranging from basic dial-ups to dedicated, high-speed (and expensive) data lines. The goal is to make a WAN that uses the expensive links for as little traffic as possible. The machines that connect the phone lines to each LAN are specialized computers called *routers*. To reduce traffic, each router decides which packets on the LAN should go out to the WAN. The router makes these decisions on the basis of the

```
C:\WINNT\System32\cmd.exe                                        _ □ ×

C:\>ping 192.168.4.253

Pinging 192.168.4.253 with 32 bytes of data:

Reply from 192.168.4.253: bytes=32 time<10ms TTL=128
Reply from 192.168.4.253: bytes=32 time<10ms TTL=128
Reply from 192.168.4.253: bytes=32 time<10ms TTL=128
Reply from 192.168.4.253: bytes=32 time<10ms TTL=128

Ping statistics for 192.168.4.253:
    Packets: Sent = 4, Received = 4, Lost = 0 (0% loss),
Approximate round trip times in milli-seconds:
    Minimum = 0ms, Maximum =  0ms, Average =  0ms

C:\>
```

FIGURE 17.11	Successful Ping in action

packets' IP addresses. Routers are most commonly used in TCP/IP networks, but other protocols also use them, especially IPX/SPX.

TCP/IP Settings

TCP/IP has a number of unique settings that you must set up correctly to ensure proper network functioning. Unfortunately, these settings can be quite confusing, and there are quite a few of them. Not all settings are used for every type of TCP/IP network, and it's not always obvious where you go to set them. There are two primary locations for TCP/IP settings, one for dial-up connections (modems), and one for direct (NIC) connections. On Windows 9x/Me computers that use a modem to access the Internet, start in My Computer and click the Dial-up Networking icon. Alternate-click the connection whose TCP/IP properties you wish to set and select Properties | Server Type | TCP/IP Settings (Windows 9x) or Properties | Networking tab (Windows Me). Figure 17-14 shows the Networking tab in Windows Me. Click the TCP/IP Settings button to configure Windows Me dial-up. The place to configure TCP/IP settings for direct connections is the Control Panel. Open the Networks applet and select TCP/IP from the list of installed protocols, then click Properties (Figure 17-15).

Windows 2000/XP makes this a lot easier by letting you configure both dial-up and network connections using the My Network Places properties. Simply select the connection you wish to configure, and then set its TCP/IP properties.

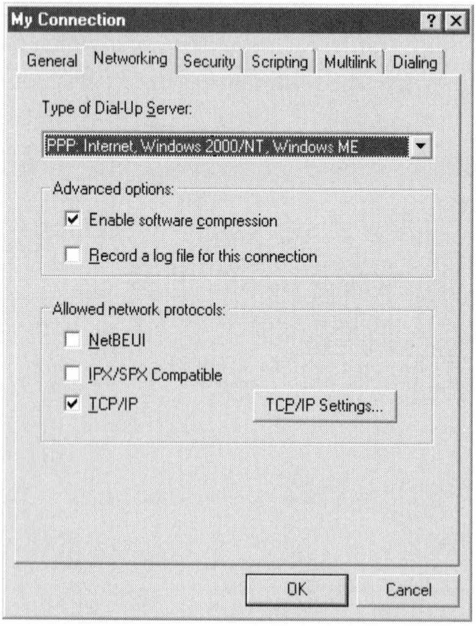

FIGURE 17.12   TCP/IP Settings button on Networking tab in Windows Me

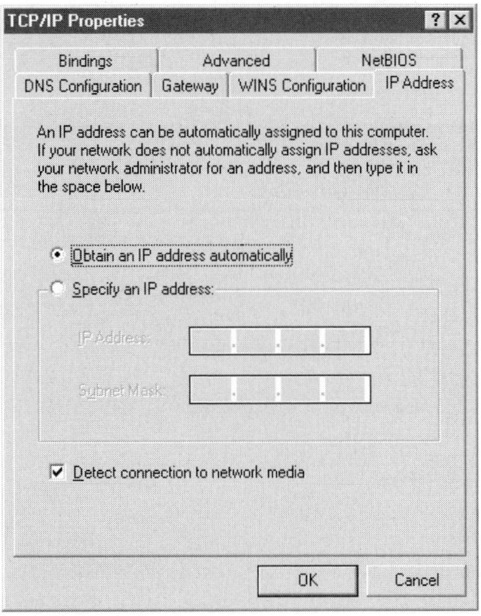

TCP/IP Properties   ? X

| Bindings | Advanced | NetBIOS |
| DNS Configuration | Gateway | WINS Configuration | IP Address |

An IP address can be automatically assigned to this computer.
If your network does not automatically assign IP addresses, ask
your network administrator for an address, and then type it in
the space below.

○ Obtain an IP address automatically

○ Specify an IP address:

  IP Address: [.   .   .   ]

  Subnet Mask: [.   .   .   ]

☑ Detect connection to network media

                        [OK]   [Cancel]

FIGURE 17.13   TCP/IP Properties dialog box in Windows Me

The A+ Certification exams assume that someone else, such as a tech support person or some network guru, will tell you the correct TCP/IP settings for the network. Your only job is to understand roughly what they do and to know where to enter them so the system works. Let's discuss some of the most common TCP/IP settings.

Exam Tip

The A+ Certification exams have a rather strange view of what you should know about networking. Take a lot of time practicing how to get to certain network configuration screens. Be ready for questions that ask, "Which of the following steps will enable you to change" a particular value.

Default Gateway   A computer that wants to send data to another machine outside its LAN is not expected to know all the IP addresses of all the computers on the Internet. Instead, all IP machines know the IP address of one computer, to which they pass all the data they need to send outside the LAN. This machine is called the *default gateway*, and it is usually the local router (Figure 17-16).

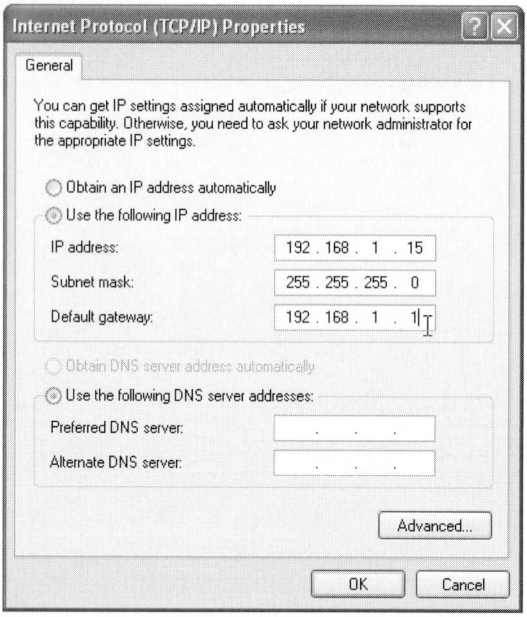

FIGURE 17.14 Setting a default gateway

Domain Name Service (DNS) Knowing that users were not going to be able to handle raw IP addresses, early Internet pioneers came up with a way to correlate those numbers with more human-friendly computer designations. Special computers, called Domain Name Service (DNS) servers, keep databases of IP addresses and their corresponding names. All the computers in a single domain (let's use TOTALSEM.COM as an example) have their individual names added to the beginning of the domain name. For example, a machine called SEMINAR1 will be called SEMINAR1.TOTALSEM.COM. A name following this convention is called a *fully qualified domain name* and will be listed in a special group called a *zone* on the DNS server. Generally, the zone looks like nothing more than a folder with the name of the domain. Thus, SEMINAR1.TOTALSEM.COM will appear as a line in the zone (TOTALSEM.COM) as SEMINAR1 with a corresponding IP address, such as 209.34.45.163. So instead of accessing the \\209.34.45.163\FREDC directory to copy a file, you can ask to see \\SEMINAR1.TOTALSEM.COM\FREDC. Your system will then query the DNS server to get SEMINAR1's IP address and use that to find the right machine. Virtually all TCP/IP networks require DNS server names to be set up, although most do it automatically for you.

The Internet has very regulated domain names. If you want a domain name that others can access on the Internet, you must register your domain name and pay a small yearly fee. In most cases, your Internet service provider can handle this for you. Originally, DNS names all ended with one of the following seven domain name qualifiers:

- **.com**   General business
- **.org**   Nonprofit organizations
- **.edu**   Educational organizations
- **.gov**   Government organizations
- **.mil**   Military organizations
- **.net**   Internet organizations
- **.int**   International

As more and more countries joined the Internet, an entire new level of domains was added the original seven to indicate a DNS name in a particular country, like .uk for the United Kingdom. It's very common to see DNS names such as www.bbc.co.uk or www.louvre.fr. The Internet Corporation for Assigned Names and Numbers (ICANN) has announced the creation of several more new domains, including .name and .info. Given the explosive growth of the Internet, these are unlikely to be the last ones!

Windows 2000 and XP systems use DNS for all network functions, not just getting on the Internet! If you have a private TCP/IP network, you can ignore all the domain name rules and call your domain anything you wish! For example, you can have a domain called DUMBNAME—just don't try to register it with ICANN!

WINS   The Windows Internet Name Service (WINS) enables Windows NetBIOS network names like SERVER1 to be correlated to IP addresses. All you have to do to set up WINS is to either type in the IP address for the WINS server or let DHCP handle it for you (Figure 17-17). Windows 2000 and XP don't use NetBIOS by default; they use DNS, making WINS obsolete. Even though Windows 2000 and XP no longer need WINS, they support it for communication with older systems.

> ### Exam Tip
> DNS is for fully-qualified domain names (Internet). WINS is for NetBIOS names.

DHCP   The last item that most TCP/IP networks require is the Dynamic Host Configuration Protocol (DHCP). To understand DHCP, we must first remember

| FIGURE 17.15 | Setting up WINS to use DHCP |

that every machine must have an IP address. This can be added manually using the TCP/IP properties menu. A permanent IP address assigned to a machine is known as a *static* IP address. Figure 17-16 has both a static IP address and a manually assigned default gateway.

DHCP enables you to create a pool of IP addresses that are given to machines when they need them and are taken away when they are no longer needed. DHCP is especially handy for networks that have a lot of dial-in systems. Why give a machine that is on for only a few minutes a day a static IP address? For that reason, DHCP is quite popular. If you add a NIC to a Windows system, the TCP/IP settings are set to use DHCP. When you accept those automatic settings, you're really telling the machine to use DHCP (Figure 17-18).

TCP/IP Tools

All versions of Windows come with handy tools to test TCP/IP. The ones you're most likely to use in the field are PING, WINIPCFG/IPCONFIG, NSLOOKUP, and TRACERT.

PING   You've already seen PING, a really great way to see if you can talk to another system. Here's how it works. Get to a command prompt and type **ping** followed by an IP address or by a DNS name, such as **ping www.chivalry.com**. Press the ENTER key on your keyboard and away it goes!

Obtain an IP address automatically

WINIPCFG/IPCONFIG Windows 9*x*/Me provides the handy WINIPCFG program. Type in **winipcfg** from the Start | Run menu option to see Figure 17-19. Click More Info to see all your TCP/IP options (Figure 17-20). The Release and Renew buttons let you get new TCP/IP information from a DHCP server.

Windows NT/2000/XP do not use WINIPCFG. Instead, you once again must go to a command prompt and run IPCONFIG. You can type **ipconfig /all** to see all of your TCP/IP settings (Figure 17-21).

WINIPCFG in action on a Windows 98 system

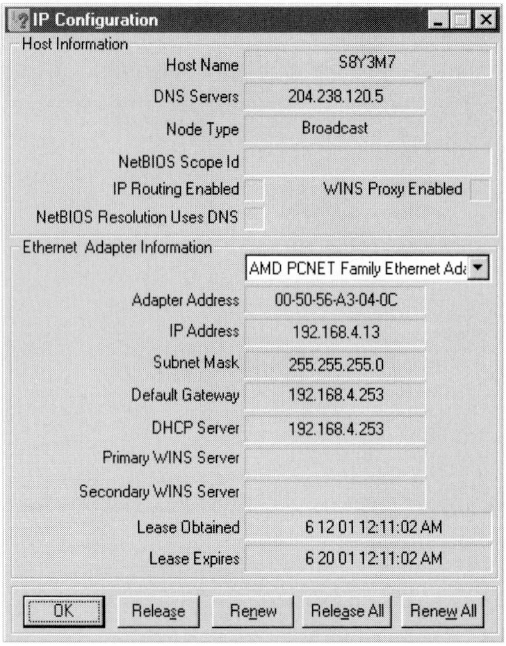

FIGURE 17.18   Advanced WINIPCFG on a Windows 98 system

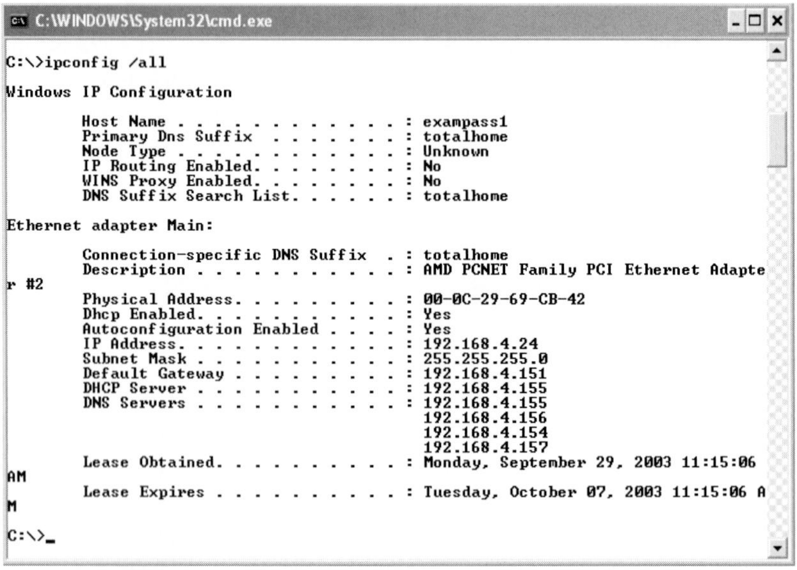

FIGURE 17.19   IPCONFIG /ALL on a Windows 2000 system

Exam Tip

Make sure you know that Windows 9*x*/Me use WINIPCFG and Windows NT/2000/XP use IPCONFIG.

In most cases, IPCONFIG and WINIPCFG are only used to perform reporting-type duties, like determining your IP address or DNS server name. However, these tools are especially helpful when using DHCP. If you're unable to connect to the Internet, try clicking the Renew All button in WINIPCFG to renew the DHCP lease. If you get a DHCP server not available error, try Release All and then Renew All. If the error persists, you may have a problem with the DHCP server. IPCONFIG has the same release/renew capabilities. Just type **ipconfig /renew** or **ipconfig /release**.

NSLOOKUP   NSLOOKUP is a powerful command line program that enables you to determine the name of a DNS server, among many other things. Every version of Windows makes NSLOOKUP available when you install TCP/IP. To run the program, type **nslookup** from the command line and press the ENTER key (Figure 17-22). Note that this gives you a little information, and that the prompt has changed. That's because you're running the application. Type **exit** and press the ENTER key to return to the command prompt.

You can do some cool stuff with NSLOOKUP, and consequently some techs absolutely love the tool. It's way outside the scope of A+ Certification, but if you want to play with it some, type **help** at the NSLOOKUP prompt and press ENTER to see a list of common commands and syntax.

TRACERT   The TRACERT utility shows the route that a packet takes to get to its destination. From a command line, just type **tracert** followed by a space and

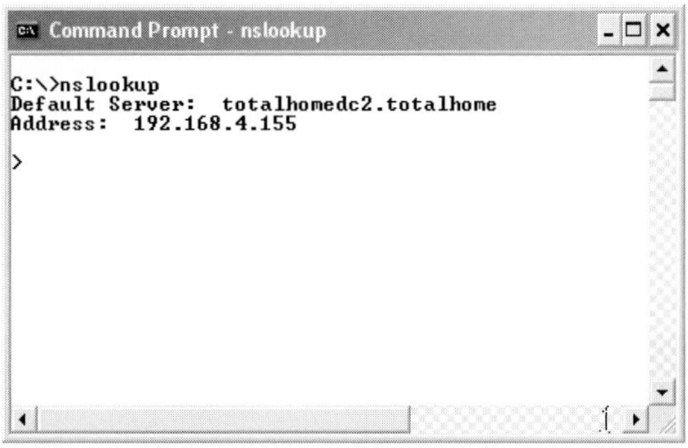

```
Command Prompt - nslookup                    _ □ ×

C:\>nslookup
Default Server:  totalhomedc2.totalhome
Address:  192.168.4.155

>
```

FIGURE 17.20   NSLOOKUP in action

an IP address. The output describes the route from your machine to the destination machine, including all devices it passes through and how long each hop takes (Figure 17-23).

TRACERT can come in handy when you have to troubleshoot bottlenecks. When users complain that it's difficult to reach a particular destination using TCP/IP, you can run this utility to determine if the problem exists on a machine or connection over which you have control, or if it is a problem on another machine or router. Similarly, if a destination is completely unreachable, TRACERT can again determine if the problem is on a machine or router over which you have control.

Exam Tip

Know your TCP/IP tools for the OS Technologies exam.

Steps for Configuring TCP/IP

By default, the TCP/IP protocol is configured to receive its IP information (IP address, subnet mask, etc.) automatically from a Dynamic Host Configuration Protocol (DHCP) server on the network. As far as the A+ Certification exams are concerned, Network+ techs and administrators give you the IP address,

```
Command Prompt                                                    _ □ x

C:\>tracert www.chivalry.com

Tracing route to chivalry.com [65.18.214.130]
over a maximum of 30 hops:

  1     2 ms     1 ms     1 ms   192.168.4.151
  2    20 ms    19 ms    21 ms   adsl-208-190-121-38.dsl.hstntx.swbell.net [208.1
90.121.38]
  3    22 ms    19 ms    19 ms   dist1-vlan50.hstntx.swbell.net [151.164.11.126]

  4    20 ms    19 ms    19 ms   bb1-g1-0.hstntx.swbell.net [151.164.11.230]
  5    22 ms    22 ms    23 ms   core1-p6-0.crhstx.sbcglobal.net [151.164.188.1]

  6    25 ms    26 ms    26 ms   core3-p3-0.crdltx.sbcglobal.net [151.164.240.189
]
  7    27 ms    26 ms    26 ms   core2-p8-0.crdltx.sbcglobal.net [151.164.242.113
]
  8    26 ms    26 ms    25 ms   bb1-p14-3.dllstx.sbcglobal.net [151.164.240.97]

  9    28 ms    26 ms    26 ms   bb2-p15-0.dllstx.sbcglobal.net [151.164.243.150]

 10    27 ms    29 ms    29 ms   sl-gw40-fw-3-0.sprintlink.net [144.228.39.225]
 11    29 ms    29 ms    29 ms   sl-bb22-fw-4-3.sprintlink.net [144.232.8.249]
 12    28 ms    29 ms    29 ms   sl-st20-dal-14-1.sprintlink.net [144.232.20.138]

 13    29 ms    29 ms    29 ms   so-1-1-1.edge1.Dallas1.Level3.net [64.158.168.73
]
```

FIGURE 17.21   TRACERT in action

subnet mask, and default gateway information and you plug them into the PC. That's about it, so here's how to do it manually.

1. In Windows XP, open the Control Panel and double-click the Network Connections applet. Double-click the Local Area Connection icon. In Windows 2000, click Start | Settings | Network and Dial-up Connections, and double-click the Local Area Connection icon. In Windows 9x/Me/2000, alternate-click Network Neighborhood and double-click My Network Places to get to your network settings.

2. Click Properties, highlight Internet Protocol (TCP/IP), and click Properties.

3. In the dialog box, click the Use The Following IP Address radio button.

4. Enter the IP address in the appropriate fields.

5. Press the TAB key to skip down to the subnet mask fields. Note that the subnet mask is entered automatically (this can be overtyped, if you wish to enter a different subnet mask).

6. Optionally, enter the IP address for a default gateway (router or another computer system that will forward transmissions beyond your network).

7. Optionally, enter the IP address of a primary and secondary DNS server.

8. Click OK to close the dialog box.

9. Click Close to exit the Local Area Connection Status dialog box.

10. Windows will alert you that you must restart the system for the changes to take effect.

Automatic Private IP Addressing

Windows 2000 and Windows XP support a feature called Automatic Private IP Addressing (APIPA) that automatically assigns an IP address to the system when the client cannot obtain an IP address automatically. The Internet Assigned Numbers Authority, the nonprofit corporation responsible for assigning IP addresses and managing root servers, has set aside the range of addresses from 169.254.0.0 to 169.254.255.254 for this purpose.

If the computer system cannot contact a DHCP server, it generates an address in the form of 169.254.x.y (where x.y is the computer's identifier) and a 16-bit subnet mask (255.255.0.0) and broadcasts it on the network segment (subnet). If no other computer responds to the address, the system assigns this address to itself. When using the Auto Private IP, the system can communicate only with other computers on the same subnet that also use the 169.254.x.y range with a 16-bit mask. APIPA is enabled by default if your system is configured to obtain an IP address automatically.

Exam Tip
A computer system on a network with an active DHCP server that has an IP address in the APIPA range usually indicates that there is a problem connecting to the DHCP server.

Sharing and Security

Windows systems can share all kinds of resources: files, folders, entire drives, printers, faxes, Internet connections, and much more. Conveniently for you, the A+ Certification exams limit their interests to folders, printers, and Internet connections. Let's see how to share folders and printers now; we'll save Internet connection sharing for the Internet section.

Sharing Drives and Folders

All versions of Windows share drives and folders in basically the same manner. Simply alternate-click any drive or folder and select Sharing. In Windows 98, the dialog box shown in Figure 17-24 appears. If you don't see the Sharing option, that means you have not enabled file sharing on the system.

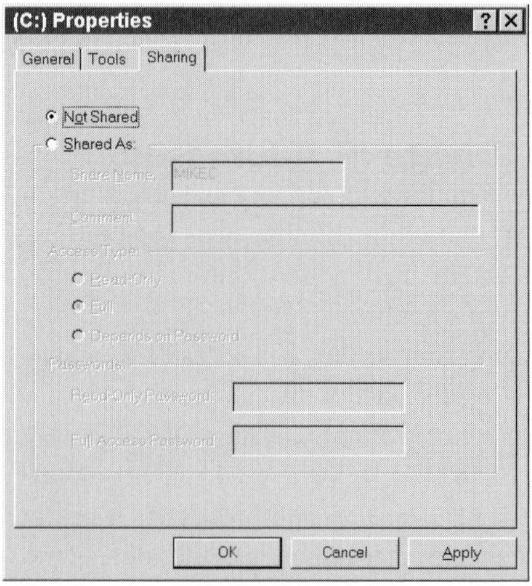

(C:) Properties

General | Tools | Sharing

- Not Shared
- Shared As:

Share Name: MIKEC
Comment:
Access Type:
- Read-Only
- Full
- Depends on Password
Passwords:
Read-Only Password:
Full Access Password:

[OK] [Cancel] [Apply]

FIGURE 17.22   Sharing tab in Windows 98

By clicking the Shared As radio button, you can add a share name. This is the name that the other workstations will see when they are looking for resources to access. The trick here is to give the resource a name that clearly describes it. For example, if the goal is to share a particular C: drive, sharing that drive simply as "C:" could result in confusing this C: drive with other shared C: drives on the network. Instead, try a more detailed name like FREDC or SALES3C. As a rule, try to keep the name short and without spaces (Figure 17-25).

After establishing the share name for the resource, note that you can determine *how* it is to be shared. Under Windows 9*x*/Me, the options are simple: Full, Read-Only, and Depends On Password. This is one of the major limitations of Windows 9*x*/Me networks. We'll do Windows NT/2000/XP next to see some real sharing power! After you select the network name and the access level, click OK to see a little hand appear on the icon; this shows that the network resource is being shared (Figure 17-26).

Windows NT/2000/XP folder shares are created the same way, with a little added complexity due to Windows NT/2000/XP's use of NTFS. When you select the properties for a folder in Windows NT/2000/XP and select the Sharing tab, you see Figure 17-27. Select Share this folder, add a Comment and a User limit if you wish (they're not required), and click Permissions to see Figure 17-28.

Hey! Doesn't NTFS have all those wild permissions like Read, Execute, Take Ownership, and all that? Yes, it does, but NTFS permissions and network share permissions are totally separate beasties. Microsoft wanted Windows 2000 and

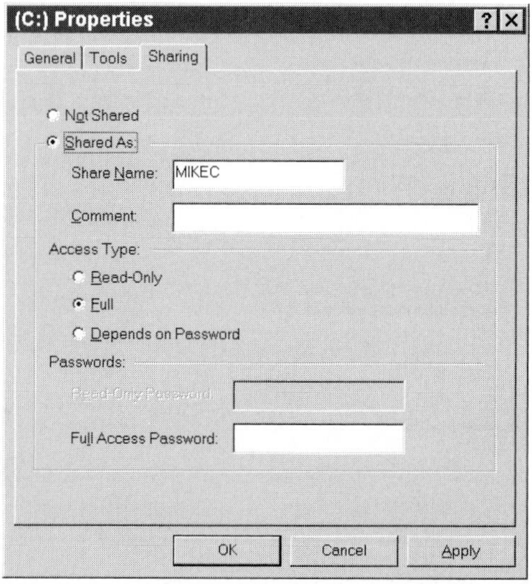

FIGURE 17.23   Sharing the MIKEC drive

FIGURE 17.24   Shared C: drive with hand icon

FIGURE 17.25   Windows Sharing tab on NTFS volume

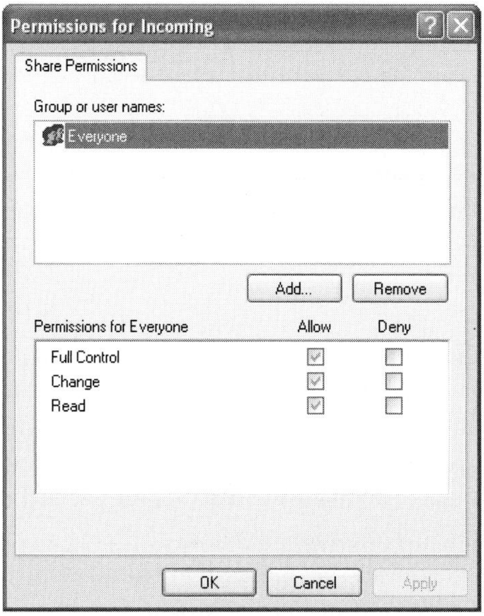

FIGURE 17.26 Network Share Permissions

XP to support many different types of partitions (NTFS, FAT16, FAT32), old and new! Network permissions are Microsoft's way of enabling you to administer file sharing on any type of partition supported by Windows, no matter how ancient. Sure, your options will be pretty limited if you are working with an older partition type, but you *can* do it. The beauty of Windows NT/2000/XP is that it gives you another tool—NTFS permissions—that can do much more. NTFS is where the power lies, but power always comes with a price: You have to configure two separate sets of permissions. If you are sharing a folder on an NTFS drive, as you normally are these days, you must set *both* the network permissions and the NTFS permissions to let others access your shared resources.

Some good news: This is actually no big deal! Just set the network permissions to give everyone full control, and then use the NTFS permissions to exercise more precise control over *who* accesses the shared resources and *how* they access them. Click the Security tab to set the NTFS permissions.

Travel Advisory

Windows NT/2000/XP has two places for setting security on files and folders: share permissions, which apply security to the folder that is designated to be a connection point to the files and folders within that folder, and NTFS security on files and folders. Share permissions affect only network users, accessing the files and folder from across a network, while NTFS security affects both network and local users.

Accessing Shared Drives/Directories

Once you have set up a drive or directory to be shared, the final step is to access that shared drive or directory from another machine. In Windows NT and 9x, you access the shared devices through the Network Neighborhood. Windows Me, 2000, and XP use My Network Places, although you'll need to do a little clicking to get to the shared resources (Figure 17-29).

Network resources can also be "mapped" to a local resource name. For example, the FREDC share can be mapped to be a local hard drive such as E: or F:. This can be done in Windows 9x/Me from Windows Explorer or by alternate-clicking a share in Network Neighborhood (My Network Places for Me) and selecting Map Network Drive. Mapping is usually done when you want a permanent connection, or to support older programs that might have trouble accessing a drive called FREDC.

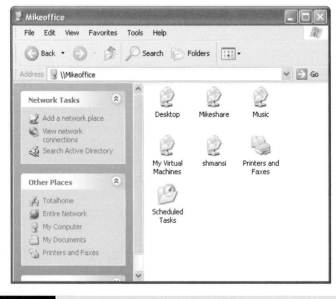

FIGURE 17.27   Shared resources in My Network Places

Windows 2000 supports Map Network Drive but adds a handy Add Network Place icon in My Network Places that lets you add network locations you frequently access without using up drive letters. Windows XP removes the icon but adds the menu option in its context bar on the left. Here's my Windows 2000 system (Figure 17-30).

Mapping shared network drives is a very common practice, as it makes a remote network share look like just another drive on the local system. The only downside to drive mapping stems from the fact that users tend to forget they are on a network. A classic example is the user who always accesses a particular folder or file on the network and then suddenly gets a "file not found" error when the workstation gets disconnected from the network. Instead of recognizing this as a network error, the user often imagines the problem to be a missing or corrupted file.

All shared resources should show up in Network Neighborhood/My Network Places. If a shared resource fails to show up, make sure to check the basics first: Is File and Print Sharing activated on the sharing system? Is the device actually shared? Don't let silly errors fool you!

UNC

All computers that share must have a network name, and all of the resources they share must also have network names. Any resource on a network can be described by combining the names of the resource being shared and the system

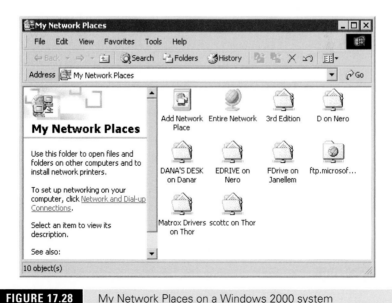

FIGURE 17.28   My Network Places on a Windows 2000 system

sharing. If a machine called SERVER1 is sharing its C: drive as FREDC, the complete name would be described like this:

```
\\SERVER1\FREDC
```

This is called the Universal Naming Convention (UNC). The UNC is distinguished by its use of double backslashes in front of the sharing system's name, and a single backslash in front of the shared resource's name. You can see this in action in Figure 17-29, where the \\Mikeoffice address shows you that you're looking at resources over a network rather than locally.

Sharing Printers

Sharing printers in Windows is just as easy as sharing drives and directories. Assuming that the system has printer sharing services loaded, just go to the Printers folder in the Control Panel and alternate-click the printer you wish to share. Select Properties, go to the Sharing tab, click Shared As, and give it a name (see Figure 17-31).

To access a shared printer in any version of Windows, simply click the Add Printer icon in the Printers folder. When asked if the printer is Local or Network,

FIGURE 17.29   Giving a name to a shared printer in Windows 2000

select Network, browse the network for the printer you wish to access, and Windows takes care of the rest! In almost all cases, Windows will copy the printer driver from the sharing machine. In the rare case where it doesn't, it will prompt you for drivers.

Before the advent of Windows 95, most network printing was done via the redirection of an LPT port. A printer would be installed and an unused LPT port, like LPT2 or LPT3, would then take all of the print information. This redirected LPT would then send the print job over the network to the proper network printer. Although this is unnecessary in most cases today, all versions of Windows still provide this option to support older applications (see Figure 17-32).

One of the most pleasant aspects of configuring a system for networking under all versions of Microsoft Windows is the amazing amount of the process that is automated. For example, if Windows detects an NIC in a system, it will automatically install the NIC driver, a network protocol (Windows 95 installed NetBEUI, but later versions all install TCP/IP), and Client for Microsoft Networks (the NetBIOS part of the Microsoft networking software). So if you want to share a resource, everything you need is automatically installed. Note that while File and Print Sharing is also automatically installed, you still must activate it by clicking the check boxes.

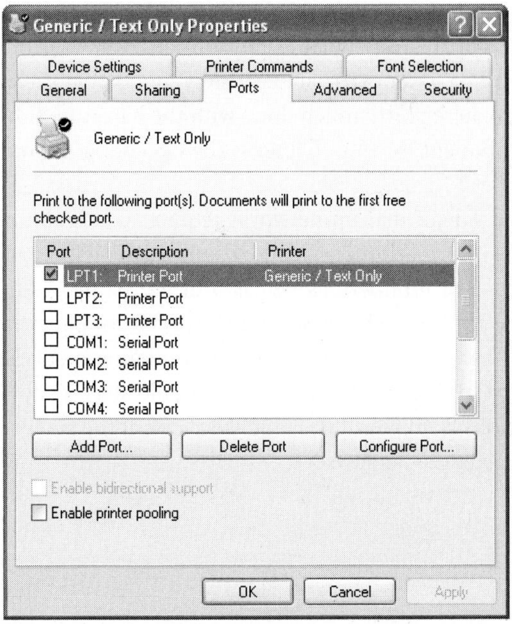

FIGURE 17.30   LPT port setting in a printer's Properties

Objective 17.03 The Internet

To use the Internet successfully, you need to connect properly and then run special applications that work with TCP/IP protocols, such as HTTP for web browsing. Let's start with connections and then hit Internet software.

PCs commonly connect to an ISP using one of seven technologies: dial-up—both analog and ISDN; dedicated—such as DSL, cable, and LAN; wireless; and satellite. Analog dial-up is the slowest of the bunch and requires a telephone line and a special networking device called a modem. ISDN uses digital dial-up, which has much greater speed. All the others use a regular Ethernet NIC like you played with in Chapter 12, so they require no special extra details here. Satellite requires you to connect via modem, but then handles downloads and sometimes uploads through an NIC. The most important configuration information here, therefore, involves dial-up, so let's take a look.

Dial-up Networking

A dial-up connection to the Internet requires two pieces to work: hardware to dial up the ISP, such as a modem or ISDN terminal adapter (TA); and software to govern the connection, such as Microsoft's *Dial-up Networking (DUN)*. Modems and TAs install like any other expansion card or device, into a PCI slot on the motherboard or to an external expansion connection such as USB. Install the drivers and you're pretty much done with the hardware side of things. The interesting component for this chapter is the OS configuration side of things, notably DUN.

The software side of dial-up networks requires configuration within Windows to include information provided by your ISP. The ISP provides a dial-up telephone number or numbers, as well as your username and initial password. In addition, the ISP will tell you about any special configuration options you need to specify in the software setup. The full configuration of dial-up networking is beyond the scope of this book, but you should at least know where to go to follow instructions from your ISP. Let's take a look at the Network and Internet Connections applet in Windows XP.

Exam Tip

Windows 9x computers have a slightly different front end for configuring a dial-up connection, using the Dial-up Network option in the Control Panel. This opens the Network Connections Wizard, which offers many of the same options found in the dial-up settings in Windows XP. Microsoft has simplified the interface in its XP operating system. In Windows 2000, go to the Control Panel and open Network and Dial-up Connections. Choose Make New Connection and launch the wizard to set it up.

Network and Internet Connections

To start configuring a dial-up connection in Windows XP, open the Control Panel. Select Network And Internet Connections from the Pick A Category menu (Figure 17-33), then select Set Up or Change Your Internet Connection from the Pick A Task menu. (If you're in Classic view in the Control Panel, by the way, simply open the Internet Options applet.) The Internet Properties dialog box opens with the Connections tab displayed. All your work will proceed from here (Figure 17-34).

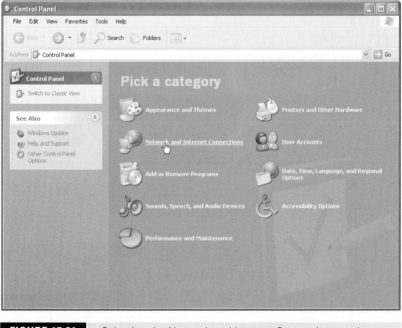

FIGURE 17.31   Selecting the Network and Internet Connections applet

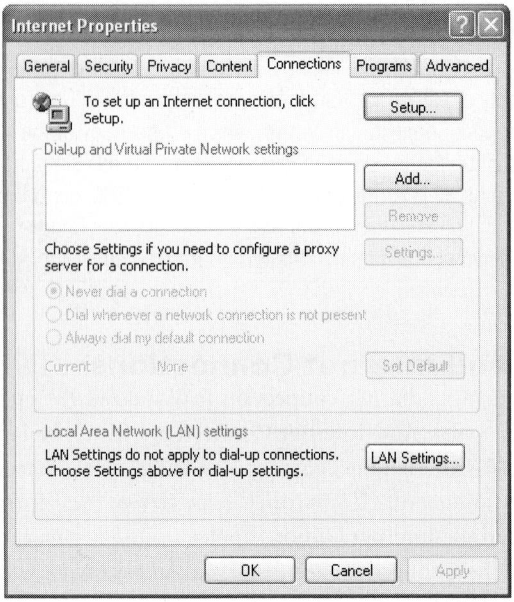

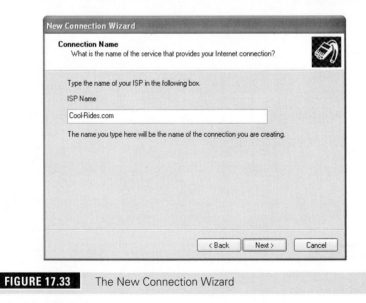

FIGURE 17.32 The Connections tab in the Internet Properties dialog box

Click Setup to run the New Connection Wizard and then work through the screens (Figure 17-35). At this point, you're going to need information provided by your ISP to configure your connection properly.

FIGURE 17.33 The New Connection Wizard

When you finish the configuration, you'll see a new Connect To option on the Start menu. Select Start | Connect To | Show All Connections to see something like Figure 17-36, which shows the option to connect to a fictitious ISP, Cool-Rides.com.

PPP   Dial-up links to the Internet have their own special hardware protocol called the Point-to-Point Protocol (PPP). PPP is a streaming protocol developed especially for dial-up Internet access. To Windows, a modem is nothing more than a special type of network adapter. Modems will have their own configuration entry in the Network Connections applet.

Modems also have a second set of settings in Dial-up Networking on Windows 9*x*/Me systems. These properties are accessed from three windows: the main Properties window shown earlier, the Server Types window, and the TCP/IP Settings window, also shown earlier.

Most dial-up "I can't connect to the Internet"-type problems are user errors. Your first line of defense is the modem itself. Use the modem's properties to make sure the volume is turned up. Have the users listen to the connection. Do

FIGURE 17.34   Connect To option in Windows XP

they hear a dial tone? If they don't, make sure the modem's line is plugged into a good phone jack.

Do they hear the modem dial and then hear someone saying, "Hello? Hello?" If so, they probably dialed the wrong number! Wrong password error messages are fairly straightforward—remember that the password may be correct, but the username may be wrong. If they still fail to connect, it's time to call the network folks to see what is not properly configured in the Dial-up Networking settings.

Dedicated Connections

Increasingly, consumers and businesses are using dedicated high-speed connections such as cable and DSL to link their LANs to the Internet. Almost all of these dedicated connections use 10BaseT Ethernet to connect a single PC or a hub/switch to a special receiver called a cable modem or DSL modem. The single PC sharing an Internet connection with multiple machines on a LAN requires some sort of software to pull off the feat. Microsoft includes such software with the latest Windows operating systems. Let's take a look.

Internet Connection Sharing

Windows 98 SE came out with a number of improvements over Windows 98, and one of the most popular was the inclusion of Internet Connection Sharing (ICS). ICS enables one system to share its Internet connection with other systems on the network, providing a quick and easy method for multiple systems to use one Internet connection. Windows 2000 and Windows XP also provide this handy tool. Figure 17-37 shows a typical setup for ICS. Note the terminology

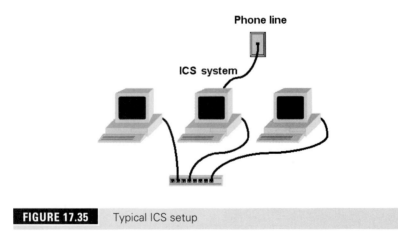

| FIGURE 17.35 | Typical ICS setup |

here. The PC that connects to the Internet and then shares via ICS that connection with machines on a LAN is called the *ICS host* computer. PCs that connect via LAN to the ICS host computer are simply called client computers.

> ### Exam Tip
> ICS works with both dial-up and dedicated connections.

To connect multiple computers to a single ICS host computer requires several things in place. First, the ICS host computer has to have an NIC dedicated to the internal connections. If you connect via dial-up, for example, the ICS host computer uses a modem to connect to the Internet. It will also have an NIC that plugs into a hub. Other PCs on the LAN likewise connect to the hub. If you connect via some faster service, such as DSL that uses an NIC cabled to the DSL receiver, you'll need a second NIC in the ICS host machine to connect to the LAN and the client computers.

Second, in Windows 98 SE, you need to install ICS in the ICS host machine. Windows 98 SE does not install ICS automatically. Most systems require that you install ICS via the Add/Remove Programs tab in Windows Setup. ICS is located under Internet Tools options.

Third, again only in Windows 98 SE, when you run ICS you get a simple client configuration floppy disk that you need to run on all the client PCs. This configuration program does little more than tell the client machines to seek the IP address of the ICS host computer (which will be 192.168.0.1) when looking for Internet services of various types. ICS turns the sharing system into a mini-DHCP server, doling out IP addresses along the same numbering scheme, such as 192.168.0.10.

Setting up ICS in Windows 2000/XP is very simple. Open the properties dialog for My Network Places, and then access the properties of the connection you wish to share. Click the Sharing tab and select Enable Internet Connection Sharing For This Connection (in Windows 2000) or Allow Other Network Users To Connect Through This Computer's Internet Connection (in Windows XP). (See Figure 17-38.)

Clients don't need any special configuration but should simply be set to DHCP for their IP address and other configurations.

FIGURE 17.36 ICS in Windows XP

Travel Assistance

Several manufacturers offer robust, easy-to-configure hardware solutions that enable multiple computers to connect to a single Internet connection. These boxes require very little configuration and provide a level of firewall protection between the primary computer and the Internet. You'll find these boxes more commonly used with DSL and cable connections than any sort of dial-up. Linksys makes a great little DSL/cable router, for example, that offers four 10/100 Ethernet ports for the LAN computers; plus, you can configure it so that to the outside world the router is the PC. It therefore acts as a firewall, protecting your internal network from probing or malicious users from the outside. Check it out at www.linksys.com.

The Windows XP Internet Connection Firewall

Once you've established a connection to the Internet, you should start thinking about security. Windows 9x, Me, NT, and 2000 require you to use some third-party tool, such as a hardware firewall, but Windows XP offers the Internet

Connection Firewall (ICF) built into the system. ICF basically stops all uninvited access from the Internet. ICF keeps track of when you initiate communication with a particular machine over your Internet connection and then allows communication back from that same machine. This works whether your connection is a single machine directly dialed into an ISP or a group of networked PCs connecting through an ICS host computer. ICF tracks the communication and blocks anything uninvited. You can implement ICF on the same screen as you would ICS, as you can see in Figure 17-38.

Travel Advisory

ICF enables you to open up specific computers inside a LAN for specific tasks, such as running an FTP server. More on FTP in the next section, "Internet Software Tools."

Internet Software Tools

Once you've established a connection between the PC and the ISP, you then still can do nothing on the Internet without applications designed to use one or more TCP/IP services, such as web browsing and e-mail. TCP/IP has the following commonly used services:

- The World Wide Web
- E-mail
- Newsgroups
- FTP
- Telnet

Each of these services (sometimes referred to by the overused term "TCP/IP protocols") requires a special application, and each of those applications has special settings. Let's look at all five services and see how to configure them.

The World Wide Web

The Web provides a graphical face for the Internet. All over the Internet are special servers called *web servers*. These web servers, in their simplest sense, provide web sites and web pages that you can access and thus get more or less useful information. Using web browser software, such as Internet Explorer or Netscape Navigator, you can click a link on a web page and be instantly transported, not just to some web server in your home town, but anywhere in the world. Figure 17-39

FIGURE 17.37   Internet Explorer showing a web page

shows Internet Explorer at the home page of my company's web site, www.totalsem.com. Where is the server located? Does it matter? It could be in a closet in my office or on a huge clustered server in Canada. The great part about the Web is that you can get from here to there and access the information you need with a click or two of the mouse.

Setting up a web browser takes almost no effort. As long as the Internet connection is working, web browsers work automatically. This is not to say that there aren't plenty of settings, but the default browser settings work almost every time. If you type in a web address, such as the best search engine on the planet—www.google.com—and it doesn't work, check the line and your network settings, and you'll figure out where the problem is!

Configuring the Browser

Web browsers are highly configurable. On most web browsers, you can set the default font size, whether it will display graphics or not, and several other settings. Although all web browsers support these settings, where you go to make these changes varies dramatically. If you are using the popular Internet Explorer that comes with Windows, configuration tools are found in the Internet Options Control Panel applet or under the Tools menu in Internet Explorer.

Proxy Server If your Internet connection runs through a proxy server, you need to set your proxy settings within your browser (and any other Internet software you want to use). A *proxy server* is software that enables multiple connections to the Internet to go through one protected PC, much as ICS does at the LAN level. It's older technology, but it's still very much in use around the world. To configure proxy settings, go to the Tools menu and select the Connections tab. Then click the LAN Settings button to open the Local Area Network (LAN) Settings dialog box (Figure 17-40).

Note that you have three options here, with automatic detection of the proxy server being the default. You can specify an IP address for a proxy server by clicking the third check box and simply typing it in (Figure 17-41). Your network administrator or a Network+ tech will give you information on proxy servers if you need it to configure a machine. Otherwise, you can safely leave the browser configured to search automatically for a proxy server.

Security and Scripts While we're on the subject of configuration, make sure you know how to adjust the security settings in your web browser. Many web sites come with programs that download to your system and run automatically. These programs are written in specialized languages and file formats with names like Java or Active Server Pages. These programs make modern web sites

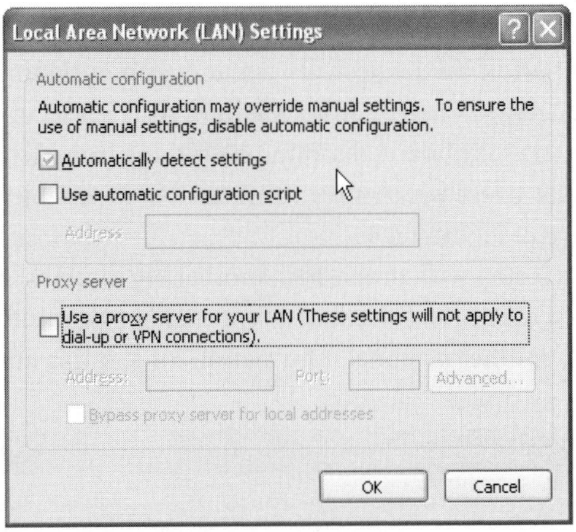

FIGURE 17.38 The LAN Settings dialog box

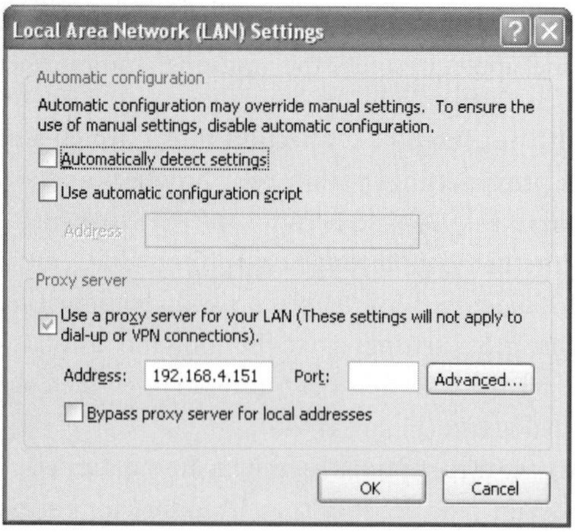

FIGURE 17.39   Specifying the proxy server address

very powerful and dynamic, but they can also act as a portal to evil programs. To help with security, all better web browsers let you determine whether you want these potentially risky programs to run. What you decide depends on personal factors. If your web browser refuses to run a Java program (you'll know because you'll get an error, like in Figure 17-42), check your security settings because your browser may simply be following orders! To get to the security configuration screen in Internet Explorer, go to Tools | Internet Options | Security tab (Figure 17-43).

Internet Explorer gives you the option to select preset security levels by clicking the Custom button on the Security tab and then optioning the pull-down menu (Figure 17-44). Changing from Medium to High security, for example, makes changes across the board, disabling everything from ActiveX to Java. You can also manually select which features to enable or disable in the scrolling menu, also visible in Figure 17-44.

Security doesn't stop with programs. Another big security concern relates to Internet commerce. People don't like to enter credit card information, home phone numbers, or other personal information for fear this information might

FIGURE 17.40   Error notice about running ActiveX

FIGURE 17.41 The Security tab in the Internet Options dialog

be intercepted by hackers. Fortunately, there are methods of encrypting this information, the most common being HTTP-Secure (HTTPS) web sites. It's easy to tell if your web site is using HTTPS because the web address will start with

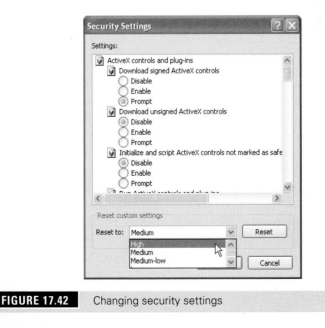

FIGURE 17.42 Changing security settings

HTTPS instead of just HTTP, and you'll usually see a tiny lock in the lower right-hand corner of the browser window.

There's one security risk that no computer can completely defend against: you. In particular, be very careful when downloading programs from the Internet. The Internet makes it really easy to download programs that you can then install and run on your system. There's nothing intrinsically wrong with this unless the program you download has a virus, is corrupted, or is incompatible with your operating system. The watchword here is common sense. Only download programs from reliable sources. Take time to read the online documentation so that you're sure you're downloading a version of the program that works on your operating system. Finally, always run a good antivirus program, preferably one that checks incoming programs for viruses before you install them! Failure to do this can lead to lockups, file corruption, and boot problems that you simply should not have to deal with.

E-Mail

You need an e-mail program to access e-mail. The two most popular are Microsoft's Outlook Express and Netscape's Messenger. E-mail clients need a little more setup. First, you must provide your e-mail address and password. All e-mail addresses come in the now-famous accountname@Internet domain format.

> **Travel Advisory**
>
> To create, access, or edit an account in Outlook Express, open Outlook Express and go to Tools | Accounts. Select the Mail tab and then click Add for a new account or select an existing account and click Properties.

The second thing you must add are the names of the Post Office Protocol version 3 (POP3) or Internet Message Access Protocol (IMAP) server and the Simple Mail Transfer Protocol (SMTP) server. The POP3 or IMAP server is the computer that handles incoming (to you) e-mail. POP3 is by far the most widely used standard, although the latest version of IMAP, *IMAP4*, supports some features POP3 doesn't. For example, IMAP4 enables you to search through messages on the mail server to find specific keywords and select the messages you want to download onto your machine. Even with the advantages of IMAP4 over POP3, the vast majority of incoming mail servers use POP3.

The SMTP server handles your outgoing e-mail. These two systems may often have the same name, or close to the same name, as shown in Figure 17-45. All

FIGURE 17.43 POP3 and SMTP information in Outlook Express

these settings should be provided to you by your ISP. If they are not, you should be comfortable knowing what to ask for. If one of these names is incorrect, you will either not get your e-mail or not be able to send e-mail. If an e-mail setup that has been working well for a while suddenly gives you errors, it is likely that either the POP3 or SMTP server is down, or that the DNS server has quit working.

Newsgroups

Newsgroups are one of the oldest services on the Internet. To access a newsgroup, you must use a newsreader program. A number of third-party newsreaders exist, such as the popular Forté Free Agent, but Microsoft's Outlook Express is the most common of all newsreaders (not surprising, since it comes free with most versions of Windows). To access a newsgroup, you must know the name of a news server. *News servers* run the Network News Transfer Protocol (NNTP). There are public news servers, but these are extremely slow. Your Internet service provider will tell you the name of the news server and provide you with a username and password if necessary (Figure 17-46).

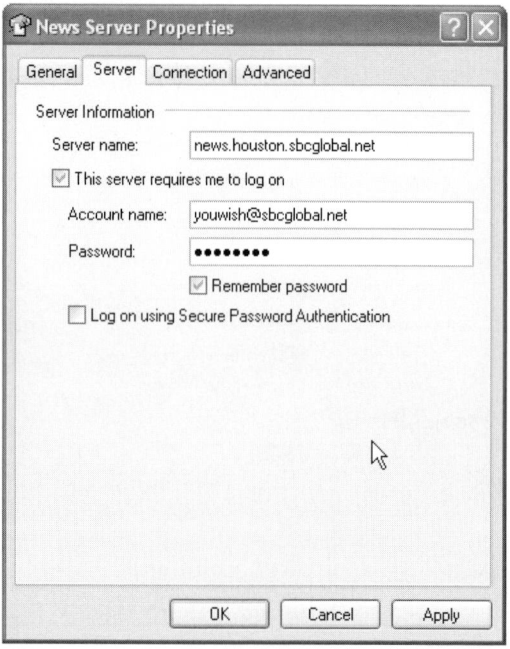

FIGURE 17.44 Configuring Outlook Express for a news server

File Transfer Protocol (FTP)

The File Transfer Protocol (FTP) can be used to access systems that you would otherwise not be able to access. FTP is also a great way to share files, but you need an FTP server. To access an FTP site, you must use an FTP client such as WS_FTP, although later versions of Internet Explorer and other web browsers provide support for FTP. Just type in the name of the FTP site. Figure 17-47 shows Internet Explorer accessing ftp.microsoft.com.

Even though you can use a web browser, all FTP sites require you to log on. Web browsers know only the most common method, using the username "anonymous" and then your e-mail address for a password. Called an anonymous logon, this works fine for most public FTP sites. However, if you need to access a site that requires a special username and password, third-party programs are preferable, because they store these settings. This enables you to access the FTP site more easily later. Figure 17-48 shows my personal favorite FTP application, WS_FTP.

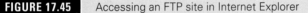

FIGURE 17.45   Accessing an FTP site in Internet Explorer

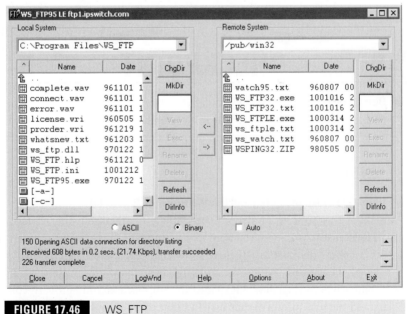

FIGURE 17.46   WS_FTP

Telnet

Telnet is a terminal emulation program for TCP/IP networks that enables you to connect to a server and run commands on that server as if you were sitting in right in front of it. This way, you can remotely administer a server and communicate with other servers on your network. As you can imagine, this is rather risky. If *you* can remotely control a computer, what's to stop others from doing the same? Of course, Telnet does not allow just *anyone* to log on and wreak havoc with your network. You must enter a special username and password in order to run Telnet.

Exam Tip
The A+ Certification exams test your knowledge of a few networking tools, such as Telnet, but only enough to let you support a Network+ tech or network administrator. If you need to run Telnet, you will get the details from a network administrator. Implementation of Telnet falls well beyond A+.

CHECKPOINT

✔**Objective 17.01: Network Operating Systems**   Network operating systems enable PCs to share resources and access shared resources across a network. They provide a network organization, such as client/server or peer-to-peer. You can make a PC a member of a workgroup or, in higher-end settings, a member of a domain.

✔**Objective 17.02: Installing and Configuring a LAN**   It takes four components at least to have a functional network: NIC, client software, protocol, and server software. First, you need to install an NIC, including proper drivers. Second, you must install client software so that the PC can see and be seen on the network. Windows installs the Client for Microsoft Networks by default when you install an NIC. Third, the NIC needs to run a properly configured network protocol that matches that of other machines. The most common protocol in use is TCP/IP, the protocol of the Internet. DHCP sets up your IP address, subnet mask, default gateway, and more, automatically. Any manual settings you'll get from a network administrator. And finally, you must enable File and Print Sharing to turn the PC into a server and make its resources available for other users across the network. Sharing resources is a matter of selecting the properties for a file, folder, or device and coming up with a share name. You use Network Neighborhood (Windows NT and 9*x*) or My Network Places (Windows Me, 2000, and XP) to access shared resources on a LAN.

✔**Objective 17.03: The Internet**   To use the Internet successfully, you need to connect properly and then run special applications that work with TCP/IP services. Many users connect to an ISP using a modem and Dial-up Networking. DUN uses the PPP protocol to enable access to remote resources. Other users connect via a dedicated solution, such as cable or DSL. Windows offers Internet Connection Sharing to enable computers on a LAN to connect to the Internet through a single machine. Windows XP offers the Internet Connection Firewall to protect the exposed computer. The TCP/IP services used commonly on the Internet are HTTP for web browsing, POP3 and SMTP for e-mail, NNTP for newsgroups, FTP for transferring files, and Telnet for controlling remote computers.

REVIEW QUESTIONS

1. Simon's Windows 2000 system can't contact a DHCP server to obtain an IP address automatically, but he can still communicate with other systems on his subnet. What feature of Windows 2000 makes this possible?

   A. Subnet masking

   B. Windows Internet Name Service

   C. Automatic Private IP Addressing

   D. Client for Microsoft Networks

2. Which of the following are true of NetBEUI? (Select all that apply.)

   A. No logical addresses are required.

   B. It is supported only on Microsoft network systems.

   C. It supports routing.

   D. It is supported by all versions of Windows through XP.

3. You need to change the TCP/IP settings on a Windows 9*x* computer that accesses the network directly through an NIC. How do you get to the proper screen to perform this task?

   A. Control Panel | Networks | TCP/IP | Properties

   B. My Computer | Networks | Server Type | TCP/IP Settings

C. My Computer | Networks | TCP/IP | Properties

D. Control Panel | Networks | Server Type | TCP/IP Settings

4. In a TCP/IP network, the two parts of an IP address are the _____ and the _____.

A. Network ID, Host ID

B. IP address, subnet mask

C. Client, server

D. TCP address, IP address

5. You need to check the status of the local area connection of a Windows XP machine on your Microsoft network. How do you get to the screen where you can perform this task? (Select all that apply.)

A. Start | alternate-click My Network Places | Properties | Local Area Connection

B. Start | Settings | Network and Dial-up Connections | Local Area Connection

C. Start | Control Panel | Network Connections | Local Area Connection

D. Alternate-click My Computer | Properties | Network Connections | Local Area Connection

6. The router that your PC uses to connect to your Internet service provider is referred to as the _____.

A. Loopback address

B. Backbone

C. IP address

D. Default gateway

7. To configure dial-up networks with Windows XP, use the _____ applet.

A. Network and Internet Connections

B. Network Neighborhood

C. Internet Connection Sharing

D. Remote Assistance

8. To check to see if the web server you are trying to reach is available or is down, you can use the command line utility called _____.

A. PING

B. ICS

   C. TELNET

   D. NNTP

9. A _____ is either hardware or software that protects your computer or network from probing or malicious users.

   A. Router

   B. Firewall

   C. Protocol

   D. Spyware

10. Liz can receive her e-mail, but she cannot send e-mail. Which of the following is most likely causing her problem?

   A. POP3

   B. SMTP

   C. IMAP

   D. UART

REVIEW ANSWERS

1. **C**   Automatic Private IP Addressing is the Windows 2000 feature that makes it possible for Steven's system to communicate with other systems on his subnet even though he can't obtain an IP address.

2. **A** **B**   NetBEUI doesn't require logical addresses and is supported only on Microsoft network systems. It is nonroutable, however, and is not available to install in Windows XP.

3. **A**   Select Control Panel | Networks | TCP/IP | Properties to change the TCP/IP settings on a Windows 9x computer that accesses the network directly through an NIC.

4. **B**   The two parts of an IP address are the Network ID and the Host ID.

5. **A** **C**   To check the status of the local area connection of a Windows XP machine on your Microsoft network, you can select either Start | alternate-click My Network Places | Properties | Local Area Connection, or Start | Control Panel | Network Connections | Local Area Connection.

6. **D**   The router that your PC uses to connect to your Internet service provider is referred to as the default gateway.

7. **A**   To configure dial-up networks with Windows XP, use the Network and Internet Connections applet.

8. **A**   To check to see if the web server you are trying to reach is available or is down, you can use the command line utility called PING.

9. **B**   A firewall is either hardware or software that protects your computer or network from probing or malicious users.

10. **B**   Liz can receive her e-mail, but she cannot send e-mail. SMTP is the most likely cause of her problem. Remember SMTP is used to send, while POP3 and IMAP are used to receive e-mail.

Maintaining, Optimizing, and Troubleshooting Windows 9*x*/Me

	NEWBIE	SOME EXPERIENCE	EXPERT
ETA	6 hours	4 hours	2 hours

CompTIA expects you to know how to maintain, optimize, and troubleshoot Windows 9*x*/Me systems, and how to install and configure both Plug and Play (PnP) and legacy devices on Windows 9*x*/Me systems. This chapter begins with the basic "housekeeping" tasks you must know in order to keep a Windows 9*x*/Me system running smoothly and efficiently, including drive maintenance and OS updates. The second part of the chapter covers the process of installing both PnP and legacy devices, including how installation works when all goes well, and what to do when it doesn't. The last section of the chapter tackles system troubleshooting issues, including boot problems, lockups, viruses, and system restore.

Objective 18.01 Maintaining and Optimizing Windows 9*x*/Me

Optimization of Windows 9*x*/Me means little more than checking the status of a few settings, which in all probability are already set properly by Windows, and making sure a Windows system takes advantage of the latest updates. Maintenance focuses on running an occasional ScanDisk, Defrag, antivirus check, system cleanup, and system backup. When installed properly, all of these functions work automatically, or nearly automatically. Let's begin with the most important of all jobs: updating Windows with service packs and patches.

Service Packs/Patches/Windows Update

There are three different ways to update Windows: patches, service packs, and new versions. Patches are EXE files that you get from Microsoft to fix a specific problem. You run these programs, and they do whatever they're supposed to do—update DLLs, reconfigure Registry settings, or whatever else they need to do to fix a particular problem and keep Windows running properly.

Travel Advisory

The order in which you install patches in Windows 95 can be crucial!

The most basic fix is called a service pack—it usually fixes a single issue. Over time, Microsoft packages these together into a single grouping of patches called a *service pack.*

Local Lingo
Security Update   Microsoft continues to redefine the names for patches. A patch that fixes a security problem is now called a "security update."

Travel Assistance
To help determine what patches or upgrades you need, visit http://windowsupdate.microsoft.com.

You need to be able to answer the questions "What service packs/patches are on my system now?" and "What should I install?" In Windows 98/Me, you can use the Windows Update utility to answer these questions (Figure 18-1). The Windows Update utility queries your system and provides a list of the updates you require.

The best way to determine the patches currently loaded on your Windows 95 system is to use Microsoft's QFECHECK. QFECHECK can be downloaded from the Microsoft web site and generates a detailed list of all patches performed on your machine. In Figure 18-2, only service packs and a few other patches have been installed, but QFECHECK breaks down the service packs to show separate patches.

Travel Advisory
You don't need every update Microsoft offers. Before you download the latest security update or service pack, let other folks test it for a few weeks, and then do a search on the Internet to see if any problems occur with that update. There's no worse feeling than installing a patch to improve a system, only to find you've made it worse!

Drive Maintenance

Drive maintenance is the single most important way to ensure the long-term health of a PC system. The three most important functions are disk scanning, defragmentation, and disk cleanup.

- **Defragmentation**   All versions of Windows 9*x*/Me come with a disk defragmentation utility called Disk Defragmenter. Many techs still just refer to it as *Defrag*—the name of the old DOS disk defragmentation utility. You access Defrag from the Programs | Accessories | System

FIGURE 18.1   Windows Update utility

Tools menu (Figure 18-3). Although the look of Defrag has changed over the Windows versions, it still does the same job.

- **Disk Scanning**   All versions of Windows 9*x*/Me also include a disk scanning program that checks for errors, just as the old ScanDisk utility used to do. As with the term *Defrag*, we still refer to any tool of this type as *ScanDisk*. In Windows 9*x*/Me, you access ScanDisk from the

Update Information Tool Properties

Registered Updates | Updated Files Found |

Windows version 4.00.1111 B

The following system file updates are registered on your computer.

Files or components designated as Invalid or Not Found may or may not affect the performance of your computer or programs. For more information, click Help.

To see information about the contents of an update icon, double-click it.

```
UPD008 System Agent update
UPD010 Printer Port update
UPD256015 Windows 95 OSR2 Q256015 Update
    IFSMGR.VXD    4.0.0.1116
W95
    UPD249973 Windows 95 Q249973 Update
        RICHED32.DLL 5.0.1461.82
        RICHED20.DLL 5.0.153.0
        USP10.DLL    1.325.2180.1
    UPD168115 Windows 95 Q168115 Update
        MSNP32.DLL   4.0.0.957
    UPD245729 Windows 95 Q245729 Update
        msnet32.dll  4.0.0.956
```

OK   Cancel   Help

FIGURE 18.2   Service packs contain many patches

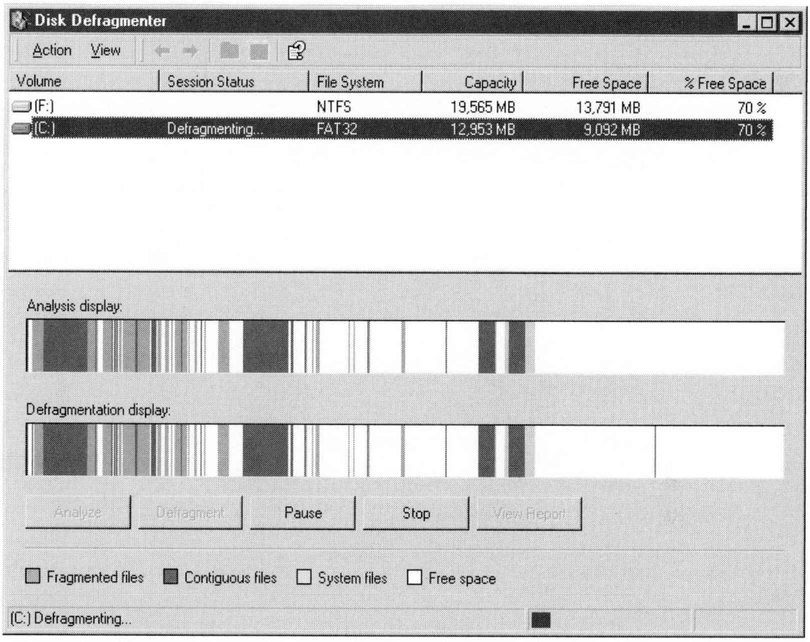

Volume	Session Status	File System	Capacity	Free Space	% Free Space
(F:)		NTFS	19,565 MB	13,791 MB	70 %
(C:)	Defragmenting...	FAT 32	12,953 MB	9,092 MB	70 %

FIGURE 18.3   Disk defragmentation utility

Programs | Accessories | System Tools menu. The ScanDisk section of the Tools tab is now called "Error-checking" (Figure 18-4).

Exam Tip

Know the difference between defragging and disk scanning.

- **Drive Cleanup Utilities**

Windows puts a lot of junk files on the system. They fall into one of six categories:

- Application temporary files that failed to delete
- Installation temporary files that failed to delete
- Internet Browser cache files
- Files in the Recycle Bin
- Internet cookie files
- Identical files in separate locations

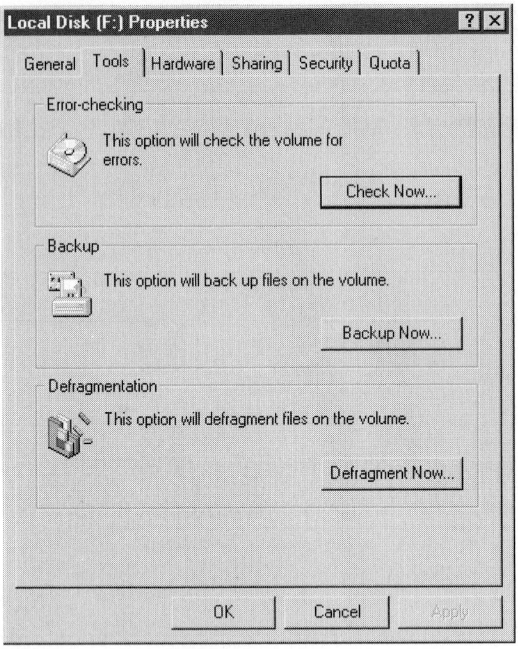

FIGURE 18.4   Windows Me hard drive Properties Tools tab

These files can take up a large percentage of your hard drive. As you begin to fill drives, you need to recover that space.

Starting with Windows 98, Microsoft introduced a built-in disk cleanup program called, cleverly enough, Disk Cleanup. There are third-party disk cleanup tools that generally do a far better job than Disk Cleanup, but it's not a bad little program (Figure 18-5). Some of the better third-party utilities are more flexible; for example, you can choose to delete only Internet cookies that haven't been accessed lately, so you won't have to type in your Amazon.com data over again.

Task Scheduling

Instead of running disk maintenance programs manually, you can use the Windows Task Scheduler that now comes with Windows 98 and Windows Me (Figure 18-6). Simply choose the program you wish to run, when and how often you want it to run, and the Task Scheduler will handle the disk maintenance tasks for you.

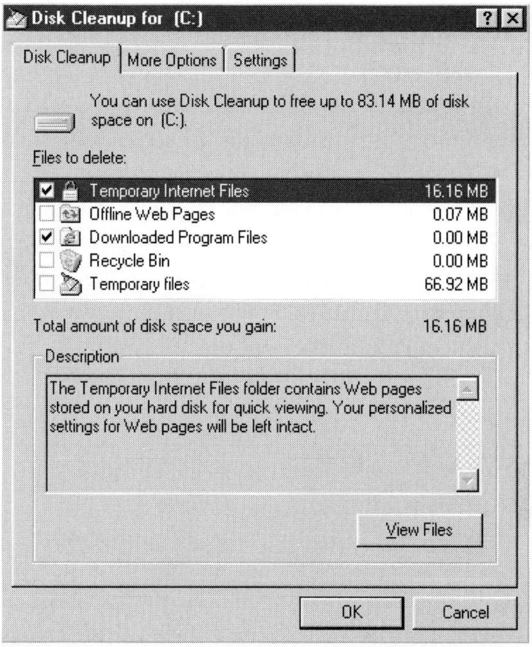

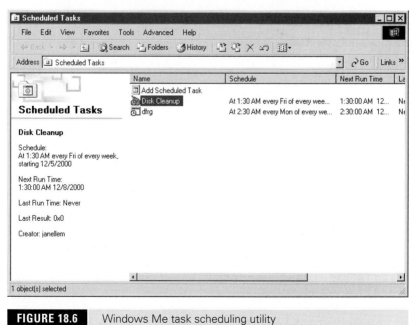

FIGURE 18.5   Disk Cleanup utility

FIGURE 18.6   Windows Me task scheduling utility

Virtual Memory

All versions of Windows use *virtual memory*—mapping a portion of the hard drive with memory addresses to mimic RAM. Windows creates a *swap file* that enables it to have more programs open on the screen than it could normally hold in real RAM. The Windows 9*x*/Me swap file is called WIN386.SWP. Windows sets the initial size of the swap file automatically according to the amount of free space available on the C: drive. To configure the Windows 9*x*/Me swap file, open the System applet in the Control Panel or alternate-click My Computer and select Properties, then click the Virtual Memory button on the Performance tab of the System Properties dialog box (Figure 18-7).

Exam Tip	
Know the name of the Windows 9*x*/Me swap file: WIN386.SWP.	

| FIGURE 18.7 | Find the Virtual Memory button on the Performance tab of the System Properties dialog box |

The most common reason for relocating the default swap file is to move it to some drive other than C:. Many systems tend to fill up the C: drive, so little or no room is left for the swap file. The swap file can use only the free space on a drive. When the space is filled, the swap file can't get any larger, resulting in the nasty "Not Enough Memory" error. To move the file, click the Let Me Specify My Own Virtual Memory Settings radio button and select another drive.

Windows 9*x*/Me sets the minimum swap file size to zero and the maximum to the size of the free space on the drive. Leaving these settings at their defaults creates swap files far larger than you really need. The current consensus is to reduce the size to two or three times the amount of RAM. Set both the minimum and maximum to the same number (Figure 18-8).

Travel Advisory

Certain programs demand large swap files. If you use programs like CorelDRAW, you will find that the "two to three times" rule won't work. Gradually increase these settings until the "Not Enough Memory" errors go away.

Disk Cache

Every version of Windows sets aside a small bit of RAM for a *disk cache*. Disk caches increase the efficiency of Windows. The disk-caching program that comes

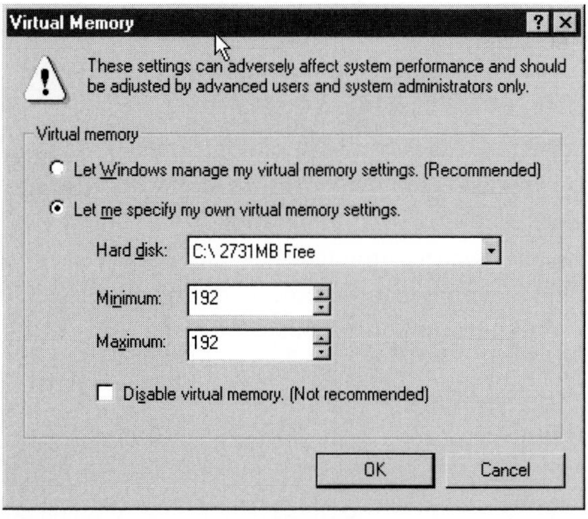

FIGURE 18.8 Setting swap file size manually

standard in Windows grabs a small section of RAM and monitors the files requested by the CPU. If the CPU starts asking for the same files over and over from the hard drive, the disk cache grabs a copy of those files. The next time the CPU requests those files, the disk caching program steps up and presents the files, much faster than the hard drive could ever respond and send.

The disk caching that comes with Windows installs automatically and is virtually maintenance-free. The size of the disk cache is roughly one-fourth the total size of the RAM. You can change these settings by accessing System Properties | Performance tab | File System button, which opens the File System Properties dialog box.

There are two settings for changing the disk cache, both found on the Hard Disk tab: Typical Role Of This Computer and Read-Ahead Optimization. The Typical role setting determines how much RAM to set aside for the disk cache holding pen. Setting this to Network Server can produce a moderate performance boost.

Read-ahead optimization determines how much to read ahead when the system goes to the hard drive. The disk cache doesn't think in terms of files; it thinks in terms of clusters. When the hard drive asks for data, it's actually asking for a number of clusters, because files tend to span many clusters. If the system asks for one cluster, the chances are good that it will come back in a few milliseconds and ask for the next cluster. So the disk cache grabs a few more clusters, on the assumption that the program will ask for them. This is called the *read-ahead*. You can adjust the read-ahead using a sliding bar. It should always be set to Full. This enables the disk cache to read ahead 64K worth of clusters, or two to four clusters ahead on most systems.

Resource Tracking Tools

Even though default Windows installations come well optimized, many Windows systems experience substantial system degradation over time, despite good disk maintenance and basic optimization. Most of the trouble stems from too many programs trying to run at the same time. The average system is stuffed with background programs that consume memory, and you need to know how to use the necessary tools to watch for these problems.

System Resources

One area that many techs look to for system resource information on a Windows 9x/Me system is the System Resources percentage on the Performance tab of System Properties (Figure 18-9). Even though the A+ Certification exams put great stock in this setting, you may find it too incomplete to be much help. Windows 9x/Me uses special memory areas called *heaps* to store many types of general housekeeping information. To calculate this value, Windows takes a snapshot of all resources' heap usage at boot time. It then monitors all heaps, dividing the current usage by the boot usage, and shows the lowest value for the System Resources usage. Many systems can run down into the low 20s with absolutely no ill effect.

Exam Tip
Know how to navigate to the Performance tab of the System applet.

System Monitor

An excellent tool for checking system problems is the *System Monitor*. It provides a graphic snapshot of a broad number of system processes. You can track free physical memory, CPU usage, network throughput—in fact, almost any process where you need to see what's happening on your PC (Figure 18-10). To open the System Monitor, click Start | Programs |Accessories | System Tools | System Monitor.

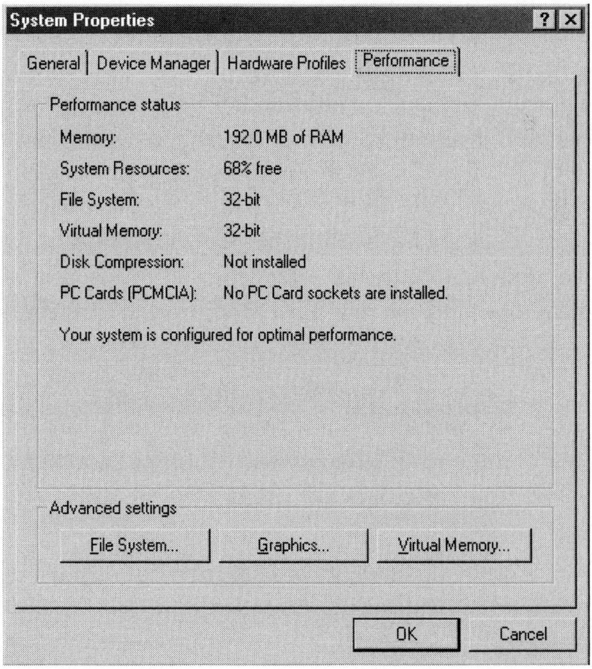

System Properties   ? ×

General | Device Manager | Hardware Profiles | Performance |

Performance status

Memory:	192.0 MB of RAM
System Resources:	68% free
File System:	32-bit
Virtual Memory:	32-bit
Disk Compression:	Not installed
PC Cards (PCMCIA):	No PC Card sockets are installed.

Your system is configured for optimal performance.

Advanced settings

File System... | Graphics... | Virtual Memory...

OK | Cancel

FIGURE 18.9   System Resources percentage

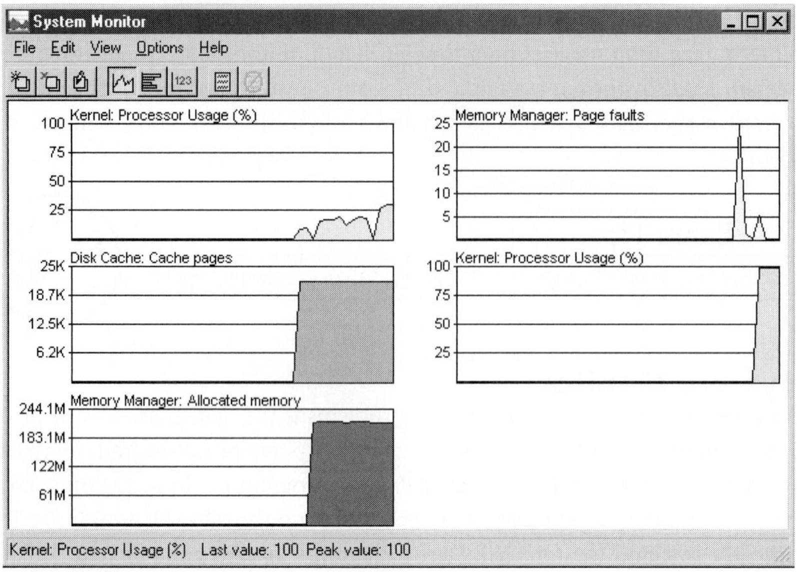

FIGURE 18.10 System Monitor

System Resource Meter

Heaps are limited in size and are prone to filling up on some systems. While sometimes an overfilled heap will provide an error, other heap overflows may lock up the system. One clear result of heap filling is substantial system slowdown. To keep an eye on your heaps, use the System Resource Meter (Figure 18-11). To open the System Resource Meter, click Start | Programs | Accessories | System Tools | System Resource Meter. Try loading the System Resource Meter if you notice a system slowdown—it runs quite nicely from the system tray. As you

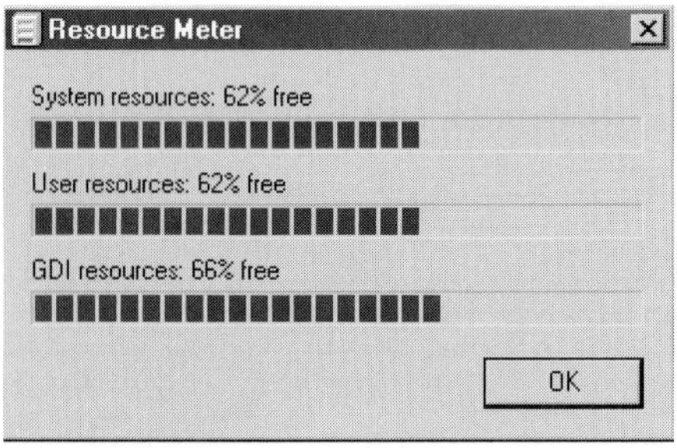

FIGURE 18.11 System Resource Meter watches heaps

load applications, see which ones are eating heap space. If you don't see any substantial heap space usage, check the System Monitor.

Task Manager

The Task Manager shows all running programs, including hidden ones (Figure 18-12). You access the Task Manager by pressing CTRL-ALT-DEL. Use the Task Manager to close background programs that defy all other attempts to close them, or to close an unresponsive program without having to crash the entire system. Don't close Explorer or Systray, as these two programs must run in order to keep Windows running.

Auto-Starting Programs

It seems that every third application installed on a PC today uses some form of background program. In most cases, this is perfectly acceptable—for example, you want your antivirus program to run constantly, invisibly inspecting the system for problems. If you encounter a sluggish system, first boot normally and open the System Monitor to check the processor usage, the available physical memory, and the size of the swap file in use. If the CPU constantly runs at nearly 100 percent, or if most of the physical memory is in use, you've got too many autostarting programs.

If you decide you need to remove some autostarting programs, first go to the System Tray and check for programs that aren't necessary. Keep the programs you need or want, but close or disable those you don't. If you have Windows 98

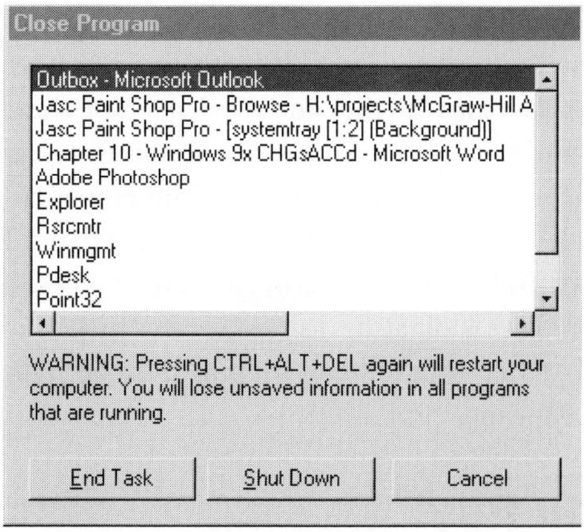

FIGURE 18.12   The Task Manager shows and can close all running programs.

or Me, fire up the System Information program, and then open the System Configuration Utility from the Tools menu. Go to the Startup tab and uncheck suspicious programs. Don't turn off the System Tray. While you're here, click the WIN.INI tab and open the Windows folder to make sure that no programs are starting under Run= or Load=. Finally, see what's running under AUTOEXEC.BAT. The TSRs rarely have much effect on Windows memory, but it never hurts to check.

Travel Advisory

The *tech* way to open the System Configuration Utility is to go to Start | Run and type **MSCONFIG**. Click OK and you're up and running!

If you use Windows 95, locate the \WINDOWS\START MENU\PROGRAMS\ STARTUP folder to locate autostarting programs. Then run SYSEDIT to check the SYSTEM.INI and WIN.INI files.

Exam Tip

Programs in the STARTUP folder load alphabetically.

Objective 18.02 Device Installation in Windows 9x/Me

Device installation has been completely transformed by the advent of *PnP*. Today, almost anyone with the "do-it-yourself" spirit and enough sense to read instructions and follow basic anti-ESD procedures can easily succeed in installing most devices. Hard drives, CD-ROMs, motherboards, CPUs, and power supplies are, or at least should be, the few components that still require PC tech skills. A number of problems do still arise, however, that require us to support device installation. Let's look at device installation first from the perfect scenario: a truly PnP device with full PnP support from both the OS—in this example, Windows 98—and a PnP BIOS.

Before You Buy

Most hardware installation failures take place long before you put a screwdriver in your hand. They take place at the store or the web site where you purchased the device. When purchasing a device, follow these basic rules.

Know What You Need

Too many people buy the wrong hardware for their needs. Never walk into a store saying, "I need a sound card." Make sure, whether you purchase the device for yourself or for a customer, that you first ask yourself, "What do I want the sound card to do for me (or the customer)?" When purchasing a device, you must juggle with four variables:

- What do I need this device to do?
- What do I expect this device to do?
- Can I afford it?
- How much do I care about this device?

Compatibility

Once you think you know what you need, you must consider how this choice will affect the system. The big question here is compatibility. Possible physical incompatibility issues include non-matching connectors and insufficient available PCI slots or power connections. System incompatibility issues are likely to involve installing new devices in a system whose BIOS, motherboard, or other components (such as the video card) are too old to support the new technology.

Travel Advisory

If you have system compatibility questions, start by surfing to the device maker's web site. Find the support area and check the *frequently asked questions (FAQ)* lists. If that doesn't give you an answer, or even if it does, send an e-mail to tech support. Between your fellow users/techs and the support guys, you're bound to find an answer to your questions, and frequently find out a thing or two you never considered!

Driver Check

Not all devices come with drivers for all operating systems—even slightly older devices may not support Windows XP, and new ones may not work well with Windows 9*x*/Me. Many devices do not ship with the latest drivers, so you should always check the manufacturer's web site for updates.

Device Installation Procedures

Here are a few things to remember when installing a device in Windows 9*x*/Me.

Create a Startup Disk

All versions of Windows 9*x*/Me can create a startup disk. A startup disk is a bootable floppy disk that, in case of an emergency, enables you to boot to an A: prompt and perform basic troubleshooting. To create one, follow these steps:

1. Click Start | Settings | Control Panel to open the Control Panel.
2. Locate the Add/Remove Programs icon and click it.
3. Click the Startup Disk tab.
4. Get a blank floppy disk and insert it into the floppy drive.
5. Click Create Disk. On some systems, Windows will prompt you for the Windows installation CD-ROM.

A startup disk must enable you to gain access to your CD-ROM. To enable a Windows 95 startup disk to provide access to the CD-ROM drive, you must copy two files and edit two others. Windows 98 startup disks *do* provide CD-ROM access, so don't do this unless you still run Windows 95!

Travel Advisory

Many techs, myself included, use Windows 98 startup disks when working on Windows 95 systems—they work just fine!

To make a Windows 95 startup disk that supports a CD-ROM drive, follow these steps:

1. Download a special device driver called OAKCDROM.SYS. Over 100 web sites provide this driver. Copy the OAKCDROM.SYS file to the Windows 95 Startup disk.
2. Locate a file called MSCDEX.EXE on your system. Most systems store this file in the \WINDOWS\COMMAND folder. Copy the MSCDEX file to the floppy disk. Once you've done this, you should see both files on the floppy disk.
3. Go to the Run menu option in the Start menu and type this command: **notepad a:\config.sys** to open the CONFIG.SYS file on the floppy disk for editing. Ignore any other text in the file; just add this line: **DEVICE=A:\OAKCDROM.SYS /D:CDROM** to the end so that it looks like Figure 18-13. Save and exit Notepad.

FIGURE 18.13   Adding CD-ROM support in CONFIG.SYS

Travel Assistance

One place you can find OAKCDROM.SYS is
http://www.computerhope.com/download/hardware.htm.
Download the Generic CD-ROM Driver.

Travel Advisory

If you have multiple hard drives or hard drive partitions in a system,
also add this line to the end of the CONFIG.SYS file: LASTDRIVE=Z.

---

4. Go to the Run menu option in the Start menu and type this command:
notepad a:\autoexec.bat to open the AUTOEXEC.BAT file on the
floppy disk for editing. Ignore any other text in the file. Just add this
line: **MSCDEX /D:CDROM** to the end so it looks like Figure 18-14.
Save and exit Notepad. The Windows 95 startup disk will now
recognize the CD-ROM and give it a drive letter.

Read Me!

Read every scrap of documentation *before* you install. Which disk holds the
drivers? What procedure do I need to follow? Check for a file on the install
CD-ROM or floppy disk called README.DOC or READ.ME or README.TXT.
These files always provide critical information and notice of late-breaking issues. Make sure you understand the setup process. Replacing one device with
another invariably requires you to delete the old device from your Device Manager before you install a new one. Video cards almost always demand this procedure. If the documentation tells you to delete a driver, jump down to the
"Device Manager" section to see how to delete old drivers.

FIGURE 18.14 Adding CD-ROM support in AUTOEXEC.BAT

Physical Installation

Now, finally, you can plug in that new device! Don't forget your antistatic procedures. Check, double-check, and then triple-check connections, power, and any switches or jumpers that the device needs. Fortunately, you read all the documentation and know all about any special issues—deal with those now. Boot the system and go to CMOS.

Driver Install

Driver installation in a PnP system is highly anticlimactic in most cases. You get to watch Windows discover the new device and show the famous "Windows has discovered new hardware" alert (Figure 18-15). Figure 18-16 shows the Found New Hardware Wizard in action.

Windows uses files with the INF extension to install a device driver. These files are commonly referred to as *INF files*. These files aren't the device drivers; instead, they're a set of instructions, used by Windows, to install the appropriate device driver.

If you're installing a new device and Windows can't find the device driver on the installation disk, check to make sure the INF file isn't tucked away in some subdirectory on the install disk. If it is, just point Windows to the right folder.

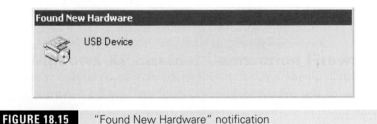

FIGURE 18.15 "Found New Hardware" notification

FIGURE 18.16   Windows Me Found New Hardware Wizard

Many systems give the "Windows has found unknown hardware and is installing software..." message. This usually comes from installing two devices at once, one depending on the other for connection to the system, like a new video card and monitor. This is fine; Windows will eventually find the unknown device, although it may take a few reboots, especially with Windows 95.

Device Manager

The first place we look to verify a good install is the Device Manager. The Device Manager is the primary tool for dealing with devices and device drivers in Windows. It displays every device that Windows recognizes. Figure 18-17 shows a typical Device Manager screen with all installed devices in good order with the exception of the mouse. If Windows detects a problem, it shows the device with a red "X" or a yellow exclamation point.

The Device Manager organizes devices in special groups called *types,* grouped under type headings. Figure 18-18 shows the Ports type opened, revealing the COM and LPT ports on the system. By double-clicking a device (or by selecting the device and clicking the Properties button) and then clicking the Resources tab, you can see the resources used by that device.

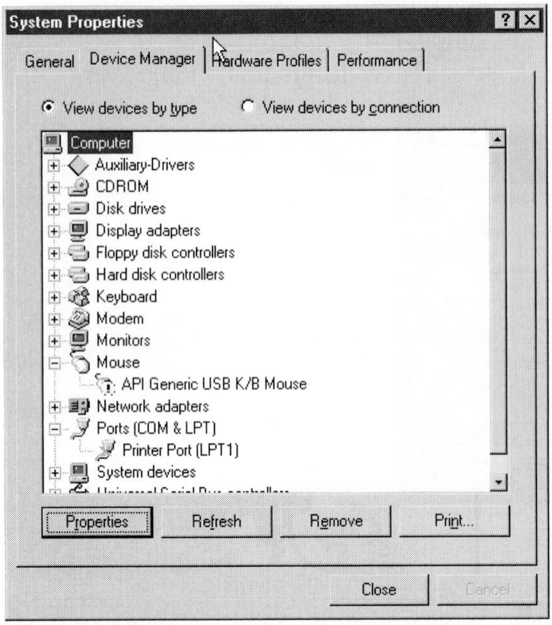

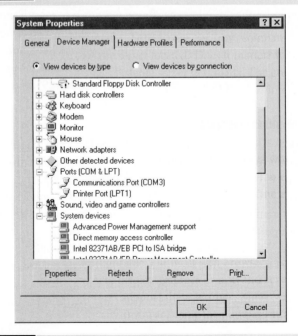

FIGURE 18.17   The Device Manager detects a mouse problem

FIGURE 18.18   Installed COM and LPT ports

Applications

Each piece of hardware that is installed in a particular PC is supported by a set of device-specific applications. These applications, some of which are included with Windows and others that are supplied by third parties, can be used to configure and "tweak" a device. We can break down device-related applications into five groups: Built-in, Enhanced, Supplied Critical, Supplied Helpful, and Supplied Optional.

Built-in

Windows has built-in applications to handle many devices. Windows has complete support for a network card via the Network Neighborhood, for example, and for a CD-ROM via My Computer or Windows Explorer.

Enhanced

Many new devices supported by Windows come with applications that greatly enhance their functionality. For example, while most versions of Windows provide basic support for Zip drives, Iomega adds extra applications that provide features such as password protection and better formatting that Windows alone doesn't support.

Supplied Critical

Supplied critical applications come with the install CD-ROM, and you must install them to make the hardware work. For example, that new USB docking station for your Palm Pilot might as well be a paperweight until you install its synchronization software.

Supplied Helpful

Supplied helpful applications are those programs you find on the installation CD-ROM that may help but are not really required. For example, a digital camera might come with a utility for doing video captures. Not required, but you may decide to install it anyway.

Supplied Optional

Supplied optional really means "supplied, but you probably won't want it." Your new modem might come with an America Online CD-ROM, but you already have an Internet service provider. Or your new sound card comes with a "Historical Tour of Musical Instruments," but you bought the sound card to play online games. Don't fill your drive with applications you will never use.

Dealing with Installation Problems

Time to jump out of fantasyland and move into the more unpleasant aspect of device installation: installation problems. Even in a perfect world, perhaps one in every five installations creates some kind of unanticipated error. Let's break these errors down and see how to deal with them.

Windows Plug and Play Can't Find a Driver

Most techs feel that failure to find a correct device driver stands as the most common PnP install issue. When you add a new device, Windows normally brings up the Add New Hardware Wizard and immediately moves to the "please tell me the location of the driver" screen, as shown in Figure 18-19. Windows PnP has queried the new device and knows that the device exists but cannot find the correct INF for that device. In most cases, you can simply click the Have Disk button and point the installer to the proper directory location, which you know because you looked this up in the documentation. If you didn't look (like that would ever happen!), you can use the Browse feature to navigate around the install CD-ROM/floppy until the Add New Hardware Wizard finds an INF file (Figure 18-20).

Use common sense when looking for the INF file. For instance, if you have a Windows 98 system and the install floppy shows the following folders, where would you look first?

> **A:\LINUX**
> **A:\NETWARE5**
> **A:\WIN2K**
> **A:\WIN95**
> **A:\WIN98**

Please tell me you picked the A:\WIN98 folder!

If you insert the wrong install disk, especially with Windows 9x/Me, you might install the wrong driver, requiring you to delete the device from the Device Manager and try again. Many times, hardware makers hide device drivers and INF files in a setup program. You must run the program to get all the files you need.

Windows Doesn't See Device

The second most common install error occurs when PnP doesn't see the device you just installed. You know this happens when you install the device and nothing happens. A fast Windows 9x system may display the install screens so quickly you miss them, and Windows Me is even quicker, so you should check the Device Manager to see if the device installed. Let's assume you checked the Device Manager, and you're positive the device is not there.

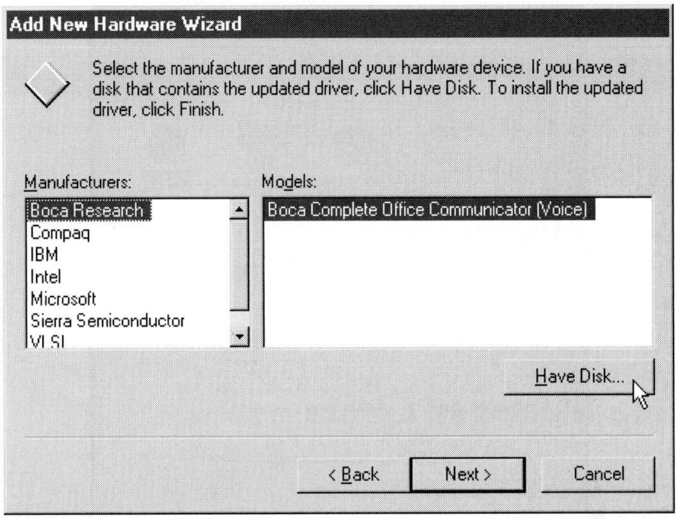

FIGURE 18.19   Windows prompts the user for the device driver.

Try Again

Assuming you know you have a PnP device, power off the system after a proper shutdown and remove the device. Reseat the device in the slot or connector and try again. PCI and AGP cards really need tight seating or they won't work. Verify all connections and make sure the device has power if it needs it. Reboot to see if Windows detects the device. Recheck the Device Manager.

Resources

Windows may fail to see a PnP device if other devices are using all its available resources. This rarely happens in PnP systems; in most cases, the Windows PnP sees the device and lists it in the Device Manager but cannot configure it. You'll learn how to resolve resource conflicts in the "Legacy Devices in a Plug and Play World" section of this chapter.

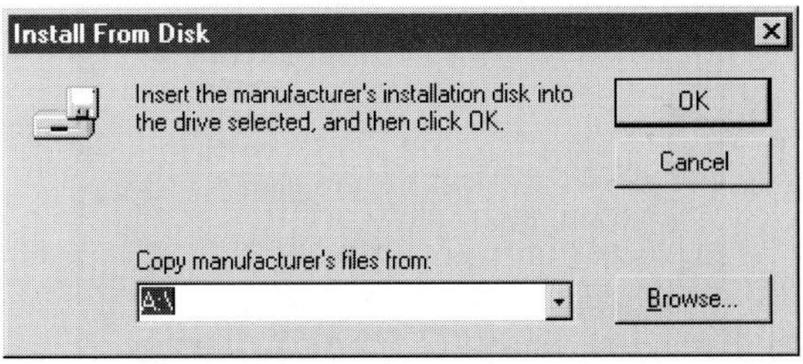

FIGURE 18.20   Browsing to find the INF file

Old BIOS

Always verify that your system has the latest BIOS. Name-brand PC makers list BIOS updates by system model. Check the motherboard maker's web site for BIOS updates for your motherboard. If your system is more than two years old, a BIOS update almost certainly exists.

Blame the Hardware?

When all else fails, blame the device. You may want to try inserting the device into another slot or port (if another one exists), but otherwise you need to point your finger at the device, return it from whence it came, and move on!

Device Manager Errors

Windows often sees a device and tries to install it, but for one reason or another fails to install the device properly. Unlike errors where the PnP simply fails to see the device, these devices show in the Device Manager, but they show one of two possible errors. If a device has a problem, it will show up with an exclamation point surrounded by a small yellow dot. A small red "X" on a device means the device has been disabled by Windows. Figure 18-21 shows an example of both problem icons.

> **Exam Tip**
>
> There are situations where disabling a device comes in handy, such as disabling an unused network card. Any device can be intentionally disabled in Device Manager in Windows.

Anyone reading the Microsoft Knowledge Base support documentation can see that probably 50 different types of problems cause these errors, but most result from one of six types of problems:

- Failure to follow install procedures
- Corruption/incompatibility with drivers or INF file
- Outdated support drivers
- Resource conflict
- Corrupted Registry
- Bad device

Failure to Follow Install Procedures

Failure to follow proper install procedures isn't really a Windows error; it's a human error that causes most of the Windows errors you're about to learn! All PnP

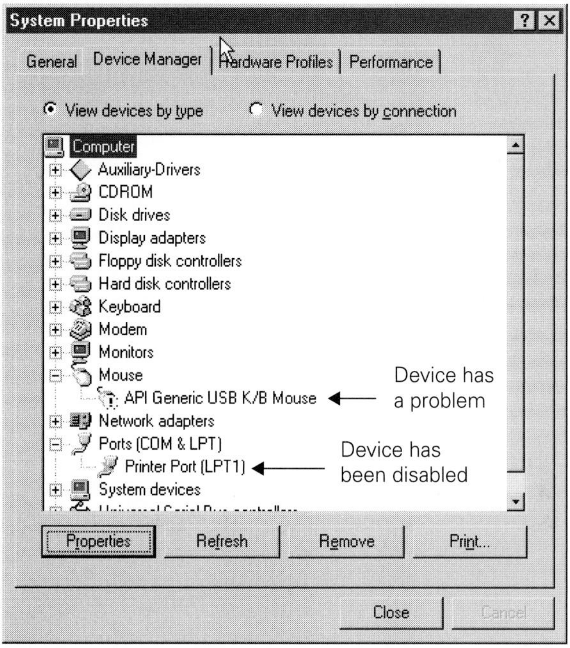

FIGURE 18.21   Improperly installed device errors

devices require a specific series of steps to ensure proper installation, particularly when you're replacing one device with a different one. Read all the documentation *carefully* before installing! Some of the more common install procedures include deleting the old driver first, running a SETUP program, checking for hardware incompatibilities, and verifying the version number of some Windows EXE, DLL, or driver.

Every device maker provides this information through documentation, but the last item, version numbers, merits further discussion here. Every device driver, Windows EXE, and Windows DLL comes with a *version number.* You can verify the driver version of an installed device by checking the device's properties in Device Manager. Select the Driver tab and click the Driver File Details button (Figure 18-22). Many times, the documentation tells you to verify the version of a certain Windows EXE or DLL before you install. Use the Search/Find utility to locate the file and click the Version tab in the file's properties to find that information (Figure 18-23).

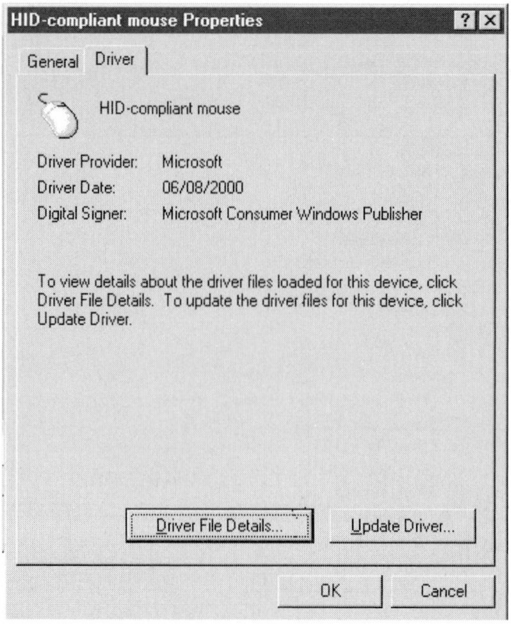

FIGURE 18.22 Driver tab for a device driver

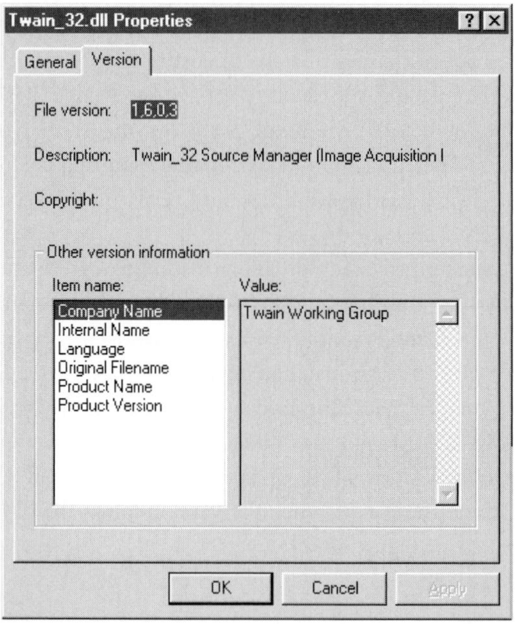

FIGURE 18.23 Verifying the file's version

Travel Assistance

When a device shows an error, you can find the specific error code number on the General tab under the device's properties in Device Manager. The Microsoft Knowledge Base (http://support.microsoft.com) lists all the error code numbers under article number Q125174. The A+ Certification exams do not expect you to memorize them.

Corruption/Incompatibility with Drivers or INF File

Let's start with the first part: corruption. Files get corrupted all the time. An install CD-ROM may get a scratch at the location of a critical driver; Windows may decide to lock up for some reason halfway through copying an INF file; or maybe Windows will decide to copy files onto a hard drive sector that dies half a second after they get copied. When you encounter error text complaining it's "not reading a driver," "couldn't find a driver," or "failing to load a driver," delete the driver, reboot, and try again. If that doesn't work, download a driver from the device manufacturer's web site. Still no good? Check the hard drive. That usually fixes it.

The Windows platform and hardware technologies evolve so quickly that incompatibilities show up constantly. The newer the technology, the more you see it. In this respect, it actually pays *not* to be the "first kid on the block" with the newest, coolest device or latest OS—at least when it's a system you need to rely upon! One of the most famous incompatibilities shows up as the always-amusing "Unknown Device" and "Unsupported Device" errors. Basically, these errors mean Windows knows that *something* is using resources, but has no idea *what*. If you see several device errors or unknown devices, incompatibility (or the wrong driver) may be the culprit.

Outdated Support Drivers

If you visualize the CPU as the center of the computer, you'll notice that almost no devices connect directly to the CPU. There's always a chipset, a controller, or some other device between the CPU and the device you install. All these "middleman" devices also need device drivers. In many cases, that exclamation point or red "X" on the device you just installed in Device Manager points to a problem with another device that your new device plugs into. Most of the time, these errors show up clearly because the support device *itself* shows an error, but sometimes it's not that easy.

Windows can provide rudimentary support for most chipsets, for example, but that doesn't always mean that the device support contains everything you need. Windows Me handles this nicely by putting a green question mark on devices that do not have optimal drivers, but that doesn't help us on 95 or 98. Windows 98 has a device error that says, "I'm not working because device X isn't working," but it's not foolproof. A clue that a support device isn't fully supported can be found in the description of the support devices under the System heading in the Device Manager. Well-supported devices always have very detailed names, whereas less-supported devices tend to get less-detailed names. Compare these two close-ups of the same Windows 95 system's System devices heading (Figure 18-24): first with Windows default support drivers, the second after using the CD-ROM that came with the motherboard to upgrade all the support devices—quite a difference!

Resource Conflict

Resource conflicts are not as rare as you might think, even in a system with only PnP devices. An ISA PnP device does not have access to every resource; the manufacturer specifies a range of resources in the INF file. Open the INF file for an ISA PnP device and see for yourself (Figure 18-25). Even if your system has only PCI and AGP devices, as long as your system uses ISA slots, resource conflicts might arise. Windows clearly reports resource conflicts in the error message, so you always know when they occur.

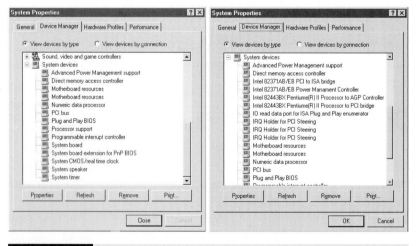

FIGURE 18.24   Default device drivers versus proper device drivers

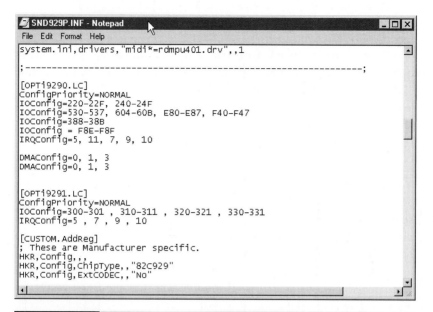

FIGURE 18.25   IRQ settings in the INF file

Corrupted Registry

In most cases, the device error will report this one very clearly: "Registry corrupted." No problem, since you kept that backup copy, right? Right!

Bad Device

After checking everything else, blame the device. Techs hate blaming hardware, primarily due to the fact that with few exceptions, no tool exists that truly tests any single type of hardware (despite the fantastic claims by a number of vendors who shall remain nameless). Unless the manufacturer provides a specialized testing tool, you cannot truly test a device.If you're not sure whether a piece of hardware is bad, you can try installing the device in another system, assuming your job description allows for such luxuries, or you can just guess.

IRQ Steering

As you've learned, PCI and AGP devices don't need IRQs. Instead, they use IRQ channels (really just advanced, shareable IRQs) that eliminate the entire issue of IRQ conflicts in these devices. ISA devices still need IRQs, however. How can the PC control interrupts if the PCI devices ignore the ISA IRQ controller? The most modern Pentium 4 still has only one INT wire. What keeps the ISA interrupt controller from trying to interrupt the CPU when a PCI device is already sending an interrupt?

Microsoft and Intel worked together to come up with a clever little function called *IRQ steering*. The basic idea of IRQ steering is based on the premise, "Who cares what IRQ we give the IRQ controller, just as long as we give it one!" With IRQ steering, PCI devices share one or more IRQs, depending on the chipset and on the function of the PCI device. When any PCI device fires an interrupt channel, the same IRQ gets sent to the ISA IRQ controller.

Windows Memory

Many people think that learning how to configure legacy devices manually may seem like a waste of time in our PnP world. Not so! Even though PnP makes device installation much easier, it comes with a price. The automation of PnP hides the reality of system resources. The gritty details of IRQs, I/O addresses, and DMA channels disappear from the normal PC support person's view. So when things go wrong (and they do), most PC techs lack the detailed skills necessary to get out of trouble. Hardly a waste of time!

A good tech needs to understand resources—not so much because you'll use that knowledge every day (thankfully, you won't), but more for those rare times when the beauty of PnP fails and you're faced with the daunting task of manual system resource configuration.

Earlier chapters already covered three system resources: I/O addresses, IRQs, and DMA; yet one more critical system resource exists: memory. Devices that need memory use a range of memory addresses. These addresses are displayed using the format XXXXXXXX-YYYYYYYY. Figure 18-26 shows the resource usage for a typical PCI video card.

Note setting D8000000-D9FFFFFF. This denotes a memory address range used by the video card. See the IRQ and I/O addresses? From the standpoint of Windows, a memory address is just another resource. If I scroll up on the same screen, you see that this device uses multiple memory addresses, as shown in Figure 18-27—a perfectly normal situation, just as some devices use multiple I/O addresses, IRQs, or DMAs.

Legacy Devices in a Plug and Play World

Installing legacy devices—those made before the advent of PnP—required techs to perform a number of careful steps to avoid resource conflicts.

1. You kept a paper inventory of used resources, in particular IRQs, because compared with DMA or I/O addresses, relatively few IRQs were available on a typical system.

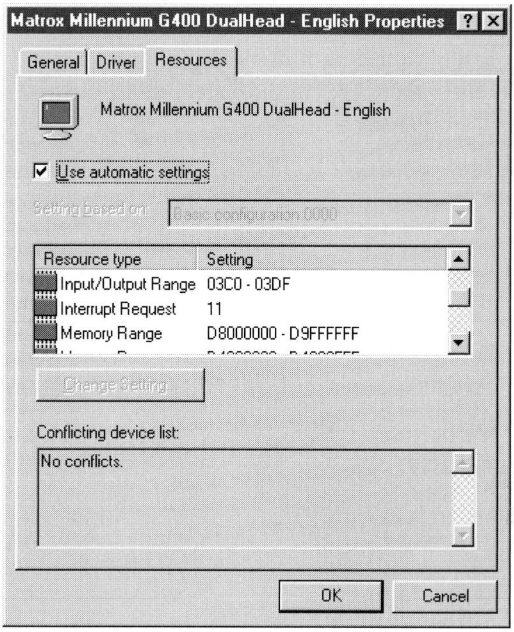

FIGURE 18.26 Typical video card resources

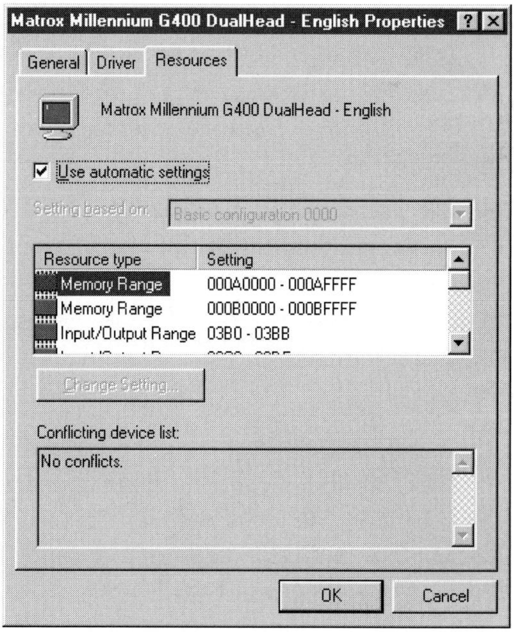

FIGURE 18.27 Multiple memory addresses

2. Lacking a precise inventory, you ran system information tools that tried to discover all the devices on the system. These DOS-based tools varied considerably in accuracy, but the better ones could find most devices.

3. You then configured the device to use available system resources. This required setting jumpers or switches on the device, or in the case of later legacy devices, running a special configuration program to set the resources.

4. You then installed the device and started the system. In the DOS and Windows 3.*x* days, the OS did not handle resource configuration. Instead, the device drivers we installed into CONFIG.SYS or SYSTEM.INI required special resource settings so that the driver knew which resources to call on to locate the device.

5. You then installed the device's application and tested. If the system experienced lockups, you assumed (usually correctly) that you had inadvertently created an IRQ or DMA conflict. If the device did not respond, you assumed there must be an I/O address or memory address conflict.

Installing a legacy device in a PnP environment creates a unique challenge. PnP does not eliminate the need to assess open resources, configure the device, or configure the device driver, although the Device Manager does make the task of determining available resources trivial. You must create an environment that enables PnP devices to avoid the fixed resources of the legacy device, and then set the resources and install and configure the driver for the legacy device.

Preparing to Install a Legacy Device

Long before you grab a screwdriver to install a legacy device, you need to answer some critical questions:

- What resources are available on the system?
- What resources can the legacy device use?
- Do you have driver support for this device?

Let's say you have a legacy sound card that must have I/O addresses 0220–022F, IRQ5 or 9, and DMA channel 1. The sound card has no jumpers and instead uses a special DOS program called UTILITY.EXE to set its resources (Figure 18-28). Before installing the card, you need to answer all three questions.

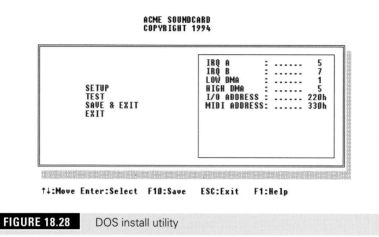

FIGURE 18.28   DOS install utility

Determining Available Resources

The first step is by far the easiest: Device Manager will display all available resources. In Windows 9*x*/Me, double-click the Computer icon at the top of the
Device Manager tree to display all resources in use by devices. This special
screen enables you to sort by any of the four resource types, making open resources obvious. Figure 18-29 shows the resources sorted by IRQ; the menu has
been scrolled past some of the lower IRQs to reveal more available IRQs—you
can see that IRQs 5 and 11 are open for use.

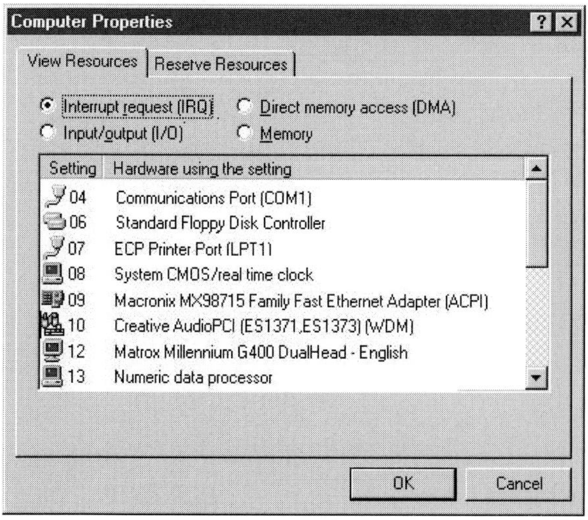

FIGURE 18.29   Resources sorted by IRQ

Reserving Resources

The makers of the legacy device and ISA PnP devices provide only so many resource options. IRQs are the serious problem in this regard, because (unlike with the other resources) there aren't many available. Referring to the preceding figure, what happens when some old sound card cannot use IRQ5 or 11? In that case, you have to kick a PnP device off an IRQ that the sound card will use and onto some other resource. You can reserve a particular IRQ for a legacy device in two places: the CMOS and the Reserve Resources tab in the Computer properties.

Reserving in Device Manager

Select the Reserve Resources tab in the Computer Properties dialog box (Figure 18-30) to tell Windows PnP to stay away from a particular resource(s). Your other option is to reboot and enter CMOS setup; you want the PnP/PCI option menu, if there is one. Figure 18-31 shows a typical Award BIOS PnP/PCI Configuration screen; however, the PnP options available in CMOS can vary widely from system to system. Every CMOS *will* have at least one of the three main PnP settings: PNP OS Installed, Reset Configuration Data, and Resources Controlled By.

PNP OS Installed

A PnP BIOS normally tries to initiate all PnP devices, including ISA PnP cards. If you set the PNP OS Installed option to Yes, the PnP BIOS initializes only ISA PnP devices required for boot, such as an ISA video card. Make sure to set this

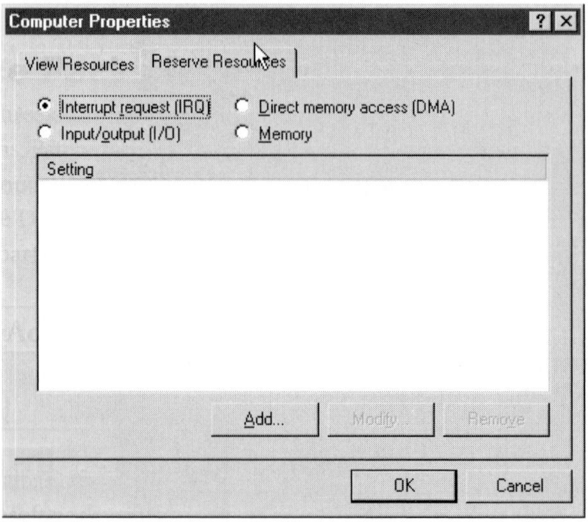

FIGURE 18.30   Reserve Resources tab in Computer Properties dialog box

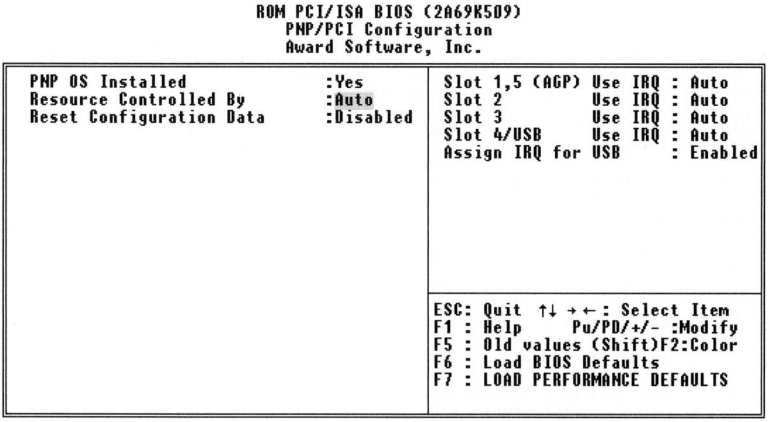

```
              ROM PCI/ISA BIOS (2A69K5D9)
                  PNP/PCI Configuration
                  Award Software, Inc.
┌─────────────────────────────────────────────────────────────────────┐
│ PNP OS Installed          :Yes      Slot 1,5 (AGP) Use IRQ : Auto     │
│ Resource Controlled By    :Auto     Slot 2         Use IRQ : Auto     │
│ Reset Configuration Data  :Disabled Slot 3         Use IRQ : Auto     │
│                                     Slot 4/USB     Use IRQ : Auto     │
│                                     Assign IRQ for USB    : Enabled   │
│                                                                       │
│                                                                       │
│                                                                       │
│                                                                       │
│                                     ESC: Quit  ↑↓ → ← : Select Item   │
│                                     F1 : Help     Pu/PD/+/- :Modify   │
│                                     F5 : Old values (Shift)F2:Color   │
│                                     F6 : Load BIOS Defaults           │
│                                     F7 : LOAD PERFORMANCE DEFAULTS    │
└─────────────────────────────────────────────────────────────────────┘
```

FIGURE 18.31   Award BIOS PnP/PCI Configuration screen

option to Yes. Some newer systems that use the *Advanced Configuration and Power Interface (ACPI)* require you to change this setting to "off."

Reset Configuration Data

This option makes the PnP reassign all resources for all devices. Set this option to Enabled after you install any ISA device, especially a legacy ISA device, to make the PnP avoid that device's resources. This option will always set itself back to Disabled at the next reboot.

Resources Controlled By

This is the traditional place to reserve IRQs and, in some systems, DMA channels for legacy ISA devices. Set this option to manual (Figure 18-32). Officially, you don't have to deal with this. If you just set it to Auto, the reserve settings in Windows will do all the reserving you need. I occasionally run across some systems where you reserve IRQs here, however, even though you have reserved the option in Device Manager. Many CMOS setup utilities have dropped this option and just count on you to handle reserving resources in Device Manager.

While you're still in CMOS, locate the Integrated Peripherals screen and turn off any unused serial ports, parallel ports, or USB ports, to open up those IRQs (Figure 18-33). You can free up a number of otherwise unavailable IRQs this way. Just remember to turn them back on if you decide to use them later!

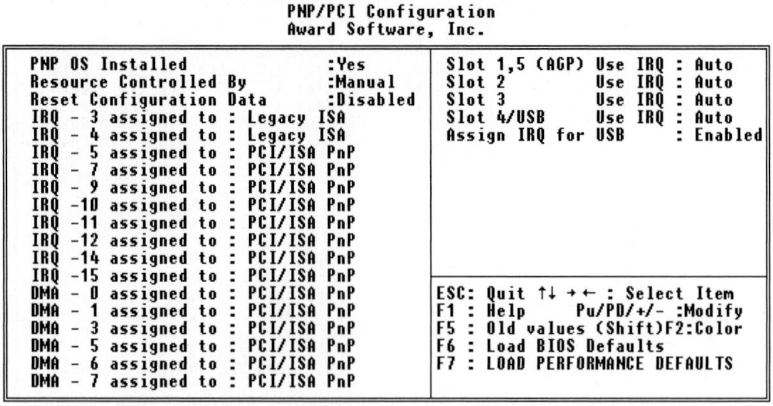

```
                        PNP/PCI Configuration
                        Award Software, Inc.

PNP OS Installed            :Yes      Slot 1,5 (AGP) Use IRQ : Auto
Resource Controlled By      :Manual   Slot 2         Use IRQ : Auto
Reset Configuration Data    :Disabled Slot 3         Use IRQ : Auto
IRQ - 3 assigned to : Legacy ISA      Slot 4/USB     Use IRQ : Auto
IRQ - 4 assigned to : Legacy ISA      Assign IRQ for USB     : Enabled
IRQ - 5 assigned to : PCI/ISA PnP
IRQ - 7 assigned to : PCI/ISA PnP
IRQ - 9 assigned to : PCI/ISA PnP
IRQ -10 assigned to : PCI/ISA PnP
IRQ -11 assigned to : PCI/ISA PnP
IRQ -12 assigned to : PCI/ISA PnP
IRQ -14 assigned to : PCI/ISA PnP
IRQ -15 assigned to : PCI/ISA PnP
DMA - 0 assigned to : PCI/ISA PnP     ESC: Quit  ↑↓ → ← : Select Item
DMA - 1 assigned to : PCI/ISA PnP     F1 : Help       Pu/PD/+/- :Modify
DMA - 3 assigned to : PCI/ISA PnP     F5 : Old values (Shift)F2:Color
DMA - 5 assigned to : PCI/ISA PnP     F6 : Load BIOS Defaults
DMA - 6 assigned to : PCI/ISA PnP     F7 : LOAD PERFORMANCE DEFAULTS
DMA - 7 assigned to : PCI/ISA PnP
```

FIGURE 18.32   Resources Controlled By set to Manual in CMOS

Device Manager

After reserving resources in CMOS (or just making sure that PNP OS Installed is set to Yes and Resources Controlled By is set to Auto), you must return to the Reserve Resources tab under Computer Properties in Device Manager to reserve the resources (Figure 18-34). Although Reserve Resources enables us to reserve any resource, in my many years of using Windows 9*x*/Me, I've only reserved IRQs.

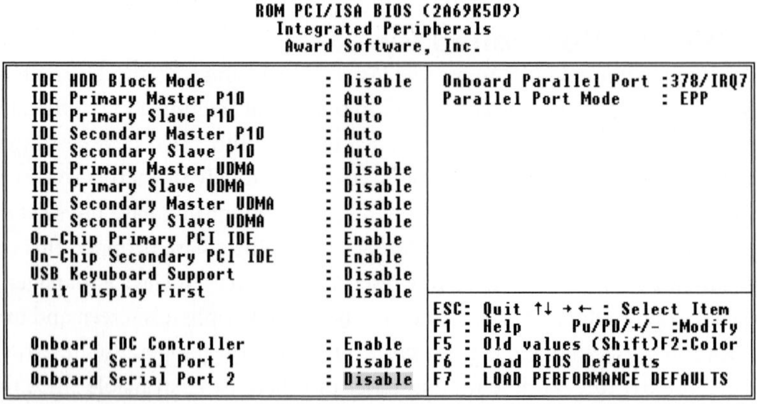

```
                    ROM PCI/ISA BIOS (2A69K509)
                      Integrated Peripherals
                      Award Software, Inc.

IDE HDD Block Mode        : Disable   Onboard Parallel Port :378/IRQ7
IDE Primary Master P10    : Auto      Parallel Port Mode    : EPP
IDE Primary Slave P10     : Auto
IDE Secondary Master P10  : Auto
IDE Secondary Slave P10   : Auto
IDE Primary Master UDMA   : Disable
IDE Primary Slave UDMA    : Disable
IDE Secondary Master UDMA : Disable
IDE Secondary Slave UDMA  : Disable
On-Chip Primary PCI IDE   : Enable
On-Chip Secondary PCI IDE : Enable
USB Keyboard Support      : Disable
Init Display First        : Disable
                                      ESC: Quit  ↑↓ → ← : Select Item
                                      F1 : Help       Pu/PD/+/- :Modify
Onboard FDC Controller    : Enable    F5 : Old values (Shift)F2:Color
Onboard Serial Port 1     : Disable   F6 : Load BIOS Defaults
Onboard Serial Port 2     : Disable   F7 : LOAD PERFORMANCE DEFAULTS
```

FIGURE 18.33   CMOS Integrated Peripherals screen

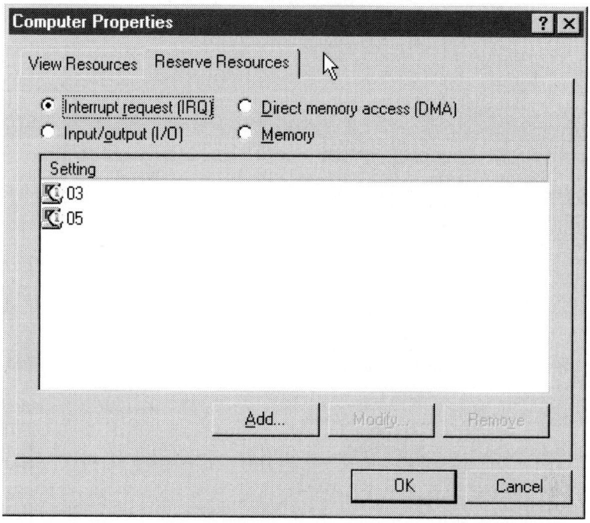

FIGURE 18.34   Reserve Resources tab showing reserved IRQs

Installing the Legacy Device

Windows comes with a powerful search function that finds most legacy devices. This confuses many techs into thinking their legacy card is PnP. Don't be fooled—it's just a neat aspect of Windows. In most cases, Windows will discover your card and will either install drivers if it recognizes the device or, in most cases, prompt you for a driver. If Windows prompts for a driver, you must hope that the disk holding the UTILITY program also contains the proper drivers for your version of Windows. Click the Have Disk button, and let Windows install the drivers. After the installation finishes, make a point to go to the Device Manager to verify that the device works properly. All of the problems discussed earlier may come into play, but as you may recall, we saved one problem for this section: resource conflicts.

Resource Conflicts

The only pleasant aspect of resource conflicts is the way Windows reports them—very clearly. If the newly installed device shows the infamous black exclamation point or red "X" error in its properties, a quick check of the device's properties will confirm the resource conflict diagnosis (Figure 18-35). Note that this error shows both the conflict text warning and the device with which the legacy device conflicts. If you failed to set the resources on the card, start over.

Communications Port Properties ? X

General | Driver | Resources |

Communications Port

Device type: Ports (COM & LPT)
Manufacturer: (Standard port types)
Hardware version: Not available

┌─Device status────────────────────────────────────┐
│ This device cannot find any free Interrupt Request (IRQ) │
│ resources to use (Code 12.)   │
│   │
│ If you want to use this device, you must disable another │
│ device that is using the resources this device needs. To │
│ do this, click Hardware Troubleshooter and follow the │
│ instructions in the wizard.   │
│   │
│   [Hardware Troubleshooter] │
└───┘

┌─Device usage─────────────────────────────────────┐
│ □ Disable in this hardware profile   │
└───┘

[OK]   [Cancel]

FIGURE 18.35   Device properties dialog box showing resource conflict error

But if you know the resources on the legacy device, you can manually configure them from the Resources tab in the device's properties (Figure 18-36).

The Resources tab differs wildly between different versions of Windows and various pieces of hardware, but almost all of its forms enable you to configure a device manually. To configure the device displayed in Figure 18-36, for example, you must click the Set Configuration Manually button and then on the subsequent dialog box, uncheck the Use Automatic Settings check box to activate the Setting Based On pull-down menu. Click the pull-down menu to see your options (Figure 18-37).

┌────────────────────┐
│ **Travel Advisory** │
└────────────────────┘
Always leave Use Automatic Settings check box checked—thus leaving the PnP manager in charge of resource allocation—unless you need to repair a resource conflict.

The Basic configurations in the pull-down menu are simply preset resource combinations used to set the device. If by some lucky chance one of these fits your resource needs, you may use it, but most of the time, you'll just scroll down and select the final Basic configuration option, which enables you to change

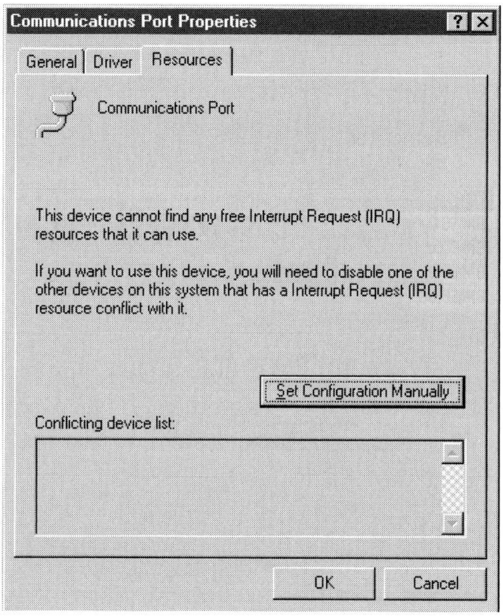

FIGURE 18.36 Resources tab of device properties

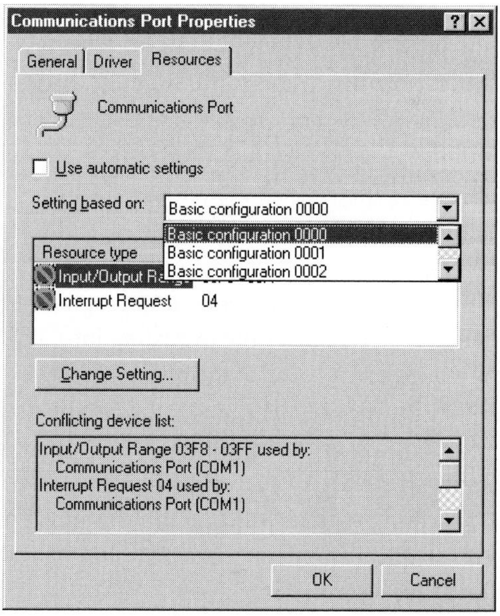

FIGURE 18.37 Resource settings pull-down menu

individual resource settings. Windows doesn't like it when you set resources manually; it throws up a big "Are you sure?" screen when you finish. Just click OK and restart the system. The device now uses the manually configured resource.

Objective 18.03 Troubleshooting Windows 9x/Me

This section focuses on some of the more common problems that seem to arise magically "out of nowhere" on a system. All these problems share one thing in common: fixing them usually requires you to restore a previously working system. Let's look at the fix first and then address the common problems.

Backups

Simply put, to make a backup of a file means to take a copy of the file and place it somewhere else so that it can be retrieved in the event of a problem with the original. To me, there are four different groups of files it may be advisable to back up (some of these overlap):

- Personal data files (usually all the stuff in My Documents)
- Personal data used by applications (for example, address book entries, favorites, or data files used by accounting programs like Quicken and Peachtree)
- Current system state files—the Registry
- The complete contents of the hard drive

Every version of Windows comes with a Backup program, and although they vary in quality, they can all do any of the preceding jobs. In a perfect backup world, users would make backups of all of their personal files every day, and they would use the export features of their contact software, account programs, e-mail, and web browsers to make daily backups of that data, too. But that's not going to happen except in the best of circumstances. Instead, Windows provides us with the handy Backup program which, when combined with a good tape backup system, will save you from data disasters and application installation nightmares time and time again (Figure 18-38).

You should choose a tape backup that can hold all your data—the popular DAT format disks are inexpensive and reliable. Since backups take a lot of time, you should schedule them to run at night. A good backup program that enables you to perform different types of backups can speed up the backup process.

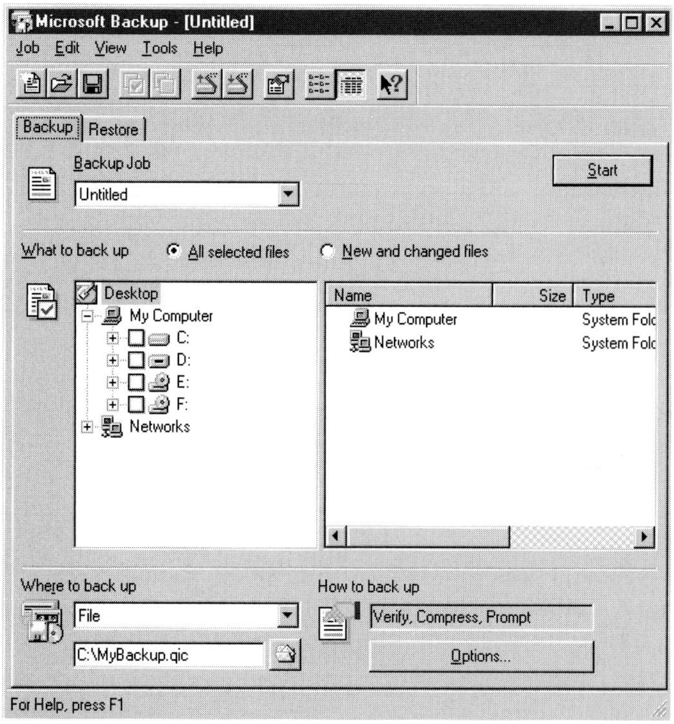

FIGURE 18.38   Microsoft Backup program

Remember the archive attribute? Backup programs use the archive bit to determine if a file has been changed since the last time it was backed up. Every time a file is modified, Windows turns on the archive bit. Backup programs use this to avoid backing up a file that's already been backed up and hasn't changed, reducing backup time.

Backups divide into four types: copy, full, incremental, and differential.

- **Copy**   Copies selected files and folders to the backup device *without* turning off the archive bit
- **Full**   Backs up *every* file and folder and turns off the archive bit
- **Incremental**   Backs up *only* files and folders with the archive bit turned on, and turns off the archive bit
- **Differential**   Backs up *only* files and folders with the archive bit turned on, but does *not* turn off the archive bit

Whoa! Copy and full make sense, but what's the deal with incremental and differential? Most businesses do a full backup about once a week and partial backups during the week. Suppose your backup program is set up to do a full backup automatically every Monday night after you close for the day, and a *differential* backup on the other weeknights. Here's what will happen:

- Monday night—Full backup
- Tuesday night—Back up of *all* files changed since last *full* backup (Monday)
- Wednesday night—Back up of all files changed since last full backup
- Thursday night—Back up of all files changed since last full backup
- Friday night—Back up of all files changed since last full backup

A differential backup requires only two tapes: one for the full backup on Monday and another tape for all the other daily backups. Each differential backup will take longer than the previous one, because it backs up every file changed since the full backup on Monday night keeps getting backed up, and each day that's more files.

An incremental backup, in contrast, backs up only the files changed *since the last backup,* whether full or partial. Here's the same five-day setup with an incremental backup:

- Monday night—Full backup
- Tuesday night—Back up of all files changed since Monday
- Wednesday night—Back up of all files changed since Tuesday
- Thursday night—Back up of all files changed since Wednesday
- Friday night—Back up of all files changed since Thursday

In this case, you need a new tape for each night because each backup stores only that day's changes. This means fewer files backed up each time, making for faster nightly backups, but if you need to restore files from backup, you have more tapes to search.

System Restore

When something does go wrong, the System Restore utility in Windows Me enables you to return your computer's system settings to a recent working configuration without affecting your personal files or e-mail. Windows Me automatically creates *restore points* each day, as well as any time you install an application, update a driver, or add a piece of hardware. You also have the option to create your own restore points whenever you want, and give them unique names that are meaningful to you. You might decide to create a restore point before tweaking a bunch of settings in the Control Panel, for example, and name the restore point *Tweak system settings.* Or, you could name it something a bit more creative, like *I hope I don't regret what I'm about to do!* All that matters is that you'll be able to remember later—while you're in a slightly panicked state—what was going on with your system when you created that restore point. If something does go wrong, you can run the System Restore Wizard, which presents you with a calendar listing of available restore points. Let's look at the process.

Creating a Restore Point

To create a restore point, select Start | Programs | Accessories | System Restore to open the System Restore utility (Figure 18-39). At the welcome screen, you choose from the radio buttons on the right side of the screen, in this case clicking the one marked Create A Restore Point. Then click Next. The next screen gives you a chance to write a description of the restore point (Figure 18-40). Don't worry about filling in the date and time, as System Restore will do it for you in a moment. Click Next to get to a screen where you can confirm the new restore point. This screen shows you the date, time, and description. Click OK and you're done!

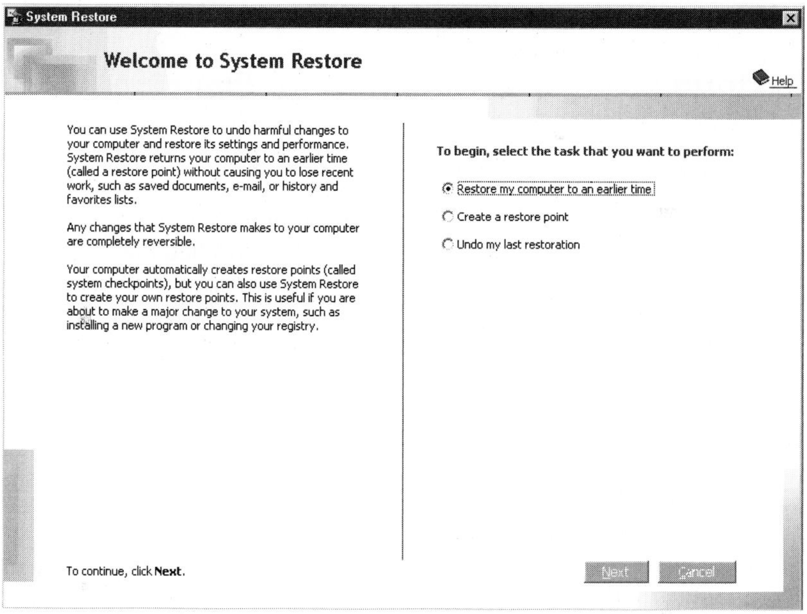

System Restore

Welcome to System Restore

Help

You can use System Restore to undo harmful changes to your computer and restore its settings and performance. System Restore returns your computer to an earlier time (called a restore point) without causing you to lose recent work, such as saved documents, e-mail, or history and favorites lists.

Any changes that System Restore makes to your computer are completely reversible.

Your computer automatically creates restore points (called system checkpoints), but you can also use System Restore to create your own restore points. This is useful if you are about to make a major change to your system, such as installing a new program or changing your registry.

To begin, select the task that you want to perform:

○ Restore my computer to an earlier time

○ Create a restore point

○ Undo my last restoration

To continue, click **Next**.

Next   Cancel

FIGURE 18.39   Welcome to System Restore

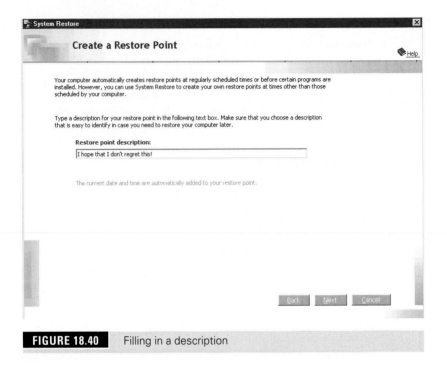

FIGURE 18.40　Filling in a description

Restoring from a System Restore Point

To use a system restore point, return to the System Restore utility, and this time select Restore My Computer To An Earlier Time. When you click the Next button, the Select A Restore Point screen displays a calendar and a listing of the most recent restore points (Figure 18-41). Using your knowledge of when your system started having problems, select a restore point and follow the prompts to complete the restore operation. System Restore is pretty powerful. Even if you crash hard and can only boot to Safe Mode, you can still run the System Restore utility to recover your system. It sure beats the alternative!

ConfigSafe

Well, that's just wonderful—*if* you have Windows Me. But what if you have Windows 98? Are you just out of luck? Don't despair—it wasn't your last hope, there is another! Solution, that is. There are a number of third-party tools available that can do for Windows 98 what System Restore does for Windows Me. One you'll find installed on many Windows 98 systems is called ConfigSafe. Let's take a quick look at it in action.

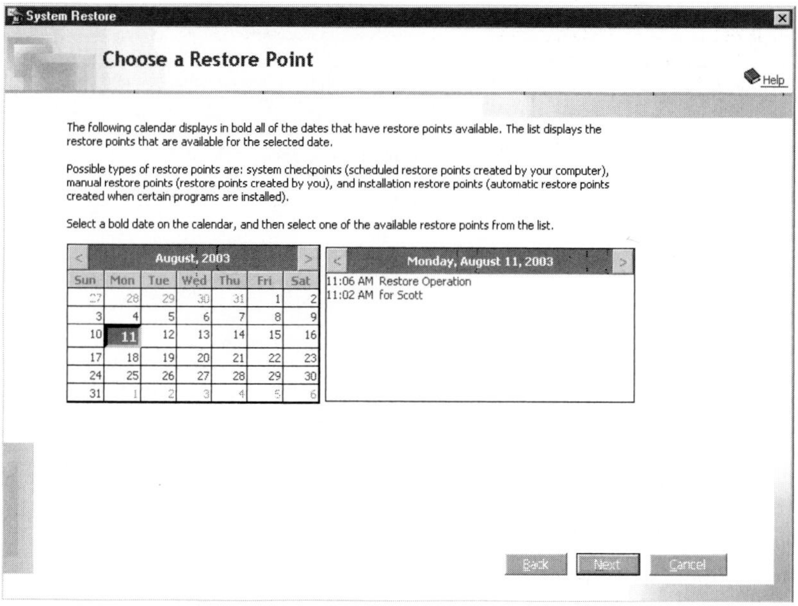

System Restore

Choose a Restore Point

Help

The following calendar displays in bold all of the dates that have restore points available. The list displays the restore points that are available for the selected date.

Possible types of restore points are: system checkpoints (scheduled restore points created by your computer), manual restore points (restore points created by you), and installation restore points (automatic restore points created when certain programs are installed).

Select a bold date on the calendar, and then select one of the available restore points from the list.

<	August, 2003					>
Sun	Mon	Tue	Wed	Thu	Fri	Sat
27	28	29	30	31	1	2
3	4	5	6	7	8	9
10	**11**	12	13	14	15	16
17	18	19	20	21	22	23
24	25	26	27	28	29	30
31	1	2	3	4	5	6

<	Monday, August 11, 2003	>
11:06 AM Restore Operation		
11:02 AM for Scott		

Back   Next   Cancel

FIGURE 18.41   Selecting a restore point to load

The opening screen (Figure 18-42) actually includes explanations of all its functions. ConfigSafe can take a "snapshot" of your system, like the System Restore utility, and then restore your system from any snapshot you've previously made. Its Advanced options enable you to see the details of any changes to your key system files in between any set of snapshots, and generate reports on any aspect of what the program has done (Figure 18-43). ConfigSafe also supports ongoing maintenance activities, allowing you to schedule snapshots at daily, weekly, or monthly intervals, or even at each startup (Figure 18-44). The ConfigSafe Install Guard feature will monitor changes to your system to help you keep your snapshot information up-to-date, either automatically or after prompting you. Not all Windows 9*x* systems will have this software, although many will.

Travel Assistance

If you (or a user you support) wants to add ConfigSafe to a system, you can buy it online from the manufacturer, imagineLAN, Inc. at http://www.imaginelan.com/configsafe/.

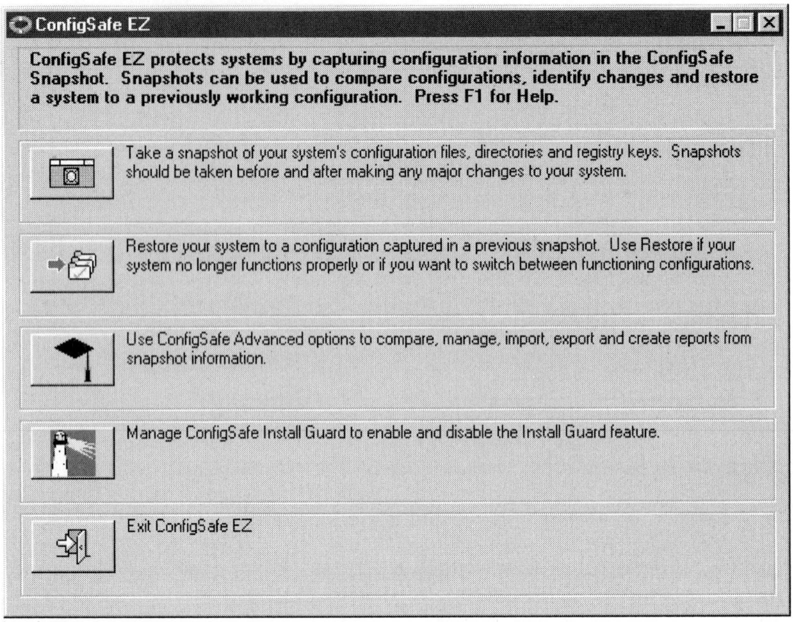

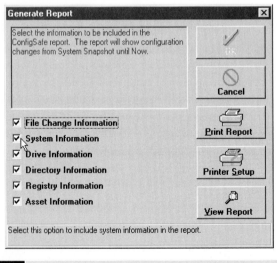

FIGURE 18.42 ConfigSafe opening screen

FIGURE 18.43 Generate reports in ConfigSafe

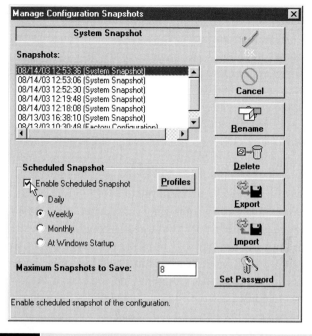

FIGURE 18.44   Schedule ConfigSafe snapshots

Recovery CDs

Many preassembled PCs from the larger computer makers like Hewlett/Packard, Sony, IBM, Gateway, and Dell ship with a CD-ROM innocuously labeled *Recovery Disc.* These CD-ROMs contain a snapshot of the system *as it was when delivered.* Every program and file is stored on the disc, so you can restore your system to its original specifications. These CD-ROMs usually come with their own special backup tool. As with any recovery tool, you'll need a good backup of your files. When the system crashes, you first rebuild the system using the restore CD-ROM; then you restore the backup, so that with luck, your system ends up the way it was at your last backup.

The problem with the Recovery CDs is that most users never make a backup of their system. If you go in to service a client's PC that's crashed hard and, upon discovering the Recovery CD, proceed to restore the client's system to its original state, *you will erase all the client's data off that PC!* Such an action is, in technical terms, a Bad Thing. If your client does not have a good backup of his or her personal data files, stay away from any Recovery CD and instead work on getting the PC up and running with more conventional tools.

Antivirus Protection

The words "I think your machine has a virus" can send shudders down the back of even the most competent PC technician. The thought of megabytes of critical data being wiped away by the work of some evil programmer is at best annoying and, at worst, a serious financial disaster. So, where do viruses come from? Just like many human viruses, they live in host bodies, in this case computers. Your computer can catch one only if it interacts with other computers, or with programs or data from an infected computer. The problem is that these days almost everyone's computer (aside from folks like the CIA) is connected to the Internet, and thereby to many, many other computers. Also, many viruses are spread through the sharing of programs or information on floppy disks or CD-ROMs.

How do you know if you've caught a virus? You feel sluggish, start sneezing and coughing, want to sleep—or in this case, the computer equivalents of those symptoms: Your computer may seem unusually sluggish, generate strange error messages or other odd emissions, or possibly even lock up and refuse to function entirely. All these are classic symptoms, but you cannot assume your computer is virus-free just because it seems fine. Some viruses do their work in secret, as you will discover here.

Virus Types

The secret to avoiding viruses is to understand how a virus works. A *virus* is a program that has two functions: *proliferate* (make more copies of itself) and *activate* (at some signal, count, date, and so on, do something—usually something bad like delete the boot sector). A virus does not have to do damage to be a virus. Some of the first viruses written were harmless and downright amusing. Without going into too much gritty detail, basically only four types of viruses exist: boot sector, executable, macro, and Trojan. A fifth type also exists that is really a combination of two others: bimodal/bipartite.

Boot Sector   Boot sector viruses change the code in the *master boot record (MBR)* of the hard drive. Once the machine is booted, the virus resides in memory, attempting to infect the MBRs of other drives such as floppy drives, connected network machines, or removable media, and creating whatever havoc its creator designed it to do. A popular method for removing a boot sector virus is to use the FDISK /MBR command to rewrite the master boot record. Before you do this, make sure the system isn't one of those that use a special disk overlay program that resides in the boot sector.

Executable   Executable viruses reside in executable files. They are literally extensions of executables and are unable to exist by themselves. Once the infected executable file is run, the virus loads into memory, adding copies of itself to other EXEs that are subsequently run, and again doing whatever evil that it was designed to do.

Macro   Macro viruses are specially written application macros. Although they are not truly programs, they perform the same functions as regular viruses. Macro viruses autostart when you run the particular application they're written to exploit, and will then attempt to make more copies of themselves. Some will even try to find other copies of the same application on a network that they can exploit.

Trojan   Trojans are true, freestanding programs that do something other than what the person who runs the program thinks they will do. An example of a Trojan would be a program that a person thinks is a game but that is actually a CMOS eraser. Some Trojans are quite sophisticated—for example, the game Trojan might run an actual functioning game, but when you quit, the secret part would take over and do bad things to your system.

Worm   A *worm* is a very special form of virus. Unlike all of the other viruses described, a worm does not infect other files on the computer. Instead, a worm replicates by making copies of itself on other systems on a network by taking advantage of security weaknesses in networking protocols.

Bimodal/Bipartite   A bimodal or bipartite virus uses both boot-sector and executable functions.

Antivirus Tools

The only way to protect your PC permanently from getting a virus is to disconnect from the Internet and never permit any potentially infected software to touch your precious computer. Because neither scenario is likely these days, you need to use a specialized antivirus program to help stave off the inevitable virus assaults.

An antivirus program protects your PC in two ways. It can be both sword and shield, working in an active "seek and destroy" mode and in a passive "sentry" mode. When ordered to seek and destroy, the program will scan the computer's boot sector and files for viruses, and if it finds any, presents you with the available options for removing or disabling them. Antivirus programs can also operate as virus shields that passively monitor your computer's activity, checking for viruses only when certain events occur, such as a program executing or a file being downloaded.

Antivirus programs use different techniques to combat different types of viruses. They detect boot sector viruses simply by comparing the drive's boot sector to a standard boot sector. This works because most boot sectors are basically the same. Some antivirus programs make a backup copy of the boot sector. If they detect a virus, the programs will use that backup copy to replace the infected boot sector. Executable viruses are a little more difficult to find because they can be on any file in the drive. To detect executable viruses, the antivirus program uses a library of *signatures*. A signature is a code pattern of a known virus. The antivirus program compares an executable file to its library of signatures. Instances have occurred where a perfectly clean program coincidentally held a virus signature. Usually, the antivirus program's creator will provide a patch to prevent further alarms. Antivirus programs detect macro viruses through the presence of virus signatures or of certain macro commands that indicate a known macro virus.

Now let's review a few terms that are often used when describing certain traits of viruses.

Polymorphics/Polymorphs   A *polymorph* virus attempts to change its signature to prevent detection by antivirus programs, usually by continually scrambling a bit of useless code. Fortunately, the scrambling code itself can be identified and used as the signature once the antivirus makers become aware of the virus. One technique that is sometimes used to combat unknown polymorphs is to have the antivirus program create a checksum on every file in the drive. A *checksum* in this context is a number generated by the software based on the contents of the file rather than the name, date, or size of that file. The algorithms for creating these checksums vary among different antivirus programs (they are also usually kept secret to help prevent virus makers from coming up with ways to beat them). Every time a program is run, the antivirus program calculates a new checksum and compares it with the earlier calculation. If the checksums are different, it is a sure sign of a virus.

Stealth   The term "stealth" is more of a concept than an actual virus function. Most stealth virus programs are boot sector viruses that use various methods to hide from antivirus software. One popular stealth virus will hook on to a somewhat unknown, but often used, software interrupt, running only when that interrupt runs. Others make copies of innocent-looking files.

Virus Prevention Tips

The secret to preventing damage from a virus attack is to keep from getting one in the first place. As discussed earlier, all good antivirus programs include a virus shield that will automatically scan floppies, downloads, and so on. Use it. It is also a good idea to scan a PC daily for possible virus attacks. Again, all antivirus programs include TSRs that will run every time the PC is booted. Last but not least, know where software has come from before you load it. Although the chance of commercial, shrink-wrapped software having a virus is virtually nil (a couple of well-publicized exceptions have occurred), that illegal copy of "Unreal Tournament" you borrowed from a local hacker should definitely be inspected with care.

Windows Boot Problems

Many Windows troubleshooting issues deal with boot problems. In most cases, these are fairly simple fixes. Here are a few of the classics.

No OS Found

This points to a corrupted or missing IO.SYS or MSDOS.SYS. Just pop in your startup disk and use the SYS program to put back the missing file. From the A: prompt, type the following command:

```
SYS C:
```

This automatically restores the IO.SYS, MSDOS.SYS, and COMMAND.COM files. If you edited the MSDOS.SYS file, you will have to restore any edits manually.

Bad or Missing COMMAND.COM

This problem is an easy one to fix. Just use your startup disk to copy the COMMAND.COM file back onto the C: drive.

Error in CONFIG.SYS (Line XX)

This one rarely happens unless you've been working in the CONFIG.SYS file or installing some older device that tossed something into CONFIG.SYS. Edit the CONFIG.SYS file and count the line numbers until you get to the one in question. Look for typos. Because most Windows systems pretty much ignore the CONFIG.SYS file anyway, just put a semicolon (;) at the very beginning of the line to comment it out. If everything runs fine for a few days, go back in and remove the line completely.

Device Referenced in Registry or SYSTEM.INI Not Found

This is exactly the same scenario as described before for CONFIG.SYS, except this usually shows the device name in question. Don't forget that reinstalling drivers here will often fix the problem.

HIMEM.SYS Not Loaded or MISSING or Corrupt HIMEM.SYS

Windows must load the HIMEM.SYS file at each boot. Because Windows does this automatically, this is rarely an issue. This error tends to result from a hard drive that needs some serious ScanDisking! As a quick fix, boot off the startup disk and add this line to the CONFIG.SYS file using EDIT:

```
DEVICE=C:\HIMEM.SYS
```

Then, copy the HIMEM.SYS file from the startup disk to the C: drive. Now boot normally and check that hard drive!

Won't Boot to GUI

Have you ever booted a copy of Windows just to get stuck at the pretty Windows startup screen? Failure to boot into the GUI can have many causes. Let's look at these in order of most to least common.

1. *The first thing to blame is a corrupted swap file.* Boot into Safe mode and disable virtual memory. Restart the system when prompted by Windows. If the swap file was the culprit, the system will boot normally, although it may run rather slowly. Turn the swap file back on and reboot again.

Travel Advisory

On systems with small amounts of physical RAM (32 MB or less), disabling the swap file might cause serious instability when you first boot. It will still solve the problem of a corrupted swap file. To open System Properties to turn virtual memory back on, however, you might have to boot into Safe mode.

---

2. *The next thing to try is the step-by-step boot option from the boot menu.* This will usually give you a good feel as to which of the following areas should be checked next.

3. *You may need to restore the previous Registry copy.* Use whatever tool you have to restore a known good copy of the Registry. If you don't have one, try replacing SYSTEM.DAT and USER.DAT with SYSTEM.DA0 and the USER.DA0. All of these files are hidden and read-only, so use the ATTRIB command from the startup disk to turn off the attributes. It would look something like this:

```
ATTRIB -r -s -h c:\WINDOWS\SYSTEM\*.dat
COPY c:\WINDOWS\SYSTEM\*.da0 C:\WINDOWS\SYSTEM\*.dat
```

If you have Windows 98, boot to the startup disk and run the Windows Registry Checker tool. From the A: prompt, type the following command:

```
C:\WINDOWS\COMMAND\SCANREG /fix
```

Try booting again. If the Registry was the problem, you should now boot normally.

4. *Resource conflicts can sometimes prevent the GUI from booting.* A quick boot to Safe mode and a check of the Device Manager should confirm this. Fix resource conflicts as described previously.

5. *A bad driver may cause problems.* For this, use the Automatic Skip Driver (ASD) tool in Safe mode. You can find it under the Tools menu in the System Information tool, or you can select Start | Run and type in **ASD**. The ASD looks over your log files and prevents any drivers that previously failed from loading at the next boot. If this works, check for a driver update or remove the offending device.

6. *Sometimes some of the core Windows files get corrupted.* If you have Windows 98/Me, you can run the System File Checker from a command prompt as follows:

```
SFC /SCANBOOT /QUIET
```

SFC doesn't show much on the screen, but it will restore any corrupted core file from its own backups automatically. You must reboot after running SFC so that Windows can reload the core files.

Lockups/Reboots

All system lockups fit into one of two groups. The first group is the lockups that take place immediately after you add a new program or device. These almost always point to resource conflicts or software version incompatibilities. Use the techniques described earlier to fix these problems. The second group is the "lockups from nowhere." These invariably point either to a virus attack or to a hardware problem, usually the power supply, RAM, or hard drive. Test/replace until the problem goes away. Spontaneous reboots always point to bad hardware or a virus. The power supply is the first item to check, followed closely by the CPU. Overheated CPUs love to reboot spontaneously. Make sure the fan works. Most CMOS setup utilities have a screen that enables you to set overheat alarms to monitor the CPU (Figure 18-45).

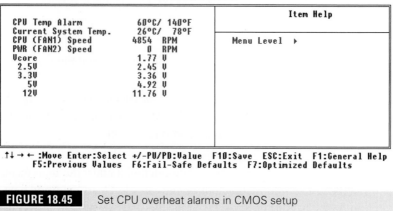

```
            CMOS Setup Utility - Copyright (C) 1984-1999 Award Software
                               PC Health Status
┌──────────────────────────────────────┬──────────────────────────────────────┐
│                                       │                       Item Help       │
│   CPU Temp Alarm        60°C/ 140°F    │                                       │
│   Current System Temp.  26°C/  78°F    │                                       │
│   CPU (FAN1) Speed      4854  RPM       │    Menu Level   ▶                    │
│   PWR (FAN2) Speed         0  RPM       │                                       │
│   Vcore                 1.77 V          │                                       │
│     2.5V                2.45 V          │                                       │
│     3.3V                3.36 V          │                                       │
│       5V                4.92 V          │                                       │
│      12V               11.76 V          │                                       │
│                                        │                                       │
│                                        │                                       │
│                                        │                                       │
└──────────────────────────────────────┴──────────────────────────────────────┘
   ↑↓ → ←  :Move Enter:Select +/-PU/PD:Value  F10:Save  ESC:Exit  F1:General Help
        F5:Previous Values  F6:Fail-Safe Defaults  F7:Optimized Defaults
```

FIGURE 18.45   Set CPU overheat alarms in CMOS setup

General Protection Faults

A General Protection Fault (GPF) occurs when one program tries to stomp on another program's memory area. Subtle incompatibilities make GPFs something we just have to live with in Windows. GPFs that always point to the same file as the culprit, however, require attention. If the system has not been changed, the named file may be corrupt. Try reloading the file from the installation CD-ROM. Use the EXTRACT command to locate the file on the CD-ROM, and copy it to the same location as the potentially bad one. Use the search function to locate the bad file.

Windows Protection Errors

Windows protection errors take place when a special type of driver file, called a virtual device driver (VxD), fails to load or unload. VxDs are used to support older Windows programs, and this error usually occurs when a program's device driver load instruction somehow ends up in both CONFIG.SYS and SYSTEM.INI or the Registry. Running SYSEDIT will show us any drivers in CONFIG.SYS. Put semicolons in front of DEVICE= lines until the problem goes away. If that doesn't fix it, check for resource conflicts in the Device Manager and then restore the Registry.

Fatal Exception Errors

Fatal exception errors are caused by software or hardware that sends a particular type of error that Windows is not designed to contain. If these arise from a new device or software, uninstall the offending beast and check the manufacturer's web site and the Microsoft Knowledge Base for known issues related to that software or device.

Dr. Watson Utility

In some cases, these problems simply defy the best of our repair attempts. At this point, you'll probably need to call tech support. But before you call, run the Dr. Watson utility and re-create the error. Dr. Watson generates a detailed report on the status of the system at the time of the error, and although the information in that report goes well beyond the knowledge of most techs, it provides critical insight to very high-level techs.

Shutdown Problems

Most shutdown problems are identical to startup issues—bad drivers, a corrupted Registry, faulty page files—but some shutdown problems are unique. Let's look at a few.

Disable Fast Shutdown (Windows 98 Only)

Windows 98 normally "turns off" every device driver at shutdown. You can choose not to turn off device drivers, however, by using a tool called Fast Shutdown. Fast Shutdown works well on most systems but gives others fits. To disable Fast Shutdown, open the System Configuration Utility, click the Advanced button on the General tab, and check the Disable Fast Save check box (third from the bottom).

Application Not Closing

Some applications refuse to close. Windows 98 does a good job of closing them anyway, but Windows 95 often needs you to close an application manually before it can shut down. Try to close the application normally, but if that fails, use the Task Manager to shut it down. If you click End Task and nothing happens, try again. I sometimes have to "End" Microsoft Word three or four times before it obeys.

Sound File

If the Windows Shutdown sound file corrupts, the system will not shut down. Use the Sound applet in the Control Panel to turn off the shutdown sound.

CHECKPOINT

✔**Objective 18.01: Maintaining and Optimizing Windows 9x/Me**   All versions of Windows 9x/Me require maintenance for optimal performance. Understand how to update Windows using Windows Updater, Service Packs, and patches. Know how to perform drive maintenance using ScanDisk, Disk Defragmenter, and Drive Cleanup. Be completely familiar with the Windows 9x/Me swap file, the System applet, and the different resource tracking tools.

✔**Objective 18.02: Device Installation in Windows 9x/Me**   Despite the advent of PnP, there are still occasions when techs must not only perform but also troubleshoot device installation. Know the procedures for installing PnP and legacy devices. Understand what the different Device Manager error symbols mean, and know the various possible causes—and fixes—for those errors. Understand IRQ steering and the resource allocation issues raised by legacy devices. Know how to prepare for, perform, and troubleshoot a legacy device installation.

✔**Objective 18.03: Troubleshooting Windows 9x/Me**   Often the fix for a problem in Windows 9x/Me involves restoring backed up software and/or data. Be familiar with the types of backups and how they differ. Understand what System Restore does, and how to use it. Be familiar with ConfigSafe and Recovery CDs. Know the different types of viruses and the terms for virus features, how antivirus programs work, and how to prevent infection. Know how and when to use MSCONFIG. Know how to troubleshoot boot problems, lockups, reboots, and shutdown problems. Be able to define and troubleshoot GPFs, Windows Protection Errors, and Fatal Exception Errors.

REVIEW QUESTIONS

1. Windows Me uses what symbol in Device Manager to indicate devices that do not have optimal drivers?

   A. A green X

   B. A yellow !

   C. A green ?

   D. A yellow *

2. The used hard drive you bought on eBay has a "PnP/jumperless" setting. What does this tell you?

   A. It's a PnP device.

   B. It's a legacy device.

   C. It won't work in Windows Me.

   D. It will work only in Windows 95.

3. What is the DOS name of the System Configuration Utility?

   A. MSCONFIG

   B. QFECHECK

   C. FDISK

   D. REGEDIT

4. What program do you run to set the resources for a newly installed legacy card?

   A. Device Manager

   B. SETRES.COM

   C. UTILITY.EXE

   D. INSTALL.INI

5. How do you access the System Restore utility?

   A. Type **SYSRES** at a command prompt.

   B. Select Start | Programs | System Tools | System Restore.

   C. Type **RESTORE /SYS** at a command prompt.

   D. Select Start | Programs | Accessories | System Restore.

6. What type of backup backs up only the files changed since the last backup?

   A. Differential

   B. Incremental

   C. Daily Copy

   D. Full

7. What program installed on many Windows 98 systems performs the functions of Windows Me's System Restore?

   A. ConfigSafe

   B. System Backup

   C. RollBack

   D. Install Guard

8. What command can you type at an A:\ prompt to automatically restore the IO.SYS, MSDOS.SYS, and COMMAND.COM files from the startup disk?

   A. RESTORE /SYS

   B. SYS C:

   C. DEVICE=C:\SYSTEM

   D. C:\WINDOWS\SYSTEM /RES

9. A _____ virus attempts to change its signature to prevent detection by antivirus programs.

   A. Stealth

   B. Bimodal

   C. Trojan

   D. Polymorph

10. Systems must have one of which two IRQs available for IRQ steering?

    A. IRQ1 or IRQ3

    B. IRQ2 or IRQ9

    C. IRQ5 or IRQ7

    D. IRQ 9 or IRQ11

REVIEW ANSWERS

1. **C**   Windows Me uses a green question mark in Device Manager to indicate devices that do not have optimal drivers.

2. **B**   If the used hard drive you bought on eBay has a "PnP/jumperless" setting, you know it's a legacy device.

3. **A**   If you type **MSCONFIG** into the Run Dialog Box, the System Configuration Utility will open.

4. **C**   You run the UTILITY.EXE program to set the resources for a newly-installed legacy card.

5. **D**   Select Start | Programs | Accessories | System Restore to open the System Restore utility.

6. **B**   An incremental backup backs up only the files changed since the last backup, whether full or partial.

7. **A**   ConfigSafe is the program installed on many Windows 98 systems that performs the functions of Windows Me's System Restore. Install Guard is part of ConfigSafe.

8. **B**   Type **SYS C:** at an A:\ prompt to automatically restore the IO.SYS, MSDOS.SYS, and COMMAND.COM files from the startup disk.

9. **D**   A polymorph virus attempts to change its signature to prevent detection by antivirus programs.

10. **D**   Systems must have IRQ9 or IRQ11 available for IRQ steering.

Maintaining, Optimizing, and Troubleshooting Windows NT/2000/XP

	NEWBIE	SOME EXPERIENCE	EXPERT
ETA	3 hours	2 hours	1 hour

Although Microsoft has made great strides in shipping products that are pretty close to optimized even out of the box, it's important for techs to know how to maintain the system to keep it in top condition, and to troubleshoot problems when they arise. This includes tasks such as

- Identifying the major operating system utilities, their purpose, location, and available options
- Identifying procedures necessary to optimize the operating system and major operating system subsystems
- Recognizing and interpreting the meaning of common error codes and startup messages from the boot sequence, and identify steps to correct the problems
- Recognizing common operational and usability problems and determining how to resolve them

In this chapter, we'll explore the tools for maintaining and optimizing Windows, learn how to maintain a healthy Windows 2000/XP system, and learn important troubleshooting procedures. Let's get started.

Objective 19.01 Tools for Maintaining and Optimizing Windows

For years, techs have accepted as their lot in life the curse of having to use dozens of different command line and GUI tools that simply did not behave in a consistent way. Microsoft addresses this issue in Windows 2000 and XP with the Microsoft Management Console (MMC). The MMC enables Microsoft, and third-party vendors, to create tools that present a consistent face while maintaining a high degree of flexibility.

Another tool that is built into Windows 2000/XP is the Task Manager. The Task Manager enables you to monitor currently running programs and processes, change their priority, and stop them if necessary. Let's look at these in more detail.

The Microsoft Management Console (MMC)

The MMC is simply a shell program that holds individual utilities called *snap-ins*. You can start the MMC by opening the Run option and typing in

MMC to get a blank MMC console. Blank MMC consoles aren't much to look at, as you can see in Figure 19-1.

The function of the MMC changes depending on what snap-in (or snap-ins) is loaded. Many of the tools in the Control Panel's Administrative Tools folder are simply preconfigured MMCs. Virtually every traditional Windows tool—and a lot of new ones—are now snap-ins. You can easily create custom MMCs with the snap-ins of your choice loaded. Let's look at how to do that by manually loading one of your most important tools, the Device Manager.

Device Manager

As you know, the Device Manager is one of the most used tools we have (oddly, not included in Windows NT). It's easy enough to get to it the traditional way—by opening the System Properties applet in Control Panel, clicking the Hardware tab, and then clicking the Device Manager button—but it makes more sense to "cut to the chase" and configure a custom MMC with the Device Manager.

Open up a blank MMC, then in Windows 2000, click Console; in Windows XP, click File. In either OS, select Add/Remove Snap-in, and then click the Add button to see a list of available snap-ins (Figure 19-2).

After you click Add, choose the computer the snap-in will manage. Select Local Computer to focus on the local system, or browse to always focus the tool on a different computer on your network, and click Finish. After this, close the Add Standalone Snap-in box. The Device Manager will be listed in the Standalone

FIGURE 19.1   Blank MMC

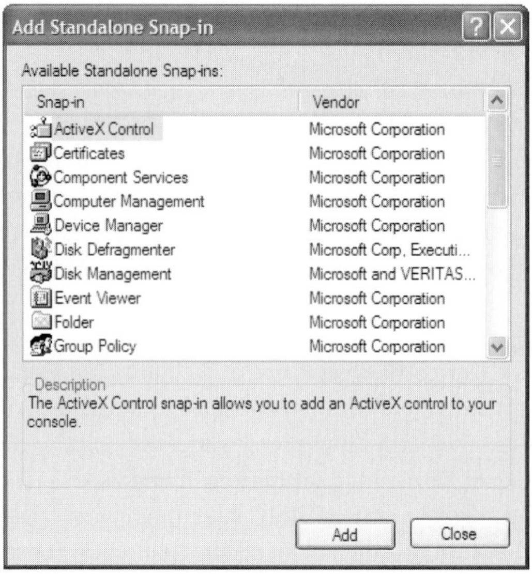

FIGURE 19.2   Available snap-ins

page of the Add/Remove Snap-in box. Click OK to close it, and then click Device
Manager under Console Root. The result should look like Figure 19-3.

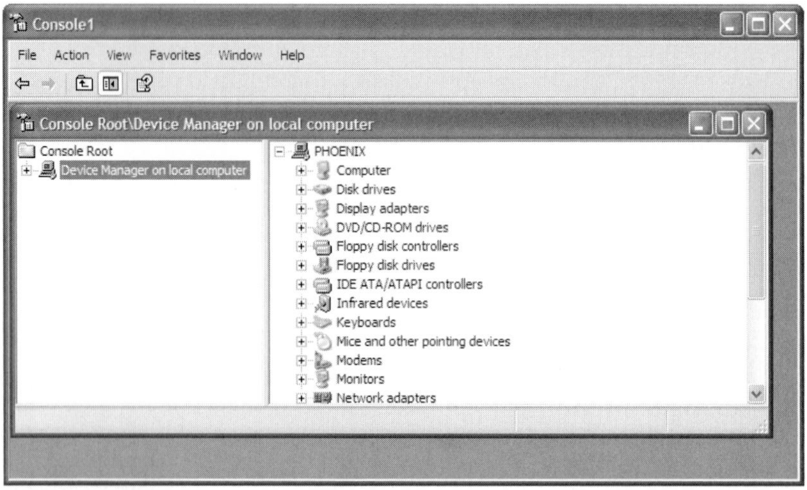

FIGURE 19.3   Device Manager as a snap-in

Once you've added the snap-ins you want, just save the console under any name you want (with the extension of .MSC). Now you're only a double-click away from the Device Manager!

Microsoft also knows that some folks like things the old way, so the company has created a bunch of premade, locked consoles for you and dropped them in the same places, or at least close to the same places, where you'd expect them to be (if you have previous experience with Windows 9x). You can open the System Information Utility in Windows 2000/XP, for example, by clicking Start | Programs | Accessories | System Tools | System Information. It's the good old System Information utility, but as you can see in Figure 19-4, it's an MMC snap-in.

The snap-in versions of the old classics all look a tad different, but they still do the same job; in fact, they usually do it better!

Event Viewer

Another important snap-in is Windows Event Viewer (available in Windows NT, Windows 2000, and Windows XP). Work with Event Viewer for a while and you'll see that monitoring various log files reveals things about the health of the operating system through the behavior (logged events) of its services and applications.

Event Viewer is usually started from Administrative Tools. In Windows 2000, open the Control Panel, double-click the Administrative Tools icon, and double-click the Event Viewer icon. In Windows XP, open the Control Panel, double-click

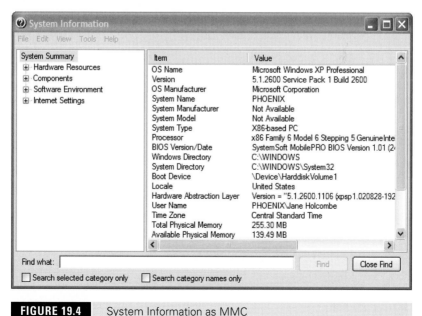

FIGURE 19.4   System Information as MMC

the Performance and Maintenance icon, then Administrative Tools, then Event Viewer. The Event Viewer will display events from three log files: Application, Security, and System. Figure 19-5 shows the contents of a System event log in Event Viewer.

Types of Events   Event Viewer displays five types of events. The System and Applications logs have Error, Warning, and Information events, while the Security log displays Success Audit and Failure Audit events. Figure 19-6 shows an Application log with three types of events displayed.

An Error event is bad news—something's broken or data has been lost. In the Application log, this can mean an entire application hung up or an operation failed. In the System log, this can mean that a service failed. A service is a special program that provides specific functionality to the OS. A warning is something that isn't critical but may mean there is trouble to come. For instance, if disk space is low, a Warning event is logged. An Information event is the only good news, because it means an application, driver, or service successfully completed an operation.

Travel Advisory

Real techs don't waste time slogging through the menus for tools they use frequently. A quicker way is to start up the console by typing its name in the Run dialog box. For example, start Event Viewer by selecting Start | Run and typing the filename of the console: EVENTVWR (the .MSC extension isn't necessary).

Event Viewer Settings   In Event Viewer, alternate-click System and select Properties. In Properties, look at the Log Size box, which defines the maximum

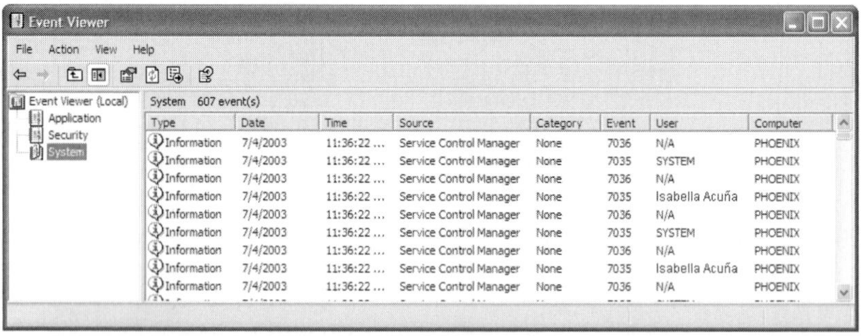

FIGURE 19.5   System event log in Event Viewer

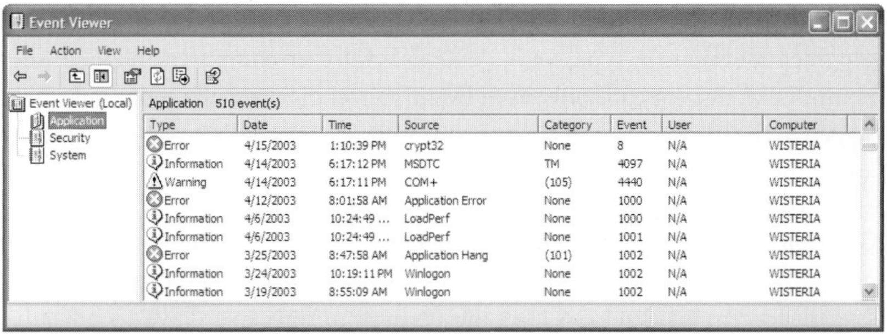

FIGURE 19.6   Application log showing three types of events

size a log file may grow to, and what action should be taken when the log file reaches the maximum. The defaults are 512 KB and Overwrite Events Older Than 7 Days. You can easily reconfigure these settings, but be aware that large log files take up a lot of space on the hard disk drive.

If scrolling through large log files makes you dizzy, you can use Filter settings to make the viewer show only specific selections. In Windows XP, simply select the Filter tab to see Figure 19-7.

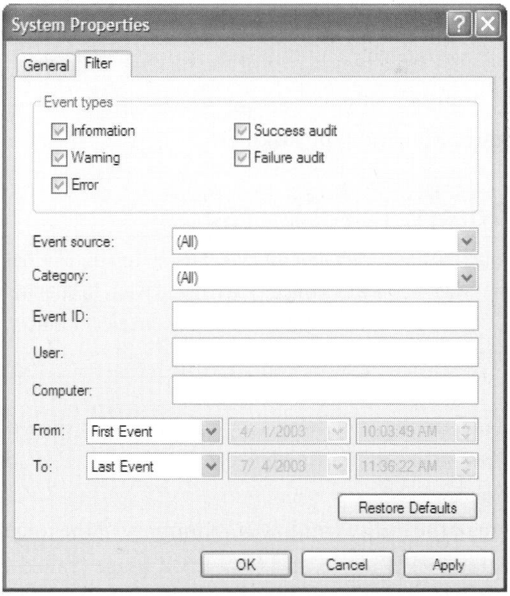

FIGURE 19.7   Event Viewer Filter settings

Change the filter settings so that when you are viewing a large log file, you can filter out events by type, source, category, ID, user, computer, and date. Keep in mind that this controls only what Event Viewer displays; all events will still be logged to the file, so you can change your filter settings without worrying about losing logged data.

Clearing, Archiving, and Opening a Log File   Clear the System Log by alternate-clicking System Log and selecting Clear All Events. You'll be prompted to save the System log. To do so, click the Yes button. You can archive a log file that you want to be able to view later by saving it with a unique filename. To open the file you just saved, click the Action menu, select Open Log File, select the file, then the log type (System, Application, or Security), and then click Open.

Task Manager

The Task Manager is another important utility in the tech's toolbox. Not an MMC snap-in, but a freestanding utility, the Task Manager enables you to monitor, in real time, your PC's currently running programs and processes and gauge overall system performance. There are several ways to look at the Task Manager. The following work on Windows NT, 2000, and XP:

- Press the CTRL-SHIFT-ESC key combination.
- Press CTRL-ALT-DEL *once.*
- Alternate-click on a blank area of the taskbar and select Task Manager from the pop-up menu.
- Select Start | Run and type **taskmgr**.

Travel Advisory

You'll notice that the Task Manager window sits on top of all other open Windows, even when you try to switch away. If you want to change that behavior, simply go to the Options menu and deselect (remove the check) from Always On Top.

The Task Manager displays three property sheets, as shown in Figure 19-8: Applications, Processes, and Performance. Windows XP also adds tabs for Networking and Users.

At the bottom of the utility window is a summary of the total number of processes running, total CPU usage, and total RAM usage (called Commit Charge in Windows XP). The paragraphs that follow describe the information shown on each tab.

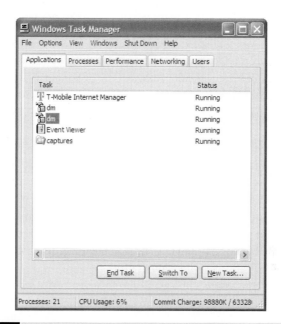

FIGURE 19.8   Windows XP Professional Task Manager

Applications

The Applications property sheet shows all applications currently running on your system, along with their active status (Running, Not Responding, or Stopped). Using the Application property sheet, you can close an application (End Task), make an application active (Switch To), or start an application (New Task).

Processes

Every program or service running on your system is actually one or more discrete process. The Processes property sheet lists processes and services currently running on the system. There's a lot you can do from the Processes tab.

Look at the Processes tab on your system and compare it to the Application tab. Notice that there's a lot of stuff showing in processes that doesn't show in applications. That's because the Application tab shows only applications started by the user. It does not show any services or any child processes started by applications or by services.

You can end a process in the Processes tab by alternate-clicking and selecting End Process from the pop-up menu. The End Process Tree option will close that process and any other processes started by that process. Notepad is a simple program that does not start any other processes, so just click End Process—Windows gives you a warning screen—then click OK.

You can do a lot more than just close processes in the Processes tab. For each process running, you will see a unique *Process ID (PID)*, the amount of CPU time that the process is using, the amount of time the process has been running, and the amount of system memory usage. One of the handiest aspects of the Process tab is the memory usage. Try starting a few bigger programs—Microsoft Word is a good example—and see how much memory they use. I think you'll be impressed!

You can also set the priority for processes in the Processes tab—a very handy way to give more important programs more of the CPU's time. The priority (we use the term "base priority") determines the order in which the threads of a process are scheduled for the CPU. To set a base priority for a process, alternate-click the process and select Set Priority from the pop-up menu, then select a base priority for the process to run at. Choices are Realtime, High, Above Normal, Normal, Below Normal, and Low. Be aware that increasing the base priority of one process may adversely affect other processes running on the system. This is especially so if you assign a process Realtime base priority, which, depending on the application, can cause the system to stop responding.

Exam Tip

You must be logged on as a member of the Power Users or Administrators group to change a task's priority.

Performance

The Performance property sheet gives you a graphical overview of the system's CPU and memory usage. You can see real-time graphs of CPU and memory usage and the total number of *handles, threads,* and other processes.

- Handles are values assigned to open resources such as files or Registry keys. Threads are discrete chunks of processes. Just as a program is made of processes, a process is made of threads.

- The Performance tab gives some very nice details on memory usage, particularly the physical, commit charge, and kernel memory statistics. To appreciate the usefulness takes a bit of explanation.

- Physical memory is the actual RAM on your system The Performance tab shows the total amount of RAM, the amount available, and the amount used for the system cache. (The system cache is basically just the disk cache.)

- Commit Charge memory is the amount of memory that is actually being used. The Limit is the total amount of both physical and virtual memory, and the Peak is the most you have used recently.

- Kernel Memory statistics show the memory used by the core Windows files. This one does vary too much and is probably the least useful.

Networking

Available only on Windows XP, the Networking tab shows the State, Link Speed, and percentage of Network Utilization for NICs installed on the system. Aside from providing a pretty graph, the Networking tab doesn't enable you to perform any real technical tasks on your NIC or network connection, however.

Users

The Users tab shows names and session status of users configured to access the PC. You can use this tab to disconnect users currently logged onto the system, or send messages to users on other systems in the same workgroup. This brings up an interesting point: the Users tab is available only on Windows XP PCs that belong to a workgroup (no domain) and have Fast User Switching enabled.

Objective 19.02 Maintaining and Optimizing Windows

Maintain Windows means keeping up with necessary patches, updates, service packs, device drivers, etc., and generally taking regular steps to ensure that the OS is running in top form. Optimizing means to improve performance of key components, such as the CPU, RAM, and hard disk drives, by making adjustments to the default system settings.

You also need to take steps to prepare for disasters. In the past, system crashes were inevitable, and the only question was "When will it happen?" Windows NT/2000/XP, however, are very robust and offer a high degree of self-correcting functionality. Nonetheless, it's important that you prepare for the worst-case scenario by maintaining good data backups, boot disks, and Emergency Repair Disks (ERDs), as well as by familiarizing yourself with Windows' built-in recovery tools. These include the Recovery Console and Automatic System Recovery utility (in Windows XP only).

Patches, Updates, and Service Packs

Windows is a work in progress, and Microsoft continually releases new software patches, updates, and service packs to address a number of issues. Windows provides handy tools to deal with these but many users don't take advantage of Windows' built-in updating features. Let's look at those features now.

Microsoft has always offered software updates via their web site, but starting with Windows 2000, they have integrated updating features into the OS through the Windows Update utility. The Windows Update utility connects to Microsoft's servers via the Internet to check for new software. It then scans your system to see if any updated patches, Service Packs, or other software items are available for your version of Windows. Depending on how it's configured, Windows Update then either prompts you to download and install any applicable updates, or grabs them and installs them automatically.

For easy access, Windows 2000 places the utility on the Start menu. Launch Windows Update by selecting Start | Windows Update. Windows XP goes one step further and automatically launches the Windows Update Automatic Update Client (WUAUCLT.EXE) when you start the system. This places an icon in your System Tray that reminds you when updates are available. You can also start the utility manually by going to Start | All Programs | Windows Update.

Launching the Windows Update utility connects you to the Microsoft Windows Update page. Click the Scan For Updates link to check your system. Figure 19-9 shows the Windows Update page in action.

Scroll through the list and review the description of each update. Click Remove to delete any unnecessary updates from the list. Click Install Now button to download and install the remaining items. Figure 19-10 shows the dialog box indicating the progress of the update process.

Travel Advisory

To take full advantage of automatic updates, your system obviously needs dedicated broadband Internet connectivity. For those relying on dial-up, Microsoft offers major updates such as Service Packs on CD-ROM.

Installing and Removing Software

The Windows OS comes with only a bare-bones selection of productivity applications preinstalled, such as Wordpad (a word processor), Calculator, and so on.

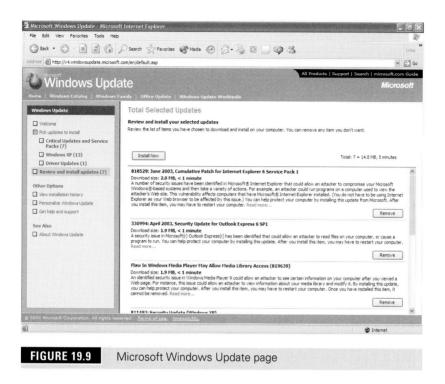

Microsoft Windows Update page

As handy as these are, they're obviously not enough to get any serious work done. As we discussed back in Chapter 14, one of the fundamental functions of an OS is to provide access and support to software applications.

FIGURE 19.10 Windows Update progress dialog box

Installing Software

Most application programs are distributed on CD-ROMs. Luckily, Windows supports *Autorun*, a feature that enables it to look for and read a special file on the CD-ROM (called appropriately, AUTORUN.INF) immediately after a CD-ROM is inserted, and then run whatever program is listed.

Sometimes, however, it is necessary to institute the installation sequence yourself. Perhaps the install CD lacks an Autorun installation program, or perhaps Windows is configured so that Autorun programs must be started manually. In some cases, a CD may contain more than one program, and you must choose which of them to install. Regardless of the reason, beginning the installation process manually is a simple and straightforward process using the Add or Remove Programs (Add/Remove Programs in Windows 2000) applet in the Control Panel.

Simply double-click the icon in Control Panel, then after it starts, click the Add New Programs button and follow the prompts (Figure 19-11). If necessary, provide the disk or location of the files.

Removing Software

You remove programs from a Windows PC in much the same manner as you installed it. That is, you use the applications' own uninstall programs, when possible. You will normally find the uninstall program listed under the application icon off the Start menu. If an uninstall program is not available, then use the Add or Remove Programs applet from Control Panel. You select the program you want to remove and click the Change/Remove button. You may then see a

FIGURE 19.11   Adding a new program from a floppy disk or CD-ROM

message telling you that a shared file that appears to no longer be in use is about to be deleted, and asking your approval. Generally speaking, it's safe to delete such files. If you do not delete them, they will likely be orphaned and remain unused on your hard disk forever (or until you clean up the hard disk drive, as we'll talk about shortly).

> **Travel Advisory**
>
> It may seem counterintuitive, but sometimes an application's uninstall program will ask you to put the app's installation CD-ROM in the drive, so be prepared.

Adding or Removing Windows Components

By default, the Windows Setup program installs a number of optional Windows components onto the PC. If you don't use these components, there's no need to keep them around. Removing these, or adding other components, is made easy using Add/Remove Windows Components.

To add a Windows component, open the Add or Remove Programs applet in Control Panel (Add/Remove Programs in Windows 2000) from Control Panel. From here, select Add/Remove Windows Components, which opens the Windows Components Wizard (Figure 19-12).

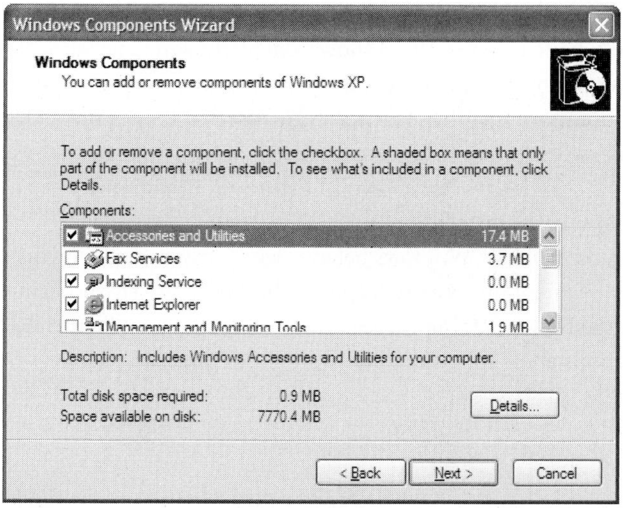

FIGURE 19.12 Windows Components Wizard

You can select an installed program to see how frequently it is used, how much disk space it uses, and (sometimes) the last time it was used.

Installing Devices

The processes for installing new hardware in Windows 2000 and Windows XP are absolutely identical to the procedures you use in Windows 9*x*, even down to the troubleshooting and backup utilities. Just remember what you learned earlier: in the case of a resource conflict, you need to reserve the resource in CMOS! If you know how to install Plug and Play (PnP) and legacy devices in Windows 9*x*, you know how to do it in Windows 2000 and Windows XP!

Driver Signing

Device drivers become part of the operating system and as such have the potential to cause lots of problems if they're written poorly. To protect Windows systems from bad device drivers, Microsoft introduced in Windows 2000 something called *driver signing*.

Signed drivers include a digital "signature" issued by Microsoft to drivers that have been tested at the Windows Hardware Quality Lab. Look on the packaging of a hardware device. If you see the "Designed for Windows 2000" or "Designed for Windows XP" logo, the driver packaged with the device is digitally signed.

Any drivers included on the Windows CD-ROM or at the Windows Update web site are now required to be digitally signed. Once a digitally signed driver is installed, you can look at the Properties of the driver to see confirmation that it was digitally signed. Figure 19-13 shows a digitally signed network card driver.

However, many manufacturers issue drivers that are not digitally signed. This does not mean that they *will not* work, just that they're not guaranteed by Microsoft to work. When an unsigned driver is detected during hardware installation, you'll see the message shown in Figure 19-14 that offers the options to stop or continue the installation.

You can control how Windows behaves when drivers are being installed. On the Hardware tab of the System Properties box, click the Driver Signing button to display the Driver Signing Options dialog box shown in Figure 19-15. The options are as follows:

- If you select Ignore, Windows will install an unsigned driver without warning you.
- If you select Warn, you will be prompted when Windows detects an unsigned driver during driver installation, and you will be given the opportunity to either cancel the installation or continue.
- Choosing Block will simply not install unsigned drivers.

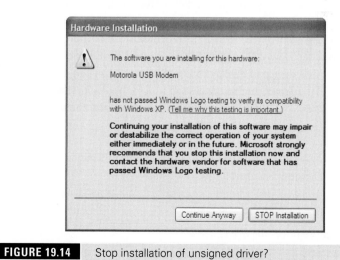

FIGURE 19.13 A digitally signed driver

The default Driver Signing setting is Warn. This also is the default setting during installation, so you will always be warned when Windows detects an unsigned driver during Windows installation.

FIGURE 19.14 Stop installation of unsigned driver?

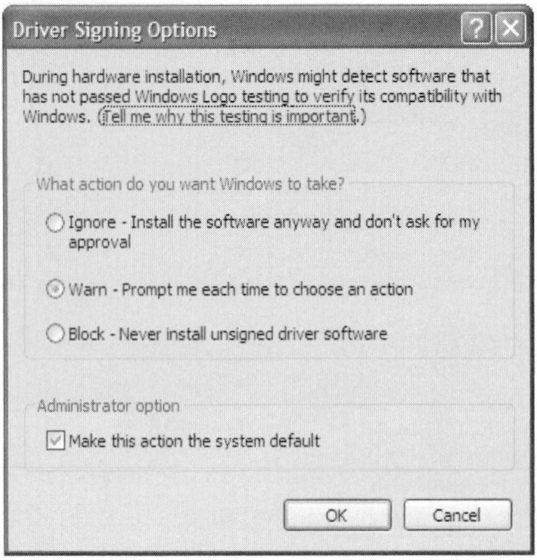

Driver Signing Options

During hardware installation, Windows might detect software that has not passed Windows Logo testing to verify its compatibility with Windows. (Tell me why this testing is important.)

What action do you want Windows to take?

○ Ignore - Install the software anyway and don't ask for my approval

⦿ Warn - Prompt me each time to choose an action

○ Block - Never install unsigned driver software

Administrator option

☑ Make this action the system default

| OK | Cancel |

FIGURE 19.15   Driver Signing options

Device Manager

We glanced at Device Manager earlier when we discussed the MMC. Device Manager is included as part of the preconfigured Computer Management MMC located in Control Panel | Administrative Tools. As a PC tech, you'll work with Device Manager extensively to install, remove, and troubleshoot devices, so this is a good time to look at its features.

Open the Device Manager to see the device tree, the list of devices installed on the system. At the root level is the computer itself. The level below that contains device nodes. Each device node in turn contains one or more devices. Figure 19-16 shows the Device Manager with a couple of device nodes expanded.

Alternate-click a device to display its context menu. You can choose to update or uninstall the driver, disable the device, scan for hardware changes, or display the Properties box. When you open the Properties box, there are buttons labeled Driver Details, Update Driver, Roll Back Driver, and Uninstall.

- Driver Details lists the driver files and locations on disk.
- Update Driver opens the Hardware Update Wizard.
- Roll Back Driver allows you to remove an updated driver, thus rolling back to the previous driver version.
- Uninstall removes the driver.

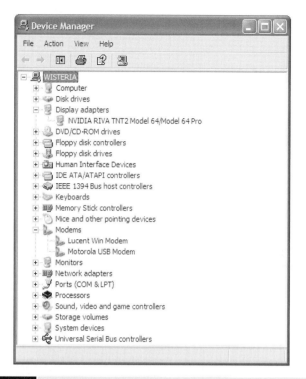

FIGURE 19.16   Device Manager with two nodes expanded

If you do decide to roll back to a previous driver version, you'll encounter a driver rollback warning that will look like Figure 19-17. That gives you one last chance to change your mind!

Adding a Plug and Play Device

It's usually a trivial matter to install a new PnP device to a Windows 2000/XP computer. You simply plug it in and Windows will detect it and install the driver. Of course, to be on the safe side, always read the documentation for the new device, just in case there is a new twist, like having to install the driver first.

FIGURE 19.17   Driver rollback warning

> **Exam Tip**
>
> The "plug" in Plug and Play really applies only to USB, IEEE 1394, and SCSI devices, which can simply be plugged in while the computer is running. When installing a PCI or ISA PnP card, you've got to power down, install the card, and power up again before Windows will recognize the device and install the drivers.

If Windows does not detect the newly connected device, use the Add Hardware Wizard, shown in Figure 19-18, to get the device recognized and drivers installed. You'll find it on the Hardware tab of the System Properties box.

Adding a Non–Plug and Play Device

As cool as Plug and Play is, a tech still has to know how to install non-PnP, legacy devices. Windows even comes with drivers for non-PnP devices, and many are also available from manufacturers. Some devices have Windows 2000 drivers, which might work in Windows XP if you're really lucky. Round up the driver beforehand, read any documentation you can find on the device, and then install the hardware. If you found a setup program with the driver, that should be your first stop.

If there is no setup program, then call once again on the Add Hardware Wizard. Click Next on the Welcome screen, and it will search for hardware that has been connected but that does not yet have a driver installed. If it detects it, select the device and the wizard will install the driver. You may have to point to the source location for the driver files. If it does not detect the device, which is very likely, it will ask you if the hardware is connected. When you answer Yes and click Next, it will give you a list of installed hardware, similar to that shown in Figure 19-19.

FIGURE 19.18   Add Hardware Wizard

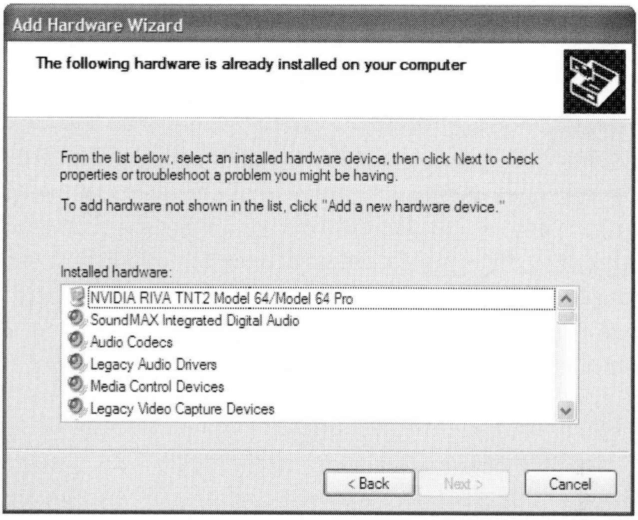

FIGURE 19.19   Add Hardware Wizard showing installed hardware

If the device is in the list, select it and click Next. If not, scroll to the bottom and select Add A New Hardware Device, and then click Next. If the device is a printer, network card, or modem, select Search For And Install The Hardware Automatically and click Next. In this case, once it detects the device and installs the driver, you're done.

But if it is not one of these devices, your best hope is to select Install The Hardware That I Manually Select From A List. In the following screens, select the appropriate device category, then select the device manufacturer and the correct model and respond to the prompts from the Add Hardware Wizard to complete the installation.

Adding Printers

In spite of optimistic predictions heard many times over the years, the paperless office is still no closer to reality than personal rocket backpacks and robot monkey butlers. Most computer users still need printers, so we'll look at the process of installing a printer in Windows 2000/XP.

Printers and Print Devices   One important bit of technospeak that you need to appreciate is the fact that Windows NT/2000/XP don't consider printers, that is, the physical devices with the paper and ink sitting on your desktop, to be *printers*. To these versions of Windows, the *printer* refers to the software object and drivers associated with the device. The physical print device is called just that, the *print device*.

This might seem like just another bit of Microsoft jargon, but it actually serves a function. You see, Windows NT, 2000, and XP enable sophisticated configurations of printers (and their attached print devices), giving you the ability to do such things as configure several logical printers that all point to the same physical print device. This enables you to assign different levels of printing priority and permissions to different groups using the same print device. Conversely, you can connect several of the same type of physical print device to the computer and, by configuring the same logical printer to address all of them, set up a *printer pool*. Once you've done this, print jobs sent to the printer are handled by the first printer in the pool that's free. This is extremely handy in offices that do a large number of print jobs!

Installing Printer Drivers   Adding a printer in Windows is really simply adding a printer driver, which you need to do whether the printer is directly connected to your computer or connected elsewhere on the network. When you install a local printer and then share it so that others on your network can use it, your computer plays the role of a print server. Remember that a printer directly connected to your computer (local) is still local even if you intend to share it on the network. Always read the manufacturer's instructions before connecting and installing a new printer. The following sections describe the most likely printer installation scenarios for installing a driver for a locally connected printer.

Plug and Play USB Print Devices   If you are installing a PnP print device using a USB cable, first run the installation program that came with the device. Then with Windows running and the printer powered on, plug in the cable. If all goes well, this is a nonevent. You might notice a quick flicker in the tray area of the taskbar, but otherwise you will have to open the Printers and Faxes console to confirm that the printer was installed.

Plug and Play Parallel Print Devices   If you are installing a PnP print device connected via the parallel port, connect the device, turn it on, and run the installation program. Respond to any prompts, and you're done. If the drivers come with Windows, or if you found drivers but no special installation program, then open the Printers and Faxes folder (called simply Printers in Windows 2000). In Windows 2000, click the Add Printer icon to start the Add Printer Wizard. In Windows XP, select File | Add Printer to start the wizard.

At the Welcome screen, click Next to continue. On the Local Or Network Printer page, choose Local Printer. Since the printer is PnP, leave the check in the Automatically Detect And Install My Plug And Play Printer box (see Figure 19-20) and click Next. The print device should be detected and the drivers

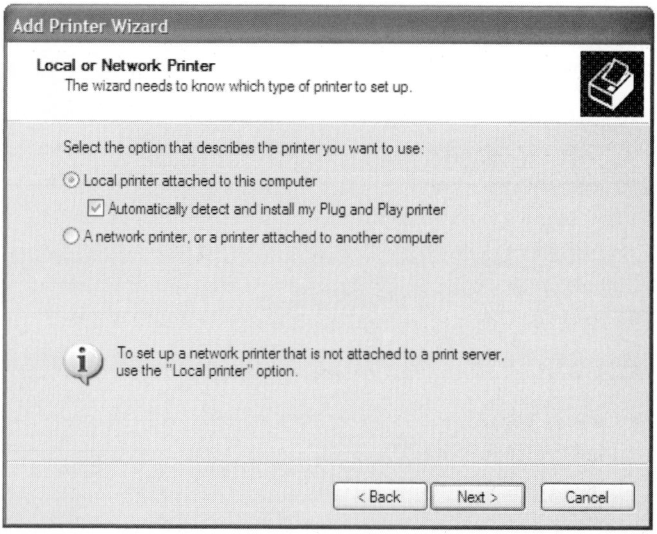

FIGURE 19.20   Local or Network Printer page of the Add Printer Wizard

installed. The most you should have to do is provide the location for drivers not provided with Windows.

For a non-PnP printer, follow the preceding instruction, but when you get to the Local Or Network Printer page, clear the check box next to Automatically Detect And Install My Plug And Play Printer and then click Next. On the Select The Printer Port page, select the port to which the printer is connected, then click Next.

On the next page, select the manufacturer and the correct printer module unless you are providing a new driver, in which case you should click the Have Disk button (see Figure 19-21) and respond to the prompts.

On the Name Your Printer page, you may enter a name that is friendlier than the model name. This is not mandatory—the default is the model name—but you may want to do this to identify how the printer is being used: for example, Brochure Printer or Accounting Printer.

On the Printer Sharing page, if you plan to share the printer on a network, select Share As and give the printer yet another name—this time a share name by which it will be known on the network. Leave the default, or enter a short, friendly name, then click Next. On the Location And Comment page, enter a location for the printer and add a description in the Comment box. Then click Next.

When the Add Printer Wizard offers to print a test page, you should accept the offer and make sure the printer works. To close the wizard, click Finish.

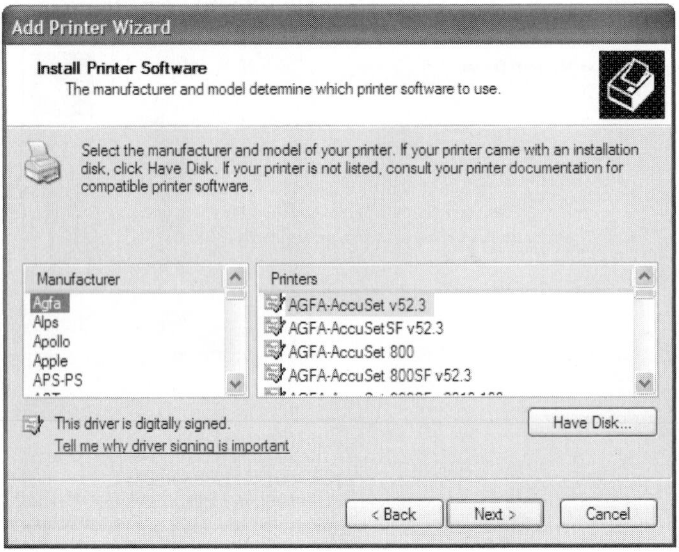

FIGURE 19.21 Install Printer Software page

Managing User Accounts and Groups

The most basic element of Windows security is the user account. Each user must present a valid username and the password of a local or domain user account in order to log on to a Windows 2000 or Windows XP Professional computer and access resources.

Each user is also a member of one or more groups of users. Groups enable the system administrator to easily assign the same rights and permissions to all members of the group without the need to set those rights and permissions individually.

Both Windows 2000 Professional and Windows XP Professional have several built-in groups, and two user accounts created during installation—Administrator and Guest—with only the Administrator account enabled by default. When you install Windows, you supply the password for the Administrator account. This is the only usable account you have to log on to the computer, unless you joined the computer to a domain or until you create a new local account. We'll focus on local accounts in this section.

Manage users and groups for either OS using the Local Users and Groups snap-in node in the Computer Management console, shown in Figure 19-22. You can open this by alternate-clicking My Computer and selecting Manage. Then click the Local Users and Groups node.

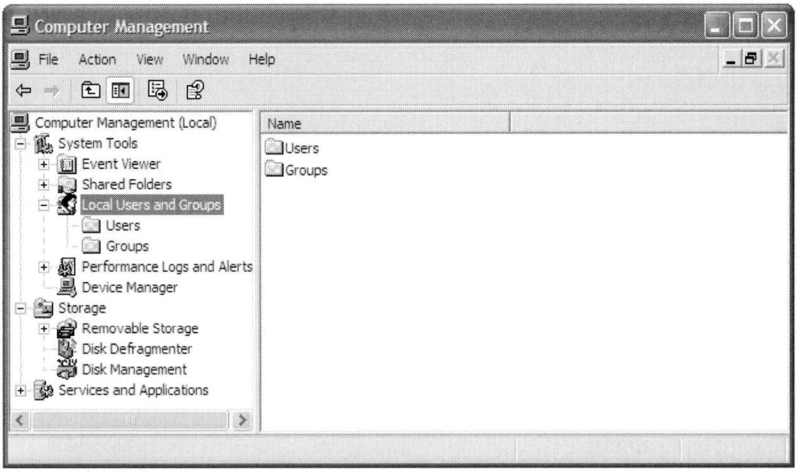
Computer Management
File
Action
View
Window
Help
Computer Management (Local)
System Tools
Event Viewer
Shared Folders
Local Users and Groups
Users
Groups
Performance Logs and Alerts
Device Manager
Storage
Removable Storage
Disk Defragmenter
Disk Management
Services and Applications
Name
Users
Groups

FIGURE 19.22 Local Users and Groups in the Computer Management console

A Word about Passwords

Passwords are a vitally important part of any security system. Most experts recommend using passwords that are at least eight characters long and that contain a mixture of numbers, letters (both upper- and lowercase), and nonalphanumeric characters. Passwords that use common words—such as the name of a pet—are easily guessed and therefore offer little in the way of real security.

Travel Advisory

Blank passwords or those that are easily visible on a sticky note provide *no* security. Always insist on nonblank passwords that are not sitting out in the open.

Using the Users and Passwords Applet in Windows 2000

When you installed Windows 2000 Professional, if your computer was not made a member of a domain, you could choose to let the OS assume that you were the only user of the computer and did not want to see the logon dialog box. You can check this setting after installation by opening the Users and Passwords applet in Control Panel to see the setting for Users Must Enter A User Name And Password To Use This Computer. Configuring this setting means that you will see a logon box every time you restart your computer.

Travel Advisory

If the user name and password requirement is turned off, anyone with physical access to your computer can turn it on and use it without entering a user name and password. It is very important to enable this security setting.

There's a second setting in Users and Passwords that's important to enable for the sake of security—the setting on the Advanced Tab under Secure Boot Settings. If checked, it requires users to press CTRL-ALT-DEL before logging on. This setting is a defense against certain viruses that try to capture your username and password, sometimes by presenting a fake logon prompt. Pressing CTRL-ALT-DEL will remove a program like that from memory, and allow the actual logon dialog box to appear.

Creating New Users   Creation and management of user accounts is done at two levels: locally and at the domain level. Local accounts are those that are created and stored on a particular PC in the Security Accounts Manager (SAM) database. Stand-alone PCs and PCs that are members of workgroups use local accounts. Domain accounts are created and stored on one or more centralized *domain controllers* in either the domain SAM (for Windows NT domains) or the Active Directory database (in Windows 2000).

- Users who log on locally enter their user name and password—their *credentials*—at the logon prompt. Windows checks these credentials— *authenticates,* in network parlance—against the accounts stored in the SAM. Assuming there's a match, Windows logs the user on and presents their desktop.

- Users who are members of a domain also enter their credentials at the logon prompt, but instead of checking against the local SAM, the PC forwards the credentials through the network to an available domain controller. The domain controller then authenticates the user and, in essence, tells the PC, "It's okay, I know this guy. You can let him in."

The process of creating and managing user accounts is very similar for local and domain accounts. At the local level, Windows 2000 gives you two tools for user management: the Users and Passwords Control Panel applet and the Local Users and Groups MMC snap-in. Windows NT user management is done using the User Manager utility. Domain accounts are managed using the Active Directory Users and Computers MMC in Windows 2000/2003 Server domains, or

User Manager for Domains in Windows NT domains. We'll concentrate on creating and managing user accounts at the local level.

To create and manage users, you must be logged on as the Administrator or a member of the local Administrators group.

Travel Advisory

The Administrator is all powerful! Never give users access to the Administrator account or group unnecessarily.

Open the Users and Passwords applet from Control Panel and click Add. This opens the Add New User Wizard. Enter the user name that the user will use to log on. Enter the user's first and last names in the Full name box, and, if you wish, enter something that describes this person in the Description box. If this is at work, enter a job description in this box. These last two fields are optional.

After entering the user information, click Next to continue. On the Password page, you will then enter and confirm the initial password for this new user. Click Next to continue.

Now you get to decide what groups the new user should belong to. Select one of the suggested options: Standard User puts the new account in the Power Users group, Restricted User puts the account in the Users group, and Other enables you to choose a group from the drop-down list. Select Standard user and click Finish to close the dialog box. You should see your new user listed in the Users and Passwords dialog box.

While you're there, let's see how easy it is for an administrator to change a user's password. Simply select a user from the list, and then click Set Password. Enter and confirm the new password in the Set Password dialog box. Figure 19-23 shows the Set Password box with the Users and Passwords box in the background.

Managing Users in Windows XP

Although Windows XP has essentially the same type of accounts database as Windows 2000, the User Accounts Control Panel applet replaces the former Users and Passwords applet and further simplifies user management tasks.

User Accounts: A Simple Tool   In Windows XP, the User Accounts applet hides the complete list of users, using a simplistic reference to account types that is actually a reference to its group membership. An account that is a member of the local Administrators group is said to be a Computer administrator, while an account that belongs only to the Local Users group is said to be a Limited account.

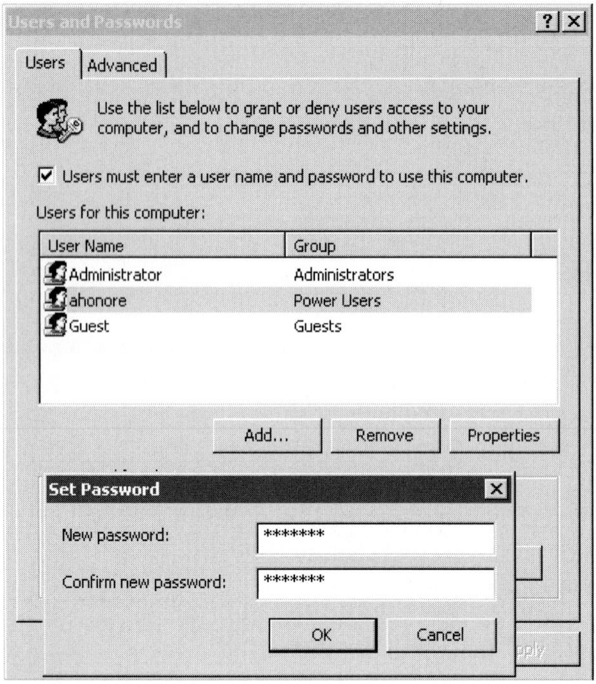

FIGURE 19.23 Set Password dialog box

What users it shows depends on the currently logged-on user, as shown in Figure 19-24.

When an Administrator is logged on, she will see both types of accounts and the Guest account. When a user with a Limited account is logged on, he or she will see only his own account in User Accounts.

Travel Advisory

When creating new user accounts on a computer for a newbie, create both a Computer Administrator account and a Limited account for the user. If you instruct him to use the administrator account only when he needs to install new software or make changes to the computer, but use the Limited account for day-to-day work, you might protect his computer from newbie mistakes.

Now let's look at how we create a new user in Windows XP. Open the User Accounts applet from Control Panel and click Create A New Account. On the Pick An Account Type page, the option for Limited is grayed out (unavailable) if this

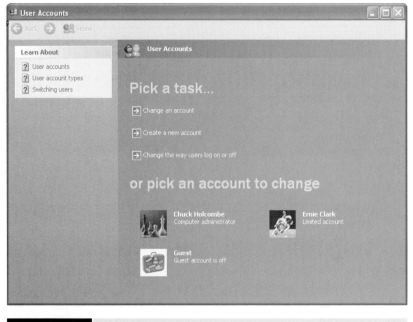

FIGURE 19.24 User Accounts showing a Computer Administrator, a Limited account, and the Guest account

is the first account you have created since installation. This first new account can only be a Computer Administrator. If you haven't created this account, create it now, following the prompts on the screen.

On the next page, the Pick An Account Type page, which looks like Figure 19-25, you can create either type of account. Once again, you simply follow the prompts on the screen.

After you have created your local accounts, you'll see them listed when you open the User Accounts applet, and it will look something like Figure 19-26.

More about Windows XP Accounts Creating users is a straightforward process. You need to provide a user name and an initial password. The user can change the password later. You also need to know the type of account to create: Computer Administrator or Limited.

Remember that if a computer is a member of a domain, users will log on using domain accounts. Therefore, local user accounts are mostly created on a stand-alone computer or a networked computer that is only a member of a workgroup. Then you should create one Limited account per user of the computer and an account that is a member of the local Administrators group (in addition to the one created during installation).

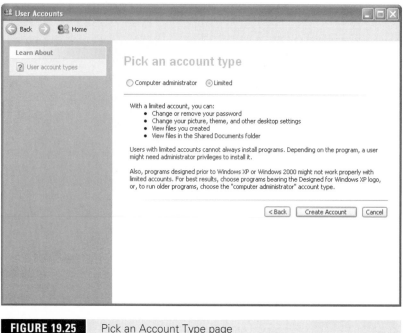

FIGURE 19.25 Pick an Account Type page

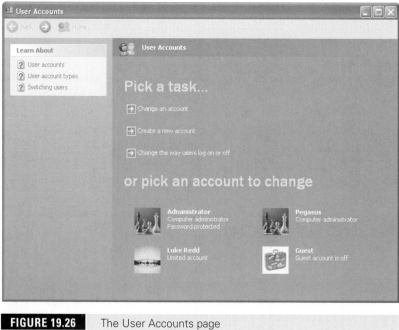

FIGURE 19.26 The User Accounts page

The reason for having two administrator accounts is that if one administrator is not available or is not able to log on to the computer, another one can—simple redundancy. Windows XP actually reminds you to do this; the first time you try to create a local account after installing Windows XP, it will allow you to create only a Computer Administrator account. After that, it will allow you to create limited accounts.

Optimizing Windows 2000/XP

Windows 2000 and Windows XP come well optimized out of the box, and there's actually very little for a tech to "tweak." However, it's still important for you to know how to set performance options and track resource usage.

Performance Options

One of the unique optimization features of Windows 2000 and Windows XP is setting Performance Options. To access these options, go to My Computer and select Properties, click the Advanced tab, and select Performance Options (Windows 2000) or Performance Settings (Windows XP).

Visual Effects   The Windows XP Performance Settings dialog box has two tab sheets: Visual Effects and Advanced, as shown in Figure 19-27.

The Visual Effects tab lets you adjust visual effects that impact performance. Try clicking the top three buttons in turn, and watch the list of settings. Notice the tiny difference between the first two choices. The third choice, Adjust For Best Performance, turns off all visual effects, and the fourth option is an invitation to make your own adjustments.

Applications and Background Services   In Windows 2000, the Performance Options dialog box shows a pair of radio buttons called Applications and Background Services. These radio buttons set how processor time is divided between the foreground application and all background tasks. Set this to Applications if you run applications that need more processor time. Set it to Background Services to give all running programs the same processor usage. You can also adjust the size of the swap file—called *paging file*—in this dialog box. Truthfully, there's no reason for you to mess with these settings; Windows handles them just fine.

In Windows XP, the Advanced tab, shown in Figure 19-28, has the settings for processor scheduling, memory usage, and virtual memory.

The previous choices of Applications and Background Services for processor scheduling are now called Programs and Background services. They work as they did in Windows 2000. The Memory usage settings let you allocate a greater share of memory to either programs or the system cache. Finally, the Virtual

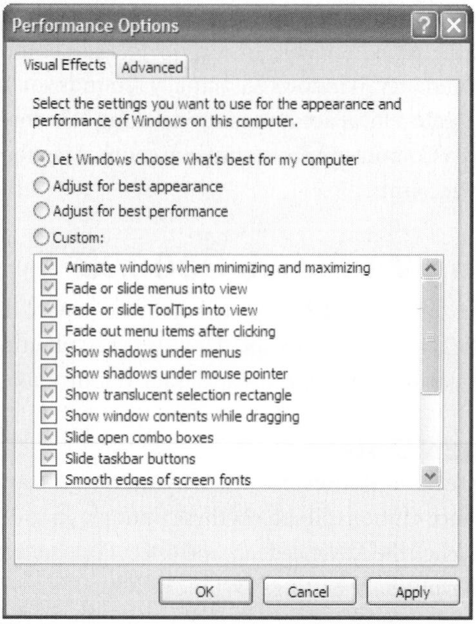

FIGURE 19.27   Visual Effects tab in Performance Options

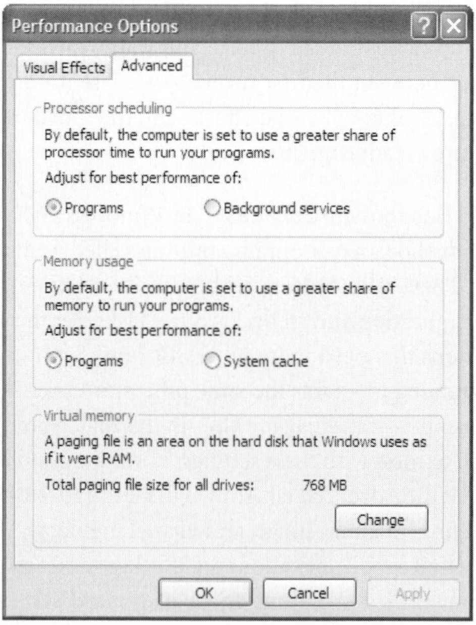

FIGURE 19.28   Advanced tab in Performance Options

Memory section of this page lets you modify the size of the paging file on disk. Again, unless you have a compelling reason (and a lot of time on your hands), there's no reason to mess with this setting!

Resource Tracking

Resource tracking is very important for solving performance problems. Let's say your Windows 2000/XP computer seems to be running slower than previously. The Task Manager and the Performance Console are tools you can use to figure out what (if anything) has become a bottleneck. Let's look at how to use them.

Task Manager   We discussed the Task Manager a bit earlier in this chapter. Let's look at how to use the Task Manager to stay on top of how your system is performing. Press CTRL-SHIFT-ESC to bring up the Task Manager and click the Performance tab, as shown in Figure 19-29.

This handy screen provides us with the most commonly used information: CPU usage, available physical memory, the size of the disk cache, commit charge (memory for programs), and kernel memory (memory used by Windows). If you know what these figures actually mean, then these numbers are useful. If not, well, it sure looks cool, doesn't it?

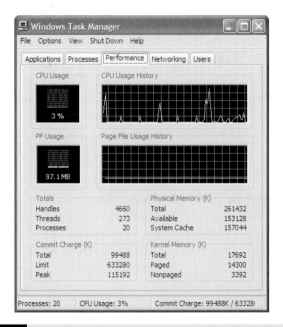

FIGURE 19.29   Task Manager Performance tab

Here's a definition of these terms:

Handles	Opening one program usually involves opening other program or data files. Handles shows all interlinks between these programs and the other programs and files they use.
Threads	Most 32-bit programs break themselves into multiple "miniprograms" called *threads.*
Processes	Any running executable programs or subsystems (usually DLLs) running on the system. These include applications and services, as well as kernel-based programs.

Performance Console Windows NT had a great tool for measuring system performance called Performance Monitor, or "Perfmon" to its friends and followers. In Windows 2000/XP, this tool has been improved upon and morphed into an MMC console.

Start the utility by either typing the MMC console filename, entering **perfmon.msc** from Start | Run, or opening the Performance icon in Administrative Tools. Now look at the Performance Console, shown in Figure 19-30.

> **Travel Advisory**
>
> You need to have a Computer Administrator account to perform Performance tasks.

As you can see, the Performance Monitor actually consists of two components, the System Monitor and the Performance Logs and Alerts. Using these tools, you can determine performance trends, identify bottlenecks (such as a buggy application or faulty component), and create performance baselines. You can also configure the system to alert you when a predetermined threshold has been exceeded by the system. Performance is monitored using *objects* and *counters,* as described next.

Objects and Counters To begin working with the Performance Console, you need to understand two terms: object and counter. An *object* is a system component that is given a set of characteristics and can be managed by the operating system as a single entity. A *counter* is something that tracks specific information about an object. For example, the Processor object has a counter, %Processor Time, which tracks the percentage of elapsed time the processor uses to execute a nonidle thread. There can be many counters associated with an object.

System Monitor The System Monitor console is a real-time graphical meter of the processes running under the hood of your system. The monitor can show

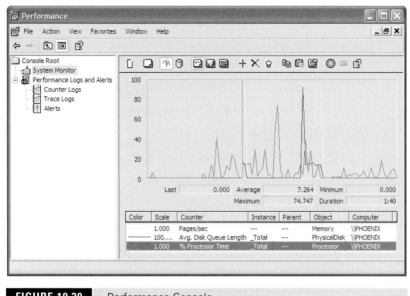

FIGURE 19.30 Performance Console

data in Graph view, Histogram view, or Report view. You'll no doubt notice that when the monitor is loaded, there are no active counters running. You must manually configure the monitor to track system processes by adding counters to the console.

Add counters to the monitor by following these steps:

1. Highlight the System Monitor node in the Console Root pane. In the alternate-hand detail pane of the console, click Add to bring up the Add Counters dialog box.

2. Click the Use Local Computer Counters radio button (default setting) to monitor the local system. You can monitor a remote system by clicking the Select Counters From Computer radio button and selecting a computer from the pull-down list.

3. System resources are tracked as Performance Objects. To track an object, select the Performance Object from the drop-down list. For an explanation of the object, highlight it and click the Explain button.

4. Note the individual counters available for the object in the Select Counters From List scrolling list. Click the All Counters radio button to track all associated counters for the object, or select them individually.

5. Note also the *Instances* listed for a performance object. Tracking object instances enables you to take readings of multiple occurrences of an object (for instance, if you are tracking the performance of two separate hard disks).

6. Click Add to add the counters for the performance object.

7. Repeat the steps to add any additional counters.

8. Click Close when finished.

There are literally dozens of performance objects and hundreds of counter combinations to choose from, and your exact choices vary slightly between versions of NT, 2000, and XP, but some of the more important objects are listed here:

- **Cache**   The file system cache is used to buffer physical device data.
- **Memory**   This counter shows physical and virtual/paged memory on the system.
- **Pages/Sec**   More than 30 pages per second is a lot of paging; add more RAM.
- **Committed Bytes**   This counter should be less than amount of RAM in the computer.
- **Physical Disk**   This counter monitors the hard disk as a whole.
- **Disk Queue Length**   This counter shows the number of requests outstanding on the disk.
- **% Disk Time**   If this exceeds 90 percent, the data/pagefile should be moved to another drive or the drive upgraded.
- **Logical Disk**   *If the Disk Queue Length* averages more than 2, drive access is a bottleneck. Upgrade the disk or the hard drive controller, or implement a stripe set.
- **Processor**   This counter monitors CPU load.
- **% Processor Time**   This counter measures how much time the CPU spends executing a non-idle thread. If it is continually at or above 80 percent, a CPU upgrade is recommended.
- **Processor Queue Length**   More than two threads in queue indicates the CPU is a bottleneck for system performance.
- **% CPU DPC Time**   This counter measures software interrupts (deferred procedure calls).
- **% CPU Interrupts/Sec**   This counter measures hardware interrupts. If the processor time exceeds 90 percent and interrupts/time exceeds

15 percent, check for a poorly written driver (bad drivers can generate excessive interrupts) or consider upgrading the CPU.

The best way to become familiar with the System Performance Monitor is to experiment with monitoring different system performance data. While the process is daunting at first, you will most likely become strangely intrigued by such subsystem minutiae as the *percentage of privileged processor time.*

Performance Logs and Alerts   The Performance Logs and Alerts snap-in enables Windows 2000/XP to create a written record of just about anything that happens on your system. Do you want to know if someone is trying to log onto your system when you're not around? The following procedure is written for Windows XP, but the steps are nearly identical in Windows 2000.

To create the new event log, alternate-click Counter Logs and select New Log Settings. Give the new setting a name—call it anything you want. Click OK and a properties dialog box for the new log will open similar to that in Figure 19-31.

Select counters for the log. Click Add Counters, and then select the Use Local Computer Counter Objects radio button. Select Server from the Performance

Properties dialog box for a new "Unauthorized Accesses" event log

Object pull-down menu, highlight Errors Logon from the list of counters, and click Add, then Close.

Back in the properties box, click the Schedule tab and set up when you want this thing to start running—probably at the end of the work day today. Then select when it should stop logging—probably tomorrow morning when you start work. Click the Log Files tab to see where the log file will be saved—probably C:\PerfLogs—and make a note of the filename. The filename will consist of the name you gave the log and a number. In the example, I named the new performance log "Unauthorized Accesses," so the file name is Unauthorized Accesses_ 000001.blg.

When you come back in the morning, open the Performance Console and select Performance Logs and Alerts, and then select Counter Logs. Your log should be listed at the right. The icon by the log name will be red if the log is still running, and green if it has stopped. If it has not stopped, select it, and then click the Stop button (the one with the black square), as shown in Figure 19-32.

To view the log, select System Monitor, change to Report view, and load the file in as a new source using the Properties box.

Hard Disk Drive Maintenance

The hard disk drive is one of the most "physical" components on the PC and as such needs regular maintenance to prevent problems. Run the Disk Defragmenter and ScanDisk (called Error-checking in the GUI) for system upkeep, and run Disk Cleanup to keep your hard disk drive organized and trash-free.

Defragmentation and Error Checking

There are several ways to access these tools; one way is to select the Properties of the drive you wish to work with. In the dialog box that opens, select the Tools tab, as shown in Figure 19-33.

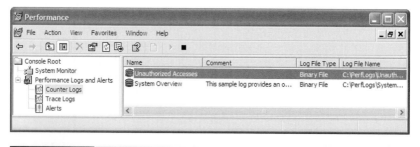

FIGURE 19.32   Counter log for Unauthorized Accesses event log

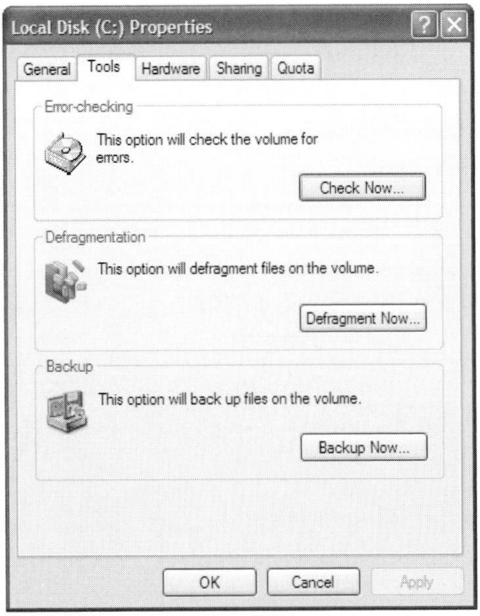

FIGURE 19.33   Tools tab of drive properties dialog box, with buttons to access Error Checking and Defrag

For the experienced tech, Disk Defragmenter is just good old Defrag, although with a much prettier front end. Run Defragmenter on a regular basis to ensure that your system isn't slowing down because of having to write files into scattered locations on the disk.

Temporary File Management with Disk Cleanup

Don't forget the occasional disk cleanup. Even though you can reach this tool the Windows 9*x* way through the menus, you can also select properties for a drive and click the Disk Cleanup button from the General tab. Disk Cleanup calculates the space you will be able to free up, and then displays the Disk Cleanup dialog box, shown in Figure 19-34.

Near the top it tells you how much disk space (maximum) it could free up. But look! The list of files to delete has only a few categories checked and the actual amount of disk space you will gain if you allow Disk Cleanup to delete only these files is much smaller than the estimate. As you select and deselect choices, watch the value for this total change. If you scroll down through the list, you will see a choice to compress old files. What do you know? Disk Cleanup does more than just delete files. In fact, this file compression trick is where Disk Cleanup really, uh, cleans up. This is one of the few choices where you will gain the most

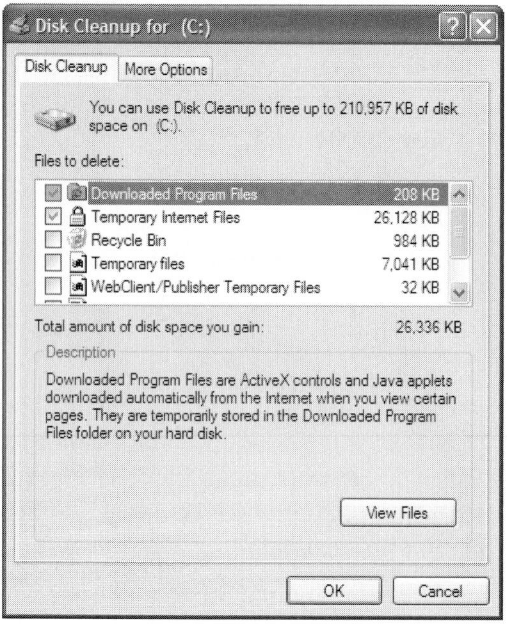

FIGURE 19.34 Disk Cleanup

space. The other big heavyweight category is temporary Internet files, which it will delete. Try Disk Cleanup on a computer that gets hours of use every day and you'll be pleased with the results.

Preparing for Problems

Being prepared for computer disasters is one of the hallmarks of a good PC tech. All kinds of bad things can cause a computer to go "blooey." Whether it's hardware failure, OS or application corruption, virus infection, or "user error," you need to know the tools that Microsoft provides to enable us to cope with problems. This includes knowing how to back up your important data in case of system failure, how to put a crashed system back in good running order, and how to restore backed-up data from your backup media.

The various versions of Windows based on the NT core offer five different tools for the job: System Restore, the Backup and Restore Wizard (called Backup in Windows NT and 2000), Automated System Recovery (ASR), the Emergency Repair Disk (ERD), and the Recovery Console. Table 19-1 shows which OS gets which tool.

| **TABLE 19.1** | Windows Backup and Recovery Tools |

Windows Version	System Restore	Backup and Restore Wizard	Automated System Recovery	Emergency Repair Disk	Recovery Console
Windows NT 4.0	No	Yes, but called "Backup"	No	Yes	No
Windows 2000 Professional	No	Yes, but called "Backup"	No	Yes	Yes
Windows XP Home	Yes	No	No	No	No
Windows XP Professional	Yes	Yes	Yes	No	Yes

System Restore

Every technician has war stories about the user who likes to add the latest gadget and cool software to their computer. Then he's amazed when things go very, very wrong: the system locks up, or refuses to boot, or simply acts "weird." Then, surprisingly, he just can't remember what he added or when.

"It was working fine before!"

Guess whose job it is to fix it?

This is not news to the folks at Microsoft, and they have a solution to this problem. It's called System Restore, and they first introduced it in Windows Me, with further refinements in Windows XP. The System Restore tool enables you to create a *restore point,* a copy of your computer's configuration at a specific point in time. If you crash or have a corrupted OS later, you can restore the system.

To create a restore point, go to Start | All Programs | Accessories | System Tools | System Restore. When the tool opens, select Create A Restore Point, and then click Next. Figure 19-35 shows the System Restore utility.

Type in a description on the next screen. There's no need to include the date and time because the System Restore adds them automatically. Click Create and you're done.

The System Restore tool creates some of the restore points in time automatically. For instance, by default, every time you install new software, XP creates a restore point. Thus, if installation of a program causes your computer to malfunction, simply restore the system to a time point prior to that installation, and the computer should work again.

During the restore process, only settings and programs are changed. No data is lost. Your computer will include all programs and settings as of the restore date. This feature is absolutely invaluable for overworked techs. A simple restore will fix many user-generated problems.

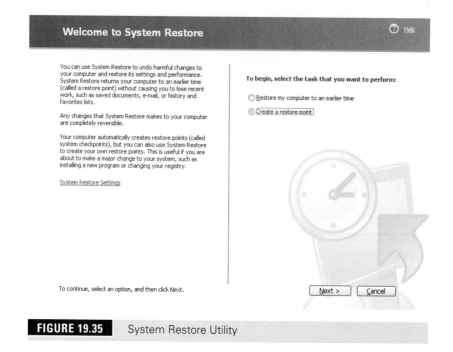

FIGURE 19.35 System Restore Utility

Backup and Restore Wizard (Backup)

Windows 2000/XP Backup provides almost all the tools we need. It has come a long way from its origins in Windows NT. It supports a greater variety of devices, allowing you to back up to network drives, logical drives, tape, and removable disks.

Travel Advisory

The Backup utility provided with Windows is great for basic archiving duties, but if you need something more feature-packed, third-party utilities such as Backup Exec are the way to go.

You can start Backup by navigating the Start menu all the way to Accessories | System Tools, or by clicking the Backup Now button on the Tools page of the local disk properties box. Alternatively, you can also go to Start | Run and type **ntbackup**. This technique works in both Windows 2000 and Windows XP and has the added advantage of bringing the XP version up in the more tech-friendly Advanced Mode (Figure 19-36), rather than Wizard Mode intended for newbies.

Both versions of Backup have three choices on this page: Backup, Restore, and a third choice that is different in each version. The third option for Windows

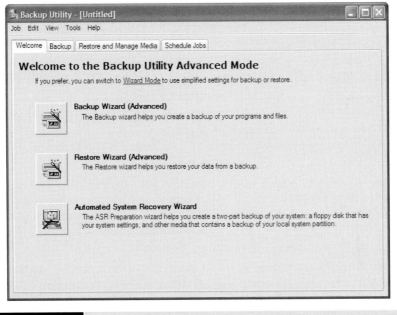

FIGURE 19.36   Windows XP Backup and Restore Wizard

2000 is the Emergency Repair Disk. The third option in Windows XP is the Automated System Recovery Wizard—a new recovery feature in Windows XP.

Let's first consider the Windows 2000 ERD. This disk saves critical boot files and partition information and is our main tool for fixing boot problems. The ERD is not a bootable disk, so to work with it, you'll need either the Windows 2000 installation CD-ROM or the four bootable floppy disks. It works with a special folder called \WINNT\REPAIR to store a copy of your Registry. It's not perfect, but it gets you out of most startup problems. You should always make a new ERD before installing a new device or program—*just in case*.

Windows XP Automated System Recovery (ASR)   The ASR Wizard enables you to create a backup of your system. This backup includes a floppy disk and backup media containing the system partition and disks containing operating system components. The restore side of ASR involves a complete reinstall of the operating system, preferably on a new partition.

As you may guess, this is not a trivial, easy solution to a system failure, but something you do as a last-ditch effort after first trying the Safe Mode Boot and Last Known Good Configuration options (described in the "Troubleshooting Windows" section of this chapter).

You run setup, pressing F2 when prompted during the text-mode portion of Setup. Follow the prompts on the screen, which will first ask for the floppy disk, then for the backup media.

Backup Wizard Data files are not backed up by the ERD nor by the ASR. Therefore, you have to manually back up data files. In the main Welcome screen of the backup utility, select Backup Wizard. When the wizard starts, click Next to see the screen shown in Figure 19-37.

You have three options here: Back Up Everything On This Computer, Back Up Selected Files, Drives, Or Network Data, Only Back Up The System State Data. The first two are fairly self-explanatory: You can back up everything or specific files of your choosing. The third option needs some explanation. The System State is another way of saving the contents of the ERD with the Registry backup. This option really makes sense for Windows 2000 Server systems because it saves Active Directory information (which your Windows 2000 Professional system does not store) as well as other critical, server-specific functions. But the A+ Certification exams may still expect you to know about it!

Creating an MS-DOS Startup Disk

If you don't have access to a Windows 9x bootable floppy disk, it's easy to make one. If you have access to a Windows 9x system, simply pop a blank 3.5-inch

| FIGURE 19.37 | Backup Wizard

floppy disk in the floppy drive and open My Computer. Alternate-click on the floppy drive, and then select Format. Create An MS-DOS Startup Disk is an option when you format the diskette. Windows 2000 doesn't have the option of creating a MS-DOS boot diskette, but the feature reappears in Windows XP, as shown in Figure 19-38.

Installing Recovery Console

Even though you can't really get Windows 2000/XP to boot to an MS-DOS environment, you can use something called the Recovery Console. You may even consider it better, because it works on an NTFS partition and pays attention to NTFS permissions.

If you have the Windows 2000/XP CD, you can start the Recovery Console by running Setup and instead of telling it to install Windows, select Repair, then Recovery Console. However, if you like to be proactive you can install the Recovery Console on your hard drive so that it is one of your startup options and does not require the Windows 2000 or XP CD to run. Instead, the Recovery Console becomes a boot option. The steps to do this in Windows 2000 and Windows XP are very nearly identical.

First, you need to log into the system with the Administrator account. Grab your Windows 2000 or XP install CD-ROM and drop it into your system. If the

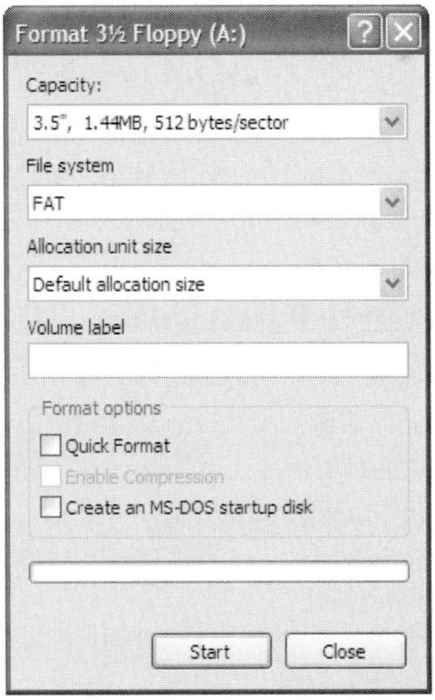

Format 3½ Floppy (A:)

Capacity:

3.5", 1.44MB, 512 bytes/sector

File system

FAT

Allocation unit size

Default allocation size

Volume label

Format options

☐ Quick Format
☐ Enable Compression
☐ Create an MS-DOS startup disk

Start   Close

FIGURE 19.38   Create an MS-DOS Startup Disk option

Autorun function kicks in, just click No. To install the Recovery Console and make it a part of your startup options, click on the Start button, then select Run, and type the following:

```
d:\i386\winnt32 /cmdcons
```

If your CD-ROM drive uses a different drive letter, substitute it for the d: drive. Then just follow the instructions on the screen. If you are connected to the Internet, allow the Setup program to download updated files. From now on, every time the system boots, the OS selection menu will show your Windows OS (Windows 2000 Professional or Windows XP) and the Microsoft Windows Recovery Console. It may also show other choices if yours is a multiboot computer.

Objective 19.03 Troubleshooting Windows

Now that you've taken proactive steps to ready yourself for a system failure, let's say that the system has, indeed, failed.

When it comes to troubleshooting tools, Windows 2000 and Windows XP have inherited the best of both Windows families. That is, they have such vintage Windows NT tools as the Last Known Good Configuration startup option for startup failures and the Task Manager for removing errant programs. Both operating systems have the new Recovery Console. The Windows 9x family legacy includes Device Manager and the Safe Mode startup options that improve on those of the Windows 9x family. Finally, Windows XP has System Restore.

Let's look at some troubleshooting scenarios.

Troubleshooting Windows 2000/XP with the Recovery Console

Start the Recovery Console as described earlier (either using the Windows 2000 or XP installation CD-ROM or selecting it from the Boot Menu). You will see a message about NTDETECT, another message will announce that the Recovery console is starting up, and then you will be greeted with the following message and command prompt:

```
Microsoft Windows XP<TM> Recovery Console.
The Recovery Console provides system repair and recovery
functionality.
Type Exit to quit the Recovery Console and restart the computer.
```

```
1: C:\WINDOWS
Which Windows XP installation would you like to log onto
<To cancel, press ENTER>?
```

Type the number of the Windows installation you want to repair (1, in this case) at the prompt, and press the ENTER key. You're now greeted with

```
Type the Administrator password:
```

Enter the Administrator password for that computer and press ENTER. You're in! Now what do you do?

Recovery Console uses many of the commands that worked in DOS as well as some uniquely its own. Table 19-2 lists the common Recovery Console commands.

TABLE 19.2	Recovery Console Commands

Command	**Description**
attrib	Changes attributes of selected file or folder
cd (or chdir)	Displays current directory or changes directories
chkdsk	Runs CheckDisk utility
cls	Clears screen
copy	Copies from removable media to system folders on the hard disk. No wildcards
del (or delete)	Deletes service or folder
dir	Lists contents of the selected directory on the system partition only
disable	Disables service or driver
diskpart	Replaces FDISK—creates/deletes partitions
enable	Enables service or driver
extract	Extracts components from .CAB files
fixboot	Writes new partition boot sector on system partition
fixmbr	Writes new Master Boot Record for partition boot sector
format	Formats selected disk
listsvc	Lists all services on system
logon	Lets you choose which W2K installation to log on to if you have more than one
map	Displays current drive letter mappings
md (or mkdir)	Creates a directory
more (or type)	Displays contents of text file
rd (or rmdir)	Removes a directory
ren (or rename)	Renames a single file
systemroot	Makes current directory system root of drive you're logged into
type	Displays a text file

You don't need to memorize all of these commands. Typing **help** at the prompt brings up a list of valid Recovery Console commands.

The Recovery Console shines in the business of manually restoring registries, stopping problem services, rebuilding partitions (other than the system partition), or using the EXPAND program to extract copies of corrupted files from a CD-ROM or floppy disk.

You can also reconfigure a service so that it starts with different settings, format drives on the hard disk, read and write on local FAT or NTFS volumes, and copy replacement files from a floppy or CD. The recovery console allows you to access the file system, and is still constrained by the file and folder security of NTFS, which makes it a more secure tool to use than some of the third-party solutions.

Troubleshooting Windows XP Using System Restore

To restore to a previous time point, start the System Restore Wizard by choosing Start | All Programs | Accessories | System Tools | System Restore. Then select the first radio button, Restore My Computer To An Earlier Time, and then click Next. Figure 19-39 shows a calendar with restore points.

Any day with a boldface date has at least one restore point. These points are created after you add or remove software or install Windows updates and during the normal shutdown of your computer. Select a date on the calendar, then select a restore point from the list on the right and click Next.

The last screen before the system is restored shows a warning. It advises you to close all open programs and reminds you that Windows will shut down during the restore process. It also states that the restore operation is completely reversible. Thus, if you go too far back in time, you can restore to a more recent date.

You don't have to count on the automatic creation of restore points. You can open System Restore at any time and simply select Create A Restore Point. This is something to consider doing before making changes that might not trigger an automatic restore point, such as directly editing the Registry.

System Restore is turned on by default and uses some of your disk space to save information on restore points. To turn System Restore off or change the

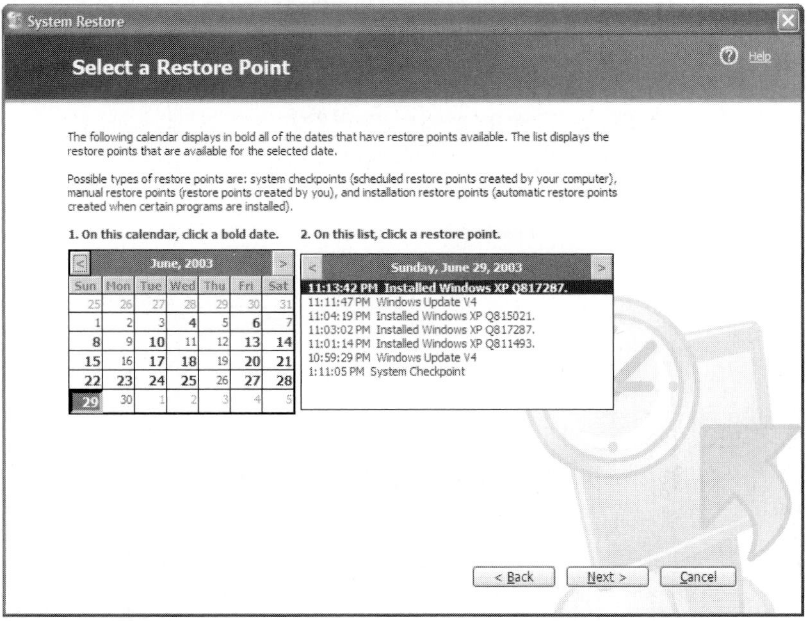

FIGURE 19.39   Select a restore point

disk space usage, open the System Properties applet in Control Panel and select the System Restore tab, as shown in Figure 19-40.

Note that with Windows XP Home Edition, System Restore is your only option for system recovery. Windows XP Home Edition lacks the Backup utility.

Troubleshooting Startup Failures with Advanced Startup Options

When Windows fails to start up, consider using the Windows Advanced Startup Options menu to discover the cause. This Windows 2000/XP menu is an improvement on the trusty Microsoft Windows 9*x* Startup menu. To get to this menu, restart the computer and press F5 or F8 (depending on your OS) after the POST messages, but before the Windows logo screen appears.

Windows 2000 and Windows XP have similar menus. Central to these advanced options are Safe Mode and Last Known Good. In all cases, you will have to log on with the local Administrator account, so be sure you know the password.

System Restore settings

There are three differences between the two operating systems in this menu: the Windows 2000 option Boot Normally is Start Windows Normally in Windows XP. In addition, Windows XP has two other options not available in Windows 2000: Reboot and Return To OS Choices Menu.

Here's a rundown of the Advanced Boot Menu Options.

Safe Mode

Safe Mode starts up without using some drivers and components that would normally be started, including network support. It loads only very basic, non-vendor-specific drivers for mouse, VGA monitor, keyboard, mass storage, and system services. Safe Mode should be your first troubleshooting step for a system that fails to start normally.

In Safe Mode, you can use tools like Device Manager to locate and correct the source of the problem. When you use Device Manager in Safe Mode, you can access the properties for all the devices, even those that are not working in Safe Mode. The status displayed for the device is the status for a normal startup. Even the network card will show as enabled. You can disable any suspect device or perform other tasks, such as removing or updating drivers. If a problem with a device driver is preventing the operating system from starting normally, you can look here for yellow question mark warning icons that indicate an unknown device or yellow exclamation mark icons that indicate conflicts with existing devices.

Safe Mode with Networking

Safe Mode with Networking mode is identical to plain Safe Mode, except that you have network support. I use these two modes to test for a problem with network drivers. If Windows won't start up normally but does start up in Safe Mode, I then reboot into Safe Mode with Networking. If it fails to start up with Networking, then the problem is a network driver. Reboot back to Safe Mode, open Device Manager, and look at network components, beginning with the network adapter.

Safe Mode with Command Prompt

When you start Windows in Safe Mode with Command Prompt mode, after you log on, rather than loading the GUI desktop, it loads the command prompt (CMD.EXE) as the shell to the operating system. This is a handy option to remember if the desktop does not display at all, a condition that, after you have eliminated video drivers, can be caused by the corruption of the EXPLORER.EXE program. From within the command prompt, you can delete the corrupted version of EXPLORER.EXE and copy in an undamaged version. This requires knowing the command line commands for navigating the directory structure, as well as knowing the location of the file that you are replacing. Although Explorer is not loaded, you can load other GUI tools that don't depend on Explorer. All you have to do is enter the correct command. For instance, to load Event Viewer, type **eventvwr.msc** at the command line and press ENTER.

Travel Advisory

Remember that typing **help** at the command line will give you a list of the commands, and typing a command name followed by **/?** will give you the syntax for that command.

Enable Boot Logging

The Enable Boot Logging option starts Windows normally and creates a log file of the drivers as they load into memory. The file is named NTBTLOG.TXT and saved in the %SystemRoot% folder. If the startup failed because of a bad driver, the last entry in this file may be the driver the OS was initializing when it failed.

Enable VGA Mode

If Enable VGA Mode works, it means that you are using the correct video driver, but it is configured incorrectly (perhaps with the wrong refresh rate and/or resolution). After successfully starting in this mode, open the Display Properties and change the settings. While Safe Mode loads a generic VGA driver, this mode loads the driver Windows is configured to use, but it starts it up in standard VGA mode rather than using the settings for which it is configured.

Last Known Good Configuration

When Windows fails immediately after installing a new driver, but before you have logged on again, you may want to try the Last Known Good option. However, you may find this to be a rather fickle and limited tool. Also, it is not available on a computer with more than one hardware profile.

Travel Advisory

Last Known Good can fix configuration problems only if you use it before a successful reboot and log on after the change. Last Known Good cannot correct problems that are not related to configuration changes in the operating system. This includes problems caused by hardware failure, and corrupted files not related to a recent configuration change.

Debugging Mode

The Debugging mode option is of little use to techs. Debugging mode is a programmatic solution that proves to be a handy option only if you happen to have a Microsoft Certified Solutions Developer (MCSD) on hand. To start in Debugging mode, you must connect the computer you are debugging to another computer via a serial connection, and as Windows starts up, a debug of the kernel is sent to the second computer, which must also be running a debugger program. Impressive stuff, but not something that you're ever likely to use in the field.

Start Windows Normally

The Start Windows Normally choice is pretty self-explanatory. Select this if you changed your mind about using any of the other exotic choices.

Reboot

Windows XP's Reboot choice will actually do a soft reboot of the computer.

Return to OS Choices Menu

The Return To OS Choices menu lets you go back to the OS Choices menu from which you can select the operating system to load.

Resetting Forgotten Passwords in Windows XP

You'd be surprised at how easy it is to lock yourself out of a Windows PC—or maybe you wouldn't! Anybody whose ever done this will appreciate a new feature in Windows XP.

Windows XP allows the currently logged-on user to create a *Password Reset Disk* that can be used in case of a forgotten password. This is very important to have, because if you forget your password and an administrator resets the password using User Accounts or Local Users and Groups, then when you log on using the new password, you will find that you will lose access to some items, including files that you encrypted when logged on with the forgotten password. When you reset a password with a Password Reset Disk, you can log on using the new password and still have access to previously encrypted files.

> **Travel Advisory**
>
> Don't use the file encryption capabilities of Windows XP unless you are an advanced user who has researched it first, or unless you have the support of skilled professionals who can take steps to ensure that your encrypted data can be successfully recovered.

Best of all, with the Password Reset Disk, users have the power to fix their own passwords. Encourage your users to create this disk soon, because you have this power only if you remember to create a Password Reset Disk before you forget the password!

If you need to create a Password Reset Disk for a computer on a network (domain), search the Help system for Password Reset Disk and follow the instructions for Password Reset Disks for a computer on a domain.

To create a Password Reset Disk in Windows XP, first get a blank, formatted floppy disk. Then open User Accounts and on the Pick A Task page select the account that you are currently logged on as. On the next page, select Prevent A Forgotten Password from the list of Related Tasks (on the left). Read the Welcome page of the Forgotten Password Wizard, as shown in Figure 19-41, and then click Next.

Now insert the disk in drive A: and click Next again to see the Create User Account Password page. Enter the current user account password and click Next. Sit back and watch the progress bar as your Password Reset Disk is created. When it's done, click Next and then Finish to close the wizard. Don't forget to properly label the disk, including the account name and computer.

Troubleshooting Using the Emergency Repair Disk

So, we've got this great Emergency Repair Disk that'll take care of all of our system repair problems, we just pop it in the floppy drive and go, right?

Not just yet. As mentioned earlier, the ERD itself is not a bootable disk. To use the ERD, you must first boot the system using either the set of boot diskettes or the installation CD-ROM.

FIGURE 19.41   Forgotten Password Wizard

The ERD contains the following files:

Filename	Description
SETUP.LOG	Copied from the %SystemRoot%\REPAIR folder
AUTOEXEC.NT	Copied from the %SystemRoot%\SYSTEM32 folder
CONFIG.NT	Copied from the %SystemRoot%\SYSTEM32 folder

The SETUP.LOG file changes any time you apply a Service Pack, install or remove Windows components, or update drivers, or else when the system state changes. You should create an updated ERD any time you perform one of these actions.

Follow these steps to repair a system using the ERD:

1. Boot the system using either your set of boot diskettes or installation CD-ROM.

2. In the Welcome to Setup dialog box, press the R key to select the option to repair a Windows 2000 installation.

3. The Windows 2000 Repair Options menu appears. You have the option of either entering the Recovery Console or using the Emergency Repair Disk.

4. Press the R key to select the option to repair Windows 2000 using the emergency repair process.

5. The next screen offers the choice of Manual or Fast repair:

   - Manual repair lets you select the following repair options; inspect the startup environment, verify the system files, and inspect the boot sector.

   - Fast repair doesn't ask for any further input.

6. Follow the onscreen instructions and insert the ERD when prompted.

7. Your system will be inspected and, if possible, restored. When finished, the system restarts.

CHECKPOINT

✔ **Objective 19.01: Tools for Maintaining and Optimizing Windows**   Windows 2000 and XP's maintenance and troubleshooting tools are standardized in the Microsoft Management Console (MMC). Two of the most-used (and most useful) snap-ins are the Device Manager and Event Viewer. The Task Manager lets you inventory, check the status of, start, and stop running programs and processes. Windows XP's Task Manager also lets you monitor your network connection and user sessions.

✔ **Objective 19.02: Maintaining and Optimizing Windows**   Keeping up with the most current patches, updates, and Service Packs is an essential part of maintaining the stability and security of a Windows system. The Windows Update feature makes it easy to download the latest versions from Microsoft. The Add/Remove Software and Add/Remove Hardware Wizards streamline the component installation and removal process. Windows Driver Signing helps you prevent untested or potentially buggy device drivers. Signed drivers are guaranteed by Microsoft to work with Windows. User and group management is handled using the Users and Passwords or User Accounts Control Panel applet, or the Local Users and Groups MMC snap-in. Using Windows 2000 and XP's advanced Performance Options enables you to optimize system performance. Using the Performance Monitor lets you track resource usage and locate bottlenecks. Regular use of the Disk Defragmenting tool, Error Checking tool, and Disk Cleanup keeps your hard disk drive in top condition. To proactively prepare for disasters, use System Restore and Backup, and install the Recovery Console as a boot option.

✔ **Objective 19.03: Troubleshooting Windows**   The Recovery Console enables you to troubleshoot problems that prevent Windows 2000 and XP from booting. These include disk errors, corrupted system files, and misbehaving services. The System Restore feature lets you take a snapshot of your Windows XP PC and return it to a previous state. This is handy if you install software that makes the system unstable. Two of the handiest Advanced Startup Options are Safe Mode and Last Known Good Configuration mode. The Emergency Repair Disk enables you to restore a corrupted Registry.

REVIEW QUESTIONS

1. Your Windows 2000 Professional system fails to boot up. You suspect that the boot sector has become corrupted. You start the system using the set of boot disks, and launch the Recovery Console. Which command should you use to write a new boot sector into the system partition?

    A. chkdsk

    B. fdisk

    C. fixmbr

    D. fixboot

2. Your Windows 2000 Professional system fails to start normally. You have not added or changed any system components. What should your first action be to troubleshoot this problem?

    A. Attempt to start the system in Safe Mode.

    B. Boot the system using the set of boot disks, and use the ERD.

    C. Boot the system using the set of boot disks, and use the Recovery Console to restore the system state.

    D. Attempt to start the system in Last Known Good Configuration.

3. Which of the following commands would you use to install the Recovery Console?

    A. Start | Run, then type **d:\i386\winnt32 /cmdcons**

    B. Start | Run, then type **d:\i386\winnt32 /rc.**

    C. Start | Run, then type **d:\i386\winnt32 /cmd:command_line** .

    D. Start | Run, then type **d:\i386\winnt32 /copydir:recovery_console** .

4. Which tool in Windows XP Home would you use to back up your essential system files?

    A. System Restore

    B. Backup and Recovery Wizard

    C. Emergency Repair Disk

    D. Recovery Console

5. Phil tried to install a printer on his Windows XP Professional machine, but found he didn't have permission. What could be the problem?

    A. Phil is logged on with a Limited account.

    B. Phil is logged on as a Local User.

    C. Phil is logged on as a Local Administrator.

    D. Phil is logged on as Guest.

6. Sendra wants to get a quick snapshot of her System Resources on a Windows XP Home machine. How does she get to the appropriate tool?

    A. Start | Run | Perfmon

    B. Start | Control Panel | Administrative Tools |Performance

    C. Start | All Programs | Accessories | System Resources

    D. Press CTRL-ALT-DEL once and click the Performance tab

7. What tool should Bill use to track who logs on and off of the busy library terminal for which he is responsible?

  A. Event Viewer

  B. Performance Console

  C. System Resource Meter

  D. Task Manager

8. Sven loaded a new video card on his system, but now everything looks very bad. What should he do first?

  A. Go to Event Viewer and check the log.

  B. Go to Device Manager.

  C. Go to the printed manual.

  D. Call tech support.

9. Tariq got hit by a virus that causes coffee ad pop-ups to appear every fourth keyboard stroke. A tech friend suggested that it was a little program that monitored his keystrokes and told him to turn it off, but Tariq sees nothing running on the taskbar or in the Task Manager, Applications tab. What should he check next?

  A. Processes tab in the Task Manager

  B. Services console in Administrative Tools

  C. Component Services in Administrative Tools

  D. Device Manager

10. James sets up a new Windows XP Professional PC for his client in an unsecured, networked environment. What's his first step for making the data safe?

  A. Make sure the user shuts the machine off every night.

  B. Require the user to log in with a password.

  C. Require the user to log in with a password composed of alphanumeric characters.

  D. Nothing. Anybody with a floppy disk can access the data on the PC.

REVIEW ANSWERS

1. **D** The Recovery Console command "fixboot" writes a new partition boot sector to the system partition. The Recovery Console command "chkdsk" runs the CheckDisk utility; "fixmbr" writes a new Master Boot Record for the partition boot sector; "fdisk" is not a valid command for the Recovery Console.

2. **A**   Attempting to boot into Safe Mode should be your first troubleshooting step.

3. **A**   Start | Run, then type **d:\i386\winnt32 /cmdcons** is the correct command used to install the Recovery Console.

4. **A**   System Restore is the only tool in Windows XP Home for backing up essential system files.

5. **A D**   Phil needs to be logged on as an Administrator, not a Limited account or Guest.

6. **D**   Press CTRL-ALT-DEL once and click the Performance tab.

7. **A**   Event Viewer is the tool he needs.

8. **B**   Always go to Device Manager first when hardware goes wrong.

9. **A**   The first place to check for a loaded program after the Applications tab is in the Processes tab. If the virus program doesn't show up there, then he should check Services.

10. **C**   James needs to make sure the user has a good password. That the system uses NTFS is assumed here.

About the
CD-ROM

The CD-ROM included with this book comes complete with MasterExam. The software is easy to install on any Windows 98/NT/2000/XP computer, and must be installed to access the MasterExam feature. To register for the second bonus MasterExam, simply click the link on the Main Page and follow the directions to the free online registration.

System Requirements

Software requires Windows 98 or higher and Internet Explorer 5.0 or above and 20 MB of hard disk space for full installation.

Installing and Running MasterExam

If your computer CD-ROM drive is configured to autorun, the CD-ROM will automatically start up upon inserting the disk. From the opening screen you may install MasterExam by pressing the MasterExam or MasterSim buttons. This will begin the installation process and create a program group named "LearnKey." To run MasterExam, use Start | Programs | LearnKey. If the autorun feature did not launch your CD-ROM, browse to the CD-ROM and click on the "RunInstall" icon.

MasterExam

MasterExam provides you with a simulation of the actual exam. The number of questions, type of questions, and the time allowed are intended to be a representation of the exam environment. You have the option to take an open-book exam, including hints, references, and answers; a closed book exam; or the timed MasterExam simulation.

When you launch the MasterExam simulation, a digital clock will appear in the top-center of your screen. The clock will continue to count down to zero unless you choose to end the exam before the time expires.

Help

A help file is provided through the help button on the Main Page in the lower left-hand corner. Individual help features are also available through MasterExam.

Removing Installation(s)

MasterExam and MasterSim are installed to your hard drive. For best results for removal of programs, use the Start | Programs | LearnKey | Uninstall options to remove MasterExam.

If you desire to remove the Real Player, use the Add/Remove Programs icon from your Control Panel. You may also remove the LearnKey training program from this location.

Technical Support

For questions regarding the technical content of the MasterExam, please visit www.osborne.com or e-mail customer.service@mcgraw-hill.com. For customers outside the United States, e-mail international_cs@mcgraw-hill.com.

LearnKey Technical Support

For technical problems with the software (installation, operation, removing installations), please visit www.learnkey.com or e-mail techsupport@learnkey.com.

Career Flight Path

A+ Certification generally serves as the base of origin for any number of career flight paths. Most IT companies big and small see A+ Certification as the entry point to IT. From A+, you have a number of certification options, depending on whether you want to focus more on hardware or go towards network administration (although these are not mutually exclusive goals). Take a look at these five in particular:

- CompTIA Network+ Certification
- CompTIA Server+ Certification
- Microsoft Networking Certification
- Novell NetWare Certification
- Cisco Certification

CompTIA Network+ Certification   If haven't already taken the Network+, make it your next certification. Just as A+ shows you have solid competency as a PC technician, Network+ demonstrates your skill as a network technician, including understanding of network hardware, installation, and troubleshooting. CompTIA's Network+ is a natural fit for continuing towards your Microsoft, Novell, or Cisco certifications. Take the Network+; it's your obvious next certification!

CompTIA Server+ Certification   Like Network+, Server+ Certification fits very nicely as a more in-depth testing of your knowledge of PC and server-specific hardware and operating systems. If you plan to go the path of the high-end hardware tech, Server+ is the next step. Plus, Server+ is a natural lead-in to Cisco certifications (see below).

Microsoft Networking Certification   Microsoft's ever popular Microsoft Certified Systems Engineer (MCSE) holds a lot of clout for those looking to work in the networking field. Microsoft NT, 2000, and XP operating systems control a huge portion of all the installed networks out there and those networks need qualified support people to make them run. The MCSE consists of seven exams: four core and three electives. Check out Microsoft's training web site at http://www.microsoft.com/trainingandservices for details. Most techs will find the Windows 2000 track the most obvious choice and almost everyone takes the Microsoft 70-210: Installing, Configuring, and Administering Microsoft Windows 2000 Professional followed by the 70-215: Installing, Configuring, and Administering Microsoft Windows 2000 Server as the first two exams towards their MCSE.

Novell NetWare Certification   Novell's NetWare may not be the powerhouse it once was, but there's still a huge installed base of NetWare networks out there! The surge of techs towards Microsoft certifications has actually created a bit of a shortage of good NetWare certified techs. The Certified NetWare Engineer (CNE) is the certification to go for if you want to get into Novell networks. Novell has a number of tracks but most techs will go for the 50-653: NetWare 5.1 Admin and the 50-632: Networking Technologies exam. Check out Novell's certification web site at http://www.novell.com/education/certinfo/cne/ for more details.

Cisco Certification   Let's face it, Cisco routers pretty much run the Internet and most intranets in the world and Cisco provides three levels of certification for folks who want to show their skills at handling Cisco products. Most everyone interested in Cisco certification starts with the Certified Cisco Network Associate (CCNA). The CCNA is only one exam (640-507) and a darn easy way to slap the word Cisco on your resume! After your CCNA you should consider the CCNP (Certified Cisco Networking Professional) certification. See the Cisco certification web site at http://www.cisco.com/en/US/learning/le3/learning_career_certifications_and_learning_paths_home.html for more details!

Index

INTERNATIONAL CONTACT INFORMATION

AUSTRALIA
McGraw-Hill Book Company
Australia Pty. Ltd.
TEL +61-2-9900-1800
FAX +61-2-9878-8881
http://www.mcgraw-hill.com.au
books-it_sydney@mcgraw-hill.com

CANADA
McGraw-Hill Ryerson Ltd.
TEL +905-430-5000
FAX +905-430-5020
http://www.mcgraw-hill.ca

GREECE, MIDDLE EAST, & AFRICA
(Excluding South Africa)
McGraw-Hill Hellas
TEL +30-210-6560-990
TEL +30-210-6560-993
TEL +30-210-6560-994
FAX +30-210-6545-525

MEXICO (Also serving Latin America)
McGraw-Hill Interamericana Editores
S.A. de C.V.
TEL +525-1500-5108
FAX +525-117-1589
http://www.mcgraw-hill.com.mx
carlos_ruiz@mcgraw-hill.com

SINGAPORE (Serving Asia)
McGraw-Hill Book Company
TEL +65-6863-1580
FAX +65-6862-3354
http://www.mcgraw-hill.com.sg
mghasia@mcgraw-hill.com

SOUTH AFRICA
McGraw-Hill South Africa
TEL +27-11-622-7512
FAX +27-11-622-9045
robyn_swanepoel@mcgraw-hill.com

SPAIN
McGraw-Hill/
Interamericana de España, S.A.U.
TEL +34-91-180-3000
FAX +34-91-372-8513
http://www.mcgraw-hill.es
professional@mcgraw-hill.es

UNITED KINGDOM, NORTHERN,
EASTERN, & CENTRAL EUROPE
McGraw-Hill Education Europe
TEL +44-1-628-502500
FAX +44-1-628-770224
http://www.mcgraw-hill.co.uk
emea_queries@mcgraw-hill.com

ALL OTHER INQUIRIES Contact:
McGraw-Hill/Osborne
TEL +1-510-420-7700
FAX +1-510-420-7703
http://www.osborne.com
omg_international@mcgraw-hill.com

Your Ticket to Exam Success

Mike Meyers' A+
Certification Passport
0-07-219363-8

Mike Meyers' Security+
Certification Passport
0-07-222741-9

Mike Meyers'
Network+
Certification
Passport
0-07-219523-1

Mike Meyers' Server+
Certification Passport
0-07-219364-6

From the #1 Name in Professional Certification Training

Mc

Sound Off!

Visit us at **www.osborne.com/bookregistration** and let us know what you thought of this book. While you're online you'll have the opportunity to register for newsletters and special offers from McGraw-Hill/Osborne.

We want to hear from you!

Sneak Peek

Visit us today at **www.betabooks.com** and see what's coming from McGraw-Hill/Osborne tomorrow!

Based on the successful software paradigm, Bet@Books™ allows computing professionals to view partial and sometimes complete text versions of selected titles online. Bet@Books™ viewing is free, invites comments and feedback, and allows you to "test drive" books in progress on the subjects that interest you the most.